Jenkins of Mexico

Jenkins of Mexico

*How a Southern Farm Boy
Became a Mexican Magnate*

ANDREW PAXMAN

OXFORD
UNIVERSITY PRESS

OXFORD
UNIVERSITY PRESS

Oxford University Press is a department of the University of Oxford. It furthers
the University's objective of excellence in research, scholarship, and education
by publishing worldwide. Oxford is a registered trade mark of Oxford University
Press in the UK and certain other countries.

Published in the United States of America by Oxford University Press
198 Madison Avenue, New York, NY 10016, United States of America.

Library of Congress Cataloging-in-Publication Data
Names: Paxman, Andrew, 1967– author.
Title: Jenkins of Mexico : how a Southern farm boy became a Mexican magnate /
Andrew Paxman.
Description: New York, NY : Oxford University Press, 2017. |
Includes bibliographical references and index.
Identifiers: LCCN 2016042218 (print) | LCCN 2017006803 (ebook) |
ISBN 9780190455743 (hardback : acid-free paper) | ISBN 9780190455750 (Updf) |
ISBN 9780190455767 (Epub)
Subjects: LCSH: Jenkins, William O. (William Oscar), 1878–1963. |
Businessmen—Mexico—Biography. | Americans—Mexico—Biography. |
Philanthropists—Mexico—Biography. | Puebla de Zaragoza
(Mexico)—Biography. | Mexico—Economic conditions—20th century. |
Mexico—Biography. | Tennessee—Biography. | BISAC: BIOGRAPHY &
AUTOBIOGRAPHY / Historical. | HISTORY / Latin America / Mexico. |
HISTORY / United States / 20th Century.
Classification: LCC HC132.5.J57 P38 2017 (print) | LCC HC132.5.J57 (ebook) |
DDC 338.092 [B] —dc23
LC record available at https://lccn.loc.gov/2016042218

1 3 5 7 9 8 6 4 2
Printed by Sheridan Books, Inc., United States of America

Contents

Introduction: The Black Legend of William O. Jenkins   1

1. Coming of Age in Tennessee   13

2. Fortune-Seeking in Mexico   44

3. How to Get Rich in a Revolution   73

4. Kidnapped, Jailed, Vilified   104

5. Empire at Atencingo   136

6. Resistance at Atencingo   172

7. With Maximino   211

8. Mining the Golden Age of Mexican Cinema   244

9. Enterprise, Profiteering, and the Death of the Golden Age   279

10. The Jenkins Foundation and the Battle for the Soul of the PRI   319

11. Jenkins's Earthly Afterlife   359

Epilogue: The Mixed Legacy of William O. Jenkins   388

Acknowledgments   395

Notes   399

Bibliography   473

Index   493

Jenkins of Mexico

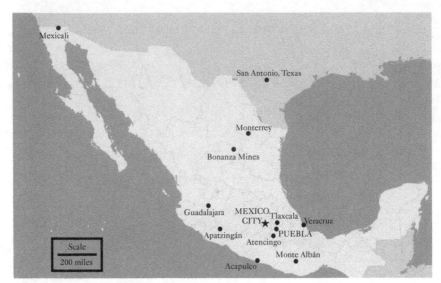

Jenkins's Mexico: Where he lived and where he mainly invested.

Yavidaxiu, "México, con división política y sin nombres," https://creativecommons. org/licenses/by-sa/3.0/. *Source:* https://commons.wikimedia.org/wiki/Category:Blank_ maps_of_Mexico#/media /File:Mexico_blank.svg.

Introduction

THE BLACK LEGEND OF WILLIAM O. JENKINS

IN THE MEXICAN city of Puebla, half a century ago, there lived an old American as wealthy as a Rockefeller. He strode the streets with a purposeful step and his head slightly bowed, as though he wished not to be interrupted. For daily visits to his country club, he had his chauffeur drive him, in one of his secondhand Packards. But he walked often enough that he was recognized by all who lived or worked near his downtown home: tall and well-built, cropped hair beneath a black fedora, and seeming always to wear the same black tie and shabby dark suit. His head was large and solid, like a marble bowling ball, the roundness interrupted by a stern jaw and heavy chin. His blue eyes were sharp.[1]

William O. Jenkins, said to be the richest man in Mexico, was an early riser. He worked all morning in the office that shared the immense space of his home: the penthouse above Puebla's leading department store. Though his assets included several hundred movie theaters, substantial rural and urban real estate, various textile mills, and Mexico's second-largest bank, his entire staff consisted of a personal assistant, an accountant, and a secretary. People who came to him for money—a farmer hoping for a loan, a businessman seeking venture capital, a state governor keen for him to finance a school—all had to climb the four flights of stairs to his rooms. Though now past eighty, he refused to install an elevator, for he was a champion of physical fitness and advancement by merit. He neither smoked nor drank. And he was frugal. On more than one occasion, visitors entered his office to find him peeling an unmarked stamp from an envelope. He would explain: "I hate to see anything go to waste."

In the early afternoon he would head outdoors. First he visited the cemetery where his wife lay buried; he had repatriated her body from California, where she had spent her final years. For half an hour he would sit on a stool by her grave. Then to the Alpha Club, for tennis. He preferred doubles, which let him partner with a local ace and usually win. Afterward he might visit his nearby ranch, where he cultivated vegetables, or take in a movie at one of the theaters he owned. Mexican comedies were his favorite; audiences knew him by his booming laugh. In the evening he dined early, together with his cook and his maids.

Weekends often found him out of town. He owned a farm two hours to the south, where he grew melon and cane. He held cotton land on the US border, and he had begun buying land in the west, to develop a second cotton estate. The old man was seldom happier than when tramping around fields, giving directions; doing so reminded him of his boyhood, on farms in Tennessee. In the passport of this titan of industry, the entry for "Occupation" still read, "Farmer." Another pleasure was to gather friends and relatives and fly to Acapulco in his secondhand airplane. He owned a hilltop mansion there, furnished with plastic chairs and an unheated swimming pool.

The casual observer might have viewed this elderly man as scarcely more than dour and unorthodox, his thrift and disregard for class distinctions quite out of step with the Mexican elite. Yet partly because he was so very rich and partly because he was so very American, he was the country's most hated capitalist. And in 1960, the clamor against Jenkins was at a peak.

Mexico, like its northern neighbor, was facing a crossroads. Fifteen years of postwar conservatism met the choice of a liberal turn. The nation had recently gained a president in his forties, and the United States was about to elect one too; both were men of charisma and energy, keen to travel to foster alliances. Most urgently, John Fitzgerald Kennedy and Adolfo López Mateos shared the Cold War challenge of Cuba: How should they respond to a socialist regime, less than a hundred miles from the shores of both countries? With confrontation, neutrality, or accommodation? The key difference was that, for the United States, the question was one of foreign policy, with consequences for relations with Russia, hemispheric leadership, and global security. For Mexico, the matter resounded at home.

Mexico's rulers styled themselves the Institutional Revolutionary Party (PRI in Spanish), the perennial keepers of a flame ignited in 1910, at the start of a decade-long civil war. The PRI was a very broad church. Its left wing wondered: How could the party of the Mexican Revolution not sympathize with the Cuban Revolution? Fidel Castro's aims were so similar: returning the economy to national hands, free healthcare and education, greater equality in land and income. To the PRI's right wing, dominant for the past twenty years, Castro was a dangerous extremist, expelling investors rather than harnessing them and eroding private enterprise. Many joined the debate: business groups placed warnings in the papers; bishops railed against Marxist godlessness; unions, teachers, and students took to the streets in solidarity with Castro, often demanding that Mexico resume its own revolutionary path. Caught in the middle, López Mateos emitted mixed signals, suppressing labor dissent while upping social spending and land reform.[2]

Mexico's debate over Cuba was a questioning of its own identity. Since 1938, when President Lázaro Cárdenas had pushed socialism to popular heights by seizing the oil sector from US and British firms, the PRI had retreated from the Revolution's promises. Hammered out in a new constitution, those promises had sought to banish the injustices of the dictatorship of Porfirio Díaz (1876–1911), when foreigners dominated the economy and white landowners gobbled up the fields of indigenous villages. Now, some of those Porfirian imbalances were returning. Despite a pledge of effective suffrage, elections at every level were won by the PRI. Despite an agrarian policy that partitioned haciendas among the poor, new estates were emerging. During a twenty-year economic "miracle," wealth had largely failed to trickle down; the 1960 census showed more than a third of Mexicans to be shoeless and illiterate and half to be living in single-room homes. In spite of a promise of Mexico for the Mexicans and decades of protectionism, foreign investors were reclaiming much of the market.

To many on the left, no one better epitomized what had gone wrong than Señor Jenkins. Cárdenas described him as a relic of the past: a "large-scale landowner," "monopolist," and "foreign capitalist"; in the language of the left, capitalist meant exploiter.[3] An influential news magazine made Jenkins its whipping boy, starting with a photo essay that blamed him for hellish conditions at a Puebla sugar mill, which in fact he no longer owned.[4] A filmmaker published *The Black Book of Mexican Cinema*, a diatribe against Jenkins and his partners. It alleged gross monopolistic practice in their film interests: favoring Hollywood over local fare at theaters, forcing producers to work on paltry budgets, having union activists murdered. It claimed that Jenkins, as a stalwart of the PRI's right wing, imposed each Puebla governor. It declared: "The world neither has nor could it have a River Jordan vast enough to cleanse William O. Jenkins."[5]

Time magazine took notice. A profile called Jenkins "a mysterious buccaneer-businessman who has built the biggest personal fortune in Mexico." It claimed that he made little money until the Revolution, when he was kidnapped and somehow pocketed half the ransom. It insinuated he grew rich by buying sugar estates in league with politicians and smuggling alcohol to the United States during Prohibition. It smirked about his "shabby office" and "broad, sometimes soiled neckties."[6] Jenkins's friends were outraged. Vanderbilt University chancellor Harvie Branscomb wrote to *Time*, protesting the article's "considerable number of errors of fact."[7] Jenkins shrugged off the matter. He had been libeled and slandered for more than forty years.

Rich, infamous, American, aloof (he never spoke to the press, never answered his critics), Jenkins was an all-purpose bogeyman. To Mexicans, he served as an incendiary symbol, with which to rally support for left-wing causes or seek economic protection; to criticize him was to advertise one's standing as a revolutionary or one's honor as a patriot. To Americans, he was a latter-day robber baron. He had managed to flourish in a land that still tolerated monopolies and crony capitalism—quite unlike the USA, of course!

Jenkins encapsulated Mexican ambivalence toward the United States: an attitude of suspicion but also of guarded respect and desire for economic cooperation. After all, if Jenkins were guilty of a tenth of the accusations against him, and if the political will existed, any president could have expelled him. But the will did not exist. The gringo had his uses.

In the 1920s and 1930s, Jenkins's sugar plantation had created jobs for five thousand and hosted one of Mexico's most productive mills. Loans and gifts of his had bolstered a chronically poor state government in Puebla. In the 1940s and 1950s, his hundreds of movie screens had brought delight to the swelling urban millions. At a time when workers were prone to strikes, his theaters soothed tempers and helped make the cities feel like home. His campaign donations had aided the rise of a political family, the Ávila Camachos, which yielded one president, two Puebla governors, and a dozen influential dependents who included the current president's right-hand man, Gustavo Díaz Ordaz. His financing had helped to build highways, automobile plants, and a top pharmaceutical company. His philanthropy had funded schools for tens of thousands, built hospitals and covered markets, brought drinking water to poorer quarters, and helped fund excavations at the ancient site of Monte Albán. All along, and especially in recent years, Jenkins had provided a lightning rod for the critique of the left. Better for the government that radicals fulminate against an American than direct their wrath at the regime itself.

Despite his singular persona, Jenkins exemplified how much the "revolutionary" state depended on the business elite: at first for its very survival, then for the ascendance and supremacy of its conservative wing, whose ideological descendants remain in power today.

OVER ITS SIX eventful decades, Jenkins's career reveals the surprising continuity of Mexican capitalism. It discloses the routes for moneymaking, during and after the Revolution, available to those with political connections. It shows the accommodations made to business by regimes from across the political spectrum. And it sheds light on the two great contradictions of the modern Mexican experience: that the ten-year Revolution, in which more than a million died or emigrated and one of the world's most radical constitutions emerged, should prove as notable for what it failed to change as for what it did and that a ruling party that called itself revolutionary should prove so friendly to the rich.

In both respects, Jenkins's story fits the reading established by Mexico's most influential historian, Daniel Cosío Villegas, who argued that the Revolution achieved far less for political democracy and social development than party-line speeches and standard histories held.[8] After a 1968 massacre of students in Mexico City, the question was voiced directly: Had there in fact been a revolution? The compromising of its radicalism, the suppression of electoral democracy, and the persistence of oligarchs has resonated with historians since.[9] A second watershed divides the socialistic Cárdenas era of 1934–40 from the rightward regimes that followed. Convention celebrated that era as the policy climax of the Revolution, after which most politicians favored foreign investors and their own bank accounts. But revisionists claimed that Cardenism achieved less than the official story maintained, limited either by the state's dependence on foreign and local capital or by a lack of cohesion due to the durability of provincial strongmen.[10]

Jenkins's career supports both rereadings. It subverts the still-popular view that the thirty years from 1910 were bad for business. Time and again Jenkins found opportunities for profit. During the Revolution he speculated with great success in property; he also kept his textile mills running.

During the two regimes that followed, he amassed huge holdings that included the Atencingo sugar kingdom, benefiting from a selective respect of property rights that favored the well-connected, a practice reminiscent of the Porfirio Díaz era; likewise, his mutually supportive relations with politicians harkened back to ties between capitalists and the cronies of Díaz. Despite the radicalism of Cárdenas, who seized his sugar plantation, he was able to use his alliance with Puebla's governor to retain the estate's mill and hence its profits. Then, after 1940, Jenkins faced various trials with labor, which showed how a state now famed for favoring business often sided with workers and advocates of public ownership. Again, the old division—radicalism up to 1940, conservatism afterward—seems simplistic.

Although a US citizen, Jenkins typified a new breed of Mexican businessman emergent after the Revolution. These middle-class climbers helped foster an acceptance of industrial capitalism as the key to prosperity. They were entrepreneurial and modernizing but also given to rent seeking, insider lending, and monopolistic practice; they disdained politicians but consented to give-and-take with the state. Unlike the self-enriching strongmen of the era, they ventured less into low-risk sectors such as real estate and took greater trouble to innovate for the domestic market. But, like those politicians, they epitomized a concentration of wealth fueled by special privileges. Jenkins's protégés fit the same mold. Many observers say the same of Mexico's billionaires today.

Herein lies a second reason for Jenkins's significance: his career reveals the interdependence of government and big business. The focus of most histories of modern Mexico—on workers, peasants, and political and social rebels—has masked the importance of capital to politics. Yet a state-capital symbiosis was vital, both to the success of the business elite and to the seventy-one-year reign of the PRI. "Crony capitalism" is the common label for such an arrangement, but the term blurs distinct dimensions of the bond: these I would call a "symbiotic imperative" between state and capital and a "symbiotic convenience" between individual politicians and industrialists.[11]

After the Revolution, state and capital needed each other. The government depended on business elites to help rebuild the economy, through investment, job creation, the paying of taxes, and the securing of foreign loans. Industrialists likewise depended on the state: to restore order, build roads, tame radicalized labor, enforce property rights, and enact laws that tempered the radicalism of the new constitution. When one president,

Cárdenas, increased expropriations and let strikes proliferate, he upset the symbiotic balance. This prompted massive capital flight, jeopardizing the economy. His need to restore that balance forced him to retreat, backing pro-business legislation and picking a moderate successor.[12]

Such a symbiotic imperative, a union of perceived necessity, is distinct from but often linked with a symbiotic convenience. A more truly crony-ish compromise, this kind of tie involves mutual self-interest without regard for anyone else. It includes such favors as covert business partnerships, no-compete contracts, and the selective application of laws. These practices pervaded the Porfirian era, re-emerged with a new set of players in the 1920s, and reached spectacular dimensions under President Miguel Alemán (1946–1952).[13]

Jenkins utilized both kinds of interdependence. In Puebla, he made loans and donations to cash-poor authorities, which helps explain how an American could safeguard vast acreages in an era of xenophobia and land confiscation. He invested heavily to help revive the state's blighted sugar sector, just as President Álvaro Obregón (1920–1924) was needing to revive the economy as a whole and hence was willing to protect large-scale agriculture. In the 1940s and 1950s, the imperative underpinned Jenkins's success nationwide, as he lent unparalleled support to the federal goal of containing the urban masses, building and operating hundreds of movie theaters, and helping finance a reactionary national cinema. In turn he was permitted a legally dubious and lucrative film exhibition monopoly. The state did not depend on Jenkins per se, but their mutually beneficial relations exemplified a bond: between elites needing to safeguard their assets and a regime needing to juggle client groups to maintain its legitimacy.

Exchanges based on mutual need often coexist with trades of convenience, and Jenkins's dealings typified this trend too. He helped his political pals get rich. Favors and joint ventures between capitalists and politicians often involved frontmen, so they are hard to verify. But the Jenkins story offers many glimpses of the infectious tango between privilege and corruption.

His story also exposes the importance of such bonds outside the capital. Mutual help tends to begin at the local or state level, where everyday exchanges between merchants and politicians are most frequent. Further, what happens regionally matters nationally. Provincial alliances were key to developing the nation, because the federal government could not simply stamp itself on the states. It had to allow some autonomy to local bosses and business cliques, especially in the chaotic 1920s and 1930s. The staple view of the single-party Mexican state as a "perfect dictatorship" ignores the messy nature of politics on the ground, including bitterly fought local elections.[14] Puebla during the Jenkins era—the state was his home from 1906 to 1963—richly illustrates these trends.

Responding to Puebla's chronic bankruptcy and recurrent seizures of the governorship by radicals, the business elite actively backed conservatives for the office. Hard-fought campaigns such as that of 1936, in which Maximino Ávila Camacho faced a popular leftist rival, show how local outcomes need to take both grassroots resistance and elite maneuvering into account. Since Maximino (as he was known) found he had to campaign hard, he solicited large wads of private-sector cash. With his victory came an entrenchment of rule that privileged business, even against federal opposition. To study Puebla at this time is to behold the jalopy of the socialist state in all its juddering complexity. It is also to behold the founding of an autonomous local fiefdom that would endure under the Ávila Camachos until the year of Jenkins's death.

The Jenkins–Maximino alliance not only held sway over Puebla; it also exerted a rightward influence at the national level. Historian Alan Knight once suggested that regional bastions of conservatism contributed to the rightward shift of the latter Cárdenas years; Puebla substantiates this still sketchy argument.[15] The strength of pro-business governors like Maximino, poised to dictate vote-counting in the 1940 election, helps explain Cárdenas's decision to back Maximino's moderate brother Manuel as his successor. The waning of Mexico's social revolution had much to do with resistance from states such as Puebla.

While this is not entirely a regional history—Jenkins's empire centered on Mexico City from the 1940s—it does cast light on Puebla's troubled past. Because of slow average growth since 1900, when it lost its ancient rank as Mexico's second metropolis, Puebla City now lags far behind the economic powerhouses of Guadalajara and Monterrey. For decades, reluctance to innovate and upgrade machinery atrophied Puebla's development, above all in its famed textile sector. When margins shrank, most mill owners reacted by squeezing labor. Jenkins had various mills, and he too declined to modernize. Economic stagnation was due in part to political stagnation. Politics ossified under the Ávila Camacho fiefdom, which hindered debate and produced inept or complacent governors. The clique owed its durability to hidebound backers such as Jenkins.[16]

Outside elite circles, Jenkins was not a popular fellow. But his questionable deeds were routinely and purposefully exaggerated. The catalogue of hyperbole and selective criticism about Jenkins amounts to a modern Black Legend. It manifests the predominant Mexican phobia: *gringopho-bia*. This is the strain of xenophobia that vilifies Americans, especially politicians and industrialists, as imperialistic, exploitative, or culturally inferior. As of the Revolution, anti-US caricatures in word, art, film, and song became common rhetorical tools within debates over capitalist ver-sus socialist paths to development. In recent times, gringophobia has con-tinued to surface, in debates over free trade, cultural influence, the drug war, and oil-sector reform.

To his critics, Jenkins embodied the grasping, guileful US capitalist. His infamy dated from his kidnapping, while a consular agent, in 1919. Facing a bilateral crisis, Mexico's fragile regime countered US charges of ineffectual government by claiming that Jenkins had plotted a "self-kidnapping"; the allegation stuck. Though exonerated, Jenkins remained so tarred by the episode that every subsequent charge of skullduggery gained a ready audience. This and further controversies—over Jenkins as landowner, monopolist, political intriguer, even philanthropist—reveal a common denominator: gringophobia as a component of leftist or national-ist rhetoric.

Observers would make Jenkins synonymous with an unethical US capitalism, which ignored how his actions equally reflected adaptation to Mexico.[17] Jenkins hired private militia to defend his haciendas; so did Mexicans. He forged cozy friendships with governors, generals, and bish-ops; so did they. His predatory lending to hacienda owners was a gambit common since the nineteenth century. He resisted unions, evaded taxes, and built state-protected monopolies. All was standard practice among Mexican industrialists; all earned the ire of the left. Yet no one drew as much flak as Jenkins. Given the similarities between Jenkins and his peers, along with his reinvestment in local ventures and his cultivation of local protégés, the American was a fairly typical member of Mexico's business elite, which affirms his usefulness as a case study. Similar things may be said of other foreign-born capitalists, such as the Lebanese Miguel Abed, the Swede Axel Wenner-Gren, the Spaniard Manuel Suárez, and the US sugar baron B. F. Johnston. Each was much criticized, but none persisted in the public eye as long as Jenkins.

His vilification belongs to a gringophobic tradition that dates at least from 1848, when the United States took half of Mexico's territory. After the Revolution, the tradition mutated: once a largely elite concern, it became a widely popular practice; once centered on Uncle Sam, the ugly architect of interventions, it equally evoked business magnates. Among them were oil barons and Jenkins. Just as British nationalism was once fostered by promoting pride in not-being-French, so Mexican nationalism owed much to reviling the gringo.[18]

The attacks on Jenkins show not only the prevalence but also the uses of gringophobia. Political benefit could be gained from assailing him, especially during the Cold War, when a battle for the soul of the PRI pitted its pro-business right against its nationalist left. Leaders could strengthen their case for a leftist turn (or divert criticism from their own conduct) by signaling Jenkins's business machinations; periodicals could polish their leftist credentials (and boost sales) with exposés of this "pernicious" gringo. In turn, Jenkins-bashing contributed to the polarizing of opinion that defined the 1960s, with its student radicalism and subsequent bloody repression.

Xenophobic rhetoric raises questions about national difference. Probing the perceived Americanness of Jenkins helps undermine easy distinctions between the two countries. *The Economist* once wrote: "Monopolies are as Mexican as mescal—and just as intoxicating."[19] But they are also as American as apple pie, as the robber barons once demonstrated. Similarly, Jenkins's career reveals parallels in business cultures, which is a useful corrective given the lack of comparative US–Mexican histories.

Some of the dubious ways in which Jenkins seemingly emulated his peers had precedent and parallel in the United States. He pursued market dominance: first in cotton hosiery, next in sugar, notoriously in film. But there was nothing uniquely Mexican about such monopolies, which thanks to the likes of Rockefeller and Carnegie loomed large in the land he had departed. His fortune owed much to alliances with the powerful. But for all the cronyism of Mexico's politicians, were these links so different from the ties capitalists were forging with mayors and lawmakers in the United States—such as Boss Crump of Memphis in Jenkins's native Tennessee?

Yet differences of business culture do exist. While deflating such myths as Latin America's "absence of entrepreneurship," historians see trends that vary greatly from those of North Atlantic business: the slower growth of managerial capitalism, the greater role of immigrants as entrepreneurs, the later emergence of corporate philanthropy.[20] Or take political self-enrichment: in the United States, the practice gained infamy during the Warren Harding presidency (1921–1923) and the subsequent Teapot Dome trial, which ended in the jailing of Senator Albert Fall. Such exposés and convictions lacked a parallel in Mexico, remaining rare until the 1980s. What emerges from comparing cultures is a need not to deny contrasts but to avoid dichotomies. Difference is very often a matter of timing or degree.

People of Jenkins's era often made coarse contrasts. They believed Mexicans were like this and Americans like that, and they based their thinking largely on prejudice. The aim here, as with the biography of any venturer abroad, is to understand the outlook of such actors from the past—that foreign country, where they do things differently—and decode their words and deeds within their twice-distant world.

THIS, FINALLY, IS the tale of a conflicted man. Jenkins devoted himself to business to please the Southern belle he married and prove to her family that they were no better than he. In time this means became an end in itself, making Jenkins a dynamic entrepreneur but a dysfunctional patriarch. He neglected his family and treated his employees as children. Yet he was remarkably philanthropic, never more so than when he left almost all his wealth to a foundation serving education, healthcare, sports, and cultural heritage in Mexico.

Why Jenkins left his fortune to charity is the most enduring puzzle of his life. Critics said he did so because of his criminal guilty conscience. Others said he was trying to cleanse his image, and yet he absented himself from the inauguration of almost every school and hospital he financed. Perhaps the answer lay elsewhere, in his complex relationship with his wife. And did he really arrange his own kidnapping? Did he indeed plot the murder of opponents? How did a man of such abstemious conduct befriend Maximino, a despot notorious for wanton living? Just how much political sway did he exercise? And why did he never return to the United States?

Compounding these mysteries is the absence of most of Jenkins's papers. His business archive had been stored in a Puebla warehouse after his death. Ten years later an earthquake struck, leaving the filing cabinets toppled and papers strewn about. The Jenkins Foundation president, Manuel Espinosa Yglesias, ordered the papers piled onto a truck, taken to wasteland, and burned.[21] Nor does much remain of Puebla state records. When stepping down as governor, Maximino sold almost the entire executive archive to a paper company, which pulped it. His younger brother Rafael, governor in the 1950s, disposed of another trove. Later, whatever survived of treasury records was also sold and pulped.[22] Such actions, and similar moves since, reflect the entitlement of a PRI regime that clung to power in Puebla for eighty-one years, a machine adverse to public accountability, given to self-enrichment, and adept at covering its tracks.

Jenkins would have been glad of such purges. He had always resisted being written about, and he seldom shared his thoughts on the past. He even destroyed his letters from his wife. Journalists sometimes approached with requests to profile him, and each time he refused. He wrote to one, who made a career of flattering the powerful: "I continue to be very reluctant to court any kind of publicity." He told another, who was proposing a full biography: "My life doesn't matter to anyone. What's more, no one ought to know about it."[23]

Here, then, is the book that Jenkins hoped would never come.

I

Coming of Age in Tennessee

*Almighty God ... has marked the American people as
the chosen nation to finally lead in the regeneration of the
world.... We are the trustees of the world's progress.*

SENATOR ALBERT J. BEVERIDGE, speech in the US
Congress (1900)

The Jenkins of Bedford County

When the United States was still in its infancy, a young man named
William Jenkins set out on his own for a mission beyond the Appalachian
Mountains. Traveling on horseback, he journeyed hundreds of miles. He
was bound for terrain quite foreign to him; it was said to be a wilderness,
inhabited by sometimes hostile natives. Some of his people had already
settled there and begun to prosper, for the land was plentiful and fertile.
Dynamic and capable, Jenkins was full of confidence. He was a Christian.
Living by faith he could count on God's favor, and the fruits of his labor
would surely multiply. And so they did. He toiled for more than fifty years,
and on reaching old age he found himself successful, wealthy, and beloved.

Jenkins hailed from Frederick, Maryland, a town founded by immi-
grants from the Rhineland-Palatinate before the Revolutionary War.
Though mostly of British lineage, Jenkins so imbibed the town's German
culture that when he decided for the priesthood he trained as a Lutheran.
After four years of study he left for Salem, North Carolina, to finish his
training. Six months later, he was licensed by the state Synod to tend to
North Carolina Lutherans who had migrated to Bedford County, in central
Tennessee. He was to minister to two existing churches and establish new
ones as he saw fit. He was just twenty-two.[1]

Two generations later, another William Jenkins set out on a trek of
his own.[2] He traveled from Tennessee to Texas, but he did not stay long;
within three months, he crossed into Mexico. Tall and muscular, he had

a piercing stare and a prominent chin, rather like those of his grandfather, the kind that point toward the future. He came with an abundance of energy and something to prove. He had a well-born spouse and very few dollars. He was just twenty-three.

Mexico was a whim at first: Jenkins wanted to please his wife with a trip to Monterrey. They would spend a couple of nights in the city and return to San Antonio. But a chance encounter changed everything. In Monterrey, a railroad man told him that well-paid work abounded for Americans and Europeans. To men of education and initiative, Mexico was a land of opportunity. And so it proved to be. In his adoptive country, Jenkins would labor at great profit for sixty years.

Yet his obituaries would differ from those of his grandfather. The Reverend Jenkins was feted as one who held "a very firm hold on the affections and confidence of his people." In Middle Tennessee he continues to be honored as the founding father of Lutheranism.[3] William Oscar Jenkins would be feted too, his death making front-page news across Mexico, his burial drawing 20,000. But his legacy was less straightforward. To some, he was a sagacious businessman and a great philanthropist. Others claimed he was an exploiter, a monopolist, a tax evader, and that, for all his charitable works, he went unloved by Mexicans. Still others felt he was the subject of a defamatory black legend. How much that legend was grounded in fact or fostered by envy or prejudice, who could say?[4]

IN THE HEART of the green vastness of the eastern United States spreads an oblong territory that colonists called Tennessee. They named it after a river that crosses it twice before linking up with the Ohio River and then spilling into the Mississippi. In the center of that territory lies a basin, 80 miles long and 50 wide, with ranges of hills on all sides. Around the time of the American Revolution, colonists of English stock, also some Scottish and German, started to traverse the Appalachians from North Carolina and head toward this central plain. Its many rivers and subtropical climate promised excellent farming. At the northwest edge of the basin, settlers in 1779 founded a town on the Cumberland River that they called Nashville, which quickly prospered as a port and eventually became the state's capital. Near the southeast edge, forty years later, settlers founded a town on the Duck River that they called Shelbyville, which grew more slowly. Throughout the plain, then entirely wooded, the colonists set about chopping down the trees. They raised cattle and planted corn, wheat, and cotton. Whatever they chose to farm, they brought numerous slaves to help them.[5]

In 1824, when the Reverend Jenkins arrived, Bedford County was bristling with frontier enterprise. He found himself part of a wave of migrants, which during that decade helped the population double to 30,000. Farms were multiplying, and some 7,000 slaves worked on them. Shelbyville already boasted a tavern, a post office, a school, and a Presbyterian church. There were doctors and lawyers, blacksmiths and masons, tailors and shoemakers. In the center of the town square stood a brick courthouse, although minor disputes were often settled by fistfight. Then came the greater challenges of the frontier. In 1830 a tornado struck Shelbyville, demolishing most of the town, including the courthouse. Three years later, a cholera epidemic swept through the county, taking one in ten with it.[6]

The young pastor was warmly welcomed.[7] He had willing constituents: two newly established German congregations rejoiced at his arrival. He also had a wealthy patron. Martin Shofner (originally Schaeffner) had emigrated as a child with his parents from Frankfurt, and the family had prospered in the North Carolina piedmont. Here many of the locals chafed against colonial authority, resenting what they felt to be onerous taxes and extortion by dishonest sheriffs. Some of the men banded together as "Regulators" and fought the British at the prerevolutionary Battle of Alamance, on or near the Shofners' thousand-acre property. Martin was twelve, too young to fight but old enough to be convinced that taxes were something to be resisted. During the Revolution he fought with the North Carolina Cavalry, and he received land in Tennessee for his service. Once in Bedford County, where he arrived with wife and ten children in 1806, he became a prominent farmer. He held hundreds of acres, well fed by creeks and springs, eight miles east of Shelbyville. On a portion of this he established a chapel for his fellow Lutherans, known later as the Shofner Church.[8]

For Jenkins, the main challenges of frontier life were logistical. The first two churches he served lay 20 miles apart, his parishioners were scattered, and his supervisory board met 350 miles to the east. Revisiting North Carolina in 1825 for the annual synod meeting, he reported: "since last Synod I have traveled 3,000 miles on horseback, preached 175 times, baptized 84 children and 14 adults, admitted to church membership 34 persons, and had 8 funerals." Eventually he would serve ten churches across Middle Tennessee.

Further testament to his success was his marrying into the family of his patron. On New Year's Day 1829, he wed Mary Euless, a granddaughter of Martin Shofner. Preaching was not his only skill. Like most ministers of his day, Jenkins developed a trade he could rely on for income. His was building carriages, and the business excelled. He also set up a school, known simply as Jenkins' School.[9] The family lived in the hamlet of Thompson's Creek, in a large two-story house a half mile from the Shofner Church. It was later said that Jenkins "drew larger congregations in his old age than in his youth." In 1859, he helped organize the First Lutheran Church of Nashville. By then, Jenkins was a father of ten and a spiritual father to hundreds if not thousands.

Two years later the United States was at war with itself. Tennessee encapsulated the larger conflagration, and Bedford County reflected it in microcosm. The aptly nicknamed Volunteer State contributed more than 120,000 of its sons to the Confederate States army and another 30,000 to the Union, the latter soldiers hailing mostly from the eastern counties where slave ownership was low. Tennessee saw more battles than any state, bar Virginia. Bedford County, where slaves made up a quarter of the populace, voted for secession, but Shelbyville remained largely loyal. Although Union troops occupied Middle Tennessee from April 1862, attacks by Rebel guerillas persisted. Banditry and vigilanteism, looting and arson, all widespread in the countryside, made daily life even worse. By war's end, much of Tennessee lay devastated. The middle counties, where loyalties were most divided, and where Union occupation and troop movements lasted three long years, had fared worst of all.[10]

How did Jenkins, as a spiritual leader, negotiate a war "when brother fought brother"? Bedford County supplied troops to both armies in roughly equal measure, and his flock enlisted on each side. Family tradition holds that his house was divided, with Jenkins himself favoring the Union. Indeed his pro-Yankee sentiments almost earned him a lynching, from which a gallant Confederate lawyer intervened to save him. His fourth son Daniel also backed the Union. When the 5th Tennessee Cavalry was mustered in Nashville he was quick to join its ranks, and he served until his side emerged victorious. The likeliest source of division was Mary, Jenkins's wife, for the Shofner clan largely sided with the Confederacy. But Jenkins was a moderate. He owned a slave, possibly a housekeeper, as was typical among the well-to-do of Middle Tennessee. Less typical was how, despite possessing a sizeable farm valued at $6,000, he did not also own several field slaves. Local lore holds that, for the sake of harmony among the Lutherans and with his in-laws, Pastor Jenkins declined to preach partiality.[11]

William and Mary had six sons and four daughters, and the family survived the war intact. They had named their youngest child, born in 1852,
John Whitson Jenkins.[12] John would raise a large family of his own, yet he
seems to have inherited neither his father's acumen nor his luck. He tried
farming in Haley, a village just north of Thompson's Creek, but to scant
reward. His misfortune was partly circumstantial: after the Civil War a
thirty-year agricultural boom—the fruit of revived production in the South,
the settling of the Great Plains, and increased mechanization—induced a
decline in commodity prices. Tennessee's yeoman farmers felt the pain as
much as any, and even hard workers lost their farms to creditors.[13] Though
Haley did not grant John prosperity, it did see his start as a family man. In
1875 he married Betty Biddle, a local girl not yet eighteen, and while her
first child died at birth, the second proved robust. This was William Oscar
Jenkins, born on May 18, 1878, and named after his grandfather.

The Reverend William Jenkins did not live to see his youngest produce
an heir, having died the previous fall. His obituary in the local *Sentinel*
spoke of the values of the era as it much as did of the man, and they were
values with which John would raise William Oscar:

> His personal habits were chiefly remarkable for energy and indus-
> try. . . . Idleness to him was a sin. When at home he was constantly
> employed in reading or writing, or attending to the affairs of his
> household. He personally superintended his farming operations
> and took great interest in having things done with neatness. His
> fields and grounds were laid out with mathematical precision. . . .
> He was remarkably temperate in all things, and as a consequence,
> with strict attention to his health and habits, he was enabled to pass
> through a long career of toil and labor. A very pleasing trait in his
> character was his systematic benevolence, for he was one of those
> who religiously believed it to be the sacred duty of a Christian to
> give the tenth of his abundance to the spread of the Gospel, and no
> one ever knew the extent of his charitable donations. The widow,
> the orphan, the poor young preacher, the Church official perhaps in
> a neighboring county, all came in for his share of his Christian sym-
> pathy and aid. Father Jenkins was emphatically a great, as well as a
> good man. He was self-disciplined, self-educated and self-made.[14]

Father Jenkins willed his estate to be divided equally among his children,
so although he was fairly wealthy, his fortune of $16,000 or so would be

split ten ways.[15] In a codicil, he desired that John should have his home, as long as he offered his siblings a fair price; he encouraged them to let John pay in installments. The Reverend must have seen that his youngest needed a hand. So John managed the family farm on behalf of his siblings and sought further income. He ran the private school that his father had set up; by the late 1880s, it was educating sixty-five boys and girls, among them his son William. Six years later he took first place in Bedford County's teacher's examination.[16] But teaching paid poorly, and John had a growing family. He signed up with the Internal Revenue Service as a tax inspector, or "revenuer," becoming deputy collector for Tennessee's Fifth District.[17] It was fortunate that John found new lines of income, for he and Betty had nine children. Seven survived infancy: after William came Percy (known as Jake), Mamie, Katherine, Joseph, Ruth, and Anne.

William was a swift learner. According to family lore, by the time he was four he could read aloud from the Bible at the same pace as his mother.[18] His childhood had the makings of an idyllic one. He lived in a large country house with an orchard behind it. He was an eldest son, with a kindly schoolteacher father and a mother who held his hand in church. John encouraged his interest in books and Betty his love of nature. When classes were over, he played barefoot with his siblings around the school building and splashed with friends and cousins in swimming holes. His father began to teach him the value of work by encouraging him to clear, plant, and tend a watermelon patch; he could keep the produce for himself.

When William was eleven his schooling stopped. He contracted tetanus from a wound. His body was wracked with spasms and fever; his mouth had to be propped open with a piece of wood to enable him to be fed. Children rarely survived tetanus then, but William somehow did. To aid his convalescence, a doctor advised his parents to withdraw him from school. Instead of long hours inside a crowded room, he should have as much fresh air as possible. So they put him to work on the family farm.

William remained an avid reader, devouring any book he could find, but he also warmed to life under the Tennessee sun. He herded cows, he mended fences, he watched the corn and clover grow. He learned to ride a horse and drive a buggy. He scythed hay, threshed wheat, and dug wells, growing to be a muscular teenager. This was a life of sweat. Wheat and melon and milk and poultry gave meager returns for long hours labored. As W. J. Cash said of the Southern yeoman farmer after the Civil War: "he must himself, along with all his sons, set hand to the plow. And whether his status was great or small, he must generally be out of bed before sun-up

... until darkness made further effort impossible."[19] Yet Jenkins sustained a passion for farming.

Nine years passed. For a young man of curious mind, an outdoor life in the remoteness of rural Bedford only satisfied in part. As a keen reader of newspapers, William cannot have failed to register that the United States was roiling with expansive and acquisitive energy. The 1890s were a "reckless decade." A financial panic in 1893 triggered the deepest depression yet, lasting four years, and still, unprecedented fortunes were being made. Captains of industry wielded monopolies and awed the public with their baronial power. The storied might of agriculture, including the millions who worked their own farms, seemed ever more overshadowed by the muscle of industry: coal, steel, and oil. During William's farm-working years, prices for the Tennessee staples of corn, wheat, and oats fell by a third, while the costs of farming rose.[20] By contrast, in 1898, the United States confirmed itself as a global imperial power. It declared war on Spain and occupied Cuba and the Philippines. That was the year in which William Jenkins, at the age of twenty, decided he wanted a high-school education after all.

Mary Street

Feeling self-conscious, William arrived early and took a seat by the window on his first morning at prep school.[21] Enrolling as a junior, he was four years older than most of his classmates, so he knew he would be stared at. He gazed out the window and thought of his mother. He was living away from home for the first time, lodging with strangers in the Lincoln County town of Mulberry, where Mr. Henry Peoples ran his small school. He was more than 20 hilly miles from home, a good three hours by horse and buggy.

The pupils had been taking their seats for some minutes when there was a commotion among the girls. William shifted around to see a young lady ascending the stairway to the classroom floor. Tall and slender, she was dressed all in white, and as she turned to greet her companions he glimpsed a wave of golden-auburn hair tipping down her back. Her oval face was gracefully contoured, with lively blue eyes. Her voice was gentle and kind, her smile sweet and affirming. "What a face!" he thought. Girls flocked around her, and from snatches of conversation he gathered she was an old friend of theirs, separated for some time. She was a week shy of sixteen and her name was Mary Lydia Street.

Mary had spent a year at Sawney Webb's school in Bell Buckle, not far from William's home. The Webb School was famed throughout the South; it may have charged too much for William's father to afford.[22] William soon gathered that Mary was native to Mulberry. He would watch for her each morning, hoping to exchange a smile. If he failed to catch it, he counted the day dull and charmless, though for close to two years he would keep that to himself. Mary was courteous to strangers, and they found they had mutual Webb acquaintances, so they became friends. They developed the custom of walking to school together, discussing their studies and the natural beauty of Lincoln County. He would carry her books. Mary, he soon saw, was exceedingly bright. As he met the challenges of Latin and literature, algebra and Greek, William found in Mary his match. Prep schools encouraged competition, each semester publishing exam results by subject and an overall ranking, and William was competitive by nature. At the end of his first year, despite his long absence from formal education, he placed overall first in exams. Mary, just 1 percent behind, came second.

For all her sociability and prowess, William came to see there was something vulnerable about Mary. The middle child of three, she had been born to John William Street, a fairly well-to-do farmer, and the wealthy Mattie Rees, a descendant of the Lincoln planter elite.[23] When Mary was three, her mother died of tuberculosis. The following year her father remarried, to Mattie's older sister Ann, but three years later he fell to the same infectious disease. Ann Rees Street lovingly raised his children, Hugh, Mary, and Donald, but not for very long. By 1895 she was battling tuberculosis as well, spending months at a time trying to recuperate in Florida. Two years later, she succumbed. It then fell to Mary's uncle, John Rees, and his wife Bettie to foster the children. This meant little hardship: there was family money, and Mr. Rees presided over a bank in Fayetteville, the Lincoln County seat. Mary made close friendships with her cousins, and Annie Rees, one year her senior, became her confidant.

The strain of losing both parents and then a beloved stepmother was not all. By her teenage years Mary found that the dreaded disease was upon her too. When the symptoms first appeared is unclear, but her absence from the Webb School register for 1897–1898 suggests she underwent a sustained attack at fourteen or fifteen. Tuberculosis would haunt her at irregular intervals for the rest of her life.

In June 1899, before leaving for the summer, William gave Mary some favorite books of his, hoping to prompt a correspondence. His plan worked spendidly. For three summers they sent each other ever more frequent letters, nearly two hundred in all. While Mary's letters are lost, William's represent by far the largest group of his personal papers that survive. Begun when he was twenty-one, the letters show through their candor the aspiring young man he was, and they suggest through their ardor the striving industrialist he became.[24]

William answered Mary's first letter with frank appreciation, and by the second his interest in its author was obvious: "To say that I was delighted to received your *very nicest* letter does not express my feelings at all," he began, later admitting he had read it "about a dozen times." They discussed William's hopes of attending Vanderbilt University, and he teased her several times for "the almost unpardonable crime of playing checkers on a Sunday"; she replied she was penitent. William plotted to contrive a visit. He had a summer job at a railroad station, so the first challenge was making the six- or seven-hour round-trip without playing truant, which he was loath to do. The second was keeping up appearances. Unwilling to make his interest plain to all, or to embarrass Mary, he recruited a friend as his call-paying comrade, whom he would pick up in his buggy en route. He made three trips that summer, two on a Sunday and one on a Wednesday that left him creeping into bed at dawn.[25]

The first of these visits inspired William to think of his future in newly bold terms.[26] On the long drive home, he gave his horse free rein and took stock of the past school year. He relayed his musings to Mary: "I am sure it is the most pleasant and the most profitable year I have ever spent. The most profitable, because it has awakened within me a desire to try to make something of myself in the world; the most pleasant because WE have had such great times there together." The one sour note was that Mary's cousin Albert Rees had disapproved of their correspondence.

In September William heard his mother had died. He was in Fayetteville at the time, his school having relocated and merged to become Peoples & Morgan's School. Little is known of the life of Betty Biddle Jenkins, but the news may well have been a shock, for William had made no mention in his letters of her health. She was forty-two and had given birth to Annie only three years before. Arriving home, to mourn and to console his family, William at first had no thought of further study. He expected his father would require him to stay and help his sixteen-year old sister Mamie raise the younger ones. Mary wrote him several letters of condolence, and the experience drew them closer. After two weeks, he requested her photograph and she complied. When, after another week had passed, his father told him he should soon return to school he was overjoyed. Neither bereavement nor a month of missed classes could slow him down, nor indeed could the increase in rivals resulting from the merger of schools. That December, William Jenkins again took first place in exams, and the champion was delighted to learn that second place again went to Mary Street. He called the results "our glorious victory."[27]

DURING HIS RURAL Tennessee upbringing, what might Jenkins have learned of Mexico, the future home that lay far beyond his conceivable horizons? And what might he have learned about his own country? Back at his father's school, like all elementary pupils, he studied using readers and histories suffused with nationalism. They included contrasts of a benign English settlement of North America with Spanish cruelty in Latin America. Most Americans regarded Spain as a degenerate country by European standards, but the prejudice had deeper roots than the scientific racism popular in the 1800s. Three centuries earlier, English and Dutch propagandists created a Protestant narrative of Catholic barbarity, later labeled the Black Legend for its exaggerations and politicized skew regarding the Spanish conquest. Textbooks of Jenkins's day perpetuated it. Said one: "Although the conquerors of Mexico and Peru displayed great courage and ability, these qualities were offset by the meanest deception, the basest treachery, and the most unrelenting cruelty." Geographies spotlighted "national character," always racially defined, with Latin Americans dismissed as cheerful, lazy, and incompetent. Such books attributed their lesser prosperity to racial mixing. One claimed: "These half breeds are an ignorant class."[28]

At Peoples & Morgan, Jenkins did well in history.[29] Almost certainly he studied the Mexican-American War, in which three US armies invaded their western and southern neighbor, one of them seizing Mexico City. It was a war writ large in the nineteenth-century mind, second only to the Civil War. The peace treaty of 1848 had sealed the incorporation of Texas and added new land from Colorado to California, altogether costing Mexico fully half of its territory. A much-reprinted high-school history had this to say of the US victory:

Mexico, the capital of the ancient Aztecs, the seat of the Spanish American empire in America—had passed from Aztec and from Spaniard to the Anglo American—the Northman of the Goths, the Saxon of Germany, the Englishman of America—the same bold, hardy, energetic, ingenious, invincible, ambitious, and adventurous being, whose genius the forms of civilization cannot confine and to whose dominion continents are inadequate. In what hour of time, or limit of space, shall this man of the moderns—this conqueror over land and seas, nations and governments—find rest, in the completion of his mighty progress?

Like all US histories of the day, the book attributed the war to Mexican provocation. It dismissed Mexico's indigenous majority as "effemi-nate."[30] Through grade school and high school, students learned to think of Mexicans as an ineffective people, lorded over by an indolent elite. These people were fated by the inexorable march of progress—that is, by Manifest Destiny—to buckle beneath Anglo-Saxon might whenever the two cultures clashed. If they knew what was best for them, they would welcome US guidance.

Peoples and Morgan likely never questioned American exceptional-ism. Like most teachers of their day, they saw themselves as moral tutors more than educators. Their chief task was to instill the virtues com-monly attached to the economic and political primacy of Anglo-Saxon Protestantism: industry, thrift, rectitude, and faith in God's providence. As well as daily devotionals, Morgan hosted Sunday afternoon lectures, where he or a guest would extol the Christian character or expound on the vices of drinking and smoking, gambling and profanity. At times William was sufficiently impressed to type up summaries to share with Mary. "Level Best Living," by Dr. Ira Landrith of Nashville, advised the following: Be a Christian ("Be a beacon of light on the moral hills to your fellow man"); Be clean; Be big; Be master of something (that is, a skill); Be active; Be healthy; Be yourself. It closed with a final injunction: "Have something to think and think it. Have something to do and do it. Have something to be and be it."[31]

What else Jenkins learned of Mexico he gleaned outside the classroom. Some of it merely rehashed the stereotypes. Consider a gem from the *Shelbyville Gazette*, titled "The Lazy Mexican Bee." This frivolous single paragraph alleged: "The bee of Mexico does not 'improve each shining hour.' As there is very little cold weather there, no necessity exists for laying in winter stores of honey, and the bee is therefore as lazy as a cockroach."[32]

Other articles—and the reminiscences of locals—conveyed wondrous tales of Tennesseans who had traveled to Mexico. The best known was William Walker. Following the Mexican-American War, California entered the Union as a "free state," prompting Southerners to eye farther lands that might be colonized and brought in, like Texas, as slave states. Private initiatives included filibustering expeditions, and Walker was the archetypal filibuster. A man of religious zeal with a knack for self-promotion, he came to be dubbed "the gray-eyed man of destiny." In 1853, Walker sailed to Mexico's Pacific coast and declared Sonora and Baja California independent. Desertions, lack of local support, and opposition from both nations' governments caused him to quit. Two years later he tried again, in Nicaragua, taking advantage of a civil war. Having backed the victor, he managed to get himself elected president, a feat that drew accolades from Southern politicians. There followed stage productions based on his exploits. His rule only lasted a year, and an 1860 attempt to regain the presidency ended in his execution. His fame as a tragic hero persisted in memoirs and narrative poems.[33]

At the end of the Civil War, a thousand or more Confederates who refused to surrender crossed into Mexico, which was then engaged in a war of its own. Napoleon III of France had imposed as emperor an Austrian archduke, Maximilian, with the support of local conservatives, but the regime met armed resistance from liberal leader Benito Juárez. The main Confederate party was a gun-toting force of several hundred under General Jo Shelby; it included four ex-governors and various other generals. Making his way separately was former Tennessee governor Isham Harris. Reaching Mexico City, Shelby offered the emperor their services, but fearing US reprisals, Maximilian turned them down. Instead, he gave the Confederates a half million acres of land in Veracruz, for he was keen to attract immigrants with agricultural expertise. Appointing Harris as their mayor, the veterans planted cotton, cane, and coffee. But a confluence of problems defeated them. The vegetation was dense, the neighbors hostile, and the negative press that the colony drew in the United States hindered the flow of needed recruits. In 1867, when Juárez deposed and executed Maximilian, the game was up. The exiles went home.[34]

Jenkins would also have heard of Tennesseans enticed southward by Porfirio Díaz, the dictator who had been ruling Mexico since 1876. Díaz lured foreign capital into mining and the railroads needed to transport goods for export. Mexico's Uncultivated Lands Law of 1883 offered surveyors one-third of any uncharted land that they surveyed, and some who heeded this call were former Confederate army engineers. All kinds of foreign investors and speculators were drawn.[35] Among them was Henry Cooper, a one-time Shelbyville schoolboy, later a US senator. Rather than seeking re-election, Cooper fixed his attention on northern Mexico, investing in a mine in Chihuahua. On a visit there in 1884 he was murdered by bandits, as his cenotaph in Shelbyville's Old City Cemetery commemorates.[36]

Perhaps the stories of William Walker, Isham Harris, and Henry Cooper served as a corrective, both to schoolroom tales of derring-do in the Mexican-American War and to proliferating reports of Mexican fortune-hunting by the likes of press baron William Randolph Hearst. Americans could not simply march down there and do as they liked. It took a special mix of guts, skill, and providence to succeed.

WILLIAM JENKINS GRADUATED from Peoples & Morgan's School in May 1900. He had completed four years of study in two, he had captained the football team, and he was class valedictorian. So his plans for Vanderbilt University were challenged, as would-be employers sought to snap him up. The previous summer, he had been offered a full-time job by the Nashville & Chattanooga Railroad. Now his commencement address drew the interest of a Shelbyville lawyer, Charles Ivie, who wrote to congratulate his father; he called the speech "the finest I have ever heard from a school-boy." For more than a year Ivie corresponded and met with William, no doubt hoping to recruit him. Later that summer a banker, Andrew Young, invited him to discuss a Bedford County branch he was setting up. Young, who already ran several banks in the state, offered to make him its general manager, if only he would pass up college. He too pursued Jenkins for more than a year.[37] Neither post quite fit the path that William was plotting.

Soon after graduation, William and Mary made their feelings clear.[38] William began his reply to Mary's first letter with unprecedented effusion: "Although last Monday was a gloomy day, though the rain came down as if the very windows of Heaven were opened, though the Sun set behind the western hills veiled in a mantle of threatening clouds, still there was sunshine in *my Heart* and joy in *my Soul*. The very birds seemed to sing more sweetly than was their wont; the flowers were more beautiful to look upon, and all the Landscape took on a brighter fairer aspect. And all this was because I had a *letter from you*."

While Mary's reply is lost, William's next shows she wrote in kind: "Oh, if you could only know the genuine, heart-felt pleasure it brought to me." He spoke of "trembling fingers" and "unspeakable joy." He declared "eternal love" for her. He quoted the pledge she made him, *I will trust you cost me what it may*, and followed with a pledge of his own: "I will never, Heaven being my helper, give you cause to think that your trust is misplaced. I will never deceive you in any way."

Their declarations made, William at once dropped the "Miss" and addressed her simply as Mary; soon she was My Sunshine, My Queen. He signed his letters with his middle name, Oscar (Williams were two-a-penny), and bid her freely use it. She, with ladylike reserve, persisted in addressing him as Mr. Jenkins for another two months. On the few occasions they met that summer, she would consent only, and only in private, to holding his hand. As society expected of a Southern belle, there was to be no kissing. Besides, if she relented, she said, he might love her less.[39]

Vanderbilt beckoned, and as the weeks passed William's determination grew. Many of his Peoples & Morgan chums were bound for the Nashville college, the state's finest, and Mary, despite her uncle's reservations, had hopes of going there too. The offer of two entrance prizes, one in English and Mathematics, the other in Latin and Greek, pricked his competitive nature; he began to study for the former. Above all, the prospect of a college education became bound up with the dream of a life with Mary. She was a girl above his station, he felt, and to prove his worth he needed riches. He was frank in this admission: "I sometimes wish that I was somebody, that I had an abundance of wealth, that I might be more deserving of you; that I might make you a Queen in name as you are The Queen among women."[40]

Love unleashed in William Jenkins a floridity of self-expression. He employed not only the usual superlatives that young lovers use but also literary quotation, Biblical allusion, lyricism of his own, and snatches of French and Latin. Whenever obstacles arose, there were passages of high drama. Reflecting on the previous year and his fear of other suitors, he wrote: "I built castles in the air and in every castle you were my queen. But alas! My jealous imagination would always picture up some dread fantasy, my castles would fall and my hopes would be buried beneath their dismantled ruins."[41]

Yet the foremost villain was no would-be rival—Mary only spoke with other pretenders to be polite—but the scourge of her tuberculosis. Further threats came from Mary's guardian, Uncle John, and her older brother Hugh. To William's consternation, all three reared their heads in the wake of his first visit that summer. Mary wrote to him shortly afterward, revealing she was unwell. She also said her uncle and brother would never consent to their match, unless William . . .—she left the condition hanging, and he assumed they meant that he needed to prove himself worthy.[42] Ever gracious, Mary would draw no connection between her health and her relatives' pressures.

Uncle John and Hugh's opposition persisted.[43] Part of the problem for William was Mary's reticence as to its cause. She once spoke of an "immovable barrier" but would not name it. After he paid her a third visit, Hugh had grown angry, and she would not let him come again. William would later try to rationalize that "her edict" owed to her need for decorum, to protect her name from gossip. But his initial reaction was more revealing: "Will you tell me what people have been saying about me? Do they say that I am a forger or a swindler or a scoundrel? If I had my way, I would pluck the lying tongue from every foul-mouthed gossip in all creation and then honest people could have peace." He went on: "But perhaps the *crime* of which I am accused is that I love you. If so I am the greatest criminal on earth because I know that very few people ever worship anyone or anything as I do you."

He then declared his professional ambition: He wrote: "a business life has a fascination for me that I can scarcely overcome." But this was not an end in itself: "I now want wealth and fame and power that I may lay it all at your feet and make you happy." He concluded: "I am going on believing until I hear the words from your own lips that *you do not love me* and even then *I shall love you still.*" Here was Jenkins in the raw: his aggressive reaction to wounded pride; his elevation of love to the superlative of worship; his goal of success in business, though chiefly as a means to satisfying his queen; the obstinacy of his heart and the strength of his will.

Patience won out. William knew that pressing his case would win him no favor with Uncle John and Hugh. It might well damage Mary's health; he feared her tendency to worry and her susceptibility to headaches. He strained to put her at ease. Meanwhile he could do nothing but work on the farm, study for his exam, and hope and dream of what he and Mary began to label "afterwhile," a time some years off when his prospects were sound and they could be together. Though he did not see her again that summer, his letters regained their humor. He joked about her move with the Reeses from little Mulberry to Fayetteville, a town of two thousand or so: "Do you feel rather important since you have become a *city* belle? I suppose you will not care to recognize your *country* friends when you see them on the streets, standing with mouths gaping, peeping into the shop windows."[44]

Beneath William's renewed composure his resentment of Uncle John and Hugh would fester. He was too proud to voice his suspicions, but he could guess that the root of the problem was class. The prejudice at work was probably mutual, and it had much to do with geography.

Bedford County people prided themselves on being more liberal-minded than those of Lincoln County, whom they regarded as snobbish. Lincoln people often viewed Bedford folk with suspicion, given the number of Shelbyville men that had joined the North during the Civil War. Old enough to remember the viciousness of the war, John Rees may well have heard that one or other of Jenkins's forebears had "turned Yankee." In fact, the counties had much in common. They both numbered among Tennessee's most agriculturally prosperous. Bedford had voted for secession just like Lincoln, and its slave-owning tradition was as strong; a quarter of the population of each was black. Still, there were documented differences. Soon after the war, the Ku Klux Klan was founded in Pulaski, a few miles west of Lincoln County, and many Lincoln men joined its brigades. Their economies differed too: Lincoln had historically hosted larger farms and thus a greater concentration of wealth and slaves in the hands of those who thought themselves Southern gentry. In Bedford, a higher ratio of blacks had been house slaves in middle-class homes, settings more conducive to tolerance between the races.[45]

John Rees and his family certainly fit the gentry mold. The progeny of antebellum planters, they always stood to attention when the band played "Dixie." Their local standing dated back to John "Peg-leg" Whitaker, a veteran of the American Revolution. Around 1800, Whitaker had wandered first to Middle Tennessee, where he founded a plantation and helped establish Lincoln County. On his deathbed, he willed his great fortune and many slaves to be evenly split eleven ways: to his widow and ten children. His eldest son, John J. Whitaker, proved able enough a farmer in his own right that by 1850 his property was worth $12,000 and counted thirty-one slaves. Within another decade, under John's widow Sarah, the estate had more than doubled in value and Sarah held another $23,000 in personal assets. Their daughter Mary married William Harrison Rees, himself a successful farmer, and these were the parents of John, Ann, and Mattie.[46] Peg-leg Whitaker, war hero and prosperous pioneer, was therefore Mary Street's great-great-grandfather, a fact of which she was no doubt frequently reminded.

Yet for all Uncle John's elitism, and despite her own conservative bent, Mary was no snob. William loved her for her beauty, intelligence, and "royal-like" demeanor but also for her cheerful devotion to others and her lack of pretense. He told her: "you are the very least affected person I ever knew. You are the same yesterday, today and forever."[47]

A *Scholar and Athlete at Vanderbilt*

Vanderbilt in 1900 was just twenty-five years old but already reputed as one of the top centers of learning in the South. As college historian Paul Conklin has put it: "Vanderbilt University, like most other American private universities, was born of an unholy marriage of piety and plutocracy." Chartered by Methodist bishops, it took its name following the gift of a million dollars from an elderly Cornelius Vanderbilt, the New York shipping and railroad titan. It so became one of various universities whose late nineteenth-century origins and ethos were tied to lordly multimillionaires and the spirit of Protestant industrial capitalism. The list included the University of Chicago, backed by oil magnate J. D. Rockefeller; Stanford University, brainchild of railroad baron Leland Stanford; and the Carnegie Technical Schools, founded by steel mogul Andrew Carnegie. Owing to their reportedly dubious approach to business—little bridled by scruple toward rivals or employees and little regulated by their friends in Congress—such men were branded robber barons. But in 1900 they inspired awe in most quarters, including on the campuses they had endowed.[48]

"I do not think that there is any other quality so essential to success of any kind as the quality of perseverance," declared Rockefeller at the time.[49] When self-made old men like Rockefeller issued opinions, young go-getters like Jenkins took note.

Perseverance might also have been the motto of James Kirkland, who set the career-oriented tone for the campus Jenkins entered. By 1900, Kirkland had served seven years as Vanderbilt's chancellor, out of an eventual forty-four. Raised in genteel poverty, he had shown himself prodigious and driven. Named chancellor at thirty-three, he took over an institution that was failing to match its founders' dreams of an elite university; lack of funds was one obstacle, the bishops' conservatism another. So with his respect for academic endeavor and his no-nonsense approach to management, Kirkland forced improvements. He cultivated a cadre of young humanities professors, keen to make their mark. He persuaded a Vanderbilt heir to bankroll the first purpose-built dorm, Kissam Hall, and he oversaw the regular admission of women. He also plotted what would prove a lengthy struggle for autonomy from the Methodist Church, to facilitate funding from Northern philanthropists. Still finding time to teach Latin, Kirkland was popular with Vanderbilt's 750 students. His salient qualities—quickness of intellect and action, fondness for power and influence, neither suffering fools nor given to flattery—would find echo in the future William Jenkins. In letters the following summer, William would refer to the chancellor by the fond nickname "old Chance."[50]

In Tennessee, a progressive institution such as Vanderbilt held great significance, for it matched the aims of the New South Democrats. These were business and political elites who attached the state's prospects for postwar revival to commerce and industry; they welcomed Yankee investment. Their vision contrasted with the devotion to agriculture, especially cotton, favored by the Bourbon Democrats, who represented the still-powerful planter class. Among Vanderbilt's vocational schools—and in contrast to many colleges founded in the late 1800s—agriculture was absent. "They saw themselves as an elite," writes Conklin of the student body, "the future leaders and shapers of a new South."[51]

Vanderbilt was well located for the new professional purposes. Since the war, Nashville had quadrupled in size to 80,000. It hosted a diverse economy: iron foundries and manufacturing plants as well as cotton mills, flour mills, and lumber yards. By the time Jenkins arrived on the campus, two miles from the city center, Nashville boasted fashionable apartment buildings and its first department store. It was also home to appalling ghettoes, with names like Hell's Half Acre and Black Bottom. Their emergence had helped prompt an incipient white flight, to multiplying suburbs served by electric streetcars. While some of Nashville's old-family whites still revered the Lost Cause of the Confederacy, the city was amenable to ambitious new arrivals. A boosterish local press loved to profile business leaders who had risen, Horatio Alger–style, from humble beginnings. These lives "tended to fit predictable formulae wherein wealth and prestige were the well-deserved rewards of personal virtues: industry, innovation, moral self-discipline"—the same values that Peoples and Morgan had taught.[52] This was a place where young men from small towns could build big dreams.

Jenkins could barely afford Vanderbilt, even with the special rate charged to sons of schoolmasters. Without letting on much to Mary, he cobbled together the fees and expenses through summer jobs, loans, and work during the semester. Then there was the prospect of the entrance prize in English and Mathematics. After three months of long evenings studying for it, Jenkins took the exam and won. The $50 prize went some way to defraying his first-year costs.[53]

He arrived on campus a week early, both to take the exam and to try out for the gridiron team. At practice on Dudley Field he mixed with fellow freshmen, and several became long-term friends. One was Frank

Houston, an eventual president of Chemical National Bank. Together they joined Sigma Alpha Epsilon, a fraternity with a proudly Southern identity that was also home to Mary's cousins Ernest and Albert Rees. William had mixed feelings about his fraternity brothers; joining ΣAE was perhaps a bid to rise in Uncle John's esteem. A second friend was John Tigert, who had attended the Webb School, where he knew Mary. Tigert was Vanderbilt royalty, being the son of a faculty member, grandson of its first Board of Trust president, and a relative of the Vanderbilt family. He would go on to be president of the University of Florida. He shared with William an equal passion for academics and athletics, and both of them ran with the track team. It was Tigert who won the entrance prize in Latin and Greek, and in seeking him out to congratulate him on his parallel victory, Jenkins sealed their friendship.[54]

Another early friend was Mexican, probably the first Mexican that Jenkins ever met. He told Mary that he found him very amusing. His name is not mentioned, but the student body that year included two from Mexico.[55] Since there were evidently Mexican families wealthy enough to send their sons to a private US university, and since these students' English was good enough for them to attend, Jenkins surely found himself modifying the negative impression he had garnered of Mexicans from history books and newspapers.

Capping William's delight at the new environment, Mary enrolled after all. One of just ten women in the sixty-strong arts and sciences class, she made an immediate impression as a very bright student, and she would bring her social skills to bear as the freshman class secretary.[56] The fact that her cousin Albert Rees was also enrolling must have softened Uncle John's reservations: his son could keep an eye on her.

During his first year at Vanderbilt, Jenkins continued to exhibit the stamina he had shown at Peoples & Morgan. Gaining greatest note were his athletic exploits, for gridiron games were already the university's most popular social events.[57] Aged twenty-two, he made the starting eleven as left tackle, earning the nickname "Bull" Jenkins. The first half of the season passed largely without merit and included a hammering by the University of Texas. Come November, the squad was grinding out impressive scores, often thanks to touchdowns by Jenkins. The Nashville press gave gleeful coverage, and Mary made clippings. In a victory over Central University of Kentucky: "Jenkins . . . a giant in strength, bucked the line to a standstill and made some of the most telling plays of the game." During a scrap with in-state rivals Sewanee, Jenkins pulled off the star turn: "With no less than half a dozen men tugging at him and hanging to his feet and body, he carried the ball and dragged the men for thirty yards amid the uproar of the spectators."

The last game was the backyard brawl against the University of Nashville. The rivalry had caused a riot four years earlier, and six thousand spectators came to witness the 1900 match-up. The city's leisured and professional classes arrived in carriages that spoke of fine social distinctions: high carts, open traps, landaus, surreys, drags and hacks, Brewsters and Victorias. They all lined up along the east side of Dudley Field, while "the working element" gathered opposite. Vanderbilt crushed its opponent 18 to 5. "The much-vaunted stone-wall line of Nashville went to pieces before the heavy rush of the Vanderbilts," declared the *Nashville American*, adding that Jenkins scored the season's final touchdown.

Academically, Jenkins also stood out. Despite his genius for figures, his love of literature and languages led him to choose the Arts program. For a BA, freshmen took Latin, Greek, English, French, and mathematics, and he excelled in all subjects. Decades later John Tigert would recall: "He was the brightest student I knew at Vanderbilt. His grades were all 100, 99 or 98." Making that performance all the greater was the length of his days, for he got up at five each morning to do menial chores for extra cash.[58]

After the excitements of the fall and the daily pleasures of seeing Mary, William found the Christmas break dull. Mary, fearful of angering Uncle John and Hugh, forbade him to visit. William wrote: "I must have my Sunshine. Without it I am dwarfed and incomplete." When Mary responded with assurances of her trust and love, he replied with words that were becoming a mantra: "I want to work for you, to make you happy, to do something to prove my Love. Why, Sweetheart, work will not be *work* but will be *play*, when it is done for you." He added: "I will drive away those dreadful old headaches."[59]

Spring at Vanderbilt, without football, brought a lighter schedule, and William began extra classes under his own steam. So great was his desire for "afterwhile" with Mary, he planned to rush through college in three years. Pursuing this scheme over the summer vacation, he took home textbooks in French and Latin with the aim of finishing those subjects through special exams in July. He hoped to skip his sophomore year.[60]

Summer, however, brought a return of the old frustrations: the shadow of Uncle John and the specter of tuberculosis. Again they loomed in unison, as her guardian's displeasure at their friendship caused Mary distress and an increase in her debilitating headaches. Still, William and Mary had allies. Though he seldom opened up to people other than Mary, William found confidants in his father and his sister Mamie. He also drew support from a Mrs. Stone of Fayetteville, with whom he had lodged while at Peoples & Morgan. Styling herself his "Make believe Mother," she addressed William as "My dear Cyclone." She encouraged him to control his jealousy at the attention Mary drew from would-be suitors. John Rees had been encouraging more socially acceptable men to take an interest in his niece.[61]

Mary's great confederate was her cousin Annie Rees. Since regular receipt of mail might draw the suspicion of Uncle John, Annie agreed to be an alternate addressee. This was one of various ruses: William concocted a fictional friend called Saidee, in whose name he sometimes wrote; he would have others address the envelopes, to disguise his hand; and Mary rented a Fayetteville post office box, to which she paid surreptitious visits. When Mary was too ill to write, Cousin Annie would keep William informed.[62]

William's correspondence was unrelenting. He had written twenty-five letters the previous summer; this vacation he wrote sixty. He also made telephone calls, though these were not daily, for the nearest telephone to the Jenkins home was in a village a mile away.[63] Letters composed on a Sunday stretched to several thousand words; sometimes he skipped church to write at extra length, preferring to worship at the altar of Mary. He was effusive in his declarations, ardent in his protests, frequently lyrical, and often funny.

William's days were taken up with farm work, and he was not above poking fun at his labors. Once he wrote of his milking a "deceitful" cow. Having congratulated himself on his ploy of giving the animal something to eat while he milked, he came a-cropper when she finished her meal. Upset that he was still squeezing, she gave a violent kick that pitched the pail over him, drenching him with the contents. Another day he wrote a letter while helping lay a country road, scribbling during ten-minute breaks between shoveling gravel into wagons. The day was hot and mosquitoes were out in force:

> I can hardly write for the "skeeters" . . . I have killed about ten since I began to write a few minutes ago, but for every one I kill, I think that about 50 must come to bury him. There! I smashed one then that they will never bury unless they pick up his scattered remains from afar. If you get a copy of tomorrow's "Mosquito Herald" you will doubtless find an obituary notice with a headline like

this: "Foully murdered! Sharp-Tooth, the great Mosquito Warrior, was foully slain yesterday while peacefully eating his morning meal of man's blood!"[64]

Occasionally a bitter note crept into his humor. He had a delicate sense of justice, and he kept score when wronged. He once told of his boyhood efforts with watermelons, which he took great pride in cultivating. As the fruit ripened, they mysteriously disappeared from the vine. When all the watermelons were gone, a pal of his confessed to the crime, thinking it a great joke. "I laughed with him at his glowing description of how good and sweet they were," he wrote. "But way down deep in my heart I vowed vengeance." This summer, that same friend was tending a watermelon patch of his own, and William was merrily pilfering a couple each day. He gloated: "Yesterday I heard him complaining about somebody stealing them, and when they are all gone, I am going to tell him who the guilty party is and remind him of that other melon patch when we were boys. Don't you think that is funny?"[65]

William and Mary met on many levels: mutual admiration, mutual friends, love of nature, love of literature. William seasoned his prose with Tennyson and Shakespeare and allusions to Roman myth and so, as far as can be inferred, did she. He passed along books to her, putting special emphasis on Mrs. Craik's *John Halifax, Gentleman*, in which he had marked some passages. A mid-Victorian bestseller, the novel told of an English orphan who through hard work and honesty grew to be a wealthy textile industrialist. Jenkins's literary hero quite embodied what Max Weber would soon term "the Protestant work ethic."[66]

As Mary approached nineteen, William's letters showed a deeper appreciation of her character. He still addressed her as his Sunshine and his Queen, he still admired her beauty and kindness, but he also spoke of her spirited nature: an independent mind, an imperious demeanor, a sometimes sharp or sarcastic tongue, and firm convictions. Counseling her on her medicines, he noted: "I feel funny posing as a *lecturer*. I usually am the *lectured*." He disliked the popular novel *Alice of Old Vincennes* for its "masculine heroine," but he believed in the worth of a woman's education and a woman's opinion. He did not want a submissive wife; he wanted a companion who would keep him professionally keen and intellectually stimulated.[67]

Tensions over Uncle John aside, for William there was only one thorny point: Mary's attitude to black folk. She did not care for the company of blacks, unless they were there to serve her, and to treat them as equals strained her imagination. Mary inherited all the prejudices common to her class, revering a semi-mythic Old South of prosperous farms and slaves who knew their place. Whereas William's favorite song was "Annie Laurie," a Scottish lament that relates a man's love for a woman whose father opposed their marriage, Mary's was "Old Folks at Home," a Stephen Foster minstrel song in which a slave pines for his former plantation. "All de world am sad and dreary," goes the chorus, "Eb-rywhere I roam; Oh, darkeys, how my heart grows weary, Far from de old folks at home."[68]

Avoiding confrontation, William worked by stealth. He told Mary he had begun to study black speech and song, and he was finding "beautiful sentiments." He quoted a chorus of theirs—"I am longing for the day to come, When the preacher shall make us one"—and said that every time he heard it his heart would beat in unison. Sometimes he used their slang: "don't you mak no goo-goo eyes," "dem watermillions smilin on de vine." After hearing a black farm worker talk of his girl, he addressed Mary as "Sugar Babe." With humor, he hoped to cultivate in Mary a greater sympathy.[69]

July presented him with a "climax to his studies." A nineteen-year-old black employee of his family had gone back on a promise to wed a girl, and her father had reacted (perhaps because she was pregnant) by having the man arrested. William ventured to visit the offender in the county jail. When the young man admitted his deception, William persuaded him to go through with the wedding and then paid his bond. Anticipating this outcome, he had already told the young woman to come to town, and so at once he took them to be married. At the ceremony, he noted, "the chocolate Juliet ... blushed very becomingly," while "her Romeo ... looked happy as a king, though a little nervous." He concluded in triumph: "And so I have been instrumental in making two more souls happy!"[70]

Or so he assumed. He had, of course, acted like he knew best. He did not regard blacks as equals. However, he lived amid the post-Reconstruction culture of Jim Crow: like the South in general, Tennessee laws had consigned blacks to second-class railroad carriages, given innkeepers right of refusal, banned interracial marriage, and effectively kept blacks from voting. In 1896, the Supreme Court put its federal stamp of approval on segregation when it upheld a state's right to mandate railroad cars that were "separate but equal," a principle it soon extended to schools.[71] By the standards of the day, the interest of this Vanderbilt man in the welfare of a poor black couple and the happiness with which he conveyed it seem quite unusual.

William took the measure of his charm offensive at the Shofner Family Reunion. This was a five-day event of camping and activities, to which were invited all the descendants of the pioneer Martin Shofner along with their friends. For weeks, William had pestered Mary to attend, and finally she did so for a day, along with Annie Rees and another cousin. Knowing that Bedford folk, including his father, considered Lincoln people uppity, William had wondered what impression she would make. In his next letter his relief and joy were palpable: "It seems you have captured the county," he crowed, adding the same could not be said for her cousins. Among the Jenkins crowd was Aunt Louisiana, a former slave who had stayed a family friend. "When you went up and shook hands with Aunt Louisiana yesterday afternoon, it captured the crowd. ... That little touch of [your] character fixed Daddy. He said that you were a most excellent young lady."

The next day he conveyed Aunt Louisiana's impression: "She said to me: 'Dat gal ain't none of yo stuck up kind. Dat gal's got sense, she has. She ain't ashamed to speak to a poor old nigger woman before the whole crowd. Dem other gals ain't like her. See here, boy, yo had better take dat gal if you kin git her. She's as purty as a picter and she's got sense, she has.' I assured Aunt Lou that I was doing my best to 'git her.' And then she laughed and said 'It shorely do look it, the way you wuz a stickin to her that day.'" Clearly, Mary could put grace before prejudice. But whether she could happily live among folk of a darker hue remained to be seen.[72]

For Mary too there was an issue. She always held William to high standards, but all the more so concerning alcohol; she sided with those who held the proper place for "liquor" was in a sentence with "evils of." The Jenkins family, despite their Lutheranism, and though a national temperance movement was gathering force, were no prohibitionists. John Jenkins's second job as a revenuer meant that during school vacations he would ride with a posse into the hill country to track down moonshiners. He had a reputation for honesty, which in this line of work did not always make for popularity; that summer two of his team were shot. But honesty did earn him the friendship of licensed producers. One of these, 12 miles to the south in Lynchburg, was a successful distiller by the name of Jack Daniel.

Daniel, fifty-two and a bachelor, informed John Jenkins of his need for a smart and energetic young man to manage his Old Time Distillery. John thought of his eldest son. In talks about his prospects, he had told William that while he would rather he pursue a "profession," he was more cut out for business. Certainly his son could make more money that way, and John felt that he filled Jack Daniel's bill. William was sorely tempted: the job paid $1,800 per year, with good prospects for a raise; such a salary would hasten the arrival of "afterwhile." Yet he was loath to quit Vanderbilt while Mary carried on, outgrowing him in intellectual maturity, and he knew she would disapprove of the trade. Without divulging its nature, William sounded Mary out on the basic principle of his entering business. When she replied with approval, he told her all about Jack Daniel, packaging the news with caveats about his distaste for the business and desire to continue at college, while repeating his "impatience and anxiety for 'afterwhile.'" [73]

Mary shot down his trial balloon with a Gatling gun. She would rather die than marry a man in the liquor business! She expressed such disappointment and disgust that William, audibly shocked, devoted much of his reply to how hurt he felt. He despaired at her "misunderstanding." He claimed to find Jack Daniel's business despicable. He said he admired her firmness. And yet he revealed a striking capacity for rationalizing in the face of ethical compromise: "The manager of this business," he argued, "is no more directly connected with the whiskey business than every farmer in the county who sells corn to make whiskey, nor my Father who collects the revenue on it. His duty is merely to buy corn, stocks, etc., keep books, and keep a general supervision over the many employees of the place."

On one thing they did agree: she too was impatient for "afterwhile." She sometimes despaired of its arrival. Fuelling her distress was a downturn in her health. She thought she might need to rest for a year, rather than return to Vanderbilt. Not for the first time, her illness elicited a bout of self-loathing. She told William she was not good enough for him. [74]

The problem was graver than William suspected. It gave Uncle John a pretext to insist on their separation. All summer long, Mary's guardian loomed over their relationship. When Mary expressed fear of a reprimand over his first visit, William bristled: "Now who am I that I should be looked on and cussed out as if I were a common thief?" He admitted that his father, on learning of the Reeses' objections, had assumed they concerned his social standing and issued a torrent of "dreadful advice." They skirted the theme for a month, until a phone call of William's, inquiring as to her health, prompted Hugh to lecture his sister on this farm boy's unsuitability. He even warned her about his probable interest in Uncle John's estate.

William seethed. Their allegations were "idiotic." If Uncle John thought the Jenkins family not good enough for his, "Father might be glad to discuss that with him." He wished he could take Mary away at once, so "we would never see them again as long as we lived." He offered to drop out of Vanderbilt and start earning a living, the sooner to marry her. He added: "I have always been anxious to pacify and appease them. I don't care any longer. I am just as good as either of them and would be delighted to prove it to them in any way."

Once Mary felt better, he wanted to meet her for a "genuine business talk." He added: "Let the old people raise the war cry if they want to. They are only bluffing. I'll make the last one of them glad some day that they are related to *us*."[75]

Their next rendezvous took place in August, just before the Shofner Reunion. Whatever was said that day, William grew bolder. He wrote to Mary at home, rather than at her post office box. He said he would marry her as soon as he graduated if she would consent, but if she wished for him to be better established he would be willing to toil for years, as the Biblical patriarch Jacob had done for Rachel. Providing for Mary materially was ever a concern: "I would like to carry you to a home like the one you have been accustomed to."[76]

During the week before his return to Nashville, William made two visits. The first was to the banker Andrew Young, still angling for Jenkins to join him. Young again promised him a job, whether or not he pursued his degree, and offered to lend him money if he did. The second visit was to Fayetteville, for some preseason coaching of the Peoples & Morgan football team. It was a pretext for seeing Mary. Her health had taken another turn, and just before his arrival she wrote that she did not care if she died. She was frail and bed-ridden, and his leave-taking on September 13 was their saddest farewell yet. "I love you more than I ever loved you in my life," he wrote on the train back home. "My heart is torn to pieces."[77]

Back at Vanderbilt, things were not going as planned. William had hoped to cross off three classes that summer, but the absence of his French teacher precluded an exam and an economics professor declined to accommodate, so despite passing his Latin exam he returned as a sophomore after all.[78]

The day after his return, William received the surprising news from Mary that Uncle John was "coming round" to the idea of their relationship. In his delight, William launched upon a eulogy of "the great old fellow," praising his "firm manhood, his integrity and Christian character." [79] There was no apparent irony in his lines. If Uncle John had aimed to instill a false sense of security, he seemed to have hit his mark.

It is there that the known correspondence ends. A final letter, in an envelope postmarked September 24, is lost. What happened next must be pieced together from a brief newspaper item and the late-in-life reminiscences of friends and family.

One evening over dinner at Kissam Hall, William approached his fraternity pal Frank Houston and told him he needed to have a word. As they walked across campus to the ΣAE House, William put his arm round Frank's shoulder and unburdened himself: he was going to quit Vanderbilt, marry Mary Street, and take her West. Doctors had determined that what would best suit Mary, for relief of her tuberculosis, was the dry climate of Texas. John Rees told her he would send her to San Antonio, and when Mary relayed the news to William, he knew that her uncle's motives were more than medicinal. His reply was unwavering: "If you have to go to San Antonio, I will take you there."

Frank asked what they were going to do for money. William replied that between them they had enough to make a new start. His sister Kate would later recall that the lawyer Charles Ivie lent him $300, and he may also have obtained a sophomore-year loan from the banker Andrew Young; certainly, for several years afterward, Jenkins was repaying debts incurred in Tennessee. Whatever the exact sum, they had more than enough to cover the 1,000-mile train ride to San Antonio and to rent accommodation when they got there.[80]

Secrecy was paramount. William and Mary likely spoke by telephone, using Cousin Annie as a go-between when necessary. The postmark on the envelope dated September 24 suggests that William briefly returned home, for a paternal blessing and farewells with his siblings. Fortunately for William, he had friends in Nashville he could trust for help with arrangements. Houston and Tigert were two of them, and his next-oldest brother Jake had just moved there to attend business school.[81] The Reeses decided that Hugh would accompany Mary on the trip to Texas. Since the semester at Vanderbilt was underway, Mary pleaded with Uncle John to let her return to Nashville and bid her friends goodbye. Hugh would catch up with her in a few days. Meanwhile William kept up appearances, attending football training and taking up his studies. On the morning of Thursday September 26, William was elected president of the sophomore class, and in the afternoon he was back at football practice.

Early that evening William slipped from his dorm. He hopped on a streetcar going downtown, headed for the McKendree Church. McKendree was Nashville's home of Methodism, Mary's faith tradition. He knocked on the door of the parsonage, where the Rev. John Mathews awaited him. There in the parsonage at 7 PM, with a Presbyterian minister as a witness, the Reverend Matthews pronounced William and Mary man and wife.

The next evening's *Nashville Banner* made public this "culmination of a very pretty romance." It praised "the doughty champion of the gridiron and his pretty sweetheart" and detailed how they had given Hugh the slip. The article concluded: "Everything was most methodically arranged, and before Kissam Hall and the 'Row' were ringing with news of the affair, 'Jenks' and his bride were rolling on their way to San Antonio. The affair is a great surprise to the students, and the main regret is that the football team is weakened so materially by the absence of Jenkins."[82]

Gone to Texas

"Tennessee is the mother of Texas," it is often said, at least among Tennesseans. By 1901, a tradition stretching some eighty years had seen people of the Volunteer State migrating to the Lone Star State or its predecessor as a Mexican territory. Sam Houston—who served as governor of both places—and Davy Crockett famously numbered among them. Of Crockett's fellow defenders at the Battle of the Alamo, the dead included more Tennesseans than men of any other birthplace. The flow continued after the Civil War. However lush the farmland of Bedford and neighboring counties, there were locals among the migrants. The average farmer sired three or four male heirs, and, while some sons headed to the cities, for those that remained there was often insufficient land to divide as standalone properties, especially with crop prices in decline. One day in 1870, no fewer than fifteen covered wagons from Bedford and Lincoln united and moved out in convoy to Texas.[83]

For migrants drawn to city life, San Antonio beckoned as a bustling metropolis. Though just two-thirds the size of Nashville, it was growing much faster. The largest city in Texas, it was thriving as a commercial hub for the border region and the Southwest, with markets for cattle and wool and supply stores for farmers and westward migrants. It hosted a military complex—Teddy Roosevelt's Rough Riders had mustered there in 1898— and railroads headed in six directions. It was more diverse than Nashville, a mix of native Tejanos and Mexican immigrants making Spanish common; German also was widely spoken. Why John Rees had picked San Antonio may well have had to do with family; various Whitakers and Reeses had moved from Tennessee to Texas, and a Street cousin lived outside the city. San Antonio also offered sanatoriums for well-off tuberculosis patients.[84]

The young couple's triumph at outwitting Uncle John and Hugh, their joy at having begun "afterwhile" far sooner than either had imagined, must have come at quite an emotional cost. Mary surely wrestled with a guilty conscience. John and Bettie had been her guardians for eleven years, and she had eloped. They were pillars of society, and she had caused a scandal.

William no doubt felt some unease of his own. He and his widowed father, now forty-eight, had drawn closer through their late-night discussions. John Jenkins's risky work tracking moonshiners caused his son to fret. "There are two people on the Earth to whom if anything should happen I could not bear it," he had told Mary that summer. "If anything should happen to my Daddy I would not care to live unless you were here."[85] William had surely considered staying in Tennessee, but the option was not realistic. Mary's health had been so delicate of late, he could hardly ignore the doctor's advice of a move to drier climes. Besides, Vanderbilt prohibited marriage between students.[86] Here too was a cause of unease: he had insisted for so long on the importance of his education. Now he had sacrificed it. But in what would emerge as a lifelong trait, William rarely looked over his shoulder. There was a future to make with Mary and a fortune to forge.

William found a job at a boys' school, teaching Latin and helping coach football. He supplemented his income by working as a ticket agent, also ill-paid, on the rail line to Laredo. Since many of the passengers were Mexican, he made his job easier by picking up some Spanish. He was a quick learner; a Vanderbilt professor, impressed with his ability, had encouraged him to specialize in languages if he ever became a teacher, and his fluency in French and Latin gave him a wide vocabulary of cognates and a sense of Spanish grammar. As he conversed with the Mexicans, he found that many were miners. There was a lot of work in Mexico's mining camps, and some of it paid better than the pittance he made teaching Pliny and stamping tickets.[87]

After the newlyweds had spent ten weeks in Texas, the chance arose for a trip to Monterrey.[88] Mary's health had evidently improved, and given William's employment on the railroad the passage would be cheap. He planned the visit as a treat for her. San Antonians regularly traveled to Mexico's northern metropolis, so he must often have heard that the city—founded in 1596 and now a hive of industry—was worth visiting. The

300-mile journey took the better part of a day, but crossing the border was easy, with no passports required.

What drew William and Mary to Mexico was the Virgin of Guadalupe. On the 12th of December each year the country celebrated the legendary apparition of a dark-hued Virgin Mary to an indigenous peasant near Mexico City, an episode said to have occurred in 1531, ten years after the Spanish conquest. In honor of the country's patron saint, a national holiday arose. Churches were decorated and special masses sung.[89] In 1901 the 12th fell on a Thursday, so the Jenkins decided to spend a long weekend seeing the Monterrey sights.

Is the coincidence ironic or poetic that William Jenkins first set foot in Mexico on the Day of Guadalupe, a date stamped into its peoples' psyche as emblematic of Mexican identity? It might imply a foreshadowing of the imperialism with which he would later be charged. Or perhaps in some symbolic fashion it suggests that this admirer of business moguls, this son of the segregated South, possessed a cultural affinity with that semifeudal and racially divided country and an intuitive sense of its opportunities.

In Monterrey, a casual conversation with an Englishman changed Jenkins's life. The man was a manager for a US railroad company. Several of these operated in northern Mexico, their proliferating networks linking the country's mines, cattle ranches, and plantations to markets in the United States. The Englishman convinced Jenkins that this was a land of opportunity. Not just the railroads but many of the mines, the banks, the public utilities, and the nascent oil fields relied on foreign capital, and their owners preferred to entrust all levels of management to their own kind. In Monterrey alone there lived hundreds of foreigners. Industry and commerce made the city the Chicago of Mexico.[90]

In fact, Mexico as a whole was open for business. Its "liberal" economic policies, renouncing the protectionism of its early decades as a nation, enticed foreigners and their cash, as did a hard-won political stability under President Díaz. Using the model of export-led growth, these policies linked the country's development to a globalizing world. Exports, from silver to vanilla, earned the dollars and pounds needed to import foundry machinery from Pittsburgh and power looms from Manchester. The trend was welcome in the United States, whose economy was growing more slowly than its neighbor's. As of 1880, labor unrest, rising costs, declining consumption, and recurrent depressions altogether caused a long decline in rates of profit for industry. Capital sought better returns abroad. Most often the first port of call was Mexico.

Bankers such as J. P. Morgan and James Stillman paved the way, building links with the Mexican state and helping direct investment. Other famous names—the Guggenheims, the Hearsts, William Cargill, Collis Huntington, and Edward Doheny—bought copper mines, cattle ranches, and pine forests, laid railroads, and leased oil fields. Thousands of settlers, including Mormons, sought a fresh start with south-of-the-border farms. By 1900, half of all US foreign investment lay in Mexican enterprises and some 30,000 Americans called Mexico home. As their enclaves grew, they offered home comforts to new arrivals: English-language newspapers, race-courses, and bars. On Sunday mornings US expatriates attended Methodist or Presbyterian churches, and on Sunday afternoons they played or watched baseball.[91]

The Englishman offered Jenkins a job. The pay was not much better than what he earned in San Antonio, indeed it may have been worse, but the prospects for advancement seemed excellent. Presumably after conferral with Mary, he accepted. And so, at the dawn of what would come to be called the American Century, William Jenkins cast his lot with Mexico. He would never again live in the United States.

2

Fortune-Seeking in Mexico

*Mexicans of all classes and affiliations agree that their
country is on the verge of a revolution. . . .*
JOHN KENNETH TURNER, "Slaves of Yucatan" (1909)

Monterrey, 1901

If Mexico were Canaan to many US expatriates, it was Babylon for its
white elite and Gehenna for most of its dark-skinned majority. The country was in the middle of a three-decade stretch of stability and growth, an
era unprecedented since independence was won in 1821. In fact, Mexico
seemed a good deal more stable than its northern neighbor; since the end
of civil wars in both countries, in the mid-1860s, Mexico had seen just four
presidents and one military coup. The United States had experienced ten
presidents, three recessions, and three presidential assassinations, including the murder of William McKinley just before the Jenkinses eloped.
However, Mexico's elite ensured that the fruits of prosperity fell mainly to
the few: the already-wealthy or the politically ascendant, along with those
foreigners able to sidle up to them.[1]

Making that prosperity happen, through their labor as miners and millhands, railroad workers and plantation peons, were the *mestizo* (mixed-
race) and indigenous millions. While a small fraction parlayed their skills
into a decent salary and middle-class status, the vast majority led lives typified by stagnant wages, a rising cost of living, de facto segregation, and,
for an untold number of country folk, the loss of ancient communal lands.
Where the arrival of a railroad made farming for export profitable, landlords would saddle small farmers with predatory loans. Venal judges then
granted foreclosures, and the farmers, whether shunned by new masters
who wanted loyal workers or embittered by their loss, often left for work
elsewhere. For many, a transient life ensued, between plantations, mining
camps, and the filthy slums of the fast-expanding cities. The five thousand

or so who poured into the capital each year found twelve-hour shifts at factories; jobs as live-in domestics with the attendant threat of rape; or, for as many as a fifth of poor young women, prostitution. Meanwhile, the landlords who had cheated them hired new hands, whom they often shackled with company-store debts. Absconders were dragged back by the police. In the far southeast, indebted peons were bought and sold like slaves.

Assuring most of the elites that all this was fair were the prevailing philosophies of positivism and social Darwinism. Imported from France, positivism held that societies worked best when governed on scientific and utilitarian grounds, hence its senior Mexican advocates came to be called *científicos*. Modernization was the mantra, even when it meant ignoring civil liberties and leaving some people behind. Its chief apostle, Auguste Comte, summarized his prescription: "Love as the principle; order as the basis; progress as the end." (The authoritarian governments his teachings inspired, from Mexico to Brazil, downplayed the bit about love.) Imported from England, social Darwinism argued that elites occur naturally. It favored government that was laissez-faire except in its aiding of industrialization. Its senior prophet, Herbert Spencer, wrote: "The intellectual traits of the uncivilized . . . are traits recurring in the children of the civilized." He coined the phrase "the survival of the fittest" and applied it to social classes and entire societies. Some kinds of both were doomed to extinction.[2]

Jenkins would have recognized such thinking. Spencer was very popular in the United States. A Spencer devotee at Yale, William Graham Sumner, had famously answered the title of his tract *What Social Classes Owe to Each Other* with "nothing." He added: "A drunkard in the gutter is just where he ought to be." Most of the robber barons, born to poor or nearly-poor families, chose to ignore such rigidly Darwinian advice. They pursued philanthropy and founded colleges and public libraries with systematic vigor. But most of the Mexican business elite, thinking themselves the crest of a white minority amid a sea of brown faces, found Comte and Spencer to their liking. Their self-regard made for ostentatious homes, Francophile social clubs, and marriage within cliques, sometimes between cousins. Their giving, often driven by conspicuous piety and prestige, tended toward piecemeal donations to orphanages and the Catholic Church. Their unwillingness to educate their darker compatriots, whether via donations or taxes, helped keep four out of five Mexicans illiterate. They looked down from their horse-drawn carriages, driven by chauffeurs in English livery, and referred to the sandaled, straw-hatted poor as *léperos* (guttersnipes). At times they had them arrested for smelling badly.[3]

Jenkins would not, however, have recognized Mexico's political system. Its social classes all seemed to revolve around a Sun King. Porfirio Díaz was lord and master of Mexico, a position he had held with a tightening grip since seizing the presidency in an 1876 revolt. Having earned his fame as a general in the 1860s, when the French invaded and the Mexicans eventually threw them out, Díaz belonged to the tradition of the *caudillo*. This was the officer-turned-politician, whose popularity rested on victorious battles and whose power rested more on coercion and patronage than on fair elections. To Jenkins, the concept was not completely foreign. He would have heard at school how Andrew Jackson, hero of the War of 1812, benefitted from a battle-hardened aura in his campaign for the presidency, and everyone knew that Ulysses Grant had been the victorious chief of the Union army before becoming president. Nonetheless, after eight years in office both men stepped down, prodded by the two-term tradition George Washington established. Díaz, by contrast, aided by bought-off regional strongmen, would win seven terms. To ensure each re-election, he jailed his critics and gave enforcers known as "political chiefs" free rein in the provinces. His longevity also drew on a patriarchal personality cult that bordered on an absolutist mystique.

Little of this perturbed the expatriates. To most US and European residents, Díaz was a grand old man, guarantor not only of "order and progress" but also of their prospects and high salaries. They knew enough Mexican history, a seeming cacophony of civil wars and invasions, along with a sustained hum of revolt and banditry, to laud him for the peace he imposed. They hailed it as the *Pax Porfiriana*. At the Mexico City Fourth of July party in 1901, the Ambassador praised Díaz, soon an annual guest of honor, as Mexico's Washington. The expatriates also praised his finance minister, José Limantour, for balancing Mexico's budget for the first time in history. And they congratulated themselves, aware that Porfirian peace and progress relied greatly on the railroads and mines they operated. More than anything, it relied on their wealth creation: not just in taxes and import duties but in directorships, shareholdings, lobbying fees, and bribes, handed to Díaz cronies and the once restless class of regional power brokers.[4]

Mexico under Díaz was not quite an expatriate El Dorado. More US ventures failed than succeeded, especially for smaller players. Mexican skilled workers seethed at how foreigners doing the same jobs earned better pay, and peasant anger simmered over haughty landlords, many of them foreigners. Critique of the dictatorship by upper- and middle-class dissidents grew after 1900. Still, bad news often got buried. Most of the press was either partial to the regime or suppressed by its threats and jailings. The leading English-language paper, the *Mexican Herald*, enjoyed a stiff subsidy from the state.[5] When Jenkins set foot in Mexico, there was little public awareness that the whole Porfirian edifice was politically rotten and socially unstable.

AFTER 1901 STRETCH a dozen years from which no almost letters of Jenkins survive. These were semi-nomadic years, in which William and Mary inhabited half a dozen homes. What can be found are fragments: anecdotes passed down through the family, occasional mentions in newspapers, the odd archival record of a business transaction, or, more usually, the actions of more established men with whom Jenkins did business. We only know for certain the identity of a Monterrey employer because Jenkins wrote on company letterhead to his sister Mamie on her twenty-first birthday and because, while Mamie died without issue, the letter was saved by the family of their sister Kate. We only know the name of a mining firm for which he worked in Zacatecas because Mary kept a lock of her mother's hair in an envelope embossed with its title and location, which somehow escaped the destruction of most of her papers. Yet from disparate crumbs of evidence and familiarity with the twenty-three-year old who departed Tennessee, we can surmise what drove him from place to place.

Monterrey surely struck him as a revelation. This was a Mexico quite different from the backward nation of US textbooks and adventurers' tales. A city of 60,000, Monterrey was comparable to San Antonio but more industrialized. As well as a large foreign-investment presence it boasted a fast-growing manufacturing sector, initiated and largely controlled by local capital. During the 1890s, the city's business leaders had set up a major brewery, iron smelters and foundries, and mills for textiles, soap, bricks, and glass. They also set up banks, department stores, and a slew of mining companies. Local capital was plentiful because Monterrey had reaped tremendous profits by trafficking in Confederate cotton during the Civil War. After the US Navy blockaded the Southern ports, Monterrey's merchants stepped up as middle men, importing the cash crop overland and shipping it to Europe, then exporting cloth and other provisions to the Confederate army. From 1867, wars of Mexico's own, coupled with a collapse in the mining sector, caused Monterrey twenty years of depression, but the city's merchant elite weathered it. In the 1880s, a US-assisted revival of mines and building of railways, along with a policy of tax breaks for business start-ups, set the stage for a second, more lasting boom.[6]

To the owners of Monterrey's small businesses and stores, the long depression had hit hard. Most of them had closed shop, and given the lack of social welfare and public education, the city's middle classes— as in Mexico as a whole—shrank in size and means. When boom times returned the pool of educated local people was shallow, so companies sought US and European managers and technicians. By 1895, some nine hundred Americans lived in the city, along with hundreds of Germans, Britons, and Spaniards. There was even an English-language newspaper, *The Monterrey News*, whose founder happened to be a Confederate colonel from Nashville.[7]

Jenkins did not linger with the railroad company, where one source claims he worked as a mechanic and made just 50 cents a day. Sometime in 1902 he switched to the Monterrey Iron Foundry and Manufacturing Company. The city's eighth-largest private employer, with a payroll of 120, the company produced machinery for mining firms. That year, at age twenty-four, he became a father. Mary gave birth to Elizabeth on July 9, the first of five children she would bear over twenty-three years, each of them in a different city. Though his pay had improved since his teaching days, William insisted on a thrifty existence, such was his determination to pay off his Vanderbilt debts. They lived in a boarding house, and it was during these years that he developed a habit of putting Mary and her child on the streetcar while he walked or jogged behind, to save the 5-cent fare. Mary took bravely to the new regimen. She learned to cook and to frugally manage the household. She even counted the sheets of toilet paper she used.[8]

In March 1903 they had a visit from Mamie, the sibling to whom William was closest. A subsequent letter reveals a deeper irony in his teasing than he ever displayed with Mary. He recalled Mamie's birth twenty-one years before as the arrival of "the blackest, ugliest, measliest looking critter that I had ever seen up to that time." (Jenkins's penchant for ironic humor would find echo among the Mexicans.) Only near the end did he lower his guard, admitting his tears at her departure that March. Otherwise he spoke of an austere present—"I would like to eat cake with you today, but will eat beans here instead"—and a destiny still to be forged: "I have many things to worry and trouble me now. A family of my own to work for, a future to build up, and thousands of plans to carry out if I can."[9]

That August, Mary had turned twenty-one and come into her inheritance, some $10,000.[10] Holding inherited wealth in dim regard, William apparently refused to dip into it, but the sum would aid an entrée into business; Mary could be his partner. While he waited for the right opportunity, the wheels of his imagination turned. Mary and he had the custom of sitting outside their boarding house at night and watching the trains go by. William discovered that some of the northbound wagons carried cotton to the United States, while southbound freight included shirts, dresses, and stockings.

The stuff comes all the way from New England, William mused aloud one evening. "They pay duty when it crosses the border . . . and I'll bet a lot of other charges too."

"Silly, isn't it?" Mary agreed.[11]

THE FOLLOWING YEAR brought another move, as William found work at the Bonanza Mines, 80 miles southwest in the mountains of northern Zacatecas. A copper mine, Bonanza was operated by the Guggenheim Exploration Company, part of the New York–based empire of Meyer Guggenheim. Having made one fortune in US mining and smelting, Guggenheim and his sons were seeking a second one in the dynamic sector of Mexican metals, where they became the top operators, employing thousands. Bonanza lay at the terminus of a line that typified the US-built railroads of the era. While they carried local passengers and connected national markets up to a point, such purposes were secondary. Like straws dangled across the border, they were built mainly to suck out the country's copper, silver, and other raw materials. As Jenkins had noted in Monterrey, they then carried US finished goods to the Mexicans.[12]

Jenkins's move cannot have meant a big step up from the foundry, because while mining paid relatively well, he got blisters on the job. Soon, however, he gained a managerial position, which came with a little stucco house. He must have seen how the mere fact of being white and a US citizen made him privileged. He must also have seen how the salary ratio between managers and mine workers, commonly 2.5 to 1 in the United States, averaged 20 to 1 in Mexico. Nevertheless, his own post was junior, with an annual salary somewhere in the low four figures. His aspirations gnawed at him. How could he make more money?[13]

Mary would not have found living and raising a child in a mining enclave pleasant. Not only remote, Bonanza lay amid dusty hills where little grew but cacti that crouched under wind and sun. Mercifully, she did not have to endure it long. A newspaper advertisement caught her husband's eye. It concerned a stocking factory in the city of Puebla, in Mexico's high plateau. The owner was seeking a manager. Even better, he was offering to sell a 50 percent stake.

In 1905 or 1906—he would later give both dates—Jenkins upped stakes again. With his wife and infant daughter, he headed an additional 600 miles south, into the Mexican heartland.[14]

The Merchant of Puebla

Decades afterward, the chroniclers of Puebla would strain to recall how that odd gringo Jenkins had surfaced in their midst.[15] None could pinpoint the year, nor could they relate with precision his activities. There was little they could turn to for reference, because Jenkins, despite all his wealth and fame, never related his career to the press. They made do with fragments and apocrypha. One account claimed a US missionary group lent him the funds to start an itinerant menswear business. Others testified to his starting off with a home-based hosiery workshop, managed by his wife. He was said to have dabbled in grain brokerage and real estate. He was rumored to have made a bit on the side selling scrap iron that he pilfered from railroad lines. What the chroniclers did agree on was that Guillermo Jenkins, as they called him, had shown an uncommon energy for all kinds of commerce and that he was often seen in the street, carting equipment or merchandise to and fro.

As far as we can tell, Jenkins began in Puebla by joining with two fellow immigrants, both producers of socks and stockings. One was Arturo Thielheim, a German. By the time Jenkins arrived, Thielheim's mill was the most productive of the eight hosiery-makers in Puebla City, for it was the only one to use electricity (a 5-horsepower motor) for some of its machines. Its workforce of fifty women and fifteen men produced more apparel than the other seven combined. Jenkins would later claim that he arrived in Puebla with savings of 13,000 pesos, roughly $6,500. The initial commitment he made to Thielheim's firm, for a one-third stake, was $8,750, so he presumably pledged to make up the difference from future salary and profits, using Mary's inheritance as collateral.[16]

His second partner was Leon Rasst, a German Jewish businessman of Russian nationality. Hard evidence of their association is lacking. Then again, Rasst was known to operate at the margins of legality, so their association may never have been formalized. By one account, they partnered in a modest mill that used rudimentary wooden machines, but it is also possible that Rasst and Thielheim's mills were one and the same, with Rasst a silent partner; Rasst is recorded as having later gained ownership of Thielheim's mill. Either way, it was Rasst, a man frequently sued for debts, who would publicly be remembered as Jenkins's first associate, and this cannot have aided the American's reputation.[17]

Textiles was a good first business for Jenkins, and the state of Puebla, home to the metropolis of the same name and a quarter of the nation's mills, a good place to start. This was an industry in transformation: in the 1890s, large mills had burgeoned across the nation, and, due to a massive importation of machinery, a majority were automated. Increasingly Mexican textiles were displacing imports. But hosiery lingered as an undercapitalized niche and so as an inviting business for those with vision and a little capital. Start-ups using manual equipment cost as little as $1,000. With the sector's reliance on sewing machines, employers used a largely female and therefore cheaper workforce. In the early 1900s, Jenkins was one of a number of Puebla newcomers to invest in hosiery. Others included Spaniards, who dominated the sector, and Lebanese, fleeing the impositions of the Ottoman Empire. Middle-income Mexicans also got involved, but their wealthier compatriots ignored the sector, considering it beneath them. One of them sniffed that hosiery was "an industry fit for the attic."[18]

Puebla offered enough stability to give a young investor confidence and enough flux to let him think he might take advantage. Governing the state, as he had done since 1892, was General Mucio P. Martínez, a proxy of Porfirio Díaz.[19] A career officer of humble origins, Martínez had fought alongside Díaz against the French in the 1860s and backed his coup of 1876. Díaz returned the favor by imposing him upon Puebla (he was a northerner), first as a congressman, then as governor. Martínez toed the order-and-progress line. He answered the press with a muzzle and dissent with a cudgel. As the gubernatorial terms clicked by, he cultivated a bushy white moustache like that of his aging friend, the president.

In his usual fashion, Díaz cemented Martínez's long-term loyalty by allowing him pieces of Puebla's pie. The governor habitually raked off funds from public works projects. He controlled a dozen illicit gambling houses and a monopoly on the meat supply to butchers. One of Puebla's main sources of tax revenue was the distribution of *pulque*, the fermented sap of the maguey cactus that was the choice beverage of the poor, and Martínez and two partners pocketed most of the take for themselves. His excesses were common knowledge and complaints frequent; even the

president tried to rein him in. A member of Díaz's inner circle would estimate that Martínez benefitted from his office by some $2 million.

Martínez was not merely venal; at times his greed bordered on the
entrepreneurial. His interests included several joint-stock companies, one
of which owned the Calipam sugar plantation. A veteran general would
recall that Martínez expanded the estate by seizing land from indigenous
farmers, while other peasants were drafted at gunpoint for seasonal work
in the cane fields. In 1904, when Calipam needed a capital injection,
four leading Puebla families paid most of the $220,000 committed. For
most of that decade, the state's top sugar producer was Calipam. Another
Martínez firm made cement. With municipal construction contracts multiplying, this was a good business to be in. For partners in such ventures,
the governor recruited a mix of Mexican patricians and Spanish textile
barons, some of whom joined his inner circle of advisers.[20]

Such relationships of convenience typified the Porfirian age. They
allowed the rich to get richer, to the detriment of less connected business
rivals and to the doubtful benefit of the consumer. This kind of interdependence differed from the imperative links that had been a governing
principle of Díaz's early years, when overcoming a legacy of political disorder and economic stagnation necessitated mutual support between these
elites. With its history of reneging on loans, the Mexican state had found
it hard to borrow abroad, so it depended on bankers and industrialists
to lend and invest; Díaz gave them the confidence to do so by awarding
monopoly concessions and protective tariffs and by letting them help
shape policy. These privileges, along with guarantees of public order and
compliant labor, made investors in turn dependent on the state. Governors
cultivated similar reciprocity in the provinces. By the early 1900s, however,
systems designed to build mutual trust, including shareholdings and seats
on company boards for politicians, had resulted in spectacular concentrations of wealth. Where once the main beneficiary was the state as an institution, the deals merely favored the pockets of individuals, undermining
the legitimacy of the government and particular politicians alike.[21]

Martínez kept Puebla stable, but he was an indifferent developer. On his
eighteen-year watch, Puebla City lost its historic rank as Mexico's second
metropolis to Guadalajara, and statewide literacy only inched up from 12
to 15 percent, falling further behind the national average. Geography somewhat hampered development, for Puebla was subject to the pull of nearby
Mexico City, which beckoned entrepreneurial Pueblans.[22] There were also
human factors, and not just the crookedness of Martínez. Puebla's famed

textile sector, which dated from the sixteenth century, grew in quantity of factories but less so in quality. In Guadalajara and Orizaba, larger mills of more than a thousand workers, backed by French capital and served by state-of-the-art machines, would prove more profitable. Only one such mill came to the state of Puebla. Martínez may have found his ability to draw investors handicapped. Puebla's textile barons were cautiously conservative: they did not readily partner with outsiders, nor were they keen to upgrade technology; they held a deep preference for protectionism; for that matter, innovators tended to be outsiders (even local hero Estevan de Antuñano, builder of the first mechanized mill, had come from Veracruz). Further, the sector hit a rocky patch after 1900, with a jump in the price of cotton. By the time Jenkins arrived, most of Puebla's mills were running on slim margins and workers were getting restless over wage cuts.[23]

A striver like Jenkins would have sensed some vulnerability here. Textiles was a business with growth potential—he had seen that Mexico was still importing some of its clothing—but populated in Puebla by a number of families who seemed to hold onto their mills for the sake of tradition or status. There was room for modernization. Meanwhile, the long arm and grasping hand of Mucio Martínez offered two further lessons. Most obviously, those who got ahead tended to have friends in high places. And to Jenkins, the son of a revenuer who had once associated tax collection with his father's honesty, it must have come as a strange epiphany that in Puebla there was something almost foolish about the paying of taxes.

PUEBLA WAS BOTH a stranger land and a sort of homecoming.[24] After four or five years in the arid climes of northern Mexico, a desert landscape intermittently inhabited, this lush and populous state might have reminded William and Mary of Tennessee. The central and temperate Puebla Basin evoked the basin of the middle counties. Subtropical rainfall nourished the landscape, where wheat and corn and fruit trees grew. Summer days, so scalding in the north, were bearable due to the state's elevation, most of it over a mile above sea level, and its afternoon rains. Tennessee is three times the size of Puebla, but in geographical variety there too were similarities. Southern parts of Puebla hosted plantations, though sugar rather than cotton was the crop, and they were worked by a sizeable dark-skinned underclass. Northern parts were home to mountainside farmers, who wanted little to do with central authority or the conservative planter class, not unlike the mountain folk of eastern Tennessee.

But volcanoes made the landscape quite distinct. Two of them, the extinct Iztaccíhuatl and the semi-dormant Popocatepetl, locally known as Izta and Popo, separated the state and its capital from Mexico City to the west. Perpetually snowcapped—Izta's summit resembling a supine woman in white, Popo's crater threatening with plumes of smoke—their peaks captured the imagination, while their piedmont harbored towns with traditions of violent resistance.

Puebla City, the Jenkinses' new home, was nearly four centuries old but offered cosmopolitan echoes of Nashville. With a matching population of 95,000, it was serviced by streetcars (if mule-drawn rather than electric) and lit by street lamps, the better to observe the finery of its many churches and mansions. Though it was proudly Catholic, its main Protestant community, like that of Nashville, was Methodist; a prominent red-brick church stood a mere three blocks from the central plaza. An attached school would educate the Jenkins children.[25] The Porfirian zeal for urban improvement, showcased in Mexico City, had recently caught on. In fact, 1906 was a banner year in Puebla for the hallowed goal of modernization. It saw the completion of a lengthy remodeling of City Hall and the erection of two monuments, one commemorating independence and the other the hero of mid-century reform, President Benito Juárez. It saw the erection of a glass-ceilinged shopping arcade, just three years after this Italian innovation appeared in Nashville, and the opening of the Pathé, Puebla's first moving-picture house. Entering as mayor was Francisco de Velasco, a French-educated descendant of two Spanish viceroys, who would serve for five years. Ardently Europhile, and the first Pueblan to own an automobile, Velasco would invest his energies, along with an unheard-of $4 million, in public funds, into beautification, sanitation, and transport projects. These included electric lights and street paving in the city center.[26]

Yet 1906 was also "the year of the strikes." Unrest flared across Mexico, and Puebla was a hotspot. A dissident Mexican Liberal Party emerged, promoting radical ideas through an underground newspaper; a new labor union, the Great Circle of Free Workers (GCOL), gained momentum in Puebla and Veracruz mill towns; and a strike at the US-owned Cananea mine in Sonora was put down by US gunmen, leaving eighteen Mexicans dead. Together with wage cuts, these factors caused a surge in textile worker militancy. During an autumn of strikes, the Puebla elite took a united stand and issued regulations to govern their mills. Most offensive to workers were bans on taking newspapers into the factories and on hosting guests in company housing without permission; both moves sought to suppress union recruitment. In December, the Puebla GCOL reacted with a thirty-mill strike. Mill owners in other states replied with a lock-out that paralyzed most of the industry. Porfirio Díaz brokered a compromise, making concessions to the GCOL while imposing a rule that workers carry booklets in which supervisors could note their conduct; the device would keep "agitators" from switching between factories. While Puebla workers accepted the deal, those at the French-owned mills at Orizaba in Veracruz, already angry over having to spend part of their wage at high-priced company stores, took exception to the notebook clause. On January 7, a riot broke out at the Río Blanco mill; managers fired into the crowd, and the company store was burned down. As looting and burning of stores spread to neighboring mills, Díaz sent troops to respond with "energetic measures." At least seventy strikers were shot to death. Six leaders were summarily executed.[27]

Never had Porfirian progress seemed so visible, yet never had Porfirian order been so challenged. Certainly, the shots fired at Cananea and Río Blanco halted dissent in the short term, but they raised public awareness of the plight of workers, and they offered grist for the mill of dissidents and plotters against the regime.[28] They would also provide long-lasting symbols of Mexican resistance in the face of exploitative foreign capitalists.

Such disturbances were unlikely to have deterred Jenkins. Any newfound reticence among textile producers to commit fresh capital surely gave Jenkins the hope of strengthening his position. What unsettled him and Mary was not worker agitation but high society. Puebla had only a tiny US colony and the British were also few. The business and managerial classes were predominantly Spanish. Through the commercial drive and communal support usual in immigrant enclaves, they had gained ascendancy even over old-money Mexicans, into whose families they sometimes married. They wore their Iberian identity like a heavy red coat: it insulated them and aided recognition. Established elites congregated at the Spanish Casino, while merchants and managers gathered at the Spanish Circle. They afforded each other mutual aid and medical services through the Spanish Charity Society. In their speech, they held on to Spain's *ceceo* (a lisping "c" and "z") through several generations. They practiced a conspicuous Catholic devotion, and they named their mills after sacred images and Christian battles against the Moors: Santiago, La Providencia, Covadonga.

They had a high opinion of themselves too. A 1901 yearbook of the Catholic Circle, which grouped the wealthiest Spaniards and Mexicans, had this to say of one gathering: "Attending the meeting were all who constitute the *crème de la crème* of Puebla society. Not only the aristocracy of money, but that of talent and honorability."[29]

Puebla's well-to-do were cool to outsiders, unless they were Spanish or French. Such aloofness was at least the usual perception; accusations of prejudice can of course form a prejudice themselves. Today it is common to hear Pueblans dismissed as *muy mochos* (very pious) or *pipopes*, an acronym for *pinches poblanos pendejos* (damned, or tight-fisted, Pueblan idiots). Earlier visitors too made claims for Pueblan distinctiveness. Around 1840, Fanny Calderón, a Scotswoman married to a Spanish Ambassador, found the city handsome and cleaner than the capital but shrouded in an almost penitential quiet, and she remarked on the inhabitants' reserved manners. Nineteenth-century visitors often noted the fine architecture—the graceful Cathedral, mansion façades inlaid with colorful tiles—yet also the constraint and piety of the people. A tourist from the United States summed up the sentiment: "[Puebla] has the name of being conservative as to social taste and customs, anti-foreign, Romanist in religion, reactionary as to politics."[30]

Religious, social, and economic traditions help explain the city's standoffish repute. Its founding myth, dating from 1531, holds that a bishop was visited in a dream by angels, who called him to create a city where (unlike the capital) no indigenous town already stood. He did so, naming the place Puebla of the Angels. A city ordinance prohibited "Indians" from living in "Spanish territory," keeping them to the periphery. While similar rules governed other colonial centers (and similarly came to be broken), the "Spanishness" of Puebla City endured for centuries in the minds of its elite. In the 1760s, the Jesuit intellectual Francisco Javier Clavijero referred to Pueblans as devout and attached to their churches. Even after independence, the Catholic Church owned four-fifths of the city's real estate and acted as the region's main bank. Complementing the belief of Pueblans that they lived in a uniquely blessed domain was their city's self-sufficiency. With its thriving industry, chiefly in textiles but also in pottery, leather goods, and flour, and a large pool of indigenous labor to work it, colonial Puebla rivaled the capital as an economic center. It was larger than any of the Spanish capitals in South America. All this fostered autonomy and insularity. Still, Pueblans were not so parochial that they would snub successful settlers. Owing to Puebla's commercial traditions, wealth, even swiftly earned, gave entrée into elite circles, as long as newcomers abided by the city's social codes.[31]

After Mexico's independence, rebellions and civil wars pitted secularizing, free-trade liberals against Church-friendly, protectionist conservatives.

Unsurprisingly, most of the Puebla elite sided with the latter. After the historic defeat of invading French forces on May 5, 1862—feted ever after as the Battle of Puebla or *Cinco de Mayo*—General Ignacio Zaragoza complained to Benito Juárez about the scant support his army had received from the city. He added: "It would be a good thing to burn down Puebla. It is in mourning for the 5th." Two years later, after the French conquest, Puebla worthies numbered among the minority that welcomed Archduke Maximilian of Austria. Napoleon III's pick for emperor of Mexico was coldly received on his landing at Veracruz, but Puebla feted him: high-society balls, firework displays, a *Te Deum* in the cathedral. Another explanation of Pueblan conservatism adds that outsiders were met with suspicion because of their very number. Lying between Veracruz and the capital, Puebla was a staging post for merchants, soldiers, and sailors on leave. Fathers would caution their sons against business ventures with transient types; mothers would hide their daughters from suitors who might not return.[32]

Gringophobia

Lacking Monterrey's proximity to the United States and its critical mass of English-speakers, and differing from a mining enclave in which Anglo-Saxons were privileged, Puebla posed fresh challenges for the Jenkins family. Its opinion of North Americans was quite distinct, based more on fleeting impressions than on familiarity, and the impressions were not pretty. As someone who had married a ward of Southern gentry, was quick to perceive a slight, and held to the gospel of advancement by merit, Jenkins found his early years in Puebla a trial.

For elderly Pueblans, Jenkins's name may have rung an unfortunate bell. During the Mexican-American War (the US Intervention, as Mexicans call it), Puebla had endured a three-month military occupation, headed by one William Jenkins Worth. The general's edicts included an advisory that troops not drink the water lest the Pueblans try to poison it, which to the citizens added insult to injury.[33] More recently, the *Pax Porfiriana* had spurred the birth of tourism from the United States, and Puebla featured on the usual trail. Travel writer Charles Macomb Flandrau, an annual visitor, noted that while most tourists were well behaved, a visible minority—"the exception by whom the others, alas!, are judged"—were loud of opinion, gauche of dress, and given to photographing the locals without consent. When Flandrau visited Puebla, near the time of Jenkins's arrival, he heard a story doing the rounds about US tourists who lunched in the Cathedral. They left their orange peel and sardine tins on the floor, and before leaving they washed their hands in the holy water.[34]

Church officials, men whose opinion weighed heavily in Puebla, were already wary of Americans. As of the late 1860s, Juárez and Díaz had opened Mexico's doors to US Protestant missionaries, deeming them good educators, and they were making small but significant inroads. It cannot have helped Jenkins's cause that his wife was a Methodist, for in Puebla the Methodists allied openly with the minority of educated folk who were liberals. Together they hosted annual commemorations of Cinco de Mayo and the death of Juárez—referred to by the city's Europhile elite as "riots"—and they had their sons schooled at the Mexican Methodist Institute. Puebla's elite was better disposed to the Spanish and the French: they were Catholics, and they hailed from the Continent of Culture.[35]

Jenkins cut a strange figure for a foreigner. Whenever he accompanied his wife to market he would put her on the streetcar and walk or jog behind it to save the fare. When acquaintances made comment, he would say he was doing it for the exercise. On weekdays, clad in dirty overalls and a battered hat, he could be seen riding a bicycle mounted with a large basket filled with spools of thread, or pushing a two-wheeled cart laden with equipment, back and forth between Rasst's mill and his warehouse.[36] To Puebla's dark-skinned majority, culturally coerced to regard whites with deference, a tall and fair-skinned man openly engaged in manual labor must have seemed amusing; it might well have earned him some employee loyalty, for it showed that he lacked airs. To the textile nabobs, however, such activities were the work of an indigenous or *mestizo* peon. "Decent people," as Mexico's whites often called themselves, would not engage in physical labor.

The Spanish had a term for it: *deshonor de trabajo*, the dishonor of working with one's hands. When tracing the colonial history of the Americas, English-language historians once made much of this notion: it complemented facile contrasts between effete Spanish settlers freighted with feudalistic mentalities and rugged British settlers blessed with capitalistic vision. In fact, Spanish colonizers were frequently entrepreneurial. The thousand Spaniards who arrived in Puebla City from Brihuega between 1560 and 1620 brought their knowledge of textiles and in many cases founded mills for mass-producing woolen cloth. Employing up to one hundred workers, these were much bigger than the artisans' shops left behind in Castile, and they helped convert Puebla into the leading textile producer of New Spain, serving markets throughout the Viceroyalty and beyond. On the other hand, their typical workforce consisted solely of nonwhites: the laborers were indigenous and the overseers were slaves. Even the managers were often *mestizos*. Spaniards were owners and executives.[37] Such distinctions would persist, little altered, for centuries.

In the Porfirian age, aversion to *deshonor de trabajo* deepened as leisure opportunities grew. During the French occupation of the 1860s, Puebla's self-described "Divine Class," like other wealthy urbanites, had developed a fixation with all things Gallic. Then, as the Porfirian boom permitted all kinds of imports, they devoted ever more time to emulating *la vie parisienne*. To be modern—the goal prescribed by Comte and his disciples— involved displaying one's modernity just as one would in France. Dinner parties became popular, as did bicycle rides. The theater, now deemed déclassé, lost favor to the opera and the symphony orchestra. The sons of industrialists attended college in Europe and returned there for winter vacations. They dreamed up French-style homes, calling them *chalets*, while their wives shopped for Parisian fashions. These men did take part in the textile start-ups of the 1890s, but they spent a great deal more time at leisure, taking exercise and conspicuously consuming. Around 1900, with the advent of the athletic club, the department store, and the automobile, the scope for cosmopolitan diversion multiplied.[38]

Some of these traits no doubt reminded Jenkins of his in-laws and the more entitled of his Vanderbilt peers. The elites of the South, too, revered the "honor of unsoiled hands" and the indulgence in hospitality that riches allowed.[39] While the Civil War and emancipation had greatly eroded both the wealth and the leisure time of Southern gentry, the fondness for lengthy social gatherings persisted. Mary's summers had been peppered with parties and the visits of friends. He had excused her such things, but he held work-shy men in dim regard.

His difficulty fitting in with Puebla's self-made Europeans and old-money Mexicans owed also to his manner. His pushy and uncouth qualities repelled those who felt themselves refined. He spoke gringo-accented Spanish, and as he was used to shouting instructions above the din of his machines, his voice took on a noted boom. He always wore the same suit and hat on days off. He was said to be driven by profit, and then there was his partnership with the unloved Leon Rasst. Worse, he was not a convivial sort. He seemed to one close friend to have "made a slave of himself." He did not drink, play domino, or take a mistress; he did not attend mass, he rarely entertained, and he retired early to bed. His best friend was his wife.[40]

Pueblan parochialism and self-regard were not all that Jenkins was up against. A suspicion of North Americans was etched into the culture of the age. Despite President Díaz's sustained courting of US investors, and in part because of it, the United States was often viewed with alarm or derision by educated Mexicans. Even those who held US innovation in high esteem—who rode the railways that US capital built or visited their northern neighbor's towering cities—would turn up their noses at Uncle Sam and his offspring. Such sentiments were so pervasive and automatic, they might well be called a phobia.

Whereas xenophobia is that irrational fear of foreigners that produces a nationalistic defensiveness, gringophobia is a Mexican variant that views the United States and its citizens as objects of fear, disdain, and blame for the country's ills. For much of the twentieth century, such sentiments were exploited for political or economic ends. They were distinct from—though often mixed with—a historical distrust of the United States as an imperial threat that was eminently rational. This was true politically, in light of a Mexican-American War, planned and executed by President Polk, that left Mexico missing the top half of its territory.[41] It was also true economically, for by 1910 the privileges extended by the Díaz regime left Americans owning much of the rail network, carting off most of its silver and copper, in position to exploit its oil, and by one estimate owning 27 percent of the country's surface area. All this it did at only irregular benefit, sometimes tangible harm, to the population.[42]

But reasonable suspicion can slide into phobia, especially when a nation's educators and opinion leaders encourage stereotypes to take hold. Regarding US businessmen, such as Jenkins, an initial ambivalence would mutate into an outright aversion. As the American economic presence grew, qualities once admired, like ingenuity and drive, were displaced in the Mexican imagination by greed and arrogance. As mass media proliferated, this negative image grew more pervasive in popular culture, where it carried a heightened emotional charge. The image also revealed a phobia in that it ignored how "typically gringo" practices and traits, from union-busting to naked greed, were common among the Mexican business elite too.

For nearly a century, gringophobia had mainly existed among elites. It had its origins in the 1820s, during Mexico's first years as a republic. The nation's leaders had good cause to be suspicious, as the first US ambassador, Joel Poinsett, meddled openly in politics. His support for the liberal president, Vicente Guerrero, earned him the wrath of conservatives, setting a precedent for their antipathy to Uncle Sam.[43] But conservative politicians adopted a deliberately harsh rhetoric, for political expediency in their rivalry with liberals. And the conservative press, during and after the Mexican-American War, tried to nurture a phobia well beyond a call to defend the fatherland. Senior ideologue Lucas Alamán distinguished Americans from Mexicans thus: "We are not a people of merchants and adventurers, scum and refuse of all countries, whose only mission is to usurp the property of the miserable Indians." A pamphleteer claimed that Protestantism led to "sedition, disorder, cruelty, blood, and death."[44]

In the 1860s, however, the conservatives' fateful alliance with the French-imposed Emperor Maximilian cost them their claim to speak for the national interest.[45] The ensuing Age of Liberalism was well disposed to foreign investment. For forty-odd years the regimes of Juárez and Díaz enticed it into railroads and mines. Mixed feelings about the influx of US capital and labor certainly found voice: elites whined about an invading "swarm of ants" that brandished revolvers and frequented barrooms; they satirized the rude manner of the Yankee workers with whom they some-times shared train compartments. But outside the contact zones of min-ing camps and railroad hubs—where resentments sometimes prompted a carnivalesque burning of gringo effigies—antipathy was not commonly shared. Schoolchildren absorbed a contradictory nationalism, which com-bined patriotic history with the general lesson that North American and European societies were superior models to which to aspire.[46]

Where gringophobia did surface at the national level, it was chiefly polit-ical in nature, notably as events elsewhere in the hemisphere rekindled fears of US expansion. Two episodes were crucial: the Spanish-American War of 1898, which brought Cuba and Puerto Rico under US control; and the Panamanian Revolution of 1903, a US-manufactured war that allowed the Americans to build a canal in a zone of their keeping across what had been Colombian territory. In response, writers referred to US empire-builders as "the barbarians of the North," "the drunken mobs," "savages." A cartoon in a satirical weekly inflamed contemporary fears with its depic-tion of President Theodore Roosevelt, bedecked in Rough Rider garb, annexing northern Mexico in the face of futile protest from Díaz.[47]

The president's suspicions of Yankee muscle gave rise to his Díaz Doctrine, a defense of Latin American sovereignty. As of 1898, when Díaz favored Britain's Weetman Pearson over American rivals with a big rail-road contract, there were tensions in the economic sphere as well. Some in the cabinet fretted that the US presence was growing too fast, although such worries did not stop the United States from overtaking Britain as Mexico's chief source of investment.[48]

As concern about Yankee imperialism mounted, Latin American elites grew wary also of US culture. This wariness gained eloquent voice in the essay *Ariel*. Penned in 1900 by a Uruguayan journalist, José Enrique Rodó, the work used characters from Shakespeare's *The Tempest* as contrasting metaphors for Anglo-America, drawn as a materialistic and unrefined Caliban, and Latin America, the spiritual, idealistic, and cultivated Ariel. Anglo societies were held to be innovative but soulless, while Latin societies were motivated by the selfless values of family and religion. A declaration of cultural independence, *Ariel* achieved enormous influence across the region.[49]

Mexicans who traveled beyond their northern border offered dichotomies of their own. The era's best-known account was *In Yankee Territory* by Justo Sierra, who became minister of education. Sierra expressed amazement and delight at US material progress, its great universities, the fine living offered in New York. But his underlying impression was negative. An early encounter with Texan rail-car segregation set the tone, Sierra both denouncing the practice as undemocratic and implying relief at not having to sit with blacks. The United States, this self-proclaimed bastion of liberty, seemed so devoted to work that Sierra found it oppressive: "the effect of hundreds of pounds of steel on my chest." He returned to Mexico with relief, finding a slow and happy life under the sun a better option than the Yankee ant-hill.[50]

Rodó, Sierra, and others gave an intellectual respectability to what nonetheless remained a phobia. The ugly images they conjured dovetailed with Mexico's nightmare scenario of US annexation, whether that took the form of further territorial mutilation or, as seemed increasingly likely, economic subjugation.[51]

Ownership was becoming the focus of nationalistic angst. The concern was seen in a new vilification of the Díaz regime's technocrats, the *científicos*, who were charged with selling off Mexico's assets to foreigners and enriching themselves in the process.[52] This transition from fear of Washington to fear of Wall Street would be halting. While, in 1909, "Big Stick" Roosevelt made way for "Dollar Diplomat" William Taft, regional interventions by US forces continued to occur. But the Yankee rogues' gallery of the future would include fewer presidents and generals and more investors and managers. It would also find more widespread and popular expression, in the press and public protest, in song and in film.

WILLIAM JENKINS WAS still some years from entering that gallery, but the language that Puebla's chroniclers would use for him reflected some of the prejudices of *Ariel*. He was described as "an uncultured man," even though his command of five languages and knowledge of the ancient and nineteenth-century classics, together with his first-place high-school graduation and his year of Vanderbilt studies, made Jenkins much better educated than all but the most privileged Pueblans. He was also described as "very poor," a misreading of his modest dress and frugal habits. One narrator went so far as to claim that this cold-hearted Anglo-Saxon had only married Mary for her money.[53]

Jenkins did well enough during his first two years in business to take his family—including a second daughter, Margaret—to Tennessee for Christmas in 1907. The one document of the trip back home that survives, a family portrait in formal attire at a photographer's studio, shows a satisfied Jenkins. His head slightly cocked and his arm akimbo, he stares deliberately at the camera. The slight jauntiness is heightened by his bushy moustache; this was the only time he would grow one, and it matched that of his father, as if he were paying him a compliment. "Pappy" John Jenkins sits in the middle, holding the two girls, showing the knitted brow, stiff posture, and tanned complexion of a farmer unused to such rituals. Mary, elegant but somewhat matronly, looks slightly apprehensive, as though worried about the return to Mexico.[54]

William very much wanted a son, but he was good with little girls and boys alike.[55] As the eldest of seven, he had had a lot of experience with small children. The month he had eloped, Ruth was eight and Anne only four. He had doted on Anne in particular, letting her climb into his lap as he wrote his letters. He had delighted in how she and Ruth quickly warmed to Mary. Having infant sisters taught him some patience, and he learned how to keep children entertained with simple games and stories.

The Tennessee visit was not simply a social call. That year, Mary's younger brother Donald had turned twenty-one, which meant he too gained his inheritance. Unlike her elder brother Hugh, who had married and moved to Seattle, Donald had never objected to Mary's match. William had big plans for the textile business, and he invited Donald to join him.[56]

Jenkins's First Million

On November 20, 1910, it is written, the Mexican Revolution began. The date is annually commemorated as though the whole Porfirian edifice was toppled that day. Yet no more did that happen than did British rule evaporate in the Thirteen Colonies on the Fourth of July in 1776. A stand was made; a long war was still to be fought; some of the building's foundations would endure. Certainly there was a cataclysm: the Revolution would oust Díaz after five months and continue to shake Mexico for another nine years, with aftershocks until the 1930s. But it would host many disparate agendas, and what happened on November 20, the date decreed by Francisco Madero for a nationwide revolt, caused less than a tremor.

Madero was a wealthy landowner and leading Díaz critic who in the summer had run for president, only to be jailed for his efforts. In imprisoning Madero and then sweeping the vote for a sixth term, Díaz only legitimized his opponent's cry for "Effective Suffrage" and "No Re-election." These slogans formed the basis for Madero's revolution, which was basically political, appealing to the small middle class and those elites resentful of Díaz's dictatorial ways. In the north, the rural and urban poor seethed at the lack of opportunities in a society rigged in favor of the large-scale cattle rancher and the foreign oil and mining companies. In the center and the south, indigenous farmers loathed the hacienda owners, who managed to grab much of their land and water supply to expand their wheat and sugar fields. In Mexico City and the mill towns, workers fumed against exploitative employers, crackdowns on unions, twelve-hour workdays, and a falling real wage. Less a tinderbox waiting for a spark, Mexico in 1910 was a series of tinderboxes. Local leaders would strike their flints at different times and for different reasons.

So it is no surprise that Madero's powers of convocation reaped a tepid response that November day. He crossed the Rio Grande, hoping to be greeted by insurgent hordes; when a mere ten men showed up, he returned with head bowed to Texas. Actions against the Díaz regime did take place elsewhere, but there was no sign of mass uprising. Six months would pass before a movement cohered.[57] In keeping with this erratic start to modern Mexico's greatest episode, the first flutter had been felt two days before. It occurred in Puebla.

Governor Mucio Martínez had heard of a local component of Madero's plot. His police began searching the homes of known dissidents, and Aquiles Serdán, Madero's point man in Puebla, got a tip-off that he was targeted. Shunning the chance to flee, Serdán convened two dozen conspirators and sent word to allies across the state: in Puebla the revolution would start two days in advance. On the morning of November 18, as the hated chief of city police crossed the threshold of Serdán's home, the rebel shot him dead. A firefight ensued as the police laid siege. Twenty rebels died. The last survivors pressed Serdán to hide in a cubbyhole, but on emerging the next day he was shot in cold blood.[58]

Word soon reached Puebla of regional uprisings gathering pace; Madero's call was finding local responses after all. In Chihuahua, a sharecropper-turned-bandit who called himself Pancho Villa had drummed up an army of three hundred, and a mule-driver named Pascual Orozco had captured a series of villages. In Puebla's neighboring state of Morelos, an indigenous small-town mayor, Emiliano Zapata, was making a stand against the sugar barons who had been gobbling up communal land; open revolt loomed. Outside Puebla City too there were clashes, as random groups of peasants and textile workers took up arms; a sugar plantation was assaulted, the Covadonga mill set ablaze. These early acts set a local precedent: in Serdán, the movement had lost its most effective urban leader; henceforth the revolt would burgeon in the countryside.[59]

By February, rebel bands were appearing over all Puebla, bar the capital. Ever heavy-handed, Martínez was losing control and losing the trust of the president. Díaz had already criticized his friend for failing to take Serdán alive: killing him had given the rebels a martyr. Martínez went to Mexico City to confer with Díaz and plead for authority over the troops based in Puebla. Instead, Díaz forced him to quit. Before stepping down on March 4, Governor Mucio P. Martínez issued a statement that he wished to spend more time with his family. Then he helped himself to a final sack of banknotes from the treasury.[60]

Rural violence mounted. The hated haciendas were a frequent target, and in April an incident at one of them would hold great consequence for Jenkins. In Puebla's torrid southwest, not far from Morelos, lay the lucrative sugar estate of Atencingo. This hacienda belonged to a wealthy family by name of Díaz Rubín, owners of the unlucky Covadonga mill. To the people of nearby villages, Atencingo was triply a target. For years it had diverted more than its fair share of river water to irrigate its sugar crop; it had seized village land along its borders; and its owners and managers were haughty Spaniards. Inspired by Zapata's early victories, a band of peasants assaulted the heavily armed estate, seizing its central mansion. They found ten Spanish managers, whom they put against a wall and shot; seven died. The atrocity caused an uproar in the capital and strained relations with Madrid. It would mark but one moment in what became a litany of vengeance against Spaniards, whom revolutionary fervor often singled out in return for years of racially tinged abuse. (Unlike gringophobia,

Hispanophobia was widespread among the poor.)[61] It would also mark the first attack of several upon Atencingo. Within a few years the hacienda lay devastated. In order to revive it, the Díaz Rubíns—their fortune drained by the war and the banks no longer lending—would need a hefty loan from a willing private lender.

To Porfirio Díaz, the Atencingo massacre paled in comparison to what happened in early May. Pascual Orozco made a stunning attack on the well-defended border city of Juárez and captured it. An insurrection that for six months had been fragmentary and confined to rural patches now claimed a major urban prize: a base at which Francisco Madero could name an alternative government, import arms, and direct the Revolution. Díaz had already made concessions, firing governors like Martínez and purging unpopular cabinet members, but to no avail. On May 25, realizing his grip on power was melting, the eighty-year-old dictator resigned. He then prepared for exile, opting unsurprisingly for France. His famous parting shot was aptly skeptical: "Madero has released a tiger. Let's see if he can control it."[62]

BY THE REVOLUTION's outbreak, and after just nine years in the country, Jenkins was well on the way to wealth. What placed him there were his personal drive, his transfer of technology, and an unusual (for Puebla) willingness to partner with whomever suited his goals, no matter their nationality or location. He also had the entrepreneur's knack of being in the right place at the right time. Put another way, circumstances not of his choosing—in this case, an underdeveloped hosiery sector—lent themselves to his making business history.

In 1908, it seems, Jenkins had bought out Rasst's share in their jointly owned mill. What inclined Rasst to sell may well have been the state of his import/export business. In 1907 a panic on Wall Street had caused the US economy to crash, and since the Díaz model of development depended on exports, Mexico's economy was dragged down with it. The two-year depression that followed, coupled with famine due to several bad harvests, heightened the inequities and tensions wrought by Porfirian progress. These proved important causes of the Revolution.[63]

When Jenkins made his purchase, Puebla's hosiery sector was still fragmented. Not only were most mills small, all except the one that Jenkins co-owned with Thielheim relied on hand-operated machines. (What happened to that partnership is unclear.) Around the same time, probably as an extension of his trip to Tennessee, Jenkins visited New England and acquired three secondhand electric machines for the spinning of cotton thread and the knitting of cloth for hosiery. The sale price included training in their operation and maintenance. When Jenkins returned to Puebla, accompanying his precious machines on the train, he brought with him two technological advantages over his competitors: he could spin his own yarn and produce garments at speed. His initiative was typical of a larger trend of textile industry automation, but within the niche of the hosiery sector he was ahead of the curve.[64]

Next he needed a new location, for his business was outgrowing the workshop he had bought from Rasst. In May 1908 he paid $2,000 for a property on the southern edge of town—allegedly he underreported the value by half, to save on taxes—and there he developed his own mill. Using part of their inheritance, Mary and Donald Street became his partners; Donald took a 25 percent stake.[65] By one account, Jenkins was so keen that the mill bear the stamp of his ambition that, with Donald's help, he laid the foundations himself. Jenkins operated one of the new machines, his brother-in-law the second, an employee the third. Presumably, workers brought over from the first mill continued the assembly work, using the same sewing machines as before. The difference was that, able to produce knitted cloth far more quickly, Jenkins could hire many more hands to assemble the garments and greatly increase output. A year or two after start-up, he named the mill La Corona (The Crown). Within five years, La Corona was capitalized at $300,000. It could boast a 72-horsepower generator and a workforce of more than two hundred.

As was common in the hosiery sector, with most processes involving detailed work on small machines, the vast majority of his workers were women.[66] Jenkins built a house next door to La Corona for his family, and, when not minding her daughters, Mary took an interest in the "girls" of the factory. The Jenkins adopted a typically paternalistic attitude, but by industry standards of the day, when few but the smallest operators lived next to their mills and managers formed an exclusionary buffer between owners and workers, the arrangement was progressive.

Jenkins was hands-on in all respects, which served his business well. He took personal responsibility for carrying the finished product to retailers. When the condition of the unpaved roads made using his bicycle impractical, he carried the bundles of garments on his back. He also handled the purchase of raw cotton. However uncouth his appearance, he developed a reputation for paying his bills on time, which distinguished him from Rasst, among others. He paid his senior workers the highest wage offered at any mill in Puebla, which no doubt benefitted the quality of his product. Business boomed and La Corona expanded. Jenkins increased its capacity and added a separate hall for spinning yarn. Taking a leaf out of Rasst's book, he had the road connecting the mill to the city center paved at his own expense. After taking care of his own street, Rasst had sought exemption from the municipal paving tax, a petition that Jenkins probably made as well. If so, here was precedent: in years to come, Jenkins would prefer to fund public works himself than pay taxes, to preempt any skimming by state officials.[67]

In a testament to his growing success, Jenkins was able to ally in Mexico City with a major player in the clothing scene, Sébastien Robert & Co. Founded by one of the various French immigrants who set up department stores in major cities, the firm owned El Centro Mercantil, a retail emporium offering imports from Paris, which stood on the capital's central square. Robert then acquired La Hormiga, a large and recently modernized factory with its own hydroelectric plant. In 1910, this mill bought out a smaller rival that was failing, and Jenkins struck a deal with La Hormiga to produce hosiery at the acquired mill. Most likely the arrangement gave Jenkins access to Robert & Co.'s retail network. Jenkins then either built or bought a third hosiery mill, 200 miles to the northwest in Querétaro.[68]

The elite families of Puebla seldom invested outside their state. Jenkins's three-mill operation not only signaled ambition, it made good business sense. The fast-rising price of cotton made economies of scale more than usually important; Jenkins could buy in greater bulk and hence at a discount. His working knowledge of railroads and mines gave him familiarity with transport logistics for raw materials and finished products and also with the potential demand from various urban markets. As the Revolution's disruptions multiplied, owning dispersed production centers became ever more advantageous.

Jenkins later recalled: "as I brought in automatic machines for knitting, and as there were only old hand knitting machines in the country at the time, I was soon able to increase the business in a most extraordinary manner ... by the year 1910, I practically controlled the cheap hosiery market in the entire country." While the claim predates his dominance by several years, most of his Puebla competitors did go out of business. In 1914 the *Mexican Herald* wrote that La Corona was the biggest stocking factory in Mexico. Jenkins also recalled that by 1913 he had banked $1 million in profits; this claim rings truer, for it would be borne out in the loans and property transactions he made soon after. Altogether, La Corona gave

Jenkins his first taste of monopoly. Back home, the government had been moving to "bust the trusts," like Rockefeller's Standard Oil. But Mexico still favored concentrated ownership: limited access to capital and thus to imported machinery meant economies of scale fell to the few, while a limited consumer class required very few large producers to satisfy demand. And the state did not stand in the way.[69]

Setting another precedent for his actions, in 1912 Jenkins began to diversify, investing $225,000 in the Commercial Company of Puebla. Founded by Americans and Swedes, the firm was a prominent dealer in animal hides and exportable foodstuffs, and it counted a number of wealthy foreigners among its shareholders.[70] Joining them gave Jenkins contacts and potential partners for future endeavors, while his handsome stake announced that he was nearing the top tier of the expatriate business community.

Jenkins also spent on arranging to move most of his family to California. When he was a child, his uncle Joseph Biddle had gone west to the town of Hanford, in the San Joaquin Valley, and taken up sheep farming and become a banker. William thought California held opportunities that Bedford County lacked. His hard-working father had never had much success, and his bad luck was compounded in 1912 when his house was destroyed by fire. Soon after, William persuaded his father, now sixty, to move to the Hanford area. He also persuaded three of his sisters, Mamie, Ruth, and young Annie, who had yet to graduate from the Webb School, to accompany him. William then spent $125,000 to buy his father a grape ranch. Mamie, who had wed before leaving Tennessee, agreed to manage the place with her husband.[71]

William's gesture was a way of honoring his father. He had always admired him for his honesty and his willingness to work long hours, making ends meet for his seven children, and doing so as a widower. He had written to Mary, on the day his father turned forty-eight: "May he be spared many more years to give to his biggest boy a chance to pay back the infinite debt of gratitude which is due him."[72] Unwittingly perhaps, William suggested by his purchase his ascension as family patriarch. Over the decades that followed, he would move family members hither and thither. He felt he knew best.

Jenkins was well on the way to fulfilling his dreams of wealth and of showing the Streets and Reeses that he was worthy of Mary. In 1912 he accompanied her on a visit to Brother Hugh in Seattle. Would he have traveled so far to see a man he had always disliked if not to feed him some humble pie? (Whatever his reaction, Hugh never joined him in any invest-ments.) In Puebla, however, his success remained unmatched by accep-tance within the upper echelons of society. Businessmen derided him as a "profiteering American, getting rich off Mexican sweat." Such snobbery and hypocrisy must have recalled old times with Uncle John and Hugh, and to similar effect: spurring him on to demonstrate that he was their equal or their better.[73]

One night, as the Jenkins were leaving after an opera performance, a member of one of Puebla's elite families barged into Mary and caused her to stumble from the sidewalk. It was probably an accident, but that did not matter to Jenkins. His sense of personal injustice was already inflamed by their manner. He assured his wife: "They're going to pay for that some day."[74] Within ten years, a significant number of that same Divine Class would find themselves seeking Jenkins's investment, in serious debt to him, or bitter that he had seized their property for failure to meet loan payments.

By 1913, Jenkins could call himself a winner. His three mills worked at capacity, and he employed several hundred. He had banked a million and, together with Mary and Donald, held at least another million in company assets. In March that year, news arrived from Tennessee that Mary's uncle John Rees had died.[75] Jenkins must have felt mixed emotions. No doubt he was sad to observe Mary in mourning for her second father, the man who had been her guardian from when she was seven until she eloped at nineteen. Yet surely he delighted that the Lincoln County blueblood had lived to see the Bedford County farm boy prove him wrong.

THE REVOLUTION TURNED much bloodier in 1913. As president, Francisco Madero had proven quite unable to satisfy all of the constituents and com-batants who brought him to power. Madero was a gentle idealist, with a vision for Mexico based on "effective suffrage, no re-election" and a right-ing of Porfirian wrongs that would be settled calmly by the courts. But the country that Díaz had overseen barely existed as a nation. There was no community imagining a common interest, trusting in institutions, prac-ticing a shared culture. As Alan Knight has put it, Mexico was "a mosaic of regions and communities, introverted and jealous, ethnically and physi-cally fragmented."[76] Most grievances were local, and Madero's regime was too weak to satisfy them. In some areas the fighting never ceased. After the iron hand of Díaz, the conciliatory and legalistic approach of Madero seemed to many a weakness.

Certainly this was the thinking of Victoriano Huerta, a general once loyal to Díaz whom Madero had tapped as his chief enforcer. A *mestizo* career soldier with a long and brutal record in the snuffing of rebellions, Huerta was an unreconstructed believer in Order and Progress. He had no time for the concessions that Madero was planning, such as to Emiliano Zapata and his rag-tag landless peasants. Encouraged by Porfirian elites and a meddlesome US ambassador, Huerta executed a coup on February 18. For good measure, four days later, he handed Madero over to a mid-ranking officer who, during a pretense of taking him to jail, shot him in the back of the head. Huerta's careless creation of a martyr only boosted rebel activity, even among those like Zapata who had fulminated at Madero's pace of reform. The United States withheld recognition of Huerta's government. Things deteriorated further as Huerta murdered political opponents and, in a rigged October election, imposed himself as president.[77]

Puebla City went largely untouched during these first three years of war, but worsening conditions elsewhere took a toll on its more sensitive residents. For Americans in Puebla, news of attacks on private properties in other states, mostly in the north but also in next-door Veracruz, had them wondering whether the contagion of rebellion might infect them too. Nationwide, droves of their compatriots were returning to the United States; others sought refuge in the capital. Puebla's more delicate souls apparently included three consecutive US consular agents, who departed Mexico in November 1911, January 1913, and September 1913, respectively. Two of them cited the health of family members. Of course, Mary Jenkins too was frail and vulnerable, but that did not stop her husband from stepping forward when the last of this trio departed.[78]

Arnold Shanklin, the consul general in Mexico City, had heard good things about Jenkins. Writing to the State Department in support of his application, he conveyed greater enthusiasm than he had over the previous two appointees: "Mr. Jenkins has been most highly recommended to me personally by representative Americans here. ... You will note from his statement that he is independently wealthy and I feel that he wishes the position only for the service which he can render the American Government."[79]

If he knew as much about Jenkins as he claimed, Shanklin was being disingenuous. While the post was unpaid and honorary, usually given to a senior member of an expatriate community, a consular agent chiefly promoted commerce. He helped importers and exporters with permits and other paperwork: every Pueblan wanting to do business with the United

States, and every US firm seeking agents in Puebla wrote to the consulate. Chambers of commerce, like Chicago's, sent its business directory; would-be exporters, such as Dodge Brothers Motor Cars of Detroit, sought market information; US buyers and Mexican vendors of cotton fabrics also wrote. In other words, a consular agent was a gatherer of information and a facilitator of trade, functions quite conducive to building networks and making more money.[80]

William Jennings Bryan, the secretary of state, transmitted his approval with a caveat: an official appointment was impracticable, so Jenkins should serve on an acting basis.[81] The issue was not with Jenkins but with Huerta; since the United States did not recognize his government, it could not formally request Jenkins's exequatur, the document of recognition by a host country. In 1913, the distinction seemed a trifling matter. To the people of Puebla, Jenkins would simply come to be known as the American Consul.

Mexico was now at full-scale war. With it came capital flight, currency devaluation, bank closures, pillage of haciendas, bankruptcies. Whatever the disruptions to business that the conflict occasioned, the prospects for advantage multiplied for those with cash, connections, and nerve. To Jenkins, revolution meant opportunity.

3

How to Get Rich in a Revolution

The best time to buy is when blood is running in the streets.
BARON NATHAN M. ROTHSCHILD (1815)

The Zapatistas and the Firing Squad

A couple of years later, as he faced the firing squad, Consular Agent William O. Jenkins was to curse the Mexican Revolution. The lengthy war, with no end in sight, had turned docile workers and peasants into "drunken soldiers . . . animals without hearts . . . howling devils." For three weeks Puebla City had been occupied by Zapatistas, rebels loyal to Emiliano Zapata. But as Jenkins wrote afterward, the trouble had only started when the Zapatistas began to leave.[1]

After Madero's call to arms in 1910, Zapata had emerged as the hero of downtrodden country folk, notably in his native Morelos and in neighboring Puebla. Zapata's early victories against federal forces helped drive out Porfirio Díaz, allowing Madero to become president. When Madero was murdered, Zapata allied with northern leaders Venustiano Carranza and Pancho Villa to oust the usurper who had him killed, Victoriano Huerta. With that goal accomplished, however, the alliance with the patrician Carranza dissolved. Villa and Zapata, believing Carranza too little interested in the plight of the poor, deposed Carranza's governors in Mexico City and Puebla in late 1914. But occupation of Puebla City was never part of the Zapatistas' project of land and autonomy for their villages. Soon, even the Villa-Zapata alliance was crumbling, eroded by third-party intriguers and Villa's vacillation. So when Carranza's army neared Puebla that winter, the Zapatistas prepared to head home.[2]

On the morning of January 5, 1915, as Carranza's forces—the Carrancistas—swept into the city from the north and the Zapatistas departed to the south, work at La Corona carried on as usual. It was a Tuesday, and the mill's full complement of three hundred women toiled at their knitting and sewing machines, while a dozen or so male workers spun thread. Despite occasional sounds of gunfire, many Zapatistas were evacuating without a fight, as Jenkins could see from his office window. They passed by in large groups and melted into the countryside, which began behind his mill and rolled down to the hot lowlands that were true Zapatista territory.

The Zapatista rearguard did not leave so easily. By choice or by necessity they fought their way out, and they made their last stand at La Corona. Jenkins later noted this was a chance occurrence: some company must have found itself cornered outside the building, because the gunfire went on for more than an hour. When the shots had drawn near, Jenkins had marshaled his employees to safe cover. Stray bullets spat and whizzed through the windows, but none of the workers were hurt. After the firing ceased, Jenkins ventured outside and counted twenty-seven dead Carrancistas and one still alive. Having sent the wounded man to the hospital, he examined the corpses and found the Zapatistas had finished off many of their foes at close quarters, sticking them with knives or blowing their heads open with expanding bullets.

That afternoon, as Carrancistas patrolled the city and picked up their dead, Jenkins was alarmed to hear it claimed that the Zapatistas had made so successful a stand by firing from within his home. Early the next morning, he awoke to banging on the front door. Thirty soldiers were there to rearrest him. First, they insisted on searching the house, including the bedrooms of his wife and two daughters. When Jenkins demanded to know whose orders they were following, they told him their rifles were their orders. Frog-marched with six of his employees to a second barracks, Jenkins found himself subjected to "the vilest invective, curses known only to Mexicans, abuses, and even blows." They shut him in a cell and sent a party to arrest Donald, whom they roughed up and jailed elsewhere. Soon they told Jenkins that he was to be shot, immediately, for helping the Zapatistas. They bundled him outside to a patio, stood him against a stone pillar, and taunted him while they readied their rifles. Giving up all hope of salvation, Jenkins asked permission to write a farewell note to his wife. The taunts only worsened.

At that moment a captain passed by and asked the sergeant in charge what was going on. Seizing his chance, Jenkins addressed the captain: he had three hundred employees who could attest to his innocence. The sergeant admitted that he had no execution orders, only a general brief to shoot snipers. The captain told him it would be a dangerous matter to execute a US consul without specific instructions. He then escorted Jenkins back to his cell. Meanwhile, Mary had rushed to find William Hardaker, the British vice-consul. Hardaker sought out the generals in command of the Carrancistas: Francisco Coss, who doubled as the state governor, and his military superior, the renowned Álvaro Obregón.[3] On being informed of the arrests, Obregón ordered the release of Jenkins, his employees, and Donald. By early afternoon they were all free, and Obregón had Jenkins brought to him. The general, Jenkins would relate, "gave me offers of all protection and guarantees, assuring me of his sincere regret of the occurrence, and offering to punish those who were guilty of such an act. He was extremely kind about it." Jenkins was so impressed with Obregón's courtesy and sincerity that he wrote later that day to thank him.

The following morning Jenkins sat at his typewriter and recounted the episode for Arnold Shanklin, Consul General in Mexico City, who would forward it to the State Department. Angered by what had befallen him and frustrated at the Revolution as a whole, he bashed out eight tightly packed pages of Consular Service letterhead, including tirades against Zapatistas and Carrancistas alike. He denounced robberies by Zapatistas at his mill the day they had entered the city, while admitting he had then arranged with a Zapatista captain to billet his platoon there for several days to secure protection. He denounced Pancho Villa for the theft in Mexico City of 800,000 pesos' worth of animal hides from the Commercial Company of Puebla, in which he was a major investor. After detailing his near-execution by the Carrancistas, he advocated an armed US intervention as the only solution to the continuing chaos. He waxed furious on the descent of regular soldiers into "animals," looting and murdering; he lamented the waste of Mexico's resources; he noted food shortages and forecast famine; he even criticized the US government for allowing arms sales to Mexicans. He predicted that violence and disruption would worsen, with further Zapatista attacks on Puebla and escalating tensions between Zapata and Villa. He said he had long opposed intervention, for reasons of Mexico's sovereignty, but now there was no other solution. He claimed that three-quarters of the Mexican civilians with whom he had contact "pray for assistance from the United States to help the country."

As for Mexico's interim president, Eulalio Gutiérrez, installed the previous October, Jenkins took a very dim view. Two weeks earlier, he had gone to Mexico City to visit Gutiérrez, only to recognize him as a former subordinate of his in the mines of Zacatecas. Jenkins was shocked. This was a man "utterly incapable of even comprehending the position which he fills, much less understanding the thousand and one difficult problems that he has to face." Here was yet another argument for intervention. President Gutiérrez, he added, would "serve no other purpose than to probably cause trouble when he is separated from his position."[4]

The war had turned Mexico "into a Hell." Soldiers had "long since lost all conception of personal privilege or property rights, and accept[ed] as authority only someone whom they fear." The Revolution was "a cold-blooded traffic in men's lives, and nothing more." All Jenkins wanted was to leave, abandoning his successful textile business, but the exchange rate and business climate encumbered his selling out. A friend of his, who hand-delivered this letter to Shanklin, reported that the trauma seemed to have aged Jenkins "twenty years in that many hours." It had left Mary "absolutely prostrated."[5]

JENKINS'S LETTER TO Shanklin, one of the longest of his that survives, provides a vivid glimpse of the Revolution's intrusion in Puebla City and multiple insights into its author's agitated mind. His heated rhetoric and flair for the dramatic aside, its narrative does not seem unreliable. Testifying before the Senate Committee on Foreign Relations five years later, a Baptist minister based in Puebla during the war gave a similar version of events.[6]

One of its many striking elements is the continued operation of La Corona, even on the day that Carrancistas were battling to oust the Zapatistas. Jenkins was forewarned of the fight. He admitted that for several days prior he had observed Zapatista chiefs deserting the city with their men, anticipating an onslaught they would be unable to resist. On the night of the fourth, he had heard gunfire. Yet on the fifth he would not close his mill, an action that might suggest disregard for his workers' safety but certainly shows unwillingness to let the Revolution interfere any more than it had done already. This obstinacy was shared by most Pueblans, rich and poor. Mill owners like Jenkins were determined to press on, making up for losses incurred through supply interruptions, merchandise theft, and outgoing shipment delays. Millhands, lacking legal right to recompense when shifts were suspended or workers laid off, needed the assurance of a regular wage, all the more so with staple foods becoming scarce.[7]

Also striking is Jenkins's emotive tone. He had a tendency to greet material losses with exaggerated woe, so laments like "I have lost immense sums . . . and will undoubtedly lose the rest of what I have made" are unexceptional. What was unusual, for surviving letters yield little evidence of bigotry, was his utter disdain for the Revolution's combatants and by extension the indigenous poor who largely made up their numbers. He repeatedly depicted soldiers as less than human: they were "drunken dogs," "insane fiends," "animals without hearts, conscience or intelligence," only wishing "to satisfy their own appetites and passions."

Jenkins was no extremist. Prejudice against country folk was routine, despite some idealizing of Zapatistas by the educated left. Conventional wisdom that many were beasts in need of taming had given rise to *México bronco*, a Porfirian term for provinces prone to violence. Felix Palavicini, Carranza's first education minister, claimed: "the ignorant, the slaves of sensual appetite and beasts of the field" would persist in their "absurd hopes" and "evil passions" if denied schooling. The foot soldiers of the Revolution conformed to cosmopolitan opinions of "sullen peoples, half-devil and half child," as Rudyard Kipling famously labeled the world's non-whites. In his letter Jenkins twice referred to rebels as "devils." His fellow Puebla landowner Rosalie Evans, a feisty American widow who hated the peons who wanted her land, repeatedly labeled them devils, while their *mestizo* leader had "the cruelest little black eyes, like a snake ready to strike."[8] Even at the best of times, wrote Jenkins, peasants were "children" who needed to be taught. His paternalism marched on: soldiers were "mentally incapable as yet to understand any possible ideal they might have"; President Gutiérrez was "a good miner to earn two or three pesos a day"; Mexico needed "some assistance in straightening out this tangle."

Jenkins's plea for intervention was also quite typical, both of the era and of the moment. It echoed Kipling's appeal of 1899, that the United States should "Take up the White Man's burden," by staying on in the newly occupied Philippines and civilizing the populace. Memories of the Spanish-American War, which had occasioned Kipling's poem and a lengthy occupation of Cuba, colored the US reporting on Mexico; at least until 1914 it clearly favored sending in troops. Like Jenkins, journalists did not advocate intervention out of a desire for annexation but from a faith in the superiority and the duty of Anglo-Saxon civilization. The US Army could do for Mexico what it had done for Cuba: aiding people displaced by war, improving infrastructure, and eradicating lethal diseases.[9]

Some Americans sympathized with the plight and fight of Mexico's poor, like the leftist journalists John Kenneth Turner, who exposed abusive plantation owners, and John Reed, who rode with Pancho Villa. But these were a progressive minority, and even Reed cast the rebels as "gentle, simple people," "delightfully irresponsible." More commonly, Americans portrayed the ferocity of the Revolution as a reflection of Mexico's national character. One reporter claimed the war exposed the rebels' dormant savagery, transforming them into "the embodiment of lust and ferocity." The novelist Jack London wrote a short story, "The Mexican," about a prize-fighter who pledges his winnings to the Revolution; his eyes are "venomous and snakelike," while a character views the boxer as a "wild wolf." In 1914, when President Woodrow Wilson sought to undermine President Huerta by sending the military to seize Veracruz, London covered the occupation. For all his socialist leanings, he favorably contrasted the healthy US forces with the beggarly local poor, and he concluded that Mexicans would "yearn for the blissful day when the Americans will conquer them again."[10]

Back in Tennessee, Jenkins had mixed well with black folks, just like his father. By the local standards of the day, his outlook had been progressive. His experience of the Revolution hardened his heart. For years to come, his views about Mexico's vast underclasses and most of his employees—with the notable exception of an interest in their education—would reflect the conservatism of elite opinion. Only in old age would he rediscover the tolerance he once learned in Bedford County.

Jenkins's language revealed a clash of cultures, a non-meeting of minds between elites and the underprivileged that was pervasive in the society in which he lived. Since he did not regard the rebels as rational, Jenkins never paused to consider their point of view. Twice he recorded their claim that "their rifles gave them their orders." To a peon-turned-soldier, once disenfranchised and landless and now a revolutionary, fighting under the Zapatista banner of Land and Liberty, this claim was an exuberant declaration of unprecedented power. To Jenkins, it was the chant of an idiot. Likewise, while he was sure he was about to be shot that January morning, it seems his captors were in no hurry to raise their rifles once they had stood him against the pillar; their repeated taunting and lackadaisical manner suggest their aim was to have some fun with a haughty *gringo*, rather than to execute an enemy of the Revolution. Jenkins reported, accurately, that the Villa-Zapata alliance was fraying, but he added that conflict between them was inevitable as "they both want the same thing, and are in each other's way." To Jenkins, each of the Revolution's factions sought control of the republic. Despite his contact with several Zapatista leaders, he failed to perceive that this movement's ambitions were local.

As for US intervention, Jenkins's assertion that most of the Mexicans he knew were in favor does not ring entirely false. Puebla's city fathers had a history of welcoming foreign powers in the hope that they would bring order: the Americans in the 1840s and the French in the 1860s. But even if his claim were true, the opinions Jenkins sounded out were surely those of the well-to-do. What did the millhands of La Corona, or the Zapatista rebels, think about a US occupation? Had Jenkins ever thought to ask them?

Like many American journalists of the day, Jenkins could fathom no rational motive for the Revolution. To veteran war reporter Richard Harding Davis, as pro-intervention in 1914 as he had been over Cuba in 1898, the struggle between Villa and Huerta was not a revolution but "a falling out among cattle thieves."[11] Jenkins wrote: "If the war was for a cause, or a reason . . . if it was for men's liberty, or a heritage for their children, we would all of us, who know Mexico so thoroughly, say that it was for the best." For Jenkins, liberty was only definable in a literal sense: freedom from slavery or colonial occupation. Freedom from debt peonage, freedom from want, the freedom to elect leaders, the freedom that comes with municipal autonomy—such freedoms were, to varying degrees, all a part of the revolutionaries' agendas. But Jenkins felt he knew better, because he knew Mexico *so thoroughly* . . .

Despite his prejudices, magnified in the heat of a near-execution, Jenkins remained a pragmatist. His admitted deal with a Zapatista captain to station troops at his home—an arrangement of billet and board in exchange for protection of property—shows his ability to secure unlikely allies. Elsewhere in his letter he mentions delivering a message from the Brazilian Legation in Mexico City (which briefly represented US interests) to Zapata's personal secretary in Puebla; he also conversed with the leaders of the Zapatista occupation. A few months earlier, Jenkins had become friendly with the young and educated Gildardo Magaña, already a senior aide to Zapata and later his political successor.[12]

As an acting US consular agent, Jenkins gained entrée to high circles. An interim and honorary post, this was a card of low face value, but he played it with ostentation.[13] He referred to his home as "the Consulate," flew the US flag, omitted to mention his interim status, and used his title to secure audiences with the Brazilian Legation, President Gutiérrez, and General Obregón. Naturally he played his little card with the Zapatistas. While dealing with the Brazilians over Villa's theft of his animal hides, Jenkins also sought the return of hides confiscated by Zapata's Puebla City commander. In response, the Zapatista secretary general urged the commander to hand back the merchandise, for Jenkins's trading company was "not an enemy of the Revolution" and it was in everyone's interest to avoid difficulties with the US government.[14]

Taken together, his dealings with the Zapatistas show that Jenkins had both the motive and the means to trade favors with them. Since his home and mill stood on the city's southern edge, they were vulnerable to rebel or bandit incursions. Quite feasibly, even before the occupation, Jenkins struck a deal with some Zapatista officer—perhaps via Magaña—in exchange for the safety of his family and business; if so, the looting he suffered that December merely reflected the loose coordination of the converging pro-Zapata troops. In 1919, Jenkins would admit to paying monthly protection money for several years to an Atlixco-based Zapatista, who safeguarded a hacienda he had acquired; rumor held he had similar arrangements with others. By then he was also friendly with the Zapatista agent in Puebla City. These covert maneuvers and friendships were not extraordinary; a number of Puebla landowners and industrialists paid off rebels who threatened to destroy or steal.[15]

In Jenkins's case, at least, such dealings set a precedent for when the war was over. Subsequent decades would confirm his skills at promiscuous politicking, as he cajoled and bought influence with governors and generals of diverse affiliation.

Weaving Profits in Wartime

Mexico's Revolution both started and ended in the state of Puebla. On November 18, 1910, Governor Martínez had preempted the uprising planned by Aquiles Serdán. On May 21, 1920, in a village in the Puebla Sierra, Venustiano Carranza was heading for safety in Veracruz when he met an ignoble death at the hands of assassins. The killing of Carranza proved the last of the Revolution's five violent regime changes. Under his colleague-turned-adversary, Álvaro Obregón, the tiger unleashed by Madero was caged.

For most of the intervening decade, Puebla was a battleground: between the forces of Porfirio Díaz and Madero, between those of Huerta and Madero's heirs, and then between the Villa-Zapata alliance and the armies of Carranza. Puebla also beheld struggles for local power, often divorced from national movements. Troops loyal to Zapata in the southwest, Domingo Arenas in the northwest, chieftains of the Sierra in the northeast, and Díaz's nephew Félix in the southeast frequently fought whichever army held Puebla City. Sometimes they battled each other. Zapatistas, above all, wreaked havoc: destroying sugar mills, burning crops, attacking trains, cutting electricity supplies and telephone lines. The forces of

Carranza, nominally at the helm of Puebla from September 1914, failed to subdue a third of the state and alienated their urban subjects with anti-Church measures and taxes. By 1920, when the Carrancistas fled, Puebla's government was bankrupt and its districts wracked by political turmoil and banditry.[16]

William Jenkins did not hunker down. He made the most of the storm's lulls, and when the sound and fury struck, he harnessed its energy. Altogether he more than doubled his fortune. Writing long afterward to the US Internal Revenue Service, he recalled: "The great Mexican Revolution began in 1910, but it did not seriously affect life and business in my section of the country until 1913, and I was able to continue to work with great profit." He went on to record that by 1913 he had $1 million in savings and roughly $1.5 million in assets and that after another four years his net worth had doubled to more than $5 million. Of this, a third reflected the stock value and reserves of his three stocking mills, held by the company La Corona; another third represented property in Puebla City and Mexico City and farmland in the states of Puebla and San Luis Potosí; and a quarter consisted of loans to a clutch of distinguished families.[17] While the motive of his letter, an appeal to the IRS for clemency during an audit, calls into question some of its details, there is no doubt as to the wartime spiral in his wealth. Two US researchers who visited him in 1918 commented on it, emphatically and disapprovingly.[18]

How did Jenkins become so wealthy during the most turbulent period in the nation's history, years of chronic instability, economic depression, and—through the sum of battlefield killing, death from disease, lost births, and emigration—a population decline of 2 million?[19] The answer is twofold: Jenkins profited in spite of the Revolution, through the almost constant operation of his textile business; and he profited because of the Revolution, by exploiting currency fluctuations and venturing into a fluid market for urban and rural real estate.

In the textile trade, Jenkins's experience affirms a revisionist take on the Revolution: industry proved remarkably adept at business-as-usual for much of the war, and it emerged from the fighting largely intact. Most historians have described the war as one of "incalculable destruction" or as a "lost decade" for Mexico, readings inherited from accounts of the Revolution written or sponsored by its victors, who liked to think of it as a mighty wind that swept away the old order.[20] What happened to Jenkins and the Puebla textile sector also affirms how damage was much less widespread than outraged victims claimed at the time. Moreover, it affirms how

individual experiences of a revolution can vary enormously, from desolation, to dogged survival, to unusual profit.

Throughout most of Mexico, the first three years of the Revolution
little affected the economy. The cotton textile industry, as Jenkins recalled
of his own experience, was barely touched. Between 1910 and 1913, average annual production was only slightly lower than before.[21] But then, as
armies mobilized through much of Mexico after the murder of Madero,
activity declined. Industrialists were obstructed by the occupation of cities,
the disruption of rail, road, telegraph and telephone networks, shortages
in the energy supply, and the fragmentation of the currency as competing
factions issued their own banknotes. Supplies of cotton from the north
were interrupted or simply stolen. Jenkins complained that in March 1914
a large amount of his cotton was confiscated at the northern rail hub of
Torreón.[22] On the other hand, having stowed his early profits in US banks,
Jenkins held the competitive advantage of access to dollars. After warring
factions drove down the value of the peso, he was able to change hard currency into local paper and reduce his operating costs by up to 96 percent.
At one point, he was paying just a dollar per rail car in freight fees from
Mexico City.[23]

By 1917, when an industrial revival began, the nation's textile workforce
had been cut by almost a third. Still, damage to the sector was limited
and recovery fairly swift. By 1920, as many mills were operating as when
Porfirio Díaz stepped down. In contrast to haciendas and plantations, the
focus of slow-boiling resentment for several decades, it simply did not
behoove rebel factions to destroy factories. These could provide a recurrent
source of cash with which to sustain and equip their armies; mills could
be expropriated, taxed, or extorted for protection money.[24] The minority
that were burned and damaged most likely suffered because their owners
refused to pay or their employees put up a fight.

Puebla's mills were targeted on occasion. Metepec in Atlixco, the largest factory in the state, was thoroughly sacked in January 1915, causing
a four-year closure, the loss of two thousand jobs, and a distaste among
local millhands for joining the ranks of the Zapatistas responsible. Several
factories were set ablaze and took years to rebuild. During the height
of Zapatista incursions a majority of Puebla mills came under attack.[25]
Damage, however, was exaggerated. In November 1914, the US Consul
in Veracruz told the State Department of sixteen foreign-owned mills in
Puebla and Tlaxcala that had been "looted and burned" over a two-day
period. The attacks allegedly involved the execution of most employees

and material losses of 45 million pesos. Yet the killings remained unconfirmed. Jenkins filed a report about the same attacks, mentioning the sacking of twenty or so factories, but confirming the destruction of just two. By May 1917, the local association of mill owners reported that forty of the Puebla-Tlaxcala region's fifty-four mills were operating. The fact that the sector revived so quickly—at a time when the credit needed for major rebuilding or machinery imports was scarce—confirms that theft of payroll and merchandise was the usual object of rebel attacks, not arson or machine smashing.[26]

Greater than Zapatista raids was the threat of internal unrest. Strikes were isolated at first, but from late 1911 they became general.[27] Expecting to be rewarded for their hand in Madero's victory over Díaz, workers grew resentful of the federal government's failure to implement reforms or to enforce those it announced, like the ten-hour workday agreed upon in January 1912 when Madero met with textile industrialists. Sector-wide strikes paralyzed anywhere from half to almost all of Puebla's mills, for weeks on end, between December 1911 and September 1912.

That March a stoppage hit La Corona. It was the men who struck, together with a dozen of the women, protesting Jenkins's failure to reduce the workday from twelve hours to a new limit of ten. The agreement Madero had brokered was not legally binding; a large number of mill owners refused to implement it, which had prompted a walk-out by nearly half the state's textile workforce in February. Jenkins's response was to seek the help of the local political chief, a federally appointed fixer with the power to solve all kinds of problems. Visiting La Corona, the political chief urged the remaining women not to join the new Workers' Union, to which the male strikers belonged, and told them the industry was too depressed for Jenkins to be able to afford concessions. His intervention apparently stopped the strike from proliferating, and it ended in defeat for the workers when Jenkins replaced the dozen striking females and threatened to bring in other women, trained as spinners, to replace the striking men.[28]

Given the unyielding reply to this unrest by Puebla's textile elite, Jenkins proved himself as stubborn as his peers. He saw how industry veterans got away with ignoring federal directives and opted to do likewise. When the situation got sticky, he obtained the help of the elite's old stand-by, the political chief. This man was evidently partial, because his claim that the industry was "too depressed" for concessions is belied by Jenkins's later admission to the IRS that until 1913 he was "able to continue to work with great profit." Already, in one respect, Jenkins was adapting to the rules of the local game, matching the wiles of his mill-owner peers. Presumably this is how Jenkins viewed and justified his actions.

But there was nothing necessarily Mexican about Jenkins's tough response. In the culture of his formative years, US unions enjoyed few legal protections, especially the more radical groups that tried to organize the lesser skilled workers. American labor saw numerous protests broken by underhand and violent means, most famously the 1892 Homestead Strike against the Carnegie Steel Company near Pittsburgh, the Pullman Strike of 1894 in Chicago, and the Lattimer Mine Strike of 1897 in Pennsylvania. Each of these involved massacres of workers. Such episodes made nation-wide headlines in a press that usually sided with management, at least until shots were fired and bodies fell. The Progressive Era that followed saw a surge in union organizing, but, at the time that Mexicans were waging their Revolution, illicit and violent attempts to break US strikes continued, notably in the mining and textile industries, the very sectors with which Jenkins was most familiar.[29] Jenkins may have emulated his Mexican peers in the methods he used to undercut the strike at La Corona, but the free-market, anti-union mindset that prompted him to do so, one that privileged an owner's right to profits over a worker's right to health, safety, and collective bargaining, was equally Anglo-Saxon.

In other ways, Jenkins was in the vanguard of management practices. By 1915, he had become one of the first Puebla mill owners to reduce work shifts to eight hours.[30] Having earlier resisted federal pressures for shorter workdays, he saw that a newly decreed eight-hour limit allowed for three shifts per day, a potentially more productive format than the standard two shifts of ten hours—he could squeeze another four hours each day out of La Corona. Most of Puebla's textile bosses were meanwhile haggling with the government, stubbornly resisting the decree by offering to reduce each shift from ten hours to nine. After the Revolution, the three-shift rotation would become common.

Jenkins's decision to hire a largely female workforce followed prec-edent at hosiery mills; it also suited his conviction (typical of his day) that women were docile. He liked to refer to his workers as his "girls." La Corona indeed experienced fewer stoppages than the average factory, but that owed at least in part to two other factors. One was Jenkins's far-sighted decision that La Corona should spin its own yarn; this capacity, not found at most hosiery mills, shielded it from strikes at factories that supplied thread. Another was his non-membership in Puebla's top business cham-ber, the Mexican Industrial Center (CIM), which represented nearly fifty textile mills. When textile workers struck or attempted to organize a sector-wide union, owners several times retaliated with mass lockouts, coordinated via the CIM. The longest of these, for three months in the spring of 1918, involved most of Puebla's mills in a concerted attempt to strangle at birth Puebla's Federation of Unions; La Corona was not among them.[31] Whether he simply shunned the CIM, or whether he applied to join and its Spanish grandees refused to admit the upstart American, Jenkins no doubt felt that with a mainly female shop floor, and what he held to be his fair-minded managing of it, he had no need of the CIM to help stave off strikes. Surely his "girls" would not try to unionize themselves. During the 1912 episode, he claimed that the dozen La Corona women who had joined the strike were tricked by the men.

His father-knows-best attitude was not all bluff. Contrary to the dark repute he later gained, Jenkins was a fairly benign employer who prided himself on running a model factory. After months of wartime disruptions to the textile trade, a CIM official reported to the Labor Department that while La Corona was operating irregularly, it kept paying its women a part of their wage on the days it was closed, a fact he would not have mentioned were the practice common. Seven times during the war, the department checked textile mill adherence to a 1912 law establishing a minimum wage, and on each occasion La Corona and its Querétaro sister mill were in compliance; close to a third of mills flouted the law.[32] Several visitors commended Jenkins for his treatment of employees. A Methodist minister found the workers well-clothed, well-fed, and content, laboring in a "very modern factory . . . well lighted and sanitary." A one-time business associate reported that the mill was equipped with baths and a schoolhouse.[33]

The school was unusual. Concerned with an enfeebled educational system and 75 percent illiteracy rate, the Puebla government passed a Primary Education Law in 1919 that obliged haciendas and factories to build on-site schools for employees' children, but violence, lack of ready cash, and intransigence among the business elite meant the mandate was not widely observed until the passage of a similar law at the federal level in 1931.[34] Jenkins was ahead of most of his peers in helping educate the less privileged, a trait that would distinguish his career.

LA CORONA WAS not only distinctively managed; it was distinctively structured as a business. Already Jenkins had cleverly developed his market dominance: identifying a niche where production was fragmented, applying new technology and economies of scale, building La Corona into the

country's largest hosiery mill, and establishing two further mills that supplied different regions. Almost all of Puebla's industrial fraternity, parochial in their outlook, owned mills in Puebla alone.[35]

The three-mill system inadvertently set Jenkins up for making the most
of the Revolution. Having mills at his disposal in Puebla, Mexico City, and
Querétaro afforded him a flexibility in wartime that few others in the textile
sector enjoyed, as he could shift supplies and orders between factories. If
cotton bales were not getting through to Puebla from plantations in the
north, the Mexico City mill might have some to spare; if rail links were cut
between the capital and retailers in Guadalajara, the Querétaro mill might
fulfill the order. To cite a concrete example, Puebla City suffered unprecedented turmoil in the second half of 1914, with invasions by Carrancistas
and Zapatistas. That semester the Querétaro mill, which had been billing
about half the sales of La Corona, generated one and a half times as much.[36]

In February 1913, Jenkins made another unorthodox move, when
he registered La Corona as a joint-stock limited-liability corporation, or
Sociedad Anónima (SA). It was only the fourth of Puebla's forty or so textile
mills to assume this legal charter.[37] The bargain required in founding an
SA—the trade-off that Jenkins was ahead of the curve in embracing—was
the sacrifice of a modicum of privacy and control, mainly in having to dis-
close financial statements, in exchange for limited liability for all partners
and greater access to new capital and loans.

Jenkins's opting for this legal model owed somewhat to circumstance.
At the start of 1913, Madero's regime was looking fragile; a need for quick
access to credit might soon arise. The move was prescient. On February
22, just three days after La Corona became an SA, Madero was assassinated, a crime that would drag Mexico into the bloodiest phase of the
Revolution. But Jenkins's willingness to embrace the SA, ahead of most of
his peers, also had to do with his formative culture. Jenkins hailed from
a nation in which the joint-stock limited-liability company arose in the
1810s, seven decades before it emerged in Mexico. In contrast, Puebla's textile elite belonged to a fairly closed culture in which networks of kinship,
intermarriage, and national origin (mostly Spanish) created bonds of trust
and facilitated private loans, so most felt little need for risk protection or
independent credit.[38] Changing La Corona's legal basis was also a sign of
ambition. In 1919, with other mills still trying to return to normal, Jenkins
would build two additional halls at La Corona, allowing more space for his
workers by separating spinning and weaving from the sewing area and
increasing the factory's number of looms.[39]

In years to come Jenkins would set up dozens of SAs, gaining another, more devious advantage. He would name associates and relatives as shareholders in his place and so conceal himself from the registration papers. Once he was rich enough to buy protection from the state government, he no longer needed the legal rights afforded by a notarized document. After all, in matters of ownership, it was physical possession of the anonymous share certificates that mattered. Thus he freed himself from Uncle Sam: the Internal Revenue Service could not possibly tax him on what he did not legally own. For Jenkins, the *Sociedad Anónima* meant anonymity in more ways than one.

La Corona emerged from the Revolution, as did most mills, with scratches but no broken bones. While typical in some respects, however, Jenkins's operations were unusually advantaged in others and so more resilient than the average firm to wartime misfortunes. Jenkins had a flexible production base and a dominant market niche. He had a largely female workforce that was treated well by the standards of the day and less apt to strike than most. He had a company that operated as an SA, which facilitated credit.

His was a more adventurous, less insular approach than that of most of Puebla's elite, for whom the textile business was a multigenerational pursuit, dependent networks that confined mutual trust to their ethnic enclaves. Since Jenkins had no sons or nephews to train, his outlook was also less sentimental. Should union activity accelerate in the sector, as it did after 1920, he might well sell La Corona and use the proceeds to expand his fortune elsewhere.

Preying Upon the Porfirians

Four months after the firing-squad incident, Jenkins at last took Mary and the girls to safety in the United States. Puebla had only become more dangerous, as had much of the republic, amid full-on war between Carranza and Pancho Villa. Factional conflict was one issue, banditry another. Americans were frequent victims, targeted sometimes out of a sense of revolutionary nationalism, more usually out of convenience. Some were kidnapped; some were murdered.[40]

There was now a healthier alternative to Tennessee, with the summer heat and humidity that had so troubled Mary: Northern California. Most of William's family had already moved there, and in 1913 the Jenkins had dispatched their daughter Elizabeth, now eleven, to a school in Berkeley.

They would all provide a community for Mary, along with her second daughter, Margaret. Nine months or so after William's departure, in a San Francisco hospital on March 20, 1916, Mary gave birth to a third daughter, Jane.[41]

For about a year, Jenkins was released of his dependents. He did worry about Mary's health, but it cannot have escaped him that, without her at home and anxious, he would be freer to move about the country. Daily operations at La Corona were being managed by his brother-in-law Donald, who was enjoying life as a newlywed; a Jenkins cousin, Annie Wells, had come to stay in September 1914, and she and Donald married the following June.[42] So amid the Revolution's chaos, Jenkins set about diversifying his assets, furthering his fortune, and, perhaps unconsciously, deepening his roots in his adoptive land.

At one stage Jenkins wrote to the Foreign Relations Ministry to inform it of his dealings with three distinguished ladies: Lucrecia Lara de Miera, Loreto Galicia de Pérez Salazar, and Doña Josefina González de la Vega de Zevada.[43] These women had all become debtors of the American, who held mortgages against houses of theirs in Mexico City and Puebla. Following a new legal requirement for foreigners acquiring property, Jenkins was surrendering right of recourse to the US government in the event of legal difficulties and requesting certification of the loans.

Details of the deals are few but resonant. The women's names speak of high social rank: most obviously Doña Josefina's lengthy appellation, and the uncommon names Lucrecia and Loreto also evoke a certain standing. One referred to herself as widowed, which was likely true of all three. Two of the mortgages, worth 23,000 and 21,000 pesos, could only have been backed by houses of desirable size or location. The history of their debts was also telling. In 1911, Doña Josefina first obtained a mortgage on her house from a Jewish immigrant, who later sold it to a third party, who in turn sold it to Jenkins; Lucrecia Lara secured a mortgage on her property from a man who, again, sold it to Jenkins.

During the Revolution, many propertied women found themselves in need of cash: perhaps their haciendas had been overrun; perhaps their husbands had expired, died in battle, or fled into exile. Often identified with the *ancien régime*, such ladies were vulnerable to the insistence of revolutionary governments that property taxes be paid in full. Long had the wealthy undervalued their mansions and estates for tax purposes, with Porfirian authorities turning a blind eye. Worse for these women, most banks were either reluctant to lend, closing up shop, or forcibly suspended from operation. To fill the vacuum, private lenders offered credit against the value of properties. Thus arose an informal market for mortgages.[44]

What befell the three ladies' houses is unknown. But given Jenkins's later admission that he speculated in real estate during the war and fore-closed on defaulted mortgages after it, and given the inability of many families to meet their tax payments, these houses very likely wound up in his hands.[45] So the transactions offer a glimpse of a major trait of the Revolution: the decline of one social elite, in which ladies distinguished themselves by the length of their names, to the benefit of a new, hard-nosed business class. Among them were a potent number of expatriates and immigrants—Lebanese, Jews, and lone wolves such as Jenkins—whose business skills and lack of sentimental ties to high society enabled them to prey upon needy Porfirians.[46]

Jenkins acquired many urban assets at this time, including a Mexico City theater and the site of the Puebla City bullring.[47] But city properties were not his specialty. Where the former farm boy speculated to far greater success, and with uncommon daring, was in the war-torn countryside.[48] During the Revolution, Jenkins bought and sold haciendas at a spectacular rate. Combining his knowledge of the nation's territory—gleaned through his textiles sales network—with the profits from his business and his access to dollars, he made speculative purchases along a 400-mile axis: San Luis Potosí, in the central north; Mexico City and its surrounding State of Mexico; neighboring Tlaxcala; and down to southern Puebla.[49] In 1918, Jenkins told a US visitor that his assets already included 100,000 acres of property outside the state of Puebla. By that time or soon after he also held six wheat-growing haciendas in Puebla's San Martín Valley, to the northwest of the state capital, and a huge mortgage on the sugar hacienda of San José Atencingo, in the southwestern lowlands.

Jenkins's bonanza began in 1913, the year of the Huerta coup, when rebel factions began printing their own currencies. The peso, worth 50 US cents, gradually devalued. That autumn, due to growing unrest and Huerta's forced loans and onerous tax policies, the banks suffered massive capital flight. This prompted a surge in demand for credit from private lenders.[50] Jenkins was primed to take advantage: his three mills were still fully operating, and he had $1 million deposited in the United States. As the black-market exchange rate fell from 2 pesos to the dollar to 5, Jenkins traded his greenbacks for Mexican paper money, to buy properties or mortgages upon them. When the currency hit bottom in 1916, he could purchase pesos for as little as 2 US cents. "It was too good to believe," he would tell a visitor. Feeling compelled to share his luck, he twice travelled home to urge friends to join the property rush. For whatever reason—reports of pitched battles, trains blown up, Americans kidnapped—none would chance it, so Jenkins continued on his own. He found he could usually buy properties at their prewar value; only near the end of his spree, as inflation increased, did he have to pay a higher peso price, but in dollar terms he still found bargains. In the latter years of the war, as the peso regained its strength, he started to sell his holdings. He later recalled: "Even at the cheapest price, I made enormous profits in the deals."[51]

In 1939, Jenkins would draw up statements claiming that his net worth reached a peak, in December 1917, of nearly $5.4 million. His data imply that over four years he almost doubled his fortune through property speculation, netting some $2.5 million. Since he was compiling this data for the IRS, it served him to massage the facts, exaggerating early gains to help him show a net loss over the next two decades. However, archival records confirm his ownership of the assets he listed. What is awry is his chronology, for he continued to buy and sell after 1917; he may have predated some of his gains so that they would fall beyond the purview of the IRS audit.[52]

Jenkins guessed that during the war no one else invested as heavily in the countryside, and he may well have been right.[53] His willingness to make deals with landowners in rebel-infested territory—landowners who were losing control over the very terrain they were seeking to sell or mortgage—says much of his bravura approach to fortune-seeking. These deals were no mere matter of signing documents before an urban notary; he ventured into the fields too. When Chester Lloyd Jones, a researcher employed by the oil baron Edward Doheny, visited Puebla in 1918, Jenkins took him for an afternoon drive through 30 miles of San Martín Valley countryside. Here he had "saved," as he put it, some 14,000 acres of fertile wheat land. They passed the burned-out shells of hacienda mansions and golden fields confiscated by insurgents, some of whom were threshing wheat in the middle of the road. Jenkins, perhaps enjoying his guest's discomfort, told Jones that there was no danger "so long as the Indians were not disturbed." Misreading local sentiment could well prove costly. A year later, indigenous revolutionaries sacked one of the haciendas that Jones visited, killing the brother of a Spaniard who was leasing the property from Jenkins. Reports said that the family had become targets because of their hard line against the land-seeking rebels.[54]

How these estates became available owed not only to the carnage of the Revolution but also to the conspicuous consumption that preceded it.

As Jenkins informed Jones, many landowners were heavily in debt, having borrowed to purchase and run their haciendas. Some of these estates were the recent acquisitions of Spaniards who had made good in textiles.[55] Owning one allowed these immigrants to confirm themselves as gentry, with all the social cachet and weekend appeal that a large landholding and country mansion implied. But many such farms struggled for profit. While the San Martín region was famous as a breadbasket, wheat had long proven an unreliable commodity for investors seeking a return. Sugar, if it were to be milled and refined as well as grown, required a lot of capital. So when in 1916 the government confiscated many leading banks, still-indebted landowners often sought to sell; they needed to pay off their loans and to gain some precious cash in hand. If they did not sell, the state—which with the Carranza Law of 1915 had both a revolutionary mandate and a legal basis to redistribute land to the poor—might well foreclose on the hacienda, delay in compensating for the balance, and undervalue the whole. To take the example of Santa Clara and Santa Ana Portales in the San Martín Valley, their owner was a Spanish immigrant who sold the two haciendas to Jenkins. By the date the deal went through, the seller had already returned to Madrid.[56]

With or without debts held by intervened banks, many landowners were forced to sell or seek private loans. During the war, such pragmatic concerns as an army's access to cash often failed to prevent rebels from laying waste to haciendas, common objects of loathing among country folk. This was especially so in the sugar-growing regions of Morelos and southwestern Puebla, where Zapatistas had exacted a terrible revenge on plantation owners for decades of abuse and theft of choice lands. The insurgents killed several landlords and managers and jailed or drove off most others; they burned most of their crops and destroyed many of their sugar mills. This much southwestern Puebla had in common with its westerly neighbor, but then their paths diverged. In Morelos, the Zapatista heartland, revolutionaries generally held onto the lands they had seized, and later President Obregón would take the politically astute step of formalizing their possession. In Puebla, where Zapatista leadership was fragmented, the pattern resembled the trend nationwide: from 1917, encouraged by a Carranza government now seeing the need to feed the nation, landowners returned to their ransacked properties and tried to revive them.[57]

Enter Jenkins. The American could offer the cash that landowners lacked. They needed him because of the depleted state of their reserves, some having spent the war in costly exile; because of the scarcity of bank loans; and because of the enormity of the rebuilding ahead. Some sold to Jenkins directly; others either obtained loans from him, putting up their properties as collateral, or leased him their land.

No doubt the Porfirian elites, with their high self-regard, were reluctant to go cap-in-hand to this American arriviste. Bridging the social gap between the two parties were mutual friends, including Puebla's public notaries.[58] Like their US counterparts, notaries were licensed by state governments to authenticate legal documents, including company charters and property transactions. But in Mexico they were far fewer—just ten of them served the million people of Puebla—and as well as providing a signature they offered a web of contacts and the stamp of community honor. During the Porfirian era, when banks were few, notaries acted as financial matchmakers, using their acquaintances to bring lenders and borrowers together; they have been termed Mexico's original micro-financiers. A notary hailed from a "good family" and put stock in personal honesty. Unlike judges, who might come and go with each governor and often appreciated bribes, notaries held their license and guarded their reputation for life. The accord that two parties made before a notary was effectively an honor pledge to the entire elite. During the Revolution, Jenkins worked with several notaries. Since times were lean, they surely valued his business.

By 1920 Jenkins had lent Puebla's upper crust at least 3 million pesos. Recipients included the French immigrant builders of Puebla's finest department store. Another was the giant holding company Viuda de Conde, named after the wealthy Spanish widow Ángela Conde de Conde (who in a fit of Pueblan parochialism had married her cousin). Much the largest loan, at 1.2 million pesos, was held by one Díaz Rubín and guaranteed by "the sugar property of Atencingo."[59] This estate would become the fulcrum of Jenkins's third major moneymaking scheme, after textiles and speculation: the production of sugar and alcohol.

The story begins with the untimely death of Spanish immigrant Ángel Díaz Rubín, at age forty-three, in 1913.[60] Together with his elder brother José, who predeceased him, Ángel had made a rapid fortune in textiles, coming to own three of Puebla's leading mills. In 1894, José had bought Atencingo, a midsize sugar plantation in southwestern Puebla, which the brothers developed into the state's second-biggest producer after the one owned by Governor Martínez. José bequeathed his assets to Ángel, who in turn left them to his eldest son, Álvaro. By then, Zapatistas had assaulted Atencingo several times. In 1914 the rebels returned and laid waste to it, wrecking the mill.[61] As hostilities subsided, Álvaro had little chance to revive the estate as he too died, a victim of the Spanish flu pandemic of 1918. Second son Pedro, recently returned from studying engineering at Cambridge, found himself head of the family. The Revolution, which had caused their mills to close for a while and inflicted three years of attacks on Atencingo, had badly depleted the family's reserves. So young Pedro turned to Jenkins for a loan.

The deal stipulated that Pedro Díaz Rubín would begin to repay the credit after the next harvest. But by 1920, Pedro faced default. Perhaps he had underestimated the damage Atencingo sustained. Or perhaps he was confounded by how, in his family's absence from the hacienda, local villagers had taken much of its land for growing staple foods, as occurred throughout the sugar region; further, Atencingo had lost some of its water supply following an old dispute with the nearby town of Chietla.[62] That Atencingo would not produce a harvest of any quantity for another three or four years reveals the extent of his miscalculation. When political conditions were propitious, after the fall of Carranza and once he had befriended the new state government, Jenkins would begin to foreclose on Atencingo.[63]

Detractors have cited Jenkins's dealings with Díaz Rubín and other elites as evidence of his pernicious nature, persuading the vulnerable to accept loans that they could never repay.[64] In the larger scheme of things, however, there was nothing unusual about sugar haciendas changing hands. Colonial records show successive families owning any given plantation, the churn owing much to sugar's price sensitivity to demand and supply from abroad. As debts rose and fortunes fell, estates were sold or foreclosed upon, the more so during periods of prolonged market decline for Mexican producers. During the bloody nineteenth century, Puebla was a frequent battleground and site of epidemics, which further eroded wealth; estates were seldom held by a family beyond a generation or two. Haciendas continued to change hands with frequency under Porfirio Díaz, in Puebla as nationwide, even as the *Pax Porfiriana* allowed cultivation to accelerate and consumption to soar. Immigrants who made fortunes in textiles, like the Díaz Rubíns, featured among the eager buyers.[65]

Nor was there anything unusual about predatory lending. Although President Díaz had fostered a formal banking sector, much loan-making remained a person-to-person activity. Private lenders charged high interest rates of 12 percent, or worse; many landowners felt asking for loans to be shameful and so agreed to pay a yet higher rate if the lender kept the transaction secret. When owners of haciendas and mills then failed to make payments, lenders typically foreclosed on them, adding coveted assets to their portfolios.[66]

So Jenkins's activities, if ethically dubious, followed local precedent. They may also have appealed to any lingering sense he held of Southern honor, which placed high value in being a creditor. As Southern historian Betram Wyatt-Brown has put it, lending and borrowing among the wealthy was a way of cementing social relations, and for the creditor it implied prestige. He adds: "A man of wealth gained authority as well as accrued interest by allowing the number of those owing him to increase."[67]

Whether or not Jenkins actively plotted to denude as many Puebla bluebloods as he could, his resentment over their initial snobbery toward him and Mary undoubtedly hardened his creditor's heart. As for the Díaz Rubíns and their kind, saddled with debt and humbled by war, they had little choice but to borrow from private lenders, and these of course required that properties be submitted as collateral. After all, Puebla's leading bank, the Banco Oriental, had been shuttered by the federal government in 1916, its assets liquidated, its reserves seized. To the hapless Díaz Rubín family this was a particular blow, for they had numbered among the bank's founding shareholders.[68]

The New Opportunists

The story of Mexican capital from 1911, when many wealthy families began to be displaced, is to some extent one of economic climbers taking their chances, by fair means and foul. This occurred little in heavy industry, but it was a marked trait in landholding, both urban and rural; it was also common in infant industry. Where the revolutionary state granted concessions or issued rulings, the playing field was favorable to the newly well-connected.

The up-and-comers who turned the war to their advantage were broadly of three kinds. First were the officers, who used the prestige, connections, and regional fiefdoms that they forged during the violence as entrées into business; often they spent time in politics en route, collecting licenses and contracts; often the federal government encouraged their self-enrichment, effectively buying them off rather than risking their rebelling.[69] One might call this "the Artemio Cruz model," after Carlos Fuentes' fictional anti-hero, who marries the daughter of a Porfirian landowner, hangs his uniform in the closet along with his revolutionary ideals and launches into a gamut of enterprises, some of them ethically suspect.[70] Eminent among them were ambitious men from the northern border states, a region of affinities and links with US capitalism. Generals all, they included several presidents: Álvaro Obregón (agribusiness, auto distribution), Plutarco Elías Calles (agribusiness, banking), and Abelardo Rodríguez (agribusiness, tourism, sea food, banking, movie theaters, and much else). They included cabinet ministers like Benjamín Hill (agribusiness, railroads), Aarón Sáenz (sugar, banking, aviation), and Juan Andreu Almazán (construction, tourism). And they included scores of state governors, although as many of these men pursued mere venality and theft as sought to create businesses.[71]

Next there were immigrants: Jews from eastern Europe and, more prominently, Arabic-speakers from the Middle East, especially Lebanon, most of whom settled in Mexico between 1900 and the 1920s. Among the latter came a fourteen-year-old boy called Julián Slim, who with an elder brother would found a Mexico City dry goods store, where hosiery from Jenkins's La Corona was sold at wholesale prices. During the Revolution, Slim invested in urban property. These were the seeds of the fortune of his third son, Carlos Slim, who a century or so after Julián's immigration became the richest person in the world. In the 1930s came another wave, Spaniards fleeing civil war and the fascist dictator Francisco Franco. What all these immigrant groups brought with them, as well as the storied work ethic and mutual-aid practices of ethnic enclaves the world over, was a decent education and (relative to most Mexicans) a fairish complexion, two powerful levers to social and economic mobility in a country so stratified by class and race. Lacking the social prejudices of the old elites, immigrants were willing to cozy up to the generals-turned-politicians. Crony relationships proved of great benefit to both.[72]

Then there were young and energetic businessmen of middle-class backgrounds, who multiplied their capital by exploiting wartime openings. They bet on fluctuations in the peso-dollar exchange rate; they played on needs of cash-poor Porfirians. Since their activities were surreptitious, such cases tend to emerge anecdotally. The Azcárraga Vidaurreta brothers, later the lords of radio and television, reportedly derived much of their initial capital from smuggling Porfirian gold and jewelry, bought cheap from desperate families and sold in the United States.[73] Emilio Azcárraga, the most successful of the brothers, had the advantages of a Texas education and years as traveling salesmen, so he had a command of English, a wide network of contacts, and the ability to move with ease between cities and across the US border.

Jenkins had things in common with both the middle-class strivers and the immigrants. Inheriting little wealth, founding his own businesses, and finding buyers nationwide for his hosiery products, Jenkins was a self-made man with an extraordinary nose for enterprise. Like many immigrants, he possessed a remarkable work ethic, which in his case compensated for the social disadvantages of being a non-native Spanish-speaker, a non-Catholic, and (probably as a concession to Mary) a non-drinker. He was also willing to trade favors with the powerful, in his case the dozen military officers who predominated in the Puebla governorship between 1913 and 1941.

Other US expatriates behaved similarly: Sinaloa-based sugar planter B. F. Johnston and Mexico City iron merchant Harry Wright, to name the best known. Johnston and Wright were better established than Jenkins by the fall of Díaz, but Johnston's story, in particular, offers a parallel. During the Revolution he played both sides, even supplying Yaqui rebels with arms; he bought out neighbors through predatory loans; and as rivals suffered ravages he saw his profits grow. The stories of Jenkins, Johnston, and Wright are unusual, however. During the war and the agrarian reform that followed, most US investors lost their shirts.[74] The exceptional nature of these three men's experiences implies an important caveat to Baron Rothschild's maxim. Blood in the streets may create opportunity, but one needs to be a natural risk-taker to exploit it.

Indeed, despite their frequent resorting to political connections, the up-and-comers were no mere horde of profiteers. Many of them had an approach to business as entrepreneurial as it was opportunistic. They often prevailed in sectors that were in their infancy and thus demanded something of a gamble, such as tourism, motorized transport, and residential real estate. Immigrants proved adept at entering established industries, applying innovation and marketing skills, and emerging after a generation or two as leaders, as would the Lebanese in Puebla's textile trade. Jenkins excelled in both respects, later by committing large sums to the capital-intensive emerging sector of film exhibition, more immediately by innovating in sugar.

In war, to depict profiteering as the opposite of entrepreneurialism is to invoke a false dichotomy. Doing business as the bullets fly and rivals alternate in the seats of power involves a good deal of risk, as well as imagination in crafting the web of relationships needed to fend off all kinds of threat. Risk and imagination help explain key questions about Jenkins's success: How could an upstart foreigner foreclose on the properties of prominent Porfirians? How could he do so given a judicial tradition that favored established landowners, the same tradition that had helped unscrupulous elites acquire much of Mexico's communal farmland? Later, how was he able to protect those assets from the expropriations of the 1920s and 1930s? The intricacies of each foreclosure are hard to ascertain. Such matters were rarely reported in the press, and the state judiciary's records for the era await cataloguing.[75] But the political arena of the day, when property rights were weak, favored the bold and the cunning. Jenkins's moves within that arena reveal an energetic strategy: he ingratiated himself with a variety of Puebla's power cliques.

Networking and Graft

Little affection prevailed between the Revolution's victors and the Puebla elite. In part the antipathy was political: liberal leaders disdained the cronies of the old regime. In part it was provincial. As of 1914, the first three governors that Carranza imposed all hailed from his home state of Coahuila. Carranza's fourth and last appointee, Alfonso Cabrera (1917–1920), was a Pueblan but of the wrong sort. He was from the Sierra, a bastion of liberalism long at odds with the state capital, and he was associated with Mexico City, where his brother Luis was finance minister. It riled the denizens of Puebla City to be ruled by outsiders, men who were anti-Catholic to boot, and the snobbery of the elite in turn riled the governors. Amid such tensions, there was ample reason for a judiciary named by Carranza's officers to rule against those who had fared well under Díaz. And at a time when officials were paid irregularly, there was ample reason for such judges to yield to lucre. As a British diplomat noted of the Carranza era: "Verdicts are bought and sold daily, like any other commodity."[76]

Still, in legal disputes, Jenkins could not entirely depend on local judges. The system worked slowly; decisions made in state courts were often stalled by injunctions gained in federal courts.[77] Besides, while Puebla's new governors did not regard Americans with the contempt they held for Spaniards, Jenkins remained a foreigner. Nor could he rely on much help from the United States. He was still a minor investor compared to those like William Randolph Hearst and Edward Doheny who had real lobbying power, and, as of 1917, per Mexico's new constitution, foreign nationals had to renounce all recourse to their governments when acquiring property.[78]

What Jenkins needed was a variety of friends, in a variety of high places, to assist him through all eventualities. So he wove a remarkable web of relationships that might protect him from the vicissitudes of the Revolution and help him navigate through, or around, the legal system. To a degree, these relationships also gave him respectability, which in the deferential and hierarchical society of Puebla City was tantamount to power.

Even before the Carrancistas took Puebla, Jenkins was working on his networking. The post of acting consular agent opened doors both commercial and political. He made friends with established expatriates, men of local knowledge and influence. One was William Hardaker, the British vice-consul, whose business of importing textile machinery acquainted him with many of Puebla's wealthy. His intervention in 1915 had helped save Jenkins from the Carrancista firing squad, and he joined his American friend in making predatory loans to bankrupt or vulnerable landowners.[79] With Diego Kennedy, a tough-minded American hacienda owner, Jenkins formed a company importing Emerson-Brantingham tractors. Their clients surely conveyed valuable information about which estates might be ripe for purchase or a high-interest loan. Kennedy was further useful as an expatriate of unusually high standing in Tlaxcala, where Jenkins acquired several estates; he had even led a coalition of landlords in a bid for that state's governorship in 1912. Kennedy's hard reputation rested on his being a vigilant, at times militant, guardian of private property, and during the Revolution he hired private forces to protect his land.[80] Later on, with Kennedy family assistance, Jenkins would copy this strategy.

He also became friendly with wealthy and influential Mexicans. Whether due to luck or an astute reading of character, he befriended men with enough savvy to emerge from the war with wealth and status more or less intact. One was Sergio B. Guzmán, a US-trained dental surgeon; his father was a doctor who had served in the Porfirian legislature of Veracruz state and later in Carranza's Congress as a senator for Puebla.[81] Best connected of all was Eduardo Mestre, an attorney as close to the old guard as anyone, having married the daughter of Puebla's former governor Mucio Martínez and served as a federal congressman. He steered through the 1910s by working for successive state governments as a negotiator of loans and by befriending the Revolution's leading general, Obregón. He offered legal counsel to Jenkins, and its usefulness can only be imagined.[82] Like Guzmán, Mestre possessed an affability the American lacked, yet from which he benefitted vicariously. They defended his name in social circles when others besmirched it, and as they were well liked their opinion counted. Mestre, in particular, was a consummate mixer, and it was largely thanks to him that Jenkins joined the Alpha Club.

Determined to act as though nothing remarkable were afoot beyond their castle walls, some of Puebla's moneyed set pooled resources in July 1914—the bloody month that saw President Huerta ousted and World War I break out—and founded a country club. Located on the fashionable western edge of town, the Alpha Club brought together a mix of textile elites, old-money Mexicans, and senior expatriates; wealth and whiteness were their bond. It was Mestre's brainchild but his stake was only 10 percent. The Conde y Conde brothers, owners of two big mills and vast real estate holdings, subscribed to more than a quarter of the shares; other textile men owned another quarter. Jenkins bought his first share in July 1915.[83] If some of the Divine Class were none too pleased at the prospect of this scruffy American joining the roll, Jenkins could count on his friendship with both Alpha's president, Mestre, and its vice president, Diego Kennedy. It cannot have hurt that he excelled at tennis, the club's main sporting activity.

At the Alpha, Jenkins could rub shoulders with whomever he pleased. He could talk business among fellow members, some of whom—the Díaz Rubíns, Conde y Condes, and the illustrious former mayor Francisco de Velasco—were among the families that would lose to him their sugar estates. Though he was not gregarious, Jenkins's Tennessee upbringing had exposed him to wealthy people who valued socializing much in the way the Puebla elite did, and if the company became overbearing he could retreat to the tennis court. Coming two years after his consular appointment, Alpha membership not only boosted his acceptance in senior circles but also implied a social contract between Jenkins, his debtors, and the club as an institution. Should a Díaz Rubín or a Conde balk at having to forfeit a property to the American, he faced the dishonor of reneging on a deal with an Alpha man.

Jenkins's ability to integrate himself into the elite, and during the Revolution, set him apart from the majority of US expatriates. Many departed during the war; many who stayed would sooner or later lose their assets, as a newly nationalistic state confiscated property.[84] Survival required, among other things, befriending a new political class. Since the Revolution's victorious generals were often drawn to high society, seeking social acceptance and perhaps an industrialist's daughter, entrée to the right clubs continued to matter. A contemporary of Jenkins, the merchant Harry Wright, used his presidency of the Mexico City Country Club to notably good effect. Despite prior attachments to Porfirio Díaz, he would cultivate Obregón and other presidents on the golf links while rising to become a steel magnate.[85]

Friendship opened some doors; others needed to be greased. Assured of anonymity, Jenkins told Chester Lloyd Jones, the Doheny researcher, that he had "made arrangements" with the head of the Local Agrarian Commission to minimize how much land he must sacrifice to radicalized peasants. (Set up by the Carranza Law, Local Agrarian Commissions were to work with state governors and the federal government to restore or grant hacienda land to indigenous communities.) He remarked: "It is only a choice of their taking your land or that of someone else, and most men think in such cases that it would be better to have the other man's land taken. This will require graft. Everybody does it." In 1918 alone, by May, he had paid the commissioner $2,400. Jenkins added: "There is no use going to the courts for justice; you have to buy it. It isn't a very high moral standard, but it is a question of living or dying."[86]

Graft was equally essential to the operation of his import business, Jenkins told Jones. To sell tractors to the state government, he had needed to pay three lots of bribes: to customs officers at the Mexican border, to railroad officials to bring the tractors down, and finally a "heavy rake-off" to Puebla's secretary of state. During the worst of the fighting, the backhanders required for transport were high. He had paid up to 300 pesos per freight car between Puebla and Mexico City and up to 1,000 pesos between the capital and the north-central hub of Celaya. Now things had settled down, yardmasters tapped just 10 to 15 pesos per car. Jenkins said he was sure that Governor Cabrera himself was getting protection money from landowners—and Jones added he was sure that Jenkins was one of those making the pay-offs.[87]

His admissions fit nicely with his later image as a dishonorable gringo capitalist. Yet were such practices unusual? His matter-of-fact description of bribery as a necessity suggests not. So does the substantial record of Yankee shenanigans during the late Porfirian era: both routine bribery and out-and-out fraud (small investors back home were the usual victims). One ambassador, David E. Thompson, spent much of his time in Mexico expanding his personal portfolio and covering up the corruption of others. Sinaloa-based sugar planter B. F. Johnston bought off judges to help him seize the estates of his neighbors.[88]

Whether US expatriates engaged in corruption any more than their Mexican peers is hard to say. Travel writer Charles Macomb Flandrau thought they did, but his conclusion may reflect his disgust at a few compatriots behaving badly. Gregory Mason, one of a journalistic minority to report on the Revolution from within Mexico (rather than from an El Paso barstool), claimed most US residents were "the kind . . . we don't want at home—plutocrats, privilege-seekers, and mining riffraff." But Mason was fond of sweeping statements.[89] Perhaps gringos were no more given to fraud and bribery than the locals, but American pretensions to the moral high ground, advertised ever since President Monroe issued his "doctrine" of Latin American guardianship in 1823, exposed their transgressions to charges of arrogance and hypocrisy.

By 1918, Jenkins was friends with the right expatriates and with some of the right Mexicans. That year he hosted at La Corona a champagne lunch on the Fourth of July, for a mix of US and European businessmen, along with local dignitaries.[90] He knew how to grease palms, both in the private sector and in state government; the graft of public officials, he advised Jones, "generally requires a long talk." But in pious Puebla of the Angels, his networking was not complete until he had befriended the Church. After all, he belonged to a tiny Protestant minority in a self-consciously Catholic city; several of his US forebears had found it good for business to convert.[91] To attain the friendship of an archbishop was to gain an ecclesiastical character reference and a substantial social blessing. Even the textile nabobs would take note.

With his conservatism and his support for schools and hospitals, Jenkins was something of a natural ally for the Church. His beneficiaries included Puebla's Latin American Hospital (a Baptist institution), its Methodist school, its Chamber of Commerce business school, and Vanderbilt. For the hospital, Jenkins gave both the land and the buildings. At his alma mater, he paid the fees of a number of boys and donated $6,000 to an Alumni Memorial Fund for a student center to commemorate Vanderbilt's Great War dead, a gift described in 1919 as the largest donation to date.[92] To this grandson of a pioneer preacher, such philanthropy was first a matter of noblesse oblige. Like the robber barons in whose United States he had come of age, Jenkins gave as a Protestant of means was supposed to; "For unto whomsoever much is given, of him shall be much required," as Luke's Gospel put it. The robber barons had also set a philanthropic precedent that was less altruistic: they made large gifts to churches, even to the Catholics, for they saw these institutions as buttressing the social order by pacifying the working class.[93]

Jenkins must have known his giving would catch the Church's eye. Certainly it did so in 1918, when Puebla encountered the Spanish flu. The contagion affected a third of the state's population and killed up to 45,000. With no effective response from the state government, and with the capital's death toll soaring past 100 per day, Catholic groups, business associations, and consuls put together a Central Charity Committee (CCC), raising funds to pay for doctors, medication, clothing, and ambulances. Jenkins appealed to the US government for medicines. In a display of efficiency that embarrassed Governor Cabrera, the CCC organized the cleaning of city streets, inspection of homes, and installation of emergency telephone and electricity services. The CCC raised 54,000 pesos during the two-month outbreak, and the largest single donor, with 3,000 pesos, was Jenkins. That sum was four times the size of La Corona's annual state tax bill.[94]

Jenkins's reputation was mixed. Chester Lloyd Jones labeled him a pushy businessman, "not particularly popular with the Mexicans." Another US researcher claimed that Puebla's American colony deemed him "a man who warranted their respect and friendship." If so, landowner Rosalie Evans dissented, for after a brush with his unforgiving business practices she called him "an awful character." But his social standing was sufficient by 1919 for Jenkins to be able to secure the Archbishop of Puebla, Enrique Sánchez y Paredes, for a service of blessing at his newly expanded mill. Respectful of local custom, Jenkins went to ask him in person, taking Mary with him. Though a strict Methodist, Mary would admit she found the Archbishop "lovely" and "broad minded," and the family was delighted when he accepted the invitation.[95]

The prelate's visit took place on Saturday, October 18, and Jenkins gave his workers most of the day off so they could decorate.[96] They festooned La Corona with flowers and evergreens and long strings of carded cotton that looked like floating lines of snow. The archbishop appeared in his coach and horses at four, greeted by twelve white-clad girls bearing tall candles. The girls led him into the main hall, where hundreds of women knelt in wait. He said a prayer before the factory altar and then followed the girls through the hall, sprinkling holy water on the machines, with Jenkins, his wife and daughters, and the chief seamstresses and mechanics close behind. The procession crossed to the new knitting and spinning halls, where the men were kneeling, and blessed them likewise. All then returned to the main hall, where the archbishop gave a homily. Finally he joined the Jenkins in their home for tea, cake, and ice cream. As he departed, women crowded to touch His Excellency's cloak. Afterward they stayed on with the men until nine, celebrating the visit with sorbets and cakes, music, and dancing.

"It was the nicest thing I ever did see and I am crazy about the Archbishop," Jenkins enthused the next day. He was writing to his daughter Elizabeth ("My dearest Piggy-Wiggy"), now at the Marlborough School in Los Angeles. "He is very nice indeed, not a bit stuck up over his high position, and great power, for you know he is the biggest guy in these parts by a jugful."

Sánchez y Paredes was the first in a succession of archbishops to whom Jenkins became close.[97] These were relationships of convenience to a point, politically advantageous to Jenkins and financially beneficial to the Church, but they were also friendships. Though no longer a churchgoer, Jenkins enjoyed the company of clergy. They offered well-informed exchanges of views and took scant interest in his businesses, so he could let his guard down a little. William Jenkins could still be convivial when he chose to be.

4

Kidnapped, Jailed, Vilified

Is Mexico Worth Saving?
US BOOK TITLE (1920)

Mueran los gringos [Death to the Gringos]
PROVISIONAL MEXICAN BOOK TITLE (1927)

A Consular Agent Is Kidnapped

Around nine that Sunday evening, the day after the archbishop's visit, Mary sensed that something might be wrong. The girls were asleep and the servants were in their quarters. The playing cards were put away and her sister-in-law Anne Jenkins, who had come to visit, retired to her room. Mary too was readying for bed, but something was keeping her husband. William liked to make a nightly inspection of the mill. He was a stickler for efficiency, so everything had to be in order for a quick start on Monday. Besides, it seemed prudent to be watchful in these times of continued unrest and banditry. Now, half an hour had passed.[1]

"Mary!" She was startled by the shout, which came from outside.

"Mary! Come to the office! I need you!" In William's booming voice, usually so self-assured, she could hear a tinge of strain.

Mary stepped out into the October night, wrapping a shawl about her shoulders. There was no sign of her husband. She made her way over to the mill house, beckoned by the sliver of light under the office door. Opening the latch and stepping inside, she found William in the company of three strange men, raggedly dressed. Handkerchiefs disguised their dark faces. They carried pistols, pointed at William, who stood with his wrists tied. On the floor sat the watchman, bound and gagged.

Mary was not one to make a fuss, but this was a nightmare come true. Ever since the Revolution had fired its first shots, she had grown in resolve that the family must leave. She had never much taken to Mexico. The random stresses of life abroad seemed to aggravate her tuberculosis. The war had only made things worse. Puebla had changed hands seven times; William had that brush with the firing squad; her brother Donald had a spell in jail. Then, having borne her third daughter, Mary had returned from California in mid-1916, hearing the violence had waned. Carranza was secure as president and rival factions were weakening. But dissident bands continued to roam, and they often raised cash by kidnapping the wealthy. Americans were frequent targets. The Jenkins family was especially vulnerable, living on the perimeter of Puebla City, and William was a multimillionaire. At long last, this year in July, Mary had persuaded him to take her property-hunting in Los Angeles. He bought a plot of land there and promised he would build on it a mansion fit for his queen. His words echoed the pledge he had made when they were falling in love, twenty years earlier.

As Mary glanced between the pistol barrels, the face of her husband, and the eyes of his captors, she heard William's voice addressing her. She forced herself to listen. These men had ransacked the company safe, stealing 50,000 pesos. Two of their band had already left with the loot. Now they proposed to take her husband hostage, but they wanted the Mexican government to pay. They had chosen him because he was a consular agent, which made them confident the US government would bring pressure to bear. They aimed not only to collect 300,000 pesos (that is, $150,000) in ransom money but also to show that Carranza was incapable of maintaining order.

Mary collected herself and began to protest. Why take her husband? Wasn't it enough to have robbed a consular agent? If they wanted treasure and publicity they could plunder the house too. William protested likewise, adding that the stress of not knowing his whereabouts would risk his wife's delicate health. But the leader of the band, distinctive with his large frame and red kerchief, said that only by taking him hostage could they strike a blow against Carranza. William told Mary she must alert the US Embassy and the local consular community. As they made to leave, Mary had the presence of mind to request they wait while she fetched her husband's overcoat. On parting, the leader warned her that any attempt to follow or trace them would result in Jenkins being shot. Then the four men vanished into the cold and gloom.

A WELTER OF activity followed, as the embassy, the Puebla authorities, the national and international press, Jenkins's business colleagues, and the governments of Mexico and the United States all got involved.[2] Carranza's Interior Ministry sent twenty-five military police to Puebla to investigate. Secretary of State Richard Lansing and Senator Albert Fall, two of the officials Mary telegrammed for help, took an active interest and made forceful declarations. The embassy sent personnel to Puebla who adopted a typically take-charge attitude, telling the police to call off their pursuit, denying officials access to correspondence with the abductors, and pressuring the governor to pay the ransom. Jenkins's friends, led by the lawyer Eduardo Mestre, mounted a private investigation to track down the kidnappers.

Everyone had an opinion on the matter and whose fault it was, and Mary soon discerned that everyone had an agenda. There were those, like Lansing, Fall, and the newspapers of William Randolph Hearst, who attacked Carranza to destabilize a regime they held to be anti-American; another senator, Henry Myers of Montana, submitted a resolution that the United States mobilize its armed forces to rescue Jenkins, while Representative J. W. Taylor of Tennessee airily proposed the annexation of a 100-mile band of Mexican territory "as indemnity for past depredations." There were those like the leader of the kidnappers, Federico Córdoba, who attacked Carranza because they detested his autocratic, centralizing leadership; many revolutionaries had fought for regional autonomy, which the government now sought to limit. Then, to Mary's alarm, there were those who attacked her husband, to support Carranza in his refusal to meet the demands of his captors and the urging of Washington that he pay the ransom. In standing firm, Carranza was snubbing the United States, but this was less of a surprise: nationalistic defiance was a chord that the Mexican President regularly struck.[3]

Most astounding to Mary were the allegations in certain Puebla newspapers that her husband had plotted his own kidnapping. Another article claimed that she was crazy and her testimony unreliable. By Tuesday, two days after the abduction, she was bed-ridden with frayed nerves. On Wednesday the family doctor visited and, finding her very weak, had her hospitalized. Later that day she received a letter from William. At least he was alive. That evening she wrote to her eldest daughter, Elizabeth, at boarding school in Los Angeles: "Pop is out in a cave in the mountains somewhere, he has no idea where himself, as he was blindfolded, and they move him from one place to another." But, she added, he had said they were treating him well. Further letters followed, in which her husband put a brave face on a worsening situation. Forced to sleep in the open on three of his nights in captivity and caught by rain each time, he was growing sickly and his right leg developed a sharp rheumatic ache.

On Friday, Mestre established contact with Córdoba, who agreed to let him see Jenkins the next day. Reaching Córdoba's camp on horseback, Mestre found Jenkins very weak, and his condition seemed aggravated by food poisoning. An affable lawyer with a knack for befriending all parties, and an experienced negotiator in matters of finance, Mestre prevailed on Córdoba to accept third-party payment for the ransom.[4] He also told him that no one had ready access to the sum of gold pesos he wanted, so payment would have to be made in installments. Aware that Carranza was refusing to negotiate, and fearing his captive might die before the president relented, Córdoba agreed.

Jenkins's co-investors in the Commercial Company of Puebla, along with British vice-consul William Hardaker, cobbled together a first installment. Signing a promissory oath, they vouched with their lives to pay the balance. On October 26, a week after the abduction, Mestre rode again to meet Córdoba, saddled with 34,000 pesos in gold coins and 20,000 in drafts. Fearing bandits, he had dressed down in an old raincoat, and as he approached the rendezvous he dismounted and hid his bags under an agave plant. On finding Córdoba, he went back for the cash.

"I know who you are," Córdoba reminded him. "If you don't deliver the rest, I'll have you taken from the train to Mexico City and hung from the nearest telegraph pole."

Córdoba threatened to do the same with the others who had vouched for Jenkins. Mestre promised the payment would be completed as soon as Jenkins could gather it. Córdoba then wrote him a receipt. At a separate rendezvous, a house with a telephone, Jenkins was allowed to call his friends and arrange for his collection. They took him straight to the Latin American Hospital, where Mary was still convalescing.

Mary's joy at her husband's release receded at the sight of his condition. He was near collapse: ill-fed, with one leg inflamed, suffering from diarrhea and intense pain in the colon. The doctor diagnosed his ailments as "nervous prostration, acute articular rheumatism, and colitis from exposure and hardship," and for five days he was hospitalized.[5] Mary confided to Elizabeth that his nerves seemed crushed and nightmares of his ordeal interrupted his sleep. She added: "It seems too bad to see a strong man broken, and when he first came back, he would just cry." Though a muscular man of forty-one, he needed a cane to walk. He spent another fortnight recuperating at home.

To the public, Jenkins maintained a steely façade. He had always despised Carranza, ever since that platoon of his had threatened to shoot him for aiding Zapatistas. Since then, Carranza had backed the 1917 Constitution, which threatened private enterprise. His government had confiscated some of Jenkins's land for redistribution to peasants. And his latest proxy as governor, Alfonso Cabrera, was unusually ineffective. Aloof, authoritarian, clueless at building bridges with Puebla elites, Cabrera had managed to alienate almost everyone.[6] Jenkins had tried to keep on good terms with him; he told the US Embassy that several times he had rendered him "valuable assistance" (possibly loans to his government, a standard practice of his in years to come). But Cabrera seemed to be building a conspiracy theory against him. Claims that Jenkins had staged his abduction, that he was spied enjoying a beer with his captors, that he was in league with Puebla "reactionaries," and that he wanted to help provoke a US invasion all appeared in newspapers known to be in Cabrera's pocket. The very day after the kidnapping, Cabrera had told a judge to start an investigation—not of the kidnappers but of Jenkins.[7]

On October 31, on leaving the hospital, Jenkins was detained for questioning. By now Cabrera's officials were openly saying they believed Jenkins had conspired with his abductors.[8] In what became a pattern of dismissive behavior toward local authorities, Jenkins only gave vague answers. He said he could not be sure who had kidnapped him, and he denied knowing how much was paid for his release. All he clarified was that his captors had targeted him because of his official position, so he held the Mexican government liable for his reimbursement.

Cabrera remained under pressure from Mexico's Ministry of Foreign Relations and the US Embassy to capture and prosecute the kidnappers, but he claimed that due to Jenkins's noncooperation he was unable to do so. Jenkins in turn said he could not trust the state judiciary for a fair hearing. His assessment was probably accurate. In early November, so investigations by the Embassy and a Mexico City newspaper would find, state authorities led by Judge Fernando Guzmán had detained a number of peons at a hacienda Jenkins owned near Atlixco, Santa Lucía, and goaded them to testify to having seen him interact amicably with his abductors. When they resisted, three of their number were successively taken outside, whereupon rifle shots were heard, and a soldier reported each execution to the assembly. The remaining peons agreed to testify, later discovering that their friends were alive.[9]

Jenkins insisted that the Carranza government cover his ransom and losses. The acting foreign relations minister, Hilario Medina, quite reasonably rejected the demand, informing the embassy that paying would encourage other kidnappings. He added that neither Mexico nor the United States would pay a ransom under such circumstances. Throughout the fall of 1919, as the diplomatic crisis unfolded, Medina's measured if sometimes sly prose would contrast with the haughty outrage of his counterpart, Lansing.[10]

Tensions climbed another notch on November 14 and 15, when Puebla police again called Jenkins for questioning. He was faced with the testimony of the Santa Lucía peons that they had seen him socializing with his kidnappers; they added that he had threatened to retaliate if they ever reported this. When Jenkins angrily denied the accusations, he was arrested for two hours, under tentative charges of perjury (for denying his presence at Santa Lucía), paying money to rebels, and attempting to defraud the state by conniving with his kidnappers. Bail was set, but Jenkins refused to pay it, believing that doing implied an admission of guilt. He insisted on complete exoneration. For the time being, Cabrera decided to let Jenkins return home.[11]

Jenkins was furious and did not care who knew it. He felt Cabrera was careless in the first place for failing to post guards on the roads leading to Puebla City; bandits could come and go as they pleased, and incidents of theft were common. He resented the newspaper attacks, which had also maligned Mary. Cabrera's officials were heavy-handed; they had even tried to remove him from the hospital, only desisting when a state-appointed doctor confirmed he really was sick. They had also arrested his friend Mestre and three of his employees, as part of an investigation that an embassy official termed "inquisitorial." His belief that Judge Guzmán and Puebla Attorney General Julio Mitchell were fabricating evidence against him was shared by Puebla's European consuls, and several Mexico City papers reported suspicions that Puebla officials were coercing witnesses. After his questioning, Jenkins repeatedly returned to the court with twenty witnesses for his defense, only to be told that the judge was "too busy" to receive them.[12]

As events unfolded, the impatience of US opinion leaders over Carranza's refusal to repay Jenkins's ransom, and over the State Department's hesitance to force the issue, made for provocative press. "If the Mexican authorities have been often negligent and sometimes impotent," sniffed *The New York Times*, the Jenkins case "should be pressed upon the Mexican government for indemnification and reparation." The

Toledo Blade huffed: "It may be that the American government is using [Jenkins] as a sort of experiment to see just how much mistreatment it is possible for one American to stand at the hands of a gang of outlaw greasers." Oregon's *Salem Statesman* cried: "Mexico is not a government. It is a riot." Hawkish elements were readier than usual to believe the worst about Mexico, for Carranza was now ratcheting up his nationalistic defense of the oil sector, ordering the army to seize the wells that US firms had started drilling without permits.[13]

Ever sensitive to personal injustices, Jenkins was openly contemptuous of the local authorities, and his attitude in turn conformed to Mexican notions of American arrogance. No doubt it facilitated the negative image that the pro-Carranza newspapers were gleefully building. In one story he was reportedly planning to leave the country to evade the Puebla judiciary; in another he was said to have received Mexican citizenship from the disgraced President Huerta.[14] Jenkins's conduct made him seem ever guiltier to the Mexicans. Unwittingly, he was laying the groundwork for his own mythification.

Lansing and Fall Bang the Drum for War

Exactly one month after his abduction, Jenkins was jailed in the state penitentiary. On November 19, Cabrera's officials formalized their earlier charges of perjury and threatening witnesses; that of colluding with kidnappers, for which they lacked sufficient evidence, was dropped. Bail was set at a mere 1,000 pesos, but Jenkins again refused to pay it.[15] Not only did he feel that posting bail implied guilt, he also seemed to calculate that staying in jail would draw support for his complaint against Cabrera and for his demand for reimbursement. Doing so also raised the heat on Carranza. But if Jenkins were upping the ante in the hope that the regime would buckle, Carranza seemed ready to match him. Keeping this insolent gringo in jail would serve his nationalistic reputation.

Hawks in Washington flew into circling mode. Secretary of State Lansing, a Democrat, and Senator Fall, a Republican, had been seeking to unseat Carranza for some time. Now they had their best chance of doing so. They professed outrage that the Mexicans should jail the American victim of a kidnapping, and a consular agent at that. Lansing sent a formal protest, requesting Jenkins be released at once. Knowing Carranza as he did, Lansing surely had little faith that his demand would be met; his note, immediately released to the press, was rather a move to start building a consensus for some kind of intervention. Similarly he gave the papers Jenkins's lengthy account of his kidnapping. Fall meanwhile geared up his push for a diplomatic break: if it did not elicit armed intervention, it could at least give Carranza's rivals the impetus to join together and overthrow him. That notion was not far-fetched. In September four leading dissidents—Pancho Villa, Gildardo Magaña (new chief of the Zapatistas), Manuel Peláez (to whom the kidnapper Córdoba reported), and Félix Díaz (a nephew of Porfirio) —issued a joint manifesto. They promised to unite their movements to form a government if the United States would recognize and aid it. By this time, all four bands had lost much of their strength, but they remained attractive to Fall for their commitment to private property.[16]

A diplomatic break would mean a step toward a US invasion. At this stage, Lansing and Fall were perhaps less eager for battle than some of their rhetoric suggested. By a War Department estimate, occupation of Mexico would require 400,000 troops. Lansing several times spoke of war but likely as part of a strategy of threatening Carranza into making concessions and less over Jenkins than over oil rights and property damages; in a diary entry he wrote of hoping for a peaceful solution. Fall had been a long-term proponent of intervention, but he surely recognized that regime change was better effected by local forces friendly to the United States.[17] Yet the two men's stoking of the public mood, via official bulletins and a compliant section of the press, made war seem a growing probability. So did the fact that the US Army, even after most of the postwar demobilizations, could count on some 200,000 soldiers hardened by service in Europe.[18] All this only added to the pressure on Carranza while giving succor to his enemies.

Generally, Lansing's inclinations were interventionist, and for years they had paralleled those of his president. Woodrow Wilson had sent the military into Haiti, the Dominican Republic, Cuba, and Panama, usually on grounds of protecting economic interests. But during the first half of 1919, while attempting to influence the Paris Peace Conference that followed the war, the Democratic president had proposed a League of Nations that would safeguard the principles of national sovereignty and equality among nations. This latter-day dovishness was not to the taste of Lansing, who opposed the League; he also resented Wilson for sidelining him at the Paris talks. However, Wilson now was bed-ridden, recovering from a grueling tour to sell the League to the American public. The president had suffered a stroke that paralyzed his left side. Lansing saw the chance to put a greater stamp on foreign policy. By threatening war, he might penetrate Carranza's "thick skull"—as he put it in his diary—and force him to meet US demands over property rights.[19]

Lansing's complaint about Jenkins's jailing met with a crafty response. His counterpart Medina wrote that the Mexican government had no more right to interfere in Puebla's judicial processes than did President Wilson in the processes of a US state; he included a lengthy account of Mexican penal procedure for Lansing's edification. Lansing was enraged. He told colleagues in the Wilson cabinet that the United States needed to "straighten out" Mexico. In language recalling arguments for the Spanish-American War of 1898, he added that invasion of Mexico would return unity and stability to US society, which was now beset with strikes, race riots, and fears of "red" agitation among the swelling ranks of the unemployed. Lansing then called in Mexico's ambassador, Ignacio Bonillas. "The patience of this country is nearly exhausted," he told Bonillas. He added that a tide of indignation among the American people might prevent further discussion and force a break in diplomatic relations, which would "almost inevitably mean war."[20]

The Wilson cabinet was divided. Navy Secretary Josephus Daniels was one of several ministers who tried to persuade Lansing to pursue a moderate line. Others were as hawkish as the leading Republicans. Interior Secretary Franklin Lane reassured Lansing that Mexicans were "naughty children who are exercising all the privileges and rights of grown ups"; they therefore required the administering of "a stiff hand."[21]

The powerful Senator Fall shared Lansing's distaste for Carranza. Fall was so close to the oil industry that he earned the nickname "Petroleum Fall." But his sentiments about Mexico were not born of cronyism alone. In recent years the navies of the Great Powers had been abandoning coal for oil, which was lighter, easier to handle, and gave ships a greater range; it also solved the problem of coal's thick smoke, which easily drew enemy attention. Fall believed that control of key petroleum supplies would determine which nation gained global supremacy. Carranza thus posed a strategic obstacle: he had several times raised taxes on oil fields; he had sponsored a constitution that threatened their very ownership; and the previous spring he had sent troops to stop the oil companies from drilling new wells.[22] Fall deemed Carranza bad news for Americans in general. Hundreds had been killed during the Revolution, chiefly on Carranza's watch, and Jenkins was only the latest victim in a catalogue of kidnappings.

To the consternation of Fall and his oil industry cronies, Wilson seemed unwilling to tackle this "Mexican problem," even with war concluded in Europe. But the tide in Washington was turning against the president, and not only due to his abortive League of Nations tour and subsequent ill health. In November 1918, the Republicans had regained control of Congress; they forced Wilson to cede them control of the powerful Senate Committee on Foreign Relations, now chaired by Wilson's foreign affairs nemesis, Henry Cabot Lodge. Two powerful lobbies emerged, hoping to push the United States into unseating Carranza: the National Association for the Protection of American Rights in Mexico (NAPARM) and the Oil Producers Association. Edward L. Doheny, oil baron and close friend of Fall's, helped direct the first and chaired the second. On July 1, 1919, NAPARM began issuing sensationalistic bulletins that pandered to US xenophobia, painting Carranza's Mexico as a barbarous failed state, rife with banditry, and host to a godless Bolshevism that threatened to seep into the United States.[23]

In September, Fall had initiated a Senate investigation into Mexican affairs, conducting hearings in Washington and border cities. This "Fall Committee," as the press termed it, would solicit testimony from 257 witnesses, on the Carranza regime in general and on damage to US lives and property in particular. Fall encouraged those who attacked the Revolution and badgered those who would defend it. The Committee, which would meet for nine months, was in part a stick with which to beat Carranza, and in part a tool for building the case for breaking off relations. It was also a Republican forum for airing displeasure at Wilson's Mexico policies and hence shaping public opinion before the 1920 presidential election. In the view of Fall and Cabot Lodge, the ideal relationship with Mexico would mirror that with Cuba: a protectorate, in which politics were subjugated to US interests.[24]

After Jenkins's jailing, newspapers and politicians chimed in. By no means all favored intervention. Prominent among those advocating restraint were the Pulitzer family's *New York World*, which hoped that "if it is ever deemed necessary for us to resort to stern measures south of the Rio Grande we shall have stronger provocation than a police-court case." But the loudest voices were hawkish. The Representative from Jenkins's home district in Tennessee told Hearst's *New York American*: "The honor of the United States is involved in the Jenkins case. It must be avenged." Americans in Mexico were "treated like dogs," wailed the *Detroit Free Press*. Cartoonists either imagined sombrero'd Mexicans assaulting US "patience" or ridiculed Wilson's government for its inaction. Carey Orr of the *Chicago Tribune* depicted Uncle Sam with a Mexican boy across his lap, prone for a spanking, and a cobweb attached to the old man's raised hand. Provincial papers resorted to stereotypes to trot out their invective. "No matador in a Mexican arena ever heckled a bull more aggravatingly than Mexico herself persistently heckles Uncle Sam in the Jenkins case," fulminated the *Grand Rapids Herald*. "When Mexican brigands can get $150,000 ransom for a gringo consul, without half trying, is it any wonder that those greasers don't care to work for a living!" frothed the *Key West Citizen*.[25]

By late November, what had been a page-three story in *The New York Times* generated front-page banners.[26] Fearing the worst, labor leader Samuel Gompers and the governor of New Mexico, Octaviano Larrazolo, urged Carranza to set Jenkins free. The Carranza government's claim that it could not intervene in a Puebla state matter was quite disingenuous. Carranza routinely overruled provincial authorities, appointing governors at will. When he summoned Cabrera to the capital for discussions, he may have considered forcing the governor to free Jenkins under some face-saving pretext. But for the time being, any such thought was quashed by the insistence of the governor's brother, Luis, who was secretary of the treasury and an ideologue of passionate anti-American sentiment. In standing up to the United States, Carranza also enjoyed support across the Spanish-speaking world. Newspapers from Colombia to Spain sided with him against US heavy-handedness. Nonetheless, Governor Cabrera and Foreign Relations Secretary Medina urged Jenkins, through third parties, to accept his freedom on bail.[27]

Jenkins, naturally, refused to cooperate. He viewed his plight in part as a matter of honor. At times, his proud behavior inconvenienced each party. Far from playing the innocent victim of wrongdoing, he wrote letters and gave interviews in which he let his candor and disdain for the governor get the better of him. He wrote to a friend (who passed on his missive to the press) that the Mexicans' handling of his case was a farce. He boasted to *The New York Times* that he had made lots of money during the Revolution. He said that by staying in jail he hoped to cause problems for Cabrera.[28]

War was in the air, and there was more to it than talk. Some 60,000 troops, deployed in August to protect the border towns, readied themselves for action; with them they had airplanes and a hundred light tanks. Texas mobilized its National Guard. The Navy was put on alert. Reconnaissance flights gauged a Mexican troop build-up along the border, and military intelligence found that Mexico planned to dynamite the railroad bridges between Nuevo Laredo and Monterrey. On December 1 the dovish *Baltimore Sun* admitted that war was likelier than at any time since Wilson recognized the Carranza regime in 1915. Fall was now ready to bet he had the momentum to force the weakened president into action. Wishing to move faster than Lansing, he played his hand. On December 3, citing both the State Department's dealings and evidence gathered by his committee that Mexican consuls were spreading communist propaganda throughout the United States, Fall introduced a motion: the president should withdraw recognition from Carranza and cut diplomatic ties. Fall's allies then introduced further motions: that more troops be dispatched to the border and that Wilson authorize the army and navy to force payment of claims made by Americans affected by the Revolution.[29]

As the US drumbeat grew louder, Mexican newspapers rang with rumors and reports of gunboats heading for Tampico and Veracruz and airplanes circling over border towns. Although a US War Department official told the *Los Angeles Times* that a full-scale invasion would take another six months to prepare, to much of the Mexican press an armed intervention seemed imminent.[30]

Three things were now clear. In the United States, amid rising tensions with a neighbor widely viewed as backward and barbarous, an incident as minor as the jailing of a consular agent could become a *cause célèbre* and a pretext for redefining foreign policy. In Mexico, the target of US incursions for more than seventy years, admonitions from Washington politicians, threats from the Hearst papers, and preliminary troop movements could make an invasion seem likelier than it was. And William Jenkins had seized the Mexican imagination as the archetypal gringo: devious, arrogant, and willing to do anything for a buck.

Mary Jenkins wrote to Elizabeth on December 4: "You fuss so much about our government doing nothing—I don't see where you get that, for my fear is that they will do too much and I don't feel quite ready to be murdered, and we would be the target."

Her fears came close to being fulfilled. Fall's resolution to break with Mexico, still under committee review on December 5, would have allowed a declaration of war to follow or enabled a massive "policing" presence of the kind still in place in Haiti and the Dominican Republic. At the very least it could have incited another prolonged chapter in Mexico's faction-laden Revolution. President Wilson had been so long out of the public eye, rumors abounded as to the enfeebled state of his mind; would such an invalid be able to resist Fall's interventionist freight train? Lansing was more cautious than Fall, unsure that the Jenkins affair was a politically viable pretext for a rupture with Mexico; congressional Democrats (Lansing's party, after all) were reluctant to back intervention. Still, he considered Carranza a "stubborn old mule" and would be glad to see him deposed. In a letter to a friend that day, he admitted how hard he had found it to "swallow one's pride and to keep ladling out soothing syrup to those Greasers while they smiled sarcastically and kept on with their insults."[31] But Fall and Lansing miscalculated. Wilson was less decrepit than they had imagined and Carranza less inflexible.

The Mexican president no doubt sensed that he had milked the episode for all its nationalistic worth, because on December 4 a man unconnected to Jenkins paid his bail and a Puebla judge ordered his release. At midnight, Jenkins was awoken in the penitentiary by the chief of police, who said he was urgently needed in court. At first he refused to go. The officer would not give any further reason and Jenkins could not conceive of a court operating at that hour. For a moment he feared he might be subjected to *ley fuga* (the law of flight) and shot "while trying to escape." When the officer led him outside it was not to the court they went but Jenkins's home. He was told he was free, though he was not informed why.[32]

Woodrow Wilson, though bed-ridden for two months, felt sufficiently healthier by December 5 to agree to Fall's insistence on a meeting. As the president knew well, Fall may have asked to hear his position on Mexico, but he was just as interested in gauging Wilson's physical capacity to fulfill his duties. Fall was to be doubly disappointed. Although the president lay in bed, he was more alert than the Senator expected and the grip of his handshake firmer.

"Well, Senator," Wilson began, "how are your Mexican investments getting along?"

Fall changed the subject. "Well, Mr. President, we have all been praying for you."

"Which way, Senator?" Wilson replied with a smirk.

Clearly this was a chief executive not liable to be pushed. Then, midway through their discussion of the Mexican situation, Wilson's doctor burst into the room bringing word of Jenkins's release. "That seems to have helped some," laughed the president. Fall's bloated hopes for a rapid break with Mexico were pricked. He soldiered on, presenting his committee's case against Carranza, but the issue of intervention was not broached.

Three days later Wilson answered with a promised memo, also released to the press, stating he would be "gravely concerned" to see Congress approve Fall's resolution to sever ties with Mexico.[33]

Afterward, one of Fall's aides wrote that the Carranza regime, in its covert arrangement of Jenkins's bail, had "outwitted" the State Department. In fact, Fall's misreading of Mexico extended further. Unbeknownst to him, his dissident coalition was unraveling, and in part through his and Lansing's heavy-handedness. Headlines warning of a US invasion had spurred the Zapatista leader Magaña to assure Carranza of his suspension of hostilities. A secret meeting between the two on November 28 sealed the truce, and over the next month a series of Zapatista chiefs in Morelos and Puebla surrendered. Republican leaders continued to blow hard about a break, returning to oil as their chief rationale, but on January 17 Carranza deflated that bubble too by issuing US firms with long-suspended drilling permits for new wells. For another four months, Fall would continue his Senate hearings and tally offenses against Americans, but his best chance to precipitate regime change had passed. By the time he finished, the Mexicans had dealt with Carranza on their own terms.[34]

By then, too, Wilson had forced Lansing to resign, in part because of his belligerence. Indeed, the Jenkins affair would mark a turning point in US relations with Mexico. Wilson's opposition to intervention, even to a severing of diplomatic ties, contrasted with his approval of the occupation of Veracruz in 1914 and the failed Pershing Raid to capture Pancho Villa in 1916. No US president would ever send troops into Mexico again. The episode offered Wilson a first chance to put into local practice the global principles of sovereignty he had famously touted in Paris. The evolution in his thinking anticipated the Good Neighbor Policy toward Latin America developed by Herbert Hoover and Franklin Roosevelt a decade or so later.

Jenkins himself was livid to learn that his freedom did not signal a dropping of charges. In fact, an American by name of J. Salter Hansen, claiming to act in the interests of peace, had posted bail on his behalf. Jenkins had never heard of Hansen. He assumed the man had been dispatched to Puebla by the federal government. The move was evidently designed to halt Lansing and Fall's war-mongering without harming Carranza's resolute image. Once Jenkins knew of the ruse, he demanded for several weeks to be let back into prison.[35]

The threat of war faded, but the case against Jenkins dragged on. Governor Cabrera evidently felt there was more political capital to be made, for Jenkins was summoned to court several more times to hear accusers. On his first reappearance he was dismayed to find that Cabrera had replaced the presiding judge, who had finally heard the testimony of his witnesses, with his antagonist from Atlixco, Fernando Guzmán. It soon emerged that the record of peons recanting their statements against Jenkins was "missing." Federico Córdoba then told the New York Tribune he had been offered 200,000 pesos to testify against Jenkins. After the Foreign Relations Ministry withdrew its recognition of Jenkins's consular status, Cabrera declared in his January state address that the American was without scruples and already proven guilty. Attorney General Mitchell announced new charges against Jenkins of bribing witnesses and foment- ing rebellion. At a press conference he swore he would "bury Jenkins in jail."[36]

Jenkins fought back in kind. He gave a lengthy account of his kidnap- ping to the New York Tribune. He met several times with Gerald Brandon of the Los Angeles Times, whom the Carranza regime soon expelled for his reporting. In a rollicking series published that March, Brandon reported that Mitchell asked him to relay to Jenkins an offer to throw out the case. It was a shake-down. Brandon quoted Jenkins's frank response: " 'Not a penny will I give the grafting ——,' he answered, with a round American oath." In court Jenkins barely cooperated, answering questions with defi- ance and refusing a handwriting sample. He accused Guzmán of brib- ing witnesses, and when the judge fined him for contempt he refused to pay.[37]

All the while Jenkins and Mestre were seeking a transfer of the case out of the hands of Puebla's politicized judiciary. Mestre argued that the defen- dant's office as a consular agent, which Lansing had raised from interim to actual status in 1918, necessitated a federal-level trial, but Foreign Relations' January 30 decision weakened his case. The Supreme Court was still deliberating the request in May 1920 when the Carranza regime fell.[38] Álvaro Obregón, suspecting that his former commander-in-chief wished to impose a de facto dictatorship, rose up in an April rebellion that quickly gathered momentum. It prompted Carranza's flight, which soon led to the president's murder. Governor Cabrera fled too.

The Supreme Court ruled in August that Jenkins's consular status was enough to grant him a federal-level hearing. That December, shortly after Obregón became president, federal judge Daniel V. Valencia cleared Jenkins of perjury and threatening witnesses, the only charges officially leveled. Two months later, his assiduous Puebla persecutors, former Attorney General Mitchell and Judge Guzmán, were arrested and charged with evidence tampering and witness coercion. One cannot attach too much to such reversals, for even the federal courts had their allegiances, but Valencia, to whom Jenkins owed his exoneration, was sufficiently respected for President Cárdenas later to appoint him chief justice of the Supreme Court.[39]

Was Jenkins Guilty?

Determining what really happened in a long-ago legal dispute is a slippery matter. What people wrote or said has to be read against the grain, tested for bias and inconsistency, and, where accounts conflict, motives must be considered. During the Jenkins affair, the principal players all had reasons for using the dispute to their own ends, irrespective of the merits of the case against the American. Many of the dozens of witnesses who testified were likely partial or bribed, and the judiciary was susceptible to political pressures, especially in Puebla.[40] So it is worthwhile setting aside accusations, counter-accusations, and even judges' rulings to reconsider the authenticity of the kidnapping on the grounds of logic.

Jenkins had favored US intervention once. He had said as much in his consular reports in 1914 and 1915. Now his signals were mixed. After his release, Jenkins told the press he did not favor intervention. During the investigation into his complicity, some of the evidence to emerge against him seemed quite damning, notably his first letter to Mary during captivity, in which he urged her to put pressure on Washington to take up the abduction with Mexico City. He had added: "We want it understood clearly that it is a band of Rebels who entered Puebla and took me away and not 'Apaches' [i.e. bandits]. I want to make the government responsible and this can be done only if Rebels are the cause—so don't fail to make that clear."[41] The desire his words revealed to undermine the Carranza regime, along with his arrogant declarations in public and his refusal to cooperate with Puebla authorities, made it easy for Governor Cabrera to cast Jenkins as the villain of the piece. It then emerged that Jenkins knew the kidnappers' second-in-command, an Atlixco-based Zapatista named Juan Ubera. Jenkins admitted he had been paying him the modest monthly sum of 50 pesos to protect Hacienda Santa Lucía.[42]

But sympathy with the kidnappers' goal of undermining Carranza is no proof of conspiracy. Equally plausible is that Ubera knew that Jenkins hated the president and so viewed him as a malleable target. It is also plausible that, once captive, Jenkins saw he had a better chance of returning home, soon and unharmed, if he helped his captors achieve their goals. If he did get along well with them, as some witnesses alleged, that may simply have reflected his ability to make the best of a bad situation and his fearlessness among insurgents, both well-established traits. His words to Mary about Rebels and Apaches are explicable inasmuch as Cabrera was in the habit of denying that anti-Carranza forces operated in Puebla, despite a wealth of evidence to the contrary.[43]

That Jenkins had been paying Ubera protection money is equally explicable. Zapatistas had often forced large-scale landowners to pay for protection; the two sides seldom met, for the payments were made by the estates' managers. An executive for a US tractor firm, who had visited Jenkins just prior to his abduction, reported on his return: "Those who live in rebel territory have to pay tribute to the rebel forces for protection and liberty to work their fields."[44]

Nevertheless, the chief of the kidnappers, Federico Córdoba, could well have seemed a likely conspirator with Jenkins, and not only because of the American's lack of animosity toward him after his release. Córdoba reported to Manuel Peláez, the wealthy political boss of the oil region of northern Veracruz. Peláez detested Carranza for his autocratic style and his impositions upon the provinces; his career, like Zapata's, is a reminder that many revolutionary leaders fought chiefly, even exclusively, for the welfare of their *patria chica*—their local homeland—not something so nebulous as the nation. Peláez had a lot of experience dealing with Americans and Britons, and for much of the Revolution he levied on their oil enclaves a de facto protection tax. Chief among his clients was the oil baron Edward Doheny.[45]

Here is where the "self-kidnapping" conspiracy theory gains greater circumstantial credibility. Jenkins's abductor took his orders from a general who was close to the most active of private-sector interventionists, who was in turn in league with Senator Fall. Furthermore, Jenkins was reported to have visited Fall while in the United States the previous summer.[46] Might not these five men have cooked up the whole episode?

As so often with circumstantial evidence, other factors suggest a coincidence rather than a conspiracy. For example, it later emerged that Peláez had commissioned Córdoba to unite rebel forces in and around Puebla (hence his partnering with the Zapatista officer Ubera) and to strike as big a blow to Carranza's credibility as possible. Córdoba's initial plan had been to kidnap the US ambassador; then he sought to abduct various Puebla consuls, including Britain's Hardaker, but he scaled back at the eleventh hour for practical reasons. Jenkins's edge-of-town residence made him an easy target.[47]

Moreover, the kidnapping of Americans for ransom was no rarity. Since July, there had been an upsurge in northern and central Mexico, with at least thirteen Americans reportedly abducted. By August the trend was pronounced enough for Carranza to order state governors to do more to protect foreign residents and for US congressman Fiorello LaGuardia to propose a State Department inquiry.[48] It is likely no fluke that the trend followed an increase in interventionist talk and in Mexican anti-Americanism.[49] Neither Peláez nor Córdoba were notably anti-American, but they would have seen that kidnappings were easily effected.

A conspiracy is far more likely to have been mounted against Jenkins than with him. Governor Cabrera had good reason to be suspicious of Jenkins, the pushy businessman whose ethically suspect activities he had observed for two years, but he also had good reason to fabricate a case against him. Like his Carranza-imposed predecessors, Cabrera was an outsider to Puebla City, deeply unpopular. By October 1919, he was more isolated than ever. The kidnapping of a consular agent from the state capital by rebels was a major embarrassment; Cabrera was already sensitive over Puebla's crime-infested image. That the US embassy had trampled on his turf, that Jenkins had gained his freedom with no help from state officials, and that the perpetrators remained free were further embarrassments.[50] Yet Jenkins was a controversial character, given to interventionist sentiments and rapacious practices, so the episode also offered a chance for the governor to repair his image.

Two days after Jenkins was taken, Cabrera telegrammed Carranza, conveying "anonymous" allegations that the kidnapping was a simulation and that Jenkins had hidden himself to provoke a conflict. A few days later, the Puebla newspaper *La Prensa* composed a speculative article linking Jenkins to the state's main opposition faction, the "reactionary" Ignacio Zaragoza Party, which allegedly wanted the United States to invade Mexico. *La Prensa*, a paper subsidized by Cabrera's administration, also speculated that Jenkins might well be back at home by now, enjoying a cognac and laughing at the government.[51] At the end of the week, a Cabrera propagandist sent Carranza a memo naming the supposed conspirators: not only Jenkins, Mestre, and Córdoba but also Hardaker, Puebla mayor Francisco Lozano Cardoso, local lawmaker Rafael Rojas, businessman Ernesto Espinosa Bravo, and post office chief Baraquiel Alatriste. While some were friends of Jenkins, all were foes of Cabrera.[52]

Cabrera and his allies continued to make accusations after Jenkins's return from the kidnapping. Although these were made in private correspondence, *La Prensa* made them public. Attorney General Mitchell issued daily press releases about his investigation, to put his spin on the story. The ongoing propaganda value of Jenkins to Cabrera helps explain why the governor devoted much of his January 1920 state address to the episode, and why *La Prensa* continued to vilify him. One day it claimed that Jenkins had said that, until he set up his mill, Mexicans did not wear socks. Altogether, the Puebla authorities fought doggedly, for six months, to retain juridical control of the case.[53]

Cabrera harbored a personal animus toward Jenkins, and not simply because he was a profiteering foreigner amid a nationalist revolution. There was his history of dealings with Zapatistas, the scourge of Puebla governors. Then, in May 1918, when replying to a Foreign Relations query about the consular agent's standing, Cabrera alleged with distaste that Jenkins was conducting "absolute espionage" in the state and disseminating Allied (World War I) propaganda.[54] As a leading participant-donor in the Central Charity Committee in 1918, Jenkins had aided the fight against the Spanish flu, actions that had thrown Cabrera's incompetence into sharp relief. And in July 1919, Jenkins had nailed his colors to the mast when, along with other wealthy Pueblans, he bought an advertisement in *El Monitor*, the main opposition organ, congratulating the paper on its first anniversary.[55]

Carranza's motives resembled Cabrera's. Both were initially embarrassed by the episode; both could benefit from its cultivation into a crisis. True, the abduction first seemed a troubling sign that Carranza had still to restore order to Mexico. But all year long the dour "First Chief of the Revolution" had seen his popularity wane, as the promises of the constitution failed to be turned into law, let alone put into practice. Meanwhile the war's great military hero, the charismatic Álvaro Obregón, had garnered only greater esteem. In June, Obregón formalized his candidacy for president. Fearing that his former ally would prove another Porfirio Díaz—a self-reelecting military dictator—Carranza cast about for an alternative protégé. At heart, the election of 1920 would pit the Revolution's greatest politician against its greatest general.[56] Eventually, in late October, Carranza settled on his new ambassador to the United States, Ignacio Bonillas. That Bonillas had no significant support base caused many to assume that Carranza had sought a puppet and would try to impose him.[57] So a crisis involving a controversial American would give Bonillas, even as he stayed in Washington, the chance to build some public credibility.

The Mexico City newspapers closest to Carranza, *El Demócrata* and *Excélsior*, were quickest to call the abduction a possible "self-kidnapping," aimed at causing problems with the United States. Referring to the large sum taken from Jenkins's safe, *El Demócrata* added the smear that Jenkins was rumored to be a heavy gambler.[58] Upon Jenkins's release, when Cabrera repeated the self-kidnapping allegation to federal officials, Interior Minister Manuel Aguirre Berlanga urged him to pursue the rumor. The minister wrote: "it is to the interest of the nation and the good name and prestige of the Government that this affair be solved in such a form that any charge whatsoever that could be made against the Government be deprived of its force."[59] Countering the growing claim that the Carranza regime lacked authority and competence meant pursuing all means to undermine the American's credibility.

With Jenkins rescued and under suspicion of conspiracy, the affair allowed Carranza the chance to whip up nationalist sentiment and present himself—once again, following the US hunt for Pancho Villa—as First Chief of Mexican sovereignty. It also allowed his candidate Bonillas to shine in the newspapers, acting in public defense of the country's honor.[60]

Belligerence shown by Lansing, Fall, and much of the American press, with their intimations of imminent war, only made the president's task easier. In fact, Jenkins was the perfect tool for Carranza's purposes. He not only had hawkish friends in high places, which rendered him a political threat, he also had a name for predatory lending, making him a symbol of economic threat. Not five days after the abduction, the Foreign Relations Ministry wired Cabrera and told him to investigate Jenkins's conduct as a businessman.[61]

And what of J. Salter Hansen—the "banker," as the Carrancista papers called him—who had defused Senator Fall's time bomb with his payment of Jenkins's bail? Two days before he did so, three wealthy New York–based Mexicans, anxious over the talk of war, wired Finance Minister Luis Cabrera to suggest that a third party might solve the impasse by paying the bond. Afterward, Lansing found that when Hansen paid the $500 bail, he had just 59 cents in his New York bank account. Fall did some digging too: his staff found that Hansen was once tried for sexually assaulting a twelve-year-old girl in a movie theater. He had also offered his mediating services to two oil industry lawyers, claiming to be close to Carranza and

Luis Cabrera; they turned him down.[62] Hardly a wealthy altruist, Hansen had functioned as Carranza's pawn.

As for the motives of Jenkins himself, David LaFrance, the leading historian of the Revolution in Puebla, has raised two compelling questions: Given that all his prior dealings show him to be calculating and astute, why would Jenkins have placed himself in physical danger for a plot whose outcome could well bring little or no political gain? And why risk an involvement whose discovery would jeopardize his vast fortune, much of it tied up in hard to liquidate loans and easily confiscated real estate?[63]

One may further ask: Would a married father of three volunteer for a kidnapping's inherent risks, such as a botched rescue by state police? Would a multimillionaire for whom business was booming, with a bonanza in property trading and a recent expansion at his mill, feel so inconvenienced by Carranza's regime to wish to take part? Would an American who regarded Zapatistas as "animals without hearts" entrust his well-being to them for a week or more? Would a man of such acumen have planned his abduction so poorly as to have let himself be exposed to the elements at chilly hillside camps? Would he have planned such an escapade for just after his brother-in-law Donald had returned to the United States, leaving Mary, his sister, and his daughters by themselves?[64] Would he have risked the frail health of his wife?

With rare exception, the many published accounts of the case have ignored this pile of improbabilities. Yet the conspiracy theory planted by the Cabrera government, encouraged by Carranza, and nurtured by a nationalistic press took root and flourishes still.

As for the ransom, the Mexicans never paid it and Jenkins never recouped it. In 1921, Jenkins pursued compensation from the Obregón regime, without success. He then filed a complaint with the bilateral Claims Commission, set up to deal with damages to US property during the war. He sought $285,000, which covered the amount of the ransom, the cash taken from his safe, and hospital and legal bills, along with textile assets stolen earlier. But his suit was half-hearted, for he did not support his claim with documents. Perhaps he felt that the months of press coverage and correspondence with the embassy constituted sufficient evidence; perhaps, having seen so much of his time absorbed by the episode, he was loath to invest further effort. In 1930 he gave up, writing to the Claims Commission that he was desisting from further action.[65]

A Black Legend Begins

In Puebla, and later nationwide, the kidnapping and jailing of William O. Jenkins, the accusations of Governor Cabrera, and the resulting diplomatic furor combined to plant the seeds of a Jenkins Black Legend. The original Black Legend, born in the 1500s and propagated for centuries by Britons and Anglo-Americans about Spain's atrocities in its conquest of the Indies, did have something of a basis in fact but featured a selective, exaggerated reading of events. The same could be said of the myth of Jenkins. It configured him as a stereotype: the devious, manipulative, arrogant, exploitative US businessman. He was never to be trusted. He was capable of the most heinous acts. He always put his interests above those of his adoptive country. For proof, one need only recall his activities during the Revolution: he had arranged his own kidnapping, brought Mexico to the brink of war with the United States, and in the process—so the evolving myth would claim—forced the government to pay a ransom that he shared with his kidnappers and that formed the basis of his fortune.

The foundational story within the myth developed fast. The Cabrera regime began planting defamatory stories in the press as soon as it had news of the kidnapping. After Jenkins was jailed, a pro-Carranza newspaper caused a sensation by printing a letter, signed "Federico Córdoba," that said Jenkins had proposed his own abduction. Córdoba himself immediately denounced the letter as a fake, subsequently proving to the *New York Tribune* that the signature printed did not match his own and accusing the Puebla authorities of planting the letter. But the additional damage to Jenkins's credibility had been done. By December, Mexican diplomats were saying that Jenkins had not only kidnapped himself but done so in order to enrich himself.[66]

Accusation became conventional wisdom, which in turn became embellished. This was done at first by word of mouth.[67] Little by little, the legend appeared in print. In 1932, *Excélsior* published a feature about kidnappings that dwelled on the Jenkins case and concluded that "in the end it proved not to be an abduction, or it was a highly dubious one." In 1943, a film industry rival tried to rally opposition against Jenkins through a newspaper insertion that recalled him having abducted himself. A union flyer posted in Puebla in 1956, complaining of Jenkins's political influence, called him a "filibusterer, harmful to our homeland, who kidnapped himself." A 1959 newspaper profile began by citing his "famous and theatrical, episodic and cinematic self-kidnapping." The following year even

Time jumped aboard: its profile of Jenkins called the kidnapping "a fortunate stroke of bad luck" that ended with Carranza paying the ransom and
Jenkins allegedly receiving "half of the booty." By this stage, journalistic
references to a self-kidnapping were standard.[68]

If reporters and columnists felt at liberty to term the incident a ruse,
and to embellish its supposed outcome, their doing so was facilitated by
Jenkins's stubborn silence. Offended by many of the articles about him,
he declined further requests for interviews, a policy he kept to his grave.[69]
It was as though, having battled to defend his honor and lost to the crescendo of rumors, he decided to focus ever after on what he did best: making money. It helped that he lived in so conservative a city as Puebla, where
self-censorship usually prevailed; there were also, no doubt, fears of repri-
sal for criticizing him, given his dominant position in the city's economy
and his close relations with the state's more authoritarian governors. In
Puebla, negative sketches were widely published only after his death.

In 1965 Enrique Cordero y Torres, doyen of the Pueblan chroniclers,
recorded in a then-standard local history that Jenkins's kidnapping ransom
marked the "beginning of his fantastic fortune." The myth was not of his
making—its appearance in *Time* and several obituaries showed it already
existed as a rumor—but Cordero's decision to claim it as fact enabled
future writers to do likewise. Later the fiction of the "kidnapping fortune"
was propagated more widely through the bestselling novel *Arráncame la
vida* (*Tear This Heart Out*), by Ángeles Mastretta.[70]

These embellished versions ignore how wealthy Jenkins had already
become, through La Corona, his other businesses, and property speculation.
It fails to register how the $75,000 that he allegedly stood to gain by split-
ting the ransom with his kidnappers (assuming an equal division of spoils)
paled beside his net worth: some $5 million by his own later estimate and
at least $3 million according to intelligence gathered by Mexico's Defense
Ministry. Even at the time, a Puebla newspaper pointed out the absurdity
of the self-kidnapping-for-money allegation, given that Jenkins had recently
paid a far higher sum than the ransom for a stake in Puebla City's leading
department store. The "kidnapping fortune" myth further ignores the fact
that the government neither paid nor reimbursed the ransom.[71]

As recounting the Revolution became less the preserve of journalists
and chroniclers and more the pursuit of professional historians, a striking
divergence arose in readings of the affair. US historians either withheld
judgment or deduced the kidnapping was genuine.[72] Mexican histories,
with one notable exception, all described the episode as an *autosecuestro*.[73]

The disparity of interpretations might suggest nothing more than patriotic biases within the US and Mexican versions of what happened. But the US accounts exhibit a wider reading of archival and newspaper records, and the ones that treat the subject at greatest length are precisely those that find for Jenkins's certain or likely innocence. The cautious tone of the American versions—"both logic and evidence indicate, though do not prove, innocence," says Charles Cumberland—contrasts with the condemnatory tenor of the Mexican historians. Bertha Ulloa ends her account with a dramatic flourish: "Jenkins could never demonstrate his innocence in the kidnapping."[74] The Mexican accounts also show an unwillingness to ponder the political agendas of Carranza and Cabrera, as though they were seeking only to redress a great wrong. Jenkins is given the role of stock Yankee villain and attention to the case's complexities seems to be judged unnecessary.

The one Mexican study that benefitted from access to US as well as Mexican archives, penned by Rafael Ruiz Harrell, concluded that the kidnapping was genuine. The fact that Ruiz Harrell framed his account as a historical novel scarcely diminishes its value, for his fictionalizing is largely confined to imagining conversations and his source material is set out in a 24-page bibliographic essay.[75]

Beyond circumstantial evidence, what helped make the self-kidnapping allegation stick in the first place was a public willingness to assume the worst of this gringo. Since his arrival in Puebla, Jenkins had cut an odd figure. He had partnered with the unscrupulous Leon Rasst. He had defied the conventions of "decent" people and risen suspiciously fast to great wealth. His predatory lending no doubt made him loathsome to certain circles. It is easy to believe the worst about a man who does not fit in, a man whose dress, customs, language, and religious affiliation all differ from the norm, and easier still when his fortune has increased at the expense of a society's elite. Jenkins's vocal contempt for local officials merely inflamed existing prejudices.

After December 1919, when the crisis abated, the kidnapping did not seem of lasting significance. Just before Jenkins's release, Ambassador Bonillas downplayed the episode as a "tempest in a teapot," and from the long perspective of US diplomatic history it might well have been. Or at least it was an incidental affair within a much larger and longer bilateral dispute over Mexican sovereignty and US reparations, in which by far the most contentious issue was oil.[76] By mid-1920, Jenkins's chief adversaries during the saga had either died (Carranza), departed (Cabrera), or disappeared from public view (Mitchell). The controversy over oil would endure.

On a symbolic level, however, the Jenkins affair helped foster an enduring, semi-mythical figure who would loom large in the imagination of a nation: Jenkins as the archetypal gringo bogeyman. Over subsequent decades, a variety of people in conflict with Jenkins—from rural activists and labor leaders to business rivals and political foes—would allege he had committed all manner of crimes, uniquely nefarious. But the actions and tendencies they denounced were similar to what other men of wealth and power were doing: buying the friendship of politicians and clergy, arming vigilantes to fend off land-seeking peasants, breaking strikes and co-opting union bosses, smuggling alcohol, evading taxes, engaging in monopolistic practice. What singled Jenkins out for special vitriol was that he was an enemy of the Revolution and an American. To enhance whatever case they were arguing, his opponents would appropriate the Jenkins Black Legend and often expand upon it, making his infamy a rhetorical weapon for all occasions.

Yet the weapon was double-edged. The belief that Jenkins kidnapped himself, coupled with memory of the US reaction to its consul's incarceration and his later exoneration in federal court, altogether gave the impression that Jenkins was above the law, diplomatically protected, potentially dangerous.[77] The notion that he had partnered with rebels to make money in the process, outsmarting the federal government, rendered him highly crafty, perhaps admirably so. This Machiavellian image would serve Jenkins well as he built his business empire in Puebla. Here was a man whom it would be unwise to cross. Gain his favor, strike up a partnership, and there was every chance of reward.

Gringophobia Turns a Corner

Although Mexico's suspicion of Americans practically dates from the nation's birth, its distrust of US economic power came much later. It began during the investment boom under Díaz and did not coalesce until the end of the Revolution. Around the same time, gringophobia began to branch out from the writings of intellectuals and the protests of mining and oiling enclaves to become a popular, nationwide phenomenon. In cyclical fashion, it has persisted ever since. The infamy of Jenkins helped propel both shifts.

With the Revolution came notorious instances of intervention by the United States. In 1913, its ambassador encouraged Huerta to oust Madero.

In 1914, its navy bombarded and occupied Veracruz to prevent arms from reaching Huerta, at a cost of two hundred lives. In 1916, General John Pershing led a brigade across the Rio Grande to begin a futile pursuit of Pancho Villa. At these times, incidents of anti-Americanism spiked, but they did not become a movement.[78] The prime targets of xenophobic anger remained the Spaniards, whose numbers included the hated managers of haciendas and company stores. In 1919, with the Jenkins case, the threat of full-scale incursion reached a peak, but Carranza was unable to make enough of the episode to improve Bonillas's prospects in the 1920 election or the viability of his regime. Each instance revealed the limited persuasive power of gringophobia in its political form.

As the war evolved into a troubled peace, the spindly figure of Uncle Sam, as well as the scornful Spaniard, began to be overtaken by the Yankee investor as the foreigner vilified most. These were years in which headlines haltingly shifted from alarm about US incursions to worries about the presence and privileges of American businesses. At first they focused on Mexico's oil and mineral wealth; later they involved the might of American commerce.[79]

If there were a tipping-point date for the broad switch from political fears to economic concerns, 1919 was probably it. The Jenkins affair marked the last realistic chance for US interventionists to have their way. That year also marked a mid-point between Carranza's first nationalistic decrees governing foreign capital (1915) and Obregón's assent to the Bucareli Accords (1923), which controversially let foreign firms keep working their oil fields.

Jenkins's own trajectory reflected the change. He was kidnapped by virtue of his political post, as a consular agent. It was his diplomatic status that drove the US embassy to involve itself, that prompted Lansing to press for his release from jail, and that moved Fall and the Hearst press to inflate the case as a *cause célèbre*. After the crisis, what kept Jenkins in the public eye were his business activities. It was the devious landowner and monopolist, rather than the devious agent of Washington, that fed the Jenkins Black Legend.

Moreover, the Jenkins affair helped shape Mexican xenophobia, associating it further with a specifically *gringo*phobia. It helped establish a popular vehicle for politically charged rhetoric: the shady US businessman. What had begun as a localized disdain became widespread. And as of the mid-1920s, when Edward Doheny withdrew his investment, there was probably no American as well-known in Mexico as William O. Jenkins.

Nurturing that contempt, and providing a tricky political terrain for Jenkins's postwar exploits, was a growing economic nationalism. Even before the Revolution, the seeds had been sown, with an industrial policy that included selective tariffs, an infant industries program, and a partial nationalization of the railroads. After Díaz's ouster emerged ideas more radical and rhetoric more visceral. A fairly constant criticism of US business activity came from revolutionary elites. New periodicals sprang to life across the country and criticized the old order of things, like industrialization that seemed to benefit foreigners first. Declarations of presidents and generals bore an increasingly economic focus.[80]

Carranza was consistently nationalistic, his policies grounded in passionate objection to the privileged status of overseas investors and a conviction that all nations were equally sovereign. He had good cause to target US investors in mining and oil, for their tax burden was far smaller than in the United States, and they had treated American and Mexican employees unequally. Still, the language with which his regime upbraided them was often inflammatory. One 1915 editorial in the state-supported *El Pueblo* insisted that the United States "has not finished its imperialist expansion" and accused President Wilson of backing "rich traitors, thieves, bankers, and large landowners."[81]

How much were these sentiments shared by the populace? To some historians, the Revolution was a war of national liberation.[82] About a third of Mexico's surface area belonged to foreigners, Americans owning three-quarters of that. But possession of land was often covert and evidence for rebel targeting of US firms and properties was slight. Victims of murder and theft were usually attacked as landowners, not as Americans. Spaniards suffered far more.[83]

This was Jenkins's experience too. In his 1915 account of arrest by Carrancistas, there is no hint he was insulted as an American, even though he flew Old Glory outside his home. Two months earlier, by contrast, he reported the sacking of Spanish mills and the refusal of a hispanophobic governor to do anything about it. As Alan Knight has summarized, the impact of the Revolution on Americans was "remarkably limited, macho assertions of mayhem notwithstanding."[84]

Widespread ill-will toward US capitalists came with the Revolution's end. Insurgent demands for land and the public ownership of natural resources were addressed in the 1917 Constitution. As the smoke cleared, Mexicans anticipated the charter's fulfillment, along with reward for their efforts in combat. But the years passed and such promises barely began to be fulfilled. In most states, the parceling out of hacienda land proceeded at a snail's pace. Foreign oil barons clung to their wells. Gringos like Jenkins retained, or even expanded, their large estates. The enraging gap between hopes and outcomes, following years of war and sacrifice, was fertile ground for economic gringophobia.

WHETHER POLITICIANS OR teachers, writers or artists, many of the Revolution's victors and sympathizers celebrated the war and polished their credentials with patriotic rhetoric. The nationalism they espoused was not always anti-American. In the 1920s, the state fostered a public spirit that celebrated mixed-race identity and shied from confrontation. Despite everything, the "Colossus of the North" was a needed neighbor: as a source of imports, investment, and, in order to access international loans, official recognition. Gringophobia coexisted with gringophilia, as leaders sought to modernize Mexico in ways inspired by the United States. This meant automobiles and airplanes, radio sets, toothpaste, and Coca-Cola.[85]

But a revolutionary rhetoric about exploitative gringos began to permeate the public mind after 1917, when the constitution enshrined the once-marginal notion of Mexico for the Mexicans. Its advance was heard in political speeches and seen throughout the media: popular literature, textbooks, muralist art, motion pictures, folk songs, and political cartoons in mass-circulation papers. It was confirmed in the recurrence of gringophobia in popular protest, including the clamor among country folk against Jenkins and other American landowners.[86] The anger directed at investors, managers, and landowners revealed a surging discontent with US economic power and the perceived arrogance and insensitivity of its agents.

On the political stage, Obregón's willingness in 1923 to make concessions to US oil companies, so to gain diplomatic recognition, prompted a backlash. Critics accused him of "selling out" the constitution. The discontent and attendant anti-US rhetoric helped fuel the bloody rebellion of Adolfo de la Huerta that December. In 1927, federal official Ignacio Muñoz advertised a critique of Dollar Diplomacy with the title *Mueran los gringos* (*Death to the Gringos*). After the US Embassy complained, Muñoz chose the scarcely less provocative *La verdad sobre los gringos* (*The Truth about the Gringos*). The book was a bestseller.[87] With the Depression, xenophobia in general increased. Especially thorny was the issue of Mexico's foreign debt, 29 percent of it held by US banks. Foreign Minister José Manuel Puig positioned himself as an outspoken critic of the international banking system, which he regarded as a heartless monster, made in the USA.[88]

While politicians were usually constrained in what they could say, writers gave full vent to their feelings. A literary excoriation of Yankee commerce proliferated in Mexico, as throughout Latin America. In novels with anti-US themes, oil, mining, and fruit companies were favorite targets. Unlike ordinary US citizens, whom novelists often absolved, businessmen were stereotyped as cold, racist, immoral, even lustful. They colluded with politicians and exploited workers. In Mexico the usual villain was the oil industry, since for the decade prior to 1923 the US refusal to recognize Mexico's government owed much to the will of Big Oil. Novels and plays about ruthless oilmen multiplied.[89]

The most important literary work was José Vasconcelos's *The Cosmic Race* (1925). Authored by a man already famed as the energetic head of the Ministry of Public Education (SEP), this essay adapted the Anglo/ Latin dichotomy popularized by Rodó's *Ariel*. Celebrating the "cosmic race" that had resulted from the fusion of Iberian and indigenous peoples, Vasconcelos stamped the spiritual superiority of Hispanic Americans over materialistic Anglo-Americans firmly and lastingly into his country's consciousness.[90]

More influential still were textbooks. Initially, in books approved by the SEP, the United States retained the compliments about productivity and personal liberty common in earlier histories. In the 1930s, under a policy of "socialist education," SEP textbooks adopted Marxist notions of exploitation and struggle. Geography lessons studied the impact of imperialist investors on Mexico's natural resources. History books fingered US greed as a cause of the Mexican-American War and emphasized foreign control of the Porfirian economy.[91]

Within the visual arts, Vasconcelos fostered politicized murals as he sought to preach the Revolution to the masses. Prominent display of these vast works—round the courtyards of federal buildings, on the walls of covered markets and colleges—gave them an instant mass audience. Reproductions in magazines and textbooks brought them further popularity. The three leading muralists, Diego Rivera, David Alfaro Siqueiros, and José Clemente Orozco, disdained international capitalism, and some of their best-known works satirized US captains of industry. In Rivera's series of frescoes at the SEP, several panels provocatively contrast revolutionary ideals with some of their most famous detractors, including John D. Rockefeller, J. P. Morgan Jr., and Henry Ford, who had recently opened an assembly plant in Mexico City. Rivera depicted the three men as wizened fiends, dining on stock-market ticker-tape, in what a US diplomat called a "'hymn of hate' against capitalists ... marked by a virulent and blatant hatred of the United States." Jenkins too would come in for vilification-by-mural.[92]

Cartoons further popularized the Ugly American. Oil barons came in for routine vitriol, sometimes by name (Doheny, of course), often as a class. A 1920 cartoon in *El Demócrata* drew four fat investors, bedecked with multiple diamond rings and Stars-and-Stripes top hats, gloating as they watched two ill-clad peons dig an oil well for them. Large girths, sneering smiles, and outsized diamond rings became routine symbols of capitalist excess in the decades to follow. Jenkins would be subjected to such caricature, as would other magnates, including local ones; satirical attacks against US investors were sometimes as anti-tycoon as they were anti-American.[93] In the medium of motion pictures, the US Exploiter, typically a businessman, emerged in the 1930s as a recurrent stereotype. As producers catered to evolving public tastes, cinematic depictions of the rapacious American would become ever more common.[94]

Most popularly conceived of all was the *corrido*, a traditional ballad designed for lament, critique, mockery, or celebration. Between the Revolution and 1942, when Mexico joined the Allies against Germany and Japan, most US-themed corridos mocked Americans for their lack of courage and manliness, their greed and cruelty, their contempt for Mexican workers. A "Miner's Corrido" viewed US bosses as animals. To another balladeer, "the gringo is very despicable / and our eternal enemy." Oil firms were again a favorite target, in corridos rich with fearmongering. One asserted that Americans wished to exploit all things Mexican, from oil and silver to "the country's beautiful women." Another alleged that US oil barons were plotting the downfall of Obregón by hiring corrupt generals to rebel. A lament spoke for laid-off oilers in Tampico: they were so angry, went one couplet, "they only want to eat gringos, raw and also roasted." Inevitably, given a business profile that grew by the decade, someone with an axe to grind would one day pen a ballad against Jenkins: "The Mexican Cinema Corrido."[95]

AMERICANS WERE NOT the only exploiters. The charge usually leveled at nonnative undesirables was *extranjero pernicioso* (pernicious foreigner). It was applied with equal prejudice to US citizens and other distrusted outsiders: Spaniards, Chinese, Arabs, and Jews. The words derived from Article 33 of the 1857 Constitution, which allowed the state to expel foreigners who failed to pay taxes or respect authorities. Awareness of the article and usage of the phrase, long confined to urban elites, widened after the Revolution. Country folk cited "the 33" when denouncing foreigners who resisted their designs on land, and their petitions often included "pernicious" or similar epithets.[96] They came to use such language whatever their complaint, as Jenkins himself would find; in other words, "pernicious foreigner" became a standard rhetorical device.[97] Ironically, this phrase did not reappear in the 1917 Constitution. That its official retraction had no bearing on its popularity affirms its xenophobic appeal.

Much of the era's radical language was anticapitalist first and nationalist second. When the SEP-funded magazine *Mexican Folkways* reproduced the Diego Rivera panel that satirized Rockefeller and company, it supplied the caption "The rich scheming to double their money" and identified the people depicted not by name, simply as capitalists both American and Mexican.[98]

However, as European influence weakened after World War I, gringos became the usual "others." Before the Revolution, though Americans were the largest foreign investors in Mexico, they were closely rivaled by the British; afterward, they gained an overall majority position. Before, they held only minor cultural influence, overshadowed by the French; after, with the rise of Hollywood, Tin Pan Alley, Detroit, and Madison Avenue, US films, music, and consumer products jointly caused an unprecedented cultural avalanche. Once Americans were a distant second to the Spaniards as the foreigners most widely distrusted or reviled; now they closed the gap.

Rising gringophobia made seizing of US property an ever more popular political move. Over the twenty years that followed the Revolution, US investment in Mexico fell from $1.2 billion to $300 million. Land confiscation caused much of the drop. At the same time, in the burgeoning cities, the state was letting the Yankees back in. Ford, General Motors, and other major firms founded subsidiaries in the 1920s and 1930s, and when they opened their plants, politicians attended as guests of honor. The double standard was logical. To rebuild the war-torn economy and pursue industrialization, the government felt it needed US finance and know-how. But it also needed to protect its legitimacy. Encouraging gringophobic speech and images—one of several genres of political theater at its disposal—helped it maintain a façade of revolutionary nationalism.[99]

The US Exploiter stereotype arose gradually. It is hard to pinpoint how and when it reached a critical mass of public acceptance. But the wild popularity of the nationalization of the oil industry in 1938—when thousands of ordinary citizens would line up with donations to help the state reimburse the affected companies—suggests that economic nationalism was by then enjoying a broad level of emotive approval.[100]

Though he was never involved in oil, no foreigner was deemed as pernicious—as often, or as long—as Jenkins. Other controversial capitalists had previously gained prominence, chief among them the British contractor Weetman Pearson. But Pearson and others who entered Mexico under Diaz, including the US oil developers Edward Doheny and William F. Buckley and the press baron William Randolph Hearst, were temporary residents or occasional visitors, and they were powerful at a time when channels of critique were limited. In the 1920s, their influence waned, as divestments and expropriations took their toll. The buyers of their assets were faceless multinationals of the managerial era: Standard Oil, Royal Dutch Shell.[101]

Jenkins, by contrast, had made Mexico his home. He would remain in the country until his death. His businesses, along with the controversy he generated, would continue to expand, his repudiation of the press only fanning suspicion. Presumptions of guilt would attend any controversy in which he was embroiled. This not to say such judgements were always wrong, for Jenkins frequently broke or bent the law, but he did so no more than his Mexican peers. Gringophobia, however, ensured he drew more fire.

5

Empire at Atencingo

A New Interdependence

The summer before his kidnapping, Jenkins had traveled to meet his wife in Los Angeles, where they hoped to find a new home.[1] Eighteen years of hard work in Mexico had given him the fortune he had always sought. Now he was starting to sell off his assets, count his profits, and consider his promise of a life of ease for Mary. West of what was then the fairly compact city of Los Angeles, for most of a 15-mile stretch to the Pacific Ocean, the terrain was crisscrossed by occasional roads but remained a country landscape. Along Wilshire Boulevard, which led out from the city and across the bean fields to the sea at Santa Monica, Mr. and Mrs. Jenkins settled on a plot of land at the corner of Irving. The place, they felt, was sufficiently far from bustling Los Angeles, already home to half a million people. They hired an established architect, T. Beverly Keim, who set about designing an elaborate Italianate mansion.

In the fall of 1920, Mary left Puebla for good, or so she assumed. Moving to California with her were thirteen-year-old Margaret and four-year-old Jane, and joining them there was Elizabeth, recently graduated from Marlborough School. Mary could at last put all the unpleasantness of the past decade behind her. In the Golden State, she would be free of the humidity that aggravated her tuberculosis. She could also keep an eye on Elizabeth. Over the past year her eldest had shown a rebellious free-spiritedness, seldom writing home and spending little effort on her studies. Her access to money and lack of parental oversight, in a city with a racy social life, seemed to Mary's Southern-gentry sensibilities to spell trouble.

It was a worry that would persist, for each of her daughters would grow up independent-minded. But Los Angeles offered William great prospects, and it brought them much closer to his relatives in Hanford. So Mary rented a house in the Wilshire district and supervised the building of their palatial home.

Back in Puebla, Jenkins gave priority to liquidating properties and recovering debts. At least that was his intention. His assets were many and manifold—hosiery mills, urban buildings, loans to numerous farmers and merchants, haciendas of thousands of acres in several states—and times were not propitious. Buyers were scarce, for bank loans were almost unobtainable, and few had the cash to make grand purchases. Legions of poor country folk, empowered by the Revolution, were targeting haciendas for seizure by means both legal and not, threatening their resale value. Complicating matters further, the state of Puebla, where most of Jenkins's wealth lay, was laboring through an unusual degree of postwar chaos. It would not even begin to emerge from chronic insolvency and violence for another seven years.

Since it was a poor time to sell, it might be a good time to continue lending and buying. That most banks were still shuttered meant a continued demand for private credit, which could lead to stakes in textile mills that might see better days. The rise of peasant activism meant that landowners reluctant to part with their estates might soon be intimidated into doing so or duped via a predatory loan. Puebla's dire finances suggested that its governors needed friends of means: people with cash and a willingness to lend it. Such a willingness might be traded for favors—particularly, in these times of radicalism, protection against strikes and land confiscation. Throughout the 1920s and well into the 1930s, the weakness of many landowners and industrialists, the militancy of peasants, and the bankruptcy of the Puebla government would combine to afford unusual openings for risk-takers.

So was Jenkins less than sincere in his assurances to his wife that he would soon be joining her? At the very least, it suited him well that his Los Angeles architect was going to take five years to finish the mansion.

MORE THAN ANYTHING, Jenkins's extraordinary rise as a landowner depended on the relationships he developed with politicians. These arrangements illustrated the return of an interdependence between government and private business, in the wake of a cataclysm that was supposed to have swept away the old order, with its cozy ties between elites.

Such a change had been the aim of the Revolution's heroes, whether radicals like Zapata and Villa or moderates like Madero and Obregón, and such was the conclusion of "official histories," the works of eye-witnesses and partial historians that proliferated for decades, feting the Revolution's progressive gains. In fact, much of the Porfirian economic edifice survived.[2]

At the heart of this interdependence lay the banking system.[3] In the 1920s, Finance Minister Alberto Pani resurrected the mutual bond between the Ministry and private bankers that had been crafted in the late nineteenth century. Needing to revive the economy, Presidents Obregón and Plutarco Elías Calles—who both entrusted the Ministry to Pani—were forced into accommodation. The Revolution's pledges could hardly be fulfilled if the industrial tax base were still meager and the few existing banks unable to lend; social policy and political stability were at stake. Revival meant restoring the confidence of investors, badly shaken by the wartime plunder of bank deposits and frantic printing of money. Pani responded with a charm offensive. He allowed the bankers to benefit from high barriers to entry, minimizing competition; he let them write their own regulating legislation; and he invited them to help create a central bank. Pani's generosity also arose from the fact that it was the bankers who had the rapport with international lenders. Foreign loans were deemed vital to recovery.

So the interdependence of the early Porfirian era—that state-capital bond based on mutual need—made a comeback. Top financier-industrialists and the Pani circle together built a bankers' alliance; it would dominate economic policy until the early 1980s. The state dealt likewise with the manufacturing elite, helping revitalize production by permitting monopolies and duopolies and protecting them with trade tariffs.

Such deals made for an economic system not unlike the US model. Just as the excesses of the Gilded Age were tempered by the Progressive Era under Theodore Roosevelt and Woodrow Wilson, so those of the Porfirian Era were tempered by the Revolution. There was now a more visible division between banking and political elites; one no longer found cabinet members on the board of top private bank Banamex. Nor was the banking sector as concentrated as before. In both nations, however, signs of crony-ish convenience persisted. In the United States, the secretary of the treasury from 1921 until 1933 was none other than Andrew Mellon, a career banker who had become one of the very richest Americans and the third highest income-tax payer in the country.[4]

Relationships of mutual need—and later of mutual convenience—also prevailed in the Mexican provinces.[5] In Puebla, William Jenkins cultivated

protection for his threatened assets, both by arguing his worth as an entrepreneur to the federal government and by making loans to the perenni-
ally underfunded state treasury, which made successive governors ever
more indebted to him. In the early years, when the government of Puebla
was highly fractious and unpredictable, it was his bond with President
Obregón, a kindred spirit of sorts, which proved the more useful. After
Obregón's term, Jenkins drew closer to Puebla's governors, especially the
conservatives. Owing greatly to the support of Jenkins and other wealthy
Pueblans, pro-business governors were able to hold on to office for longer than their radical counterparts. All the while, Jenkins rounded out his
strategy by befriending additional power brokers: military chiefs, archbishops, and gun-toting rural bosses.

Buying Atencingo, Selling La Corona

Jenkins's main outstanding loan comprised the 1.2 million pesos he
had granted to the Díaz Rubíns to help them revive the sugar estate of
Atencingo. The prospects for its swift redemption were feeble. The Díaz
Rubín siblings were young and inexperienced, and due to the association
of their forebears with the old Porfirian order, they were vulnerable. They
faced prolific challenges in trying to rebuild a devastated mill and revive a
plantation burned to the ground. New machinery needed buying. A vast
network of irrigation ditches needed unclogging. Even then, a sugar crop
would take at least eighteen months to grow.

Whatever dreams Jenkins had of Los Angeles, the Hacienda San José
Atencingo must have fired his imagination. Nestled in Puebla's southwestern Matamoros Valley, the state's chief sugar region, Atencingo was one
of nine large haciendas whose cane fields basked in the hot lowland sun.
Their thirst was satisfied by rivers streaming down from the mountains to
the north, the majestic volcanoes Popocatepetl and Ixtacihuatl. Atencingo
encompassed roughly 16,000 acres, close to half of that irrigable flat land,
and the Inter-Oceanic Railroad ran conveniently through it.[6] Most of its
neighboring sugar estates were equally laid to waste, equally awaiting
repair. Like the Díaz Rubíns, the elites that owned them were finding postwar life tough. One day, they might be persuaded to sell.

The Matamoros Valley was more than the former farm boy could resist.
By mid-1920, Jenkins must have felt drawn by a vortex of opportunities.
Some were sentimental: to become a farmer in his own right, to divest
Puebla's arrogant Spaniards of their haciendas and show them who was

who, to prove to his blue-blooded in-laws that he too could run a plantation. The social dynamics were familiar to him. The plantations and larger
farms of the Tennessee that he left behind had employed many blacks as
laborers or sharecroppers, some of them former slaves. Even his father
had hired several black workers to help with the family farm. The plantations of Puebla depended for their labor on "Indians," as indigenous
Mexicans were termed, many of whom were former debt peons. In both
cases—despite the respective triumphs of emancipation and revolution—
relations between white landowners and their dark-skinned workers
remained segregated and deeply paternalistic. Having grown up in one
semifeudal society, Jenkins was about to assume control of another.

The times favored a takeover. That May, President Carranza had
boarded his last train and Governor Cabrera had fled into exile. The state
judiciary would soon be replaced by a governor with no axe to grind over
Jenkins's kidnapping, in turn reducing legal obstacles to his foreclosing on
Atencingo. Following a September election, Obregón would be president;
he was much less anti-American than Carranza. Global conditions were
also enticing. In January, the US and UK governments had lifted wartime
price controls on sugar, causing a speculative spiral in world markets. By
May, the price reached a record 23 cents per pound. Fortunes were made
within weeks, in what was tagged "The Dance of the Millions." Although
the price were to tumble to less than 5 cents by December, it would stay
substantially above its prewar level.[7]

In October, responding to reports that he was selling out and leaving,
Jenkins announced that he was staying and investing further. That very
day, he said, he had closed a deal to buy the Atencingo estate, paying 1 million pesos, and he would invest another million to improve it.[8] His unchar-
acteristic announcement, one of the very few times he would speak to the
media after the kidnapping scandal, was a statement of defiance. It was as
if to say that whatever the Carrancistas had thrown at him, whatever bad
press he had endured, he was challenging Mexico to respect his efforts as
a businessman.

The Atencingo deal was not in fact closed. The estate was worth much
more than the 1.2 million pesos lent, and Jenkins wanted to cover the difference by trading smaller farms rather than paying cash; negotiations
with the Díaz Rubíns would not reach a legal conclusion for a year or
so. But Jenkins did not wait for the niceties to be tied up before setting
his shoulder to reviving the estate. At first he worked in tandem with the
Díaz Rubín family.[9] Then, in late 1921, the Díaz Rubíns were forced by

a court ruling to agree to a trade that ceded Atencingo to Jenkins, along with a large annex called Lagunillas. In exchange, they gained the cancellation of the debt, three houses in Puebla City, and three haciendas growing wheat.[10]

What Jenkins needed first was professional help. His tractor-importing partner, Diego Kennedy, had died during the war, but he persuaded his son Diego Jr. to temporarily administer the estate. Kennedy knew how to keep agrarian activists at bay, and it was probably he who advised Jenkins to hire gunmen to defend his boundaries, just as the Kennedys had done.[11] However, Diego Jr. was a wheat farmer, and sugar required a special expertise. So Jenkins soon employed a sugar agronomist, a no-nonsense Spaniard called Manuel Pérez.

What Jenkins needed second was money. Since his wealth was tied up in property, he had to find buyers. Among the first assets on the block were La Corona and its sister mill in Querétaro. Jenkins found a willing customer in William Hardaker, the British vice-consul, who ran a firm importing textile machinery. Initially, Hardaker and his son entered La Corona SA as Jenkins's partners and company managers. Jenkins stayed on for a while as president, but he ceased to oversee the mill and moved to a home in the city center.[12] He cannot have parted lightly with La Corona, which he had spent fifteen years cultivating, nor with its workforce of four hundred, who were both his employees and his neighbors.

Yet in a hallmark of his career, Jenkins chose a good time to sell. Urban labor had begun to flex its muscles with unprecedented cohesion, energized by strikes during the Revolution, emboldened by the new constitution and close relations with Obregón. Arguably the world's most radical worker charter at the time, the constitution's Article 123 fixed the workday at eight hours and guaranteed labor the right to organize, bargain collectively, and strike. In 1918, delegates from the capital and seventeen states founded the powerful Mexican Regional Worker Confederation, known by its acronym CROM. Under the portly and nattily attired Luis Napoleón Morones, who had a talent for radical rhetoric and a taste for high living, the CROM eventually came to be seen as a corrupt, corporatist machine in the service of the state. But during its first ten years its impact on the textile workforce was invigorating, helping secure better working conditions and a near-doubling in the average wage. In Puebla, the six mills of Atlixco were organized within two months in 1919. Strikes proliferated, as did bloody clashes between union and nonunion workers. For most of the next five years, Pueblan textiles were in turmoil.[13]

Jenkins experienced the new militancy in November 1920. He had called a halt to production, citing a cotton shortage and an excess of unsold product. Some at La Corona claimed the halt was a pretext for culling workers newly unionized by the Sindicalist Confederation of the State of Puebla (CSEP), a CROM affiliate. The claim was credible. Jenkins had shown his intolerance of activism during the strike of 1912. Shutdowns were now a proven bartering mechanism used by owners to expel union ringleaders. Donald Street having returned to Tennessee, Jenkins had a new manager named J. C. Riach. When Riach reopened La Corona after a few days, he allowed only fifty workers back inside, all of them nonunionized; a clash broke out between workers entering the mill and CSEP members trying to stop them. Riach was pelted with stones and four others were wounded. In contrast to 1912, those involved were mostly women; a number of Jenkins's "docile" charges were no longer willing to be deferential. In response to the riot and petitions by the CSEP, the Labor Department in Mexico City began to mediate. His hand forced, Jenkins rehired most of the eighty or so unionized workers. By year's end, all but eight or ten, presumably the "trouble makers," were back at their machines.[14]

The radical genie was now out of the lamp. Newly empowered, La Corona's women petitioned for a pay raise; the matter again went to the Labor Department, upon which Jenkins agreed to 10 percent. Along with the CSEP, the women militated for the reinstatement of the remaining union members. In February 1921, the CSEP organized a city-wide mill strike and a march. The protesters, mostly women, carried placards proclaiming: "We are victims of foreign exploitation," "If you are Mexican, don't buy stockings from La Corona," and "Only beasts carry the yoke." Yet this action, typical of labor's new assertiveness, would reveal the limits of the confederation's power. Owners threatened to close their mills, claiming that constant agitation meant they had not operated for a full week in six months. Within a few hours, the state government forced the CSEP to back down.[15]

Despite the turbulence and the promises of Article 123, protection for Puebla's unions had not quite arrived. The owner-worker balance of power would shift more decisively in 1925, when union influence reached its zenith. The CROM had organized most of the textile industry, along with other sectors, and Morones now doubled as Industry Minister. Morones brought owners and unions together in a nationwide Textile Convention (1925–1927). It spent eighteen months hammering out an industry détente that gave workers various protections, along with a minimum wage of 2 pesos, and granted owners a less conflictive environment. The days of 100 percent profit margins were over, noted a US observer; optimistic owners foresaw 40 percent profits and pessimists none at all. Further, the sector's inefficiencies and reluctance to modernize would render it vulnerable to recessions until the boom of World War II.[16]

Even in this troubled sector, Jenkins's activities did not match his master plan. Far from getting out, he forged new ties, although often his hand was somewhat forced, when his loans turned bad and he felt compelled to foreclose. By 1923, he was owner or co-owner of another three local mills. Each was small but represented a useful connection. One called Los Ángeles was a finishing plant for the sizeable La Trinidad mill in Tlaxcala, whose owners, the Manuel M. Conde Co., had come to him for a 300,000-peso loan during the Revolution. Jenkins probably assumed Los Ángeles as collateral; certainly the Conde Co. had trouble repaying him, for he would later take over La Trinidad too. La Paz he leased to several operators, one of whom, Miguel Abed, would become the most powerful man in Puebla's Lebanese enclave. San Joaquín he obtained in an apparent exchange of favors with another Lebanese.[17]

The American's persistence in textiles, like the growing presence of the Lebanese, was an irony typical of an era in which increasing foreign or immigrant ownership belied nationalist government rhetoric. By 1930 only 75 of Mexico's 205 mills were wholly Mexican-owned. Of course, many of the "non-Mexicans" were immigrants who became citizens; like Jenkins, they repatriated little or no profits. But the Revolution heightened ethnic sensitivities. Enclaves were considered "foreign," respected for their abilities, suspected for their differences.[18]

Meanwhile Jenkins would continue to shift his focus to sugar. It would prove a wise move. The activist unions were in the cities, not the countryside. The vast majority of country folk were illiterate, so they were less exposed to radical ideas. In Puebla, at least, sugar millworkers would not start to organize independently until the late 1930s, and peons, those who cut the cane and dug the ditches, would lack an effective union until the mid-1940s.

As for the promise he made to Mary, its malleability is confirmed by a curious detail from 1921. Jenkins wrote to United Artists, seeking a Mexican distribution franchise. This Hollywood studio had recently been founded by four of the biggest names in film: Douglas Fairbanks, Mary Pickford, Charlie Chaplin, and D. W. Griffith. United Artists preferred to set up its own distribution arm rather than use a contractor, so it turned down Jenkins's request.[19] But his inquiry foreshadowed his interests of two decades later: already he sensed that motion pictures were a business of the future and that Mexico was fertile ground for this most urban of entertainments. And already he was placing his zeal for new ventures above concern for his wife and daughters.

President Obregón Lends a Hand

The Revolution's greatest military hero was General Álvaro Obregón. The battles he had won in the war's middle years helped topple Huerta and marginalized Pancho Villa. (He lost just 200 men to Villa's 10,000 killed or captured at the crucial Battle of Celaya.) He had enabled Carranza to claim the presidency. To show for his exploits he had a missing right arm, which became a badge of honor. But for all his battlefield heroics, Obregón was much more approachable than the aloof Carranza. Famed as a raconteur and a joker, he could equally poke fun at himself and at the grasping tendencies of many fellow officers. Hence his famous phrase: "There is no general who can resist a cannonball of 50,000 pesos."[20]

Obregón was also a pragmatist. His devastated nation needed tax revenue, its people needed jobs, and they also needed food, three reasons to be cautious toward the sugar planters. On his presidential watch, land seizures would only occur where politics made them necessary. But in October 1920, when Jenkins declared he was staying on, Obregón was only president-elect, and though his manifesto had welcomed foreign investment, the bold nationalism of the constitution remained a concern.[21] So Jenkins took a gamble that the general would welcome a gringo's help in reviving the sugar sector.

In January 1922, a month after closing on Atencingo, Jenkins wrote to Obregón, seeking protection from radicalized country folk. The town of Chietla had provisionally obtained tracts of Atencingo land. The villagers were claiming the constitutional promise that land would be redistributed from haciendas to create or enlarge communal farms. So Jenkins sought guarantees for the plantation's sugar-growing core. As things turned out, the appeal marked his first parry in a battle of more than twenty years against activist peasants. These were *agraristas*, the name given to—and proudly worn by—those who sought land by any means possible.[22]

For Jenkins, it was a battle fought in the name of private property, social order, and material progress, values that the Porfirians had held sacred and that the revolutionary state, whatever its socialist rhetoric, would find hard to renounce. For the *agraristas*, it was a battle fought for "Land and Liberty," to quote the Zapatista slogan. Land meant the fields out of which their forefathers had been cheated. Liberty meant release from the grip of oppressive landlords and freedom to govern their pueblos with minimal state interference.[23]

Jenkins began his letter by extolling Atencingo's potential. It was an estate that once produced 20 to 25 million pounds of sugar per year and generated significant taxes. Now it was starting to yield its first harvest since its destruction in 1914. To date he had spent 1.5 million pesos on its reconstruction and he intended to spend more. The problem was the people of Chietla. They had requested land from Atencingo yet were failing to cultivate their own. He was in favor of redistribution in principle, as a way of creating a middle class; he had voluntarily divided up two of his estates between villages and given up parts of other properties. Besides, there was much abandoned land elsewhere in the area. He denied he was pleading as foreigner, but still he was asking for the same protection that Obregón had given El Potrero, a heavily capitalized plantation in Veracruz owned by US investors.[24] The very life of Mexico's great sugar industry was in the president's hands.

Jenkins's letter was an exercise in exaggeration and provocative lobbying. He inflated Atencingo's historical output, more than doubling the totals. Any redistribution had been entirely pragmatic: giving away land of his own choosing or declining to litigate against its seizure was a tactic for fending off *agrarista* designs on more fertile, irrigated land.[25] The abandoned land was a sly allusion to neighboring estates, whose owners lacked the capital to revive them; if further weakened by *agrarista* incursions, they might well opt to sell out to him. His letter was also shaped by a frankly capitalistic mindset. When he claimed that Chietla's townsfolk failed to cultivate their land, Jenkins was thinking of their subsistence farming; to him, "cultivation" meant generating a surplus and accumulating capital. As for favoring redistribution, a bigger middle class was the sole justification he could find. He was blind to the rural bond between landholding and personal integrity. He could not envisage any peasant wishing to remain one.

As well as making his case in writing, Jenkins asked his lawyer Eduardo Mestre to visit the president and plead for him. Obregón's response was emphatic, telling Mestre: "I wish that all the things we burned down while fighting each other could be rebuilt. Certainly I'll give him my approval." The twin approach, a sign of deference, did the trick: Jenkins secured an

audience. Obregón gave him his assurances that Atencingo would be protected, adding that regulations would soon formalize the rights of large
landowners.[26] Obregón's actions were not especially a matter of favor, for
Carranza had already established a precedent of exempting sugar estates
from division. But the president's personal attention gave Jenkins the confidence to carry on investing. It also sent a message of caution to Puebla's
governor, the *agrarista* sympathizer José María Sánchez, who was making
provisional land grants elsewhere in the Matamoros Valley. Five months
later, Obregón's guarantees for Atencingo became public knowledge.[27]

Jenkins's alliance with Obregón was built on ideological compatibility,
pragmatism, and sheer luck. It was by coincidence that the future president had been in Puebla on January 6, 1915, the day Jenkins faced the firing squad, from which Obregón helped save him. It was fortuitous that
his kidnapping occurred little more than a year before Obregón began
seeking US diplomatic recognition; this was a task made arduous by the
preconditions of the combative Albert Fall, now a cabinet member under
Warren Harding, who insisted on guarantees for US investors in Mexico.
That task would become still harder were Puebla's famous consular agent
to suffer more deprivation. It was also somewhat by chance that Jenkins
had an advocate in the genial Mestre, who befriended Obregón during the
Revolution and mediated for him in labor disputes during his presidency.[28]

Yet all this luck would have counted for little were not Obregón a realist
and a believer in private agro-industry. He was a farmer himself, having
made a small fortune in chickpeas. In a congressional debate just before
his inauguration, he had made himself clear: awarding land to peasants
was a noble goal, and he would sanction it to a point, but, carried to the
extreme advocated by Antonio Díaz Soto y Gama, the leading Zapatista
legislator, it would cause the destruction of agricultural credit, great loss
of taxes, risk of famine, and the flight of foreign capital "which at this
moment we need more than ever." No, the rural reforms needed most
were technical advancement and higher productivity. Other countries had
seen such changes, reaping increased agricultural wages and a reduced
price of food. He cited the example of the United States.[29]

There was another connection: Jenkins and Obregón had a great deal
in common, whether or not they spent enough time together to discover
how much. Both were sons of farmers who had fallen on hard times; both
were raised between small towns and the country; both had toiled in manual jobs—Obregón as a carpenter, mechanic, and by coincidence at a sugar
mill. Both exhibited calm in the face of danger. Alan Knight's description

of Obregón as a " 'self-made man': practical, mobile, opportunist, endowed with an eye for the main chance" might equally apply to Jenkins. To historian Jean Meyer, Obregón was both "a nationalist and an americanophile ... and he was to run the country like a big business."[30]

Though this was not an interdependence of equals, Jenkins represented the *kind* of investor that Obregón needed, as did the owners of El Potrero. He was an entrepreneur, ready to risk his capital, and he was proposing an ambitious scheme to help revive a vital sector and create many jobs. He did not represent a politically awkward concentration of wealth. Despite the president's admiration for the United States, Jenkins's citizenship was unlikely a decisive factor, for Obregón would expropriate a number of US estates, including several owned by such high-profile firms as Cargill Lumber.[31]

Obregón showed his appreciation of Jenkins by being attentive to his needs. One case involved his Hacienda Pozo de Acuña in San Luis Potosí, which that state's military strongman, Saturnino Cedillo, had seized to give his soldiers. Evaluations by the War and Agriculture Ministries offered 300,000 pesos in compensation. Jenkins felt it was worth more, so he and Mestre asked the president to adjudicate. Obregón dispatched a third expert, who gave an estimate of 325,000 pesos. Jenkins argued that 340,000 would be more just. Obregón at once agreed and instructed payment for that amount. Ingeniously, Jenkins had requested to be paid not in government bonds, the usual and little-desired compensation for expropriated land, but with the right to assume a mortgage, held by a state bank, upon the Hacienda Tatetla in Puebla's Matamoros Valley. Obregón and Jenkins thus did each other a favor. The state got rid of a loan it might well have had difficulty collecting, while Jenkins became a creditor of another sugar plantation, close to Atencingo, which put him in a position to take it over.[32]

While he was haggling with the president, Jenkins felt confident to ask him another favor. Despite Obregón's promise of protection, *agraristas* were continuing to agitate at Atencingo. In July 1922, a dispute over a fifty-acre tract produced a fracas that left three of Jenkins's men dead. In December, it emerged that Puebla's Local Agrarian Commission might recommend for expropriation some Atencingo land that included cane fields.[33] So Jenkins told Obregón of his petition before the National Agrarian Commission (CNA) to have Atencingo declared an Agricultural-Industrial Unit, which would legally exempt its cane fields from seizure. Wishing to dedicate himself "with greater zeal" to the hacienda's development, he asked the president to have the CNA hurry the certification. Obregón telegrammed the CNA's director the next day. Within weeks, *agraristas* complained about Atencingo's newly exempt status: it ignored the government's "obligation to give land to Mexicans before gringos." Obregón replied testily that the law respected rights, regardless of nationality.[34]

Other Puebla landlords were more at the *agraristas'* mercy. Spaniards, victims of the worst xenophobia, were most vulnerable.[35] Having forfeited Atencingo, the Díaz Rubíns suffered further bad luck with the San Martín Valley wheat farms they received from Jenkins. This trio of haciendas was eroded by redistribution, leaving the family suspicious that Jenkins had duped them into taking properties slated for seizure.[36] But Pedro Díaz Rubín, in his mid-twenties and now the family patriarch, had neither the political connections of Jenkins nor the Machiavellian savvy of Marcelino Presno, a Spanish multi-industrialist who was the valley's largest landowner. Presno used all manner of ploys to ward off expropriation: transferring estates to family members, selling plots on credit to villagers, spreading rumors that agrarian reform was a false promise and that anyone falling for it would suffer disastrous consequences. Like Diego Kennedy, he armed his employees, having them expel *agraristas* and scare off government surveyors. He also struck a deal with the commander of the San Martín garrison. In a 1921 clash, its troops fired upon *agraristas*, leaving six dead and many more wounded.[37]

Especially at risk were Puebla's sugar planters. With the destruction of their mills, much of their property lay unfarmed, so *agraristas* could make claim to fields citing a 1920 statute, the Law of Idle Lands. The planters had few allies in the region, having largely neglected to cultivate village leaders who might have safeguarded their estates in their absence. Some could not even trust their own peons, since numbers had joined the Zapatistas.[38] Meanwhile they were faced with heavy property taxes. For two well-endowed widows, Herlinda Llera de la Hidalga and Angela Conde de Conde, losses mounted to the point that they risked losing everything.

Under Porfirio Díaz, the De la Hidalga family had become the leading landlords of the Matamoros Valley. They controlled three haciendas totaling 87,000 acres: Colón, Rijo, and Matlala. Like the sugar planters of Morelos, Vicente de la Hidalga and his neighbors enlarged their domains through foul play as well as fair, increased their control over rivers, kept their cane-cutters in the virtual slavery of debt peonage, and altered the Valley's population by drawing extra labor from elsewhere. These moves helped to foster the varied resentments that would explode in the Zapatista rebellion. For all its association with Morelos, Zapata's movement was as much at home in southwestern Puebla, as a recruiting area and as a frequent sanctuary.[39] Just as befell the planters of Morelos, so the De la Hidalgas met the Zapatistas' wrath. The rebels wrecked their mills and tortured the manager of Matlala to death.[40]

By 1922, Herlinda Llera de la Hidalga was in a fix. Village mayors were encouraging *agraristas* to occupy her estates, citing the Law of Idle Lands. José María Sánchez, the radical governor, sanctioned these moves and made provisional land grants. Allegedly, the beneficiaries were then exceeding the portions to which they were entitled. According to Llera's lawyer, seven of Puebla's sugar estates were suffering illegal land-grabs, but the region's military chief was protecting only one of them: Atencingo. He also claimed that *agraristas* were burning down the houses of peons loyal to the landowners and even killing them. The Spanish manager of Colón added that pueblos bordering Llera's estates were cutting their water supply, while a group of five hundred armed with Mausers were threatening any peons who refused to down tools and join them. *Agraristas* counter-lobbied, accusing the manager of using federal troops to shoot at the villagers, murdering one of the leaders.[41]

Matters improved little under Sánchez's moderate successor, Froylán Manjarrez. He partitioned more of Llera's land among villages, which also took much of the water supply. An appeal to the government for 5 million pesos in property damages, dating from the Revolution, yielded only 1 million. Worse, the Finance Ministry informed her that the value of her land was insufficient to cover her tax debts. In October 1924, with creditors at her heels and four children to care for, Llera would turn to a capable man who agreed to lease the estates: William Jenkins. But two months later the young widow remained distraught, enumerating her woes to the president. The deal with Jenkins meant forfeiting much of her profits. Many of her sharecroppers were not working, due to *agrarista* death threats. The land risked total abandonment and thus legal seizure. It was ever more likely she would have to sell.[42]

Angela Conde de Conde was Llera's Matamoros Valley neighbor. Or rather she would have been had either of them lived there. (Llera had lobbied the president, in a five-page telegram that refused to economize by using ellipses, from an address on Reforma Avenue, the Champs-Élysées of Mexico City.) Angela Conde owned the sugar estates Tatetla and Teruel. Through a holding company, she also owned stakes in at least six other haciendas, various urban properties, two large textile factories, and much else. In 1922, the conglomerate's assets were valued at 10 million pesos, making it perhaps the largest locally owned enterprise in the state. So it caused a sensation in June that year when it ceased making payments to creditors. Beset by contraction in the textile sector, the destruction of its sugar mills, and multiple land expropriations, the holding company was bankrupt. A two-year liquidation of its assets would produce a settlement with 131 creditors.[43]

One of them was Jenkins, thanks to his deal with Obregón over the San Luis Potosí estate. The mortgage he held against Tatetla was insufficiently large for him to foreclose. But in 1927 Tatetla too would go on the block, after failing to cover a bank debt. As for Teruel, another Spaniard took temporary charge. As receiver of Conde's businesses, he continued the hacienda's restoration. He managed to get the mill working again, but his was an uphill battle. In January 1923, at the start of the annual sugar harvest, *agraristas* stormed the fields and burned the cane. Reportedly, their aim was to clear the land so they could claim that it was empty and then invoke the Law of Idle Lands to request its expropriation.[44]

By summer 1923, the only Matamoros Valley sugar mills successfully revived were the Maurer family's Raboso and Jenkins's Atencingo. The latter was much the most impressive, producing 5,000 metric tons of sugar, almost triple Raboso's output and superior to the 4,000-ton peak under the Díaz Rubíns.[45] Pueblans surely questioned the American's success. Had he struck a deal with the state government too? Had he even done so with the *agraristas*?

AFTER A FEW years, Jenkins needed to reassess. Obregón's tenure would end in December 1924, and it was becoming clear that his successor would be the Interior Minister, Plutarco Elías Calles. Jenkins did not know Calles, and his fixer Eduardo Mestre found this stern atheist much less approachable than the incumbent.[46] Whatever protections Obregón had afforded, including Atencingo's status as an Agricultural-Industrial Unit, the state of Puebla was still in turmoil and federal authority over it, as for most of the provinces, remained tenuous. Jenkins would have to rely on alliances at the state and local level if he were to retain all of his cane fields—even more so if he were to buy out Atencingo's neighbors, and they were tenacious in clinging to their estates. What he had achieved so far was significant, taking Atencingo's productivity to record levels. Perhaps, after all, it was time to sell out and leave.

His Los Angeles home, 641 Irving Boulevard, was nearing completion. The mansion offered sumptuous space, if somewhat less tranquility than William and Mary had foreseen. Beyond its garden walls, a newly widened Wilshere Boulevard had become a thoroughfare, as the city hurriedly expanded westward. Over the four years since the Jenkins had bought their plot of land, others had built nearby. Streetcars whizzed past at 50 miles per hour. Los Angeles had continued to proliferate, due to a surging film industry and another oil boom. With the rise of the automobile and a new water supply, real estate developments were multiplying across the coastal plain. At gaps between the trees, one could look north to the hills where realtors with a genius for marketing had just erected a sign in bold white capitals, 50 feet high, lit up at night by four thousand bulbs. The letters spelled HOLLYWOODLAND.[47]

Jenkins's mansion reflected the extravagant optimism of 1920s Los Angeles. More than a home, it was a statement, a neo-Renaissance declaration of a fortune rapidly gained.[48] The property's high walls enclosed two acres of landscaped gardens and a tennis court. The residence boasted fourteen rooms and six bathrooms, each with its own unique shape. There was a large entrance hall into which descended a wide, curved staircase. There was a conservatory and there was a ballroom. The floors were of mosaic oak, the paneling of walnut, and the carpets were Chinese. Imported tile covered the bathrooms from floor to ceiling. Grillwork of hand-wrought iron covered the bookcases. The staff of ten included three gardeners, a butler, and an English cook. Determined to provide Mary with the queenly lifestyle he had always promised her, Jenkins spent $250,000 on the place, $3 million in today's currency. He would never live in it.

Puebla's Decade of Chaos

"The fecund State of Puebla has been ruined by a succession of atrocious governors—murderers, thieves, or drunkards." So wrote the left-wing US journalist and future senator Ernest Gruening, in his classic tome *Mexico and Its Heritage*.[49] In the 1920s, the one-time editor of *The Nation* spent many months in Mexico, anxious to correct the negative view that Americans commonly held of their southern neighbor. With credential letters from Obregón and Calles, he interviewed politicians, intellectuals, industrialists, and union leaders. He deemed the federal government admirable, but the provincial powers much less so. Visiting twenty-four of the states, he recorded all manner of fraud and foul play: impositions of governors by departing incumbents, looting of state treasuries, polling-day violence, assassination. Puebla, he found, was prodigious in its dysfunction. He continued:

> the governorship has been going from worse to still worse: General José María Sánchez, author of the attempted assassination of Morones in the chamber of deputies in November, 1924, in which affray an innocent bystander of a deputy was killed; Froylán Manjarrez, who after looting the state joined the de la Huertista rebellion in search of still more loot; Alberto Guerrero, a drunkard; Claudio N. Tirado, who stole at least a million pesos by the simple device of paying no one and keeping the state revenues, seeking immortality by cutting his name on every new stone erected in the state during his term; and General Manuel P. Montes, the agrarian agitator. In March, 1927, intoxicated, he entered the Palacio de Cristal, and began to quarrel boisterously with political enemies dining there. When he drew his pistol they retired, but not to be denied his fun the governor shot up the mirrors which gave the restaurant its name.

However satirical his tone, Gruening captured a state of affairs typical of postwar Mexico, especially the more populous central states.[50] While federal government was relatively orderly, the vast majority of governors failed to finish their four-year terms. But Jenkins's adopted home was especially troubled. During the 1920s, Puebla was overseen by sixteen governors, more than any other state. Some held power for mere days.[51] Within months of Gruening's sketch, Montes was not only deposed but dead, his murder attributed to his federally imposed successor, Donato Bravo Izquierdo, a man "renowned for brutality."[52]

This was the political chaos through which Jenkins rose to substantial fortune and power. The disorder heightened the vulnerability of much of Puebla's elite. At the same time, it increased the state government's financial dependence on the business sector, especially those up-and-comers whose revenues were multiplying. It made for an environment in which industrial progress demanded toughness, guile, and at times—to the thinking of those who lived through it—a willingness to meet violence, or the threat of it, with violence.

While the corruption and incompetence observed by Gruening played their part, Puebla's political disorder had origins more fundamental.

A faction-driven power struggle pitted elite moderates against the *agrarista* forces inspired by the Revolution, and these were fragmented by regional allegiances. Second, governors were vulnerable to federal meddling, as Obregón and Calles either molded their regional support base to manipulate presidential elections or tried to impose order when provincial authority waned. Next, bankruptcy persisted, due to the state's inability to collect sufficient taxes. Finally, Puebla was riddled by constant violence, from prolific banditry to aggression between landed and landless. While a revolving-door governorship prevailed in Puebla City, the law of the gun prevailed in the countryside.

Agraristas found champions in José María Sánchez and Manuel P. Montes, both rural power brokers. Becoming governor offered them the chance to hasten land redistribution and garner greater autonomy for their homelands. But their bases were geographically limited and their allies fickle. Their clumsy attempts to enforce radical policy, including their approval of *agrarista* land-grabs rather than steer petitions through official channels, met concerted and often violent resistance.[53] Landowners such as Jenkins used injunctions, political lobbying, payments to the military, and their own gunmen to reclaim their fields. Beset by such pushback, reviled by most Pueblans for their heavy-handed leadership, and wearing presidential patience thin, the governors' authority proved ephemeral. Sánchez lasted from June 1921 to March 1922. After a pilgrimage to Soviet Russia, his attempt in 1924 to reassert himself as governor failed within a few weeks. Montes fared no better, lasting from November 1926 to July 1927.[54]

Equally tenuous was the hold of the elite moderates. The first post-Carranza governor, General Rafael Rojas, son of a wealthy Porfirian family, fell victim to the electoral machinations of Obregón within two months. Obregón imposed the patrician labor leader Vicente Lombardo Toledano (four months in 1923–1924) but then removed him when his tenure appeared ineffective. Claudio Tirado (most of 1925–1926), though supported by Calles, lacked the popularity to resist the machinations of the radical Montes, who conspired in his ouster to gain the seat for himself.[55] In sum, Puebla's governors could not build enough of a coalition, or retain enough presidential backing, to resist an unscheduled exit.

Both cause and effect of this fragmentation was a debilitating dearth of cash. The Carrancistas, after nearly six years of government, bequeathed a bankrupt state to future regimes, which put any new governor in a quandary. This was a vicious circle: governors inherited an empty treasury, struggled to administer effectually, failed to reward or buy the loyalty of sufficient supporters, and, succumbing to power-hungry rivals, often took the contents of the state coffer with them as they quit. Efforts to raise revenue found all manner of obstacles. The state lacked qualified accountants. Records had been destroyed to cover up fraud. The state's finance ministry employed just twenty-one tax collectors to traverse a hilly state where highways were few. The pitiful pay accorded these men, as low as two pesos per day, out of which they had to pay their expenses and feed their mules, gave plenty of motive to embezzle or take bribes.[56]

Each governor's suspect legitimacy further hindered tax collection. As these officials came and went, Pueblans withheld their payments. The prospect that a regime might not survive was a strong disincentive to pay, even among its supporters.[57] Many new incumbents inadvertently stoked this disinclination by announcing that their predecessors had left little or nothing in the treasury.[58] Allegations of embezzlement were fueled by spectacles of new wealth. Unfortunately for the peasantry, whose interests they represented, *agrarista* governors were among the worst culprits— although it might be fairer to say that, with fewer friends in the business community, they were less able to disguise their booty.

Sánchez, after his second stint in office, was accused with unusual directness of taking 72,000 pesos home with him. He obtained some choice properties, including a ranch abutting Puebla City. Montes staffed his executive team with friends, who all acquired new automobiles. He himself bought a 240,000-peso hacienda in the San Martín Valley, and on departing he pilfered the treasury books to cover his tracks.[59] Such corruption was typical of the times. Though a persistent trait from the Porfirian age to the present, self-enrichment by governors was especially overt during the 1920s and 1930s.[60]

All told, Puebla's average annual tax haul by the mid-1920s was a measly 2.5 million pesos, about a dollar per head. Ten years later the sum was scarcely more respectable, at 4.1 million, which given currency devaluation still meant little more than $1 million. Beyond issues of gubernatorial legitimacy and administrative inadequacy, there were two fundamental problems. The first was that after the Revolution the federal government gradually eroded the ability of the states to collect tax. This was a deliberate policy to help bring governors into line and to centralize authority in Mexico City.[61]

The second basic problem was a woefully inadequate tax base. The largest sources of revenue—liquor, sugar, textiles, property—were stifled one way or another. Real estate had traditionally been assessed at a third or even a tenth of its value. In the case of sugar, since many fields and mills were burned and destroyed, several years passed before the sector returned as a major tax source.[62] When it started to do so, from 1923, governors were torn between cultivating its fiscal potential and satisfying the demands of *agraristas*. They had to weigh concerns about the productivity of *ejidos* (the traditional communal farms favored by most *agraristas*) with the political capital to be reaped from awarding hacienda land to the former officers, soldiers, and allies of Zapata. Peace and stability beckoned too, for otherwise the Zapatistas were given to land-grabs and bloody confrontation. Such was the calculus facing governors as they mulled taking land from Jenkins. Such was the need for Jenkins, for whom cane acreage was sacrosanct, to sway the governors in their thinking.

Violence took multiple forms. By no means was all the killing within Jenkins's sugar dominion attributable to him or his minions, as some have alleged.[63] Statewide, there was violence between village-based bosses, known as *caciques*. There was violence between rival unions. There were inter-village feuds with ancient origins that the Revolution had revived. There were assaults by bandits on travelers and by suspicious villagers on well-meaning visitors. There was violence experienced as a part of general rebellions against the federal government.[64] Amid all this occurred clashes between landlords and *agraristas*. Owners like Presno, Kennedy, and Jenkins defended their land by arming employees, creating private militia, even summoning detachments of federal troops, while former Zapatista generals and other *caciques* goaded armed peasants into claiming their rightful prize by invading desirable fields, or worse.

One hot day in 1925, Roberto Maurer was killed in cold blood by *agraristas*. Maurer was one of six sons of a French immigrant who owned the sugar-producing Hacienda Raboso, not far from Atencingo, and his murder caused a heated debate in the federal Congress. The respected radical Soto y Gama defended the killing, which some attributed to General Fortino Ayaquica, a Zapatista *cacique*. The Maurers had exploited and terrorized the Atlixco region for generations, he claimed; the man's death was an act of divine justice. Against Soto y Gama's wishes, Congress approved a committee to investigate. During a banquet that night at the Soviet Embassy, which he attended as guest of honor, Soto y Gama told President Calles of his firm desire to protect General Ayaquica: "My General, I'd rather our balls be cut off than we let our brother be punished."[65]

With chronic unrest pervading Puebla, landowners felt justified in arming themselves. Foreigners were often targets, and radical politicians tended to exonerate their assailants. Within just five years, murder victims included Maurer, a German landowner, a Lebanese landowner, at least three Spanish hacienda managers, and the combative American widow Rosalie Evans. On an August afternoon in 1924, while riding with her driver in her mule-drawn buggy, Evans met an *agrarista* ambush. At that moment she happened to be reciting a poem by Goethe, and she barely managed to reach for her pistol before she died in a cacophony of bullets.[66]

So Jenkins had ample cause to carry a gun. But he chose not to, even when bringing sacks of cash from Puebla for the Atencingo payroll.[67] It was a point of pride, even a conscious projection of feeling himself untouchable, that he would not be cowed into carrying a weapon by the threat of sundry peasants, bearing rifles or machetes and a grudge.

Atencingo itself was well fortified, however. The manager and submanagers were always armed, and for most of the Jenkins era a batch of federal troops was garrisoned at the mill, a rare privilege. Atencingo also employed full-time gunmen to patrol the fields, deterring sabotage and land-grabs.[68] Ironically, such private militia, found throughout Mexico during and after the Revolution, often included former *agraristas*. These militias' reputations for vigilante violence, and their obvious challenge to the competence of the state, led governors to make repeated and unconvincing denials of their existence.[69]

In the absence of a local *caudillo*, a charismatic military strongman of the kind that stamped order on other states, Puebla's violence and disarray caused the business elite to crave political influence.[70] Seeking a return to Porfirian "order and progress," old-money Pueblans and climbers such as Jenkins tried to shape a conservative revival. What they desired above all was an iron hand in the governor's office, clamping down on bandits, radical unions, and *agraristas* alike. The political class, meanwhile, needed to supplement the state's deficient revenues, to enact policy and consolidate their power. Conditions were ripe for interdependence.

Governors: More Friends in High Places

Ten days after Governor Cabrera fled, in May 1920, the press had revealed that state coffers were virtually empty. Cabrera and his bureaucrats had taken the contents and, in the quixotic hope of a return to power, tried to set up a temporary capital in the Sierra. The news was an ominous welcome for Rafael Rojas, who became interim governor the day of the report. Nonetheless, after seven weeks, Rojas was able to chalk up a surplus of

70,000 pesos. Making the healthy balance possible was his successful appeal to businesses to advance their tax payments. These included sums from William Jenkins.[71]

Unlike the Carrancista governors, Rojas was a known quantity in Puebla City, a local businessman and revolutionary moderate who came from a Porfirian-allied family. Politically experienced, Rojas cemented the trust of the elites by settling strikes and returning confiscated property to the Church. As it turned out, the general's conservative background would be used against him in a power play by Obregón, who wished to emplace personal allies in state governments ahead of the presidential election, ready to rig the results where necessary.[72] But Rojas's short tenure established a crucial precedent: incumbents could ensure a degree of stability by obtaining credit from the business elite.

Puebla's governors looked often to the industrialists, as the paltry tax haul faced disproportionate demands. Bureaucracy consumed most of the budget, and further amounts needed to be allotted for the upkeep of federal troops. This left little for fulfilling the mantra of modernization: laying highways, paving city streets, providing sanitation and drinking water, and building and staffing schools. No statistic better captured the gargantuan task than Puebla's 82 percent illiteracy rate.[73] In response, the business class gave financial support to conservative incumbents, reached compromises with moderates, and withheld aid to radicals. So doing, it selectively bolstered gubernatorial tenure. Conservative and accommodationist governors proved increasingly able to meet Puebla's needs and see out their terms. Over the years to come, Jenkins would become the leading private participant in Puebla's conservative turn.

Deals between politicians and businessmen were usually covert, going uninvestigated by a generally timid press. So the evidence is fragmentary, often coming to light only decades later. We know of Rojas's borrowing only because Jenkins mentioned it in a dispatch to the US Embassy. We gain another glimpse from a late-in-life interview with Vicente Lombardo Toledano. Recounting his short spell as governor, the veteran labor leader told of how, as a young idealist, he had been determined to kick-start agrarian reform but found his path obstructed by Jenkins. The problem was that Puebla was beholden to the American because he had been lending it money.

While this assessment of the American's political sway is an exaggeration, the manner of their meeting suggests that Jenkins already considered himself on equal terms with any governor. One day, Lombardo recalled, he was working in his office when the door swung open and a stranger walked in. He announced: "I am William Jenkins."

"Who gave you permission to enter?" asked Lombardo, incredulous.

"For me the door is always open in the government of Puebla," Jenkins replied.

"It *was*. Today that's not possible. I can't receive you without an appointment." Lombardo pressed a bell to summon an assistant. "Get this man out of here."

Although the bravado of the twenty-nine-year old radical (if embellished in the retelling) carried the day, forces were marshalling against him. Not four months after taking office, obstructed from carrying out land and labor reforms by local congressmen and the Spanish textile elite as well as by Jenkins—but also having irked Obregón by staffing his offices with his union cronies—Lombardo quit his post under presidential duress.[74]

As for Jenkins's arrogance, it was more a reflection of his attitude to politics in general than an expression of racial elitism. He never cared for politicos, Mexican or American. His close proximity to later governors he would put down to necessity.[75] In his distrust of politicians, he cannot have failed to notice how, just when he was dealing with Lombardo, his interventionist acquaintance Albert Fall was deeply mired in the Teapot Dome scandal. Teapot Dome was a messy saga of Big Oil and bribery, which would result in Fall's imprisonment for influence-peddling. According to prominent social critics, in the cold sea of US politics Fall was only the tip of a tawdry iceberg. Not long before the scandal, essayist H. L. Mencken had this to say about the average US congressman: "he is incompetent and imbecile, and not only incompetent and imbecile, but also incurably dishonest."[76]

Private-sector support for the treasury did sometimes surface in the newspapers. In 1925, just after his inauguration, Claudio Tirado secured a 300,000-peso advance from the industrialists, equal to 12 percent of the budget. Four months later, Jenkins saved the state university from closing; in relocating one of his businesses to Puebla, he ensured that the annual 30,000 pesos due upon it in taxes would allow the state to cover the professors' salaries. In the late 1920s, Donato Bravo requested that sugar and alcohol producers, among whom Jenkins was by far the leader, make half of their annual tax payment each preceding autumn. Tirado and Bravo, both conservatives, lasted long in office: twenty-two and nineteen months, respectively, three times a Puebla governor's average that decade.[77] Already business was shaping politics to its advantage.

Central to the Mexican state's modernization program was road-building, to unite the nation and its distinct communities, and governors needed help with the costly task. In 1927, aiming to halt misuse of public funds for paving Puebla City's pothole-ridden streets, Bravo created a committee of "distinguished citizens." The so-called Paving Board included Jenkins, several other consuls, and chamber of commerce chiefs, who together proposed a special tax on businesses to support the work. A year later, business leaders praised Bravo for the Board and for putting its budget, a healthy 100,000 pesos, beyond the reach of state officials. Meanwhile Jenkins and other industrialists dipped into their pockets to subsidize new highways, including those leading from Puebla City to Matamoros and to the state's second city, Tehuacán.[78]

Jenkins gained further capital with acts of civic charity. Two came to light in December 1929, when he donated to a guard house at a city park and a committee planning Puebla's four-hundredth anniversary. A year earlier, after recording how he helped a store-workers' association buy a mansion for its headquarters by persuading the bank that owned it to lower the price, a paper claimed that Jenkins "is always hunting down good works, to carry them out with his powerful business influence, without making any show of it at all."[79] The claim for his low-profile approach rings true. Jenkins appeared only rarely at inaugurations or other public events, preferring to send a representative. Unlike his fast-rising Lebanese peer Miguel Abed—who gave handouts to his workers and even took them and their families to the beach, in each case ensuring his generosity generated press—Jenkins cared little what the public made of him.[80] What mattered was that he fulfill noblesse oblige, his duties as a wealthy Protestant in the tradition of Carnegie and Rockefeller, and that the authorities were on his side.

On doing such favors, Jenkins and his peers were unlikely to receive a direct quid pro quo, although there may have been example of that in the arrangement with Tirado, who in exchange for their tax advances reportedly promised edicts against *agraristas*. In most cases, the dealings probably contributed to a common understanding that when the state wrote laws or issued a ruling, the interests of business would be foremost. Given the new sense of revolutionary entitlement among peasants and workers, Puebla's industrialists and landowners needed less to gain a governor's guarantees about resolving a specific strike or land-grab—after all, the man might be gone in a few months—than to cultivate a climate of reciprocal obligation, which would transcend changes in office.

First as a creditor, then as a landowner, and later as a multi-industrialist, Jenkins needed the protection of the Puebla judiciary and bureaucracy, and all such officials were typically under the governor's thumb. Jenkins needed the terms of his loans enforced when debtors defaulted, so he could foreclose on their properties without a lengthy lawsuit. He needed his estates to be safeguarded from the leftists who gravitated to Puebla's Agrarian Commission; with the federal government slow to gain hold over the provinces, local officials tended to wield greater influence over land reform than their Mexico City counterparts.[81] As violence and property disputes continued to flare, he needed his lands and his personnel shielded from *agrarista* invaders and bandits. From the late 1920s, as Jenkins diversified by allotting venture capital to cement manufacture and automobile assembly, and by reinvesting in the textile sector, he needed favorable rulings from the state's Conciliation and Arbitration Board at times of labor unrest.

Apparently such protections were forthcoming. Accounts of Jenkins's property gains mention no protracted legal battles. This suggests the complicity of local judges, who were appointed by the governor.[82] Judges were also widely held to be purchasable. The Atencingo ruling of 1921 may well provide an example. A month later, a newspaper made the daring claim that a 43,000-peso tax on the purchase had failed to reach the treasury. The report implied that Governor Sánchez, whom it sarcastically called "a Quijote in matters of honor," had stolen or waived the tax; a waiver involving a pay-off, to both judge and governor, would seem most likely. Financial favors were probably not the only factors. When judges sided with Jenkins in debt disputes, they may also have been swayed by the history of ties between the debtors and the Porfirian establishment. Former Atencingo owners the Díaz Rubín family, like many textile barons, had enjoyed warm relations with the discredited Governor Mucio Martínez, who had pampered such investors and shared in their creation of wealth.[83]

Official actions against *agraristas* were more blatant. When peasant farmers took over fields belonging to Atencingo or a sister property without due process, governors usually dispatched officials and troops to evict them. Three different governors, in 1922, 1924, and 1925, intervened with force to reverse the encroachments of country folk on Jenkins's land.[84]

Concentric Rings of Protection

Jenkins also cultivated Puebla's next most powerful men, the military chief and the archbishop. Military chiefs were the generals placed in charge of the zones into which Carranza had divided Mexico, to secure his victory; later presidents retained the zones, to secure the peace. Jenkins's relations with these generals are hard to pinpoint, for the post was rotated almost every year. Yet many of them believed that the Revolution had granted them privileges. Two military chiefs from the state of Coahuila, Cesáreo Castro (1917–1919) and Fortunato Maycotte (1920–1921), set the kleptocratic tone. They spent their terms acquiring haciendas, raising cattle, and, at least in Castro's case, producing liquor.[85] They were men with whom one could do business.

It is telling that a batch of federal troops was permanently stationed at Atencingo, housed within the mill compound. (By the early 1930s, each of the Jenkins sugar estates had military protection.)[86] It is also telling that many other haciendas tried but failed to secure similar services. Since the army's budget was stretched, an on-site company of soldiers might be obtained with the offer of a billet, tortillas, and beans. But the severity of rural violence meant there were never enough troops to shield all the haciendas that wanted them. What could make the difference was a willingness to pay cash. Jenkins, two generals later attested, paid well.[87] Of course, the expanse that he controlled by the mid-1920s, up to 200,000 acres along a 25-mile axis, meant he could not rely on a single posse. At times, reinforcements under the military chief and regional forces under the governor played supplementary roles, while on a day-to-day basis Jenkins deployed a private vigilante force.

With the archbishop, Jenkins built on the rapport he established in 1919 during Sánchez y Paredes's visit to his mill. A year later, he offered to contribute whatever was necessary to complete renovations at the Archbishop's Palace. The Catholic Ladies Union, in charge of the fundraising, gleefully released the news to the press. As a token of thanks, Sánchez y Paredes gave Jenkins a book of lectures by an English Jesuit, inscribing it: "To the highly esteemed gentleman and honorable consul Mr. William Jenkins, with particular affection."[88]

After Sánchez y Paredes died in 1923, the Jenkins family befriended his successor, Pedro Vera y Zuria. The new archbishop would preside during two periods of religious persecution, the Cristero War of 1926–1929 and a more legalistic repression during the mid-1930s. Both reflected the anticlericalism of the nation's political elite, to whom the Catholic Church was a foe of the Revolution and an obstacle to social progress. In 1927, when tensions between the state and the Church were at their peak, Vera was forced into exile in the United States. Before long, several Church dependencies were shut down, including the Puebla City orphanage. Mary came to the rescue, taking in many of the orphans and nuns at the spacious house that the Jenkins now occupied at 6 Porfirio Díaz Street, one of the stately mansions of downtown Puebla. She then found and rented a dedicated home for them. Among the girls she took in was Amelia García, known as Mía, who joined the home permanently as a maid, becoming in turn a nanny, a cook, and eventually the domestic anchor of the Jenkins household. William made a key contribution during the second period of repression by paying for men from the shuttered Palafoxian Seminary to continue their studies at the Montezuma Seminary in New Mexico.[89]

Despite the rise of anticlericalism and bouts of persecution, in the pious city of Puebla the Church remained a revered symbol and potent social force. This is what led Calles, on his presidential campaign tour, to sniff that the city was "churchy." Popular piety was evident on the eve of Vera's investiture, when crowds of thousands greeted his train and escorted him from the station to the cathedral, prompting the Mexico City press to comment on Puebla's "profound Catholicism."[90] The help that his American Protestant family afforded the Church during its times of trial was a signal that, whatever his faith in the Church as a tool of social control, Jenkins took seriously his duties as a wealthy Pueblan. In Archbishop Vera, he had the most eminent of advocates. Vera might convince a Spanish widow that this American would make a trustworthy creditor; he might inform a left-leaning governor that this landowner showed a real concern for the poor—behold his aid for orphanages and schools—and so should not be singled out for tax reassessment or land confiscation.[91]

Lacking among Jenkins's advocates was Uncle Sam. For one thing, Mexico's constitution forbade meddling by other nations in property disputes. For another, Jenkins would have been well aware of the failure of his neighbor Rosalie Evans to recruit the US and UK governments to good effect; such strategies to defend her hacienda had only antagonized Obregón.[92] Moreover, some at the US Embassy disapproved of Jenkins. They frowned on his aloofness. One ambassador was aggravated at Jenkins's hacienda-buying; unaware of his friendship with Obregón, he misread the purchases as an affront to Mexican authorities. By 1927, exasperated at a decline in Jenkins's consular dispatches, a consul general was urging for his appointment to be terminated. Franklin Roosevelt's ambassador to Mexico, the left-leaning Josephus Daniels, would also express a low opinion of Jenkins.[93]

Very likely, Jenkins felt that his high-profile playing of the consular card during the kidnapping episode had not served him well; it had cost him in the wallet and in reputation and allowed nationalist politicians to use him as a punching bag. Whatever the case, State Department and other records reveal little contact between Jenkins and his embassy after 1920 and none involving requests for help.

AROUND ATENCINGO, JENKINS wove concentric rings of protection. Only a few of them involved the rule of law and guarantees of property rights that supposedly applied to everyone. True, two of the rings were institutional safeguards: Atencingo's protected status as an Agricultural-Industrial Unit and its legal identity as a limited-liability company. Rather more involved muscle, not only the governor, with his judiciary, his troops, and his police but also the federal military chiefs and the plantation's private militia. Others involved "soft power," such as friendship with archbishops, donations to charity, and erection of rural schools.[94] There was the Local Agrarian Commission, whose surveyors, though often more sympathetic to *agraristas* than their federal counterparts on the National Commission, were also susceptible to bribes. There were prominent local strongmen, political heirs of Zapata and proconsuls of agrarian reform, who sometimes proved willing to compromise. And there was the physical ring of hills and rain-fed land that enclosed the sugar-growing core, a large quantity of peripheral terrain that could be surrendered piecemeal by way of appeasement.

Jenkins's ability to defend the heart of Atencingo no doubt owed something to the jerky pace of agrarian reform during the 1920s, when neither Obregón nor Calles was committed to the process. But he would continue to shield it in the 1930s, when more radical leadership redistributed private land with revolutionary fervor. Fundamentally, it was his multipart strategy, a reliance upon a gamut of mutually beneficial relations and hegemonic practices, that explains how an American succeeded in developing an unusually large and productive plantation in an era when most large landowners, especially foreigners, suffered depletions. Holding onto property was a Darwinian game. It favored those who were equal parts wealthy, connected, and willing to suspend their scruples.

His success contrasted starkly with the fate of many families whose identity as Porfirian elites, and often as Spaniards, lingered as a liability; now they were targeted by *agraristas*, radical governors, and tax assessors. With the textile sector also sluggish, their debts mounted. Their social prestige counted for little in the new political order. The luckless Díaz Rubín family could not prevent the erosion of the estates they had received in partial exchange for Atencingo; by the early 1930s, they were left with nothing but the haciendas' main houses.[95] Bankruptcies ensued, such as that of the Conde y Conde family. Even the wily Marcelino Presno, primary landlord of the San Martín Valley, found his Porfirian-accented vulnerability catching up with him. In 1932, to cover his mounting debts, he was forced to sell the luxurious downtown Puebla home he had bought just before the Revolution. He had lost a nine-year battle to retain it, and he died five months later.[96]

Jenkins's rise contrasted also with the decline of families whose fortunes were urban. In 1921, the Spanish widow Adela Méndez de Gavito, owner of three textile mills, declared bankruptcy. In 1924 the Matienzo family, prominent since the colonial era, lost their storied mill El Patriotismo to Miguel Abed, who was aided by a loan from Jenkins.[97] Owing to another bankruptcy, Jenkins claimed the crown jewel of Puebla retail, La Ciudad de México.

A short step from the central plaza, this French-owned department store was the epitome of Porfirian opulence, a marvel of *modernité*. Sixteen years in the planning, built with wrought-iron stanchions imported from Paris, La Ciudad de México had two spacious floors, linked by a grand, bifurcated staircase. The store was bedecked with French and British fashions, along with beauty products, household goods, furniture, and oriental rugs. *Le tout* Puebla came there to shop. Unfortunately for its backers, this palace had opened in the inauspicious year of 1910. The very next year, spooked by the war, most investors dropped out. Adrian Reynaud remained, and though a very wealthy man he needed a partner. Leon Signoret, one of the country's richest Frenchmen, came first to the rescue, but after seven years of losses he too bailed out. With no banks able to lend, Reynaud turned to Jenkins, who in 1919 loaned 500,000 pesos. Reynaud later fell victim to embezzlement by a fellow Frenchman, and in 1927, bankrupt, he had to close the store and relinquish the building to Jenkins. Eventually Jenkins found another clothier to lease the space. By then, he had registered the holding company under a new name, the self-assurance of which cannot have been lost upon the Pueblans: Imperial Building, Inc.[98]

The Sugar Empire of Atencingo

The mid-1920s were a crossroads for Jenkins. Although his protector Obregón was stepping down, the rings of protection he had woven around Atencingo looked strong enough to hold off the *agraristas*; some rings depended on relationships, but its status as an Agricultural-Industrial Unit shielded its heartland from seizure, as did its importance to the Puebla treasury. So the estate might well seem safe enough to some buyer. If Jenkins were still sincere about selling up and rejoining Mary, this was surely the time to do it. On the other hand, Atencingo was starting to fulfill its potential as a money-spinning giant of the sugar industry.

On a visit to Los Angeles in 1924, Jenkins saw for the first time in years his old Vanderbilt friend John Tigert, and once back home he wrote: "if I can only arrange my business in such a way as to permit me to leave Mexico in a more definite way than I have been able to do heretofore, we will try to bring about more frequent reunions." The following April he told Tigert that, while his work had been "especially heavy these last months," he and Mary planned to move into their California home "later on in the year." In 1927 he admitted he had not visited Los Angeles in two years. He added that "in all probability" they would move in "next year."[99]

Jenkins did try to find buyers for Atencingo, or so he later claimed, but evidently he found no takers at a price he thought fair. He had invested around $5 million, so presumably he wanted at least that in return.[100] Exactly who, beyond the government or a foreign investor, had sufficient capital for such a purchase is unclear. Well-connected generals like Aarón Sáenz and Abelardo Rodríguez could have shown an interest—they could have bought using inside access to public finance—but Puebla's volatile politics might have deterred them.

The greater obstacle to selling out was that things were simply going too well. Output and productivity were soaring. Atencingo had overtaken Calipam to become Puebla's top sugar producer. Jenkins was a farmer at heart, and the growth of Atencingo, in size and yield, must have thrilled him.[101] Doubly so, for his old-money neighbors were starting to quit.

One by one, undone by *agraristas*, bankruptcy, and competition from Atencingo, the Spanish grandees of Puebla (or more often their widows) surrendered their estates to the American. William and Mary would later tell their daughters that there was justice in all this, as these were the same snobs who had once rebuffed them. From southwest to northeast, up the wide Matamoros Valley, Jenkins came to own nine contiguous haciendas.

These began with Lagunillas, an annex of Atencingo; then Atencingo itself; and after it Jaltepec, which he bought in 1924. The sellers were two Spaniards who had lost interest after seven villages were granted pieces of it. In fact, Jaltepec was typical of the new fluidity in real estate; the brothers had only acquired it the year before, foreclosing on Francisco de Velasco, Puebla's last Porfirian mayor.[102]

Proceeding northeast from Jaltepec lay Colón and Rijo. These were leased from Herlinda Llera in 1924 and purchased seven years later. After Rijo came Tatetla and Teruel, which Jenkins would soon obtain from the bankrupt Angela Conde de Conde.[103] West of Jaltepec lay two further targets, later rounding out the chief estates of what came to be known as the Atencingo System. The nearest was Tolentino, once owned by a diplomat who died in Parisian exile during the Revolution, leaving the estate to his wife. Beyond it lay the Maurer family's Raboso, which they had bought for less than half-price during the war.[104]

How large an area Jenkins controlled is hard to define. Since he gave up swaths of some estates before he took over others, the Atencingo System never reached the much-cited total of 123,000 hectares, or 300,000 acres. A likelier sum is a still impressive 220,000 acres, owned or leased at one time or another. Of that, 37,000 were irrigated cane fields, which left a lot of rain-fed land that Jenkins could surrender piece-meal, in negotiations with *agraristas*, with little loss of revenue. The repeated claim that Atencingo represented "the greatest concentration of land under a single owner in the history of Puebla" is untested but feasible. Similar concentrations of sugar estates were taking place across the country, as planters took advantage of a federal willingness to put food production above land redistribution.[105]

With his politicking and his predatory lending, Jenkins evinced monopolistic instincts, but his efforts at farming were decidedly entrepreneurial. Given the sheer size of the combined estate, Jenkins and his manager Manuel Pérez performed a Herculean labor. To begin, instead of rebuilding all the mills the Zapatistas had destroyed, they concentrated the milling and refining at Atencingo, salvaging machinery from the others to augment the central mill. To ferry the cane from the annexes to the mill, they built a narrow-gauge railroad and bought three locomotives and rolling stock secondhand. The private line ran parallel to the Interoceanic Railroad and connected with it, but having their own railway cut operating costs. For one thing, they no longer had to bribe station masters so often to secure services.[106]

Some of Jenkins's other investments offered synergies. His farm machinery firm gave him cut-rate access to steam tractors. He bought a substantial stake in the Puebla Light and Power Company, which likely gave him cheap electricity rates. This company had a side business selling irrigation pumps, which it would have sold to Jenkins at a discount. His accumulation of land made for economies of scale on multiple levels. He was said to buy fertilizer—nitrates from Chile—by the boatload.[107]

Of all the assets that Jenkins applied to Atencingo, the most important was his Spanish lieutenant. Manuel Pérez doubled as manager and chief agronomist. Born in Galicia in 1874, Pérez had sailed for Cuba as an adolescent and worked in the island's thriving sugar industry. Drafted into the Spanish army during the Cuban War of Independence and forced to leave upon Spain's defeat, Pérez then worked at plantations in Mexico.[108] The Jenkins-Pérez partnership began around 1921. The match was decisive to Atencingo's phenomenal long-term growth, to the employment of most of the valley's workforce, and, it would transpire, to the repression of that workforce and the suppression of local *agraristas*.

Pérez's expertise, along with his rigorous (some say despotic) management, earned him a reputation as Mexico's best cane agronomist. Right away, he knew what needed to be done. To help him revive the mill and its fields, and later the land that Jenkins annexed, Pérez hired from rival estates a band of mechanics, smiths, and carpenters. Jenkins brought in a team of Cajun sugar technicians from Louisiana for each harvest, and Pérez employed various foreigners full-time: an American and a Briton to help rebuild the refinery, a Canadian sugar chemist, a Belgian to run the locomotives, several Spaniards as annex administrators, another Spaniard as chief mechanic, and a German, who "drank beer like water," to supervise the tractors.[109]

Pérez repaired the estates' irrigation systems, supplied by rivers and wells, and expanded them by building aqueducts and small dams. Other fields, too swampy for use in the past, he drained by cutting trenches with mechanical diggers; still others, strewn with volcanic rocks from ancient eruptions, he cleared and irrigated. He experimented with species of cane to draw the best per-acre yield; this depended on factors he could not control, like regularity of rainfall and the chemical balance of the soil, and on those he could, like irrigation and fertilizers. He imported superior cane varieties untried in Mexico, from Hawaii, Indonesia, and the Philippines. Jenkins paid for him to visit Cuba, Louisiana, and Hawaii, to learn of new developments and fetch the best seed. His massive use of nitrate fertilizers was unprecedented in Mexico and helped achieve spectacular results. By the early 1930s, he was harvesting double what Atencingo yielded before the Revolution. Manager of the Atencingo System for twenty-five years, Pérez turned it into the most productive sugar plantation in Mexico.[110]

Jenkins frequently accompanied Pérez as the Spaniard revamped the mill and the fields. Unlike many predecessors, he was not inclined to leave all the work to his manager. One weekend in 1922, in letter to her Los Angeles housekeeper, Mary bewailed his regular absences: "Mr. Jenkins is down on that pesky old sugar farm—in fact he is either there or in Mexico City so much of the time that I had almost as well be in L.A." Five years later, Mary had developed a grudging enthusiasm for the place: "I have to go down as often as I can for there's so much to see there." But with her husband still spending half of his time at the plantation, Mary's visits were in part a matter of not wanting to be left alone.[111]

Even in the 1930s, when Jenkins visited only weekly, he would make a full day of it. After delivering the moneybags to the paymaster and conferring with Pérez in his office, he spent the rest of the day with the field managers, riding on horseback round the canefields and tramping beside the irrigation ditches.[112] He gave no thought to the honor of unsoiled hands.

Yet his forte was assembling protection for his estates and obtaining finance for their development. To fund Atencingo's revival he needed to sell haciendas elsewhere, along with urban properties and La Corona. Atencingo was probably generating a profit as of 1924, but then the new challenges posed by reviving Jaltepec, Rijo, and Colón and acquiring further sugar estates would require new sums. Fortunately, Jenkins's need to borrow coincided with advances in Mexico's financial markets, thanks to US diplomatic recognition and the founding of a central bank. During the 1920s, private banks rose in number from ten or so to fifty, including branches of the Bank of Montreal, National City Bank, and Chase Bank. The painfully high interest rates of up to 36 percent that prevailed until 1925 started to fall, down to 12 percent by 1928.[113] To take advantage, Jenkins changed his plantation from a private business into a joint-stock partnership, whose shares (issued "to the bearer") could be deposited as collateral for loans. In January 1926, his Matamoros Valley investments— the central mill, the estates, and an alcohol factory—became the Atencingo Civil & Industrial Company, valued at $5 million.[114]

The Atencingo Company was also a safeguard, for Jenkins was suspicious of Calles. Writing to John Tigert the year before, he had worried about the president: "It is quite true that the present tendencies here are very strongly radical, and while some pretend to see in the new Government a certain reaction against these principles, I can't say that I do."[115]

Calles's support for labor and repression of the Church aside, his radicalism was more bark than bite, but Jenkins was not the only American to mistake his nationalism for policy goals.[116] At any rate, rolling his business into a partnership gave it a legal foundation as a Mexican enterprise, which could prove useful were Atencingo to prick the interest of one of Calles's left-wing bureaucrats. The partnership was a safeguard in a second sense, too: it protected Jenkins's profits from the gaze of Uncle Sam. Though he remained a US citizen (as was typical of American expatriates), he paid no US taxes on his Mexican income. The Atencingo Company gave him a ready pretext: he could argue that he reinvested all of its profits in the business, that it never paid a dividend, and that its net value was actually in constant decline due to expropriations of tracts of his land.[117]

A year later Jenkins made another clever move, setting up a corporation, the Investments of Puebla Company, to handle most of his other activities. Founded with a modest 1 million pesos, Investments of Puebla would function as Jenkins's real estate and venture capital vehicle. It would enter a host of sectors, from urban development to the fledgling chemical industry. It also held properties in California: the mansion he had built for Mary, apartment buildings in downtown Los Angeles, and the fruit ranch in Hanford he had bought for his father. Since the ranch lost money and the Los Angeles properties could be amortized over time, and since some of the corporation's Mexican investments were funded by loans, Jenkins might claim that Investments of Puebla could not yield dividends and so should not be taxed.[118]

On the sales side, Jenkins saw that instability in prices—subject to global markets and the uncertainties of weather and competition from other states—could be tempered via a regional trust. In 1926 he joined with Harold Skipsey, an English planter in Veracruz, to form a wholesale cartel for both states. Though Skipsey was president, Jenkins dominated. The need for alliance was pressing, as sugar was in the middle of a three-year glut and the southern mills faced cut-rate rivalry from planters in the north and west. The cartel was not a great success, as the emergence of other regional cartels fomented competition between them, driving industry-wide prices lower.[119] Still, Atencingo more than made up for price oscillations with its soaring output.

Under Jenkins, the Atencingo System became the largest enterprise in Puebla, measured by both investment and workforce. By 1927, it had a payroll of 3,500: overseers, technicians, millworkers, and most numerous of all, cane-cutters. Mostly indigenous, these men hacked at the fat stalks with their machetes under the tropical sun for five months; some then stayed on to clear ditches and dig new ones.[120] In 1928, Atencingo became the second-largest sugar producer in Mexico, outranked only by Los Mochis of Sinaloa, the property of B. F. Johnston. Output was 12,000 metric tons, having more than doubled in five years. Successive harvests continued to surge, reaching 29,000 tons in 1931. The larger the Jenkins-Pérez operation grew, the harder it was for neighbors to compete. So the Maurer family found. When Jenkins foreclosed on Raboso in 1935, their surrender signaled the end of the valley's independent mills.[121] The sugar empire of Atencingo was complete.

BEYOND ALL THE vision and hard work, beyond all Jenkins's exchanges with Obregón and calibrated dealings with local power brokers, there was another factor behind Atencingo's success: the menace and perpetration of violence. At best, this meant a willingness on the part of Jenkins, Pérez, and their men to meet guns with guns. At worst, it meant premeditated killing. Almost no one writing about Atencingo has failed to mention threats or murders instigated by Jenkins or Pérez. This violence, carried out by private militia and hired assassins, is said to have served both to goad neighbors into selling out and to intimidate or eliminate troublemakers: *agrarista* leaders, union organizers, or peons who refused to fall in line.[122]

Newspapers and archival records make clear that many were killed in the Matamoros Valley, and the majority of them were poor. It is also true that Jenkins frequently had something to gain. But it is equally true that, as the subject of a growing Black Legend, Jenkins tended to be suspected of complicity whenever a body was discovered, whatever the evidence might suggest. It is further true that the Atencingo region, like much of Puebla, was bristling with firearms and echoing with violence: uprisings, banditry, xenophobic assaults, feuds ancient and modern over land and water, and the everyday killings that people anywhere commit, spawned of jealousy, adultery, drunkenness, insult.

Less clear is how much violence actually owed to Jenkins. The archival record of accusations is much slighter than one would expect for a man of such ill repute. Neither is it clear, when violence benefitted the Atencingo Company, where in the chain of command the orders originated; some assaults may have been the work of young guns hoping to curry favor. Nor is it clear that a peasant riddled with bullets was always and only a victim. Murder was common currency in the Matamoros Valley. Country folk were alienated from each other along all sorts of lines: hacienda worker versus *agrarista*, garrisoned soldier versus villager, loyalist of one local boss versus loyalist of a rival, member of one union versus member of another.

Decades after Jenkins was gone, a ninety-year-old former peon recalled: "There was plenty of killing. We were thoroughly divided."[123]

6

Resistance at Atencingo

Don Manuel: "And the 11,000 arrobas of sugar, my lord
Count? I'll have to whip the blacks harder. I'll have to put
many blacks in the stocks."

The Count: "Why tell me that? It's your business! You're
the overseer!"

TOMÁS GUTIÉRREZ ALEA, La Última Cena (1976)

Blood in the Sugar Fields

One summer day in 1922, Jenkins saw three of his men shot to death
by *agraristas*.[1] A conflict had arisen in early June, six months after he
closed on Atencingo, when villagers from Lagunillas took over a fifty-
acre expanse after the mayor of Chietla declared it unused. Under the
new Law of Idle Lands, such fields could be granted to the rural poor.
The law offered safeguards for landowners, like exemption for fields left
fallow between plantings, and petitions had to proceed through state
and federal channels. So Jenkins appealed against the Chietla edict, and
Governor Froylán Manjarrez, intent on due process, ordered the villagers to leave his land. They refused and carried on planting their corn.
After a month of stalemate, Manjarrez dispatched his brother to solve
the problem.

David Manjarrez arrived at the disputed fields on July 3 with an
intimidating entourage. With him were Jenkins, the Atencingo manager
Diego Kennedy Jr., various employees bearing arms, and several others driving tractors. Manjarrez announced he was putting a stop to the
field work, and Jenkins's men began to measure the area already planted
so the peasants might receive compensation; later, his tractors plowed
up the fields to destroy the seedlings. Among the villagers present was
Celestino Espinosa, a rancher from Chietla who had earned a reputation
as a defender of peasant rights.[2] He and two others present, Margarito

Rodríguez and José Campos, had often dealt with the state's land-granting Agrarian Commission. The three of them argued the villagers' case, but Manjarrez was adamant. Then came along a former Zapatista general, Gil Vega. Claiming to be Lagunillas's chief representative, Vega joined the argument, but Manjarrez refused to recognize his authority.

Stung by Manjarrez's rebuke—and, said one report, stirred by drink—Vega drew his gun, and Rodríguez and Campos drew theirs. They shot at Jenkins's men and gave chase to Kennedy. When the smoke had cleared, one of Jenkins's men was dead, two were fatally wounded, and the assailants had fled for Chietla. No report mentioned casualties among the *agraristas*.

Remarkably, the most detailed account comes from Vega himself. Vega wrote to his former commander, Francisco Mendoza, requesting he plead his case before President Obregón. Previously one of Zapata's senior officers, Mendoza was a general in the federal army. In soliciting such a man's help, Vega must have felt that honesty was the best policy. He took responsibility for the three deaths. He admitted Manjarrez's intent to compensate the ousted peasants. He even admitted that the ruling that the land was idle only came from the mayor of Chietla. Mendoza in turn portrayed Vega as an honorable man who had fought well under his command during the Revolution. Obregón replied that he could not pardon Vega; it would set a bad precedent to decree impunity to those who deemed legal process inferior to use of force.[3] But neither, apparently, did the president insist he be brought to justice. Fourteen years later, Vega would be mayor of Chietla.

Tensions persisted. The peasants of Lagunillas continued to target the unused land, now through formal channels. Then there were those who occupied land close to the mill, having arrived during the war when Atencingo was in ruins, moving into huts built for its workers. Jenkins wanted to clear the huts to expand the sugar fields. But by the autumn he found Froylán Manjarrez, an unusually fair-minded governor, less disposed to help him. He also suffered a setback when the state legislature approved the Lagunillas petition for *pueblo* status, a political upgrade that would give it a legal basis for seeking hacienda land. In a move standard among landowners, Jenkins reacted by obtaining an injunction against the ruling.[4]

Soon enough, blood was spilled on the other side of the ledger. That autumn, an *agrarista* named Ramón Ariza was murdered. Ariza had represented peasants of the Atencingo-Chietla region in their efforts to secure land grants, and he was said to have bad relations with Jenkins. His killer was an Atencingo peon.[5] Had Kennedy or his replacement, Manuel Pérez, dispatched the laborer to do the deed? Or was the gunman acting on his own initiative, seeking to ingratiate himself with his bosses? Maybe he acted out of a wider self-interest, fearful that seizure of part of the Atencingo estate would deprive him and his friends of jobs and homes. Whatever the trigger—and any of these answers are feasible—Ariza's killing was but a foretaste of the political murders to come, in and around the fields of the Jenkins sugar empire.

AT LEAST SINCE the time of Columbus, sugar farming has wrought a legacy of inequality and a history of violence. For four centuries, most American sugar plantations—from Cuba to Brazil, from Louisiana to coastal Peru—involved large quantities of capital, applied by small circles of landowners, who relied on the labor of slaves. When slavery was eventually outlawed, planters still subjugated their workforces. To achieve the economies of scale that such capital required, and to meet soaring demand from Europe, investors sought ever more land on which to plant. If rains were only intermittent, they sought ever more river water to irrigate it. And so, in the supreme calculation of white settlers and their heirs, sugar demanded not only captive labor but also the removal of villages and the theft of their resources.[6]

In 1524, three short years after conquering the Aztecs, Hernán Cortés set up Mexico's first sugar mill, in Veracruz state. Within a generation, cane was growing in southwestern Puebla, and plantations spread across much of the country over the next 250 years. In the nineteenth century, with the rise of European sugar beet, the price for cane sugar trended downward. From the 1870s, however, the Díaz regime enabled planters to reap profits anew: the *Pax Porfiriana* boosted rural investments; multiplying railroads hurried bulk products to markets and ports; and a pre-existing law that privatized communal land now encouraged predatory lending to country folk. Lying between the capital and Veracruz, Puebla was well placed to benefit, and in 1890 a branch line of the Interoceanic Railroad was extended from Atlixco to the sugar hub of Izúcar de Matamoros. The demand for land adequate to cane production intensified, as did the thirst for the water to irrigate it. Indigenous farmers, who had worked their land communally since time immemorial, tended to lose on both counts, until the Revolution.[7]

During the 1920s and 1930s, in a quest for growth and profits that echoed that of his Porfirian forebears, Jenkins met resistance on all sides. Often moved by resentments dating from the previous century, country folk sought the redistribution of his land. The Revolution had given them the legal tools to request it: the Carranza Law of 1915 and its various improvements, the creation of Agrarian Commissions, the Law of Idle Lands. It had granted them a sense of empowerment that came of fighting under Zapata, sacking haciendas, and briefly occupying the capital cities of the nation and the state. It had also given them a moral authority: the Revolution promised an end to the abuse of their class by the wealthy and a Mexico for the Mexicans. Yet here, in the Matamoros Valley, Spanish overlords were making way for a North American and land reallocation was glacially bureaucratic.

Agraristas had limited patience with the law. Often led by former Zapatista chieftains, they responded to the lethargy of agrarian reform as "land invaders," grabbing fields by stealth or force of arms. Jenkins, holding property rights sacred, considered these moves outrages. But *agrarista* leaders were good tacticians. They preferred those fields already under review at the state's Agrarian Commission, hoping that possession might quicken a process that could take five or ten years. Sometimes the governor would turf them out, but often he lacked the resources or the will to do so. So a land-grab was a clever gambit, especially in the early years, before Manuel Pérez had fully marshaled his militia. If not evicted, *agraristas* could use possession as a bargaining chip. Since they were legion, bargaining is what Jenkins did.

Jenkins also met resistance at senior levels. Radical governors winked at land-grabs, for they favored their rural base and hated hacienda owners with a righteous passion. Most populists were friends of the peasants too; nothing improved a governor's standing like the mass awarding of land. But, given Puebla's fiscal penury, they recognized their need for cordial relations with the private sector. Finally, in the mid-1930s, by which time his wealth had become nationally conspicuous, the American would face challenges from two presidents, Abelardo Rodríguez and Lázaro Cárdenas. The former would confront him over contraband alcohol; the latter would threaten the entire Atencingo System.

The cover that Jenkins gained through his interdependent relationships—with Obregón, Puebla's governors, its military commanders, its archbishops—does much to explain his success in consolidating Atencingo and keeping its sugar-growing core. But such protections only accounted in part for its productivity, its command over workers, and its neutralizing of unions. Profits depended on finely balanced practices of discipline and negotiation, charity and intimidation, always in the face of peasant activism and resistance.

This is the story of what happened on the ground.

Zapatistas and Their Power Brokers

Country folk of the Matamoros Valley often called themselves Zapatistas. Many had fought under Zapata, or affiliated leaders, but their grievances stretched back for generations. Much unrest was a legacy of the Lerdo Law of 1856. Authored by treasury minister Miguel Lerdo and backed by Benito Juárez, both committed liberals, the law tried to boost agriculture by privatizing corporately held land: the holdings of the Catholic Church and farmland owned communally by thousands of indigenous villages. The liberals hoped that by bringing vast amounts of arable land into the market economy and encouraging folk to farm for surplus rather than subsistence, output would increase, fostering an economic growth that had eluded their war-ravaged nation since independence. They hoped to turn Mexican peasants into US-style yeoman farmers, who would produce profit and use it to become consumers.

The Lerdo Law was doubly flawed. It tried to dismantle a landholding system common to indigenous peoples since before the Spanish conquest; communal ownership, like other collective practices such as religious festivals, was central to their culture. "Modernization," an elite project to reform Mexico's economy in the image of the United States, France, or Britain, was not an aim shared by most rural people. Worse, the Lerdo Law came to be exploited by landed elites and foreign investors, who through purchase or predatory lending, and often with the aid of a venal judiciary, obtained vast amounts of land. Exploitation reached its peak under Porfirio Díaz. Figures are uncertain, but by one estimate communal villages saw their collective ownership of Mexico's arable land slip from 25 percent in 1850 to 2 percent in 1900.[8]

Historians long attributed the massive rural participation in the Revolution to anger over land losses and debt peonage. But much of the conventional wisdom about Díaz's reign owes to "official" histories, which saw the Revolution as an inevitable mass response to exploitation. Reasons for joining the fight were in fact quite diverse; in some cases, self-rule was a much more pressing issue than land.[9] However, the villagers of the Matamoros Valley held resentments over land and water that fit the traditional narrative of dispossession.

The hamlet of Lagunillas, whose quest for fifty acres spurred the bloody confrontation of 1922, had been seeking this particular plot since before the Revolution, when it belonged to Ángel Díaz Rubín. Evidently he had gained it from their forebears by duplicitous means. Vicente de la Hidalga and his son Agustín, the Matamoros Valley's most powerful landlords, similarly took advantage of the Lerdo Law to enlarge their haciendas. They also gained control over several of the valley's rivers and ensured their peons were bound to their estates by debt.[10]

The most detailed history of the valley in the Jenkins era, by anthropologist Francisco Gómez, unearths numerous cases of landlords buying tracts from smallholders and acquiring water rights from villages in the Porfirian era. As to the legality or ethics of such moves, the paper trail is more suggestive than conclusive. Gómez speculates, for example, that Agustín de la Hidalga was able to buy river water rights from three *pueblos* in quick succession because the state government forced the village leaders' hands. In light of De la Hidalga's friendship with Governor Mucio Martínez (they were co-investors in the Calipam plantation), that deduction is quite credible. Similarly, the frequent purchase of land by middle-class townspeople in Izúcar or Chietla, who in turn sold their tracts to landlords, reveals moves that, while not illegal, deprived peasants of a fair price; in fact, these speculators may well have been predatory lenders. The Díaz Rubíns were another family that exploited the Lerdo Law. Before acquiring Atencingo, Ángel's elder brother José bought a slew of fields and orchards from two indigenous *pueblos*.[11]

Evidence of abuse is at times more concrete and more damning. In one 1896 case, confirmed by the federal government, Hacienda Raboso illicitly altered the flow of a river to increase its share of water at the expense of barrio dwellers on the edge of Izúcar. In 1912, Hacienda San Nicolás Tolentino cut off much of the water for the village of Tatetla, merely because the manager considered its supply to exceed its needs.[12] Even when the poor managed to recover their rights, as they did in the Izúcar case, such episodes can only have sown distrust and hatred between haciendas and neighboring communities.

From William Jenkins's perspective, the history of the land and its waters was irrelevant. He paid good money for his properties, he had the legal documents to prove his ownership, and if there was any trouble he had many an authority on his side.

AFTER ZAPATA REVOLTED in early 1911, many Matamoros Valley villagers joined his movement. In their aims they resembled their Morelos neighbors: regaining ancient land and rivers, seeking vengeance on the haciendas where they had been forced by deprivation or debt to work. But in their warring there was an important difference. Though Zapata flirted with a nationwide program, at heart his goals were tied to his home state.[13] This strategy left his Pueblan allies in political limbo. They would have to forge "Land and Freedom" for themselves.

The problem for Puebla's Zapatistas was that theirs was a much larger state than Morelos, its economy more diverse, its terrain more fragmented. Northern sierras, central plains, southern hill country, and the sugar zone that was the Zapatista base all threw up distinct leaders, disjointed by ideology as well as geography. Further, due to resistance to orders from Morelos, Zapata had failed to appoint a field marshal for Puebla.[14] Since few leaders commanded allegiance beyond a day's horse ride, the postwar map of the southwest comprised dozens of well-armed fiefdoms. Most were run by a "general," whose power might rest as much on his social status before the war as his victories in it. These strongmen, as found in towns throughout Mexico, were the *caciques*.[15]

Once a Caribbean island term, *cacique* came to be applied by the conquistadors to any indigenous chieftain in the Americas. These men (female *cacicas* existed but were rare) mediated between the colonial state and the people. Some intermarried with Spaniards, giving their line the distinction of lighter skin.[16] After independence, as towns elected mayors, the term evolved into broader label for power brokers; they held office at times but persisted as bosses who controlled the vote; they held sway over communal economies but sought personal profit through town stores. Relatively rich, often holding private land, they bequeathed their status to their sons. After 1910, the more ambitious *caciques* took the Revolution and the power vacuum of its aftermath as opportunities to expand their domains. At first they used the gun, later the ballot box. How much their motives involved Zapata-style altruism versus dreams of grandeur is often hard to gauge, but no *cacique* could hope to do well without delivering land. This often required violence, so *caciques* came to be known in the urban press as "lords of the noose and knife."[17]

Land was not everything. Beneficiaries needed credit to revive and farm it. Private banks would not lend to *agraristas*, and federal financing only became available (inadequately) in 1926. However, loans might be obtained from private lenders: landowners such as Jenkins, who after all had agreed to pay Zapatistas for protection during the Revolution. So lay the path to negotiation, and from there to compromise. Most *caciques* started out as *agraristas*; over time, many allowed their ideals to slide and their assets to climb.[18] Whether great or modest in might, they preserved support through a mix of benevolence, force, and populism. Land-grabs, with their so-so rate of success, were crowd-pleasing gestures as much as tactical ploys.

As carrot-and-stick populists, who imposed mayors and enriched themselves while bringing material benefit to their base, *caciques* differed little in practice from the political bosses of many a US city. Jenkins, with his general disdain for politicians, surely recognized the type. His home state of Tennessee boasted two of the most eminent and grasping: Edward Crump of Memphis and Hilary Howse of Nashville.[19] The main difference, aside from the larger populations of those US domains, was that Mexico's bosses were hardened by battle and not squeamish about personal involvement in violence.

Among the *caciques* of southwestern Puebla, a handful could project power beyond their birthplace. One was Sabino P. Burgos of Chietla, the town nearest the heart of the Atencingo System.[20] More locally confined bosses whose activism affected Atencingo included Gil Vega of Lagunillas, the trigger-happy leader of the skirmish of 1922. Then there were those who, though neither generals nor *caciques*, gained prominence in the struggle for land, notably Celestino Espinosa and Dolores Campos, in Chietla. All these people had reason to loathe Jenkins. The gringo represented the persistent disgrace of foreign-born landowners: he had friends in high places and resisted *agrarista* claims to land and water. Not all of these people, however, remained pure in their antipathy.

Sabino P. Burgos dominated the valley between Izúcar and the Morelos border. Little is known about his military career, only that he fought under Zapata and gained the common Zapatista rank of general. He then returned to Chietla, where some of his land bordered Jenkins's. After the war the federal budget was too stretched to maintain a full army, so Obregón let many *caciques* keep a personal contingent, to be called upon in time of need; thus the president hoped to retain their loyalty. Burgos was one such beneficiary, permitted fifty men under arms.[21] By 1927, Burgos was in the federal Congress as alternate deputy to none other than Soto y Gama. Press reports said that he controlled Chietla's town council, that his soldiers terrorized the populace, and that he charged bribes for everything.[22] So Burgos was a man worth befriending.

After suffering yet another land-grab, in 1925, Jenkins told President Calles he would surrender 42,000 acres from the Atencingo and Jaltepec estates to the communal farmers of Chietla. Having rejected such overtures in the past, the *agraristas* involved said they accepted Jenkins's offer and would respect his cane fields. This was a highly unusual move for Jenkins, as he made an issue of every acre. He was unlikely submitting to *agrarista* pressure, for doing so would set a bad precedent, and anyway the land he was surrendering included none of the irrigated tracts the *agraristas* most desired.[23]

The American's offer involved a deal with Burgos. With Obregón gone and the governorship a revolving door, a well-armed local ally was crucial. Jenkins could respond to land-grabs by summoning troops or making piecemeal grants, but it was better to preempt them, and if anyone could control the *agraristas* it was the *cacique*. Invasions of his estates more or less ceased. During the 1927 Gómez-Serrano rebellion, when discontented officers rose up against Calles and the fighting spilled into Puebla, it was Burgos who defended Atencingo against ransack by rebels. Most tellingly, Burgos tried to extend his power in 1933 by founding a Puebla-wide Peasant Social Union, which critics derided as an effort to undermine the more radical Emiliano Zapata Peasant Confederation (CCEZ). The CCEZ's paper responded by publishing a copy of the lease for the Burgos union's offices. Signing as guarantor was William O. Jenkins. An accompanying article accused Jenkins of giving Chietla's peasants nothing but barren ground and Burgos of betraying the agrarian cause by accepting Jenkins's bribes and forming an association that sowed division. Burgos, it said, possessed "the grim face of Judas."[24]

Burgos may well have offered Jenkins further uses. It was later claimed that Jenkins had stirred *agraristas* against his neighbors, ratcheting up their economic hardship, from which he would then offer himself as a rescuer. In taking loans from him, the old elite unwittingly set up their haciendas for future foreclosure. There is no proof of such plotting, but circumstantial evidence is suggestive. One may recall the plight of the De la Hidalga widow, Herlinda Llera, who after repeated *agrarista* aggressions leased her haciendas to Jenkins. And Burgos was but one of four or five Zapatista generals who collaborated with Jenkins.[25]

Doña Lola

Alliances with *caciques* set Jenkins's reign apart from that of the Porfirians. Ensconced in their city mansions, the Díaz Rubíns, Condes, and De la

Hidalgas had shown little interest in such politicking, which helps explain the attacks on their estates during the Revolution.[26] Jenkins's local strategy complemented his bond with state and federal governments; it formed the innermost ring of protection around Atencingo. Yet his collusion with ex-Zapatistas did not put an end to *agrarista* ambitions. Country folk were no flock of sheep, willing to be goaded by whichever "general" held sway. In the Matamoros Valley, many were suspicious of Burgos and his ilk. They were not content with land that, if not entirely barren, was merely rain-fed, when 35,000 acres of irrigated cane fields lay tantalizing nearby. If anything, Jenkins's recruitment of *caciques* worsened divisions, deepening distrust between those who would compromise on Zapata's ideals and those who would not.

Chietla was a hotbed of unrest and factionalism. The tensions that accompany any sugar economy had long made it so. Power plays by Burgos stirred trouble anew. During the 1920s, two of Chietla's police chiefs were murdered, and when a third was gravely assaulted the attackers were said to be nephews of Burgos. In all three cases no one was caught. Some *agraristas* threatened those that resisted their calls to join land-grabs. At one point, a Chietla mayor tried to hit a number of Atencingo peons with 50-peso fines; they had refused to take part in political agitation. Of course, division was already sown by the mere existence of the Atencingo System. Much of the population of the Chietla municipality lived not in the town but in settlements on the estates where they worked: Atencingo, Lagunillas, Jaltepec. These resident peons could vote for Chietla's mayor but could not, by law, petition for hacienda land, so their loyalties tended to cleave to their source of wages.[27]

Prominent among Chietla's true believers was Celestino Espinosa.[28] A successful middle-aged livestock rancher, Celestino was radicalized by the Revolution into supporting the landless. It was an unusual stand, for Mexico's small and upwardly mobile class of ranchers rarely sided with the impoverished majority in their quest for communal land.[29] When Huerta seized the presidency in 1913, he retaliated against the Zapatistas by ordering partisan villages be burned, and Celestino, his property damaged by Huerta's scorched-earth tactics, only grew more resolute. Moving his livestock into the hills, he carried on supplying Zapata's local forces, and after the war Soto y Gama encouraged him to help Chietla-area peasants gain land. In some twenty villages and hamlets, he and his supporters organized groups to petition for hacienda tracts. Though a radical,

Celestino was no hothead; in the Lagunillas skirmish of 1922, he was the only one of the four *agrarista* leaders present who did not draw his gun on Jenkins's men.

As driven as Celestino was his wife, Dolores Campos. Her name—quite aptly, given the road she was to travel—might translate as Sorrows of the Fields. Dolores had learned writing and arithmetic from a kindly woman whom she served as a maid when young. Able then to help her father, who rented out horses, she traveled with him throughout southwestern Puebla and learned how to handle a gun to fend off bandits. Married in 1895, she raised a son, Rafael, and during the Revolution served as secretary to Celestino, who like the vast majority of rural Pueblans was illiterate; Celestino wished to encourage Zapata's troops with inspirational letters. Her secretarial skills were put again to use within Celestino's lobbying campaign: she studied agrarian laws and helped draw up the documents with which hamlets like Lagunillas could qualify for land grants by first being recognized as *pueblos*. Lagunillas was one of their success stories, for Governor Manjarrez overruled a Jenkins injunction, arguing that it merited *pueblo* status due to its population size, and in 1924 it gained its first land grant. The villagers' descendants would claim that neither Dolores nor Celestino charged them for their help.[30]

Celestino's work became more official when many communities named him their representative before the state's Agrarian Commission. In 1923 he took time off to lead three hundred men in helping put down the De la Huerta rebellion, thus earning the favor of Obregón. By 1924, despite death threats and the murder of several activists and agrarian officials, he had obtained a number of grants for his clients. Presumably his success was a factor behind Jenkins's decision to surrender the 42,000 acres. But late that year he died from an illness. Had Celestina Espinosa lived, Chietla's peasants might not have had to settle for grants of so much barren terrain from Jenkins. It fell to his wife and son to continue his work.

Rafael Espinosa, now twenty-eight, inherited his father's mantle and the enmity of the hacienda managers. Jenkins's right-hand man, Manuel Pérez, had already emerged as the most powerful and feared of these. According to local lore, Pérez first tried to win Rafael over with bribery, next hired a gunman to kill him—a plot that failed when Rafael killed the assassin—and then arranged to have him jailed. Dolores, very ill at the time, refused an offer from Pérez to secure Rafael's release in exchange for her cooperation. In 1929, walking down a Chietla street with his mother one evening, Rafael was gunned down by killers in the hire of Sabino P. Burgos.[31]

Dolores was wounded in the same attack but remained undaunted. Aided by her daughter, she pursued the peasant struggle for farmable land. Around 1930, she helped establish a clandestine association of mill-workers and cane cutters at Atencingo, the Karl Marx Union. The name mirrored her deepening convictions, for both she and her daughter were covert members of the Mexican Communist Party. Before long, Manuel Pérez managed to co-opt the union by having its radicals chased away and, allegedly, its leaders murdered. This rendered it a *sindicato blanco*— literally, a white union (as opposed to a red, socialist union).[32] Still Dolores pressed on, and as her ideology took shape, so did her willingness to meet fire with fire. One year she tried to rig the Chietla mayoral election. Months later she was accused of arranging the murder of a councilor. Her fame now transcended the Matamoros Valley, and country folk gave her the honorific used for women respected and beloved: *Doña* Lola.[33]

Doña Lola had a key ally in her struggle, the general who had been quick on the draw at Lagunillas: Gil Vega. As *cacique* of that village, Vega had a much smaller base than Chietla's Burgos, but he proved himself a thorn in Jenkins's side. He instigated a number of land-grabs, and he and his followers clashed frequently with Atencingo employees and guards. His reputation for violence would grow further in 1930, when an anti-*agrarista* political party claimed that Vega had burned down the house of one of its members and murdered another.[34]

By then Vega himself was lucky to be alive, for a year earlier Burgos had plotted to kill him. In April 1929, Burgos traveled to Morelos to meet a man he thought he could trust, one S. M. Bonilla. Burgos boasted of his success in the murder of Rafael Espinosa. He then asked Bonilla to kill Vega and several others. The job was worth 500 pesos. To show he meant business, Burgos handed him a letter of introduction to Crescenciano López, a crony of his, who would pay Bonilla once the deed was done. The letter instructed López to talk with either Manuel Pérez or Jenkins to claim the 1,500 pesos that "he offered" to anyone who would elim-inate the area's chief *agraristas*. Burgos added they had the support of the president of the Republic.[35] (Whether the "he" referred to Pérez or Jenkins is unclear. Burgos was likely thinking of Pérez, since he handled Atencingo's day-to-day running, but included Jenkins's name to give his note greater weight, for which reason he also made the dubious reference to the president.)

Burgos badly misjudged Bonilla. Some days later, having mulled the cost of defying the *cacique*, Bonilla wrote to Vega and warned him of the plot. He said he would never betray a friend and colleague, which suggested they had fought together as Zapatistas. He enclosed Burgos's letter as evidence. Unhinged by his encounter with Burgos, Bonilla planned to leave at once for the state of Guerrero; his mother had already fled. In 1934, Vega would hand the letters to local political activists, to bolster their complaints to President-elect Cárdenas against Burgos and Jenkins. Whether or not their lobbying had much effect, one year later Vega managed to get himself elected as mayor of Chietla.[36]

Vega's electoral triumph, a joy shared by the stalwart Doña Lola, would mark a major victory for the region's landless peasants. That is, until Jenkins co-opted Vega too.

The Wasp

By the early 1930s, when Atencingo had incorporated most of the estates it would subsume and was setting national records for productivity, Jenkins was spending less time in the Matamoros Valley. Mexico was in the grip of the Depression, and the greater challenge for sugar planters was no longer production but sales, for demand was stagnating just as output was spiraling. Then, once the glut subsided, Jenkins focused on diversifying his assets. So instead of being hands-on for days at a time, he would travel down from Puebla City every week or two, carrying the payroll and sometimes bringing his daughters. Now more than ever, Atencingo was the domain of its overseer, Manuel Pérez.

Jenkins was cheerful when he visited. Ten years of hard work were paying off. He had proved to himself, Mary, and her family that he could build and run a plantation. On the train from Puebla City, once it passed through Atlixco and made the shallow descent into the Matamoros Valley, he was lord of almost all he surveyed. Lush expanses of sugar cane, up to three meters high, stretched out to the hills on either side of the Interoceanic Railroad. He was practically lord of the rails, as well. Sugar made up almost half of all rail freight in Puebla, and three-quarters of that quantity came from Jenkins's mill.[37]

One day, a guest of Jenkins at Atencingo overheard a subordinate telling him there were no freight trains available that day. "For *me*, there is a train," he replied. Another day, as Jenkins and his daughters rode down to the plantation, his daughter Mary dropped her rag doll out of the carriage window. The passenger train was promptly brought to a halt, so that some unfortunate ticket inspector could descend to the track and run back to find and fetch the doll.

Atencingo was an adventure playground for the children. Jenkins now had five, all daughters. Jane, in her early teens, and the two youngest, Mary and Tita, spent their visits being driven around on tractors or playing in the old plantation house. Built in the shape of a U, the home housed Manuel Pérez in one wing and the offices in the other, with a communal dining room in the middle where as many as three dozen senior managers and technicians ate. Jenkins added an upper floor for family and guests. The girls developed fond memories of Pérez, who gave them horse-riding lessons and discussed books with Jane.[38]

Millworkers and peons saw another Pérez. He was, above all, a man of *mano dura*: an iron hand. Six-foot tall and thin, with piercing eyes, prominent eyebrows, and swept-back hair, he had the aspect of a gaunt eagle. His unmistakable Iberian bark struck the fear of God into his subjects. He was a stickler for order, quick to anger, and he suffered neither fools nor drunks. Children were taught to cower before him; if playing in the street when Pérez approached, they had to stop their game and stand at attention. No father risked displeasing the boss, for Pérez fired millworkers and peons at will and then ran them out of their homes. If they were especially troublesome—trying to organize a union, campaigning for an *agrarista* for mayor—they might vanish altogether. No one saw Pérez kill a man. But from time to time pairs of strangers were seen in Atencingo, men said to be from Morelos, and their arrival would coincide with the disappearance of someone who had defied the manager. It is said that years after the Pérez regime had ended, workers laying foundations for an extension at the rear of the mill discovered a series of skeletons, the remains of the missing. Owing to his temper and his habit of carrying his pistol tucked into the back of his pants, Pérez was dubbed *La Avispa*: The Wasp.[39]

Even Pérez's family was afraid of him. He made his wife stay in Puebla City with the children. This arrangement had two advantages: it kept his four sons from under his feet until old enough to work for him as submanagers, and it allowed him to keep a mistress at Atencingo, with whom he sired a second family. At weekends, Pérez would travel up to Puebla City to visit his wife, but these were not happy reunions. He applied discipline to his boys as to his workers, yelling at them, humiliating them, tolerating no disagreement. His wife adopted the habit of lighting a candle to the Virgin each Friday, praying that this weekend there would be peace.[40]

If Pérez was a hard and hardened man, much of that came from the risks he ran as a Spaniard in rural Mexico. Hispanophobia, deep-rooted since the War of Independence, had been reinvigorated by the Revolution. Numbers of his countrymen had been killed, often hacienda stewards like himself. When the Spanish administrator of San Bernardino, 20 miles east of Puebla City, was killed by intruders in November 1929—a murder soon followed by that of two Spanish farmers elsewhere in Puebla—Pérez can only have doubled his resolve that if danger arose, it was better to kill than be killed. His life was often threatened. While some of those threats were made idly, The Wasp met them all with defiance. Told that the rural activist Porfirio Jaramillo had boasted he would bump him off, Pérez was heard to scoff: "I'm not afraid to die. The one who'd better watch out is Jaramillo."[41]

Spaniards like Pérez, in positions of authority or successful in commerce, also faced calls for their expulsion. Opponents were quick to tag them "pernicious foreigners." Close to four hundred Spaniards were expelled between 1911 and 1940, more than any other nationality; about twenty lived in Puebla. In 1931, a Chietla official wrote to the President with a litany of complaints against Pérez. He claimed the Spaniard liked to boast that he and Jenkins had enough money to buy off every Mexican, from the president on down, and had paid three times Atencingo's worth in bribes. He alleged that as well as opposing agrarian and labor groups, Pérez commanded the local army garrison, forbade federal and state inspectors to set foot on the hacienda, and had killed several people. Conditions were so bad for the peons that in some cases huts of forty square feet were sheltering five families. Further, Pérez had established a company store of the price-gouging kind common before the Revolution and now outlawed. He was paying workers and peons in vouchers, obliging them to shop there, and its profit margins were 40 percent. In sum, this Spaniard should be expelled from Mexico.[42]

For all its technological modernity, Atencingo indeed smacked of Porfirian times. Resident peons formed the backbone of the workforce, and while no longer tied by debt bondage they remained subject to the steward's whims. They could build huts of straw, nothing more; if they used adobe bricks, Pérez would have the homes destroyed. There was a modern twist to this: permanent homes on hacienda property had legal implications. If settlements became large enough, they might petition for *pueblo* status, as did Lagunillas, and hence the right to grants of land. Millworkers mostly lived in the Atencingo village, which was not a *pueblo*.

Pérez ran it as a company town, with its own school, general store, and worker housing. Drinking was the most common solace, though Pérez tried to curb that through organized sport. And Pérez himself evoked the past: the dictatorial Spanish manager had been a staple of the Porfirian hacienda.[43]

Perez's regimental obsessions had an ancient precedent. Ever since sugar was introduced to the Americas, along with the slavery and peonage on which its profits depended, the doctrine of a plantation steward was efficiency, order, discipline.[44] To develop each square meter of irrigable land, to command when to sow and when to reap, to use every hour of daylight during the harvest, to govern the boiling and setting of cane juice to the particular minute. To enforce the clock and crack the whip and keep the master happy.

AND THEN THERE were the guns. In his ardor to fend off land-grabs and keep peons and millworkers in line, Pérez kept a large posse of vigilante guards. Private militia multiplied on haciendas during and after the Revolution, a response to the frailty of government and to the conflicting signals over land reform between federal, state, and local authorities, which prompted *agraristas* to take matters into their own hands. These paramilitaries came to be known as *guardias blancas*, or "white guards."[45] Most were stationed in the fields, some inside the mill, a few at the alcohol factory. Typically they came from the ranks of resident field hands; their dependence on the hacienda for a job, a home, and in some cases parcels of rented land, gave them an interest in protecting the estate. Given Jenkins's cozy relationship with Sabino P. Burgos, some of them were probably former Zapatistas, experienced with weapons. The posse was more numerous than the mill's small garrison of federal troops and much more feared. The guards resisted invasions and maintained order with zeal. When cane-cutters built homes of adobe, it was they whom Pérez sent to smash them.[46] At times, they did more than defend and police.

Beyond the usual postwar score-settling and the clashes between *guardias blancas* and *agraristas*, there was a further reason for violence in the valley. While most of Atencingo's sugar fields were the core holdings of the haciendas that Jenkins bought from the likes of Díaz Rubín, some of his acreage was more forcibly acquired. According to Jenkins's capitalistic pragmatism, land that was irrigated or irrigable should be brought into the Atencingo System and used for cane. That was the most productive use for it. That would also generate the most jobs; everyone would benefit. Peons could grow their corn and vegetables on rain-fed land. In fact, because all irrigable land was to be used for cane, with each acquisition Jenkins moved any settlement that hindered maximum productivity. After Jenkins bought Lagunillas in 1921, he shifted two of its resident hamlets to peripheral terrain, "uprooting them as one would a plant," as a grandson of one of the families put it. Later on, Pérez's guards took charge of these relocations. A member of the Maurer family, once owners of Raboso, claimed Pérez wiped out whole villages.[47]

Jenkins did not content himself with the haciendas of the old elite. Local lore claims he forcibly took over many smaller ranches, with Pérez and his gunmen spearheading his efforts.[48] Given that Jenkins's use of violence to press farmers into selling out is one of the most enduring stories about him, evidence for it is remarkably thin. In the presidential archives, abundant peasant complaints about Jenkins contrast with an absence of protests from ranchers. Nor do the intelligence archives mention the issue, despite dozens of agents' reports from the region during the Jenkins era.[49] Many of the claims may involve a mix of supposition and myth, a further facet of the Jenkins Black Legend. Force was certainly not, as some have implied, a blanket policy. Villages were often persuaded to part with select tracts in exchange for the building of a school or a municipal office. With several of the larger ranchers, Jenkins struck deals by which they supplied their cane for him to mill. In the case of the Maurers' Raboso, the last of the haciendas that Atencingo absorbed, the foreclosure was settled without rancor.[50]

By contrast, surfacing with frequency in the written record are reports of everyday murder. Individually, they are often inconclusive; excepting Burgos's confidential admission of having plotted the killing of Rafael Espinosa, neither Pérez nor his senior personnel are ever found holding a smoking gun. Taken together, the records show how *agraristas* and labor organizers, though sometimes the perpetrators, bore the brunt of the bloodshed. At best, that makes for a damning indictment of a culture of tit-for-tat violence that Pérez let fester. At worst, it suggests a systematic policy of eliminating troublemakers, effected through a chain of command extensive enough to afford plausible deniability to Jenkins.

By 1934 the phrase "regime of terror" had crept into the press; one such report related the disappearance of five men opposed to a mayor of Chietla who was allied with the mill. Even if only a minority of murders were committed by guns-for-hire, a sense of victimhood among *agraristas* and pro-union workers was widespread. In 1935, a peasant organizer wrote to the President denouncing Jenkins and Pérez over the murder of sixty locals; he requested their expulsion. The missive was forwarded to the Interior Ministry, which replied it would need some evidence, and the correspondence ended there.[51] The exchange was typical. On one hand, activists were convinced of the brutality of the Atencingo System; on the other, due to uncooperative local authorities, judges handpicked by governors in debt to Jenkins, and their own tendency to inflate their claims, activists were unable to back up their accusations.

Evidence or no, as Matamoros Valley villagers petitioned for land grants, frequently they argued their case by highlighting the nationalities of *el gringo* Jenkins and *el gachupín* Pérez, and then citing their sowing of division in peasant ranks, employment of paramilitaries, and responsibility for murders.[52] Such accusations became conventional wisdom; eventually they made their way into print. They were also a lobbying tool, and in the late 1930s a Mexican president, Lázaro Cárdenas, would finally pay them heed. Meanwhile, unconcerned about public relations, neither Jenkins nor Pérez made a point of denying them.

HOW INVOLVED WAS Jenkins in all this killing? Did he plot or request specific murders? Did he approve plans by Pérez to dispose of opponents? Or did he merely give Pérez *carte blanche*, preferring not to be told of the particulars and declining to comment when killings occurred? Perhaps he cloaked his complicity in ambiguity, wishing aloud, like Henry II deploring Thomas Becket, "Will no one rid me of this troublesome peasant?"

Certainly Jenkins was feared, as decades of written complaints about him attest. The conspiracy theory that he once planned his own kidnapping and squeezed Carranza for the ransom ironically served his reputation as a man not to be trifled with. He helped cultivate a general fear in his refusal to deny allegations. He could be theatrical too. Later on, his insistence on working from home in a penthouse for which he refused to install an elevator meant that anyone wishing to request a favor had to climb more than ninety fretful steps to see him. Jenkins then made a home movie for Mary, once she was back in California, to illustrate his daily routine. In one scene he acted out a meeting with Pérez. Sitting before his manager, he barked orders and pounded his desk and showed the most terrible frown, his brow so deeply furrowed, the corners of his mouth so far turned down, that his face became a mask of malevolence.[53]

Jenkins was unlikely to have plotted killings, most of all because he did not need to. In Pérez he had a right-hand man with a dictatorial bent, a boss rigidly devoted to order, so much so that ambitious employees may often have anticipated his wishes, gun in hand. In staying above the fray, Jenkins could follow the ancient practice among sugar planters of refusing to dirty their hands while letting the despised overseers wield the lash. The more harshly the steward acted, the more benevolent the owner often seemed. This was a precedent deep-rooted in Mexico; not for nothing, when the Zapatistas rose up, were Spanish managers the first to meet the whirl of machetes. It was a precedent similarly rooted in the plantation culture of the US South, including Tennessee.[54]

An ability to distance himself helps explain why Jenkins never carried a gun. It was not merely a display of bravado. He saw himself inhabiting a higher plane, one that existed above violence, where hard work and benign supervision were the norm. These were the values in which he was raised, the values he shared with Mary. With Pérez, Jenkins could buffer himself from Atencingo's violence and inhabit the world of the white elite with a clean conscience.

There were traces of moral myopia in some of his daily habits. His favorite films were light comedies, simple escapism, and for an hour before bed he would read murder mysteries and other pulp fiction.[55] Agatha Christie and the like were leagues from the sensibilities of his youth, when he quoted Virgil and Tennyson in his letters to Mary. Literature raises complex questions, asking readers to evaluate the way they live their lives. Jenkins no longer read literature. He no longer wished to wrestle with ethical dilemmas.

Decades later, Jenkins's grandson would recall of Atencingo: "It was like the Wild West down there. Everyone had guns." His grandfather no doubt felt likewise. Peasants were peasants. They lived by the gun and died by it. They had their ancient feuds and their scores to settle.[56] One had to be armed and ready. Look what happened to Roberto Maurer, Rosalie Evans, and quite a few local Spaniards. Look at Morelos, where no one imposed a firm hand: once a sugar cornucopia, the state had produced next to nothing since Zapata's rebellion. So much for the celebrated breaking up of its haciendas. Now Morelos sugar workers were flocking to Atencingo.[57] So, as long as they had jobs, peasants should be grateful and know their place. Those that didn't—Pérez would sort them out.

Soft Power and Schools

Cast into relief by Pérez, Jenkins could hardly fail to seem kinder.[58] For many a millworker, he was *Don Guillermo*, the benevolent lord of the hacienda, the demanding but jovial gringo who arrived whistling to himself. He would salute his workers by name and ask after their families. He would poke fun. Among retired millhands, a favorite anecdote recalled how Jenkins was once being driven from the train station to the mill when one of his money bags fell off the buggy. A peon found the bag and, expecting reward for his loyalty, took it to the office where Jenkins was talking with Pérez. Don Guillermo thanked him and handed him a five centavo coin. The peon looked up in surprise at the paltry token.

"Take it," said Jenkins, "and go buy some rope to hang yourself, for being such an idiot! You could have been rich!"

The joke showed that Jenkins grasped the darker side of Mexican humor, for which cruel irony and laughter at misfortune are mainstays, and where those who fail to get ahead when they have the chance—ethics be damned—are prime objects for ridicule. It also showed his ability to pander to Mexican sensitivity over hierarchy: the joke was on a lowly peon, while the audience that found it funny consisted of semiprofessional millhands. For similar reasons, workers thought it amusing when Jenkins addressed a senior employee as *pendejo* (dumb ass). Jenkins applied the insult liberally. Often this was in jest, sometimes not. Once, when his patience was stretched during a meeting with several managers, he exclaimed: "I've worked with a lot of *pendejos*, but never with all of them at the same time!"

There was purpose in this language. Jenkins knew that Mexican humor can undermine a man's masculinity for the amusement of others. The manager of the Jaltepec estate, a loyal employee for decades, was a tough rancher named Facundo Sánchez. Jenkins was tickled by his unusual name, and he subverted it by addressing him as Facunda, as though he were a woman. He was often heard calling out for him in his distinctive gringo bellow: "Facunda! Facunda!"[59]

Jenkins was astute enough to see that distinguishing himself from Pérez, and heightening the distinction through humor, would generate loyalty. It was one way among many, for Jenkins employed a variety of "soft" tactics to show he was a boss who cared about his workers and that when it came to their welfare he knew best. He gave them proper jobs. He treated them with humor. He built them schools and hospitals. He sponsored sports teams and religious fiestas. With all this, what need did they have of unions?

DESPITE THE OBVIOUS political advantages of building facilities for one's workers, Jenkins's interest in schools and hospitals had its roots in the baronial duties that came with being a rich American. He had shown this conviction during the Revolution, when in 1919, he began a lifelong association with the Latin American Hospital. Founded by a Baptist missionary using buildings donated by Jenkins, it was reputed as Puebla City's leading hospital. Jenkins made friends with Dr. Leland Meadows, who took charge in 1925, while also becoming the Jenkins family physician. Meadows had a knack for knowing when to ask his benefactor to pay for equipment, fund a new building, and so forth. The huge Atencingo workforce inevitably met with industrial accidents, and when injuries were too serious for the mill's on-site doctor to handle, Jenkins would send the wounded to be treated on his account at the hospital.[60]

While Jenkins was in the vanguard of health practices, some of his other employer tactics were more traditional. The most valued and loyal workers earned the right to live in new, stone-built houses along the nearest section of Atencingo's main street, leading to the mill. By contrast, employees who fell out of favor, or retired, had to vacate their homes to make way for men more deserving. These houses were sizeable by the standards of the day, roomier than those that Porfirian employers had built at their Atlixco textile mills.[61]

As an advocate of a sound mind in a sound body—who at forty-two had climbed the 18,000-foot volcano Popocatepetl and in his fifties was still winning the Alpha Club tennis cup—Jenkins naturally made use of sport.[62] In Porfirian times, British miners had imported soccer and Americans baseball and basketball. While these sports were initially the preserve of Anglo-Saxon employees, company teams soon included Mexicans, and after the Revolution the rosters were wholly local. It became obvious to owners that sponsoring a team was a way of fomenting "loyalty to the (company) jersey," among both players and their workmates who came to watch. Sport was also a way of channeling the potential threat of workers' excess energy.[63]

Manuel Pérez launched a basketball team by 1930, and further sports followed. By the 1940s, Atencingo fielded two baseball teams—one of mill-workers, the other of cane-cutters—as well as a men's soccer team and a women's volleyball team. The Atencingo Company provided uniforms, equipment, and fields to play on. Baseball was much more popular than soccer in Puebla, and the state association counted seventy-four teams across nine leagues, divided into four tiers. (Perhaps Pérez did not allow much time for practice: in June 1944, the mill team sat bottom of one of the fourth-tier leagues, with six defeats in six games.) The company also subsidized musical bands, the best-known being the marimba-based Atencingo Tropical Orchestra.[64]

Then there were national and religious festivals, for which Jenkins provided food, drink, and extra days off. For Independence Day, Pérez had his carpenters build wooden replicas of Mexico City's best-known patriotic monuments along the main street, while every building was adorned with paper flags, a festive backdrop for the horseback parade. The next day there would be a baseball game, at night a dance for which Pérez would hire a band, and the following weekend two days of bull-fights. The hacienda's saint's day, the Feast of San José, featured a mass and a dance, horse races and fireworks, and then another weekend of bullfights.[65]

Of all of Jenkins's soft-power tactics, school-building was his passion. Providing education in the Matamoros Valley not only generated loyalty at a time when the state could not fulfill its promises but also inculcated values of hard work and self-improvement. Mexico would always have its peasants, Jenkins felt, but he was keen that the brighter of their number should strive for material success.

In 1928, Jenkins built a school next to Atencingo's factory gates for the sons and daughters of millhands. One February day in 1930, two schools opened for the children of peons in the villages of Ahuehuetzingo and Pueblo Nuevo. By April of the following year, he had finished three more and rebuilt another, replacing its scorpion-infested thatch roof with a metal structure. Even before the 1931 passage of the Federal Labor Law, which ordered industrialists to provide schools for their workers' children, Jenkins had built seven or eight schoolhouses in the valley, as many as those built by the state government.[66] He later built at least another three, and in 1942 he would back his sister Anne Buntzler in founding Puebla City's American School.[67]

The ten or so schools that Jenkins paid for were much more than functional. They were built to last, and some operate still. One in particular was designed with flair. The school at Ahuehuetzingo, in the heart of the Atencingo-Lagunillas cane land, resembled a miniature castle in Andalusia. It boasted three turrets, triangular crenellations, and a series of two-tone Moorish arches on top of slender white columns. The walls were white, interspersed with decorative bands of brick. The gate was wrought iron and topped by a crescent moon. The building could accommodate 120 pupils.

Just as its design intended to impress, its February 2 inauguration emanated significance. The event showed how Jenkins could use a public occasion to foster the kind of patriotism and good will that might persuade peons that the boss was not such a bad sort. The date was the feast of La Candelaria, a choice that reflected his closeness with the Catholic hierarchy and his grasp of local devotion to Mary, whose legendary apparition in the Canary Islands the day commemorated. As each year, a large and festive crowd milled around the village church and the plaza—and now the new school. This day also honored earthly authority, with the attendance of Jenkins, Pérez, and state and federal officials. Jenkins's presence was not typical. He tended to delegate such affairs to Pérez or his older daughters. Yet on this day he issued a triple statement of his commitment to education: with this inauguration, that of the school at Pueblo Nuevo, and his announcement that he would work with a federal adult-education program to set up evening schools throughout the valley.[68]

These acts of charity involved exchanges of favor. Ahuehuetzingo was said to have been given the most magnificent of schools because it was the village that had given Jenkins shelter when Gil Vega chased after him during the Lagunillas skirmish of 1922. So went one version; another added that Jenkins was further moved to build the school because the locals had let him run water conduits through the heart of their village to supply the Lagunillas estate. A third version held that Jenkins lay ill in bed one day when he was visited by two women who asked him to increase the village's water supply. Jenkins said nothing but soon found himself healed. Later visiting the local church he spied two icons of Mary, the Virgin of the Ascension and the Virgin of Solitude, and recognized them as the women who had visited him. Believing himself miraculously cured, he built the school in gratitude.[69]

So the perception among the locals was that the school was somehow deserved, that they had earned it through their own efforts (or those of their saintly protectors). This kind of understanding would not have perturbed Jenkins. If the villagers worked hard and cooperated, they would reap extra reward. In turn, the villagers devoted an ever larger amount of their cornfields to growing cane, which they supplied to Jenkins's mill.

Such reciprocity helped win Jenkins respect, albeit of the grudging kind, and the sentiment has persisted. One hundred-year-old peasant, a former Zapatista soldier, had this to say about Jenkins in light of his gift of the school: "He was a good man, but he was the second God of the region, as he acquired so much power." An eighty-something former mill-hand reminisced: "Jenkins wasn't so bad. It was Pérez who was the real tyrant."[70]

The American's ability to buy favor had its limits. The ever-combative town of Chietla gained a state school in the 1920s but needed further facilities for its growing population. Jenkins proposed to build another two schools, but his offer went unwelcomed. Reportedly this was due to bureaucratic disorganization, but since Jenkins's allies controlled Chietla's mayors at this point, a likelier reason was opposition among the general populace, which had after all borne a spate of murders. In loyal Ahuehuetzingo there persisted a faction of villagers opposed to the mill and resentful of its encroachment on ancient water rights.[71] There was even some resistance to Jenkins's schemes from Manuel Pérez.

Eusebio Benítez was fourteen years old when his classes came to a halt. One day in 1935, the mistress instructed Eusebio and the other older boys to line up outside the school building, quiet and orderly, because Mr. Pérez was coming to visit. Along came The Wasp, and as the boys stood at attention he gave them a little speech.

"I'm going to tell you what I want. I don't want professionals, I don't want accountants, I don't want lawyers, I don't want journalists .... All I want are *hands*."

Pérez went down the line, asking the boys their age. He picked out those who were thirteen or fourteen or looked tall enough to be so. "Tomorrow you are to report to me at the mill. Then I'll tell you where you're going to work."

That was the end of Eusebio's education.[72] It could have been worse. Most boys were made to work as apprentices within the mill, so they learned marketable trades: mill operation, electrical work, mechanical repair, and so on. To finish school at fourteen was standard, and more than half of Puebla's children received any schooling at all.[73] But it was the manner in which Eusebio and his friends met the world of work, shunted into the mill like Dickensian urchins, that seems at odds with Jenkins's design. It was as though Pérez thought the boss a bit soft. His school was useful in supplying boys who could read, write, and count, but taken any further it might spoil the Atencingo machine. It might give the Mexicans ideas.

JENKINS SURELY VIEWED his commitments as a success. He continued to fund schools in Puebla, ever larger and costlier constructions, for another thirty years. He was not simply investing in the favor of his subjects or rewarding their loyalty; he was, as he saw it, undertaking the mission of the enlightened and fortunate to liberate backward country folk from their culture of vice and violence. It was surely with some pride that, in complying with a 1938 industrial census, he was able to state that only three foreigners besides Pérez remained on the Atencingo payroll. Most of the Americans and Europeans he had hired as technicians and mechanics in the early 1920s had gone, their jobs now held by the Mexicans they had trained.[74]

Jenkins's philosophy differed little from the federal government's. Until the early 1930s it continued to attribute the problems of rural Mexico to the character of its people, rather than to any political and economic structures that might suppress them. Although the state termed itself revolutionary, the policy of its Public Education Ministry (SEP) bore striking resemblance to Porfirian norms. It sought to boost the productive capacity and consumerist tendencies of Mexicans, with the United States as its model. Textbooks, still saturated with positivism and economic liberalism, praised Anglo-Saxon achievements and linked indigenous culture with backwardness. They instilled acceptance of a society stratified by class.

Jenkins must have nodded in approval when scanning the standard fifth- and sixth-grade history text, which told its readers: "The Anglo-Saxon world is today at the head of the most active, most progressive, most inundating culture. What is the secret of such superiority in a race and their expansive power? We ought to study this to imitate it." The answer to the secret, the author revealed, lay in the Anglo spirit of enterprise, usefulness, and hard work.[75]

But the early 1930s saw a fundamental turn at the SEP. The ministry came to champion "socialist education," a project to rid schools of clerical influence and distribute textbooks promoting social revolution. It hired teachers to double as community activists. Fanning out into the countryside, these men and women would preach agrarian reform, sex education, and other radical ideas; some would encourage land-grabs. Undoubtedly spurred by his friend Archbishop Vera to fend off such affronts to decency and capitalism, Jenkins may well have sped up his efforts, thinking that if he built the schools he could vet the teachers. If so, his plans again met resistance from Doña Lola, who helped secure a corps of left-leaning teachers for the region.[76]

No event more gravely reflected a remoteness from the modernity that Jenkins and the state—each in their own way—were seeking to build than the fate of Edgard Kullmann.[77] No event could have more unnerved Puebla's foreigners or more disgusted its self-appointed civilizers. And none could have convinced them more deeply of the need for education to free the poor from what they termed "the chains of ignorance and superstition."

Kullmann was a Norwegian scientist, traversing the country gathering material for a book, and shortly before Easter 1930 he arrived in Puebla. His visit coincided with an upsurge of interest in the exploits of Pablo Sidar, an aviator who had become a national hero by flying around the Caribbean. Since Charles Lindbergh had flown his *Spirit of St. Louis* from Washington to Mexico City in 1927, airplanes had captured the imagination of Mexico's ruling elite and urban public. Feats of aviation became a staple of the press. To the educated, airplanes symbolized the very zenith of modernity. To the rural poor, however, they meant the threat of the unknown, the imposition of the outsider. For them, transport was a matter of horse or donkey; most had yet to ride a bus. Economic depression, which prompted a spike in xenophobia and rural violence, fertilized such fears of foreign inventions. And so, in the spring of 1930, illiterate villagers across Puebla came to associate the disappearance of various boys and girls with Sidar's fantastic flying machine. The pilot was conducting test flights in the region, and his habit of flying at night made the sound of his approach all the more sinister. The rumor ran that Sidar was feeding the missing children as fuel to his airplane's motor.

Kullman's travels took him to Amozoc, just east of Puebla City, to inspect the crafts. The day was hot, and he asked some children where he might bathe. They were leading him through the town when he was halted by a woman's shouting. She yelled that this foreigner had come to steal their children, to kill them and use their body fat to fuel Sidar's airplane. As onlookers gathered, Kullmann protested his innocence. He tried to show his papers: he held letters of safe conduct from the president and the governor. But the townspeople were not interested in what they could not read, and they pelted Kullmann with stones. When the odd-looking white man ran away, a growing crowd gave chase. At the edge of town, they caught him. Soon numbering in their hundreds, they held a brief inquisition. Finding him guilty, they beat him, stabbed him, and hacked him with machetes. They dragged him with a rope around his neck and threw him down a hundred-foot well. The day was Holy Thursday, and the townspeople then went to mass.

With Almazán, a Populist of the Left

Jenkins had another motive for building schools: to add to the store of political capital he had accrued by lending to the state government. From 1929 this tactic was especially important, as Puebla had a popular governor who styled himself a leftist. He was a friend to workers and peasants and a believer in education for all. This governor, member of a powerful clan that would later launch a bid for the presidency, was Leonides Andreu Almazán.

Known by his maternal surname, Almazán was an unorthodox idealist. Though born into a wealthy landowning family, he had fought along with Zapata. He then studied in Mexico City and Paris and dedicated himself to medicine. But politics beckoned. Thanks in part to his elder brother Juan, a career general and the military chief of Monterrey, Leonides gained the backing of President Calles for Puebla's gubernatorial race of 1928. He triumphed by a wide margin.[78]

Almazán lived up to his revolutionary billing, and he was a man for the times. His tenure coincided with a radical turn in agrarian politics: the promises of the Revolution would be fulfilled more quickly and emphatically than under Carranza, Obregón, or Calles. Almazán would redistribute an unprecedented 520,000 acres, some of it irrigated farmland. Helping him fulfill his agenda was the coincidence of his first year with reform-minded President Emilio Portes Gil. Interim premier from December 1928 to February 1930, after the reelected Obregón was assassinated, Portes Gil oversaw land distribution at a rate twice that of Calles.[79]

In a further taste of things to come, Almazán empowered the have-nots. He backed the grouping of the peasantry within a powerful confederation. He supported labor, specifically a radical union that broke with Morones's increasingly corrupt CROM. With this record, coupled with his Catholic sympathies, Almazán alienated Calles—the power behind the presidential throne—and unsuprisingly he met with an assassination attempt. En route to Mexico City in October 1931, his car was sprayed with bullets.[80]

Almazán seemed to be bad news for the business elite and for Jenkins in particular. Broad swaths of the Atencingo System were expropriated as the petitions of Doña Lola and other *agraristas* gained attention, to the benefit of forty towns and villages. By the mid-1930s, once Almazán's final land grants had been formalized, the domain was nearly 90 percent smaller than the original extent of its nine haciendas. The vast majority of what Jenkins lost or surrendered was rain-fed land, but around 9,000 acres was precious irrigated fields. Almazán was partly, if not largely, to blame. Jenkins's consolation was that most of the best terrain remained in his hands: the heartlands of the haciendas, 28,000 acres of cane fields.[81]

THE ALMAZÁN YEARS were a testing time for Jenkins, and for Mexico as a whole. The Great Depression sharpened the pain of an economy already wounded by yet another war. This was the Cristero War, born in reaction to federal repression of the Church and the most disruptive revolt since the Revolution. Depression caused a sugar glut, just as Atencingo climbed to second place in national output and should have been posting fantastic profits. There were tough negotiations to be had with Industry Minister Aarón Sáenz, who was trying to coordinate a nationwide distribution cartel; Jenkins wanted no part of any monopoly he did not control. Depression also prompted labor agitation—for the first time, Atencingo faced strikes—and a spike in ill-will toward foreigners. The government pressed the US Embassy into terminating Jenkins's consular appointment. Banditry and violence surged in the countryside, with conflict-ridden Puebla leading the nation in bloody incidents.[82] Investing much of his energy in Atencingo, Jenkins contracted malaria and was bed-ridden for weeks.

"We are in the most terrible financial state," his teenage daughter Jane wrote in her diary. "Damn Atencingo anyway!! It keeps Pop away from Los Angeles and pleasure and keeps us in a constant state of wondering where our next meal is coming from. . . . Oh God!! Please get someone to buy this darn old place quick!!!"[83]

Even within the family things were slipping beyond Jenkins's control.[84] On New Year's Day, 1930, at a party in Los Angeles, Mary suffered a hemorrhage. At the age of forty-seven, the tuberculosis-related decline she had feared since childhood was upon her. Over the course of the year she convalesced but stayed largely confined to her mansion. She would spend much of the rest of her life in bed. At least she had her daughters for company, and in November 1930 she hosted a wedding. Margaret, her second daughter, married a jeweler, Robert Anstead. Jenkins was too busy with Atencingo to attend.

Margaret's marriage, her second inside a year (the first was soon annulled), was as hastily conceived as the first. While she bore a son, whom she named William, she and Anstead divorced within eighteen months. These matches may have been doomed by earlier events in Puebla. Margaret had fallen in love with a Mexican. On finding out, her parents forbade the romance and dispatched their daughter to Los Angeles. Mary was particularly opposed, insisting that Margaret find someone "suitable." Jane soon suffered a similarly doomed romance.

Elizabeth met a suitable man of her own: Lawrence Higgins, a charming Harvard graduate and an officer at the embassy in Mexico City. By 1931 he had been posted to Honduras, where they married. For reasons unknown, Jenkins did not make the trip. He was especially fond of his eldest daughter, so the wedding may have been precipitous. Or he may have disapproved of the match, for Higgins had caused a scandal several years earlier through an affair with a high-society Boston woman whose husband had brought suit. Inauspicious beginnings became awkward routine when Higgins revealed he had no intention of being faithful. He encouraged Elizabeth to take lovers too. It was the modern thing to do, he told her. They pursued a bohemian existence through a number of consular postings, among them Oslo and Paris.[85] Try as she might to emulate her husband's dalliances, she was seldom happy. Elizabeth sought solace in drink, as would her sisters Margaret and Tita.

The Jenkins daughters would marry a total of nine men, all of them non-Mexicans. Mary did not want it any other way. Sending her girls to Los Angeles boarding schools had kept them within an Anglo sphere. She feared Mexicans would pursue them for their money; within their Los Angeles social set, most were already wealthy. Yet eight of the marriages would fail.

Jenkins would attend only one of his daughters' weddings (Margaret's fourth, held at his Puebla home). Tita would later say that though he was a kind and attentive father while they were young, "the minute we got interested in boys we lost him." Elizabeth had grown up in Los Angeles with little supervision, Margaret was irregularly supervised too, and by the time the younger girls came of age—Jane in the early 1930s, Mary and Tita in the early 1940s—their mother was usually bed-ridden. With an emotionally and physically absent father and a mother too weak to enforce discipline, the Jenkins girls were left to find their own way in the world. When they needed something, their father felt, they could ask him for money.

His own father, whom the family visited each Christmas, was close to eighty and growing frail. Never a success in business, John Jenkins saw the California fruit ranch his son had bought for him go bankrupt in the Depression. Not wanting to hurt his father's pride, William covertly channeled funds via his sisters Mamie and Ruth to rescue the farm. He then persuaded his brother Joe, a former baseball player also mired in bankruptcy, to move from Los Angeles to Hanford and help run the property.[86] When any relative needed help, and sometimes when they did not, William sent them money or moved them around. His millions gave him authority.

IN ALMAZÁN, JENKINS met his match. This was not a man who could be bought, quite unlike his predecessor. Donato Bravo Izquierdo had reportedly acquired several homes and ranches, three Packard limousines, and (making for business dealings with Jenkins) a sugar mill. Giving these allegations credibility was Bravo's earlier record, during a military campaign, of having fleeced electricity and oil companies, traded in arms and medicine, operated a brothel, and run a newspaper that he forced his soldiers to buy.[87] Reliable accusations of self-enrichment never touched Almazán.

Yet Almazán's four turbulent years involved a striking series of compromises, with Jenkins and with others. After threatening businesses with new taxes, or insisting indignantly on the payment of arrears, the governor would settle for small amounts.[88] While cultivating an ambiance of anti-capitalist rhetoric and expropriating much of Jenkins's land, when strikes loomed or erupted at Atencingo, he was quick to mediate. The truth about Almazán is that although he was a leftist he was also a populist.

The art of populist rule is the well-timed concoction of podium bluster and back-room deals. Rage first; accommodate later. Here the exercise was almost necessary. Puebla had endured fifteen governors in nine years, and if Almazán were to survive he knew he must forge alliances.[89] His broad-church approach also mirrored events in the national arena, where in March 1929 former president Calles engineered the founding of the Revolutionary National Party (PNR). The PNR was to be a "party of government" that would carry the torch of the Revolution and appeal to all classes, while reining in provincial strongmen. Accounting for two changes of name, the PNR would endure as Mexico's ruling party for an uninterrupted seventy-one years.

Almazán knew that intransigence with the private sector could backfire, for a business resentful of tax increases could seek an injunction in federal court and cease payment altogether while the case dragged on. On the other hand, he held the counter-weapon of loyal masses, who could be bade to down tools and strike. Almazán could make demands of the business elite but not dictate to them. In his toughness he hammered out deals with the equally tough Jenkins.

Almazán codified in law the informal practice of seeking advance tax payments from the sugar sector. He established a governor's legal right to demand them and then mandated that the mills pay 50 percent of their bill each autumn before it was formally due.[90] Effectively, as of September 1929, sugar producers were obliged to hand the state an annual interest-free loan, and since Jenkins accounted for three-quarters of Puebla's output, he footed three-quarters of the credit. In exchange for his compliance, the evidence suggests, Jenkins gained the governor's promise that land grants from the Atencingo System would cause little damage to its cane-growing heartland and that labor agitation would be contained.

In 1930, as the sugar glut approached a crisis and much of the crop had to be warehoused, Almazán granted tax relief to mill owners, to help their product compete in the national market.[91] In September 1931, with oversupply at its worst, news surfaced that the Atencingo Company had reverted to Porfirian practices banned by the constitution, putting its workers on a three- or four-day week and paying them a quarter of their salaries in vouchers for the company store. A month later, the PNR newspaper *El Nacional* defended the practice, reporting that the vouchers were redeemable for cash within ninety days, once all the sugar crop was sold, and that both Governor Almazán and the workers had approved the measure. The story was disingenuous. Given the glut, there was no guarantee that all the harvest would be sold. The denial that Jenkins was running a company store was false; in June, Chietla officials had written to the president protesting it, and a secret service agent would find company stores operating on each of the Atencingo System estates. The claim that workers had approved the measure ignored how Manuel Pérez had co-opted their union. That payment in IOUs was necessary for the mill to avoid bankruptcy was faintly preposterous. Atencingo had spun profits for years—its absorption of further sugar estates was testimony—and it later emerged that Jenkins held a 4 million-peso bank account, to say nothing of savings parked elsewhere.[92]

Where the article did not mislead was in Almazán's approval of the IOU scheme. The new president, Pascual Ortiz Rubio, was not pleased. He told Lázaro Cárdenas, then interior minister, that Atencingo's use of letters of credit must be stopped. But Almazán must have defended the practice, because Jenkins would settle another pay dispute the following January by again issuing IOUs.[93]

Like all planters, Jenkins had difficulty selling his crop in the fall of 1931, and come November he was trying to trim workers' wages. In reply, some eight hundred Atencingo laborers downed tools. Prime mover behind the strike was the Emiliano Zapata Peasant Confederation (CCEZ), which Almazán had recently helped create. His intention was to bolster his standing with the peasantry, co-opt many of the state's *caciques*, and create a corporatist unit that would adhere to his Socialist Party of the East, an affiliate of the PNR.[94]

At February's State Peasant Congress, where the CCEZ was founded, the radical rhetoric had flown fast. The Congress passed a motion favoring the arming of peasants and the disarming of private guards. Speakers assailed the press for cozying up to landowners. Charges were voiced against Jenkins, with the request he be expelled under Article 33, the so-called "pernicious foreigner" motion. Almazán, presiding over the closing session, was exalted by peasant leaders as a governor who gave preference to the "humble classes." Though communist activists were not welcomed at the Congress, the CCEZ devised for itself a Soviet-style logo: a corncob with a machete, to evoke the hammer and sickle, plus a Zapatista bullet belt.[95]

In light of such political theater, the irony of an Almazán-backed union calling a strike at Atencingo was not so great. It gave the governor an opportunity to step in as a peacemaker. His mediation naturally served his repute as a leader who balanced interests and got things done. Two days after the strike broke out, the eight hundred returned to the fields, Almazán having resolved the crisis. Unrest resurfaced in February, when Jenkins proposed more wage cuts and workers threatened a new strike. Again Almazán rode to the rescue, negotiating a compromise that saw the lowest-paid peons lose 5 percent of their salary and the highest-paid lose one-quarter.[96]

So, when times were good, Jenkins raked in the profits, channeling them into expanding the Atencingo System, diversifying his portfolio, and banking what was left. When times were tough, he expected his workers to share the burden. His justification is easy to picture: Why pay peasants very much anyway? They don't know how to save; they only waste their income getting drunk; it does them better service for him to profit and then channel a fraction into building schools for their children. Perhaps he also felt justified by doing some belt-tightening of his own. He removed his third daughter, Jane, from her dorm at Los Angeles's Marlborough School and arranged for her to board with friends.[97]

ALMAZÁN'S POPULIST JUGGLING act came apart in the end. In February 1932, the CCEZ complained of his meddling in elections, among them the mayoral vote in Chietla. The union told Calles that Almazán was imposing antipeasant councils; these belonged to a party linked to Almazán's political machine. Under duress, Almazán backtracked, allowing new elections in several towns. In Chietla, the moderates withdrew in protest, handing victory to a candidate backed by the CCEZ and Doña Lola.[98] Almazán had founded the Confederation only twelve months before, and already it had broken its leash.

When trying to sway the election of his successor, Almazán again failed to rope in the CCEZ. It backed its own candidate rather than Almazán's, and this rupture of the left helped a conservative, José Mijares Palencia, to win.[99] The arguably avoidable outcome—only arguably, for Mijares was backed by Calles, Puebla's PNR officials, and the business elite—spelled a tragedy for the *agraristas* of the sugar zone. Soon after Mijares took office, they would suffer another wave of murders. After four contentious years, the balance of power in the Matamoros Valley was about to swing back in Jenkins's favor.

But not before frictions peaked with Almazán. Fearing losing influence over the valley's peasants altogether, the governor reneged on his pledge to Jenkins and made grants that included precious cane land.[100] Then, at the insistence of Calles (now contemplating the governor's ouster), Almazán got dragged into a dispute between Jenkins and Aaron Sáenz over the new sugar cartel, Azúcar SA Neither Jenkins nor B. F. Johnston, owners of Mexico's two biggest mills, wanted to submit to Sáenz's production quotas. Jenkins was a strict Darwninian: the way to reduce output was to let the least efficient mills go under. To that end, he was happy to continue a price war with the Sinaloa-based Johnston; they had been dumping sugar in each other's backyards for years.[101]

Industry Minister Sáenz had the welfare of the people to consider. Mexico's population was growing, and its demand for foodstuffs had soared. True, the Depression had caused sugar consumption to fall off, but over the next ten years Sáenz expected demand to double, so all mills were needed. Sáenz also considered his own welfare: he owned the up-and-coming sugar mill El Mante, in partnership with the son of Calles. He had been subsidizing its rapid expansion in the usual revolutionary fashion, by dipping into the public purse.[102]

Sáenz threatened Jenkins: comply with the quota or face Atencingo's closure for five years. But the minister could not force him to back down.

Jenkins likely guessed the threat was idle; with Atencingo closed, Puebla would lose one of its biggest tax sources and have five thousand angry workers on its hands. So Calles called a meeting with Almazán and he in turn met with Jenkins. His head in Calles's noose, Almazán threatened Jenkins with expulsion from Mexico. Within days, Jenkins submitted to the quota.[103]

Four weeks before his term was up, Almazán resigned. Opposition from Calles to his land reform was part of it. Then there were his vain efforts to block the state legislature from ratifying Mijares as his successor; in seeing his favorite lose, Almazán felt the PNR had rigged the ballot. As a true populist, and with far greater success than any predecessor since 1911, he had retained power through a fine balancing act. He had cultivated labor and the peasantry, but he had also observed the symbiotic imperative, drawing crucial cash from the business elite in exchange for allowing it to prosper, despite occasional sacrifices. Still, Jenkins and his peers were loath to repeat the experience, so they threw their weight behind Mijares.[104]

Jenkins Jailed Again

There is something about the selling of liquor that fosters the dodging of taxes. Al Capone was famously convicted not for murder or bootlegging but for tax fraud. The trait has touched licensed producers. In 1875 former senator John Henderson, special counsel to the White House, helped expose the Whiskey Ring. Henderson found that scores of distillers were underreporting sales and splitting what they saved in taxes with Treasury officials, with kickbacks going to the Republican Party. Henderson was fired after he issued one indictment too many, namely to the private secretary of President Ulysses Grant, and then accused the Hero of Appomattox himself of blocking the investigation.[105]

Not long afterward, Jenkins's father became a revenuer, collecting distillery taxes and rooting out armed moonshiners. After the Whiskey Ring debacle, Washington wanted a more reputable class of recruit, and John Jenkins was the son of a Lutheran patriarch. But a few decades later, John's eldest son was engaged in the activity that he had risked his life to suppress. "I would rather die" than marry a liquor producer, Mary had told William just before they wed. Jenkins himself remained teetotal; perhaps that helped him rationalize his disloyalty.

The business in question was Atencingo's alcohol factory. While it legally supplied pure alcohol to stores, Jenkins built a side business in contraband.[106] Much of that untaxed product was sold in Puebla, but some traveled farther, allegedly even to the United States. During Prohibition, Mexican distillers, like the Canadians, helped to quench the thirst of the American public. They had easy access, for the Prohibition Bureau assigned just thirty-five agents to the 2,000-mile border. At a Senate hearing in 1925, a senior enforcer estimated that of all the liquor smuggled into the United States, only 5 percent was intercepted.[107] Did Jenkins claim a piece of the action? There were mills farther north in Sinaloa, and others in coastal Veracruz, much better placed for export. US archives have yet to yield any trace of Jenkins as a bootlegger.

Nonetheless, not only detractors but family and friends all claim that Jenkins profited from Prohibition, some say handsomely, despite his own denials. Whether or not he did so, the perception of Jenkins as a rum-runner flourished, part of the Black Legend to some, part of the Jenkins mystique to others. By one account, his alcohol was shipped via the Port of Veracruz to New York, earning him millions of dollars. By another, Jenkins pumped large amounts of liquor into Texas through a cross-border pipe-line, known to employees as "the alcoduct."[108]

Closer to home, contraband allegations had more substance. They first made news in 1932, under Abelardo Rodríguez, who like other postrevo-lutionary presidents waged a temperance campaign. Finance Ministry inspectors intercepted 240 crates of Atencingo alcohol lacking the req-uisite tax stamps. Nonpayment had evidently gone on for years. With the aid of railroad employees in Atencingo and Puebla City, Jenkins had alleg-edly defrauded the treasury of hundreds of thousands of pesos. Somehow the matter died down for seven months, until a federal judge ordered Jenkins's detention for a similar offense. A railroad inspector at Atencingo had discovered that the mill was transporting alcohol disguised as corn shipments. Again there was no arrest and no apparent follow up. It was as if junior officials would no longer take bribes, while senior officials were still happy to do so. A newspaper story on *agrarista* killings offered a possible reading: "The gold produced by Atencingo's alcohol has silenced justice."[109]

Government lost patience with Jenkins in June 1934, the Finance Ministry shutting down his alcohol factory. Delivery trucks had been detained, the drivers failing to show the necessary papers, and Finance Minister Marte Gómez declared Jenkins was evading taxes systemati-cally. Jenkins telegrammed President Rodríguez, asking that judgment be withheld pending investigation. Meanwhile his foes at the CCEZ also telegrammed the President. As they had done at their inaugural congress, they asked that Jenkins be expelled "for being a pernicious foreigner" and that Atencingo be placed in the hands of its workers.[110]

Matters worsened in August. The Finance Ministry imposed an extra levy on Jenkins's salary, to make up for an income tax on the Atencingo System that it had vainly been trying to collect since its founding. In response, Jenkins simply canceled the 2,000-peso monthly sum he had been paying himself as chief executive. Gómez and Rodríguez had had enough. Though the investigation was not yet concluded, Gómez declared that Jenkins owed 90,000 pesos, and for a second time the American found himself in a Mexican prison.[111]

The jailing made front-page news in Mexico City, and *El Universal* gave it a banner headline. To add to his shaming, the papers recycled the legend that he had kidnapped himself in 1919. Jenkins responded with stoicism. The Puebla City prison, under the aegis of the governor, allowed him to set up an office. His private secretary, Manuel Cabañas Pavía, was jailed alongside him, and people wishing to visit the American were informed by the prison guards that they would first have to speak to Cabañas in the cell adjacent: "Is Mr. Jenkins available?"

There was no contrition on Jenkins's part. He frankly told his family that he avoided taxes whenever possible. As he once said to his daughter Jane: "Why should I pay taxes, when someone's going to steal them, and the money is not going to public use?" It was better, he felt, to invest in public works directly: in schools, hospitals, and rural roads. That way, he could supervise the contractors himself, ensuring no one raked off a percentage.[112]

Rarely was anyone jailed for tax evasion. Such matters were settled behind closed doors, with graft. So Jenkins's incarceration had ulterior motives. For President Rodríguez, jailing the infamous gringo was a way of polishing his suspect credentials as a leftist and maybe drawing attention from his own fantastic enrichment, some of which came from alcohol smuggling.[113] Jenkins was a perfect target: already laden with a dubious reputation; no longer a consular agent, and so deprived of embassy protection; well-enough entrenched in Mexico that a little humiliation would not prompt him to sell out and take his entrepreneurship with him. As was the case in 1919, the controversial capitalist was being used as a political football. Jenkins, seething at the president's hypocrisy, and Rodríguez, angered by this American who flouted his nation's rules, became enemies for a quarter century.

After fifteen days, Jenkins walked out on bail. There would be no conviction. The tax inspector overseeing paperwork at the factory had "made
a mistake." Gabriel Alarcón, a grocer who sold Atencingo pure alcohol,
claimed the embargoed trucks were his, submitting "proof" that he had
paid the required taxes. (Was Alarcón a reliable witness? The year before,
tax agents had confiscated eighty-two contraband crates of his own.)
Investigation of the larger issue of systematic tax evasion lasted for another
year, with the alcohol factory kept closed, but at last Jenkins was cleared.
The distillery reopened. And the illicit alcohol shipments resumed, the
trucks now traveling by night.[114]

Jenkins later told his friend Sergio Guzmán that to get out of jail he had
palmed a federal minister 100,000 pesos. The likeliest recipient was Marte
Gómez. A posthumously published letter of his contains an implicit admission that he and a colleague had sought some "crumbs" from Jenkins's tax-
evading profits. It was, Jenkins said, the biggest bribe he ever paid.[115]

BY THIS TIME Mary had left Mexico for good. She had made several visits from Los Angeles, only to suffer another breakdown in 1933. Family
pressures were probably part of it, starting with Margaret's embarrassing
return to Puebla, accompanied by her baby son Billy but *sans* husband. As
there was a divorcee in the family, some of the Jenkins's society friends
would no longer receive the family in their homes. Then there was news
of Elizabeth's troubled marriage. The economy was reviving, but Puebla
remained a violent state. Besides, Mary had truly never cared for Mexico.
She could appreciate what William was doing at Atencingo, but she had
not warmed to the Mexicans in general and her social circle was small. At
the Methodist Church the services were in Spanish so she rarely attended,
in spite of having made a large donation toward a new building when a
fire destroyed the old one. For all her prowess at high-school French, she
had never mastered more Spanish than she needed to direct her maids.[116]

Before leaving, Mary wrote to congratulate Jane on graduating from
Marlborough. Surely recalling her own commencement—the love of her
life by her side, his promises lightening the burden of her illness—she
wrote: "always keeping in mind the happiness of others and eliminating
self, life will be happy and peaceful and worthwhile."[117]

William sent Mary to see the Mayo Brothers at their famous clinic in
Minnesota. He had Elizabeth take her there. Once Mary began to conva-
lesce, the Mayos recommended she move to Arizona for its dry climate.
Mary registered at Barfield Sanatorium en Tucson. When it transpired she

would be there for a while, William built a home for her and the girls; he called it Half-Way House. Mary would spend five years at Barfield. This left Jane, aged seventeen when they moved in, as head of the household, raising her younger sisters Mary and Tita, who were nine and eight. Margaret had trouble coping as a mother, so Jane also looked after her little nephew Billy. These responsibilities were a maturing experience. In adult life, Jane became the daughter most given to disagreeing with her father and the only one of the five to marry happily.[118]

Mary's world now consisted of a bedroom, her books, and a radio, with visits after school from the girls. William would come up several times a year, when work allowed, and stay for six days. Or three, if there were pressing matters in Puebla. At times Mary made jottings in a notebook. Some were verses from Scripture: "Lo, I am with you always"; "Let not your heart be troubled."[119]

One sleepless night in 1938 she wrote:

alone in bed in Tucson with stores of precious thoughts crowding the hours of the night. . . . Suddenly recapturing those far distant impressions, caught out of the mist of childhood—purple lilacs, once laden with snow on an April day—patch of blue larkspur in a great field of yellow wheat on a sloping hill before our eyes—the "youth's companion" coming each week to thrill us with simple stories, in the country of rolling green hills and valleys and winding creeks and country roads and friendly people. Then "afterwhile"—our tenderest memories recaptured and our fondest hopes come true!

After Mary moved to Tucson, the California mansion her husband had built for her stood silent. As the years passed, 641 Irving Boulevard came to be known as the Phantom House of Los Angeles. In the late 1930s Jenkins would sell the property to the oil tycoon J. Paul Getty. His decision put an end to the fiction that he would one day return to the United States. Despite the many declarations he had made to his sweetheart—promises he tried to fulfill in a home fit for his Queen—and despite his wife's chronic illness and need for companionship, Jenkins was too much in love with the business of business. And he retained his pretext for staying behind: he was unable to sell Atencingo.[120]

As for 641 Irving, Getty lived there with his second wife, but before long they were divorced, and Mrs. Getty took the house as part of their settlement. Thanks to her, in 1950, millions of people around the world came to behold the Jenkins palace, after she rented it to Paramount for the filming of *Sunset Boulevard*. In Billy Wilder's haunting drama, the titular street harbors the abode of Norma Desmond, a half-crazed silent movie star, and we first see it through the eyes of Joe Gillis, a young screen-writer. As Gillis surveys the mansion from its unkempt garden, we hear his thoughts in voice-over:

> It was a great big white elephant of a place, the kind crazy movie peo-ple built in the crazy twenties. A neglected house gets an unhappy look. This one had it in spades . . .

With Maximino

*Liberal North Americans are congenitally unable to deal
with charismatic Latin Americans—precisely because
they project upon the latter their own criteria for leadership. One might almost venture that the shape and feel of
politics in the southern United States equips the Southern
conservative better than it does the Northern liberal to
understand the political life of Latin America.*

RICHARD MORSE, "The Heritage of Latin America" (1964)

Getting to Know the General

With Mary gone from Mexico, Jenkins's closest friend was Dr. Sergio
B. Guzmán.[1] Son of a distinguished doctor, Sergio was a born athlete.
Among his father's patients were the teachers at Puebla's Methodist
College, who in gratitude helped arrange for Sergio to attend a Methodist
high school in Evanston, Illinois. Next he went to Northwestern University,
where as a tall and muscular undergraduate he captained the basketball
team. He stayed on to earn a doctorate in dental surgery. When not drilling
teeth, he also boxed, rowed, and flourished his cape in amateur bullfights,
tallying some thirty kills. On Puebla's tennis courts he met Jenkins, who
recognized in Sergio a younger version of himself: athletic, hard-working,
cosmopolitan, teetotal. The main difference was that Sergio was not much
interested in making money.

With his pedigree and his *don de gentes*, or sociability and charm, it was
expected that Sergio would enter public service. His father, Daniel, had
served in the Veracruz state legislature and, after relocating to Puebla, in
Carranza's federal Congress as a senator. An elder brother, Roberto, had
been private secretary to the interim president who preceded Obregón,
Adolfo de la Huerta; another, Salvador, was a delegate to the Constitutional
Congress of 1917 and then a diplomat. At the age of forty Sergio finally ran

for office and served for two years in the state legislature.[2] But he did not care for politics, so he returned to his dental surgery, down the street from Jenkins's home. In 1935, however, two generals approached him and compelled him to change his mind. One was former governor Donato Bravo Izquierdo, who suggested he should seek the mayorship of Puebla City. The other was the state's new military commander, who had political aspirations of his own: Maximino Ávila Camacho.

Maximino—known by his first name to tell him from his brother Manuel, a rising star in the Defense Ministry—had known the Guzmán family since his childhood in Teziutlán, in the Puebla Sierra. People from the Sierra called themselves *serranos*; they thought themselves hardier than lowlanders and more independent-minded. So Maximino prevailed upon his *serrano* friend, asking if he could help him raise money from the city's wealthy to fund a campaign for governor. Sergio, through his dental practice, family connections, and membership in the Alpha Club, was friendly with all the right people.

Maximino could be charming, but his request must have given the doctor pause. While the two men's politics were similarly conservative, Sergio was scrupulously honest. Maximino, the rumors ran, was less so. Perhaps the bonds of family friendship were such that honor was at stake. Perhaps Guzmán recognized that the general was a man to whom one said "no" at one's peril. Or perhaps he made a calculation: Maximino was an appointee of the new president, Lázaro Cárdenas, and his brother Manuel was one of Cárdenas's closest aides, so the Ávila Camachos were clearly in the political ascendance; Maximino's campaign was likely to succeed. If they were to hold office together, with Guzmán as mayor, he might exert a moderating influence. At any rate, the two men agreed that in the 1936 elections they would support each other. The doctor set about introducing Maximino to men of wealth and influence, and one of their first visits was with Jenkins.

The general had begun his charm offensive during the Revolution. Coming from a family of modest means, Maximino flattered his way into the favor of whichever military superior he felt could advance his career. By the war's end, he had scraped the rank of colonel. Once promoted to brigadier general in 1924—following a display of valor during the De la Huerta revolt—he received his first command of a military zone. Thus he began to involve himself in politics: first in Chiapas, without much success and to the anger of the local legislature; from 1926 in Zacatecas, where his interference again met objection but found more fertile ground; and from 1931 in Aguascalientes, by which time he had risen again in rank, was a political player of some weight, and received overtures from Puebla regarding his interest in running for governor.[3]

In each state, Maximino built friendships with the rich by using his command to obstruct agrarian reform. In each state, he nurtured his personal wealth. Many military commanders lined their pockets, but Maximino's methods were unusually shameless. During his Cristero War postings, he gained fame not only for mercilessly crushing Catholic radicals but also for profiteering and plunder. He was said to be selling federal arms to the rebels, seizing property from people only remotely connected to the Cristeros, developing a beef distribution monopoly based upon stolen cattle, even kidnapping priests to hold them for ransom.[4]

By one count, Maximino collected at least two houses in Mexico City and one in Guadalajara, three ranches with cattle and horses, and several cars. According to his last surviving son, by the mid-1930s he had a collection of nine or ten children by five or six different women.[5] Now, using his military, political, and business connections, he intended to collect the governorship of Puebla. But there was a hitch: obstructing him was a popular leftist of impeccable revolutionary standing, a teacher-turned-career politician by name of Gilberto Bosques.

MISSING FROM MANY electoral accounts is the tricky question of cash. Until 1993, when an exposé of a PRI-convened "billionaires' banquet" blew the lid off elite fundraising, neither journalists nor historians paid much attention to campaign finance. Journalists were long cowed by a culture of self-censorship not to pry into such matters. Historians have documented violence and fraud, but how goons and votes were paid for they have seldom inquired. So the bearing of business elites upon Mexico's political processes has been much underplayed.[6]

That the peso weighed heavily in Puebla's gubernatorial race is affirmed first of all by precedent. In 1932, four years before the Maximino-Bosques contest, José Mijares Palencia had faced stiff competition. Although Mijares was backed by former president Calles, and although the ruling PNR had rubber-stamped him in the primary as its official candidate, he was new to Puebla politics. His opponents had sizeable bases. Lauro Camarillo was the chosen candidate of the popular incumbent, Governor Almazán. Manuel Palafox had served as a general under Zapata and was backed by a leading peasant confederation. So the support of Calles and the PNR was insufficient to guarantee Mijares victory. Enthusiasm would have to be generated on the ground and power brokers bought off. Here,

Mijares held the right cards: the business elite, tired of Almazán's radicalism, were ready to donate. Afterward, his campaign manager attested that Mijares raised a lot of funds from businessmen, in Puebla and even in California. During the campaign, Palafox criticized the PNR president for "arranging everything on the basis of money."[7]

Then there is tangible evidence. During the 1935–1936 campaign, Maximino regularly wrote memos to his ally Guzmán on the back of his presentation cards, asking him to convey his thanks to this donor or the other. Some of these survive. On one card he wrote: "Sergio: Give thanks on my behalf to our friend Manuel Concha for the five hundred pesos that he delivered to you for help with our costs. Avila C." On another he wrote: "Sergio: I beg you give thanks to our friend Luis Cué, for the five hundred pesos he delivered to you for help with our costs. Avila C." Concha and Cué were Puebla industrialists, but not all businessmen were so forthcoming. A Spaniard named Jesús Cienfuegos, a pulque merchant and tax collector, was approached by Maximino but refused to chip in, a decision that would return to haunt him.[8]

Jenkins, so Guzmán would later tell his son, was Maximino's chief donor. Conversing with the US Consul General, Jenkins would admit to having made a donation—not the 500-peso sums that members of Puebla's cash-poor textile fraternity were chipping in, but 40,000 pesos.[9]

His gift to Maximino cemented a bond that transcended the personal, illustrating a mutual and sector-wide interdependence. Jenkins needed Maximino as a new safeguard against land reform, now that an avowed leftist held the presidency; a radical like Bosques would double the danger to Atencingo. Puebla's textile elite, facing the unprecedented might of organized labor, had similar concerns. Maximino needed Jenkins and his kind to back him because he had two obstacles to overcome: a tough opponent and his own dubious reputation. Hence the PNR high command, which preferred Maximino to Bosques, needed that financial assistance too.

The Jenkins-Maximino partnership would prove powerful—and prophetic. Under President Cárdenas, socialism may have held sway on the national stage, but the Cardenist project was much less monolithic than official histories once supposed.[10] Outside the capital, in Puebla and several other regions, radicalism was already receding. The support of activist industrialists like Jenkins for conservatives like Maximino would help build an influential right wing within the ruling party, in turn helping ensure that when Cárdenas chose his successor he would pick a pro-business moderate.

An Election Is Purchased

Although the PNR—the ancestor of today's PRI—was hardening its national hold in the 1930s, a number of races were bitterly fought, and in a couple of states its preferred man lost. Maximino's campaign of 1936 would be a slog, rather like Mijares's in 1932. But this time the outcome would hinge on the PNR primary election.[11]

As Puebla's military chief, Maximino had spent most of 1935 traversing the state, suppressing banditry, snuffing out strikes, and protecting landowners. He developed a base among wealthy and middle-class conservatives and rural *caciques*. Crucially, he had the backing of President Cárdenas, who had appointed him zone commander so he might function as one of various strategically placed assets in a planned showdown with Calles. This fight, by which Cárdenas aimed to free himself from man who for a decade had more or less controlled Mexican politics, had its first bout in June 1935: he purged Calles loyalists from his cabinet, and Calles himself retreated by airplane to his native northwest. At this juncture, Maximino played the role of counterweight to Mijares, lest pro-Calles governors such as he try to unite in revolt. With Calles marginalized, Mijares likely felt compelled to back Maximino.[12] Having Cárdenas behind him and Calles out of the way, Maximino could count on the backing of the PNR, both its federal and its Puebla apparatus. The latter, headed by his brother Rafael, would tabulate the votes.

But Maximino's heavy hand as zone commander had created a reservoir of popular resentment. Notoriously, in April 1935, his troops suppressed a general strike by the Regional Front of Workers and Peasants (FROC), a radical group affiliated with Vicente Lombardo Toledano's powerful Confederation of Mexican Workers (CTM). Three men were shot to death in Puebla City. Several months later, Maximino declared martial law in the mill town of Atlixco, upon the murder of the FROC secretary general. The general was also reported to have fostered private militia in the service of hacienda owners. This claim brought a typically emphatic and lengthy public denial from Maximino.[13]

So the FROC threw its weight behind Bosques, a man who had worked in the Education Ministry and the Treasury and was serving a second term in the federal Congress; he was sufficiently respected to be named president of the Chamber of Deputies.[14] At the time, the FROC had overtaken the Regional Confederation of Mexican Workers (CROM) as the state's leading labor federation, a power seen to yield results when the FROC won the mayoralty of Puebla City for 1936. Its backing of Bosques, along with Lombardo's support at the federal level, meant the primary would be a battle. Next, seventeen locals from the state's chief peasant association, the CCEZ, voted to split from the Maximino camp and support Bosques. Strengthening his hand further, he was running alongside the popular ex-governor Leónides Andreu Almazán, who joined the Bosques ticket to campaign for senator. Bosques also enjoyed the backing of *La Opinión*, Puebla's newspaper of record and a sympathizer with the left.[15]

Given Bosques's strategic and popular strengths, the PNR's (often weak) supervision of the voting apparatus was insufficient to fix a win for Maximino. A blatantly fraudulent result might well result in revolt, especially in light of Puebla's fractious history. In other words, Maximino had to campaign for votes. Concern that he might lose was evident two weeks before the poll, when a gunman from his camp tried to assassinate Bosques at a rally. Failing in his attempt but killing a sympathizer in an ensuing scuffle, the shooter took refuge in the home of the local *cacique*, a candidate for state Congress in alliance with Maximino.[16]

In the end, two factors besides the hand of Cárdenas steered the election: fear and Jenkins's money. Intimidation shook the whole campaign. Beyond the attempt on Bosques, killings took place across Puebla. In the countryside private militia were said to be bullying peasants into supporting Maximino.[17] In Atlixco, where the FROC and CROM had bloodied each other over control of mills since 1929, violence erupted again, with two FROC members slain in February. The CROM, a diminished corporatist machine in search of new patrons, was backing Maximino. In March, a similar tussle at a Puebla City cigarette factory left another two FROC members dead; then troops arrived, beat back the FROC faction, and led the CROM aggressors to safety.[18] No doubt such clashes helped convince the middle classes, perhaps the unaffiliated poor too, that what Puebla needed most was the iron hand of a general.

Money was essential: for funding campaign events, buying influence, printing propaganda (including a daily newspaper), and bringing out the vote. But Maximino's own wealth was largely tied up in property, and the state government was always short of funds. Of course, shortfalls in 1936 may have owed in part to subsidies for Maximino, but the budget was so small to begin with, at barely $1 million, it is unlikely that Mijares had much discretionary cash to offer.[19] Jenkins's donation was therefore vital, allowing Maximino to spend a good deal more than his opponent. The general's campaign was lengthier than that of his rival and reached farther afield.[20] Town rallies all required an outlay—not just the transport and lodging of a candidate and his entourage but also the cost of enticing folk to hear predictable speeches by politicians they barely recognized and whose predecessors (barring Almazán) had largely failed to fulfill their promises. At the very least, a free meal was in order. His lack of widespread support among workers and peasants, by far the majority of the electorate, surely forced the general into a great deal of vote-buying, with handsome payoffs to mayors and *caciques.*

The day before the April 5 election, in a vision of ballot-rigging expense, Maximino's team bused in thousands of "political tourists" to inflate his vote. According to one report, seventy buses and thirty-four trucks arrived from Mexico City, and having dropped off their cargo they sped to neighboring states to scoop up further voters. One driver, whose bus was fire-bombed by Bosques sympathizers, admitted to having been contracted in the service of Maximino.[21]

Both sides claimed victory, but from the PNR there was silence. The tallies must have needed further massaging, and the timing was not propitious, for the party was unwilling to stir a wasp's nest in Puebla while it still had a hornet to dispose of in the capital. Calles had returned in December, seeking to rally what support he could. A second bout with Cárdenas culminated on April 10, when Calles, clutching his copy of Hitler's *Mein Kampf,* was packed onto a plane once again, this time bound for Los Angeles and a five-year exile. A few days later, the PNR national committee said it would summon Bosques and Maximino so they might make their cases and voice their complaints. At 11 PM on April 29, it declared Maximino the winner.[22]

That the PNR took three weeks to declare the result only affirmed that Maximino either squeaked ahead of Bosques or required "electoral alchemy"—as the massaging of results would come to be known—to claim his prize. Massive protests followed. A May Day march in Puebla numbered 25,000; another march brought 20,000 to Mexico City, just as a general strike brought Puebla to a halt. Bosques himself stayed away. Whatever words he had exchanged with Cárdenas remained in confidence. The president deeply respected Bosques, but he held a debt of loyalty to Maximino over the Calles showdown and he wanted to preserve friendship with Maximino's politically talented brother Manuel.[23]

From there the rivals' paths diverged. Five years later, having raised his bank balance by several million pesos while governor, Maximino was still sleeping under a portrait of Mussolini. He planned to impose himself on the Ministry of Communications, which would offer new avenues of venality. Gilberto Bosques, meanwhile, was toiling to save persecuted Europeans from fascist terror. As the Mexican consul in Marseilles, he engineered the flight of thousands of left-wing Spanish exiles and thousands of fugitive Jews, issuing Mexican residency visas, arranging secure board and lodging, and finding ships to carry them from France.[24]

Interdependence Becomes Convenient

Puebla's poll of 1936 foreshadowed the national vote four years later, when Maximino's brother Manuel captured the presidency. Both contests were violent and tainted by covert fundraising and fraud. Both signaled a shift to the right, initiating an era of overt alliance between pro-business political elites and industrialists. This bond between state and capital was equally significant to each. In Puebla, it consolidated stable rule amid a climate of persistent violence and helped establish a right-wing dynasty that would endure for decades, and it shielded capitalists like Jenkins and the state's textile barons from property seizures and strikes. At the national level, the bond cemented the dominance of the ruling party, which showed itself increasingly tolerant of monopolies and complicit in a general concentration of wealth.

In the chaotic wake of the Revolution, interdependence had been considered necessary by most political and business leaders; historians would tend to concur. But was it still? Certainly, from Maximino's point of view, there was no other course but his, that of the open hand toward business and the iron hand toward workers and peasants, by which Puebla might achieve stability and growth. Once in power, he would continue to find alliances with business elites to be imperative, relying on them to satisfy many a need. These stretched from day-to-day favors, such as access to their bullrings and theaters for mounting displays of populist demagoguery (after all, order depended on unity) to longer term ones like supplements for Puebla's inadequate budget to build roads and to generate jobs.

Seen from the left, however, or from the viewpoint of electoral democracy—the stand Madero made in 1910 when he cried for "effective suffrage"—Maximino's victory was not imperative at all. It was merely convenient. It evinced a pact between a would-be autocrat and an already-privileged coterie of capitalists. Peace in Puebla might have been better achieved by fulfilling the Revolution's promises of land, liberty, and democratic representation. A similar question could soon be raised of state-capital alliances at the federal level, where after 1940 the threat of another violent regime change all but disappeared.

Making Maximino's election an instructive crucible in which to observe the nature of elite alliance is its timing. At his inauguration, Cárdenas had promised state intervention in the economy would be "increasingly great, increasingly frequent, and increasingly profound." Strike activity spiraled. Business leaders fretted about an advent of communism.[25] To the Puebla elite, the 1936 ballot might allow continuity with Mijares's conservatism and a buffer against the socialists in Mexico City, or it might bring a turn to the left, giving those radicals free rein, nipping the state's recovery in the bud. Of course, the president's paradoxical support for the brutal but useful Maximino, rather than his ideological soul mate Bosques, was a major factor in the outcome, but so was that economic imperative that impelled Jenkins and his peers to open their checkbooks.

A pressing need for cash also marked Maximino's years in office. Despite his pro-business ideology, the dire condition of the state coffers meant that one of his first decrees was to raise various taxes. A report about his decree added that those "who do not submit to his dictates will see their businesses converted into cooperatives." While there is no evidence that any such measures were applied, tax revenue did rise under Maximino. Over his first two years in office, the state budget grew by 25 percent.[26]

But incremental success proved insufficient for Maximino's needs. First, the state posed immense challenges. The 1930 census showed Pueblans were still undereducated, with 68 percent of the population illiterate, against a national average of 59 percent. During the electoral campaign, the National Economy Ministry released figures showing that, in the past three decades Puebla City had grown much more slowly than its rivals. Its population was up by a mere quarter, to 115,000, versus a tripling of Mexico City's (to 1 million) and an approximate doubling in size of Guadalajara and Monterrey (to 180,000 and 133,000, respectively). Within a generation, Puebla had fallen from Mexico's second-most populous city to fourth.[27] To reverse the relative decline of city and state, the governor needed the help of the private sector.

Maximino also wanted help because his vision of leadership insisted on self-enrichment. In part this was sheer greed. In part it was a matter of maintaining an aura he felt to be fitting of the office. Hence his expensive suits, his flashy automobiles, and his hosting of foreign dignitaries. Hence the largesse he bestowed at his annual birthday celebrations, when the public was invited to the city bullring and entertained for free.[28] To fund the satisfaction of these tastes, the imperative that motivated his alliance with businessmen and persisted through his reign was complemented by ties of convenience. Industrialists like Jenkins not only made campaign donations, loans, and tax advances; they subsidized the governor's lifestyle and partnered with him in business.

Most of the evidence for such relationships is lost. At the end of his term, Maximino sold almost the entire executive archive to the Peña Pobre paper company, to be pulped and recycled as newsprint.[29] What remains are the surmise of historians, the narratives of chroniclers, the memories of the living, and fragments of documentation.

Historians agree that Maximino used political office to feather his nest, first in Puebla and from 1941 as head of the Ministry of Communications and Public Works. Stephen Niblo wrote that in mid-century Mexico "money and political protection formed a symbiotic union" that was best illustrated by Maximino's links with Jenkins. He added that their bond "saw Jenkins offer Maximino business opportunities and financial rewards all the while that Maximino provided political cover for Jenkins." But here, as in other histories, details are lacking.[30]

Evidence from witnesses is likewise sparse, although there is consensus as to Jenkins's complicity. In a 1939 dispatch, Consul General Stewart (to whom Jenkins revealed his campaign donation) wrote that Maximino was "undoubtedly a secret partner of Jenkins," implying that the governor held a stake in the Atencingo Company. Decades later, at a dinner convened for Puebla's chroniclers by Enrique Cordero y Torres, elderly doyen of the group, the guests pooled their knowledge of Maximino's assets and frontmen. Jenkins was first to be named, followed by his private secretary and his two closest partners. Recalling that occasion, Cordero's son would record that Maximino had a stake in Atencingo and in Puebla's movie theaters. He also noted that Jenkins and Maximino bought 50,000 acres of land at risible prices just south of Puebla City, anticipating the construction of the Valsequillo Reservoir. Whatever land was to be flooded they sold to the federal government at inflated prices, while the rest was transformed into valuable irrigated farmland, once Valsequillo began to operate in 1944.

Maximino's last surviving son, Manuel Ávila Camacho López, swore that Jenkins was one of the men with whom his father held covert partnerships. He said he had the documents to prove it, but he died before retrieving them. Jenkins's eldest grandson, while silent on the issue of partnerships, conceded that his grandfather did favors to ease Maximino's personal cash flow, in several cases buying houses that the general owned in Mexico City. By Jenkins's own admission, this kind of favor worked both ways. He told Stewart that Maximino had made him business loans, from out of his personal account, of up to 100,000 pesos.[31]

The Atencingo Compromise

Maximino's assumption of office, in February 1937, came not a moment too soon for Jenkins. The American was facing the possible loss of Atencingo.[32] In October 1936, with Calles out of the way, Cárdenas had accelerated his program of land reform. He began with an assault, overseen in person, on the industrialized cotton estates of the fertile northern region of La Laguna. First affected was Manuel Pérez Treviño, former governor of Coahuila and president of the PNR, who bore the double misfortune of having rivaled Cárdenas for the presidential nomination and having scaled the party's echelons as an ally of Calles. After packing Pérez Treviño off as ambassador to Spain, Cárdenas seized his massive plantation. At least in part, agrarian reform was driven by score-settling and splashy headlines. Some seizures were aided by the popular xenophobia that had spiked with the Depression and stayed potent through the decade. Several of the biggest expropriations would be made at the expense of foreigners.[33]

As owner of Puebla's largest agroindustrial enterprise, as an American, and as a man famed for snubbing the rule of law in Mexico, Jenkins knew he was a target. "I have prospered greatly in the last five years," he wrote to his Vanderbilt friend John Tigert. "I have a very large business now, and of course all large business enterprises in radical countries like this are very dangerous. We never know when we will be kicked out."[34]

Jenkins was prone to alarmism, but these remarks were prescient. Weeks earlier the veteran *agrarista* Dolores Campos—Doña Lola—had secured an audience with Cárdenas. So far, aided by Campos and other courageous activists, some forty pueblos had won land, in the face of slow-moving bureaucrats, gun-toting private guards, and Jenkins-friendly *caciques* like Chietla's Sabino P. Burgos. Indeed, it was Burgos's death in 1935 that provided the opening Doña Lola needed to push for resolution over Jenkins's most valuable terrain. Amid the ensuing power vacuum, her ally Gil Vega won election as mayor of Chietla.[35]

Vega's support for his townspeople's petitions during 1936 helped them gain Mexico City's attention. Their persistent complaint was that very little of the land so far granted them was irrigated, and much of it was hilly. Then a setback: Vega lost his fighter's appetite after his year in office. There were hints he was unhappy at having failed to cash in as a *cacique*. He opted to side with Jenkins. This might in turn explain why, shortly after Doña Lola's visit to Cárdenas, Vega would be riddled with bullets one night while sleeping.[36]

In her meeting with the president, Doña Lola argued that the people of Chietla, along with other villagers who lacked arable land, should receive the valley's economic engine: the 28,000 acres of sugar-growing heartland. Cárdenas was familiar with the Matamoros Valley from a brief stint as Puebla military chief in 1932. In his diary he had described the region as one in which depressed and often drunken laborers of the Atencingo Company contrasted with their communal-farming neighbors, who seemed happy and healthy. Whether or not his sketch was fair—for Manuel Pérez had little tolerance for public drunkenness, while the diary was likely written (and edited) for posterity—the attractiveness of the proposal was plain. Atencingo might be the next showcase of the Revolution, a testament to peasant productivity, like La Laguna. The president told Doña Lola that he would consent to her plea. In May he ordered the Agrarian Department to arrange the seizure and partition.[37]

Jenkins responded with a clever legal ploy. He would take advantage of a 1934 change in the law, which permitted haciendas' resident field hands to petition for land on the same basis as all other country folk. To effect his plan, Jenkins enlisted two powerful men.

The first was Maximino. The governor ordered a study of Atencingo, which concluded that its resident cane growers should have first claim; after all, they already occupied the land yet owned nothing, whereas the villages already possessed land grants and were merely seeking enlargements. Maximino used this study to lobby Cárdenas. He also argued that the division of Atencingo into communal *ejidos* could have seriously negative tax repercussions for the state. Later, he protested that the commissioner handling the matter was inviting people from far-off villages, even from Morelos, to take part in the redistribution. In July, Cárdenas responded favorably and issued a suspension of his seizure order. Overriding the Agrarian Department, the president entrusted Maximino with determining how Atencingo should be divided.[38]

Jenkins's second ally was the unlikely person of Blas Chumacero, a vocal leader of the radical FROC, the worker federation. Chumacero had become a state lawmaker in January, and there were signs that he and fellow deputy Francisco Márquez might temper the conservatism of the new establishment, for the rest of the legislature were self-declared Maximino loyalists. Only eight months earlier, Chumacero had strode at the head of the Mexico City march against Maximino's theft of the Puebla primary. He gave a vivid speech, recalling the machine-gunning of striking FROC members at the general's orders in 1935 and culminating with the declaration: "General Ávila Camacho, candidate imposed on the governorship of Puebla, is at the service of the clergy, capitalism and the [fascist] Gold Shirts." Yet within weeks of entering the legislature, both he and Márquez found it expedient—and quite possibly helpful for their health—to cast their lot with the governor. This produced a schism within the FROC, and Chumacero persuaded Jenkins to let the Atencingo union join its new, pro-Maximino wing.[39]

Chumacero in turn helped Jenkins devised nine commissions to represent each of the former haciendas in the Atencingo complex. On August 25, on behalf of the resident peons, these made a formal petition to Maximino for the land.[40]

Very soon came more good news for Jenkins. While on tour in the Yucatán, Cárdenas issued regulations that clarified the rights of peons to the lands on which they toiled. As the president sailed back, Maximino, Chumacero, and various agrarian officials hurried down to Veracruz to intercept his boat. In an audience on August 26, they convinced him of the resident peons' right to Atencingo.[41] Cárdenas's acceptance of this proposal met with outrage in Chietla, but no violence ensued, only an all-day drinking binge. This signaled a hiatus. By no means was it the end of anti-Jenkins activism.

Nor did it mark the end of Jenkins's string-pulling. By coincidence, a few weeks earlier, Jenkins had hosted his old Vanderbilt friend John Tigert. As president of the University of Florida, and formerly Commissioner of Education under Presidents Harding and Coolidge, Tigert was well connected. He gathered from Jenkins that Ambassador Josephus Daniels was unsympathetic to his plight. Indeed, the left-leaning Daniels had become close to Cárdenas, and he shared his disdain for Jenkins. In his memoirs, he would trot out the Black Legend version of the kidnapping as though it were fact.[42]

So Tigert began to lobby. First, for propiety's sake, he wrote to Daniels, who replied with boilerplate language ("We have followed developments in Mr. Jenkins's case with interest"). Next he petitioned his contacts in New York and Washington: US Ambassador-at-Large Norman Davis, a fellow Vanderbilt alumnus; the director general of the Pan American Union;

and a counsel for the Special Mexican Claims Commission (SMMC). He even offered to go to Washington and visit President Roosevelt. The thrust of his efforts was not to protect the Atencingo estate, for in September Cárdenas had nixed the legal clause that had protected Agricultural-Industrial Units from expropriation, so Jenkins was resigned to losing his land. Rather, Tigert sought proper financial compensation for his friend.[43]

Tigert's diplomacy came to naught, and Jenkins did not urge him to visit Roosevelt. The basic fact was that, unlike US claims for compensation relating to the Revolution (filed with the SMMC), there was no formal mechanism yet in place to negotiate claims arising since 1920. Further, the State Department was well aware that the land expropriations enjoyed massive public support. With Ambassador Daniels unwilling to push the matter, Jenkins and Tigert could see that there was nothing to be done for now. By one account, Jenkins therefore decided to earn some political capital by making a formal gift of Atencingo's land to Cárdenas. If the account is true, it was a disingenuous move, for the following year Jenkins would petition a new American-Mexican Claims Commission for compensation.[44]

Meanwhile a struggle was taking place over the nature of the land grant. Maximino, Chumacero, and Jenkins proposed that the lands become a single, collective *ejido*, dedicated to cane growing. It would be administered by a cooperative society and supplied by the mill company with the necessary credit, for which the cane crop would serve as collateral. Lombardo Toledano, the national labor leader and a close adviser to the president, agreed that the complex should continue to produce sugar and be farmed collectively. But Lombardo differed on the crucial matter of the mill, advocating that it too be expropriated. The idea was not outlandish, for a similar model prevailed across the state line in Zacatepec, Morelos. Here, Cárdenas was already plowing 14 million pesos into the building of a giant mill that would enhance the existing peasant cooperative.[45] Maximino moved quickly to neutralize Lombardo's influence. On October 5, according to due process but also reflecting the governor's autocratic rule, Puebla's Local Agrarian Commission submitted its report: it favored a single communal land grant without the seizure of the mill. Maximino stamped his approval the very same day. He then assured Jenkins that he would force the beneficiaries to continue planting cane.[46]

In a ceremony on December 20, 1937, Maximino gave the peons of Atencingo provisional possession of their 21,170-acre *ejido*. Jenkins was legally permitted to retain just 370 acres, although with the aid of incompetent or corrupt surveyors he managed to keep another 7,200 acres of peripheral land on the sly. The following June, Cárdenas would confirm the governor's resolution, awarding definitive possession of the land to the 2,043 members of the "Ejidal Cooperative Society of Atencingo and Annexes."[47]

As he signed the documents that formalized the transfer that December, Jenkins wept. The one-time Tennessee farm boy still felt a special connection to the soil, above all this soil, to which he had devoted the better part of his energies for seventeen years, to which he had demonstrated a greater commitment than he had shown even to his wife. Farmer was the occupation written in his passport, and farming continued to absorb his imagination.[48] Now the soil of Atencingo was no longer his.

Still, the Maximino connection brought Jenkins long-term victory. The terms of the land grant bound the Atencingo cane growers to a series of obligations that served Jenkins very well: they must work collectively, only produce sugar cane, and only sell it to the Atencingo mill; only the field hands and mill employees of the Atencingo Company, the least mobilized peasants and workers in the vicinity, could qualify as *ejido* members; funds for the crops were to be provided on credit, with interest, by Jenkins, rather than by the federal Bank of Ejidal Credit; and the Atencingo Company manager, Manuel Pérez, had the right to select the manager of the Ejidal Cooperative Society, the *ejido*'s administrative organ, which oversaw work schedules, wages, and the sale of the harvest. In practice, Jenkins and Pérez came to control the appointment of all posts within the communal farm. Altogether, little changed in the way that the business was run, and Jenkins was granted enormous legal influence over his former peons. The biggest operational change was that Jenkins now had to pay for his cane, but as sole buyer he could more or less fix the price. Better still for him, the *ejido*'s legal constitution blocked further designs on the plantation by Doña Lola and her *agraristas*. This did not stop them from trying to seize parcels of land, but when they did so, as occurred amid bloodshed in 1939, Maximino would be quick to defend the integrity of the new cooperative and arrest any intruders.[49]

Exchanges of favor over Atencingo did not end there. During the debate over the plantation's future, the US State Department had contacted the Mexican government to express its concern that so large an American-owned asset faced expropriation. The State Department's note prompted what was probably Jenkins's biggest favor to Maximino since his campaign donation.[50] As he afterward recounted to Consul General Stewart, the governor had immediately sent for him, "in a panic," and confessed his worry that the US government might retaliate by confiscating Mexican deposits in American banks. He said he therefore intended to transfer his US savings into Jenkins's account. No doubt worried about the red flag that this might raise with the IRS, Jenkins protested the idea. But Maximino, like many a dictator, was prone to paranoia; he would not be dissuaded, and so, for several months, Jenkins felt obliged to harbor $250,000 of Maximino's ill-gotten fortune. Jenkins closed his tale of this episode with a rare display of public self-examination, which Stewart, in wry understatement, conveyed thus: "Mr. Jenkins says that sometimes he thinks his relations with the governor may be too close."

Then, in May 1940, a return kindness: Maximino proposed to his legislature that it withdraw the funds of the state welfare department from its bank account and invest them in the Atencingo Company, where he claimed they would earn a higher return. That July, following a congressional study, the proposal was approved, while going unreported in the press.[51]

Other major US landowners, less adept at politicking, fared worse. Jenkins's closest rival had been B. F. Johnston of Sinaloa, whose United Sugar Companies dominated production in the northwest. But Johnston died on a trip to Hong Kong in 1937, leaving his family to confront the expropriation of his Los Mochis estate a year later. Like Jenkins, they retained both the mill and an exclusive supply and credit agreement with the *ejido*. Unlike Jenkins, they failed to retain control over the cane-growing cooperative. Profits were siphoned off by self-interested leaders; know-how dissipated; production declined. Over the next fifteen years, despite extending the cane fields by a quarter, the *ejido* saw its cane yield fall by a fifth. A few years after that, the Johnston heirs quit, selling their mill to the politician-businessman Aarón Sáenz.[52]

Until after World War II, Jenkins would continue to reap profits from Atencingo. Cane productivity in tons per hectare remained high. The millworkers and cane growers stayed subservient and—except during the 1939–1940 presidential campaign—fairly peaceful. The federal government maintained a price cap on sugar, but wartime demand far outpaced supply, so like other mill owners Jenkins managed to sell massive amounts on the black market. For Jenkins, these sales were allegedly handled by his shopkeeper friend Gabriel Alarcón. Jenkins also continued his covert shipments of large quantities of contraband alcohol. The state government turned a blind eye to both practices. Referring to the expropriation, Jenkins later told a friend: "I came out on top."[53]

Labor leader Chumacero also came out on top. The pragmatism he showed in abandoning radicalism for accommodation may have been born of awkward necessity. Yet it also foreshadowed the daily compromises of a very long career under the umbrella of the ruling party. He would serve as federal deputy for Puebla six times, a national post-1940 record. He would be elected a senator twice, and he would rise to No. 2 in the Confederation of Mexican Workers (CTM), the perennial accomplice of labor's dictator-for-life, Fidel Velázquez. Famed communist labor leader Valentín Campa, for one, never trusted Chumacero. He later recalled observing him at the CTM's founding: "a pseudo-peasant . . . in an English cashmere suit."[54]

Maximino came out on top as well: politically, economically, personally. He scored political points by negotiating to the president's satisfaction a prickly agrarian problem, marked by three decades of violent tussles. He secured a productive future for the largest private unit within the state's economy, an employer of five thousand, a major source of taxes, and an investment option for state-controlled moneys. He preserved a relationship of sufficient convenience with the state's leading industrialist that he maintained a safe harbor, when he needed one, for his loot. And if Consul General Stewart is to be believed, he also preserved for himself a lucrative covert stake in the Atencingo Company.[55]

The Atencingo compromise had its losers, chiefly Doña Lola and her hundreds of land-hungry followers. While various historians depict her as the thwarted heroine of the tale—the brave opponent of a dastardly rich American—contemporary reports claim she plotted murders and ruled by fear like many a *cacique*. Tough as she was, she could not match the Maximino-Jenkins alliance. After spending time in jail for complicity in further land-grabs, she left for exile in Morelos. In 1945, at the age of sixty-four, she would be about to return to Atencingo when she fell to an assassin. Her legacy would endure, however, in the ground she prepared for a young associate, Porfirio Jaramillo, to organize resistance to Jenkins the following year.[56]

Mary Jenkins and her younger daughters must also be counted among the losers. Had Cárdenas sided with Lombardo Toledano and confiscated the mill, Jenkins's chief reason for staying in Mexico, and the cash cow that allowed him to invest in other businesses, would have evaporated. Very possibly he would have returned to Mary and sought opportunities in Los Angeles, where he retained several rent-producing properties.

Pangs of conscience told him he should. Staying with Mary in Tucson over Christmas 1939, he wrote to John Tigert that her health had improved somewhat. She would now move back to Los Angeles, where Mary and Tita were at boarding school. William had bought a new home for her, "a knock-out I might add ... right close to Hollywood." He went on: "I plan to try and spend more time in Los Angeles than I have spent in Tucson for the past years. In the first place, if this son-in-law of mine [Elizabeth's husband, Lawrence Higgins] is any good, I will have someone down in Mexico to help look after things, and then again, I am getting too darned old to try to do everything myself."[57]

It was a pipe dream. Son-in-law Higgins *wasn't* any good. He would supervise a few enterprises, never to much effect, and soon the world war would remove him from Mexico. More to the point, Jenkins's protestations of age were a sham. Though now sixty-one, he had just fashioned for himself a new luxury home: the vast upper story of the Imperial Building in Puebla, above its leading department store, a perch higher than City Hall. He had just initiated a trio of partnerships in the film industry. He had no intention of slowing down.

With Maximino, a Populist of the Right

For all the brutality of his rise, Maximino Ávila Camacho was a master populist. He needed to be. As he fastened his rule during his first year in office—gaining unanimous loyalty within the state Congress, staffing the judiciary and labor arbitration board with allies, co-opting the main newspaper *La Opinión*,[58] containing *agrarista* activism—Puebla's stability was secured. The symbiotic equation that helped bring him to office saw him backing the business elite in conflicts with workers and peasants. His bloody crack-down on the FROC general strike of 1935 had heralded his modus operandi. His continued persecution of that hard-left union, to the benefit of the CROM, left it decimated and marginalized; between 1938 and the presidential election of 1940, the murder of FROC members averaged more than one a month.

Puebla's investment growth, meanwhile, contrasted with the economic sluggishness at the national level. Jenkins and friends were often involved. In one high-profile example, Jenkins invested in Romulo O'Farrill's automobile dealership, enabling it to start assembling luxury Packards. At the opening of the Packard plant, O'Farrill praised effusively Maximino, "who offered me all facilities and help without limits."[59]

Order and progress came at a cost, and not only to the FROC. Room for dissent all but disappeared. Maximino was self-aware enough to know that his hard line and his coziness with capital risked fueling public discontent. He craved popularity, not only to bolster his regime but also to assist his dream of becoming president of the Republic.[60] Hence he constructed a populist façade, behind which he could do his deals and, as he felt to be his due, enrich himself.

In the arsenal of the populist, the heaviest weaponry is rhetorical. So it was with Maximino. At his investiture—staged at the Variedades movie theater, where more could attend than at the state Congress—the governor declared: "I desire to be in direct contact with the masses, so that the efforts of my government coincide with popular aspirations, which have known how to encourage the revolutionary movement of the country." He called for unity and harmony among classes. His government would emphasize efficiency, firmness, honesty.[61]

Atencingo was another site for grandstanding, at the act of expropriation that December. "We come to redistribute, not to destroy," Maximino announced, with comfortable use of the royal we, the confetti sparkling on his shoulders. Thousands of cheering millworkers and peons had gathered at Jenkins's mill to hear him. "I will be the guardian," he told them. "I will not permit that either you or the person who'll supply you with credit [Jenkins] fail in your contracted obligations, because what is most important is the future that the fruit of labor forms." (The rhetoric was typical Maximino: reassuring and exhorting, with a substratum of threat.) The next day's headline ran: "The Promises Made by the Revolution to the People are Fulfilled, Yesterday in Atencingo." Maximino would milk this "revolutionary act" for years to come, ensuring it featured as a singular achievement in each of his State of the State addresses.[62]

Maximino's rhetoric, in classically populist fashion, was often visual. He had his investiture filmed, and five months after he took office the reel began to tour the state's main towns. At his annual birthday celebration each August, he invited the public to a free *fiesta brava* at the city's new 20,000-seat bullring. On occasion one of the attractions was Maximino himself, atop a white stallion, dressed in masculine *charro* finery, taking part in the bullfights as a lance-wielding *rejoneador*. Before leaving office he would dress up and mount up for the cameras, when a US documentary team came to town.[63]

Another weapon was the edict. Shortly after taking office, the governor announced that the College of Puebla, which traced its founding to 1587, would become the University of Puebla. The name sounded suitably modern, but there was little difference. The state paid for a swimming pool and a billiard hall, and Maximino donated forty horses so the students could learn "the healthy sport" of polo. As rector Maximino imposed a reactionary crony, Manuel L. Márquez. Far from a proponent of liberal education, Márquez acted as legal adviser to the local chapter of the Gold Shirts, Mussolini-inspired nationalists who called for the expulsion of Jews and eradication of communists. After a year of student outrage, Maximino felt obliged to dump Márquez; indeed he publicly humiliated him.[64]

Public works are a time-honored tool of the populist, for their ribbon-cutting photo ops and their vote-pulling power. Though Maximino raised the state's tax haul and pledged large amounts to new schools and highways, his scope of action chafed against its still-paltry levels—and against those kleptocratic tendencies that would earn him the nickname "Mr. Fifteen Percent."[65] Often where there was a shortfall, Maximino had a helping hand from Jenkins.

Sometimes he made donations, as with the continuation of his school-building program in the Matamoros Valley. After he once incurred damage to his car on the crude track from Puebla to Izúcar de Matamoros, Jenkins had his Atencingo employees help lay a proper highway.

Other times he made loans. The son of auto dealer O'Farrill would recall: "Jenkins helped Maximino a lot. ... When times were tough and the state's resources were low, Maximino would say to Jenkins, 'Look, can you help me out?' And Jenkins would make him a loan." The nephew of a former councilor of Tehuacán would relate how the councilors once approached Maximino about a new sewage system. The governor approved the project but said no funds were available. "However," he added, "if you walk round the corner and visit Don Guillermo Jenkins, perhaps he can help you." So the delegates did just that. They convinced Jenkins of the project's viability and signed their names as guarantors of the loan. Puebla congressional records confirm that Maximino approved a Tehuacán sewage project, funded by a loan, in 1938. Jenkins's lending for specific municipal projects would continue under Maximino's successors.[66]

In key respects, Maximino's reign recalled that of Leonides Andreu Almazán, Puebla's best-remembered populist of the left. A matter of style as much as of substance, populist leadership, while vocally privileging "the people" over "the elite," seeks to satisfy everyone.[67] It papers over the gaps between promises and results with more promises. Like Cárdenas, Almazán championed the poor, above all in the mass granting of land. Like the postwar president Miguel Alemán, Maximino embraced capitalists and defanged the unions, while still claiming to represent the Revolution.

Where for Almazán populism had served like a fortress in a warring province, for Maximino it was a wall behind which to hide his allegiances. Yet the bricks in each construction were similar.

Both governors proclaimed a commitment to education, and both permitted new schools to be named for them while still in office.[68] Both men trumpeted their support for workers and peasants, although Maximino was much more successful in co-opting the CROM and dividing the FROC than was Almazán in fostering the Emiliano Zapata Peasant Confederation. Both granted substantial tracts of farmland—much more in Almazán's case, but Maximino's bluster obscured the gulf. And both offered protections, in exchange for financial support, to Jenkins.

Perhaps the greatest difference was of conviction. Almazán believed in the Revolution. He tried to enact the pledges of its constitution. Maximino believed in his own advancement; enacting any leftist program was but a means to an end. In the rhetoric of the day, any real or suspected opponent of Maximino could be tarred, with an Orwellian flourish, as "reactionary" or "antirevolutionary." The greatest reactionary was Maximino himself. His program of repression, his use of co-optation, his favoring of business elites, and his profiteering in partnership with them altogether recall Puebla's final boss of the Porfirian era, Mucio Martínez.

To a conservative American, both Almazán and Maximino were satraps to be tolerated. Jenkins was closer to Maximino, but he cozied up to both to get things done. "Maximino was the biggest son-of-a-bitch I've ever known," he later told a son-in-law. The need to flatter and accommodate was especially true with Maximino, since his ego and his power were colossal, and he would handpick his two successors. But if Jenkins had stayed in Tennessee, his experience may have differed little. Memphis, for example, was under the heel of Boss Ed Crump, who having served as mayor from 1910 to 1915 remained the puppet master, effectively appointing every incumbent for the next three decades and helping swing governors' races. Like Maximino, Crump ran a corporatist political machine that delivered votes in return for favors. He used populist rhetoric but put business first, aiming to ensure that labor stayed docile and cheap. He had a love of publicity and a taste for graft.[69]

Americans of the day often comforted themselves that whatever the Depression might throw at them, theirs was a strong democracy. Mexico belonged with the fragile states of the southern hemisphere, prone to insurrections and ruled by dictators. Machine politics, vote-rigging, self-enrichment, and political dynasties, all common in the US South (along with some outstanding examples in Chicago, New York, and Boston), gave the lie to that dichotomy.[70] The major difference was that in Mexico the strongman tended to be the governor rather than the mayor. Autocratic governors did emerge, most famously Huey Long in Louisiana, but the US petty dictator was more commonly found at City Hall. Mexican mayors were relatively feeble, although Maximino would bear testy witness to an exception.

JENKINS WORRIED ABOUT his proximity to Maximino, but he chose to swim with the current. One who refused to do so was the general's former campaign ally—and Jenkins's closest friend—Dr. Sergio Guzmán.[71] During his two years as mayor, Guzmán charted his own course. While previous regents had bilked the treasury for kickbacks to the governor, Guzmán insisted on rectitude: it would protect his name and reduce Maximino's dipping into the till. After a year of building revenues and effecting public works, Guzmán became the first mayor in Puebla City history to request a federal audit. The Finance Ministry gave him a glowing review.[72]

Maximino still considered Guzmán a friend. That first summer of their parallel tenure, they had traveled together to their home town of Teziutlán for a trade fair, where both showed off their bullfighting skills to great applause.[73] But the doctor's refusal to concur that "to the victors belong the spoils" irked the general no end.

Maximino was in the habit of giving jewelry to his paramours and then sending the receipt to City Hall. Guzmán, choosing his battles, tolerated this behavior to a point, yet matters came to a head toward the end of his mayoral term, in January 1939. Maximino was hotly in pursuit of the Colombian starlet Sofía Álvarez (soon to appear as "Velvet Rosa" in the Mexican picture *Cabaret Fodder*).[74] After Maximino presented Álvarez with a diamond necklace, Guzmán received a bill for 50,000 pesos. He refused to pay it.

Two things induced in Maximino an erratic behavior that to some observers bordered on psychosis: money and women. The next day, Guzmán found that his car had been stolen from outside his office. Later, one of Maximino's goons told him he had orders to kill him, but he was tipping him off because he held him in high regard. That evening Guzmán stole away, and his letter of resignation appeared in the morning paper. "Special circumstances affecting my health impel me to withdraw," he wrote; "I need to absent myself from this city to undergo a medical treatment of some duration."[75]

There would be no more pushback from City Hall. Soon after, Maximino hosted a banquet for Fulgencio Batista, head of the Cuban armed forces, and awarded him the keys to the city.[76] The next mayor of Puebla would be Maximino's brother Rafael.

A few years later, as minister of communications, Maximino invited Guzmán for dinner. The general was in a jocular mood that night. He could not resist ribbing the doctor about their contretemps of 1939: "You're lucky you're not six feet underground!"

"Oh, I don't believe you, Maximino," Guzmán graciously replied.

Enter Espinosa: Adventures in Film

In the summer of 1938, Jenkins embarked on an adventure that would make him richer than ever, perhaps richer than anyone in Mexico. He agreed with three Puebla entrepreneurs to invest in a trio of start-ups, each designed to catch a mounting wave of public interest in motion pictures. Within a decade, Jenkins would be the single most powerful force in the Mexican film industry, by then enjoying a golden age of high output and awards at festivals. While most film fans were likely oblivious, Jenkins came to own the country's largest collection of theaters, to indirectly control film distribution, and to oversee much of the financing for production. His dominance would cause insiders great distress. Filmmakers would curse the surge of foreign films that his theaters seemed to favor and lament their own meager budgets. Rival theater owners would claim they were being muscled out of the business by a Machiavellian Yankee.

The year 1938 is not remembered as an opportune time for investors, especially for those US and British firms that lorded over Mexico's oil industry. Recession in the United States was having a knock-on effect, and Cárdenas's wildly popular act of oil expropriation—Mexico's "economic emancipation," as the president disingenuously termed it—exacerbated an existing problem of capital flight, forcing a 30 percent devaluation of the peso. Further, per later polls conducted by Nelson Rockefeller, Franklin Roosevelt's Latin America point man, the land and oil conflicts of the Cárdenas era led to Mexicans becoming "predominantly anti-American."[77]

But the year still held its attractions. The president, worried about a prolonged recession ahead of the 1940 election, felt compelled to comfort investors. He eased off on land seizures and reduced permitted strikes. Proposals for new taxes were watered down, and an infant-industry decree permitted five-year tax breaks to business of all sizes. Furthermore,

Cárdenas increased deficit-spending to rekindle the economy in Keynesian fashion, stepping up his road-building, electrification, irrigation, and agricultural credit programs. One could tell the positive impact on consumers from how much beer they were drinking. Despite the various economic woes, national beer production rose in 1938 by a relatively healthy 7 percent; in 1939, it rose 24 percent.[78] For businessmen with cash to spare and strong nerves, 1938 was a year of opportunity.

Movies were opportunity par excellence. Driven by Hollywood talkies— three-quarters of all films released in Mexico during the 1930s—theaters were banking enormous receipts. Even though dedicated movie palaces were still few, Mexico was almost as large a market for Hollywood as Canada. Production was also enticing, as it advanced toward industrial levels. In 1936, Fernando de Fuentes's rural musical melodrama *Allá en el Rancho Grande* (*Out on the Big Ranch*) had become a genre-establishing blockbuster; in turn it was Mexico's first big cinematic export, a hit from Cuba to Argentina. In 1937, cashing in on this "ranchland comedy," producers cranked out another twenty like it.[79]

For a reactionary like Jenkins, *Rancho Grande* was further alluring for its departure from the social realism and revolutionary themes that occupied filmmakers over the previous few years. Anticipating the paternalistic and nostalgic strain of nationalism that became a mass-media staple from the 1940s, *Rancho Grande* celebrated a mythical Mexico in which landowners were benevolent patriarchs and peasants knew their place. In a dig at the radicals of the Cárdenas regime, the hero's communism-spouting stepfather was a clownish drunk.[80] Such traditionalist escapism would persist as a mainstay of Mexican cinema until the 1960s, when these pictures would gain renewed influence through primetime television.

When Jenkins came to be bitten by the film bug is not known, but as early as 1921 he had written to United Artists, offering to handle Mexican distribution of their pictures. Sometime in 1938, Sergio Guzmán introduced Jenkins to his brother Roberto, recently back from Hollywood. Roberto had gone to Los Angeles as private secretary to the exiled Adolfo de la Huerta and found success acting in Spanish-language features. Following a face-lift that went awry, Roberto returned to Mexico, looking to work behind the camera. He pitched a project called *Alma Norteña*, and Jenkins agreed to back it. Released the following year, it proved a modest hit. A number of older Pueblans, teenagers in the 1940s, remember Jenkins as an avid moviegoer, his presence in the theater made known to all by his booming guffaws during comedies.[81]

DIMINUTIVE BUT DYNAMIC, Manuel Espinosa Yglesias led the most established of the investor groups that approached Jenkins. Four brothers, of which Manuel was the second, they had inherited a movie business from their father, who had used to play chess with Jenkins.[82] The Espinosas had dominated film exhibition in Puebla, owning a bona fide movie palace called the Variedades and leasing a second venue. They had theaters in another four cities and a distribution company that serviced several states. But with the 1930s came a rival: the Cinema Guerrero, built by a well-connected Basque immigrant, Jesús Cienfuegos, in a plum location on Puebla's central plaza. By 1938 a nationwide boom in theaters was starting. Manuel saw that the distributors in Mexico City were supplying their better product to the larger circuits, so long-term survival necessitated expansion. The Espinosas began building a third theater in Puebla, the Coliseo, but they felt that by the time they had recouped their investment and were ready to expand further, the game might well be over.

Manuel and his brothers needed capital, and fast, so they sought out their late father's friend. They knew that Jenkins was already exploring the theater business, in tandem with two other partners. One was Cienfuegos, for whom he financed new venues in neighboring Veracruz. The other was the shopkeeper and alcohol merchant who had come to his aid during his 1934 arrest: Gabriel Alarcón.[83]

Jenkins was sufficiently impressed with Espinosa's record and vision to partner with him and his brothers in a new company, Ultra-Cinemas de México. The two parties constituted the firm by each committing 50,000 pesos, and Jenkins also pledged a loan of 1.2 million pesos.[84] Years later, Espinosa would recall a follow-up meeting, in which he and one of his brothers asked Jenkins for a portion of that loan. It was for the first new theater they were going to build, in Guadalajara. To his great surprise, Jenkins handed them 300,000 pesos without requiring they sign a receipt. "When we asked him what we should sign, he told us, 'Nothing. If you are capable of stealing that money, you are not your father's sons.'"

Repeatedly Jenkins made loans to men he knew he could trust, often the sons of friends. His dismissal of paperwork demonstrated his below-the-radar approach to joint ventures. He could not be taxed on what he had not put his name to, and as a US citizen he continued to fear that a leftward shift in political winds could prompt expropriations. Jenkins became a routine user of so-called *prestanombres* (literally, name-lender) arrangements, registering almost all of his assets under other peoples' names, often those of his private secretary and his accountant.[85]

Manuel Espinosa later grew concerned about the imbalance of capital in Ultra-Cinemas and the brake this might put on expansion, should the Espinosas be obliged to repay Jenkins's loan before committing fresh funds to new construction. Manuel proposed that the family roll its existing brace of Puebla theaters into a new company and offer Jenkins a 50 percent stake in it to clear their debts. Jenkins agreed. He thus became part-owner of a promising circuit of theaters, in addition to those he co-owned with Cienfuegos and Alarcón.

Soon the trade press was paying attention. In January 1939, the US show-business bible *Variety* reported on Jenkins's financing of five provincial theaters. In an April 1940 story on Mexico's construction boom, it highlighted "William Oscar Jenkins, reputed to be the wealthiest American in Mexico." Two months later, the Espinosas opened their theater in Guadalajara, a 4,500-seat palace named after their Puebla flagship, the Variedades. With two balconies and state-of-the-art air-conditioning, it was by far the city's premier venue.[86] Manuel's brothers opted to leave the business after a couple of years, which forced Manuel to propose that Jenkins buy the family out. Jenkins countered by lending him the funds to buy out his brothers. So, by 1942, Jenkins and Manuel Espinosa were practically on their own as partners, the Pueblan gradually repaying him from his share of the profits. After the Atencingo expropriation, Jenkins always insisted on having at least one local partner in his businesses. His accord with Manuel afforded him a *prestanombres* who could shield his ownership role from public view.

Jenkins's diversified approach to theater building was evidently another clever ploy. His three partners were driven to compete, and hence excel, by virtue of the fact that they despised each other.[87] Social provenance was part of it. Though Espinosa would later cultivate a Horatio Alger image, he was an old-money Pueblan. His father had been a Porfirian mayor as well as an owner of hotels and of half the stock of the telephone company. The family home was a neoclassical mansion on the downtown thoroughfare of Reforma Street.[88]

Alarcón hailed from a remote village in Hidalgo with an indigenous name. At fourteen, he had journeyed to Puebla City to seek his fortune. When he hopped off the bus, his capital consisted of three years of schooling and a bundle of clothes tied up with string. But he also carried a sackful of energy, and his curly-haired good looks attracted many a glance from the city's high-society daughters. He worked in an uncle's hardware store and before long struck out on his own. By the time he was twenty, a newspaper ad for his grocery could boast of its numerous clientele. Three years later, he was prominent enough for his promise not to raise prices in the face of recession to make front-page news. Rumor later had it that he was Jenkins's smuggler-in-chief. Some said it was he who handled liquor shipments to the United States.[89]

Cienfuegos was a *gachupín*, as Mexicans derisively termed Spaniards. He had made two small fortunes already, one as a licensed vendor of pulque to Puebla's cantinas, a dozen of which he owned, the other on commission as a tax collector (while avoiding taxes himself). Not only were such pursuits socially gauche, they required political favor.[90]

The mutual loathing was especially true of Espinosa, sly and well-spoken, and Alarcón, brash and bearish. Within months of Alarcón opening his Cinema Reforma in August 1939, *La Opinión* ran articles praising his theater and deriding Espinosa's, a bias explained by the fact that Alarcón advertised in the paper while Espinosa did not, and by the likelihood that Alarcón was paying for these stories. The first of them pilloried Espinosa's Coliseo, which opened not long after Alarcón's Reforma, alleging its temperature fluctuated so severely that numerous patrons, "known to be honorable," were complaining that the place caused them breathing problems. "Do You Want Pneumonia?" sang the headline, "Go to the Cinema Coliseo."[91]

THE ARRANGEMENT WITH Cienfuegos, Espinosa, and Alarcón completed a shift into delegation. Jenkins had employed managers before, such as his brother-in-law at La Corona and Pérez at Atencingo, but he had remained a hands-on executive and the majority or exclusive owner. The year he entered the film business he turned sixty. Having partner-managers working under him (just as he himself had worked back in 1906), ensured that Jenkins could hand off day-to-day oversight. He could focus on arranging the financing, dealing with Sáenz at the sugar cartel, politicking with Maximino, and overseeing his other assets. The partnership model he used with his theaters was a deliberate attempt to grow businesses quickly by giving his associates a vested interest in their success.

Jenkins's other assets were numerous. In part he was diversifying in response to Cardenist policy: until 1937 or so with the threats of its radicalism, as of mid-1938 with its recession-driven goodwill toward investors. But there were also opportunities in the fragility of new businesses, the vulnerability of old ones, and, as in the case of O'Farrill's Packard plant, the rise of friends into Puebla's pro-Maximino elite.

In 1935, he bought into a bank. At the request of prominent Mexico City banker Salvador Ugarte, Jenkins stepped in to save Puebla's fraud-crippled Banco Mercantil. This was an affiliate of Ugarte's Banco de Comercio. The major stake that Jenkins acquired in this local bank would eventually lead to his becoming one of Mexico's top financiers.[92]

That same year, Jenkins took a majority stake in La Trinidad, a midsize textile mill in neighboring Tlaxcala. Here again was Jenkins gaining the upper hand over the Porfirian set that once had snubbed him. La Trinidad belonged to the Morales Conde family, who by the end of the Revolution were indebted to the American to the sum of 300,000 pesos. Given the parlous state of the local textile sector for much of the 1920s and 1930s, it was probably a foreclosing of that loan that gave Jenkins the firm's ownership. When the company was reconstituted, it was Jenkins's most regular *prestanombres*, his accountant Manuel Sevilla and secretary Manuel Cabañas, whose names appeared in the Property Registry.[93]

The two trusty employees appeared as shareholders in further textile companies. These likely involved further foreclosures; prior to the outbreak of war, there was little reason for Jenkins to have looked to return to this low-rent sector, which was beset by labor troubles and, with the local reluctance to reinvest profits, hampered by outmoded machinery. The first was a joint venture with another US expatriate, Simon Utay, a Jewish textile engineer from Dallas; this firm owned the midsize San Juan Xaltepec mill, near Tehuacán. Another was La Moderna, SA (1938), with investors including Indalecio Canteli, a Spanish immigrant who became Jenkins's point man in the mill town of Atlixco. A third was Textil Poblana, SA (1943), in union with Edmundo Cobel, his favorite tennis partner.[94]

The biggest foreclosure of all involved La Concepción, a large factory in Atlixco with a workforce of nearly seven hundred. That town's oldest textile mill, it was acquired during the Porfirian era by Angel Díaz Rubín, father of Pedro, whose borrowing from Jenkins had led to the family's loss of Atencingo. Perhaps Pedro never learned his lesson, for by the 1930s he was in debt to Jenkins again. He and his siblings had taken a 200,000-peso loan from the Bank of Montreal to keep La Concepción afloat, but it was Jenkins, as one of the local branch's largest clients, who had approved the credit. The Bank of Montreal closed its branch in 1932, at which point Jenkins persuaded the bankers to let him retain the Díaz Rubín loan. In 1935 he moved to foreclose it, apparently sealing the takeover during the Maximino years.[95]

In total, Jenkins found himself owner or co-owner of at least five mills by the outbreak of World War II. That cataclysm, causing a huge overseas demand for military uniforms, would give Puebla's risk-averse textile barons—Jenkins soon among them, growing similarly averse to risk—an immense profiteering boost. Complacency and stagnation were almost bound to follow.

Although Jenkins was responding to Cardenist policy and opportune openings, it seems he also sensed a broader zeitgeist. In 1938, with land reform slowing and infant mortality falling, urban growth was about to soar. Each of Jenkins's new ventures catered to a populace concentrated in cities. Thanks to union-won wage gains, workers were more able to buy clothes and go to the movies. An expanding middle class, much of it salaried by a ballooning federal bureaucracy, was more able to open bank accounts and buy automobiles. Jenkins never lost his love for farming, but he anticipated Mexico's evolution from an agricultural society into an industrial one, having witnessed the same process in Tennessee. His fortune would grow with it.

Business remained a highly political pursuit, however. Jenkins's ability to diversify with equanimity, cultivate a legally dubious monopoly in Puebla film exhibition, force the foreclosure of bad loans, and retain his lucrative mill at Atencingo after facing its confiscation—all this owed much to Maximino, who in turn controlled the state judiciary. Throughout Maximino's term, their alliance typified the governor's dealings with Puebla's industrial elite.[96]

Jenkins, though he never surrendered US citizenship, was an integral part of that elite. Like contemporaries who singled him out as an exploitative gringo, posthumous accounts have sometimes missed this point. Film historians, for example, have cast Jenkins as an agent of US foreign policy and "Hollywood interests." Such inferences are misleading. By 1940, he had spent thirty-nine years in Mexico. He had forged high-level friendships with politicians, businessmen, even the Catholic Church, friendships often involving a degree of financial dependence, with Jenkins as creditor, partner, or maker of donations. He had reinvested almost all of his sugar profits in Mexican ventures. Though he had functioned as a consular agent until 1930, he retained little contact with officialdom; memos dispatched by the State Department during the Atencingo affair were an exception and had little apparent impact. There is no evidence of his partnering with US interests, let alone the Hollywood studios, in the film industry.[97]

Even socially, Jenkins preferred the company of Mexicans. Simply put, he was too savvy to let himself be pigeon-holed as another Yankee investor and too well connected locally to need much help from Uncle Sam.

The Ávila Camacho Fiefdom

When Cárdenas designated Manuel Ávila Camacho as his successor, brother Maximino was not exactly happy. "Manuel is a piece of steak with eyes!" he scoffed of his portly sibling. Maximino took offense that, as an eldest son, he had been passed over for the job, especially since he thought himself greater presidential material. He had taken the scorpion's nest that was Puebla and pacified it. Manuel, by contrast, was a safety-first bureaucrat who had never been elected for anything. Maximino was not alone in his slight regard for his brother. Jenkins, having committed as a campaign donor, came away from his first meal with Manuel thinking he lacked caliber. A US journalist noted that Manuel had all the charisma of a slab of halibut.[98]

On calming down, however, Maximino came to see the nomination as a blessing in disguise. Whom else would Manuel handpick in turn than Maximino himself?

Once Manuel became candidate for the Party of the Mexican Revolution (the PRM, as the ruling PNR had recently become), the influence of William Jenkins began to be felt nationally. In part this owed to the fact that during the campaign of 1939–1940, Jenkins made the future president a whopping loan of $400,000.[99]

The presidential race was closely and harshly contested. Rival candidate Juan Andreu Almazán, brother of Leónides, enjoyed deep popular support. This made Maximino so nervous that the first Puebla newspaper editor to declare support for Almazán was murdered within days; few doubted the identity of the mastermind. Further murders peppered the campaign, notably so in Puebla but also nationwide. Almazán's eventual loss in the July 1940 poll was widely held to be rigged, a belief affirmed for many by a ludicrous lopsidedness in the tally: 2,476,641 votes for Ávila Camacho against 151,101 for Almazán.[100]

The closeness of the contest on the ground—in rallies, in the murder of activists—suggests again that an Ávila Camacho's access to plentiful campaign funds was crucial. Financial considerations also smoothed matters afterward. Had Almazán called for an uprising, many would have joined him. Instead he retired to Acapulco. He had made a dubious acquisition of seafront real estate, on which he was building the luxurious Hotel Papagayo, and Cárdenas and Ávila Camacho opted not to question the project. As one insider put it, Almazán was too "fat, sick, and rich" to chance a rebellion.[101]

There were, in a sense, two Ávila Camacho dominions, and Jenkins supported both. In the short run, Manuel and Maximino lorded over the federal landscape in the first half of the 1940s. Not long after his term was up in Puebla, Maximino imposed himself on the Ministry of Communications, ousting the incumbent minister at gunpoint.

In the long run, Puebla endured what came to be known as the Ávila Camacho fiefdom, as Maximino's *cacique*-like hold was perpetuated by his clique for several decades. Appointees of Maximino while he was governor, whether serving as local lawmakers (in theory elected but in most cases hand-picked), as judges, or in some other capacity, would yield another six governors, ruling consecutively to 1969. The clique also included an ambitious lawyer who, when only in his twenties, served as head of Puebla's Arbitration Board and then as a judge on the state Superior Court. This man was another future president, Gustavo Díaz Ordaz.[102]

THROUGH THEIR INTERDEPENDENCE with Puebla's state government, Jenkins and his peers had played a decisive role in shifting it to the right. It was only from 1933, with the accession of the pro-business Mijares, that Puebla's governors managed to serve out their terms. Under Maximino, *agraristas* were kept at bay, unions defanged, banditry suppressed. Deference to the governor prevailed. (The electoral season of 1939–1940 was the exception, when grassroots support for the Almazán brothers could not be contained except by violence.) Maximino's political machine was so dominant, future gubernatorial polls went all but uncontested for decades. Therefore, with few rivals, rebels, or radicals to worry about, the state-capital alliance became a series of symbioses of mere convenience. For business leaders, matters of need became matters of privilege. Monopolies were permitted and cossetted; fewer and fewer strikes were ruled legal; a real-estate boom favored the connected few. For governors, money-making became standard practice, via investment with cronies or mere embezzlement.[103]

Maximino had Puebla under his jackboot. So Jenkins, whatever his distaste for the general's methods, had much less need for the time-consuming rings of protection he had woven around Atencingo in the

1920s. He could devote himself more fully to his portfolio. For the governor, his largely covert alliance with Jenkins helped him look "revolutionary," in being better able to bring tangible benefits to the people, while allowing him quite a bit of business on the side, as did his friendships with Gabriel Alarcón and the Lebanese immigrant Miguel Abed. These crony relationships harkened back to the Porfirian era, but they also offered a prototype, if a crude one, for a more entrepreneurial abuse of authority that became widespread at the federal level under President Miguel Alemán, after 1946.[104]

Bonds between Puebla's business and political elites also showed how provincial alliances could influence the federal government. A number of conservative bastions emerged in the late 1930s: in Veracruz, Nuevo León, Sonora, San Luis Potosí, and elsewhere. The strength of business-backed governors such as Puebla's Maximino and San Luis's Gonzalo N. Santos, all well poised to manipulate vote-counting in the 1940 poll, helps explain Cárdenas's pragmatic decision to back the centrist Ávila Camacho as his successor, rather than the leftist early favorite Francisco Múgica, the president's mentor, friend, and communications minister.[105] And so provincial alliances between state and capital help explain the rightward drift in Mexico's national politics. In bolstering regimes that favored magnates and monopolies, and, in helping to deny voters the chance to hold any politician accountable, these alliances played a key role in perpetuating inequalities.

The state-capital alliance was increasingly a marriage of convenience nationwide. The financial imperative that had driven the state to pact with business elites diminished, as did the need of Jenkins and his class for protections from revolutionary radicalism. As late as Ávila Camacho's presidential campaign, the ruling party could argue that its continuity in office was necessary to fend off the rebellions led by malcontent generals that had plagued Mexico for two decades, most recently the revolt of Saturnino Cedillo in 1938. But as of 1940, neither Almazán nor any other general would rebel, and the economy was about to receive an enormous boost through US investment during World War II. The PRM, later renamed the PRI, would enjoy another sixty years of rule. Certainly it faced challenges, most immediately the mounting masses who left the countryside for the cities and proved ready to strike for better pay; the state would recruit the private sector to help contain them. Viewed objectively, however, the old symbiotic imperatives had receded.

The fruits of the marriage between state and capital would include a culture of self-enrichment among office-holders and a concentration of wealth among a few hundred families. The middle decades of Mexico's twentieth century are conventionally remembered as a "golden age" of prosperity and urban comforts, especially for the new middle classes.[106] Yet the greatest beneficiaries were a tiny class of well-connected captains of industry.

Mining the Golden Age
of Mexican Cinema

*In Puebla everything happened in the arcades, from court-
ships to assassinations.*

ÁNGELES MASTRETTA, *Tear This Heart Out* (1985)

Chronicle of a Stabbing

It was dusk on the second day in January and Jesús Cienfuegos was chatting outside his Puebla theater.[1] The Spaniard struck his usual jaunty pose,
leaning against a pillar, hands together behind his back.

"How's the year looking, Don Jesús?" asked his friend Samuel Kurián.

"Well, it seems the cash won't flow. Hardly anyone came to the bullfights yesterday. I lost 20,000 pesos!"

Cienfuegos was one of few Pueblans who could afford to lose such a
sum in a day's dealings. If business were down at his bullring, he had his
movie palace and pulque bars to rely on, along with his new theaters in
Veracruz, where he was partnered with William Jenkins.

The pillar against which the Spaniard was leaning belonged to the
arcade that hemmed City Hall. This handsome construction leased part of
its ground floor to the popular Cinema Guerrero, and it was Cienfuegos's
custom to stand outside in the evening, watching his customers arrive and
conversing with one or other of Puebla's ascendant bourgeoisie. From where
he stood, he could survey the trees and fountains of the plaza, three sides
of it lined by arcades, and facing him was the grand seventeenth-century
cathedral. At this hour, the colonial heart of Puebla was echoing with the
sounds of a modern weekday winding down. The screech of a rolled-up
metal storefront, pulled from its awning to be fastened at the ground. The
voices of American tourists, debating which restaurant they might choose
for dinner. The honk of a Packard, its chauffeur taking his lady home after

shopping. Students, beckoned by the posters of the Guerrero, discussing if they had enough pennies to see *All This and Heaven, Too.*

The year was 1941, a good time to be an immigrant businessman in Mexico. The xenophobia of the 1930s had subsided. The economy was booming. After the prickly nationalism of the Cárdenas years, there was a conciliatory moderate in the presidential chair. The Spanish liquor merchant-cum-impresario and the Jewish clothier had ample reason to view the new year with optimism, the more so given that the rule of a venal and violent governor would soon be a thing of the past. In four weeks Gonzalo Bautista would be sworn in, a moderate successor to Maximino Ávila Camacho.

At about 6:30 PM, a man rushed up to Cienfuegos and, exclaiming "Happy New Year!" he made as if to embrace him. Instead, the man stabbed him in the chest and the stomach with a dagger. Don Jesús, his hands clutching his abdomen, tumbled face-first to the ground, sprawling at Kurián's feet. The first stab had severed his aorta, and his blood seeped out from under him. By then, the assailant had fled; a tall brown man in a hat and jacket, he ran off through the crowded arcade. Kurián, transfixed for several seconds in shock, began to cry for help. He managed to flag down a taxi. Cienfuegos was breathing and might still be saved. Hauled out of his dark pool, his robust constitution just keeping him alive, the victim was whisked to a nearby hospital. Fifteen minutes later, Cienfuegos was dead.

Leads were promising, had the police chosen to follow them. There were witnesses. The dagger was a Finnish import and still bore its price tag. The killer's jacket, dark gray and felt-lined, was of a brand rare in Puebla, and an official from the state attorney's office claimed to know the murderer by sight, having often seen him wearing it. But there was little effort at investigation. No one was ever arrested. The press declined to speculate. Not until forty years later did the old guard of Puebla chroniclers begin to recount the events of that day.

For decades following the Revolution, guns abounded. Despite confiscation campaigns, homicide rates involving firearms remained high. And yet Cienfuegos was stabbed. If a shooting offers near certainty of death, a stabbing offers more satisfaction to the mastermind: the thought that the victim will die in agony, not in an abrupt flash; the idea that, as he clasps his hemorrhaging body he will have time to rue the choices that led to his demise, time to realize that, had he only played by the rules of the game, he would not have left his children orphans and his wife a widow. Should the victim by chance survive, such messages would lose none of their clarity. A stabbing speaks of lengthier premeditation, of resentment building to boiling point.

Two men resented Cienfuegos very much. One was Maximino. Back when starting to campaign for governor, the general had included a request to Cienfuegos among his entreaties for donations. Citing the constitutional bar on foreigners meddling in politics, the Spaniard declined. The following year Cienfuegos unveiled his Puebla Bullring: a wonder in reinforced concrete, able to seat 20,000. This too drew Maximino's attention. The bullring would form the symbolic showroom of his governorship: a place for his saint's day celebrations, a forum for the election of his Carnival Queen daughter.[2] To the governor it seemed only right that he should own it himself. Cienfuegos, proud entrepreneur that he was, refused to sell.

Shortly after Maximino took office, signs emerged that the governor was pressing Cienfuegos to change his mind. His legislature began investigating his lease for the Cinema Guerrero, where he was known to be making a killing. It held a twenty-five-year tax exemption that the Spaniard had somehow procured from City Hall. The Congress unearthed all manner of irregularities, but it did not vote to rescind the tax exemption for three months, time enough for Cienfuegos to weigh his options.[3]

On the failure of this tactic, the governor took to harassment. Inspectors would visit the theater and the bullring, issuing fines for infractions real and imagined. An evening's double-bill might be cancelled. Cienfuegos might have difficulty assembling a bullfighting slate. In May 1938, the entire Congress addressed a petition to President Cárdenas, asking that Cienfuegos be expelled from the country on grounds of illicit commerce, tax evasion, and various other sins. They gave the story to the press, adding Cienfuegos was making donations to the fascist General Franco of Spain. For good measure, they had the Guerrero closed for a week, on "safety" grounds. Later Cienfuegos was subjected to a federal audit.[4] In 1939, the Spaniard had the temerity to screen the documentary Natalidad (Birthrate), which promised to "reveal the secrets of conception and birth." Maximino answered the outrage of the Catholic Ladies Association by confiscating the box-office take and briefly shuttering the theater again.

Cienfuegos soon had another enemy. Gabriel Alarcón became a rival that year, with his Cinema Reforma. After its splashy opening it failed to turn a profit, putting Alarcón in danger of defaulting on his loan from Jenkins. The problem was that Cienfuegos and Manuel Espinosa Yglesias had tied up the supply of the Hollywood distributors. Espinosa would later say that Jenkins told each of them to share some pictures with Alarcón and that, while he acceded, Cienfuegos refused. To Espinosa's surprise, Cienfuegos counter-proposed that the two of them join forces against the American; the Spaniard railed at the interest rates Jenkins was charging and alleged the American's aim was to own all of Puebla's theaters. According to a chronicler, meanwhile, Alarcón proposed a deal to Cienfuegos: since Espinosa was dominant in Puebla the two of them could redress the balance by coordinating their business. Cienfuegos, whose theaters in other cities already gave him commercial leverage, rejected the offer.

So Alarcón, the story goes, complained to his friend Maximino, making sure to pique his envy. The governor replied, "I'm going to get that *gachupín!*," a remark that might be dismissed as improbable were it not for Maximino's fame as a hothead and a bully.[5] The threat was intended to be overheard, and friends were soon advising Cienfuegos to abandon the Cinema Guerrero. His reply was typically stubborn: "They'll have to take it from me over my dead body."

THE MURDER ACCOMPLISHED, Maximino took the bullring. Or so it is alleged; he was never so cavalier as to register it in his name.[6] But he was typically indiscreet. In the wake of the murder, some wag circulated a joke:*¿Quién es el mejor bombero de Puebla? ¡Max vale no decirlo!* The jest was a pun on the names of victim and suspected mastermind. The question, "Who is the best firefighter in Puebla?" played on Cienfuegos, which literally means one hundred fires. "Better not say," came the reply, except that, punning on the Governor's nickname, *"Más vale. . ."* became the sinister *"Max vale . . ."* It was a joke that, at private lunches with his buddies, Maximino himself liked to tell.[7]

As for the Cinema Guerrero, Alarcón became president and manager of its operating company on February 1. In March, he also assumed the presidency of Cines Unidos, which owned the three Cienfuegos-Jenkins theaters in Veracruz. A few years later, Alarcón took over the bullring too.[8]

Where was Jenkins in all this? In years to come, accusations would surface that it was he who had plotted the murder, driven by designs on the Guerrero. But the accusers seemed unaware that Jenkins and Cienfuegos had been partners.[9] Even if it is true that Cienfuegos was unhappy with their Veracruz joint venture, his alleged expression of fears about a Jenkins takeover sounds dubious, because for many years the American had favored partnerships over outright ownership. He might have given tacit approval to the murder of *agraristas*, rationalizing this as the price of protecting land and jobs, but would he plot the killing of a fellow business-man, a fellow expatriate? Would he do so over a single theater, one whose prestige had been eclipsed by newer venues? The accusations smack of the Jenkins Black Legend.

Jenkins's trespasses, as so often, were less of commission than of omis-sion. Premeditated murder had been committed. As his partner Alarcón swooped to claim the booty, Jenkins could have opted to have nothing to do with it. But the Property Registry shows that when Alarcón assumed the Guerrero, Jenkins's regular frontmen, Manuel Cabañas and Manuel Sevilla, took seats on the company board, a sure sign of the American's presence as a co-owner. Alarcón likely gave him half of the Guerrero's shares, thereby canceling debts to him from the Cinema Reforma. The following year, Alarcón matched Espinosa in the Puebla City market at three theaters apiece, when he added the Colonial, another Jenkins joint venture.[10] Alarcón was becoming a local player of stature, a useful rival to Espinosa. As Jenkins backed them both, he helped develop their mod-est chains of Puebla theaters into a nationwide duopoly that would clutch exhibition and much film production too.

Perhaps Alarcón was guiltless, merely the recipient of a windfall oppor-tunity. But if the stabbing of the Spaniard was Maximino's plot alone, there was no attempt by Jenkins to distance himself. On May 9, 1942, when the general was minister of communications, their relationship acquired new public prominence and symbolic weight. Jenkins joined an impressive assembly of dignitaries at the wedding of his daughter Hilda to the son of industrialist Rómulo O'Farrill. Maximino's brother, the president, was there, as was Governor Bautista. Prior to the church wedding, these men signed as witnesses at the civil ceremony, and so did Jenkins.[11]

This action conferred on Jenkins the exalted status of *compadre*, or inner-circle friend, of Maximino. As a public figure, to invite a man to be one's *compadre*—whether as godfather to a child or witness at a daughter's wedding—was to offer a formal bond of friendship, the bond's closeness exceeded only by its visibility.

The Gringo and the Golden Age

The film monopoly planted under President Ávila Camacho, which would mature under his two successors, was an anomaly and a paradox. Cultivated while local filmmaking was at a creative zenith, yet owned by a US citizen, it seems to contradict the patriotic spirit that the Golden Age of Mexican Cinema embodied. How was a foreigner allowed to gain dominance in a sector that Mexico deemed culturally strategic and symbolic of nationhood? How was this permitted of someone from the United States, whose cultural industries many nations were already straining to keep from swamping their own? And not just any US citizen, but a gringo of great notoriety? How did all this happen within a generation of the Revolution, whose victors had boldly expropriated foreign assets and continued to call themselves "revolutionary"?

These questions point to the true economy of Mexico at mid-century, the arrangements behind the rhetoric. The answers involve elite interdependence. While Jenkins employed great business acumen in building what proved to be his most profitable enterprise, he also used political alliances that allowed his skirting of the law to proceed unchecked. Ávila Camacho engaged in a balancing act: the pursuit of a growth-led, pro-business, US-friendly economic policy, set against a need to let labor score limited victories. Under pressure from the unions, with rapid industrialization causing inflation that in turn eroded wages, he took a high-profile stance in favor of workers at Jenkins's sugar mill and his second-largest textile factory. In exchange, he gave Jenkins free rein to expand his film dominion, allowing him the privileges and exemptions that made a monopoly possible. Of further benefit to Ávila Camacho, by building or improving scores of theaters and helping finance many of the films they screened, Jenkins entertained the people with cheap and often patriotic diversions from daily strife and also eased the adaption of millions of country migrants to city life.

Very likely, Ávila Camacho and Jenkins both felt themselves driven by a parallel imperative: a political need to assimilate rural masses and calm underpaid workers; a financial need to invest in a costly sector without fear of foreign-investment and monopoly laws strictly applied. To a degree, both were acting on behalf of institutions and thus the greater good: the president as the head of a government having to juggle the interests of the usual colliding constituencies, labor and capital, and also the pressures of a wartime alliance with the United States; the businessman on behalf of the Mexican film industry, which needed more theaters in order to be viable and which depended in part on production advances from those theaters.

Yet the symbiosis between the two was as much a matter of individual convenience. It began with the American's illegal campaign loan of 1939, to aid the victory and cement the favor of a friend. It continued with the president turning a blind eye to Jenkins's repeated skirting of the law, sometimes at the cost of his rivals. This was true especially in the film sector. But he also looked away as Jenkins evaded taxes, dodged a price cap on sugar sales and, in breach of the constitution, bought nearly half a million acres of farmland next to the US border.

CONCEPTIONS OF MEXICAN film's Golden Age vary enormously, from a giddy fondness for icons like Pedro Infante and Dolores del Río to a cynicism as to whether it ever occurred. One popular survey traces a span from 1936—year of the ground-breaking *Allá en el Rancho Grande*—until 1965. More commonly, histories define the era as lasting until the late 1950s. But Mexico's best-known film chronicler, Emilio García Riera, offered a more sobering judgment: "It's usual to talk of a Golden Age of Mexican cinema with greater nostalgia than chronological accuracy. If that Age actually existed, it was . . . 1941 to 1945."[12]

The variety of definitions reflects a vagueness as to what exactly was golden about the age. Without a doubt, a slew of mid-century pictures captured the hearts of the country and the imagination of audiences throughout the Americas. The best of them combined popular appeal with durable artistry and won prizes at Cannes and Venice. By output, Mexico hosted the third-biggest film industry in the world, after the United States and India. But historians have conflated the sector as a whole, including its theaters, with the success of Mexican production. "The national cinema evolved and matured into the nation's third-largest industry," goes a typical claim, which ignores how more than half of industry revenues owed to films from Hollywood and Europe.[13] And while "Golden Age" suggests a high level of quantity and quality, those values did not always match. Some films were so shoddy that exhibitors refused to screen them. Production outfits lurched along, unable to attain a Hollywood mode of creative, self-financing efficiency.[14] Annual output would stabilize at one hundred or so features in the 1950s and stay high for another three decades, but chiefly thanks to slim budgets and generic formulas.

Least disputable was the boom in attendance. Film was by far the favorite ticketed entertainment. By 1946, Mexicans were spending eight times as much on movies as on bullfights, the number-two draw.[15] However, the main beneficiary of each box-office peso was the theater owner, who typically retained half, while state and municipal governments took up to 15 percent in taxes. Of the remaining 35 cents, the distribution company might keep 20. That left, at most, a sixth of the ticket price to the filmmakers. Forced to compete with the Hollywood production line and its distribution networks, Mexican films rarely turned a profit; most relied on state subsidies. Rivalry was intense. In 1949, when producers mustered a record 107 releases, they had to compete with 246 imports from Hollywood and 88 from elsewhere.[16]

As moviegoing became the national pastime, the bullion mined during the Golden Age was plentiful, but the vast bulk of it either left the country or entered the pockets of exhibitors—above all, William Jenkins. No one knows how much of his fortune flowed from his theaters, but close witnesses attest that of all his businesses, exhibition was the most lucrative.[17]

Profit distribution was the dirty secret of the Golden Age. It contradicted its egalitarian image, as immortalized on the façade of Mexico City's Insurgentes Theater. Here Cantinflas, the era's best-loved comic, takes money from well-dressed patrons with one hand and gives it to the poor with the other. Most accounts have feted the industry's rich creative side: the pictures and the awards they reaped; the international stars; the directors, writers, cinematographers. They have paid much less attention to film as a business, an enterprise shaped by the jostling interests of financiers and producers, distributors and exhibitors, unions and the state.

Of course, Jenkins did not lend himself to scrutiny. He operated his theaters through hands-on partners, Espinosa and Alarcón. He registered his shares in the names of these and other frontmen, as a safeguard against the US taxman. He counted his cash in the shadows.

From Provincial Players to Monopolists

When Ávila Camacho became president, Mexican cinema was still a cottage industry. Production in 1940 reached just twenty-seven films. Apart from Cantinflas, Jorge Negrete, and Fernando Soler, bankable stars had yet to emerge. There were no Hollywood-style studios capable of hosting more than one shoot at a time. The exhibition sector was booming but fragmented. All this would change during the six years that followed, but contrary to popular belief the state had little to do with it.[18] The Golden Age depended much more on World War II, when a Hollywood slowdown elicited demand for something else, and on the backing of Mexico's business elite.

In December 1941, following several years of government promises to help finance the industry, Ávila Camacho approved the creation of a Film Bank. But this was a largely private-sector bank, the state committing just

10 percent. Ávila Camacho's minimal support for the Film Bank owed something to his fairly laissez-faire philosophy and also to how, thanks to the wartime economic boom, Mexico's captains of industry were flush with cash and private banks brimming with deposits. Those disposed to dabble in filmmaking, like banker Luis Legorreta of Banamex, auto indus- try pioneer Gastón Azcárraga, and Jenkins himself, were wealthy conserva- tives; they had little need either of subsidies or of ideological supervision. Men such as these were the Film Bank's chief backers. Jenkins placed his eldest daughter Elizabeth on the board, and within a couple of years he had acquired a substantial minority stake.[19]

The Film Bank lent 5 million pesos during 1942, helping boost out- put to forty-seven pictures.[20] Soon it began to appeal to Jenkins as a take- over target. But what made it attractive was not its aid in film production (where it often lost money), but its 25 percent stake in the capital's leading theater circuit, the Compañía Operadora de Teatros SA (COTSA); Jenkins already owned 25 percent himself. The brainchild of another US expatri- ate, Theodore Gildred, COTSA was unable to make a profit. It still lost money even after leasing theaters from two other companies to create an unprecedented chain of twenty Mexico City venues, backed by several pri- vate banks and said to control more than half the local box-office take.[21] Still, COTSA offered domination of the capital and a platform for forging a presence nationwide.

According to Manuel Espinosa, who quite unlike his publicity-shy mentor would pen a prideful memoir, there was a danger that another investor might beat Jenkins to buying out the Film Bank. So Espinosa took it upon himself to seek a shareholder willing to sell; he found one in Adolfo Grovas, persuading him to surrender over whiskeys at a cantina. By Espinosa's self-serving account, his deft maneuver gave Jenkins control of both the Film Bank and COTSA. The facts are more complex. COTSA's recent expansion had left the Film Bank's stake at 12.5 percent, so Jenkins needed another 12.5 for 50 percent control. Three other banks held stakes of that size, and the obvious candidate for negotiations was the Banco de Comercio. Here Jenkins did not need Espinosa's help; he had saved its Puebla affiliate from bankruptcy and since become a prominent share- holder in the parent bank. One inside maneuver at a board meeting, we may infer, and the additional 12.5 percent was his. By June 1944, Jenkins was able to replace COTSA's manager with Espinosa. That autumn, Jenkins traded his shares in the Film Bank for further shares in COTSA that were owned by Nacional Financiera (Nafinsa), the state development bank, possibly with a green light from the president. This gave him a clear majority. Rolling their theaters in Puebla, Guadalajara, and elsewhere into the operations of COTSA, Jenkins and Espinosa now ran much the most powerful chain in the country.[22]

The striking matter of the Film Bank/COTSA dealings is their covert nature. The press reported neither takeover, which explains the episodes' absence from film histories. Even the perspicacious *Variety* was kept in the dark, so much so that it later referred to Elizabeth Jenkins (a fixture of the film-industry party circuit) as "probably the top femme exhib in the world," mistaking her father's assets for hers. The stealthy approach suited Jenkins. As a foreigner, his ownership of a bank might raise issues of legality (while Elizabeth was Mexican-born). In June 1944 a presidential decree required that corporations be 51 percent Mexican-owned, putting COTSA itself in a legal gray area, the more so in 1945, when the state categorized motion pictures among sectors that could not obtain an exemption.[23]

Less is known about Jenkins's activities with Gabriel Alarcón, but the pair developed a second powerful circuit. The Jenkins-Alarcón operation focused first on Puebla and Veracruz and then the north. In 1949 it began to catch up with COTSA when it bought an established circuit in Mexico City, and still richer pickings lay ahead. Working with Alarcón, Jenkins applied the same *modus operandi* as with Espinosa. Tackling new markets, the American provided most of the expansion capital, bidding his lieutenants to work toward a fifty/fifty ownership of each holding. They would gradually repay their debt to him from their share of the profits.[24] Importantly, Jenkins established a separate limited-liability company for each market, rather than incorporating everything into COTSA or a single Alarcón-run enterprise. The motive was to minimize tax payments. At the time, and up until 1965, personal income in Mexico was taxed on a schedular rather than a global basis, with earnings divided into separate categories. The rich reported their gains in small fractions, thus lowering their tax exposure.[25]

The Jenkins Group, as the trio came to be known, was said by autumn 1944 to have more than sixty theaters. In 1950, its collection reportedly totaled 220, a figure that likely omits another 100 or so with which it held leases or affiliate relationships. Together, this comprised about a quarter of the national total, not yet a monopoly (nor a monopsony) but big enough to press distributors into favorable terms and to bully operators of smaller chains into selling out.[26]

Movie palaces were a high-stakes business. Beyond the cost of choice real estate, theaters needed to be built to order and then equipped with multiple imported projectors, a sound system, and comfortable seating. In Mexico City, the combined cost for a first-run venue might total $400,000. How Jenkins expanded his collection so quickly no doubt owed somewhat to his status at the Banco de Comercio; insider lending at the time was common and legal.[27] His rapid expansion also owed, ironically, to the loss of his precious land at Atencingo.

Like hundreds of other Americans, Jenkins had filed a claim with the American Mexican Claims Commission, a body set up by both governments to adjudicate land reparations. The commission agreed on a settlement of $40 million, which US officials then apportioned among the claimants. In 1943, after five years of correspondence, Jenkins heard he would receive $2.27 million. It was the second-highest award that the commission made. It also represented a much higher proportion of the sum requested than most other recipients gained, at 62 percent of the claim. The Johnston family, heirs of the Los Mochis sugar estate, got 39 percent. Since Jenkins was as apt to inflate his losses as anyone, what made the difference may well have been an intervening word from his friend President Ávila Camacho.[28]

Jenkins got a further cash boost when he sold the government a 438,000-acre estate in the Mexicali Valley. This was land he had gained in a 1944 trade with Harry Chandler, publisher of the Los Angeles Times. In exchange for Chandler's Colorado River Land Company (CRLC), he had given Chandler the Los Angeles apartment buildings that Elizabeth used to manage, plus $360,000. The CRLC, which had once owned 850,000 acres in the region, had only developed a small part of the estate, but the land offered great potential for cotton. Across the border, in California's Imperial Valley, cotton plantations had flourished once the Colorado was tapped as a source of irrigation. However, Mexico's constitution forbade foreigners from owning land within 100 kilometers of the country's borders.[29]

Jenkins's purchase flagrantly broke the law. An equally odd matter was that he owned the land for just fourteen months, far too short a time to develop it. Why had the government not simply bought the land from Chandler? Very probably the president had tried to do so, and Chandler, resentful over Cárdenas-era expropriations, refused to sell to him. In a time of war, with the United States its key ally, Ávila Camacho could hardly have wished to press the issue against one of the most powerful US press barons. Jenkins, by contrast, would have offered Chandler a higher price, without any affront to his dignity. But why he would buy such a vast estate, in defiance of the law, thus risking public embarrassment to his friend the president?

Jenkins was doing Ávila Camacho another favor. At the president's request, he bought from Chandler in order to sell to the state when both parties found it convenient. Once Chandler died in September 1944, his newspaper was less likely to complain about the maneuver. More to the point, in April 1945 the US Senate ratified a United States–Mexico Water Treaty, which increased Mexican rights to the Colorado River for irrigation use. The value of the Mexicali land rose, making Jenkins confident of a profit when he agreed to sell his tract the following month. Ávila Camacho, in turn, could bask in the fanfare as the long-distrusted CRLC was officially dispossessed and a large acreage of borderland returned to the nation.

In 1946, the financial terms were set: state bank Nafinsa paid Jenkins $2.1 million for the CRLC. The contract only specified the Mexicali estate. Jenkins, who had twice issued himself a fat dividend during his short tenure as owner, kept the CRLC office buildings, its stake in a local bank, some farms in Chiapas, and all its other assets. Just as he had sneakily done at Atencingo, he also kept a swath of the Mexicali land, intending to farm his own cotton.[30]

IN CRAFTING HIS exhibition empire, Jenkins wisely bet on a duopoly. Rather than creating one towering enterprise, he opted to help Espinosa and Alarcón develop two distinct clusters of assets. The decision was a crucial factor in the Jenkins Group's success, exemplifying how the American was more than a mere "rent seeker," profiting thanks to the right connections. Entrepreneurship was crucial and shrewd business management a critical component of it.

First, the dual approach avoided the appearance of monopoly, which was barred by Article 28 of the constitution and outlawed in specific terms in 1934.[31] Eventually the truth of the matter became common knowledge, as is clear from satirical cartoons that later appeared in the national press, depicting Jenkins as an octopus, or linking him, Espinosa, and Alarcón in a procession of *gringo* king and Mexican courtiers.[32] But during the crucial early expansion phase of the 1940s, when the presidential cabinet still included powerful leftists, the strategy was surely advantageous. Making the appearance of competition more credible and the overall operation more efficient was Espinosa and Alarcón's continued mutual loathing.[33] They strained to out-do the other. Though out of spite they sometimes erred by building rival theaters too close to each other, the overall result was a pair of fast-expanding enterprises. The fact that with each new venture they began with a loan from Jenkins pushed them to generate a profit as soon as possible. They would enjoy no dividends until their debts to Jenkins were paid.

Often the Jenkins Group's methods were not monopolistic, just born of good business judgment. When Espinosa took the helm at COTSA, he saw that Mexico City was oversaturated with "first-run" theaters, venues that tried to draw wealthier moviegoers by consistently hosting premieres. The fault lay at home: in a splashy attempt to draw more patrons, Theodore Gildred had designated fifteen COTSA venues as first-runs. The liability was that whenever such theaters screened premieres, the Hollywood distributors charged higher rental fees, whether or not a picture was a proven US hit, and so box-office returns for lesser movies often failed to cover costs. Boldly reversing Gildred's strategy, Espinosa converted half of the first-runs into second-runs, reducing the capital's premier venues to a viable total of eight and increasing the options for middle-income patrons, since tickets were always cheaper at second-run venues. The reduced fees that Espinosa paid to distributors allowed his firm to make a profit, and at the end of his first year he handed shareholders—chiefly Jenkins—a 15 percent dividend.

Espinosa then modernized the concession stands. Patrons entering COTSA entrance halls were greeted with an artificially generated popcorn smell, to whet their appetite, and by circular candy stalls, offering just a limited selection of sweets, so they would choose quickly and move on. Espinosa may also have been the first Mexican exhibitor to engage in branding: using the name of the flagship venue that his father had built in Puebla, he unveiled a Cinema Variedades in Mexico City, Guadalajara, Acapulco, and nine other cities. All these measures boosted theater revenues. Within a few years, COTSA dividends reached as high as 90 percent.[34]

On the other hand, exhibitors were deliberately squeezed out of the business by the Jenkins Group. As early as 1943, Tampico exhibitor Vicente Villasana was voicing protest as he fretted about the impact of a Jenkins-backed movie palace on his antiquated chain of theaters. Here, in fact, was a provincial pot calling the larger kettle black, as Villasana dominated exhibition in the Tampico area, with eight or nine theaters, hyping his business through his local newspaper. Essaying the art of commercial gringophobia, he railed against "The Trust of the notorious Yankee" and reported as fact that Jenkins had once kidnapped himself. A year later, he placed an open letter in the Mexico City press attacking Jenkins for strong-arming distributors into favoring him in Tampico by threatening to boycott their pictures at all his other theaters. Villasana depicted himself waging a "patriotic" struggle against a "foreign" monopoly. Provincial exhibitors, lacking broad circuits with which to convince distributors to treat them on equal terms, gradually succumbed and sold out to the Jenkins Group. In 1955, even the Villasana family would throw in the towel, selling their theater chain to Alarcón.[35]

At this stage, how much Jenkins controlled production was harder to define. There were two issues here, the commercial and the cultural: which production companies did the Jenkins Group control, and what influence did it have over their creative processes? As to the first, Espinosa, like many Mexican exhibitors, had dabbled in cofinancing films since the mid-1930s, as a way of securing promising product and as a hedge against bullying by the Hollywood distributors. Then Jenkins cofounded the Film Bank. But when he offloaded his shares in the bank he also sold the stake he had gained through it in CLASA Films, then Mexico's leading producer. Perhaps he deemed the production side of the business too risky. In 1942 the Film Bank had partnered in giving newly formed Grovas SA a million pesos to play with, touting it as "the most powerful film company in Latin America." Making a prolific eight pictures that year, Grovas failed to turn a profit, leaving the bank to absorb the loss.[36] A few years later, the Jenkins Group's involvement in production would become more consistent.

Its creative influence was initially nebulous. Complimentary portrayal of US characters was not necessarily evidence of a Jenkins imprint. The undercurrents of Golden Age cinema were already influenced by Ávila Camacho's desire to be a "good neighbor" to the United States and by the efforts of US propagandists to foster a united wartime front.[37] Between a film's director and Jenkins existed a multitiered hierarchy of producers, executives, and company board members, so it is unlikely that Jenkins reserved the right to green-light productions. Unlike the radio magnate Emilio Azcárraga, Jenkins was not a hands-on executive; the only activity for which he did roll up his sleeves, so to speak, was farming. In the 1950s, however, the Jenkins Group's impact on creativity would become easier to spot—and easier for his critics to denounce.

The Force of Labor and a Quid Pro Quo

It must have seemed to many of his peers that Jenkins was untouchable. In film, sugar, and textiles, he seemed to hold all the right cards, or at least an immunity to laws restricting foreign ownership, banning monopolistic practice, and guaranteeing labor the right to organize. With a friend on the presidential throne, a *compadre* in the federal cabinet, and another ally as governor of Puebla, Jenkins had three aces up his sleeve. Certainly this is how things looked within the film industry, as his critics later recorded. Yet Jenkins would encounter several drawn-out disputes with labor in which he came off decidedly the worse.

By the standards of the day, Jenkins's newfound troubles with workers were not unusual, for Ávila Camacho's term suffered a record spike in stoppages. Despite the president's calls for national solidarity on Mexico's 1942 entry into the world war, high inflation and tumbling real-terms wages caused strikes to proliferate. Besides its frequent agitation over the rising cost of living, Mexico's industrial workforce was fast growing and much given to factionalism. In 1940's violent election campaign, some unions had backed opposition candidate Almazán.[38]

However, the fact that disputes at the La Trinidad textile mill and Atencingo were resolved to labor's benefit seems odd in light of Jenkins's chumminess with the Ávila Camachos. The pressing demands of labor only partially explain the contradiction. At a given moment, a president had any number of favors and secret incentives he could dole out to whomever was causing the greatest headache. So why would Ávila Camacho inconvenience one of his staunchest and wealthiest allies when there were many more distant capitalists whose interests might be compromised to keep labor leaders happy? And why would he do so when this ally was proving himself useful once again, with a theater expansion plan that suited state interests?

The apparent contradiction owed to a calculation by Ávila Camacho that operated on two levels, one overt and pragmatic, the other tacitly reciprocal. On the visible level, the Trinidad and Atencingo disputes both involved workers who had long agitated for a fairer deal. To side with labor in such cases not only afforded specific workforces tangible gains but also promised the president good publicity and an infusion of political capital in his dealings with labor.

At the covert level, there was a quid pro quo. Ávila Camacho would allow Jenkins vast gains in one field at the expense of lesser losses in others. In the film business, he would let Jenkins develop a highly lucrative, commanding position. (The deal concerned film rather than sugar, for the latter sector was much more the dominion of Aaron Sáenz, who controlled the sugar distribution cartel.)[39] In return, Jenkins would render forfeits that benefitted labor, both directly and symbolically, and thus serve Ávila Camacho's political balancing act. Such forfeits might also enable the president to assure the many left-wingers in his cabinet—which included former president Cárdenas as defense minister—that he was not in thrall to the gringo.[40]

There is no documented evidence of this quid pro quo. No such arrangement would ever be put in writing, and even in conversation it may have lacked specifics: Jenkins would simply owe favors that Ávila Camacho could choose when to collect. But such an understanding would entirely conform to the face-to-face nature of dealings between elites and to the personalistic nature of Mexican presidential leadership. It would also conform to the state-capital symbioses—arguably necessary during World War II but increasingly of convenience—that proliferated at the national level in the 1940s and 1950s.[41]

LA TRINIDAD WAS a storied site of conflict. This midsize textile factory in the state of Tlaxcala had experienced labor agitation since the Porfirian era.[42] After Jenkins became its chief owner he left its running to his partners, the Morales Conde family. Then, in 1941, management tried to impose on the workforce a "minority union": a syndicate embracing a minority of workers, more owner-friendly than the majority one. This was a typical ploy toward establishing a *sindicato blanco*, a company-loyal union comprising all hands, so the tactic met immense resistance from the majority faction, which was affiliated to the CROM. In August 1942, on the pretext of an arcane dispute over the union's right to govern three white-collar posts, an all-out strike began. That the strike should obtain recognition from the Federal Arbitration Board, in a year in which it recognized only 19 of 133 petitions, made it unusual. The board's ruling was doubly odd in that the grounds for the strike were a blue-collar complaint concerning white-collar employees; the two sides of the workforce were organized in separate unions. More unusual still was the length of the strike, twenty-three months, one of the longest of the Ávila Camacho era.[43] Management efforts to end the stoppage through injunctions came to naught. Textiles were enjoying a wartime boom, so the two-year closure of a 470-worker mill implied an aggravating forfeit of profits for Jenkins. Was the state sending a message that the gringo was not invulnerable after all?

The stakes rose in May 1944, when the Supreme Court granted the owners an injunction against a board ruling that they were liable for a million pesos in back pay to the strikers. The National Worker Council immediately responded by threatening a general strike in sympathy with La Trinidad. Set up by the president in 1942 to reduce interunion disputes during wartime, the council incorporated most labor federations, including the CROM and the Confederation of Mexican Labor (CTM).[44]

Since the reasons for the strike had been well aired for two years, the widely reported events that followed suggest signs of orchestrated political theater, though this is not to deny the sincerity of the workers involved. First, at the president's urging, the Labor Ministry intervened, summoning the CROM leadership and the mill's manager for talks. Then another labor federation, the FROC—usually the CROM's arch-rival—threatened a sympathy strike of its own. Over subsequent days, scores of unions at businesses throughout Puebla, from bakeries to public baths, made similar announcements, garnering further local headlines. The strikers were then dealt a setback when a federal judge suspended legal recognition of their strike, a ruling that encouraged the management to send in a contingent of scabs, escorted by private guards, to occupy the mill on June 20. In response, Ávila Camacho sent his labor minister, Francisco Trujillo, to evaluate the situation. The military zone commander accompanied him.

Speaking later to the press, Trujillo waxed lyrical: "Something Dante-esque, something exceptional among the class struggles that I've known, did I observe at La Trinidad," he began. Headline-baiting aside—and the papers of course led with "Dante-esque"—the conditions he described were credibly disturbing, arising as they did from twenty-two months of worker perseverance without salaries. They testified to the sheer will of labor in its refusal to be co-opted by management. Trujillo had met with gaunt, ragged men who held their heads high when questioned, replying "I'm with the strike, against the unjust boss, as long as I'm still alive." Reportedly, ten had already died. Others had lost children to starvation. Some of the saddest figures remained defiant, shouting their allegiance to the strike "until death!" That sentiment was not universal; between supporters of the minority union and those who had simply had enough, the minister counted 153 workers. But 247 favored pressing on. Trujillo was moved. "One has to admire this group of workers," he concluded. "One has to respect them."[45]

The very next day, on the minister's approval and with the strike-breakers removed, red-and-black flags were rehung outside the mill and soldiers helped to keep the scabs at bay. Simultaneously, the National Worker Council announced its postponement of the general strike, expressing confidence that the president would solve the dispute. On July 7 came the climax: Ávila Camacho announced a government takeover of La Trinidad. The mill renewed operations the next morning, employing most of its original workforce.

Ávila Camacho's decree generated headlines in the national dailies and jubilation in the labor press. Dozens of congratulatory telegrams reached the president from unions as far away as Mexicali. CTM chief Fidel Velázquez acclaimed the actions of Trujillo and defended him from the attacks of the business elite. The CTM paper, *El Popular*, contrasted the president's "very eloquent reply" with the "clumsy and antipatriotic pig-headedness" of the owners; a follow-up headline chimed: "Neither misery nor death conquered the workers of the mill La Trinidad." The centrist *El Universal* published an atmospheric feature about a new mood of hope at the factory; it began: "La Trinidad is now a symbol of Shangri-la." Weeks afterward, editorials continued to fete the president's decision, *Rebeldía* taking the unusual and provocative step of fingering Jenkins as the mill's owner and calling the outcome a "triumph of the proletariat."[46]

The final moves toward state intervention may have taken Jenkins by surprise, not least because of Ávila Camacho's conciliatory style.[47] Throughout the dispute he had let the mill's manager handle talks with the authorities. On July 3, however, he telegrammed the president from California, informing him (more probably reminding him) of his ownership of the mill. He noted the Supreme Court's ruling that the company was not responsible for back pay during the strike, and he protested a contradictory Labor Ministry threat that the mill would be confiscated were half of the back pay not met. Two days later, the company's executives in Puebla placed a protest letter in *Excélsior*, claiming that contrary to Labor Ministry declarations the Federal Arbitration Board had annulled the strike's legality two weeks before.[48] On the face of it, Jenkins's private and public requests for presidential favor fell on deaf ears, and the CROM, with Ávila Camacho's help, scored a historic victory.

Matters were not so simple. While the stamina of La Trinidad's strikers necessitated some form of state intervention, there were signs throughout that the affair was stage-managed. The strike's legal recognition, on debatable grounds, suggests that factors beyond the merits of the case were involved. The contradictory rulings of judicial bodies and the efforts of Trujillo allowed for high drama and purple prose. Even the harm to

Jenkins's pocketbook was less than it seemed. Since he owned another four mills, at least some of La Trinidad's work orders could be reassigned. It is also telling that his July 3 telegram was his only missive to the president about the dispute. In contrast to previous administrations, when he telegrammed presidents fairly often, Jenkins rarely wrote to Ávila Camacho. One may well imagine that, whenever urgency arose, he telephoned his *compadre* Maximino and asked him to take up the matter with his brother. His being out of the country that summer was hardly an issue, for telephone links between Los Angeles and Mexico were well established.[49] No doubt such calls preceded and followed the telegram. Sooner or later he would have been assured that the decree in labor's favor would prove less drastic than headlines suggested.

And so it was. To begin with, the edict pledged to indemnify the owners, in that any net profits would remain theirs. Then, two years later, the state reversed the seizure. In August 1946, three months before Ávila Camacho stepped down, Jenkins and the Morales Conde family regained La Trinidad. It was still in decent shape, as the books showed an 11 percent profit margin under state management, although two-thirds of that sum went to cover the strikers' back pay. This time there was no announcement and little press coverage.[50]

Three Deaths

The biggest blow to Jenkins in 1944 was sentimental. On January 15, Mary Street Jenkins passed away.[51] She was sixty-one. The cause: tubercular meningitis. Jenkins had only just left her to return to Mexico, assured by her doctors that she would pull through her latest downturn. His failure to be with her during her final hours shook him to the core. He returned to California at once and leaned for support on Jane, his capable middle daughter. "My father is clinging to me like a child," Jane wrote a fortnight later, "I don't even think of leaving him."

For four years Mary had lived in the splendor of Beverly Hills. When she was ready to leave Tucson, William had bought her a grand mansion on Doheny Road called The Woods. It came with a fifteen-acre garden. (The staff, fourteen in number, included six gardeners.) Mary had a favorite spot by a sunny upstairs window where she would sit every morning, slowly brushing her long red hair. She had her old-time musical shows on the radio, and she drew comfort from her Christian tracts. She often had her three youngest daughters for company; at times all five of them were there, and there would be parties, with minor Hollywood stars. But usually she stayed upstairs, and doctors' concerns with contagion meant that her daughters could only enter her room for fifteen minutes each day. Mary once counseled Jane: "The best lesson you can have in life is to learn how to be alone."

Mary had frequent letters from her husband: he had mailed a typed sheet of news almost daily. And she had his Sunday night phone calls: they would talk for three minutes (if she wanted to talk longer, she had to ring back). Yet she seldom had William in person. When he came he would joke with her and make her laugh, but he only visited twice a year. Toward the end of each week-long stay, his daughters would sense him itching to return to Mexico. "My father loved the *thought* of the existence of my mother, rather than the actual fact," Tita surmised.

But Jane would claim: "The day that Mother died, something died in Pop too." This might have surprised anyone outside his immediate circle. To everyone else, the sixty-five-year-old captain of industry seemed as committed as ever. His drive for domination in film exhibition only gathered pace. Initially, the only visible concession he made to widowerhood was to don a black suit and tie. Even then, Jenkins had always shown such dull sartorial taste that few could say for sure whether he had not always worn that color.

Gradually it appeared that something indeed had changed. After a few more years, he developed a less demanding schedule and a more contemplative demeanor. He devoted his afternoons to tennis, chess, or cards with friends, and he treated their offspring to trips to his movie theaters. He built a seaside holiday home. He spent more time with his daughters and still more with his grandson Billy.

Jenkins had always wanted a son. After Mary bore a fifth daughter, he wrote to John Tigert: "we were visited again by the stork, and in spite of all my earnest pleas to Lady Luck, it was another girl." Perhaps he thought of John D. Rockefeller, who after siring five girls fathered a boy, but Mary lacked the vigor to endure another pregnancy. So Jenkins took a close interest in Margaret's son, Billy. Since the father, Robert Anstead, was largely out of the picture, Jenkins became the boy's surrogate parent. In 1943, when Billy was eleven, he had a lawyer friend draw up a new statute for Puebla that would let him adopt the boy as his own. Billy now had an active father, a still-energetic man who took him on fishing trips and visits to his farms and taught him about accounting, all the while trying to resist the grandfatherly urge to spoil him.[52]

Jenkins's philanthropy changed too. So far, it had meant fairly modest sums, and while consistent with his belief in the importance of education, it had clearly bought him political gain. Now the donations involved substantial amounts. Politics never faded entirely from view, but his giving assumed a new altruism. Often it brought him no discernible benefit at all.

A few months after Mary died, Jenkins began to aid the eminent archaeologist Alfonso Caso in his excavation of Monte Albán. This Zapotec capital, crowning a hilltop outside the city of Oaxaca, had lain more or less unexcavated for 1,500 years when Caso started work in 1931. Jenkins's donations supported the final stages, and Caso sent him annual reports illustrated with photographs of the dig. Just as Jenkins would have insisted, he also sent him booklets of receipts showing how every peso was being spent.[53]

Jenkins retained an attachment to his birthplace, which prompted several Tennesseans to fly down in the hope of tapping his largesse. After he pledged $200,000 for a swimming pool at Vanderbilt in 1947, the chancellor himself paid Jenkins a visit. Harvie Branscomb hit it off with Jenkins over lunch in Mexico City, and an invitation to holiday with Jenkins in Acapulco followed. Before long, Branscomb would have Jenkins elected to Vanderbilt's board of trustees. Around the same time a doctor came calling from Shelbyville, eliciting his support for a sixty-bed hospital for Bedford County. A new act of Congress promised matching funds for such projects, and the county was planning a bond issue. Jenkins committed $100,000.[54]

But his adoptive state of Puebla remained the chief beneficiary. As well as continuing to support public works, Jenkins underwrote the expansion of the American School. He and his sister Anne Buntzler had founded it in 1942, at the US government's request, as a wartime alternative to the prestigious German School. Jenkins gave 2 million pesos for a dedicated site and building, by far his biggest donation so far, and the new facility opened in 1949. Jenkins also revitalized the Alpha Club, which had declined in popularity. Over several years he bought out most of the shareholders and paid for additional tennis courts, a bowling alley, a pool, and a gym. Together with Puebla's Rotary Club, which also owned a stake, he would turn the Alpha into a nonprofit foundation, established in 1954. Under Jenkins's guidance, the Alpha became more of a sporting center, shedding some of its old exclusivity.[55]

For the rest of his life, schools and hospitals received the lion's share of his giving. These were understandable priorities, sentimental ones.

Mary and he had met and excelled at high school. They had romanced at Vanderbilt and, despite having dropped out, continued to believe in education. Mary had spent so much of her life confined to hospital beds. An observer might have reasonably asked whether the widower Jenkins, who kept most of his donations quiet, were not trying to atone for something.

A year later, back from a visit to Los Angeles, Jenkins wrote to Tigert: "Mary rests in the Garden of Memories of Forest Lawn Memorial Park of Glendale. It is one of the most beautiful spots one can imagine. I enjoy going there and spending as much time as I can with her."

HIS NEXT GREAT loss was political. On February 17, 1945, Maximino Ávila Camacho took a turn for the worse at a series of events held in his honor, hosted by the mill unions of Atlixco. In some pain, the general had himself chauffered back to his mansion in Puebla. He was lying on his bed, an assistant struggling to remove one of his boots, when he expired. To many his death was quite unexpected, for he was only fifty-three.

Suspicions abounded. Puebla's just-departed governor, Gonzalo Bautista, was so sure it was murder, and that Maximino's cronies would take him for its plotter, he had his wife and children picked up by loyal agents and whisked away into hiding. A popular conspiracy theory claimed that the indomitable mill-hands of Atlixco managed to poison Maximino's Coca-Cola.

The general had in fact battled illness for some time. He had coped with diabetes since his thirties, along with a fractured right leg that in later life caused severe rheumatism. He also suffered from a worsening heart condition. After 1940 his hair grayed rapidly, and he sometimes walked with a cane, though he took care not to be photographed with it. In late 1944, Puebla's *La Opinión* carried reports of Maximino in various stages of convalescence (read: ill health), which found him in Mexico City, Acapulco, and a spa in Michoacán. It was whispered that this kidnapper of teen damsels, lover of actresses, and father of fourteen children by seven women (fourteen that he recognized, and there were said to be three dozen he did not) was heavily syphilitic and could no longer "perform." A triple heart attack is what finished him.[56]

The following winter came a third blow. Manuel Pérez, Jenkins's right-hand man at Atencingo, was summarily forced into retirement. For at least fifteen years, Pérez had kept his fields in the agronomical vanguard, posting Mexico's highest per-hectare yield of cane. In mill productivity too he helped keep Atencingo in first place, as measured by tons of sugar produced per hectare of cane harvested—a ranking the mill would now lose.[57]

What happened to The Wasp must have seemed to those who toiled under him an act of God. The man whose voice had struck fear into the hearts of hundreds of millworkers, thousands of cane growers, and even his immediate family, woke up one morning unable to speak. Assailed by a kind of paralysis that also affected his limbs, Pérez stayed in bed for several days, trying to recuperate. His body partially recovered but not his speech. So he left the mill where he had reigned for a quarter century, left his local mistress and the children he sired with her, and returned to Puebla City. There in the family home his long-suffering wife could keep a careful eye on him. A year later he was dead.[58]

Jenkins had suddenly lost two key allies in Puebla. Nevertheless he could still count on several powerful friends: the new state governor, for example, and the president of the country.

The Quid Pro Quo, Part II

A year to the exact day after Maximino died, Atencingo witnessed what old-timers had surely doubted would ever come to pass: the founding of an independent union. The two events were not unrelated. With Maximino's passing, Jenkins lost his most fearsome ally. The general had been especially antagonistic toward the CTM, whose founder, Vicente Lombardo Toledano, had been a personal foe since childhood.[59] Were Maximino still alive, and Manuel Pérez still in sound health, the CTM-affiliated National Sugarworkers' Syndicate (SNA) might not have dared to organize the Atencingo mill.

Even then, Local 77 was almost over before it began. February 17 was a Sunday, and as they congregated at the Atencingo sports field for the founding assembly, many workers brought their wives and children with them. Just as the men were lining up to sign the charter, Fernando Pérez, one of Manuel's sons, showed up with a dozen private militiamen. At the sight of their machine guns, a number of people began to run away. An activist named Adalberto García shouted for them to stop: "Don't run, comrades! They can't kill us all!" The SNA delegate echoed his cry. People returned to their places.

Pérez then summoned police to take the names of everyone present. He declared those who signed would lose their jobs at the mill. The SNA commission had earlier visited the military zone commander, who agreed to provide support to guarantee the peace, but his promised troops never appeared. Despite everything, the workers kept on signing.

When the SNA later complained to the president, Puebla's new governor, Carlos Betancourt, showed his true colors by responding disingenuously. He claimed his investigation had found no evidence of anti-union aggression. In terms reminiscent of his patron Maximino, he hotly denied the existence of private militia at Atencingo.[60]

Betancourt lacked the political base his two predecessors had enjoyed, especially after the death of Maximino, on whose coat-tails he had ridden to the governor's mansion. He also lacked the iron fist. To save the day for Jenkins, Maximino would probably have dispatched agents provocateurs recruited from the CROM, along with soldiers to arrest the right people once the fighting broke out. Betancourt was too patrician and too nice for that sort of thing.[61]

Circumstances boded well for union activism that February. The SNA, formed nine years earlier, had grown quickly by organizing workers at many of the big mills: the Johnstons' Los Mochis, Aaron Sáenz's El Mante, the communally owned Zacatepec. Owing to Jenkins's politicking, Atencingo was perhaps the last major mill still harboring a company-run union, and the SNA now had the critical mass to push for total unification. In addition, the CTM was taking a more aggressive tack in its dealings with the government. It had supported Ávila Camacho's policy of a wartime wage freeze, but by 1946 real minimum wages in the capital had fallen 29 percent in five years. Its most powerful constituent unions were getting restless. In February, the CTM organized a nationwide work stoppage to protest the curse of inflation, and it would continue pressuring the government until June.[62]

The year's presidential contest gave the CTM extra leverage. Ruling-party candidate Miguel Alemán faced former Foreign Minister Ezequiel Padilla. The CTM had thrown its weight behind Alemán, but such support for a man who was hardly a friend of labor no doubt came at the price of various concessions.[63] All told, allowing Atencingo's workers to organize was a favor the state had good reason to concede to the CTM—or, put another way, a favor it had good reason to charge against Jenkins's account.

What in February 1946 was a setback for Jenkins felt like emancipation to the workers. Within a few months, Local 77 and the SNA were suing Jenkins for a million pesos, alleging systematic underpayment over the previous two years. Mill electrician Mario Ortega could scarcely believe how much his salary improved thanks to the local's efforts. Sixty years later he would claim it had doubled, perhaps an exaggeration but equally a reflection of the union's impact on the collective memory of his community. "In my pay packet there were peso bills I'd never even seen before," he recalled. "I didn't know how I would spend so much money!"[64]

The new assertiveness also arose in response to acts of terror, as Fernando Pérez tried to subdue the activists. One August evening a local leader, José Lima, was chatting with a union colleague in the street when two men came walking by. They were strangers, but they knew whom they were looking for: they took out their guns and shot them both, Lima fatally. Friends nearby reacted at once, killing one of the hitmen. The other managed to run away, but he did not know the area and hid within the disorienting forest of the sugar cane. The union organized a posse to sweep the fields. Tracking the assassin down, they dragged him back to the entrance of the mill, where they hoisted a rope. Hearing the commotion, a priest appeared, and he persuaded the mob not to lynch the man. So they took him to a field next to the union building, tied him to a post, and questioned him. Then they lynched him anyway, throttling him with a tourniquet.[65]

Eusebio Benítez, whose education had ended when Manuel Pérez plucked him from his schoolyard, found that he and his friends had been kept ignorant of their rights.[66] It was as though the Federal Labor Law, issued in 1931, had at long last landed with a thud in Atencingo. Two Spaniards ran the company store, a business of high mark-ups and dubious legality, and not long after the union's arrival Benítez saw them packing their cart and preparing to leave.

"What's going on?" he asked them. One of the merchants replied: "You people finally opened your eyes."

SIMILAR THREATS TO Jenkins's control were underway at Atencingo's *ejido*. This was the communal farm that supplied the mill, where sugar had been grown on a supposedly independent basis since Cárdenas forced Jenkins to surrender the land. Most *ejido* members, or *ejidatarios*, resented the company's continued control of their cooperative society. They wanted to be able to grow other crops besides sugar, such as corn, their staple food. Many wished the *ejido* to be subdivided into individual plots.

Porfirio Jaramillo, brother of famed agrarian activist Rubén, returned to the region from Morelos at the invitation of senior *ejidatarios* in early 1946. He and his associates hastened to mobilize the nine Atencingo estates. They drew support from landless peasants—many of them, like Jaramillo himself, veterans of the campaigns of Doña Lola—who wanted to become *ejidatarios.* Manuel Pérez's successors, including his son Fernando, were too inexperienced and too little feared to slow the tide. Jaramillo then made simultaneous appeals to the National Peasant Confederation (CNC) and the federal Agrarian Department. Both responded sympathetically, dispatching a joint team of investigators in June.[67]

Equivalent to the workers' CTM and thus another corporatist pillar of the ruling party, the CNC was led by Gabriel Leyva Velázquez. Leyva was the consummate political insider: a veteran officer of the Revolution, former senator, and Ávila Camacho loyalist. He took an interest in the Atencingo cane-growers' grievances and brought to bear his knowledge of other cooperatives where *ejidatarios* enjoyed greater autonomy and higher wages. The Agrarian Department was headed by Silvano Barba González, an inner-circle Cardenist. His left-wing convictions drove his activist approach to curtailing Jenkins's power.[68]

The Agrarian Department report on Atencingo was damning. It described the *ejido* as a feudal dominion, in which the mill administration exploited the peons, terrorizing any who tried to assert their rights. Dissenters, it found, were usually dismissed and sometimes evicted from their homes. The report relayed the *ejidatarios'* demands and advised strong measures, lest violence erupt against the mill company. Such findings became the basis of a briefing and list of recommendations, backed by the CNC, that the department submitted to the president. On July 31, 1946, Ávila Camacho gave the department the go-ahead to reorganize the *ejido* cooperative society as a more autonomous unit, freer from mill domination, and to help it negotiate a new supply contract with the Atencingo Company. Tellingly, the president made this decision just a day after authorizing the return to Jenkins of La Trinidad.[69] Whatever his favoritism toward him in the film industry, Ávila Camacho evidently felt obliged by loyalty to sugar any pill he might wish an ally to swallow.

Jenkins telegrammed the president a few weeks later, alleging that the department and the CNC were supporting agitators "hostile to all order and discipline."[70] He made a predictably dire forecast that, should these elements proceed unchecked, production would fall by half within a year. He asked that no reorganization take place before the submission of a pending report from the Ministry of Agriculture; the ministry oversaw cane production and was less sympathetic than the department to Jaramillo and the rebel *ejidatarios.* This telegram was longer and much more strenuous in tone than the one Jenkins had sent in 1944 regarding La Trinidad. Maximino was no longer around to plead his case. Devoted as ever to farming, Jenkins felt that his carefully constructed sugar kingdom was about to be laid to waste by its serfs.

The telegram did not prevent the Agrarian Department from convening an *ejidatario* assembly the next day. It hosted a first-ever election of councils for the *ejido*. In November, as a novel sense of empowerment pervaded the fields, workers at eight of the nine Atencingo estates went on strike, claiming Jenkins had delayed distributing revenues from the harvest. Reporting the strikes, *La Voz de México*, a communist newspaper subsidized by the ruling party, stoked the new fire. In a report replete with the gringophobic epithets that were its stock in trade, the paper called for an end to official tolerance of "the assassin of Mexican peasants, William Jenkins" and the expulsion of "so terrible a Yankee landowner." Atencingo's sugar growers should be treated as Mexicans, it added, not as how some Yankees treat their blacks.

Autonomy was confirmed on January 1, 1947, when the reorganized cooperative was officially recognized. The next month, Porfirio Jaramillo took office as its manager.[71]

By then Jenkins was effectively out. He had initiated the sale of the Atencingo Company, his greatest creation to date, in early December.[72] His loss of control of the *ejido* and the unionization of the millworkers made a sale the logical move; he may also have tired of butting heads with the national *cacique* of the sugar sector, Aarón Sáenz. But he was able to sell his newly disadvantaged property for a decent $7 million, a price related to the fact that its buyers included Espinosa Yglesias, his main film-sector partner. Espinosa, who assumed part-time management of Atencingo, and two Spaniards, Lorenzo Cue and Moisés Cosío Gómez, took 30 percent each. Espinosa presumably felt that while the commodity value of sugar was in decline, loyalty obliged his purchase.[73] After all, it was largely thanks to Jenkins's capital that he was now one of the generals of the film industry.

For Atencingo's cane-growers, the promised autonomy failed to equal that of the millworkers. Jaramillo's five-year leadership made gains in wages that barely matched inflation. Nor was there flexibility for those wanting to plant staples rather than cane. Despite his devotion, Jaramillo had little training and made an indifferent manager. After three good seasons, mostly a legacy of Jenkins's team, production tumbled and the cooperative's debts soared. That said, Espinosa was partly to blame, as the mill repeatedly broke down on his watch, and he refused to let Jaramillo sell elsewhere the cane that Atencingo could not process; justifiably, the cooperative felt that Espinosa was sabotaging their leadership. Rafael Ávila

Camacho, governor from 1951, could now more easily contrive Jaramillo's ouster. Mexico City would side with him, tacitly giving him the right to name a new manager. So Rafael forced Jaramillo to resign and named in his stead a military officer who would satisfy the interests of the mill. The contrasting experience of millworkers and *ejidatarios* would typify Mexico's postwar social development: modest improvements for the moderately poor, paralysis for the poverty-stricken.[74]

Strikingly, during both conflicts at Atencingo, the president made no discernible effort to protect his ally. This was more remarkable than the confiscation of La Trinidad, as Atencingo was a much larger business. But once again the loss to Jenkins was less than it seemed. By 1944, after the acquisition of the COTSA chain, his profit center was shifting. With the death of Mary that year, he may also have harbored new guilt over Atencingo, since it was largely his devotion to this property that had led him to renege on his promise to leave Mexico. Well before then, the Atencingo land divestment had eroded his attachment to the company, and it more or less freed him from the consuming concerns of landowners: the relentless hassle of land-grabs, water disputes, official rulings, and lawsuits. As of 1938, Jenkins not only had the money for a sustained assault on a separate bastion of business; he had the time. Now he had $7 million more to plow into the fertile terrain of film.

Compared to the advantages he was enjoying in cinema, the reversals Jenkins suffered under Ávila Camacho were acceptable. Beyond the tax breaks and other small favors he no doubt received when building theaters, Jenkins went unrestrained by laws against foreign majority ownership and monopolies. Losing control over labor at Atencingo and operations at La Trinidad—no matter how galling at the time—made for a fair deal as a quid pro quo. In years to come, moreover, Mexico's sugar sector would decline in profits while experiencing ever more intervention by the state.[75] The setbacks Jenkins had once protested and that moved him to sell his sugar mill surely struck him, like the earlier land expropriation, as blessings in disguise.

The Many Uses of Film

For Jenkins and Ávila Camacho, the dealings with labor went deeper than the quid pro quo. Their exchanges of favors were part of a wider symbiosis, in which a Jenkins-dominated film industry served the state as a provider of patriotic entertainment, an employer of thousands, and a stalwart supporter of the ruling party. In addition, like many in the private sector, Jenkins helped out with various federal projects. The state takeover of the Colorado River Land Company was one example. Another was development bank Nafinsa, which Jenkins reportedly aided once by buying an entire $5 million bond issue.[76]

Such interdependence was increasingly the Mexican norm. The bankers' alliance, established in the 1920s, continued to hold sway in a laissez-faire governance of the financial sector. While the Ávila Camacho regime relied upon the Jenkins Group in film exhibition, it let Emilio Azcárraga and his partner Clemente Serna monopolize radio, similarly aiding its rapid expansion. In return, the state enjoyed a second dependable medium for disseminating political messages, consumerist values, and a cohesive, sentimental nationalism.[77]

Jenkins's service to the state as a mass entertainment provider, like Azcárraga's, was especially valuable because he invested for the long term. He did not dabble in the film business—as he did as a venture capitalist in other sectors—but committed the bulk of his capital to it for two decades. His theaters helped spur a massive boom. Across the nation, between 1938 and 1948 alone, theater totals grew from 863 (with fewer than half in regular operation) to 1,431.[78] And so the public came, the sheer number of venues ensuring a wide variation in ticket prices that catered to all kinds of audience. The capital's nine first-run palaces charged 4 pesos, more than the minimum weekly wage, and drew an upscale clientele. Second-run houses catered to the middle classes, who usually had to wait a just week or two for a picture after its premiere. The poor flocked to local houses known to their owners as "lice theaters." Here a triple-bill might be seen for eighty centavos. In provincial cities, prices were cheaper still. Balcony seats at Puebla's middle-ranking Cinema Guerrero could be had for 25 centavos, or 5 US cents.[79]

Yet did the state really need Jenkins? Might not his hundreds of theaters have been built anyway? Perhaps they would have been, but not so quickly. Building and equipping movie theaters was an expensive pursuit. It required unusually deep pockets and ready access to hefty bank loans (as Jenkins had at the Banco de Comercio), all the more so to build with the rapidity the state desired. Nor was it a risk-free venture. Despite the Mexican public's spiraling demand for movies, a theater might not prove profitable. If the terrain were leased rather than bought, the rent might go up, contract be damned. A rival might erect a venue in close proximity. Contracts for every Hollywood film had to be negotiated with the notoriously hard-nosed US distributors. Even COTSA lost money in its earlier years.

Still, the state's need of Jenkins was more perceived than real. Given the solidity of the political apparatus and the economy, the need for interdependence was dissipating into mere convenience. Theaters played a key propaganda role by including newsreels with each feature, so it suited the state that they be owned by people known for party loyalty. That Jenkins was a foreigner was an exploitable pressure point; should he prove troublesome, the state could threaten to expel him. It was also convenient for the state to deal with a single magnate, rather than with a host of competitors. (This was true of any sector, which helps explain the ruling party's long affection for monopolies.) If the president wanted to ban a film, axe a newsreel scene, reserve a theater for a minister's speech, or prevent a union boss from doing likewise, he only had one phone call to make.

Convenience was also prevalent at the personal level. From Ávila Camacho on down, the government winked at Jenkins's sale of sugar above the official price cap, his evasion of alcohol taxes and other levies, his joint purchase of the paper *Novedades* (illegal for a foreigner), and so forth.[80] Jenkins's film empire almost certainly offered something in return. The scope for favors was huge: real-estate deals, construction contracts, bulk purchase of equipment, insurance policies, funding for production companies. All offered chances to thank (or woo) politicians, at the federal and state levels, with a slice of the pie. Then there was the option of offering stakes in the theaters themselves. Concrete evidence of such dealings is lacking; clues are not. Maximino had been widely believed to hold an interest in the Jenkins Group's Puebla theaters. His brother Manuel would be an obvious suspect; reportedly he inherited some of Maximino's assets, departed the presidency a very rich man, and left his widow a billion-peso fortune. As for Alemán, his reputation for self-enrichment, in league with various private-sector frontmen, was well established even while he held office. Afterward, Jenkins would continue to meet with him—he once confided to his family—to discuss their affairs.[81]

WHAT THE PUBLIC saw when the lights went down and the curtains drew back were stories thick with emotion. At the lice theaters, where Mexican fare outdrew Hollywood, this was especially true. Golden Age movies shied away from contemporary realism or "social cinema"; they even shied from hailing the gains of the Revolution. The accent was on melodrama, comedy, and romantic musicals. So Jenkins's service to the state was to channel a heady mix of escapism, contentment with one's lot, national pride, and imagined community.

The Roman adage about the people's craving for bread and circuses was popularized in Mexico by a rhyme: *al pueblo, pan y circo*. A medium that offered cheap diversions was a natural ally of the state, whose priorities were social stability and economic growth. But the very factor that did most to boost growth threatened stability: World War II had caused a price spiral in staple goods and thus a surge in strikes. So cinema, Hollywood and Mexican alike, offered distraction from daily woes. Since it upheld family values and public decency, fostered stability between rich and poor, and encouraged consumerism, so much the better. Some in the labor press claimed to see the ploy. "What does Mexican Cinema do for Mexico?" asked a columnist, going on to berate producers for stupefying audiences with puerile films.[82]

Rampant urbanization was a related state concern: the cities' capacity to absorb a myriad annual rural migrants, both physically and culturally. Films, especially Mexican films, could play a role, shaping frustrations into laughter, homesickness into reverie. Mario Moreno took the street smarts and subversiveness of Charlie Chaplin's tramp and added a layer of verbal dexterity to create his comic screen persona, "Cantinflas." The adventures of this plebian jack-of-all-trades idealized the resilience and quick-wittedness of the proletariat, often in the face of superciliousness and corruption.[83] (Jenkins adored Cantinflas; he loathed city snobs and grasping bureaucrats.) Jorge Negrete became a singing *charro* in the vein of Nelson Eddy's singing cowboy. Handsome and honey-voiced, he gave the new urbanites a comforting, dream-like connection to the pastoral landscapes they had left behind.

Pedro Infante appeared in a hit musical trilogy as Pepe el Toro (Joe the Bull), who reminded the ill-paid proletariat of the nobility inherent in being poor. Pepe endured the turmoil of city life and the schemes of its corrupt and crooked. He resisted its sexual temptations. His dignity and selflessness met reward, while adversaries discovered that crime does not pay. For audiences to get to that point, Pepe had to endure deception, beatings, a jailing, rejection by those he loved, even the death by fire of his blue-eyed infant son. Each film in the trilogy put audiences through the wringer. (Politicians might well have reassured themselves: Who would have the energy to take to the streets after *that*?) Said a slogan at the close of *We the Poor* (1948): "One suffers . . . But one learns!" This was catharsis with a jackhammer.

Throughout his Pepe el Toro trilogy, Infante's persona also suggested that to be nobly poor was to be Mexican; there was something cold-hearted and *malinchista*, too keen on foreign customs, about the rich. The nationalism implicit in these films was a crucial characteristic of Golden Age cinema: despite an occasional lampooning of the wealthy, it was an inclusive nationalism. The indigenous and their cultures were prettified, most famously in *María Candelaria* (1944), featuring Dolores del Río as a humble flower farmer, paddling to market in her canoe. Jalisco's mariachis strummed their way into musicals no matter where they were set. And as Ávila Camacho and Alemán sought friendship and investment from Roosevelt and Truman, it was a nationalism largely free of the old resentments of the United States.[84]

Political elites deemed Jenkins's venues vital, for they believed mass media could mold the people. In 1938, Cárdenas had used radio to announce the oil nationalization, and on the overall usefulness of radio he opined: "Our people are profoundly auditory, and radio can be a factor of invaluable effectiveness for the integration of a national mentality." In 1943, while honoring Hollywood honchos Walt Disney and Louis B. Mayer for helping improve bilateral relations, Foreign Minister Padilla claimed film was able to penetrate "directly into the heart of the masses." In 1946, when Ávila Camacho submitted a bill proposing a film-industry commission, his preface noted Mexican cinema's ability to foster "feelings of unity and cohesion."[85]

While feature films promised a variety of seductions, Jenkins's theaters were also conduits for a more direct propaganda: newsreels, documentaries, and public service announcements. In wartime such conduits were more desirable than ever, for the United States did not strike Mexicans as their natural ally. Once Ávila Camacho declared war, after the Germans torpedoed a Mexican oil tanker, a common fallacy claimed it was Americans who had sunk it. Some small-towns listeners reacted to the declaration with cries of "Viva México! Death to the gringos!"[86] Clearly, in the parlance of the day, some "orientation of the masses" was in order.

Newsreels and shorts were a regular part of an evening's program, most of them US-made. Roosevelt's wartime office for Latin America, under Nelson Rockefeller, produced and subsidized much cinematic propaganda. Rockefeller had US producers tailor their reels for Latin markets by including items of regional interest, to advance wartime goodwill. Latin American content rose from 1 percent of all newsreel items in 1939 to 23 percent in 1944, reportedly to public enthusiasm.[87] Mexico's own newsreel makers had close ties to the state: EMA counted ex-president Abelardo Rodríguez among its shareholders, while the federal bank Nafinsa took a majority stake in CLASA, whose investors included former cabinet members Alberto Pani and Aarón Sáenz. EMA and CLASA received generous subsidies, and politicians would pay to have them film their speeches and ribbon-cuttings. As such political payola increased, news became submerged beneath a sea of hype.[88]

Secret police would report on public reactions to newsreels. In April 1944, an agent viewed a reel at Jenkins's second-run Cinema Lindavista and noted that the two items featuring the president were greeted with murmurs of admiration; a few people clapped. A day later, the same agent reported on a reel at the upscale Cinema Iris and noted that when Ávila Camacho appeared on screen there was complete silence, as was usual at "first-class" movie theaters. By implication, the moderate applause at the Lindavista was typical of middle-class viewers, which suggests that the newsreel cog in the propaganda machine was working to satisfaction that week.[89]

Mexico's audiences were certainly not passive receptacles, either of the sentimentalism and consumerism ingrained in Hollywood films, the patriotism and didacticism of local features, or the propaganda of the newsreels. Nor did all ticket-holders seek the same escape. Theaters were sites of conduct freed from social restraints: unmarried couples would kiss and cuddle in the privacy of darkness; teenage gangs appropriated balconies as their dens. Under Alemán, police dispatched to monitor newsreels would report as early as 1948 a waning enthusiasm for the president; at some Mexico City theaters, footage of his State of the Nation speech that year met with outbreaks of whistling.[90]

Yet the collective and repeated experience of Golden Age moviegoing, at a time when most city-dwellers were country-born, undoubtedly created congregations whose differences were lessened by the act of communal spectatorship. This was a global phenomenon.[91] Certainly, some patrons whistled at the newsreels, and others were busy necking. But for most of their shared time in dark, the melting-pot majority laughed together, cried together, felt their pulses race together, and then left Jenkins's theaters with their troubles tempered.

IN LATE NOVEMBER 1946—not two months after *María Candelaria* took a top prize at Cannes—some three hundred Americans converged on Mexico City to help celebrate the investiture of a president. Now a metropolis of more than 2 million, the capital had many of the trappings of a modern city, including seventy-three movie theaters and an airport with service to Los Angeles. Miguel Alemán, inaugurated on December 1, was keen to prolong the good-neighborliness that his predecessor had cemented. Ever image conscious, he was also keen to rub shoulders with some of the most famous Americans, including the banker-philanthropist Nelson Rockefeller and media magnate William Randolph Hearst. Three months later, Truman himself would visit.

And it would not have suited Alemán—a career politician of broad smile and jovial charisma—without some Hollywood razzle-dazzle. Thirty stars and studio chiefs attended, adorning the parties, symphony concerts, fashion shows, bullfights, and military parades, which lasted for five days. MGM's Louis B. Mayer, Fox mogul Spyros Skouras, and RKO topper Peter Rathvon were there, as were Orson Welles, Tyrone Power, Ann Sheridan, and John Wayne. *Variety* enthused that the whole inaugural gala was "organized with North American efficiency plus Latin grace plus Hollywood production."[92]

Mexico's film community must have viewed the exalted Los Angeles presence with mixed feelings. It affirmed they were all part of a bilateral brotherhood of entertainers and cultural ambassadors. But it also suggested that the president was a little too gringophile for comfort. There was business at issue, for the end of the world war had threatened the Golden Age. In autumn 1946, with European and Hollywood studios showing renewed vigor, Mexican producers found access to theaters much harder than before. They clamored for a screen quota. Ávila Camacho and Alemán both refused.[93]

With Mexican production soaring and some of it quite poor, these rebuffs definitely benefitted the Jenkins Group. At the capital's first-run theaters, most now operating as homes to the Hollywood majors, such a regulation would have been especially onerous. With the war over, there was less of a need to refrain from protectionism; in fact, Alemán would soon opt for generalized import restrictions. So the state's rejection of screen quotas hints at further favoritism toward the American.

Or a return of favors. After all, Jenkins had recently lost control over the workers and field hands at Atencingo. Following precedent, he had surely contributed to Alemán's campaign, both directly and via the sugar cartel; when the election was still a year away, cartel president Aarón Sáenz reportedly collected 700,000 pesos from the sugar barons.[94] Altogether, Alemán's fondness for Hollywood would have inclined him against quotas. But there were also quite pragmatic reasons why the president would have wished to start off as friends with the powerful Señor Jenkins, private banker to politicians and lord of Mexico's silver screens.

The graduation portraits of Mary Lydia Street and William Oscar Jenkins, Peoples & Morgan School, Fayetteville, Tennessee, 1900. Having quit school at age eleven due to illness, Jenkins returned nine years later and graduated at twenty-two, top of his class. Courtesy of Rosemarie Eustace Jenkins.

At Vanderbilt University, Jenkins (middle row, third from right) was quick to make an impression on the gridiron. He made the starting eleven as left tackle and was dubbed "Bull" Jenkins. From the Vanderbilt yearbook *The Comet 1901*. Courtesy of Vanderbilt University.

At Vanderbilt, Jenkins (third from top at left) also joined Sigma Alpha Epsilon, a proudly Southern fraternity that was also home to Mary's cousin Ernest Rees (far left) and his younger brother Albert (third from bottom at right). From the Vanderbilt yearbook *The Comet 1901*.

After six years in Mexico, Jenkins returned to Shelbyville, Tennessee, in late 1907. There he introduced his father, John Whitson Jenkins, to his daughters Elizabeth (age five) and Margaret (eleven months). Courtesy of Rosemarie Eustace Jenkins.

Jenkins, brother-in-law Donald Street (front row, second from left), and the senior staff of La Corona, his first business, c. 1918. This Puebla mill, along with sister mills in Mexico City and Querétaro, dominated Mexico's cheap cotton hosiery market within a few years of its founding in 1908 and continued producing throughout the Revolution of 1910–1920. Courtesy of Rosemarie Eustace Jenkins.

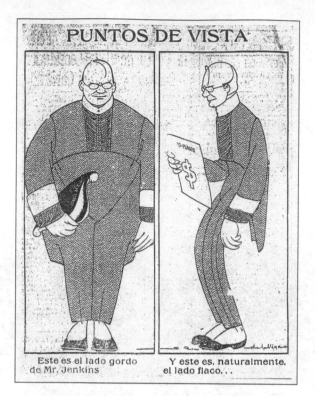

Jenkins's kidnapping in 1919 brought distinct reactions from Mexican and US papers. *El Heraldo de México* shows Jenkins's image as a consul belied by his alleged intent to profit from his abduction, while the *Los Angeles Times* depicts Uncle Sam preparing a formal protest over Jenkins's treatment after issuing many others due to revolutionary assaults on US lives and property.

W. O. Jenkins House, Los Angeles   *T. Beverly Keim, Jr., Architect*

Completed in 1924 at a cost of $250,000, 641 Irving Boulevard in Los Angeles was the dream home that William Jenkins had long promised to Mary. He would never live in it. A quarter century later, after he had sold it to oil tycoon J. Paul Getty, it would feature as the lair of Norma Desmond (played by Gloria Swanson) in Billy Wilder's *Sunset Boulevard*. Top: House featured in *Architectural Digest*, vol. 6, no. 1 (1926). Bottom: Filming *Sunset Boulevard*. Paramount Pictures.

Jenkins with daughters Elizabeth and Jane at the Hacienda Atencingo, Mexican Independence Day, 1926. Jenkins bought the estate after Zapatistas destroyed it during the Revolution, and together with Spanish agronomist Manuel Pérez (at left) he turned it into Mexico's most productive sugar plantation. Courtesy of William Anstead Jenkins.

Much of the project's success owed to economies of scale; to achieve them, Jenkins bought another eight nearby sugar estates, including the Hacienda Colón, and linked them by private railroad to the main mill at Atencingo. Courtesy of Manuel Pérez Nochebuena.

Over twenty-three years, William and Mary Jenkins had five daughters: (left to right) Jane, born in San Francisco, 1916; Elizabeth, born in Monterrey, 1902; Mary, born in Los Angeles, 1924; Margaret, born in Mexico City, 1907; and Martha, known in the family as Tita, born in Puebla, 1925. Courtesy of Rosemarie Eustace Jenkins.

Three generations in 1932, in Hanford, California, where Jenkins bought his father a fruit ranch. Having failed to sire a son, Jenkins adopted his first grandchild, William Anstead, as his own, following his daughter Margaret's divorce. Courtesy of Rosemarie Eustace Jenkins.

Maximino Ávila Camacho (center, with scroll) became governor of Puebla in 1937, thanks in part to a large, illegal campaign donation from Jenkins. Soon after taking office, he posed with Puebla City mayor Sergio B. Guzman (to the right of Maximino); his cabinet, which included future president Gustavo Díaz Ordaz (second from right); and editors of the state's main newspapers. Courtesy of Sergio Mastretta Guzmán.

In 1939, Jenkins moved his family into the top floor of Puebla's leading department store, Las Fábricas de Francia (formerly La Ciudad de México), a building he had acquired by foreclosing on a loan made during the Revolution. Courtesy of William Anstead Jenkins.

A living room the size of a tennis court: Jenkins is just visible at the far end, with adopted son William and daughter Margaret. Courtesy of William Anstead Jenkins.

Jenkins did not like parties, but he would not refuse an invitation from Maximino (back right). Along with Ezequiel Padilla (soon to be minister of Foreign Relations), Maximino's wife Margarita Richardi (front right), and the wife of Senator Noé Lecona, they toasted the marriage of Maximino's daughter Alicia, August 1940. Courtesy of the Acervo Fernández Chedraui.

In 1940, Maximino's brother Manuel Ávila Camacho (center) was elected president, with financial assistance from Jenkins, and with Miguel Alemán Valdés (right), himself a future president, serving as campaign manager. Maximino and Alemán both became covert business partners of Jenkins, and Manuel likely did so too. Courtesy of the Acervo Fernández Chedraui.

A 1941 portrait of Mary Street Jenkins. Stricken with tuberculosis, she had left Mexico eight years earlier, to go first to the Mayo Clinic in Minnesota, then to Tucson, and finally to Beverly Hills. She would die, while her husband continued to work in Puebla, in 1944. Courtesy of William Anstead Jenkins.

Two years after losing Mary, Jenkins lost the services of Manuel Pérez, the fearsome Spaniard who had managed Atencingo and its five thousand workers. Within a year, Jenkins negotiated the sugar mill's sale. Courtesy of Manuel Pérez Nochebuena.

Jenkins's fourth daughter, Mary, on her wedding day at the family's Beverly Hills home, in 1946. As was his custom, Jenkins refused to attend. Between them, his daughters married nine times, eight of those marriages ending in divorce or separation. Left to right: Jane, Elizabeth, Mary, Tita, Margaret. Courtesy of William Anstead Jenkins.

As a widower, Jenkins gradually chose to spend more time with his family. He built a three-story weekend home in Acapulco on an old hilltop gun emplacement (top left), completed in 1950. Courtesy of William Anstead Jenkins.

In Acapulco, Jenkins became a keen fisherman, buying a series of ever bigger and more powerful boats, each named *Rosa María*, after his favorite granddaughter. Courtesy of Rosemarie Eustace Jenkins.

Actualidades en el Cine

In 1950, by when Jenkins held a near-monopoly in movie theaters, director Miguel Contreras Torres (center) launched a crusade against his influence; this 1951 cartoon in *El Universal* depicts "Don Guillermo" Jenkins as a Hydra—whose heads comprise his partners Gabriel Alarcón, Emilio Azcárraga, Manuel Espinosa Yglesias, and Luis Montes—towering over a sleeping government official.

Despite President Alemán's enactment (1949) and revision (1952) of a film industry law, Jenkins's influence—critics would say stranglehold—over Mexican cinema only grew, as this 1953 image from *Excélsior* reflects.

In the early 1950s, Jenkins's man at Puebla city hall was Nicolás Vázquez (second from left), his long-serving notary. Vázquez ran an exemplary administration, publishing annual accounts, which included subsidies for public works from Jenkins. Here they attend Puebla's Cinco de Mayo celebration in 1951, accompanied by US Ambassador William O'Dwyer (left) and labor leader Martín Rivera (right). Courtesy of José Luis Vázquez Nava.

His film assets largely managed by Manuel Espinosa and Gabriel Alarcón, Jenkins spent much of his time in the 1950s attending to his farm near Matamoros, southwestern Puebla. When Cárdenas expropriated the Atencingo estate in 1937–1938, Jenkins slyly retained seven thousand acres—typically registered to frontmen—on which he continued to grow cane and melon. Courtesy of William Anstead Jenkins.

In 1954 Jenkins set up the Mary Street Jenkins Foundation, Mexico's first US-style endowment-based charity. The board members consisted of (left to right, top to bottom) Jenkins; his right-hand man Manuel Espinosa; sugar industry colleague Felipe García Eguiño; his old friend Sergio Guzmán; his private secretary Manuel Cabañas; and his twenty-three-year-old adopted son and biological grandson, Bill. Courtesy of William Anstead Jenkins.

Jenkins spent much of his free time in his later years with Sergio Guzmán, seen here at the 1958 opening of the dental practice of his son Teto. Despite that friendship he remained a lonely man, visiting his wife's grave each afternoon, sitting on a stool, and reading to her. Courtesy of Sergio Mastretta Guzmán.

A last trip home: Jenkins made a final visit to Shelbyville, Tennessee, in 1962, for the eightieth birthday of his closest sister, Mamie (bottom right). Joining them were siblings (left to right) Kate, Ruth, Joe, and Anne. Courtesy of Rosemary Eustace Jenkins.

For many years after his death, Jenkins was remembered with services at his graveside on June 4. Those present at the 1965 event included (middle row, left to right) Felipe García Eguiño, Manuel Espinosa, Governor of Puebla Aarón Merino Fernández, Bill Jenkins, Puebla Mayor Carlos Vergara Soto, Sergio Guzmán, Nicolás Vázquez (elected to the Jenkins Foundation board on Jenkins's death), and Manuel Lara y Parra, rector of Puebla's state university. Courtesy of José Luis Vázquez Nava.

Jenkins lives on today in the name of Puebla City's convention center (depicted), the UDLAP Jenkins Graduate School in Mexico City, the Jenkins Foundation Wellness Center at the capital's American School, and countless plaques across the state of Puebla and elsewhere, registering Jenkins Foundation support for the restoration of churches, building of schools, and creation of sports facilities, parks, and monuments. Photo by Andrew Paxman.

Enterprise, Profiteering, and the Death of the Golden Age

Mexican cinema is at once one of the best and one of the worst in the world. For every film of artistic and folkloric value like Roots, María Candelaria *or* The Pearl, *there are hundreds of bad imitations of Hollywood which present a false, ridiculous Mexico.*

ERICO VERISSIMO, *Mexico* (1957)

Acapulco

In late 1946, quite by accident, William Jenkins discovered Acapulco.[1] He had just fixed the Atencingo sale when he fell ill with a nagging pneumonia. His doctor advised him to head to the coast and spend some time convalescing. So Jenkins had his chauffeur drive him down to Veracruz, the favored seaside spot for vacationing Pueblans. The city was famous for its café culture and the Caribbean accent of its music. But on arriving they encountered a *norte*, a harsh Gulf wind that strikes the port from time to time, whipping up the sand and making the sea too choppy for swimming. Jenkins loved to bathe in the sea, so he and his chauffeur turned round. They made the lengthy trip back up to Puebla, crossed the central plateau, and took the highway that snaked down to the Pacific Coast through the corrugated state of Guerrero.

When Jenkins first beheld it, Acapulco was barely awakening from more than a century of slumber. In colonial times, it had been the destination of the Manila Galleon, bringing spices, porcelain, ivory, and silk from China and India. At the Acapulco dock, the goods were packed onto mule trains headed for Veracruz. There they were loaded onto the treasure fleet, bound for Seville. But at independence, trade with Spain collapsed. By the Revolution the port was still a backwater, most of its 10,000 inhabitants, many the mulatto descendants of slaves, perched upon sleepy hills that overlooked a decrepit harbor. Yet revival was soon afoot. Mexico's revolutionary modernizers, ever alert for lucrative real estate ventures, perceived Acapulco's new potential in tourism. They built a highway from the capital in 1927 and began snapping up beachfront for themselves. Six years later the Hotel Mirador was opened, with its view of the La Quebrada cliffs. Guests could gawp at Acapulco's bravest fishermen, recast for tourists as "cliff divers," defying death 150 feet below by timing each plunge with the sea swells. During the 1940s, as President Alemán made Acapulco a pet project, the town would triple in size.[2]

Jenkins loved Acapulco at once. He fell for the balmy climate and beautiful views, the easygoing people, the respite from the demands and the din of Puebla City. He foresaw fishing trips and having friends and relatives to stay. The place could be a panacea for Margaret, his second and most vulnerable daughter, in between her sad marriages and battles with the bottle. That winter he roomed in the house of a friend, on a hillside above the municipal beach. It had a view to the west of Acapulco Bay, then a pristine six-mile curve of sand with no sign of life but the odd fishing hut. When his host mentioned that the house was for sale, Jenkins bought it. Soon he had guests; one of his first was José Ignacio Márquez, Archbishop of Puebla (to the family: *Padre Nachito*). But this home was only temporary.

Jenkins's next acquisition was a prime patch of realty. On the very summit of the same hill lay a disused artillery emplacement. Jenkins somehow convinced the authorities to part with the property, and there he erected his ideal holiday home: a large building of three tiers, with wrap-around balconies and eight bedrooms on the top floor. It could sleep up to thirty guests and servants. There was a garage for several cars and a large swimming pool. When it was finished, in 1950, the press took note. In Puebla, Jenkins boasted a half-acre apartment from whose third-story windows he could survey much of the city that was his fiefdom. In Acapulco, he again dwelt on high. From much of Acapulco Bay and many points within the town, one could raise one's gaze to that rotund hill and see the house of Mr. Jenkins, perched on top of it like a happy nipple.

Acapulco was a tonic for Jenkins and a salve for his family. Forty years of hard work in Puebla, with weekly trips to Atencingo and the capital, had earned him one of Mexico's biggest fortunes, but the routine had separated him from his wife and distanced him from his daughters. As a widower, he tried to be a family man again.

Easing this task, ensuring he was not the only man among women and children, was his new son-in-law.[3] Ronnie Eustace was a jovial Englishman, handsome and tall, who had met and charmed Jane on the ski slopes of Switzerland. Once his country was at war, Eustace joined the Royal Air Force, which posted him to Canada for training. When on leave, Ronnie would meet up with Jane at the Jenkins home in Beverly Hills, or in Montreal, and in the latter city they were married. Jane then had to endure four anxious years as her husband piloted bombing missions over Japanese-held Burma. By war's end, the strain of separation and opposite goals—Jane wanted to move to England, Ronnie to move to Mexico—had grown to breaking point. Ever strong-willed, Jane flew to Montreal to ask for a divorce. Her father talked her out of it. He liked the sound of Ronnie, and in time his instinct was vindicated. Jane and Ronnie would be spouses for more than sixty-five years. Only Jane, the least spoiled of the five daughters, the one who parented her siblings more than she had been parented herself, had the selflessness and stamina to ensure her marriage was a happy one.

For Ronnie, postwar England was a dour place: cities half-ruined by the Luftwaffe, basic foods still rationed. He saw more opportunity in Mexico, where he could seek a job from his father-in-law. So in early 1946, he and Jane drove from Canada to Puebla, where for several years they lived with Jenkins. Later they made their home on a hill in the upper-income enclave of La Paz, a new subdivision in which Jenkins had invested. In the affable and confident Ronnie, Jenkins hoped he might have a new associate, someone he could cultivate like Espinosa and Alarcón. In the meantime, he was happy to have his company at chess or fishing.

Since Acapulco was a ten-hour trek from Puebla by automobile, Jenkins acquired an airplane. He could now take his expanding family, his favorite guests, such as his best friend Sergio Guzmán and his tennis pal Luis Artasánchez, and their families too. Whoever came, he always brought Mía (Amelia García), the household cook who had been with the Jenkins since Mary took her in as an orphan the 1920s. In these later years Mía was his most regular and faithful companion. So often were they seen together, it became a joke among the Puebla elite that this plump, dark, and pretty woman was Jenkins's mistress. Ever frugal, Jenkins got the plane secondhand—it was a US wartime cast-off—and he split the purchase with his friend Rómulo O'Farrill. He also bought a fishing boat, which he named after Jane's infant daughter, Rosemary. He moored the *Rosa María* at Acapulco's nascent yacht club, where his booming, Anglo-accented Spanish would signal his arrival to everyone.

Trips on the *Rosa María* became the focus of each visit, with guests told to be up at six to head out for a productive day on the water. Jenkins applied the same industrial vigor to fishing as he had to planting cane or building theaters. There was no time to waste, and each guest was to handle his or her own line. Since some preferred to bask in the sun the lines sometimes became tangled, to much grumbling from their host. Jenkins's desire to catch ever greater quantities meant that every few years he would replace his vessel with a bigger one: *Rosa María II, III* and eventually *IV*, which could sleep several people and make trips up the coast. Whatever tuna and dorado the guests could not eat, which was the vast bulk of it, would be packed in ice and stowed on his plane for the flight back to Puebla. Jenkins would make gifts of the fish to the nuns of the Trinitarian Order and their orphanage. Mary had always supported the Trinitarians.

Each of these boats was captained by an amiable local named Héctor Morlet, whom Jenkins treated with utmost respect, insisting his guests do likewise. Morlet came from a well-known Acapulco family but lacked the fair complexion that would mark him as upper crust. When once on a fishing trip Elizabeth patronizingly scolded Morlet, Jenkins dressed down his daughter in front of everyone. When the president of the yacht club refused the dark-skinned Morlet admission to the clubhouse, supposedly on account of his attire, Jenkins dispatched Ronnie to Mexico City to talk with club bigwigs and have the policy reversed.

For some of the adults, Jenkins's lust for productive fishing became a bit of a chore, so his most frequent shipmates came to be his teenaged grandson Billy and his two young godsons: Oscar, Gabriel Alarcón's second son, and Luisito, son of Luis Artasánchez. For the boys, the boat was all adventure. There was the crash of waves, the spray of salt water, the wrestling to land a big tuna. There was freedom from parents, and Jenkins let them drink as much Coca-Cola as they wanted. As he reached seventy, Jenkins discovered the grandfather within. Far from the fearsome businessman, or the stern father of five women, in the company of children Jenkins was tender. When Oscar and Luisito stayed in Acapulco, they shared a bedroom, and they would play the old trick of opening their door a fraction and placing a paper cup of water on top. Called to the room, Jenkins invariably responded. He knew what was coming but he always walked in, and he always laughed when the splash came.

The house was spartan, the pool unheated, and Jenkins did not serve alcohol. When they were not fishing, guests found themselves swimming or playing cards or chess. In the evenings their host would prepare

Tennessee iced tea. His healthy regimen was not to everyone's taste, but over the years he hosted a range of visitors, from his sisters—Mamie, Kate, and Ruth would visit annually—to senior executives and state governors. Vanderbilt chancellor Harvie Branscomb and his wife came once or twice a year. Guests who did not know Jenkins well, especially children, who held this bear-like man with the fearsome name and thunderous voice in awe, were often surprised at how lightly he behaved: his frequent laughter, his lusty singing of the "Toreador Song" from Bizet's opera *Carmen* as he pottered about in his swimming trunks. They were struck by how he treated his servants with affection, even as equals, especially Mía. She would scold him when she caught his unsubtle cheating at cards and tease him about the fruit he had brought from his ranch in Puebla. "Sir, your melons are terrible!"

Jenkins was adamant that his Acapulco home be a retreat, one where everyone could feel at ease. As on the tennis courts of the Alpha Club, he did not mix business with pleasure.

There was one exception. During each visit his local manager, Pepe Aguirre, would come calling. Aguirre ran the Acapulco Investments Company, which Jenkins set up to bet on the resort's development. Through it he bought a long band of property named Costa Azul, parallel to the beach but slightly set back from it, at the east end of the main bay.[4] The constitution banned foreigners from owning property within fifty kilometers of the coast, but—as with his Mexicali cotton lands buy a few years before—this did not stop Jenkins, either from joining Acapulco's tourist boom or from owning a hilltop home that everyone could see. He could count on frontmen to hold his assets. He could also count on the friendship of the president.

Emissary of Enterprise

If Jenkins took a slight turn in December 1946, Mexico took an emphatic one. The month in which he sold Atencingo and encountered Acapulco was the month in which Alemán became head of state, and the nation's political trajectory veered markedly to the right.[5] Alemán would clamp down on labor activism and force most unions to adhere to the ruling machine, which had just undergone a second facelift to become the Institutional Revolutionary Party (PRI). He would also adopt the United States' anti-communist agenda and model an intelligence apparatus on the FBI, its chief function being to spy on Mexicans who did not adhere to the PRI.

Alemán embraced monopoly in many forms. His corporatist state tolerated almost no opposition victories, even at municipal levels. It imposed governors upon the states with regularity. It insisted that workers, peasants, teachers, bureaucrats, and even businesses join unions and associations allied to the PRI. This political monopoly found something of a mirror image in the private sector. Industries came to be concentrated in the hands of one or two firms.

In tandem with Alemán's policies of repression, co-optation, and centralization, and partly because of them, corruption rose to chronic proportions. There had always been graft among the ruling elite, but under Alemán it evolved: it was more blatant and more entrepreneurial. The venal rapacity of Maximino became the investor savvy of Alemán and his circle. Mexico's new leaders were no longer satisfied with rake-offs; they wanted stakes in start-ups whose fortunes they could manipulate with contracts, tax breaks, and subsidies—nest eggs from which they would further benefit after their maximum six years in office. They took symbiotic convenience to new heights. And they continued to call themselves revolutionaries.

"I shall either save the Mexican Revolution or sink with it," declared Alemán after taking office. When his interlocutor relayed these words to a national congress of communal farmers, the acclaim was clamorous. Alemán then met his pledge by issuing protections for private farms and pouring millions into dams to benefit agroindustry. Agricultural output shot up and the profits benefitted the few, politicians notable among them. As early as 1947, the intellectual Daniel Cosío Villegas pronounced: "the term revolution has now lost its meaning." Later on, the historian Enrique Krauze would label Alemán "The Businessman President."[6]

The course on which Alemán took the country was much to Jenkins's liking. Though not as close personally to him as to his predecessor, Jenkins was closer ideologically, and he and Alemán shared a basic contradiction in their approach to capitalism. The new business-friendly political culture prompted a slew of start-up companies, eager to compete for the wallets and purses of the middle class but also a concentration of ownership in existing sectors that helped make the wealthy much wealthier. These conflicting impulses were manifest in Jenkins's career from the 1940s onward. Even as he strengthened his film industry dominion, he continued to diversify his investments, and here his venture capitalism took on a missionary aspect. He lent capital to a large number of people, many of them Puebla friends or their sons, with a view to cultivating them as industrialists. These were far from the predatory loans he made decades earlier. The interest rates were reasonable, and he was no longer so hard-hearted about securing a return, let alone foreclosing. Jenkins became, in effect, an emissary of enterprise.[7]

This strategy originated in his first investments in movie theaters. As of 1938, nearly all of his businesses were joint ventures. While in some ways this let him minimize risk—danger of seizure, exposure to the IRS—Jenkins usually assumed most of the financial liability. He did not expect his partners, always younger than himself, to bring much cash to the table, so he lent them all or most of their 50 percent stake on the understanding they would repay him from future profits. Whether making an investment or a loan, Jenkins applied the same principle to smaller ventures, which he initiated with men of less experience than Espinosa or Alarcón. Except for his daughter Elizabeth, who dabbled unsuccessfully in film production, they were always men.

To Eduardo Mestre's son Manuel, Jenkins loaned a sum to help him build a sugar mill, Pedernales, in Michoacán. Adolfo "Chops" Casares, a chess-playing friend, borrowed 500,000 pesos to set up a Puebla City store selling electric appliances and a further sum to establish a chain of tire dealerships. Edmundo Cobel, a tennis partner, gained capital to build a thread-making mill after his family's clothing store went bust. Joaquín Ibáñez, a lawyer friend, obtained a 500,000-peso loan to help develop a residential neighborhood, Chulavista. Rarely did these moves smack of political favors; an exception was a 270,000-peso investment in a clinic founded by Gonzalo Bautista O'Farrill, son of Puebla's recently departed governor. Jenkins also aided men of lesser means, including some of his nonwhite employees. These were acts not of paternalistic charity but of belief in advancement by merit. Once he agreed to a proposal from his chauffeur to co-invest in a pig farm. Another time he provided his farm overseer Facundo Sánchez, a rancher in his own right, with introductions to Puebla's bank managers.[8]

Jenkins also tried to foster enterprise within his family. To his son-in-law Ronnie Eustace, he loaned capital for a Dr. Pepper franchise. He thought this would help the young Englishman find his feet in Puebla. But it launched after various soft-drink bottlers had set up in the city and failed within a couple of years.[9] For Lawrence Higgins, Elizabeth's husband, Jenkins made major contributions to two ventures: a Mexico City assembly plant for Nash cars, opened in 1947, for which he complemented US financing by putting up $1 million, and the national distributor for

Studebaker, begun in 1949, in which he invested $200,000.[10] While neither proved successful, Jenkins later loaned $150,000 to his nephew Paul Buntzler Jr. for a stake in Promexa, an assembler and distributor of Volkswagens. This was a much better bet, as it was the forerunner of the huge Puebla-based automaker, Volkswagen de México.[11]

Jenkins did not merely invest; he encouraged. He liked to get his charges thinking about the wise use of capital when they were still young. The sons of his friend Sergio Guzmán, Sergio Jr. and Alejandro, were two such pupils. While at college, they started personal investment accounts with Jenkins, depositing some $1,000 apiece in his care. Every three months, Jenkins would tally their profits, type up a statement of accounts, and hand the note and the sums to Guzmán for passing on to his boys. Of course, the sums were a pittance to Jenkins. What mattered was that his friends' offspring grew up learning the lessons of capitalism.[12]

How many firms Jenkins cofounded is impossible to say. Every investment and loan he made he jotted down in a little black book, which he kept in a safe in his office and which has since disappeared. But it is doubtful he was aware of every purpose to which his money was put. He made loans and investments on instinct. An entrepreneur visited him in his office, pitched his idea, and, if Jenkins trusted him and thought the proposal viable, he reached for his checkbook. There was no due diligence, no market research, and little follow-up, apart from occasional visits by the partner to make a report and hand over a share of the profits—that is, if profits were forthcoming, for Jenkins's wits sometimes failed him in later years. As he entered his eighties, his trust would be abused more often and he would grow remote from some of his ventures. Did he know, for example, that one of his partners invested in a couple of Mexico City nightclubs? Did he know that one of those clubs, the Safari Bar, was a hook-up joint for homosexuals?[13]

Ironically, while he was guiding young capitalists, Jenkins became more of a monopolist in film and more of a rent-seeker in textiles. In exhibition, by far his largest enterprise, he continued to muscle out rivals and consume their circuits of theaters. At his textile mills, he made minimal investment in upgrades, relying for profits on backroom deals with union leaders, off-the-books sales, and a manipulation of bankruptcy laws that let him fire workers almost at will. Jenkins was able to get away with such practices due to the symbiotic links he had long cultivated with politicians, relationships now very much of convenience, not necessity.

Jenkins's contradictory approach to business, in the Alemán years and after, was at one with the postwar *zeitgeist*. It reflected the capitalistic thrust of an era in which new businesses multiplied, stimulated by unprecedented consumerism, yet in which wealth became increasingly concentrated in the hands of the business elite. Of Jenkins's twin strategies, the missionary-capitalist and the monopolistic, the latter had much the greater impact.

To a great extent, the 1940s was the decade in which contemporary Mexico was shaped, with all its disparities of wealth. There were oligarchs before, and some of the big-business families of the Porfirian era were still powerful fifty years later. But the Revolution, and the peak of its social project under Cárdenas, had opened wide the gates of wealth creation, redistributing land, raising wages, and greatly enlarging employment in the public sector; it notably expanded the middle class. From the 1940s, those gates began to narrow. Social and economic hierarchies resumed some of their old rigidity, with the poorest quarter of the population mired in an extreme poverty that went unchanged, and arguably worsened, by 1970.[14]

Atencingo Revisited

Jenkins's missionary capitalism and his charity drew approving comment. As early as 1946, a newspaper noted—flatteringly but not inaccurately— that in all Jenkins's dealings, "his generous hand is extended, with the aim that Puebla City has intense activity in its commercial, banking and industrial sectors." Years later, his private secretary Manuel Cabañas would write: "He organized numerous partnerships, partly with the purpose that other people would participate in the economic benefits of his businesses." Cabañas then reeled off a list, far from complete, of seventeen companies, in sectors ranging from road-building to ice-making.[15]

Although Jenkins was long past caring about his reputation, his good deeds, as mediated by the sycophancy of the local press, were helping sow the seeds of a White Legend—a benign narrative that would grow alongside the long-established Black one. This newer mythification, largely confined to Puebla at this stage, also drew on his multiplying acts of charity.

When *La Opinión* got wind of Jenkins's designs for a huge orphanage, it splashed the headline "Jenkins Donates to Puebla Thirty Million Pesos." In fact, the project was barely in the planning stage. When Octaviano Márquez was invested as Puebla's archbishop in 1951, Jenkins numbered among the event's *padrinos* (patrons). The title implied his financial support for the Catholic Church; it also implied Octaviano's blessing upon this American Protestant.[16]

Jenkins's hobnobbing with sacred and secular hierarchies lay open to local interpretation. Just as it bolstered his standing among conservatives as a member of the Great and the Good, so too it cemented his reputation in socialist quarters as a Bad Gringo and a plutocrat, an ever-scheming capitalist with the power to impose his choices for governor and Puebla City mayor. By the end of the decade, such conflicting views about Puebla's richest individual would fuel a growing social division in the city between left and right, a tension that would spiral into protest and violence. In and around Atencingo, this sort of violence was already happening, and it owed a great deal to divisions among the millworkers once sown by Jenkins and Manuel Pérez.

One Friday in January 1949, the labor activist Adalberto García boarded a bus in Atlixco, homeward bound for the Matamoros Valley.[17] García was the worker at Atencingo who had stood up to Fernando Pérez and his gunmen at the founding of its independent union. Since then, his tenacity had earned him election to the state Congress. As a representative he was vocal, making him a thorn in the side of the Betancourt regime. His criticism often targeted the CROM, the labor federation that since the Maximino era had drawn strength from its coziness with the state government. That week Betancourt had called García for a meeting, and the governor had been quite cordial. A friend warned García to stay alert, for the CROM had recently issued threats against its enemies, but Betancourt's calm manner set him at ease.

García settled in a seat near the front and opened a newspaper. Not long after, the bus made an unscheduled stop and three men in workers' clothes climbed aboard. One sat near the driver, another in the middle, the third at the back. García, examining the news, paid them little heed. After the bus resumed its journey, the workman sitting in the middle stood up, took out a pistol, and fired into García's cranium, splattering his brains onto the sports pages. The workman near the driver then stood and fired at García's crumpled form. Both gunmen emptied their chambers into his body. The assassins yelled at the driver to stop, and as he screeched to a halt they jumped off and headed back toward Atlixco. Soon a taxi picked them up and whisked them away, but its driver was recognized: a local tough guy nicknamed El Chorizo. The men were never seen again, nor was the bus driver. The police claimed he had likely been killed as the gunmen later covered their tracks. García's friends guessed it was the police who had handled the disappearance. The official version, as relayed by a federal agent to the Interior Ministry, held that El Chorizo and other known accomplices were members of the CROM.

García's assassination was only the most spectacular among the killings that shook the region in Jenkins's wake. When the Atencingo millworkers had formed their independent union three years before, they had affiliated with the CTM. This decision displaced the CROM, which for several years had collaborated with Jenkins and Pérez to keep the mill in line. The CROM's affiliates were not habitually subservient to a company; they too pushed for better pay and benefits. But given the CTM's nationwide ascendance at their expense, they were willing to pact with capitalists. At Atencingo some CROM loyalists remained, enough to give the underdog union the sense that the plant might be retaken.[18] So the struggles at the Atencingo mill in the late 1940s and 1950s were at heart an inter-union turf war.

Nonetheless, local people attributed the killings—of García and other activists—to Jenkins. Such assumptions had a certain appeal, for the shadow of the American lingered long at Atencingo, leading many to believe he still owned the mill. Espinosa's three-year management stint in the late 1940s was part of it; everyone knew he was Jenkins's right-hand man. Then there were Jenkins's continued visits to the region to inspect his lands. These were the patch that the expropriation had officially let him keep; a much larger tract of some 7,000 acres that he had retained in secret; and several thousand further acres that he had subsequently bought on the quiet. These tracts he now held through several *prestanombres*, frontmen he felt he could trust, such as Sergio Guzmán's young son Sergio Jr., Sergio Jr.'s wife, and two former Atencingo field managers, Facundo Sánchez and Facundo's younger brother Manuel. The ownership was not much of a secret at the mill, for in addition to melon and other fruit, Jenkins persisted in growing cane, which was then carted to Atencingo for processing. A former millworker would recall being cautioned by his supervisor one day: "Be careful with that sugar. It belongs to Jenkins."[19]

If anything, Jenkins's presence would seem to strengthen over time, for in 1957 a new governor appointed Manuel Sánchez to head the Atencingo cooperative. Facundo's brother was a local wheeler-dealer, who had used his family relationship to Doña Lola to gain credence with the cane growers, while he also worked for Jenkins. His ability to play all sides helped him get elected (that is, selected) as mayor of Matamoros, after which he entered the state Congress. But his climb up the greasy pole of politics hit an especially slippery patch at Atencingo. Although he obtained high outputs of cane, his unctuous style inspired little respect among the peasants, and his regime embezzled 2 million pesos. As protests against Sánchez rose, cane growers cited his proximity to Jenkins—whom many still believed to be Atencingo's owner—as one of their complaints. Before an audit could reveal his fraud, the clamor of the cane growers, incensed at low dividends from the 1960 harvest, would force Sánchez to resign.[20]

On the other hand, vilification of Jenkins was often a deliberate rhetorical strategy, a way of fortifying community solidarity and stirring local passions at opportune times. In 1950, when the true believer Porfirio Jaramillo was still in charge of the cooperative, the Mexican Communist Party hired Arturo García Bustos, who had studied under Frida Kahlo, to paint murals at the cooperative's new office building. The commission was to show the historic struggle of Mexico's cane growers. One panel feted Emiliano Zapata and his soldiers, riding abreast under a banner of "Land and Liberty." But the panel that caused a commotion, including death threats that forced Bustos to leave town before he had finished it, depicted Manuel Pérez paying off a blindfolded gunman, while a peasant family bore away the body of a white-clad loved one. Half-hidden behind Pérez, as though whispering orders in the manager's ear, stood Jenkins.[21]

In 1957, the town erected a monument to the mill's independent union, marking the place where the constituent assembly had convened on February 17, 1946. The plaque read: "Gathered here, the people of Atencingo, encouraged by the presence of national leaders and colleagues from sister locals across the country, demanded justice and respect for our laws, so to emancipate themselves from the capitalist oppression that for so many years held them in misery."[22]

In their demands to federal authorities, cane growers would single out Jenkins. A 1954 petition to the president, also published as an open letter, named "the North American William O. Jenkins" as Atencingo's former "feudal lord" and blamed him for many of their problems. As late as 1959, some were claiming he still owned the estate; one such petition from landless villagers ran: "We have no schools, communications, lands, water, houses, food—but we do indeed have bosses, *caciques*, oppression . . . others who have tried to speak have been assassinated by the henchmen of Jenkins, the dreadful jackal who has to drink the blood of our race in order to bathe himself in wealth."[23]

A mix of resentment and xenophobia, the rhetoric of the Atencingo region sought to sway a federal ruling class that still used the lingo of revolutionary nationalism. Complaints against Jenkins had won them land in Cárdenas's day, so why not now? But in the 1940s and for most of the 1950s, a time of rapprochement with the United States, gringophobia became a device of limited usefulness. Presidential pronouncements about the promises of the Revolution and the sovereignty of the nation were not supposed to be taken literally.

Besides, the Mexican state had higher priorities than to cater to the complaints of communal farmers. Alemán had set in motion a policy shift in favor of large-scale agro-industry, and his successors would follow suit. The era coincided with the start of the Green Revolution, a global movement to increase food output through intensive use of pesticides, fertilizers, and high-yield crops in the developing world. Mexico was an early and enthusiastic participant.[24] Peasants who wished to farm their own land as they saw fit, and for whom dignity was as much an incentive as profit, were an afterthought. As far as the federal government was concerned, when it came to feeding the nation, the Green Revolution trumped the Mexican Revolution.

Jenkins's Film Monopoly: A Failed Assault

The mightier Jenkins grew in the film industry, the more his sins piled up. So believed Miguel Contreras Torres, who in 1960 published *The Black Book of Mexican Cinema*, a 450-page compendium of Jenkins's wrongdoings. This entertaining but unreliable exposé emitted the ardor and the odor of an embittered cineaste. It was the culmination of a decade's lobbying, demanding presidential protection for Mexican film, in which Contreras cast himself as a lone David slinging stones at the gringo Goliath.[25] Its chief allegations were that Jenkins and his partners killed off the Golden Age by depriving the national cinema of adequate funding and screen time, and that they did so for easy profits, in cahoots with Hollywood distributors. Absent any dispassionate analysis of the American's role, Contreras's allegations became conventional wisdom among critics and historians.[26]

Contreras was a maverick.[27] Born to a landowning family, he left home at fifteen to join Carranza's army, becoming a major by the end of hostilities. He then parlayed his good looks and charisma into a career as an actor-director-producer. He also wrote the scripts, directed photography, and edited the footage. With the advent of talkies, he limited himself to bit parts, preferring to direct and produce. He specialized in patriotic dramas, such as *Juárez and Maximilian*. Some of these starred his European wife, Medea de Novara, whose real name was the less alluring Herminne Kindle Futcher. He even put her in a *Maximilian* remake, *The Mad Empress*, surrounding her with Hollywood actors and aiming at the US box office (where it flopped).[28] During World War II his budgets grew bigger as he wrought biographical films about Latin American independence heroes. He had access to generous financing because, with his revolutionary background, he knew the right generals. Contreras was an embodiment of Mexican cinema, in all its nationalist glory and some of its internationalist pretensions. His were not the kind of films that won prizes but most of them did make money.

When Alemán took office, Contreras's luck changed and his creativity waned. Here too his career mirrored industry trends. Unlike his predecessors, the president was not an officer; military connections ceased to count so much in Alemán's modernizing Mexico. By 1950, Contreras was having trouble financing his pictures. That decade he would direct just seven films, half of what he made in the 1940s. The problem was that the Jenkins Group constituted the biggest purse, and for commercial reasons the Group and the Film Bank declined to finance more of his historical epics. From that moment, Contreras crusaded against Jenkins.[29]

He was the loudest malcontent but not the first. After the war, isolated criticisms had merged into a crescendo, as Jenkins used his Mexico City dominance for leverage with distributors. His growing muscle in what was now a buyer's market allowed Espinosa and Alarcón to dictate terms. As exhibitors, they could offer a lower percentage of the box-office peso to Mexican distributors. As financiers, they could force leaner budgets on producers. Since these distributors and producers were often the same people, they found themselves squeezed at both ends, so they clamored for subsidy support and screen quotas.[30]

In 1947 the newly constituted Mexican Academy of Film Arts and Sciences launched an annual awards ceremony, modeled after the Oscars, and in a swipe at Hollywood's renewed box-office dominance they named their prizes the Ariel. The allusion was to the famous essay by Rodó, which had celebrated the aesthetic spirit of the Latin Americans as superior to the efficient but soulless culture of the United States.[31] As at Atencingo, postwar gringophobia was creeping into film industry rhetoric.

That year Alemán threw the vociferous producers a bone by nationalizing the Film Bank—now the National Film Bank—and doubling its capital to 10 million pesos. But the Jenkins Group continued to loom large, both as theater operators and as financiers for producers needing to complete their budgets.[32]

Criticism swelled again in 1949. The year saw a record 108 films made, a 50 percent increase in three years, so competition for screens was at a new intensity. More alarming still, the Jenkins Group had only grown in power, Alarcón having captured the Rodríguez Brothers Circuit, the largest exhibitor in and around Monterrey, and Espinosa having built another six theaters in the capital. In turn, independent northern exhibitors lobbied Alemán, claiming Jenkins and Alarcón were hurting them through monopolistic practices. One alleged tactic was to press Películas Nacionales, the main distributor of Mexican films, to withhold product. Lack of access to Mexican fare, especially popular in the provinces, augured bankruptcy for many theaters. By April, when Monterrey's independents gained an audience with Alemán, their Mexico City counterparts were voicing similar complaints.[33]

Creative personnel were equally alarmed. José Revueltas, a prominent screenwriter, fired a two-page broadside in *Hoy*, the leading newsmagazine: "Jenkins is Strangling the Film Industry!" In very frank language for an era when the wealthy were rarely criticized by name, Revueltas assailed "the sinister figure of Jenkins," called Espinosa and Alarcón "traitors" to the country and exposed the dark side of industry economics. He echoed the Monterrey claim that the Jenkins Group was bullying Películas Nacionales. Its ploy, he wrote, aimed to harass rivals into surrendering, either selling out or submitting to a merger. Worse, the Jenkins Group was deliberately "burning" Mexican films: giving them the briefest of premieres, regardless of their popularity, before shipping them to less desirable theaters; it was a cost-cutting move, and Hollywood product would fill the gaps. Distributors refusing to play by these rules, opting to deal with the independents, risked a blanket boycott of all of their films by the Jenkins Group.

Revueltas feared that these practices would enable Jenkins to take over the industry's production side. He called for state assistance to resist "American capital" and "the darkest and most aggressive interests that exist against the Mexican fatherland."[34]

Alemán was compelled to act. Since his inauguration, he had projected himself as patron of the national arts. He liked the company of movie stars and to be seen with them for public relations purposes. It was widely rumored that he slept with some, including the biggest diva of them all, María Félix.[35] So Congress concocted a first-ever film act. It promised protections, including the holy grail of screen quotas. But the Film Industry Law, enacted in 1949, was only an opening gambit. Like any Mexican law, it had to be followed by regulating language and then by actual enforcement. Initial steps were not encouraging: the Interior Ministry declared that all one-theater towns be subject to a 50 percent screen quota. Since Mexican pictures outmatched foreign fare in small towns anyway, the rule was an empty gesture.[36]

It was then that Contreras Torres harnessed his typewriter. Fearing the government would capitulate, and frustrated in his efforts to fund his latest picture, the patriotic producer-director shot the opening salvo in his Ten Years' War against Jenkins. He bashed out the first of 120 polemics, all about "the MONOPOLY," for newspapers *Excélsior* and *El Universal*. He wrote a letter to the president about the National Film Bank, claiming it was confining its support to producers in the Jenkins camp. He concocted an audacious letter to Jenkins himself, claiming his actions had reduced the industry to such penury that its workers were vulnerable to communist ideas. The intrepid veteran demanded a face-to-face meeting with the magnate, adding that if he got no reply within forty-eight hours he would make his letter public—and so he did, publishing it in three dailies. Three weeks later, Alemán gave him an audience, an occasion the polemicist used to request Jenkins's expulsion from the country, on account of his "shady dealings."[37]

In the short run, Contreras's campaign seemed to be working. Before 1950 was out, Alemán had commissioned former president Abelardo Rodríguez to mediate. Rodríguez devised a plan to consolidate producers' distribution efforts at home and abroad. In 1951 the state at last issued its regulating legislation. It looked more promising: the 50 percent screen quota would apply across the nation.[38]

Hollywood was battle-ready. Its studios had already resisted quotas in Britain and France. In cahoots with the Jenkins Group they forged a twin strategy. The studios, having conferred with the State Department, threatened that the quota would be answered with restrictions on Mexican films in the United States. The prospect was daunting, for Mexico made a much higher portion of its film revenues in the United States than vice versa. Meanwhile, fifty Mexican exhibitors sought an injunction, claiming the quota was unconstitutional. The stay was granted.

Alemán knew Hollywood well and surely predicted its belligerence. He had taken the nationalistic stance expected of him. Maintaining the façade, he let the quota remain, without imposing it. At the end of his tenure, Congress would approve a revised Film Industry Law, retaining the quota: another safe move, as the Supreme Court had not yet ruled on the issue. It would fall to Alemán's successor, Adolfo Ruiz Cortines, to decide whether to enforce it.[39]

HOW MANY OF the allegations against the Jenkins Group were true? Certainly leverage over distributors was a critical dimension of its ability to expand at the expense of rivals. According to Contreras—and circumstantial evidence supports him—it was through such bullying that it forced Emilio Azcárraga to part with his precious Cadena de Oro, a twenty-venue circuit in Mexico City. Espinosa told both Mexican and Hollywood distributors that if they carried on supplying to Azcárraga's flagship Alameda Theater, he would refuse to screen their product at his theaters in the capital and all other cities where he dominated. Offering a little carrot to go with the stick, he pledged the distributors an extra 5 percent of the box-office take if they agreed to the boycott. As a result, Azcárraga was reduced to showing second-rate Mexican films and Hollywood reruns. In 1949, after a period of losses, Azcárraga sold stakes in six of his largest theaters to Jenkins and Alarcón. Two years later, focusing his resources on the infant industry of television, he surrendered control of the Cadena de Oro.[40]

Espinosa and Alarcón had an agreement to take turns picking whichever title they deemed likeliest to prove the blockbuster of the week. Espinosa, who had grown up in the business, showed a knack for choosing the right pictures. There came a day, however, when Alarcón felt he had been outfoxed once too often. Unannounced, he burst into Espinosa's office, yelling and brandishing a pistol, and demanded that Espinosa yield on some Hollywood hit. An armed Alarcón was not to be trifled with. He was a championship marksman; in rifle-shooting he had qualified for the Berlin Olympics. Following this contretemps, Jenkins suggested his lieutenants divide the distributors between them, three or four studios apiece. Hollywood was generally happy to work with Espinosa and Alarcón because they were building, or buying and improving, the best theaters. Their first-runs began to sign exclusive deals with individual studios to premiere their pictures.[41]

With the cream of US and Mexican output more or less taken by the Jenkins Group and its affiliates, independent exhibitors were left little more than the dregs: rereleased Hollywood fare and whatever European and Mexican films had not secured a major distributor. The larger the

Jenkins empire grew, the more it was able to engineer boycotts of attractive assets. Once Azcárraga's Cadena de Oro capitulated, there remained only one strong independent: Abelardo Rodríguez, the former "millionaire president," who held a fifteen-venue circuit in the capital and dominated the northwest, controlling fifty theaters from Mazatlán to Tijuana.[42]

On the production side, the Jenkins Group's influence was becoming substantial. This was an easy task for the sector was highly fragmented. As early as 1944, more than forty production outfits were active. Confusingly, some producers used multiple banners, which were often jumbled by the press. Jesús Grovas, a recurrent partner of Jenkins, owned Producciones Grovas, Cinematográfica Grovas, Grovas-Oro Films, Jesús A. Grovas y Compañía, Grovas SA, and (for a change) Dyana Films.[43] (There was a logic here: smaller companies offered lower tax exposure.) Decades later, when the Golden Age came to be chronicled, it still embarrassed most producers to admit they had gone cap-in-hand to the infamous gringo. Raúl de Anda, responsible for 128 pictures, gave a wide-ranging two-day interview about his career in which he mentioned the American as the builder of a theater monopoly and as a threat to Mexican distributors. Somehow he neglected to mention his regular receipt of Jenkins Group funding.[44]

Not unlike Hollywood, where Jewish immigrants and their sons famously created "an empire of their own," Mexico's film industry included prominent Jewish financiers and producers, and these too consorted with the Jenkins Group. One was Sam Wishñack, who in 1941 set up Filmex. Led by Wishñack's co-investor and coreligionary Gregorio Walerstein, Filmex produced some four features a year, many of them hits. When Jenkins took a stake in Filmex is unclear, but by 1953 he was writing to Walerstein about a contractual dispute involving the company, and from his language it was clear who was calling the shots. Walerstein later admitted he had to back down as Jenkins and Espinosa held 51 percent of the company's shares.[45]

Piecing together disparate sources, it is clear that under Alemán the Jenkins Group began operating at mass-production levels. Film finance was changing. Once the war ended, Mexico's private banks had cut back their lending, alarmed by poor returns and tardy repayments; a tendency among producers to inflate their budgets and line their pockets with the difference did not help. In 1947, the National Film Bank ostensibly became the biggest source of funding, but producers were still expected to come up with much of their budgets themselves. As they cast around for cash, they increasingly looked to exhibitors, seeking advances on box-office returns in exchange for exclusive screening rights. Espinosa and Alarcón were often happy to pay. They may have had the same backer, but they would be damned if they let the other snare the next María Félix melodrama, the next Pedro Infante swoon-fest. An article in 1953 claimed that Jenkins provided 80 percent of film finance. Though fanciful, the figure gives a sense of his towering stature. So does Espinosa's later recollection that he and Jenkins funded some four hundred films.[46]

As for Jenkins's hands-on involvement, any evidence is strictly anecdotal. He was a regular moviegoer, especially enjoying the comedies of Cantinflas, with whom he was friendly; in Acapulco they were neighbors and the actor would sometimes drop in. Jenkins liked to invite his grandchildren or the offspring of friends to the movies. One frequent invitee recalled that after seeing a film in which he had a stake he would telephone Espinosa or Alarcón from the box office, to discuss whether the investment had been a good one.[47]

In 1948 Jenkins tried to buy CLASA, which in owning sound stages was Mexico's closest equivalent to a Hollywood studio. Co-owner Salvador Elizondo was keen to resist. Letting Jenkins own Mexico's top production house, he said, would be as bad as "putting the Church in the hands of Lucifer." Four years later Elizondo withdrew from CLASA, and not long after he bumped into Jenkins. "Why don't you make some films for me?" Jenkins asked. The producer said he had quit the business but when Jenkins insisted he agreed to form a company. The financing arrived in the form of a check, delivered by Jenkins's chauffeur. Attached was a note, handwritten on scrap paper: "Salvador, I'm sending you the check for four million. I put it in your name because I don't know what your company is called."[48]

Jenkins may have kept an eye on his movies when they premiered, but his approach to production was cavalier. What mattered was that producers deliver quantities of content to help fill his theaters. Possibly he favored comedy, and there may have been indirect influence, in that the occasional character was altered, so as not to risk displeasing Don Guillermo. But Jenkins was foremost a financier. If his theaters made money, he was happy, for the exhibition side of the business was the most lucrative. If his movies fared poorly, his producers would presumably ensure that the National Film Bank took most of the financial hit.

WHY ALEMÁN ALLOWED Jenkins to tighten his grip on exhibition, privilege Hollywood fare, and expand into local production is a question with as many answers as there are limbs on an octopus, to recall a symbol of monopoly common at the time. Alemán was ideologically supportive of big business, unperturbed by monopolies, and admiring of the United States. The Mexican industry, for all its griping, was highly productive, averaging 95 features per year, up from an annual average of 64 under Ávila Camacho and 35 under Cárdenas, so Alemán could feasibly respond that Mexico's film community had never had it so good.[49]

Then there was the matter of mutual institutional convenience. The Jenkins Group theaters served Alemán, or purported to do so, just as they had served his predecessor: as a cheap escape for the proliferating urban millions, most of whom were still seeing their purchasing power eroded by high inflation; as forums for local films suffused with nationalist, conservative values, and as outlets for newsreel propaganda. Furthering Jenkins's usefulness to the regime, his other investments served the ongoing policy of Import-Substitution Industrialization (ISI).

Begun under Cárdenas but pursued with greater vigor by his successors, ISI encouraged foreign firms to reach the Mexican market not by exporting to it but by producing within it. Jenkins's backing had made possible the Nash and Packard auto-assembly plants in Mexico City and Puebla. He bankrolled smaller ventures including Puebla's Dr. Pepper franchise. He provided a significant investment in Nacional de Drogas, a leading pharmaceutical distributor (known today as Nadro), from soon after its founding in 1943. (He later expressed doubts about this business, feeling it paid its workers too generously.) He was also a shareholder in the airline Aero Transportes, which soon merged with the nation's leading carrier, Mexicana. All such moves served the ISI aim of replacing reliance on imported goods and services with an industrialization drive that would generate higher-paying jobs, boost purchasing power, facilitate technology transfer, and improve the country's self-regard. So did Jenkins's purchase of bonds from the bank Nafinsa, which was the state's main financing mechanism for ISI.[50]

Jenkins and Alemán were friends, besides. How close is hard to say, but they had known each other at least since Jenkins made his 1940 electoral loan, as Alemán had been Ávila Camacho's campaign manager. A sign of their proximity emerged in 1951, when several senators publicly criticized Jenkins, as a foreigner, for opining about Mexican politics. Amid speculation that Alemán was seeking to prolong his six-year mandate, the president had confided to Jenkins that he would not do so. Jenkins had evidently relayed this to a friend, and somehow the word got out.[51]

A year later, Jenkins admitted to a friend that he and Alemán had joined Rómulo O'Farrill in buying *Novedades*. There was little profit in newspapers, but this one had a lucrative side-business in comic books for adults, and the purchase came at a politically useful time, just weeks before Alemán's 1946 election. Jenkins asked his friend to be discreet with the news. He added: "It is not generally known that I am a shareholder, and I do not take any part whatever in any of the paper's activities. I am sure that if I did it would cause very unfavorable comment."[52]

Given Alemán's acquisitiveness and Jenkins's history with politicians, it is probable that the two shared interests elsewhere, such as in the nascent television sector, Acapulco real estate, and the film industry itself. As for Mexico's other leading media mogul, Emilio Azcárraga, Alemán had personal reasons for letting Jenkins strong-arm him and then gobble up his theaters. In the presidential campaign of 1940, Azcárraga had backed the opposition candidate.[53]

How to Enjoy Bankruptcy

Four years after the wartime textile boom ended, two of Puebla's most prominent mills declared bankruptcy.[54] La Concepción, the oldest factory in Atlixco, and El León, outside the same town, were relics of the Porfirian past. Owners had included some of the state's richest immigrants, and the clattering machinery on which they ran was of Victorian vintage. Like the entire sector, both mills had scored huge sales during World War II and then suffered a sharp decline. What set these two mills apart was that, having declared their insolvency, both continued to operate and to some extent profit for another decade or so, all the while remaining officially bankrupt. They were also distinguished by having the same owner, William Jenkins.

Textile workers had gained in wages and rights since the Revolution, but their industry remained inefficient. This was especially so in Puebla, where the average mill was smaller than in Veracruz or Mexico City. Workers often knew their machines better than their managers, many of whom were elite-family "juniors," who unlike their immigrant grandfathers were loath to dirty their hands. Accounting practices were backward. Protective tariffs worked against making product fit for export, as did a federal brake on machine imports. Owner complacency was one root problem, the intransigence of the CROM labor federation another, and tolerating both was the state, which prioritized keeping the peace. Owners backed the policy on imported machinery, dreading the entry of new rivals who might buy it, so they agreed to honor collective contracts with labor in exchange for the import controls. This was fine by CROM chief Luis Napoleón Morones, who feared upgrades would create unemployment. His union's workers, reveling in their security as clients of the state, gained a name for ill discipline. Truants could no longer be fired without union consent; some states forbade managers from docking their pay. Failing to modernize, the sector endured intermittent crises until 1939.[55]

By the time Germany invaded Poland, Jenkins was well placed to enjoy the ensuing bonanza, for in recent years he had foreclosed on various mills. With his takeover of La Concepción, in 1939 or so, he held three midsize factories and at least three smaller mills. Driving up orders was surging demand from the US military, which would put 16 million people in uniform. As a local chronicler put it: "Puebla put to work all the textile-producing junk of the Porfirian era ... even those who improvised as textile men made money."[56]

Allied victory over Japan in 1945 hit Mexico's textile barons like a cold shower. Within three weeks of the destruction of Hiroshima, Puebla's mill owners were lamenting their lot to Miguel Alemán, then visiting the state on his campaign tour. Their warehouses overflowed with unsold product. Great Britain, the world's biggest exporter of cotton textiles, had said it would ramp up production and install new machinery. A couple of Puebla's textile barons, recognizing the need to modernize, announced imminent upgrades. Otherwise the news was bad, as mills cut their work rate, sought legal permission for a three-day week, or shut down altogether. Sometime in late 1945, it seems, Jenkins foreclosed on El León.[57]

Overall, Puebla's textile sector was gripped by inertia, which contributed to a statewide economic stagnation that would persist for twenty years. Geography was partly to blame, for Puebla City was just two hours from the capital, now an industrial and demographic vortex. It cannot have helped that during the 1930s and 1940s some of Puebla's most ambitious entrepreneurs—Manuel Espinosa Yglesias, Gabriel Alarcón, Rómulo O'Farrill, Alejo Peralta, and Miguel Abed—relocated to Mexico City in search of bigger opportunities.[58]

Modernization barely registered in La Opinión. Editorials never discussed it. Reporting was naively boosterish, hyping the promises of politicians. Advertising was dominated by soft drinks and realty firms; the latter offered fancy homes in suburbs populated by American-looking families. It was as though Puebla wished to enter modernity—a Westernized, consumerist modernity—without tackling the initiatives that would pay for it. Apart from items about the rising cost of living, the paper oozed complacency.[59]

The textile barons seemed equally complacent. For twenty years Mexico City had cosseted them with tariff protections, shielding them from foreign competitors and impeding the founding of new mills. Puebla too had treated them with deference; witness Governor Bautista's action in 1944, following complaints about a new federal tax, in which he offered to forgo the share that was due to his treasury, as if industrialists enjoying a wartime boom needed relief. Their refusal to admit any Lebanese onto the board of their trade association, a prejudice that would persist until around 1960, again smacked of a sector atrophying in its conservatism.[60]

Some Pueblans did seek new machinery but found their plans hampered, partly by a scarcity of international supply and partly by Alemán. The president favored larger factories—found in other states—with the few import permits he was willing to award. His favoritism may have been more than logistical. During the previous administration, his arch-enemy and rival for Ávila Camacho's blessing as his successor had been the president's brother, Maximino, who had championed the Puebla elite. As a general policy, Alemán sought to keep all sectors happy and make them dependent upon the state.[61] In textiles, as in film, mediocrity resulted.

Union inflexibility was another roadblock. Taking the short view, the unions still equated modernization with job losses. Yet they were hurting from a real-terms drop in wages since 1940 of as much as one-third. Labor's resistance was especially stubborn in Atlixco, a legacy of the twenty-year turf war between the CROM and the CTM. The struggle culminated in April 1948, when four CTM-aligned mills (including La Concepción) bowed to intense pressure and switched their allegiance to the CROM.[62]

That date was significant, for 1948 was the year of the *charrazo*, Alemán's move to rein in the strong-willed Mexican Railroad Workers' Union by fixing the election of a conservative to lead it. The *charrazo* signaled a watershed, after which union opposition to the state was seldom tolerated.[63] The Atlixco power play, backed by the president and Governor Betancourt, signaled another Machiavellian scheme, ensuring for the politicians a counterweight to CTM influence in Puebla and promising tidy corporatist control of Atlixco. It also rewarded the union boss who had been first in the state to endorse Alemán for president. This leader, the CROM's heir apparent to Morones, was a jocular and cunning bully called Antonio J. Hernández.[64]

THE JACKAL, AS Hernández was nicknamed, was something of an out-sider.[65] His father hailed from Querétaro. Vicente Hernández, a former rancher, had fled to Puebla after catching his wife in bed with a farmhand; as they lay sleeping in postcoital bliss, he bashed in both of their heads with a corn-grinding stone. Remarrying with an Atlixco girl half his age, he took a job at the Metepec mill, the town's biggest employer. Once the Revolution broke out Vicente joined up, leaving eight-year old Antonio, the oldest child, to support the family by taking his place. After the war, Antonio had a lucky break. A well-to-do uncle put the toughened teenager in charge of one of his Puebla City cantinas. He also paid for his primary education at the elite Methodist Institute. On graduating, Antonio had little desire to return to the loom. Seeking outlets for his ambition, he set up a barber shop, joined the Communist Party, worked as a mailman and then as teacher. In his twenties he at last returned to Atlixco, entering Metepec as a cotton spinner and switching from the Communist Party to the CROM.

With his appetite for reading Hernández stood out from his illiterate peers. Armed with learning and a jovial charisma, he scaled the ranks of the Metepec union. Between 1928 and 1933, the CROM suffered several corrosive splits, many unions breaking off to back Lombardo Toledano in what would become the more radical CTM. Hernández stayed loyal to Morones. By now a stocky man in his early thirties, he was union boss at Metepec. This local standing and his opposition to Lombardo put him in good stead with Maximino Ávila Camacho, who loathed the CTM founder. In 1935, when the CTM's Puebla affiliate launched a general strike, Maximino suppressed it with the help of Hernández and his goons. The Jackal's star continued to rise, and he found himself serving as a federal congressman, representing Puebla in tandem with Gustavo Díaz Ordaz, the future president. They became friends, inclining to the right of the ruling party and splurging their year-end bonuses at the same high-class brothel.

Hernández's proximity to Maximino made him a potential ally of Jenkins. But the two men had clashed in the early 1940s, when Jenkins's mill La Trinidad began its lengthy strike. It was CROM workers that led the stoppage, which dented Jenkins's wartime profits for four years. Hernández had yet to consolidate his Atlixco dominion, so it scarcely served his political ends to be accommodating to management. Quite the contrary, he styled himself as a leader who would combat foes with the same ferocity he applied to internal dissent. In Atlixco he had created an "action group" to kill anyone who defied him.[66] His combativeness paid off in 1948 with the final purge of CTM locals. Hernández not only bossed Atlixco's textile workforce, several thousand in number, but through economic sway and armed persuasion also he lorded over much of the town's daily life, from the buses and taxis to the sports teams. Remaining committed to education, he used his union funds to build four schools and a technical college.

A year after cementing himself as Atlixco's *cacique*, The Jackal was again at loggerheads with Jenkins. Indalecio Canteli, the Spanish general manager of Jenkins's Atlixco mills, said he could no longer pay the workers at El León and La Concepción. Initially the CROM made up the difference, an unusually helpful move from a union, but one that let Hernández fortify loyalties at the recently affiliated La Concepción. The situation was grave. La Concepción, familiarly known as La Concha, had dispatched an order to Canada that was sent back on account of shoddy workmanship. Both mills were hampered by the age of their machinery, and the whole sector was in trouble. Puebla warehouses held 40 million meters of unsold cloth.[67]

Governor Betancourt intervened in October, meeting with Jenkins and brokering talks between Hernández and Canteli. But the industry outlook continued to deteriorate. Reportedly, only a credit of 13 million pesos would prevent management from closing La Concha and El León, each an employer of more than five hundred. Meanwhile the CROM continued to prime worker loyalty, opening sports fields and other facilities at El León. El León's union officer said the arbitration board should rule in labor's favor, "over the bastard purposes and ambitions of a mere few potentates." Betancourt at last fixed a sit-down between Jenkins and Hernández, but they reached no deal. The next day, December 1, El León and La Concha declared bankruptcy.[68]

The conflict escalated fast: Jenkins closed the two mills; the CROM blamed the crisis on bad management; Jenkins threatened to shut another mill; the CROM began a strike at La Concha and El León.[69] Jenkins held the initiative—the loss-making mills meant much more to Hernández— but he made a symbolic concession by delegating his son-in-law Ronnie Eustace to replace Canteli and continue talks with Hernández. It then appeared that the workers had consented to return at reduced wages. Both mills reopened on January 4.[70]

How the conflict ended was never clarified, but further hints of a union back-down soon emerged. *La Opinión* congratulated Hernández on the occasion of his saint's day, saying he enjoyed "great prestige," whereas a month earlier it had mocked his "lack of intelligence." Governor Betancourt left for ten days' rest in Acapulco, as Jenkins's house guest. Since he and Jenkins were never very close, the invitation suggested Jenkins was grateful for his support in pressuring Hernández. Apparently Jenkins struck a deal with Hernández, agreeing to reopen both mills in exchange for both the wage cut and the union leader's pledge to abstain from strikes.[71]

La Concha and El León resumed work under bankruptcy protection and stayed that way for at least a decade. Companies usually emerge from that status as soon as they can, for bankruptcy limits their access to credit and blots their reputation. That blot loomed large in Mexican practice, for the status became part of a firm's designation; at meetings of Puebla's textile trade association, El León was now registered as The Bankrupt El León, SA But Jenkins cared little for matters of repute. And as for credit, he was his own financier, since he now owned a large stake in the Banco de Comercio, one of Mexico's leading banks.[72]

Ronnie Eustace was new to mill administration, but he learned from his father-in-law how to negotiate the rules.[73] One advantage of bankruptcy was that it tempered federal labor laws. While the Labor Code required employers to pay laid-off workers a month's wages for each year's service, bankruptcy removed this obligation. By keeping the mills in bankruptcy, even when they made a profit, Eustace could fire troublemakers and truants almost at will.

Another advantage was to lessen debts. When a firm went bankrupt, it could legally offer its creditors measly repayment. This was a wonderful opportunity, because the entire industry operated on credit, not simply bank loans but also credits from cotton merchants and machine-parts importers. Even retailers afforded credit, by paying in advance for goods. A bankrupt mill could not simply dismiss all debts, for that would invite lawsuits claiming fraud.[74] For Eustace, the trick was to gauge what percentage of an outstanding debt he could get away with paying. He did not want to burn bridges with suppliers, but he could be fairly stingy, because his suppliers all knew that he acted on behalf of Jenkins, which in turned implied the favor of the governor and by extension the partiality of state judges. Usually Eustace offered 40 percent.

Jenkins's privileged history of symbiosis with the state government and inside access to finance explain why other Puebla mill owners were unable to pursue the same long-term ruse, at least as far as written records reveal. After all, bankrupt companies answered to the local judiciary, which according to standard practice was packed with gubernatorial appointees. A more common scam that Eustace learned was off-the-books sales. The practice reduced a firm's tax liability, and everybody did it. His predecessor, Canteli, had proven himself a master of contraband at La Concha during the war. Afterward, Canteli continued the practice, making it easier for Jenkins to declare bankruptcy, since the mills' balance sheets looked even less healthy.

Antonio J. Hernández, for all his fearsome reputation, proved an amenable ally. As a standard-bearer of the Revolution, he had great incentive to spill the beans about managerial trickery, but he kept quiet. Throughout Eustace's tenure, until the early 1960s, neither La Concha nor El León suffered a strike. There was once a spate of robberies, as workers hoisted bundles of finished product onto the roof, or threw them over the walls, returning by night to collect them for sale on the black market. Hernández and his loyalists were summoned by Jenkins to Puebla City. Lecturing them on the topic of theft, he told them, "I want you all to know that you are my eyes." Hernández did his bit by posting gunmen to the rooftops.

Still, he liked to play the radical. Once a CROM newspaper ran a cartoon of Eustace and Jenkins, drawn as beasts sucking the blood of the workers. Enraged, Eustace went straight to see Hernández. The Jackal had his lair at the vast Metepec mill. Guards stood outside the office, cradling submachine guns. But Eustace had flown twenty bombing missions through Japanese flak; he was not going to be ruffled by a couple of goons. He marched into Hernández's office, waving the paper and demanding to know what the hell was going on. Hernández offered an excuse. He had to allow such things from time to time; he had to keep up appearances.

So had The Jackal sold out? In the words of one labor historian, Hernández converted the Atlixco CROM into "a ghost, docile and submissive to government policies."[75] Yet Hernández's hands were largely tied by the sorry state of the industry. Jenkins could easily have walked away from both mills, shuttering them and selling the iron machinery for scrap. That he did not do so partly owed to his wish to test Eustace. If this young Brit could squeeze money out of two antiques, he might be capable of greater things. Contraband sales, vastly reduced debts, and a compliant union all aided Eustace in returning the mills to profit. But his success as a manager was limited. La Concha revived in the short term, thanks to orders from the Middle East, but otherwise it barely broke even. El León made money, although less so in the long run.

Except for improvements to La Concha's finishing plant, Jenkins refused to modernize. Despite import restrictions and CROM resistance, he could have improved his mills had he wished. He had the president's ear and the governor's support. He was on a federal waiting list for new machine permits, but in a gesture of loyalty to his former Atencingo manager Manuel Pérez, he let one of his sons, who was keen to start his own mill, take his place in line.[76]

Jenkins's nonchalant approach to his mills typified the risk aversion among Puebla's older generation. Why invest in upgrades, incurring the wrath of the unions, when there was easier money to be made elsewhere? For many, the soft option was real estate.[77] So Puebla's textile sector, its pride since colonial times, became a mix of moribund Porfirian factories, mostly owned by the descendants of Spaniards, and start-ups, mostly run by energetic Lebanese. The latter mills, exploiting new niches like rayon and denim, were not yet large enough to make up for the former mills' decline. While Mexican manufacturing grew 30 percent between 1945 and 1955, manufactures in Puebla, of which textiles made up more than half, grew a paltry 2 percent.

In the 1960s the old mills would begin to close, even Hernández's beloved Metepec. As much as anything, their workers were the victims of a culture of complacency among the older owners, who for more than two decades were coddled by the Ávila Camacho political machine. These traditional industrialists might blame the unions, but the famed obstinacy of labor was less than met the eye, as The Jackal had demonstrated. Besides, when Lebanese owners offered both to modernize their plant and to raise wages, they gained union support. As of the mid-1960s, the more entrepreneurial Lebanese would dominate Puebla textiles.[78]

Jenkins's Film Monopoly: A Second Failed Assault

One day in early 1953, Mexico's two leading dailies were strangely missing most of their movie advertising. Excélsior and El Universal carried front-page notices, apologizing for the absence, which would endure for a month. At the time, newspapers compiled no film listings of their own, so the lack of display ads was both an annoyance to readers and a major revenue loss. The apologies blamed the intransigence of certain theater chains. Two days later, a blitz began. El Universal assailed Jenkins's film empire for its rapaciousness, urging the new regime of Adolfo Ruiz Cortines to do something. The next day, its front page blared: "Against the

Film Monopoly the Battle Has Begun." *Excélsior* chimed in with "Concrete Charges against the Monopolist Jenkins."[79]

Jenkins had not borne so much vitriol since his kidnapping. For a full week, the papers kept up a barrage of front-page attack pieces. They castigated the Jenkins Group for monopolistic practice in exhibition, intimidation of distributors, and its growing control of film finance, which allegedly forced producers to deliver cheap genre pictures. Editorials pressed hard for governmental action. In *Excélsior*, a caricature depicted Jenkins as an octopus—a traditional metaphor for US monopoly—entrapping and strangling a sensually drawn woman, the vulnerable embodiment of Mexican cinema.[80]

The immediate reason for the attacks, it transpired, was a 25 percent hike in ad rates and Jenkins's refusal to meet the increase. By imposing his own boycott, he hoped to force the papers to back down. Instead, they joined forces with Mexico's disaffected film producers and hit back. Why they did so had a lot to do with December's change of government, ushering in Ruiz Cortines. Although he had previously served as Alemán's interior minister and handily won the 1952 election as his designated disciple, Ruiz Cortines set out to distance himself from his predecessor, taking a public stand against the corruption that had flourished under Alemán.[81] He would expect honesty. Pilfering by politicians, anticompetitive practices, and the speculative hoarding of foods would not be tolerated. The press was freer to adopt a critical tone; "monopolist" became a staple term of rebuke. The new openness seemed to embolden *Excelsior* and *El Universal* to turn their glare upon Jenkins.

Never was the sense of a new rectitude more apparent than on February 7, the final day of the PRI's annual convention, which coincided with the anti-Jenkins crusade. Addressing the floor, Jacinto B. Treviño dropped a bombshell. This general, senator, and former cabinet minister departed from the customary banalities and launched a blistering attack upon the direction of the Revolution. The PRI had lost its way, he claimed, citing its imposition of governors and mayors against the people's will and the self-enrichment of officials. Ignoring attempts by party loyalists to shout him down, he cited the massive fortunes of former president Abelardo Rodríguez and, of course, William Jenkins. He claimed the current government was clean and would no longer permit such excesses. The speech grabbed headlines and generated debate for weeks.[82]

Abelardo Rodríguez, no doubt incensed by Treviño's attack on his good person, tried a diversionary tactic. Seeing that the wolves were mostly out for Jenkins, he joined the hunt, summoning journalists and treating them to a tirade against the American. He said that when he was president, twenty years earlier, he had stripped Jenkins of his consular rank and expelled him from Mexico as a "pernicious foreigner." He claimed that for three years he had led the fight by independent exhibitors against Jenkins, and he advocated state action against him. Rodríguez's nationalistic acts of the 1930s were now reported in the press and recycled for decades to come.[83]

But Rodríguez had lied. The claims were nothing more than wishful nostalgia on the millionaire general's part. First, Jenkins had ceased to be Puebla's consular agent twenty-one months before Rodríguez took office.[84] As for alleged expulsion, there is no evidence that it occurred. During Rodríguez's presidency, neither the national nor the Puebla press reported any such news. Nor is it mentioned within files on Jenkins in either the Foreign Relations Ministry, the foreigners' registry at the Puebla Municipal Archive, or Rodríguez's presidential records in the National Archive. Jenkins's descendants could recall no such expulsion, nor is there trace of it in Rodríguez's personal archive. There is, on the other hand, plenty of evidence of Jenkins's presence in Mexico throughout the Rodríguez administration.[85]

At a time of soul searching within the PRI and discomfort over the wealth of certain revolutionaries, Rodríguez needed a lightning rod. He correctly bet that that "the boys from the press," as journalists were then known, would not bother fact checking. To claim that he had ejected Mexico's richest and most powerful gringo was an easy way of shoring up his reputation, easier still given Jenkins's custom of refusing to talk. The Treviño speech at the PRI convention had voiced an open secret: Rodríguez was spectacularly wealthy, in large part via dubious means. Jenkins was a convenient decoy, and the newspaper campaign offered a chance to press for action against him that would suit Rodríguez's business interests.[86]

That summer saw the launch of *Siempre!*, which through independent-minded leadership, plural viewpoints, and polemical topics would become Mexico's top newsweekly. Soon it ran a Jenkins exposé. Among other things, it claimed that he provided an incredible 80 percent of film production funding. Without noticing the apparent contradiction, it then alleged that the "true purpose" of this "foreign monopoly" was to "exterminate the national film industry." In subsequent months, the papers caricatured Jenkins several times more, once depicting him as "His Majesty William

I," riding atop a tank, with three of his investor partners marching behind, holding the train of his royal robe.[87]

However, the spat over advertising prices that started the whole affair had since been settled—apparently in Jenkins's favor. Film publicity returned to the pages of *Excélsior* and *El Universal*, and a friend wrote to congratulate Jenkins on having "licked the newspapers." Worse for the industry itself, in April the Supreme Court ruled against the 50 percent screen quota for Mexican films.[88] The media blitz against Jenkins had come to naught.

THE ATTACKS BY *Excélsior* and *El Universal* may have failed in their objectives but they opened the floodgates of criticism. In the past, it was the rare person who had publicly critiqued Jenkins. As of 1953, for the rest of his life, Jenkins became a routine target of editorialists, reporters, cartoonists, union leaders, and leftist-nationalist politicians. He was attacked because he was a monopolist, but also because he was an American. He was attacked for ideological reasons and business motives, but also because it was expedient to do so. An attack on Jenkins was a way of bolstering one's revolutionary standing at a time when the political elite was tarnished by scandal, of positing oneself as a nationalist in the face of US economic hegemony, or merely of raising the circulation of one's periodical.

A degree of press liberalization under Ruiz Cortines was part of it. So was a yawning divide within the ruling party. Treviño's speech articulated a deep vein of resentment within the left wing of the PRI at the turn taken since the radical zenith of the Cárdenas years. Alemán they held as particularly to blame. Since both of these ex-presidents remained powerful figures, and since they embodied opposite poles within the PRI, an internal struggle arose between left-wing Cardenists and right-wing Alemanists. Later on, as Castro came to power in Cuba and Cold War geopolitics impinged on Mexico as never before, these rival currents would make open rhetorical warfare.[89] In turn, the name of Jenkins became an inflammatory weapon of the left.

Yet the PRI generally strove to present a united front. Its priority was to centralize power in the presidency and the party's executive committee. While it had won the 1952 election quite easily, the near-defeat of 1940 lingered as a specter, as did the battle for the PRI nomination between Alemán and Ezequiel Padilla in 1945–1946. In certain regions of the country central control was incomplete and dynasties held sway. Not least was the Ávila Camacho machine in Puebla, where Maximino had "unveiled" two successors, Gonzalo Bautista and Carlos Betancourt, and where a third Ávila Camacho brother, Rafael, became governor in 1951.[90]

Given the simmering discontent within the PRI over Alemán's legacy and a simultaneous desire for unity, it behooved Ruiz Cortines to use the press as an escape valve. He was not the first to do so. Coordinated press campaigns, against some venal official or other, occurred under Ávila Camacho and Alemán and were interpreted as having presidential approval.[91] According to this tradition, the anti-Jenkins campaign of 1953 was pure theater, a drama geared toward catharsis: the release of film industry tensions and the cleansing of the image of the state.

But if the media barrage were to be believed, Ruiz Cortines had a film industry to revive, and there was substance to the complaint. While output was still strong, the number of Mexican films gaining theatrical play dates was receding; from a record 112 releases in 1951, the figure would fall to 83 in 1953. Quality showed a more serious decline. Under Alemán, the industry had begun focusing on formulaic B-pictures for lowbrow consumers, such as mawkish family melodramas and tear-jerkers about fallen women in cabarets.[92]

The state replied to complaints about Jenkins—and about the threat of television, which had debuted in 1950—with an overarching plan to revive Mexican film. Launched by Eduardo Garduño, director of the National Film Bank, the initiative upped the per-picture credit limit, suggested an import quota of 150 films per year, gave producers control of state-run distributor Películas Nacionales, and liberalized prohibitions on cinematic content. Earlier the bank had covered 50 or 60 percent of an approved budget; that subsidy could now reach 85 percent. Producers started to narrow the gap with Hollywood by switching from black-and-white film to color. Several spiced their pictures with "artistic" nudity. There was a brief vogue of dramas featuring painters and their nubile models.[93]

The Garduño Plan bombed. Most producers carried on making B-movies, which catered to the working classes and failed to draw middle- and upper-income patrons. They still drew their subsidies and they still profiteered by padding their budgets. Genres broadened to include vampire pictures and melodramas about masked wrestlers, but most such films were equally shabby and predictable. The directors' union heightened the creativity crisis by largely refusing to admit new members. Further compromising his plan to raise quality, when Garduño issued new shares in Películas Nacionales, seeking to bolster the distributor's finances, most of the stock was gobbled up by proxies for Jenkins. By late 1953, Jenkins-affiliated producers were again claiming Film Bank credit. A newspaper cartoon nailed the paradox, depicting Garduño offering the gringo both a harsh rebuke and a sack of cash.[94]

HAD RUIZ CORTINES really wished to move against Jenkins, new pretexts continued to present themselves. A high-profile murder, for example.

In August 1954 labor activist Alfonso Mascarúa was gunned down outside his Mexico City home. It was eight in the evening, just before dusk, and there were various witnesses. Mascarúa had been a radical member of the Syndicate of Film Industry Workers (STIC), a union largely comprising theater personnel, which had struck for six days that July over the effects of the recent peso devaluation. At a STIC assembly, one speaker rallied the troops by reminding them of Puebla impresario Jesús Cienfuegos, killed thirteen years earlier, and blaming the murder on Jenkins. Despite the union's defiant talk, Mascarúa had fallen out with STIC leader Pedro Téllez Vargas, accusing him of capitulation to the Jenkins Group. He challenged Téllez for the STIC leadership, and once he lost he accused him of using intimidation to get himself reelected. Along with fifty fellow dissidents, Mascarúa was booted from both the STIC and his job. Seven weeks later he was shot. Suspicion at once fell upon Téllez, with Mascarúa's widow openly accusing the STIC leader and columnists deploring union gangsterism. But it was unclear why the boss would have ordered the murder of someone he had already ousted.[95]

After a few weeks, the spotlight switched to Gabriel Alarcón. Several precedents made him a suspect, not just his rumored role in the demise of Cienfuegos. In 1951 two film union activists were murdered in Orizaba, and Alarcón was locally said to have ordered the hit. Further, Mascarúa was a native of Puebla, where he had first worked as a union organizer.[96] In September, the police investigation led to the arrest of three men in Puebla, each reputed to be enforcers of Alarcón's. Within a week, federal and state arrest warrants were issued for Alarcón himself, who responded by seeking injunctions and making himself scarce. When agents showed up at his home in Puebla, he escaped in the trunk of a friend's car. Over subsequent weeks he used several hideouts, including a textile mill owned by his brother-in-law and the top floor of the offices of *El Sol de Puebla*, directly above the paper's newsroom.[97]

For months the presidency was deluged with telegrams from unions demanding justice. Once Alarcón was implicated, Jenkins became a target of suspicion too. At a November meeting of one of the STIC locals, a chant of "Death to Jenkins!" arose from the floor. Meanwhile Alarcón's wife, Herminia, obtained an audience with Ruiz Cortines. Sinking to her knees, she wrapped her arms around the president's legs and tearfully begged him for clemency. Ruiz Cortines was moved to call off the search.[98]

Though remanded in custody *in absentia*, Alarcón was never arrested, and as the year drew to a close it seemed the case would not be solved. Just four days after the murder, a cartoonist for *El Universal* had presciently sketched a parody on the temptation of Eve, with the serpent offering a smirking Lady Justice an apple in the shape of a money bag. By the spring of 1955, Alarcón was conducting business as usual. But his reputation then suffered a further setback when it was reported that he had paid several sums of 200,000 pesos to members of the Federal Security Directorate (DFS), Mexico's FBI, to obtain a secret service badge and thus immunity in the Mascarúa investigation. A memo between Ruiz Cortines's staff confirmed the main allegations. Recent research has shown that the gifting or selling of coveted DFS badges to select politicians and businessmen was routine.[99]

In September, a Mexico City penal court produced a remarkable verdict: all three detainees were condemned to twenty years for the murder and Alarcón was sentenced (again, *in absentia*) to an equal penalty. Three months later, however, a higher court overturned all four convictions. In Puebla the rumor ran that Herminia Alarcón had paid another visit, this time to the presiding judge, leaving him a million pesos richer.[100]

SOON RUIZ CORTINES had another chance to stand firm against Jenkins, when his last major rival threw in the towel. Abelardo Rodríguez had given the industry his best shot. Having entered the ring in the early 1940s, the former president built an empire that included several hundred theaters, finance and distribution companies, stakes in production houses, and a share in a film studio.[101] His near-monopoly in the northwest and his circuit in Mexico City gave him enough clout with Hollywood to secure a flow of product. But in the mid-1950s his strategy unraveled when he bet big on CinemaScope, the wide-screen format pioneered by Twentieth Century-Fox.

Rodríguez built dedicated theaters to handle the new technology, including two on Jenkins's home turf. In Puebla, Rodríguez's 3,000-seat Cinema México opened in 1954, followed in 1955 by his Cinema Puebla, which caused a scandal when he demolished half a colonial mansion to construct it. Neither was successful. Fox was simply not producing enough CinemaScope epics to keep a circuit busy. In between times, Rodríguez was reduced to scraping the odd picture from Universal or Paramount and showing standard-format Mexican fare. Once the Cinema Puebla opened, the rival theaters run by Espinosa and Alarcón dropped their ticket prices. In spring 1957, Rodríguez called quits. The Cinema México became part of Espinosa's circuit, the Cinema Puebla part of Alarcón's, and Rodríguez sold out nationwide to Jenkins.[102]

Ruiz Cortines could hardly continue pretending the Jenkins Group was not a monopoly power, and still he did nothing. After Rodríguez sold out, other independents evidently did likewise, for a *Variety* profile in December 1958 revealed the full extent of the Jenkins empire. Espinosa's COTSA and affiliated companies owned or leased 900 theaters and was grossing $16 million in annual box office revenues. Alarcón's Cadena de Oro and its affiliates owned or leased around 700. That left just 400 or so independent theaters, many of them small-town flea pits. With nearly 80 percent of venues under his control, it had become difficult for Mexicans to go to the movies and not make Jenkins richer.[103]

Ruiz Cortines's reluctance to act presumably echoed that of his predecessors. Jenkins was providing a huge and efficient public service. His theaters entertained the urban millions, and thanks to price caps on tickets they did so cheaply. With his partners, Jenkins had contributed decisively to an impressive boom in venues and moviegoing: in Mexico City, venues doubled from 67 in 1938 to 133 in 1958; nationally, those totals rose from 863 (less than half of them operating daily) to 2,100.[104] Next, to restrict so high-profile an American would have sent the wrong signal, for the state policy was to entice foreign investors to set up Mexican plants. Whatever his rhetoric, Ruiz Cortines was not a foe of monopoly. In 1955, he gave Mexico's three infant television networks permission to merge.[105] Then there was the likelihood that senior politicians owned stakes in Jenkins's theaters. Finally, Black-Legend Jenkins functioned as a handy lightning rod for leftist or nationalist anger. The media could let off steam about social injustice and corruption by railing against Jenkins; politicians could offer remedies, like the Film Law and the Garduño Plan, which made them look like they were doing something.

Jenkins was also likely protected by the fact that he did not repatriate profits. As was clear to anyone who looked closely, Jenkins could not accurately be tagged a Porfirian throwback, nor likened to the oil giants whose assets Cárdenas expropriated, because the money he made in Mexico stayed in Mexico. He invested in the building and buying of theaters, in auto assembly plants, in an array of start-ups.

Then he made himself useful in other ways. When the Mexico City to Querétaro stretch of the Panamerican Highway fell behind schedule for lack of funds, Jenkins came up with a completion loan, and from 1954 a company of his built a large stretch of it. Some months after taking over the project, he told his family: "I sure am crazy to tackle a job like this, but apparently there was no-one else to do it, and the President told me that he wanted it very badly, so maybe he will remember it at some other time when I want him to."[106]

Of increasing importance to Jenkins and to the country, he invested in the Banco de Comercio, Mexico's second-largest bank. Though not yet a majority shareholder, Jenkins held the largest individual stake in the bank by the start of the Ruiz Cortines era. He substantiated that commitment at the time of the 1954 peso devaluation. Although the state undertook this surprise measure to boost the economy and improve the balance of trade, it prompted a crisis of confidence in the banks. Major deposit-holders at the Banco de Comercio, fearing the state might take the bank over, withdrew large sums. At once Jenkins offered the equivalent of $8 million to stabilize the bank's finances. As things turned out, the state stepped in with fresh credit, so his funds were not needed, but in the financial world the promise of extra security at times of economic turbulence can itself be worth millions.[107]

There was self-interest in Jenkins's offer, but after more than fifty years living in Mexico, the American had developed a loyalty toward his adoptive country that would have surprised his detractors. It was apparent in his gestures of missionary capitalism, cultivating the business instincts and start-up companies of his younger friends. It was evident in how he wrote at length in 1951 to the Vanderbilt board of trustees, trying to persuade it that investing part of the university's endowment in Mexico would guarantee a healthy return.[108] When it came to Mexico's economic prospects in the postwar era, Jenkins was a believer.

All in all, the convergence of Jenkins's business initiatives, vested political interests, and economic policy considerations weighed too powerfully for Contreras and other critical voices to sway the president. Like their rural counterparts in the sugar lands of Atencingo, the underdogs of Mexico's film industry employed gringophobic rhetoric in vain. Circumstances would radically change, however, when Ruiz Cortines stepped down at the end of 1958. Massive labor disturbances on the home front and a revolution in Cuba would quickly invest nationalistic rhetoric with uncommon power. Jenkins would take another beating in the press, and this time there would be tangible consequences.

Who Killed the Golden Age of Mexican Cinema?

Jenkins became the shadowy lord of Mexican cinema. But did he kill the Golden Age? Did he, as Miguel Contreras Torres and others have alleged, use his control of theaters to the privilege of Hollywood, squeezing out local fare? Did he use his leverage over producers to bully them into working on the cheap, making movies that were formulaic and ever less exportable?[109]

By the strictest definition of the Golden Age, the creative peak of 1941–1945, the answer is clearly no. At the end of World War II, the Jenkins Group was prominent but not dominant in exhibition, Mexican pictures were well represented on screen, and the Group's production activities were scattershot. The crisis of 1946 came with the revival of European cinema and a ramping up by Hollywood, along with the reluctance of Mexican banks to carry on loaning to producers, who already had a reputation for inflating budgets and making tardy repayments. Matters were not helped by a three-year postwar recession. Producers began to trim their budgets before the Jenkins Group's theater purchases of 1947–1949 raised its status to that of a de facto monopoly. Emilio Azcárraga, one of the wisest voices in the entertainment industry, declared the budget-cutting was a mistake, but he went unheeded.[110] If anything, the nationalization of the Film Bank in 1947 was a pyrrhic victory for the industry, for the consequent increase in subsidies worked to solidify bad habits. Loss-making films were written off by the state and the same producers kept on producing.

By more liberal definitions of the Golden Age, which extend it even to the 1960s, Jenkins was party to a crime of many perpetrators. Two or three years after the war, Espinosa and Alarcón were prioritizing supply deals with the Hollywood majors. These tied up the best theaters, leaving Mexican films to compete with European ones for whatever was left. There was no malice here, just business: Hollywood had built a well-oiled studio system that promised safe returns. It turned out a foreseeable number of pictures per year, carried around the globe by a sophisticated distribution-cum-publicity machine. Hollywood did not yet rule Mexican hearts; in the late 1940s, national features claimed more than 40 percent of screen time in Mexico City and an even higher proportion in the provinces, thanks to public demand. Nonetheless, Hollywood's massive output gave it a competitive advantage, and it is true that its studios engaged worldwide in "block booking," forcing exhibitors to accept quantities of B-pictures in order to secure proven hits.[111] Faced with such practices, and with the Jenkins Group playing it safe by giving Hollywood first pick of its movie palaces, it was logical that the state should respond with subsidies. But effective administration of these monies was lacking.

In production, the fundamental problem was inadequate finance. Jenkins preferred lean budgets and was more interested in quantities of pictures than quality. He contributed to a dumbing down, a drive toward predictable genre fare that seemed to satisfy the masses, along with their low-income cousins in the United States, but held little appeal for middle- and upper-income Mexicans and zero attraction in South America or Europe. The budget-cutting trend was already in place when Jenkins became the dominant source of funding, but he exacerbated it.

Contemporary critics of Jenkins often omitted to mention other systematic weaknesses, which were plenty. Not only did producers tend to inflate costs, they failed to reinvest much of their profits, either in technology or in budgets for subsequent productions. Doing so would have helped keep the industry from falling ever further behind Hollywood.[112]

Directors, meanwhile, instituted a cartel. The directors' union admitted fourteen names in 1944, but only one was let in a year later. This closed-door policy persisted until the 1960s, so directors' accusations about Jenkins's monopolistic practices were thoroughly hypocritical. In stark contrast to Hollywood, the Mexican industry deprived itself of the regular entry of younger talents who could have kept its vision fresh, pushing existing genres in exciting directions. The situation worsened over time, so that for the period 1956–1960, two-thirds of Mexico's 570 films were shot by just twenty men. The well-connected director dashed off three or four films a year, with an average shooting time of three weeks. No wonder creativity stagnated.[113]

Federico Heuer, National Film Bank chief under President Adolfo López Mateos, would sum up the postwar torpor: "for 20 years now, [producers] have been hiring the same directors and the same screenwriters . . ., with the same artists who generally sing the same compositions and perform the same roles as leading men and starlets that they did 20 years ago."[114]

There were further flaws in the Jenkins-bashing. Contreras and others alleged that the Jenkins Group kept budgets too small, yet they also complained that the National Film Bank favored those affiliated with Jenkins. So did producers such as Walerstein, Elizondo, Grovas, and De Anda have too much cash or too little? Their prolific postwar output included so few films of merit, these men surely bore substantial responsibility for the general drop in quality. Easy access to finance, with little incentive to repay loans from the Film Bank, may well have dulled their hunger for excellence. Critics also failed to note that Espinosa and Alarcón, while backed by the same partner, competed with each other bitterly. While they divided parts of the republic between them, in Mexico City (where the average film made half of its gross) they went head-to-head, as did they in Puebla and elsewhere. Theoretically, producers with promising projects could encourage Jenkins's partners to bid against each other, to the benefit of their budgets. But their tendency to ally themselves, working consistently with one of the two, suggests a preference for coziness and favors rather than an entrepreneurial spirit.

State efforts to support film consistently proved ill-executed or half-hearted.[115] The Film Laws of 1949 and 1952 failed to rein in Jenkins's monopolistic practices. The Garduño Plan of 1953 wound up as another example of symbolic politics: a scheme launched with fanfare to restore quality to cinema and contain the Jenkins Group, which through lack of political will achieved the reverse of its objectives or simply had no impact. Far from the mooted 150-film quota, imports averaged some 340 pictures per year during Ruiz Cortines's term.[116]

Contreras remained blinkered in his critique. He ignored how great directors continued to make great films, and that these were buoyed by decent budgets. As so often in filmmaking, where there was a will and an original vision, there was a way. Luis Buñuel and Roberto Gavaldón worked some of their greatest artistry in the 1950s. Their films were profitable too. Gavaldón's *film noir* folktale *Macario* (1959) ran in Mexico City for sixteen weeks.[117]

Still, a major structural obstacle against which any drive for quality foundered was the four-peso cap on ticket prices, introduced when Ruiz Cortines took office and more or less enforced for twenty years. A populist move, the price cap upheld the high frequency of moviegoing but deepened the inclination of producers to shoot on a shoestring. By the mid-1960s, thanks to these price controls and further urbanization, Mexico had the joint-highest rate of film attendance in the world. Noted a *Variety* correspondent: "cheap film entertainment for the masses is deemed a must to offset inequities of income. . . . The analogy to 'bread and circuses' has often been made."[118]

For a dozen or so years, Jenkins and his partners indeed profiteered and the film industry declined. But there was a lot of blame to go around. The nationalization of movie theaters that awaited in 1960 would underscore the problem of only blaming Jenkins. With the industry under state control (for studios were also nationalized), the long decline of Mexican cinema continued. So the denouement of our mystery, Who Killed the Golden Age?, resembles that of Agatha Christie's *Murder on the Orient Express*. There were many hands that plunged the dagger.

The Jenkins Foundation and the Battle for the Soul of the PRI

The man who dies thus rich dies disgraced.
ANDREW CARNEGIE, "The Gospel of Wealth" (1889)

The Politics of Philanthropy

"During her life, we made many projects for charitable works in this city, which due to her death we could not do, but she left it up to me to accomplish some of them." So wrote William Jenkins about Mary, as he applied to Puebla's Charity Board to register his new foundation. He added: "The idea is to do anything which will improve the standard of living, moral as well as material, of the inhabitants of our state of Puebla."[1]

In 1954, ten years after his wife's death, Jenkins publicly honored her memory by setting up the Mary Street Jenkins Foundation. It was the first charity of its kind in Mexico. Modeled on the great US endowments left by the robber barons, Jenkins's charity was an enterprise, whose profits would entirely be distributed as gifts. It would support schools and hospitals, public works and sports clubs, and scholarships for Mexicans to study at home and abroad. It would prioritize his adoptive state. With an initial $7 million in assets, the Jenkins Foundation was probably Mexico's largest private charity.

It was certainly the least understood. Its operating model was completely foreign to Mexicans, for whom philanthropy meant one-time gifts to the Catholic Church or the founding of a school or orphanage. Many viewed the foundation as another Jenkins ruse to avoid taxes.

It cannot have helped that Jenkins set up his charity while his reputation was taking a beating. The attacks over his film monopoly and the ongoing scandal over the Mascarúa killing encouraged the public to think the worst. For the rest of his life, Jenkins would be hammered: as an

American, as a monopolist, and as a friend of reactionary forces. He would become a political symbol, a target of leftists disgusted at the turn that politics had taken. Their passions found fuel in a belligerent US foreign policy. As the Cold War developed a new theater of conflict in Latin America, Jenkins happened to be the most visible gringo in Mexico.

He was still a builder of businesses. In his final ten years, he became more prominent than ever in banking, and he started a cotton plantation in Michoacán. His dominance in film continued to strengthen. His philanthropy brought health and education to thousands. But it was as a target and tool of gringophobia that Jenkins stood out most.

HOWEVER MUCH JENKINS promoted and participated in industrial development, however much he gave to charity, there remained a massive blot on his record. He was a serial avoider and evader of taxes. Everybody knew it, and usually—except for his 1934 jailing for dodging alcohol taxes—he got away with it, thanks to his symbiotic relationships. After that jailing the alcohol trafficking had continued. When the state capped the retail price of sugar, Jenkins black-marketed this product too. Among friends and family, it was common knowledge that he bent over backward to elude the taxman. Some efforts had in mind the US Internal Revenue Service, such as his routine use of frontmen to hold shares in the firms he founded. So ingrained became this habit, he even registered his secondhand cars under other people's names.[2]

Other efforts included underreporting revenues, with the help of off-the-books sales, and cajoling the agents of Mexico's Finance Ministry. These were the usual tricks employed by many a business. Agents arriving to inspect a company's books would be taken out on the town, wined and dined, shown a good time at some cabaret, and finally presented with a cash-stuffed envelope. Senior businessmen such as Jenkins usually delegated such nocturnal tasks to sons and nephews. Besides, by 9 PM, the American was usually in bed with a crime novel.[3]

Then there were more elaborate schemes. Property records suggest one: as the Jenkins Group bought out movie theaters, the companies were reregistered in Puebla City.[4] Why would Espinosa and Alarcón go to such trouble, and why do so in Puebla, now that both lived in Mexico City? Surely, because they and Jenkins had closer relationships with the governors and mayors of Puebla than they had with the bigwigs of the states where the theaters were located. Each time they brought a company into Puebla's jurisdiction, it effectively gained a tax exemption.

Puebla's authorities were happy to play along, waiving fiscal claims upon Jenkins, as it was by now well established that Don Guillermo occupied a class apart. He did not pay taxes conventionally, but he did subsidize the state and city budgets with project-specific donations. He built rural schools and supported Puebla City's Latin American Hospital and the American School. He made loans and gifts toward a host of public works. And ever since his fat donation to Maximino's electoral campaign, he had been a pillar of the Ávila Camacho political edifice.

His usefulness to Puebla authorities reached new heights as of 1951, when both city and state welcomed incoming leaders: Nicolás Vázquez and Rafael Ávila Camacho. Vázquez was a close friend of Jenkins, long functioning as his notary public. A self-made man of modest origins who despised corruption, Vázquez entered office with the guarantee of Jenkins's support. During his three years as mayor, his treasury received an annual subsidy from Jenkins of some 500,000 pesos, equal to 10 percent of the budget. This came to light because, as part of his honesty drive, Vázquez took the unusual step of publishing yearly accounts in the press. The additional monies funded covered markets, built to new standards of hygiene, and expanded the water system to the city's poorer neighborhoods.[5]

Rafael Ávila Camacho, a younger brother of Maximino and Manuel, used Jenkins's support for his grand designs in education. The most ambitious schools initiative in Puebla history foresaw primary-through-preparatory Schooling Centers catering to thousands in each of eight or nine cities. The governor was confident he could deliver on his promise because of Jenkins's financial backing.[6] It was a worthy scheme, because Puebla's literacy levels still lagged behind the national average, and many children received little or no formal education.

It was also a political scheme. Like his two elder brothers before him, if more discreetly, Rafael harbored presidential ambitions. Again like them, he was a general-turned-politician, with an eye upon posterity.[7] The completion of each Schooling Center would afford a grandiose inauguration, attended by dignitaries and amply covered by "the boys from the press." So as Schooling Centers opened around the state, the schedule was staggered for maximum exposure. Each event was freighted with as much political symbolism as Rafael could stack upon it. In 1952, he scored a personal coup by persuading Miguel Alemán to come and inaugurate the first of them, in Cholula, which in a blatant act of bootlicking he had named for the president. The next he opened himself, in the Ávila Camacho home town of Teziutlán, on the Day of the Constitution; this one he named for his brother Manuel. Rafael also liked mid-January inaugurations, as they coincided with his State of the State address. In January 1955 he scheduled openings on consecutive days in Ciudad Serdán and Matamoros, the latter town's school named for Lázaro Cárdenas. None other than Cárdenas himself came to open them. This brought Rafael's flattery count of former presidents to three.[8]

Rafael's *pièce de résistance* was Puebla City's own Boy Heroes of Chapultepec Schooling Center, which he opened on January 15, 1957. It was the day of his final gubernatorial address, and he delivered it inside the school's 4,000-seat auditorium, with another 15,000 people reportedly listening via loudspeaker outside. The school's name commemorated the six cadets who, according to lore, had wrapped themselves in the Mexican flag and thrown themselves from the ramparts of Chapultepec Castle rather than surrender to the US Army during the Mexican-American War. Puebla's compliant papers omitted to note the irony that a third of the school's million-dollar cost had been footed by a *yanqui*.

But they did lavish space on the campus. They ran aerial photographs, marveled at its six thousand student capacity, and waxed lyrical on its landscaping. "The buildings' rooftop gardens are beautiful," effused one reporter, "so beautiful that they render poorly made and lacking in splendor the Hanging Gardens of Babylon, built to flatter the sight of Semiramis."[9]

WHATEVER JENKINS'S AID to the patriotic education of Puebla, federal powers moved to bring the old gringo to heel. As a fellow US businessman of the era would recall, "The authorities had his left nut in a vice. They knew he'd never paid taxes, and with all the movie theaters and the alcohol and so on, he owed the government a lot of money."[10] An early sign of this duress came in 1950, when Jenkins gave $100,000 to Mexico City's National Institute of Cardiology, for the addition of a fourth floor. This hospital was a component of the government's modernization drive, but it was not a project close to Jenkins's heart. Despite Alemán's friendship with Jenkins, his finance minister, Ramón Beteta, allegedly pressed him into making the gift.[11]

Under Ruiz Cortines, pressure from the Finance Ministry mounted. Rather than face a lengthy audit, Jenkins countered with a compromise: he would formalize and increase his commitment to charity. Instead of continuing to donate haphazardly and often secretly, he would set up a philanthropic foundation, its books notarized and accountable to the State of

Puebla. He had been studying the structure of the great US foundations—the Rockefeller Foundation in particular—and he proposed an institution along similar lines.[12]

Since foundations had no precedent in Mexico, Finance Minister Antonio Carrillo Flores needed to be persuaded. Most of all, Jenkins had to convince him of the propriety of ceding to it his companies and gaining tax exemption for them. In his petition he added: "I intend to increase the importance of this Foundation by transferring other property and securities to it and, at my death, to leave my entire fortune to it." Carrillo Flores agreed to the request. As its initial endowment, Jenkins donated shares in his movie-theater real estate firm worth $7.2 million. These would yield annual earnings equivalent to $650,000.[13]

In its uniqueness the arrangement was widely misconstrued. To several local commentators, the foundation was little more a tax shelter, helping Jenkins augment his profits.[14] Such criticism missed the point: a foundation was *supposed* to make money. It was tax-free profits, not the principal, which would support charitable works, a financial structure allowing it to donate indefinitely and so have a far greater impact than a single large gift.

In October 1954 the foundation was born. His naming of it for Mary concealed the fact that Mrs. Jenkins had never taken to Mexico. It hinted at the guilt her widower felt at having left her to live in California and to die there alone. But it also reflected an agreement they had shared since their early years: whatever fortune he made beyond the family's needs would ultimately go to charity. Here was the noblesse oblige they had imbibed in 1890s America, just after the steel baron Andrew Carnegie had written his famous essay on wealth, arguing that "the man who dies possessed of millions of available wealth, which was free and in his hands ready to be distributed, will die disgraced."

This is what Jenkins had meant when he wrote to Elizabeth back in 1919, advising her to be thrifty: "for you know I am not going to leave any of you anything when I check in."[15]

ELIZABETH WAS MUCH on Jenkins's mind this year. His eldest daughter had grown distant from her husband. Lawrence Higgins had continued his philandering and always refused to have children. She had grown distant from her father too. He had cut her out of the film business when he saw that people were taking advantage of her and her alcoholism. In 1952 she had left Mexico for the last time. One evening in May 1954, Elizabeth was alone at home in Washington, and a mix of alcohol and sleeping pills, on top of a heart weakened by heavy smoking, caused her to expire in her bathtub. She was just fifty-one.

Jenkins never spoke about her death. It became a taboo subject, which permitted false rumors to circulate; one held that she had died in a traffic accident in Los Angeles. He had long had a testy relationship with her. She was strong-willed and liked to defy him. In conservative Puebla City, she had become a "woman with a reputation." Yet he had harbored a special feeling for Elizabeth. She was his first-born, and she was the only one of his daughters he entrusted with any business dealings. All the same, had he neglected her? Her premature death surely strengthened his resolve to increase his commitment to charity.[16]

Elizabeth's death nixed the chance of any woman serving on the foundation board, for his other daughters were never candidates. Jenkins generally held to the notion that women with access to money were liable to be duped. As for his sons-in-law, he held a low opinion of Higgins, finding him untrustworthy, and their joint venture as national distributor of Studebaker cars had folded the year before. Ronnie Eustace was learning the Mexican ropes but had yet to evince a gift for business. Jenkins had barely begun to know Margaret's new husband (her fourth), an engineer named Tom Poole. He found work for him as a construction manager on his Panamerican Highway project.[17]

His two youngest girls had stayed in Los Angeles. Both of them had married good-looking charmers, whom they met at the parties their elder sisters hosted at the family's Beverly Hills home. Mary, the prettiest of the daughters, had signed an acting contract with Twentieth Century-Fox, but her career went nowhere. She fell for a droll former Hollywood publicist who called himself Robert William (he was in fact Russian-Jewish), who in a moment of candor confided to her sister Tita that he wanted to find "a nice girl with money." After realizing this goal with Mary (for which, at Jenkins's insistence, he converted to Christianity), Robert bought a pasta factory. Jenkins supplied him with the necessary credit. The company would prove a success, but Robert never took an interest in Mexico.[18]

Tita's husband, by contrast, was professionally mobile and did know Mexico a little. But he had disqualified himself from any post requiring integrity by plotting a jewelry heist, for which he had served time at San Quentin Penitentiary.[19]

Calling himself Robert Lord III (he was actually a Greek orphan), this tall and muscular playboy had met Tita when she was nineteen. Tita was mesmerized by his tanned good looks and easy patter, although he seemed not to hold a full-time job. When her father heard of their engagement he had Lord investigated. On his next visit to Los Angeles, Jenkins read her the findings and advised her to return with him to Puebla. Sensing she would not follow his wishes, he left without saying goodbye. Hurt and headstrong, Tita doubled her resolve to marry. Only then did she realize the report had been right: Lord was a Hollywood gigolo. The first night in their new home, he went out to service some older woman. As Lord pursued this career, Tita felt there was little she could do. She was in thrall, and Robert could be violent. In one of their fights he broke her foot. During the day he would lie on the couch like a second-rate Gatsby, listening to classical music and improving his conversation by reading the *Encyclopedia Britannica.*

After seven years of marriage, Lord devised a caper with several associates to steal and sell $600,000 worth of jewels. This would finance an expedition to northern Mexico, where he had heard about a buried hoard of Yaqui gold, said to be worth $2 million. They planned to smuggle it back to the United States on a surplus Air Force bomber, and they would be set for life with the proceeds. Lord also talked of a get-rich-quick Plan B: he would kidnap Jenkins for a ransom! Ever loyal, Tita postponed her divorce petition while Lord remained behind bars at San Quentin, so as not to hurt his chances of parole.

The poor choices that most of the Jenkins daughters would make in or after marriage spoke of insufficient parental attention and an inability to discern a gold digger. Perhaps Jenkins observed their calamities with a grim sense of his rightness about women with access to money. But he never admitted that the problem was much of his making. He would rather blame his late wife. Several years later, after young Mary had put her marriage under stress through indulgent overspending, he would write to her husband: "The fact that our children have been allowed to grow wild reveals a most shocking failure of a mother's responsibilities toward her children."[20]

AS DIRECTORS OF his foundation, Jenkins opted for the men he felt he could trust the most; after he was gone they would pursue his priorities. He chose Manuel Espinosa Yglesias, his old friend Sergio Guzmán, his private secretary and perennial *prestanombres* Manuel Cabañas, and Felipe García Eguiño, a sugar industry colleague. Showing his latter-day sentimental streak, Jenkins also named his twenty-three-year-old grandson, Bill.[21]

Conspicuous by his absence was Gabriel Alarcón, then lying low after the Mascarúa murder. Jenkins never voiced an opinion about the incident, but his actions spoke loudly enough. For many years the two saw little of each other. Invitations to Acapulco dried up. They stayed partners in existing ventures, but the firms that Alarcón founded afterward lacked any sign of Jenkins or his frontmen in their registration papers; instead, he found associates in Mexico City or among younger Pueblans. Alarcón greatly resented Jenkins's refusal to stand by him or use his influence to get him off the hook. Explaining the estrangement to his wife, he blithely told her that Jenkins had grown envious of his success and so had plotted the hit on Mascarúa and framed him for it.[22]

The foundation soon made its local presence felt. While helping pay for the flagship Schooling Center, it spent $240,000 on a new building for the state capital's Red Cross Hospital. There followed a $150,000 gift toward a hospital in Izúcar de Matamoros. Once opened in 1960, it would provide free treatment to the cane growers of the Atencingo cooperative. A more complex project, taking seven years, was a second nonprofit Alpha Club, catering to a middle-class clientele and including an Olympic-sized swimming pool. It opened its doors in 1962 after an investment of nearly $1 million. Another long-term goal, the most ambitious of the American's charitable career, was an internationally recognized cancer hospital.[23]

Despite his multiple acts of largesse, or even because of them, some would doubt Jenkins's motives. As well as claiming the foundation was a tax dodge, they alleged an equally self-serving purpose: this infamous exploiter of workers and peasants, friend of tyrants, and creator of monopolies was trying to clean up his image. This idea likely says most about the ideology of its purveyors.[24] Believing himself defamed by the press ever since his kidnapping, Jenkins had long ago adopted the Duke of Wellington's maxim: "Publish and be damned!" When the media libeled him he kept mum. Juan Posada Noriega, a journalist who made a career of flattering the powerful, once sent him his latest work, which referred to him in glowing terms. Jenkins wrote back that it gave him no pleasure:

"For many years, it has been my invariable custom not to seek publicity in any form, and even less to defend myself against the constant attacks of which I have been a target for more than twenty years." He added: "I naturally cannot distribute copies of your book as you would like, because everyone will say that I'm doing it because you mention me in it."[25]

In the early 1930s Jenkins had attended one or two openings of the schools he funded, but afterward he stayed away. His managers, his daughters, and later his foundation directors took his place.[26] His reticence was never clearer than when two presidents came to Puebla to inaugurate the fruit of his philanthropy, for Jenkins still would not be drawn. When Ruiz Cortines arrived in 1957 to open an annex to the Red Cross Hospital, it was a trio of foundation directors who welcomed him; the press obliged by confining itself to say that the building was donated by "a wealthy gentleman." When López Mateos arrived in 1960 to reopen the city's eighteenth-century Principal Theater, whose restoration was two-thirds funded by the foundation, Jenkins again stayed home, designating his secretary Cabañas in his place.[27]

If the Mary Street Jenkins Foundation served a secondary purpose, it was neither as a profiteering ploy nor as a PR machine but as a political mechanism allied to the PRI. It was a coffer into which Puebla's governors and mayors could dip—once they convinced Jenkins of the worth of their projects—to help them fulfill campaign promises and bolster their reputations. By the same token, the foundation strengthened Jenkins's hand in the selection of candidates. Both Nicolas Vázquez (1951–1954) and Rafael Artasánchez (1957–1960) were widely held to have been handed the PRI's shoo-in candidacy for mayor on account of the American's backing. Some labeled them "impositions" of Jenkins, alleging governors had chosen them only because he promised to subsidize their tenures. Even here, however, philanthropy trumped politics: Jenkins main concern was the betterment of Puebla, not the perpetuation of a well-entrenched party. He judged candidates not on their devotion to the PRI but on their competence and aversion to corruption.[28]

There were limits to his power. Though he still made campaign donations to would-be governors, he did not appoint them. In 1956 a union accused Jenkins of plotting to control Puebla by foisting on it his "frontman" Rómulo O'Farrill. But Rafael Ávila Camacho opted to impose as his successor the gray bureaucrat Fausto Ortega, whom he felt he could better control.[29] Nor, after 1940, was Jenkins again able to influence the presidential succession. Convenient though it would have been to see his conservative friend Rafael become president, in November 1957 it was López

Mateos, the ideologically flexible labor minister, whom Ruiz Cortines chose to be the PRI candidate.

The Politics of Banking

Jenkins's party loyalty would serve him very well when he took over Mexico's second-largest bank.[30] The Banco de Comercio, today's BBVA Bancomer, was the brainchild of Salvador Ugarte, a merchant from Guadalajara who with several partners created the bank out of nothing in 1932. In a feat unparalleled in the postrevolutionary financial sector, Ugarte built up its business so that it overtook such venerable institutions as the Bank of London & Mexico, founded in 1864.[31] By the mid-1950s, it held 18 percent of Mexican deposits. Only the Banco Nacional de México (today's Banamex) was larger, with 30 percent.

Backing the Banco de Comercio were three powerful financiers who joined with Ugarte in forming the BUDA Group, an acronym of their surnames. These were silver magnate Raúl Bailleres, one of Mexico's richest men; Ugarte himself, the bank's chairman; Augusto Domínguez, who separately owned another bank; and Ernesto Amescua, an insurance mogul. Collectively, the BUDA quartet had grown used to working with the state to shape financial policy. By wealth, Jenkins inhabited the same lofty league as these men; by reputation, he fell rather short. So it was a shock to the entire financial elite when Jenkins, together with his wily lieutenant Espinosa Yglesias, emerged in 1954 as the bank's majority owner. The move has been called Mexico's "first large-scale hostile takeover."[32]

Although the buy-out was sudden, it built on years of stock accumulation and took place with no little stealth. Jenkins had first taken a stake in 1942, when the bank traded shares for his majority position in its Puebla affiliate. In 1945, he increased his position when a key client, Nacional de Drogas, suffered a postwar collapse in revenues as the pharmaceutical market was flooded with competing product; its solvency threatened, the bank issued shares to raise capital, and Jenkins bought heavily. He bought further shares from the families of two founders when inheritance disputes occasioned their sale. Subsequent capital increases by the bank, funding its expansion as it sought to catch up with Banamex, allowed Jenkins yet more purchases. How aware the board was of all these moves is not known; Jenkins typically bought via third parties.

By 1950 Jenkins was by far the biggest single shareholder, owning 41 percent, and he placed Espinosa on the board to represent him. The bank's other directors were reconciled to the presence of this outsider. They did not think themselves threatened because the Law of Foreign Investment forbade foreign control of banks and because Jenkins, on naming Espinosa as his mouthpiece, had subscribed to a gentlemen's agreement that no shareholder would seek a majority. They did not count on the machinations of Espinosa. By 1954, the slight but ambitious Pueblan was eying pastures greener than the box office, where profits were in decline due to price caps. Much as he had done ten years before, when sniffing out a stake in the Film Bank that would give Jenkins control of the COTSA chain, Espinosa cast around for a weak link among the bank's main shareholders. This time, he acted behind Jenkins's back.

Espinosa settled on Manuel Senderos, who had inherited a 10 percent share, enough to give Jenkins outright control. Espinosa prised the stake from him through calculation, fortuity, and guile. He offered Senderos a premium, 9.5 million pesos for a holding worth less than 8 million, and he did so just as Senderos was prioritizing other businesses. Further, Espinosa told him that the buyer was Jenkins's new foundation, which was seeking investments for its endowment. As it turned out, the shares indeed entered its books, but as Jenkins controlled the charity he also assumed the voting rights to any shares it owned. The purchase, made in March 1954, put Mexico's number-two bank in American hands.[33]

While Espinosa was ecstatic—"few times in my life had I been so happy," he would write in his memoirs—Jenkins was decidedly not. His partner of sixteen years had furtively effected a deal that put him, as a foreigner, in a position of illegal control. Jenkins had a history of skirting laws, but nothing as audacious as owning a nationally prominent bank. Following the press barrage of 1953, the last thing Jenkins needed was to be target of another nationalistic onslaught. Espinosa did not admit it in his memoir, but he forced his partner's hand: Jenkins would have to relinquish his ownership, yet the bank's lucrative potential meant he would surely wish to keep it within his sphere of influence. Inevitably it would fall to Espinosa to assume its titular control.

Espinosa would run the Banco de Comercio as a personal empire for twenty-seven years. For the time being, however, he depended on Jenkins. He did not yet have the capital to purchase Jenkins's 51 percent, presumably worth some $4 million.[34] He traded his shares in COTSA's sister company, which owned the theater buildings, for some of Jenkins's shares in the bank, but that still left a large portion in the hands of the American and his foundation. By 1961, Espinosa still owed Jenkins more than $2 million.

In the meantime it seemed to the public that Espinosa was the new owner-manager of the bank—he imposed himself as CEO in March 1955—while in elite circles the rumors pointed to Jenkins.

Sometime after the buyout, while on vacation in Acapulco, Jenkins's teenage godson Luisito Artasánchez heard a guest ask his host point-blank: Was it true that Espinosa Yglesias owned the Banco de Comercio? Jenkins was silent for a while, contemplating his chessboard. "Yes, it's true," he said eventually, "but I own Espinosa Yglesias."[35]

For all their efforts to disguise the bank's ownership, Espinosa and Jenkins were widely known to be partners, and the business-community perception was that Espinosa often fronted for the American. So how did the two men get away with the takeover? How so, moreover, when most of the BUDA Group and their boardroom allies were militating against it? Once CEO, Espinosa was repeatedly assailed from within. Bailleres, previously the bank's largest single investor, was incensed that a majority share-holding and executive power were concentrated in a single person. The bank's success had always drawn from a careful balance, the founders all accountable to one another and day-to-day operations led by an independent general manager, Aníbal de Iturbide. Espinosa's assumption of near-dictatorial control was a huge step backward for corporate governance. Worse, he was not even a banker but an upstart from the movie business! At first Bailleres tried to force Espinosa to resign his executive directorship and sell his shares by threatening the mass exit of most of the board, a move that would prompt important clients to abandon the bank. A cooler head among the directors, seeking a compromise, obtained a collective threat of resignation that only insisted Espinosa surrender his executive post. Backed by Jenkins, Espinosa still refused to budge.

In the summer of 1955 tensions spiked again. Iturbide approved a multimillion-dollar purchase of bonds from board member Carlos Trouyet's cellulose firm without consulting Espinosa; this prompted him to request Iturbide's resignation. It was the size of the sum, not the then-routine insider lending, which upset Espinosa. Iturbide quit, and so did Trouyet. "Aníbal de Iturbide's resignation creates a serious problem for the Banco de Comercio," gloated a headline in the left-wing *El Popular*; the article claimed many clients had withdrawn their deposits.[36] An exodus was understandable, for Iturbide was president of the Mexican Bankers' Association and Trouyet was a millionaire multi-industrialist of great repute.

A third crisis blew up in 1956. Seeking to turn the Banco de Comercio into a multifaceted financial institution, Espinosa wanted Baillères and

Senderos to sell to it the investment bank and insurance company they respectively owned. At the same time, tensions were worsening between the CEO and the more independent-minded directors, as Espinosa barked orders and threatened their business interests. He was faced with a wave of resignations: ten board members quit, some accepting the invitation of Iturbide and Trouyet to join a rival bank.

El Popular took the gloves off. "The gangsterish methods that for many years have been the watchword of the group formed by the multimillionaire William O. Jenkins have invaded the important circle of the private banks," it declared. Thanks to the "brute force" of Jenkins, Espinosa, and Alarcón, the Banco de Comercio had already lost its "soul," Aníbal de Iturbide. Now it was seeing the exit of Bailleres, Domínguez, and Amescua, which endangered the accounts of its clients, sowed doubt among the public, and so threatened the country's economy. The Finance Ministry might well intervene, because Mexico's development could not be put at risk by Jenkins, "who employs the methods of the sadly famous Al Capone."[37]

The Finance Minister indeed intervened, but not in the manner the paper advocated. Behind the scenes, Antonio Carrillo Flores had all along been giving Espinosa his assurances, and when most of the BUDA Group and its allies quit he recommended respected men to replace them. These included Juan Sánchez-Navarro, a senior executive at the Modelo brewery (makers of Corona) and later a great ideologue of the private sector. According to Espinosa, Carrillo Flores and other ministers expressed their confidence in his leadership, in part because Ugarte remained president.[38] These ministers would be vindicated, for Espinosa would lead the bank to new heights of profit and market share. But there was a lot more to the state's complicity.

The BUDA Group were active members of the opposition National Action Party (PAN). The PAN called for a much more free-market path of development than the state-centered model pursued by the PRI, which having nationalized the oil sector and railroads was eying further strategic industries. The PAN was also allied with the Catholic Church. When government policy veered to the left, BUDA and their allies were critical. This much is well-known.[39]

What is not is the extent of PRI concern about BUDA's power. In 1949, Alemán had entrusted his Federal Security Directorate (DFS) with spying on them. In language reflecting state fears of a resurgent PAN—which had nearly swayed the 1940 election by backing the opposition—DFS agents concluded that the BUDA quartet not only sustained the party financially but was also gearing up an antigovernment campaign. It had placed loyalists at the head of the National Banking Commission and various business associations. These were using their member networks to distribute PAN propaganda and build a vote-gathering apparatus. The Banco de Comercio, in particular, was employing its network of affiliates as "tentacles" of the party and buying firms whose employees could be molded into PAN loyalists.[40]

Given such precedents, the willingness of Ruiz Cortines and Carrillo Flores to allow a controversial American and his *arriviste* partner to buy the country's number-two bank makes a great deal more sense, for Jenkins and Espinosa were PRI loyalists. Here again the new form of symbiosis was at play, perceived by its players as imperative but in fact a matter of convenience: to preserve its political monopoly, the PRI needed to contain the PAN's sphere of influence, while Jenkins needed the state to turn a blind eye to foreign ownership restrictions and approve a purchase to which powerful rivals were adamantly opposed. This was no small favor given the growing perception that, despite Espinosa's visibility, Jenkins was the power behind the bank.[41]

Decades later, when interviewing Carrillo Flores for a book about her father, Espinosa's eldest daughter asked him about the Banco de Comercio acquisition. The former finance minister told her that Bailleres and other senior shareholders had tried to persuade him to halt the takeover, arguing that Espinosa was just a movie theater operator and knew nothing about banking. But the minister had turned them down because of their links to the PAN.[42]

Bill and Mary Return to Mexico

William Anstead Jenkins, known to the family as Bill, was much in love with his eighteen-year-old bride Chacha. They had met a year earlier, not long after Bill had returned to Mexico from service in the Marines and entered the insurance business with Espinosa. Educated at Dartmouth, he had grown up to be an easygoing young man, and his prospects were good. Chacha was slender, beautiful, feisty, and loyal. She spoke excellent English, after two years of boarding school in England, but she did not put on airs. None of this detracted from the fact that their marriage, in June 1958, glistened with social symbolism.[43]

Despite the Protestantism of Bill's family, the wedding took place at the Mexico City Cathedral. Officiating was the Archbishop himself, the

Excelentísimo y Reverendísimo Miguel Darío Miranda y Gómez. Attending were captains of national industry, among them Aarón Sáenz, Emilio Azcárraga, Salvador Ugarte, and Juan Sánchez-Navarro; the cream of the Puebla business elite, including Espinosa, Alarcón, and O'Farrill; and a mix of names evocative of the old Porfirian hierarchy, unseated a half century before: De Landa, De Mier, Casasús, Limantour.

Then there was the matter of the bride's social provenance. Young Chacha—full name: Elodia Sofía de Landa Irízar—was a granddaughter of Guillermo de Landa y Escándon, mayor of the capital under Porfirio Díaz and said by some to be the richest Mexican of his day. The society reporter at *El Universal*, perhaps forgetting there had been a Revolution, heralded the bride as a member of "the Mexican aristocracy." The wedding report, guest list, and photographs dominated Monday's society pages.

William Jenkins had long been close to the prelates of Puebla, but to persuade the Archbishop of Mexico City to officiate at his grandson's marriage was to gain a final stamp on his social acceptance. (The fact that, two years earlier, his foundation had begun making gifts for the Cathedral's restoration could have had something to do with it.)[44] There might seem to be a contradiction here, given Jenkins's contempt for public relations; however, it was not good press that he was after but rather another confirmation that an elite that had once rejected him now welcomed his company—and that of his adoptive son. In similar fashion it must have amused him that Bill should marry a De Landa, especially since most of that family's fortune had evaporated. When the Revolution broke out, Guillermo de Landa had accompanied Porfirio Díaz into exile in Paris. By 1958, Chacha's widowed mother had so little capital there was no private banquet to follow the wedding. Jenkins did not like big parties, so the family and guests dined at a restaurant.

In the 1920s and 1930s, many revolutionary officers had married daughters of Porfirian elites fallen on hard times. It was a way for rough-hewn men of provincial origins to gain public cachet and learn social graces, while their wives could benefit from the talent of these strivers for turning power into wealth. There were echoes of this exchange in the Jenkins-De Landa wedding, except that Ivy League–educated Bill needed little refinement. But the match did serve as a reminder of the new order of things, a postrevolutionary order so far removed from the war that had brought it about that an American magnate loathed by the left could command attention in the spiritual heart of the country and be congratulated for it in the press.

AMONG THE GUESTS that evening were two athletic-looking Americans who had befriended Jenkins a few years before: Rex Applegate and Phil Roettinger.[45] They had set up a gun dealership, Armamex, and Jenkins helped them with start-up capital—or so young Bill assumed. From time to time they would visit Jenkins in Puebla. Bill was not in on those meetings, but he became friendly with Roettinger, a fellow ex-Marine. Roettinger sold him several guns over the years and then offered his services as Bill and Chacha's wedding photographer.

Forty-four years later, Bill would come across Roettinger's obituary, and what he read made him spill his morning coffee. Roettinger was CIA. Or at least he had been, until a guilty conscience led him to quit in 1964. He had helped with the US-engineered coup against Arbenz of Guatemala, and for the next ten years he had meddled in Mexican politics. "I realized we weren't fighting communism at all, we were fighting the people," he later confessed.

Applegate too had been a CIA agent. He was dispatched to Mexico City after World War II, where he helped train Alemán's FBI equivalent, the Federal Security Directorate. Applegate's expertise included close-quarters combat and crowd control in riot situations. He had written a lauded training manual: *Kill or Get Killed*. Armamex was part of Applegate and Roettinger's cover. The firm had gone so far as to request, and receive, an infant-industry tax break.

Were those meetings in Puebla strictly business, or was Jenkins briefing the men on local left-wing activities? Since the CIA will neither confirm nor deny that it has a file on Jenkins, one can only guess. But precedent suggests that Jenkins was a cooperative Cold Warrior.

In the summer of 1954 the Mexican-Russian Institute for Cultural Exchange planned a festival of Soviet cinema in Mexico City. It booked a number of films into theaters operated by Oscar and Samuel Granat. But the Granat brothers soon found that their leases to the theaters had been rescinded, ownership of the buildings having changed hands, and the Russian film series was cancelled. Once the US Embassy had got wind of the festival, it contacted Jenkins and asked him to sabotage it. Alarcón and Espinosa then bought the respective real estate, which enabled them to dictate its use.[46]

FOUR MONTHS AFTER Bill's wedding, Jenkins arrived with several old friends at Puebla's Notary No. 13, where they were to witness his will.[47] He had always said he would give his fortune away. He had pledged to do so in the first version of his will, drawn up with Mary in 1937. Now he would add various clauses and make it official.

Jenkins stated his identity: he was known as Guillermo Jenkins, and he was a farmer and a widower. Originally from Shelbyville in Tennessee, he had been a resident of Mexico since December 12, 1901. He was an immigrant, as inscribed in the National Register of Foreigners (i.e., he was still a US citizen). He was father to five daughters, the eldest now deceased, and adoptive father to a son whom he considered legally his own. Next he spelled out his rationale:

> The testator declares: he has always had the firm conviction that, for the good of their children, parents should not bequeath them large fortunes, but rather should teach them and help them work so that they themselves earn what they need, for the testator believes that no one capable of working should spend money that he has not earned by his own effort; and following this principle he states that it is not his will to leave his children riches or fortunes but rather to help them work so that they can build their future by their own efforts.

He then outlined what assistance he had given so far. He had bought a house for Margaret in Mexico City and was aiding her husband Tom Poole with a construction business. Jane's husband Ronnie he was helping set up a thread-making factory, having lent him several million pesos at 6 percent interest, a preferential rate. (The mill, Hilos Superfinos, was one of Puebla's largest postwar textile companies and represented a rare late-career commitment by Jenkins to innovation in the sector.)[48] To his adoptive son Bill and to Mary's husband Robert William he had made loans on the same terms, to help launch financial services firms and a pasta factory, respectively. Finally, he had invited Tita and her new husband to Puebla, to set them up in business there, but they had rejected his offer and returned to Los Angeles; "hence the testator no longer plans to help them establish their own business."

Jenkins noted he had already donated large sums to the Mary Street Jenkins Foundation and that it was his wish to donate the rest. He did not say so, but this was a slow process because much of what he owned was held under the names of others or bound up in joint ventures, which

meant finding buyers. Should he die before the transfer of assets was complete, he hereby named the foundation as the "sole and universal heir to all
his properties, rights, and shares."

There followed several exclusions: small fractions of his wealth the
foundation was to hold for other purposes. His domestic staff should be
pensioned for life so they need not work again, with all medical expenses
covered. The foundation should fund the education of his grandchildren,
including board, lodging, and twice-yearly travel expenses should they
study abroad. He set a monthly support, of no more than $1,000, for any
of his children should they fall on hard times and added that their medical
bills be paid. He also wished to preserve his family home in Tennessee,
which his grandfather the Reverend Jenkins had built; the Lutheran
church he had attended as a child; and the cemetery alongside it, where
his ancestors were buried. This was the will of a patriarch, mindful of his
debts to the past and his duties to the future.

There was another proviso, for immediate action: Jenkins charged
the foundation with bringing his wife home. The remains of Mary Street
Jenkins were to be brought from Los Angeles, "to be buried in this City of
Puebla, together with those of the testator, for it is his desire that they be
united . . . where both spouses lived and worked for so many years."

And so, a quarter century after her departure, Mary returned to Mexico.[49]
Her coffin was disinterred from the spot she had chosen at Forest Lawn,
and Jenkins hired a plane to transport it to Puebla, where he had bought
a large private plot at the French Cemetery. Jane was furious, wanting her
mother to remain in the States. She knew Mary had not shared William's
love for Mexico, and she resented him for failing to move back to be with
her. Jenkins did not care what Jane thought; he had always found her too
opinionated. On the designated day, all the Mexico-based family joined
him at the airport for Mary's arrival. Much to everyone's embarrassment,
the coffin broke open as it was lowered from the plane; as it passed the
assembled family there was a terrible smell. Jenkins was already in tears.
No one breathed a word.

After the reburial, the family gathered at the big downtown apartment for refreshments. Jenkins made himself scarce. Jane's daughter
Rosemary, now fourteen, found him in his bedroom. Again he was weeping. Rosemary sat next to him on the bed and took his hand in hers. "I
made a great mistake," he sighed. "I should have been with her."

Thereafter, Jenkins altered his afternoon routine. Instead of going
directly to the Alpha Club, where he continued to swim and play tennis,

he would make a stop at the cemetery. Sitting on a stool by Mary's grave he would read to her, choosing poems and passages from her favorite novels. He would not fail, even in the rain.

Gringophobia and the Soul of the PRI

When Adolfo López Mateos became president in 1958, he inherited a slowing economy and an agitated labor movement. He also stepped into a Cold War climate about to get rougher, for Castro's rebels had captured most of Cuba and Havana was about to fall.[50] Buffeted by circumstance, he oscillated with his policies. First he met protest with an iron hand, repressing striking rail workers and jailing their leaders. Then he showed sympathy for the poor, with greater social spending and land redistribution. Unlike all other Latin American leaders, he refused to sever ties with Cuba after Castro declared his revolution communist in 1961. Yet he stayed friendly with the United States, careful not to hinder investment. He welcomed both President Kennedy and Cuba's President Osvaldo Dorticós to Mexico. If there were consistency to López Mateos's tenure, it was less conservatism or socialism than a deeply rhetorical nationalism.

Contradictions in policy and prevalence of oratory were part of a delicate balancing act, for the era was equally fraught with storms at home. The PRI's pro-Alemán right wing and pro-Cárdenas left wing battled for the soul of the party. The tussle spilled into the streets, as a mushrooming student population took sides. So did the business elite, the Catholic Church, and the unions. Alemanists wanted more of the policies that had helped drive growth, like low taxation, and they condemned the global rise of socialism. Cardenists claimed the Revolution had lost its compass, citing the return of monopolies as evidence; they demanded renewed efforts to redistribute wealth. Statistics supported both sides.[51] The economy had expanded at a dramatic annual average of 6 percent since the early 1930s. But the fruits of growth had vastly fallen to the elite. The middle class, as a fraction of the population, had ceased to grow for twenty years, and the poor were relatively poorer. A 1960 survey found that income inequality in Mexico, despite its famed Revolution, was higher than in the rest of Latin America and getting worse.

With US foreign policy and the Castro coup inflaming passions, the debate between Alemanists and Cardenists developed a Manichaean tone. Left-wingers goaded crowds to chant *"¡Cuba sí, Yanquis no!"* Right-wing crowds countered *"¡Cristianismo sí, Comunismo no!"* Leftist cartoonists satirized the business class with ugly caricatures; conservatives depicted Cárdenas as a flunky of Castro, brainwashed into a stupor by communism.[52]

Amid the bombastic swirl stood the aging but still-notorious target of William O. Jenkins. As a capitalist, a monopolist, a cultural imperialist, a flouter of rules, a citizen of the United States, and the subject of public critiques since 1919, Jenkins (or rather, his persona) offered leftists their most visible local vehicle for gringophobia. With the shift in the political winds, Jenkins-bashing returned as a persuasive tool for those pushing for a leftist-nationalist policy shift.

GRINGOPHOBIA HAD VERY much waned after Cardenism reached its radical zenith in 1938. The oil expropriation removed the biggest bone of contention between Mexico and the United States, and the moderate reactions of President Roosevelt and Ambassador Daniels gave further salve to historical resentments. Then the Second World War, coinciding with the centrist presidency of Manuel Ávila Camacho, occasioned a profound change in bilateral relations. The title of a study of this new entente, marked by the entry to Mexico of major US firms, encapsulates the shift: *Yankee Don't Go Home!* State censorship, wartime propaganda, and US support for the film and radio sectors further minimized negative views of Americans.[53]

But the rapid growth of industrial capitalism, and with it high inflation, caused a backlash by the late 1940s. Suspicion of US motives returned. There was concern that, with the transition from antifascist to Cold War geopolitics, the United States had lost interest in being a Good Neighbor. After 1959, when Washington opposed the Castro regime, backed the Bay of Pigs invasion designed to oust it, and supported right-wing dictatorships across Latin America, apprehension grew. Further, the postwar surge in Hollywood movies and the advent of rock 'n' roll caused consternation in elite circles, as did the apparent ignorance of surging numbers of US tourists. They and an influx of business managers brought Mexicans face to face with Americans as never before. Grudges festered over their superior pay scales and insensitivities. Writers and artists geared up their attacks on the triple threat of US influence: political, economic, and cultural.[54]

Daniel Cosío Villegas, a giant of Mexican letters and usually measured in his views of the United States, could not refrain from tarring American tourists as "noisy, stupid, meddling, inconsiderate, and childish." Popular historian Ignacio Muñoz reissued his bestseller *The Truth about the Gringos*. He added Jenkins to his vignettes about Yankee miscreants, offering the lie that he had once owned "almost half the State of Puebla and a large part of Morelos." There was renewed popularity for Rodó's *Ariel*, with its glorification of Latin spirituality and critique of soulless Anglo pragmatism. The most infamous US investor prior to Jenkins, oil baron Edward Doheny, received a reburial in *Doheny, The Cruel*.[55]

Elite disdain found echo in popular culture, where depictions were more visceral. In film, Yankee bloodsuckers appeared more often than ever, embodying the supposed values of US business. Only a minority of Mexicans would have had personal dealings with American executives, yet with the huge popularity of moviegoing, cinema both perpetuated the caricature and reflected how a public appetite for such villains was growing with each decade.[56]

López Mateos evidently let gringophobia grow. It distracted from domestic troubles and fostered national unity. It allowed people to believe that his repression of the railroad workers had been an aberration, for Mexico was a country in which protest was permitted. It functioned as an escape valve for discontent among dissidents, especially the Cardenists. It complemented a foreign policy that trumpeted Mexico's independence from Cold War partisanship, to mask the conservatism of domestic policy, and it fostered the impression that the president would not be browbeaten by the United States. The confrontational stance was not limited to bombast; there were nationalistic actions also. But, like the refusal to sever ties with Cuba, these deeds were mainly symbolic.[57] The rhetorical and political treatment accorded Jenkins under López Mateos provides a vivid illustration of this calculus at work.

WITH THE MONOPOLY-RELATED attacks of 1953, Jenkins had regained prominence as the gringo that leftists and nationalists loved to hate. Press coverage of his film and banking activities, including paid insertions from filmmaker Miguel Contreras Torres, kept him in the public eye.[58] Under López Mateos, a periodical could pronounce its patriotism, attract new readers, and distract them from everyday troubles by joining the critique.

Opinión Pública, a muckraking monthly full of leftist-nationalist hyperbole, published the lengthiest sketch yet, in 1959.[59] Stirring the Jenkins Black Legend and adding seasoning of its own, it provided a recipe for future profiles. The magazine heralded the piece with a full-cover caricature, satirizing Jenkins as a despotic monarch with a toy-like crown on his head, and a headline that blared: "William Jenkins, Lord and Master of Mexico."

"Mexico would be happy without foreigners," the piece began, "for they come to serve their respective nations of origin and not our country." It named Jenkins as "owner of the state of Puebla" and one of the Big Men controlling the nation's political and economic life. He had accrued the greatest fortune in Mexico. In Puebla he retained the most bloodthirsty private militia in all the country, murdering everyone who opposed his will. It was not the Ávila Camachos who had ruled Puebla for the past twenty years but Jenkins, picking governors, senators, deputies, and mayors. In owning the Banco de Comercio he exploited thousands of employees, for they worked outside the protection of the Federal Labor Law, and the fact that 70 percent of them were female made Jenkins "a great national pimp." It was a mystery as to why "the most pernicious foreigner that we have" was allowed to stay in Mexico, so it must be because he had bribed past presidents. The presence of this "formidable filibusterer" jeopardized the Good Neighbor relationship. Like many voices before, the magazine called for his expulsion.

Jenkins was not the only foreigner so targeted. *Opinión Pública*'s tone was more generally xenophobic than gringophobic. Swedish industrialist Axel Wenner-Gren and Spanish contractor Manuel Suárez also met with the "pernicious foreigner" treatment. But this organ's brand of reportage involved singling out a body for flagellation and continuing to whip it. No foreigner was as often flailed as Jenkins. Later articles assailed his farming in Michoacán ("now he's extending the tentacles with which he is sucking the blood of the peasants"), his refusal to donate to the First Lady's children's charity ("God has punished him, for he cannot eat more than a little leg of chicken each day"), and the production of "terrible films that denigrate Mexico abroad by presenting us as a people of drunks, *pistoleros*, and shouters of 'songs.' "[60]

Éxito, a new tabloid newsweekly, also profiled Jenkins in 1959. The article's tone was less visceral but more embellished, as though the American's villainous exploits made him reprehensible and admirable in equal parts: "Since his famous and theatrical, episodic and cinematic self-kidnapping, William Jenkins, the gringo of Puebla, has been captured in tradition and legend as someone of whom to be careful, like a character . . . from a picaresque novel." A man who seems "to be older than Methuselah himself" (he was eighty-one), Jenkins added "color, and sometimes blood, to the era." He was an "ambitious son of Gringolandia" who sheltered himself in consular immunity and with his iron will dominated politicians. He fired "little cannon blasts of up to 100,000 pesos" at governors, attorney generals, military officers, and judges. (There was some truth here, and

Ronnie Eustace saw that he kept a bag of gold coins in his office, which he would distribute "whenever someone needed persuading.")[61]

In 1960, Jenkins-bashing reached a new peak. Another debut periodical made Jenkins a target, the left-wing *Política*, which would gain quite an influence during its seven-year run.[62] At times its language was brazenly anti-American. Its third issue featured a photo essay about Atencingo, "A Hell on Mexican Soil." It claimed the sugar estate was still controlled by Jenkins, of whom it said: "the greatest devil is blond." (Before Jenkins turned gray his hair had been dark, but Mexican caricatures of US businessmen always rendered them fair-haired.) Later *Política* reported criticisms of Jenkins's Michoacán land purchases and attacked his film monopoly.[63]

Miguel Contreras Torres, the American's nemesis-pretend, then weighed in with his rancorous *Black Book of Mexican Cinema*. In the words of the director's biographer, the book revealed Contreras to be "located outside reality," but journalists were quick to quote it.[64] Just before the *Black Book* there emerged a "Mexican Cinema *Corrido*." Published as an eight-page booklet, this satirical ditty bore the Contreras Torres hallmarks: vilification of the Jenkins Group and repudiation of almost every producer and director of note, since all had "sold out." But the *corrido*, under the mask of pseudonymity, added fresh allegations. It had Alemán protecting Alarcón in illicit dealings and Ruiz Cortines aiding Jenkins's monopoly in exchange for a stake. It claimed the entire press was on the Jenkins Group payroll, and it ended with Jenkins boasting: "Governors have I imposed, / Presidents I manipulate, / And that is how I never pay my taxes."[65]

A panel cartoon in *Excélsior* during the 1960 census furthered Jenkins's infamy as a tax evader.[66] A census-taker finds Jenkins dressed like a dandy, in a housecoat, cravat, and slippers, with a giant diamond ring appended to his nose. "How much do you earn?" asks the official. Jenkins drops to his knees: "I swear, almost nothing. I'm bankrupt. Movie theaters that charge four pesos are no business." The census-taker wipes his tears as he departs—"Poor man! We have to help him"—while Jenkins has retreated behind his door: the portal of a bank vault.

Cárdenas joined the chorus that same week. Speaking one evening at a small-town school in his home state of Michoacán, the former president lambasted Jenkins as a *latifundista* (large-scale landowner) and monopolist. Citing the American's purchase of 3,700 acres near Apatzingán, Cárdenas called on farmers not to sell him any more. Pounding the table, he exhorted his listeners: "Neither sell your properties nor do business with foreign capitalists!" Ill-tempered, so the report said, he went on to claim that if monopolies were allowed to develop Mexico would not be safe from another revolution. Most remarkable about the episode is that the audience barely numbered a hundred, and yet the speech ran at the top of page one in *Excélsior*.[67]

Why a leading paper would generously cover so minor a speech reflected the battle for the soul of the PRI. A year earlier, inspired in part by the Cuban Revolution, Cárdenas had returned to the national stage. Breaking with a tradition of postpresidential silence that he observed so closely some had dubbed him "the Sphinx," Cárdenas gave speeches and made declarations. A year later he would co-found the Movement for National Liberation, a pressure group conceived to reorient the ruling party to the left. This activity lasted for four years, a time of growing criticism of the PRI's authoritarianism and its embrace of big-money capitalism.[68]

Cárdenas's targeting of Jenkins was a deeply symbolic act. As a foreign investor, a monopolist, and a *latifundista*, he embodied the resurgence of three of the chief ills that the Revolution, in the view of the left, had promised to curtail. Cárdenas's recourse to xenophobia emphasized the dangers that Alemán-style capitalism posed: to pursue the current path risked returning Mexico to its dark Porfirian past. The complaint had some basis. Despite the massive creation of communal *ejidos* under Cárdenas, twenty subsequent years of favoring large-scale agribusiness meant that by 1960 just 3 percent of farms controlled 55 percent of production.[69]

There was another angle, revealing Jenkins as yet more of a rhetorical tool than met the eye. Was it not strange that he was buying land in Cárdenas's backyard? A statement by the right-wing National Sinarquist Union raised that very question. It pointed out that Michoacán was a "Cardenist feudal terrain" and also noted that Cárdenas had attended a banquet in his honor hosted by Jenkins's partner Alarcón. The union asked: "What's going on behind all this?"[70]

The answer is that Cárdenas gave Jenkins a green light. The American had proposed a huge investment, involving clearance of scrubland, emplacement of irrigation, purchase of an ice factory, and laying of extra railroad. Melon would be packed in ice and exported to the United States; cotton would be grown for the domestic market. Several million dollars would be committed and hundreds if not thousands of jobs created. For Cárdenas, who retained great power in Michoacán, spent a dozen years supervising an irrigation scheme in the very region where Jenkins was buying, and could easily have barred Jenkins's entry, it was a win-win proposition. First, it would boost his homeland's economy. Second, the American's presence in the state—hidden until he had bought enough land—would provide Cárdenas with a whipping boy. He could rail against this pernicious gringo in public and welcome his money in private.[71]

AFTER ALL THE rhetoric—including denunciations of the Jenkins Group in Congress—there was action. On November 29, 1960, Finance Minister Antonio Ortiz Mena announced the nationalization of Jenkins's movie theaters. How much that year's barrage of criticism prompted the act is hard to gauge, but it would have suggested how popular the move might be, which in turn raises the possibility that the López Mateos regime encouraged it, to shape the public mood and then gain greater plaudits. The president, a capable orator, was a master of mind games. In a speech that summer he had appeased the left wing and alarmed the right by stating that his regime was "within the Constitution, a government of the far left."[72]

The state seized 365 theaters, at a cost to the taxpayer equivalent to $26 million. These were only a quarter of what the Jenkins Group controlled, but they were the core assets, the big-city, big-ticket venues that Jenkins owned with Espinosa and Alarcón. A plethora of editorials, columns, and open letters praised the expropriation.[73]

Jenkins told his friend Branscomb that the buyout was a "disaster." To his free-market mode of thinking, he must have found it galling to have built a second empire—as at Atencingo, creating thousands of jobs in the process—only to see it snatched in a fit of presidential populism. But "disaster" typified his vocabulary of complaint. He had not put up much of a fight, and for good reason. Over the past seven or eight years, profits had shrunk, squeezed by rising costs and the ticket price cap. The $26 million in compensation tempered the loss, as did the fact that the state did not buy the actual theaters; it took the operating companies but leased the buildings. The Jenkins Foundation would still receive rent. Besides, Jenkins was devoting his remaining energy to philanthropy and his fruit and cotton farms in Puebla and Michoacán.[74]

State intervention failed to alter Mexican cinema's decline. Its market position did not improve at home and virtually collapsed in South America.[75] The old corps of decrepit directors persisted, its guild loath to admit new members. Producers still inflated budgets and avoided risk. Mexican and foreign fare was never so far apart. Bedroom farces, generic melodramas, and shoddy wrestler capers, the majority in black-and-white, vied with *Lawrence of Arabia*, *The Sound of Music*, Stanley Kubrick, and Sergio Leone. Patrons of the more profitable theaters would continue to entrust their entertainment to Hollywood.

So the theater seizure proved a theatrical act. As such, it somewhat resembled that year's electricity takeover. The US and Belgian power plant owners in fact wanted to sell, for generation was dominated by the state and had ceased to be lucrative, while the takeover allowed López Mateos to make crowd-pleasing comparisons to the oil nationalization of 1938. Yet the cinema move was the more purely symbolic. Unlike the power companies, Jenkins had not repatriated profits, nor were Mexican jobs at stake.[76] And while the former belonged to anonymous investors, Jenkins was notorious.

Pipe Dreams and Protests

Apatzingán was an unlikely place for Jenkins's final venture. Situated in the western state of Michoacán, four hundred miles from Puebla, the town lay in a region known as the *Tierra Caliente*, or Hot Lands. Scarce rains and a low elevation keep temperatures very high, and the natural landscape is a scrubland of low trees and tall cacti. A visitor like Jenkins could have been forgiven for thinking that *caliente* also reflected the region's history, one of heated resistance to outside authority since colonial times. Borrowing from local wisdom, Michoacán historian Luis González would describe the Hot Lands as sufficiently torrid to make devils flee, a place where men liked to drink and to kill each other for honor.[77]

Jenkins entered the region through produce dealer Wally Alston, an Arkansas native who sold his Puebla-grown tomatoes in Mexico City. Alston was already active in the Hot Lands, sourcing fruit for the US market, and around 1956 the two men formed a partnership to increase production there, providing credit to fruit and cotton farmers. Jenkins liked Alston and he liked visiting the Hot Lands; it was another way of reconnecting with his farm-boy roots. He also liked to think big and to own the land he helped cultivate. But given his reputation, his moves required investment by stealth.[78]

Over several weeks in April and May 1960, a succession of men showed up at the same notary public in Mexico City to register land purchases around Apatzingán. They each bought modest tracts, averaging two hundred acres, such as a midlevel rancher might own. But the properties were all contiguous, lying next or near to the Tepalcatepec, the river that snakes through the Hot Lands. And the men were all friends of Jenkins: Espinosa Yglesias, Sergio Guzmán Jr., Luis Artasánchez, and so on. It was a veritable parade of Pueblan *prestanombres*. Nothing of this came to light until Lázaro Cárdenas made his anti-Jenkins speech that July, by which time the swath of land in the American's possession was enough to start a plantation.[79]

After the Cárdenas speech, various authorities inveighed against Jenkins. The Department of Agrarian Affairs echoed the former president's call for a halt to land sales. The governor of Michoacán, Franco Rodríguez, said the American's actions imperiled the state's economy. Blared *La Voz de Michoacán* the next day: "Popular Clamor in Apatzingán against the Maneuvers of Jenkins." The state's main paper assailed the "runaway ambition of the pernicious Yankee," which threatened to transform the region into "an empire at the service of the USA." Dripping with gringophobia—"the voracious and unscrupulous Yankee," "the personal whims of the Yankee," "the gringo and his empire"—the article expressed outrage that Jenkins was enjoying the gains of the Revolution to the detriment of country folk.[80]

Then the president weighed in. On the occasion of his "government of the far left" speech, López Mateos was asked what he made of Jenkins's acquisitions. The president said that the matter "could be investigated." He had advised Governor Rodríguez that if Jenkins were proven to have bought via frontmen, the state of Michoacán "might legally intervene."[81]

As the president's noncommittal language hinted, the declarations that summer were political theater. Drought afflicted Michoacán, threatening an agricultural crisis, and Governor Rodríguez needed a distraction. No move was made, either to divest Jenkins or to interfere with his scheme; he would subsequently buy further tracts. The crux was that Jenkins was plowing millions of dollars into a very poor region. Much of the land he bought was scrub, which had to be cleared with bulldozers before anything could be planted. Local irrigation had to be laid, to connect to the River Tepalcatepec. Rail links to the trunk line had to be built, so the cotton and melon could be transported. And, as Rodríguez admitted, the ranchers who had sold out had made good money. The governor in fact conducted a business-friendly policy throughout his term.[82]

Two years later, *Política* would report that Jenkins's sway in Apatzingán was greater than ever. He was financing 1,500 communal farmers to grow cotton for him, with the complicity of the Bank of Ejidal Credit. It also claimed that Governor Rodríguez was tolerating all this, due to his "strong bonds of friendship" with Jenkins. Confirming his freedom to expand,

Jenkins would tell his family of his efforts to clear another 6,000 acres of scrubland. Altogether, he would either own, lease, or finance some 12,000 acres.[83]

Then *Siempre!*, which had once assailed Jenkins as "Emperor" of the film industry, dispatched Roberto Blanco Moheno to find out what was going on. Blanco was famed as a declamatory muckraker, and true to form he first dispatched an attack piece: "Jenkins: Lord of Michoacán." A potted survey of the state's problems, the story led with the emergence of "a series of despicable chiefdoms," among which "the repugnant presence of William Jenkins" stood out. This perpetrator of "hundreds of crimes" was exploiting farm workers in conditions "worse than zoological." Blanco ended by pledging a sequel: "Jenkins, his life and his empire."

That article did not appear as advertised. Blanco must have left his Morelia hotel and done some actual reporting, because he now offered balance. Jenkins indeed used frontmen to buy land and lease plots from communal farmers; he was indeed a pernicious and exploitative foreigner. But what choice did humble country folk have but to rent their lands to him, when the official institution that was supposed to make them loans, the National Bank of Ejidal Credit, either rarely did so or charged them usurious rates? The Ejidal Bank, "the most hated of national institutions" and employer to thousands of embezzlers, was the real villain. Also to blame were Mexico's own industrialists. While benefiting from the president's efforts to find export markets, they refused to invest in Michoacán, making Jenkins's presence all the more necessary. Blanco admitted he had changed his mind: he would not call for the American's expulsion after all.[84]

Unlike at Atencingo, Jenkins's presence in Apatzingán brought little protest from local workers. There would be no reports of land invasions, union-related violence, or radicalized field hands killed by zealous managers. Perhaps Jenkins had learned from his mistakes; perhaps his more philanthropic vision would not permit a heavy hand.

Violence did occur, yet it was inflicted on the bodies of workers not by pistol but by pesticide. For all the productivity gains of Mexican agriculture between the 1940s and 1960s, the Green Revolution wrought great collateral damage among the men and women who toiled in the fields. As they sprayed the crops against insects and diseases they ingested all kinds of poison. It entered their pores and their lungs, often concealing its real harm for months or years.

Jenkins's administrators felt fumigation necessary because there were so many pests. The plantation was visited by plagues of beetles and flies, so harming profitability that the project was in danger of failing. Workers were sent off to spray without adequate protection, as was standard practice in Mexico, and number had to be hospitalized. The combination of 100-degree heat and chemical toxicity caused some to faint in the fields. There were several deaths. Once a field hand inhaled so much insecticide he expired on the job. His corpse was only found the next day. Rigor mortis had set in, and since he had died doubled up in pain, his body would not fit into any coffin.[85]

How aware Jenkins was of such problems, and whether he tried to improve conditions for his field hands, is hard to say. He developed his project before Rachel Carson drew global attention to the dangers of DDT and other pesticides in her bestseller *The Silent Spring*. Then again, over six or seven years he often visited Apatzingán. He must have heard something. But it would have been in keeping with his character if Jenkins had responded that without pesticides there would be no plantation and therefore much less work for the many underemployed of the Hot Lands. Even so, his grandson Bill would recall, the venture lost millions.[86]

APATZINGÁN WAS ONE of several disappointments. Two other projects failed to be realized despite years of planning. As of 1952, Jenkins had mooted a grand Puebla orphanage, housing a thousand children. To Jenkins, bigger was always better. Presumably, in time, someone with experience of caring for orphans convinced him that more intimate environments worked better. Although Jenkins dropped the idea, he continued to support the reform school for young women run by the Trinitarian Nuns. To encourage the school to be self-supporting and to teach the girls a trade, he supplied sewing machines and obtained a contract for them to make sugar sacks. He built them a little movie theater and paid for a choirmaster.[87]

Jenkins's grandest philanthropic dream was of a Puebla cancer hospital. It would have no equal in Latin America, and he budgeted it at $2.4 million. It was a dream he shared with his old friend Dr. Feland Meadows, head of Puebla's Latin American Hospital. Meadows and he would meet frequently to plot its design and facilities. As construction began in 1957, on a choice plot of land in the affluent west side of the city, Jenkins sent Meadows on a fact-finding trip to the United States and Europe. Meadows chose to model the facility on the Rhode Island Hospital. By early 1963, the building stood finished and much of the equipment was ready to install. But then Jenkins fell ill.[88]

A cancer hospital may not have seemed an obvious choice for Jenkins's grand charitable design. Certainly its completion would bring renown to Puebla, but perhaps the reasoning was somewhat personal. For many years now, Jenkins had been suffering from prostate cancer.

As early as 1951, Harvie Branscomb had urged him to have it operated on, whether at the Vanderbilt Hospital or the Mayo Clinic, but Jenkins was reluctant. Prostate cancer is too slow-growing to require attention in most cases, and Jenkins likely thought that an operation was not worth his time or effort. However, in April 1962, his doctors insisted on treatment, so at last he flew to the Mayo Clinic. They confirmed that the cancer had spread beyond the prostate. Jenkins must have known that his time was running out, but he refused to dwell on it. At eighty-four, he continued to make weekly visits to his ranch near Atencingo and regular trips to Acapulco and Apatzingán. His letters to family members retained their light-heartedness, with tales of his cook and confidant Mía bossing him around and ironic remarks about the midterm elections under Kennedy.

"The people should not have the vote anyway," he noted, after his favored Republicans had failed to make significant gains. "A few of us who are really on the ball should run things. That's the way we do it here in Mexico anyway, and it works."[89]

THE WHIRLWIND OF Cold War politics was to whip Jenkins up one more time. In the early 1960s the national argument between left and right was spilling into the streets, and in Puebla the infamous Yankee once more became a symbol invoked by leftists to rouse the masses. Cuba's revolution and the increasingly hostile US response to it had them energized. So the United States became their global villain, with William Jenkins its manipulative local henchman.

The main battlefield, as so often during the 1960s, was the campus.[90] As Puebla's state apparatus was controlled by the Ávila Camachos, the University of Puebla had emerged as the main forum for political debate and rivalry. Hence a tug of war arose over its control, pitting the intelligentsia and sons of the old elite, proudly Catholic, versus liberal professors and the offspring of the middle classes that the Revolution had made. As tensions grew, leftist rhetoric about right-wing students, business elites, and the United States had a polarizing effect, as did conservative warnings about Cuba and its liberal and left-wing supporters. Each position grew in intolerance, a process similar to what was occurring in cities across Mexico and around the world. With student numbers booming, the university was now an alternative power center to the state government. As of 1961, it would be dominated for decades by the left.

Tussles over Puebla's university had an ancient history.[91] Since the 1930s it had borne the heavy yoke of the Ávila Camacho dynasty, which appointed every rector. In 1956, Rafael Ávila Camacho responded to student pressure by renaming it the *Autonomous* University of Puebla (UAP); the rector would be named by an Honorary Board of seven faculty members. But the board was composed of the governor's appointees, mostly conservatives. These included Jenkins's notary Nicolás Vázquez, whose term as mayor the American had subsidized, and Gonzalo Bautista O'Farrill, whose private clinic he had funded. The first rector under the new arrangement was related to Puebla's hard-right archbishop, Octaviano Márquez, another member of the Jenkins circle. State control over the UAP did wane, but that was due to the political weakness of Governor Ortega, while the business elite and the Church saw their influence climb.[92]

In a sign of things to come, the divisive subject of Jenkins arose at a pro-Cuba rally in July 1960. As hundreds of students gathered outside the UAP's main building, a speaker called on them to march in support of Cuba. The president of the student union then climbed on the hood of a car and interrupted him, warning everyone that such support could endanger current plans to build a new campus: Mr. William Jenkins might take offense and withdraw the funding he had offered for it. (With students ever more squeezed into buildings downtown, the UAP was seeking land for a dedicated site.) The first speaker countered that Jenkins had made his fortune by exploiting the people of Puebla, so students should turn their back on him and march. The radical voice won the day. Participants would relate that it was the Jenkins factor that had swung the crowd. Until the student union president spoke up, the organizers' efforts had met with mockery, but once it appeared that Jenkins was using financial leverage to threaten free speech—and that this student leader supported him—the crowd grew indignant.

A majority of the students then marched through the city center, chanting "*Viva Cuba!*," "*Viva Fidel!*," "*Cuba sí, Yanquis no!*," and insults against President Kennedy. A dissident group countered with chants against Castro, Cuba, and Russia.[93]

Raising tensions the following year was the Bay of Pigs invasion. That very day, April 17, 1961, some two thousand students reacted to the news by holding a Cuban solidarity rally. Their passions inflamed, some attacked the building of the paper *El Sol de Puebla*, a constant critic of Castro. Police intervened and a riot ensued.[94] Subsequent days occasioned further rallies, orators mixing support for Castro with criticism of right-wing influences at the UAP and calls for educational reform. When the conservatives of the University Anti-Communist Front (FUA) held a counter-rally of their own, some of the leftists responded by attacking and damaging a Catholic college. This provoked the business elite to close private schools and firms to declare their nonpayment of taxes until order was restored.[95] It was hard for Pueblans not to take sides.

Amid the din two voices emerged. Once reformists seized the UAP's main building on May Day, they named Julio Glockner as *de facto* rector. A former member of the Mexican Communist Party, Glockner was now of the center-left. He was also a charismatic and humorous speaker. Conservatives found their most effective advocate in Archbishop Márquez. Within a week of Glockner's appointment, Márquez denounced events at the UAP as part of a global plot against Christian civilization. When the Church organized anticommunist rallies nationwide, the one in Puebla stood out for its size and impact. *El Sol* and the business elite worked to promote it, and Catholic faithful from across the state showed up in droves. On Sunday June 4 they packed the Cathedral's outdoor atrium and spilled out into the city's main plaza. The event featured a speech by Márquez and ended with chants of *"Cristianismo, sí! Comunismo, no!"*[96]

Jenkins's friendship with Márquez was well-known. The American had cosponsored his investiture and more recently, in a gesture as symbolic as aesthetic, paid for exterior illumination at the cathedral. Unsurprisingly the two became joint targets in the language of the left. The poet and journalist Renato Leduc responded to the rally of June 4 with a satirical ditty, "Puebla 1961," first published in the radical *Política*.[97] It began: "The lord bishop preaches in the atrium. / The people listen to him on this Sunday / under the threat of Jenkins the gringo."

Governor Ortega offered a compromise that largely catered to the UAP's liberal majority. It included the installation of a liberal (rather than socialist) interim director and the abolition of the Honorary Board. Given his Ávila Camacho affiliation, Ortega might have sided with the conservatives, but he had fallen out with Rafael, whose continued influence he resented; each accused the other of embezzling the treasury. Favoring the liberals was a way for Ortega to declare his independence. But pressure from the business elite, including a threatened closure of city stores, caused Ortega to rescind several measures. Then the right-wing FUA insisted on removal of the new rector. This prompted a street battle between conservative and liberal students, in which a storekeeper shot and wounded two of the latter. Now the army moved in.[98]

While the military occupation of the city center put an end to the conflict, the bitterness between left and right persisted in Puebla's body politic. Soon it would force a governor's ouster. It would prompt a splintering in the educational system, with private universities setting themselves up as conservative options, while the UAP (which retained its liberal interim rector) embraced a leftist identity. A similar trend would affect Mexico City, with private colleges drawing the children of the elites away from the ever more Marxist-oriented National Autonomous University of Mexico.

Central to the disturbances was the role of rhetoric. Each side pelted the other with exaggerations, depending on their position vis-à-vis Cuba and the UAP: liberals and reformists became "communists" and "traitors"; conservatives and traditionalists became "fascists" and "terrorists." The middle ground, and the space for dialogue, almost disappeared. Consequences were tangible: in the short term, violence, and in the long term, the growth of political groups that would wrestle for control of city hall and the university, as the Ávila Camacho dynasty finally lost its hold.

Attacks on Jenkins nurtured the identity and intransigence of the left, even though he took no visible part in the conflict. Abelardo Sánchez was more prominent: he led a Puebla Citizens' Coordinating Committee, which managed the response of the trade associations and raised 85,000 pesos to run a press campaign and finance the FUA's propaganda. It was Sánchez who was most often criticized that spring and summer. But Sánchez was a known friend of Jenkins; the American had signed as a witness at his wedding, and Sánchez's Committee was reportedly created by the Board of Moral, Civic, and Material Improvement, a body that Jenkins had helped establish to oversee new public works and advise on cultural policy.[99] So Jenkins remained the *éminence grise*, whose name evoked dark puppetry. When Sánchez disappeared from the news, the old gringo reemerged as everyone's favorite pariah.

The magazine *Siempre!*—less an autonomous voice than one of state-sanctioned complaint—claimed Jenkins had called the shots all along. An editorial, "Puebla, Under the Claw of Jenkins," posed the question: What accounts for all the extremism, with each side threatening or engaging in violence? The answer: "there is only one factor capable of explaining things: that factor is called William Jenkins." (Here again was Jenkins as lightning rod, drawing heat away from the authorities.) Holding extraordinary economic power and absolutely lacking in scruples, Jenkins was not a classic *cacique*, relying on brute force, but a subtler operator, keeping his opponents from bank loans and employment. UAP reformists, knowing that without Jenkins's approval no graduate would ever go far, had risen up against his dictatorship. The UAP might be a minor part of the Jenkins kingdom, but he would not tolerate the smallest fissure in its structure. The private sector would not dare to resist him, lest he ruin their businesses. This old fox Jenkins had kept a low profile lately, while his propaganda machine converted the conflict into one of Christianity versus communism. The column closed with a challenge to Pueblan readers, using the words of President López Mateos: "*Caciques* last as long as their subjects want them to."[100]

The Cárdenas-backed Movement for National Liberation issued a booklet on the events. It concluded that the conflict reflected a nationwide problem, pronounced in cities like Puebla whose "reactionary forces" were powerful, whereby the United States was conspiring to restrict freedom of expression and to control Mexico's economy and foreign policy. In Puebla, those forces were industrialists who admired the Spanish dictator Franco and a nucleus within the Catholic Church. Both took their lead from the "sinister political personage who is W. Jenkins."[101]

Closer to home, Julio Glockner, the former interim rector of the UAP, gave a lecture that October on the reform movement, presumably to clarify his version of events. According to the secret service agent who attended, the talk featured attacks against Jenkins: he was a *cacique* and an agent of Yankee imperialism. Glockner also claimed that Jenkins had offered him—or the university—money to abandon his struggle.[102]

The King and His Daughters

Sixty-one years after his elopement with Mary, William Jenkins undertook a final visit to Tennessee. The occasion was the eightieth birthday of Mamie Moore, his favorite sister.

Jenkins had not been neglecting his origins. He had footed much of the bill for a Bedford County hospital and funded the swimming pool at Vanderbilt. He often paid to fly down his sisters for visits. He provided for the upkeep of his boyhood home and the Shofner Church. Then, in 1961, he spent $10,000 to relocate the grave of Martin Shofner, his Revolutionary War ancestor. Shofner and his wife had been buried in a hilltop cemetery, now overgrown. So Jenkins paid for a handsome memorial close to the church entrance, wrought in marble and adorned with a plaque recording

Shofner's military service and patronage of Lutheranism. Mamie protested this extravagance, feeling that their ancestors were happily at rest
where they lay. But William wanted his Shofner and Jenkins forebears all
collected together.[103]

For half a century, he had been moving his family around. He brought
his brother-in-law Donald to Mexico; relocated his father, Mamie, Ruth,
and Annie to Hanford; sent his daughters to schools in Los Angeles; and
moved Mary to the Mayo Clinic, then Tucson, then Beverly Hills, and
finally, postmortem, to Puebla. He had also tried to recall his daughters,
but not all were happy to come back on his terms.

There still was time for one last act of familial orchestration. Jenkins
told his other siblings he would return unannounced to give his sister a
birthday surprise. Mamie had no children, but among the Bedford County
Jenkins she was the grande dame, and William wanted shower her with
family love.

October 7 was a Sunday, and when Mamie returned from church, getting out of her car and heading down the path to the Jenkins family home,
the front door opened. Her youngest great-nephew came out to greet her
and wish her a happy birthday. Then came the next oldest, to do the same.
And then came the next, and so on and so on. Then came a succession of
nephews and nieces, all emerging in turn to greet her, all in genealogical
order. Then came her youngest sister, Annie, then Ruth and Joe and Kate.
And finally, when Mamie thought she could be overwhelmed no more,
came her eighty-four-year-old brother, William.[104]

CHRISTMAS 1962 WAS a mixed season for Jenkins—one of political satisfaction and personal malaise. The governor-elect, General Antonio Nava
Castillo, was a true conservative. He was also the first governor imposed
by Mexico City since the 1920s. López Mateos saw that the Ávila Camacho
dynasty, encumbered by infighting, had to be brought in line. But Nava,
an authoritarian, was good news for Puebla's elite. Surely he would make
amends for Fausto Ortega, who had allowed radicalism to fester at the university. Nava was also a man of ideas, promising to expand the stagnated
industrial base with the help of outside investors.[105]

Nava's appointment was a sign of the times. The Cuban Missile Crisis
that autumn had struck while López Mateos was abroad, and the response
of his Interior Minister to the US request for support—maintaining
Mexico's pledge to the sovereignty of nations but agreeing the missiles
posed a regional threat—pleased the president. He decided then that this

minister, Gustavo Díaz Ordaz, would be his successor. Díaz Ordaz believed in civil order and capitalistic development, and his rise in favor reflected the president's satisfaction that containment of the left had succeeded. López Mateos had nationalized high-profile industries (if to little tangible consequence) and given more land to peasants than his three predecessors put together (albeit land of often dubious quality). He had stopped the Movement for National Liberation from coalescing into a viable opposition party and marginalized its ideologue, former president Cárdenas. By late 1962 the battle for the soul of the PRI was over and the right had won.[106]

If order and progress were reasserted in the outside world, within Jenkins's palatial penthouse there was anything but. As the family gathered in its cavernous living room, the mood was uncertain. Pop, as they called their patriarch, was slowing down. He never talked about his cancer, but his moments of low energy were more frequent, and his Christmas cheer lacked its usual gusto.

"He is lonely many times," Jane had told her sister Mary earlier that year, "and of course he never asks for company." That Christmas, Bill and Chacha's first girl was learning to walk, and Chacha observed how Pop followed the little girl's movements with tears in his eyes. She surmised he must be thinking of his own daughters when they were that age.[107]

"He was fine when we were very young," Tita would later reflect. He had indulged her then. He let her roller-skate around the house, making lots of noise. When she had diphtheria, he let her sleep on a day-bed in his room, where she felt cocooned in his presence. Thirty years later, on one of her last visits to Puebla, when she told Pop she wanted to discuss a problem he had simply replied: "I don't want to hear it."[108]

Jane's daughter Rosemary, home from boarding school, sensed there was something amiss. She and Pop were close. In long discussions he had revealed his suspicion of riches: "Wealth is what you have inside you, what you keep in your head. It's not what you wear." She sought him when he was alone, finding him on a couch with his feet up, and she sat beside him. He reminisced about Mary. As he had done three years earlier after her reburial, he shared his guilt at having let her die on her own. She had seemed fine when he departed after that last visit. She had passed so suddenly. Again the tears came, and soon he was weeping with great heaving sighs. As Rosemary hugged him, she felt the sobs wrenching his massive frame.

Jenkins's confidence seemed to be failing, along with the certainties that supported it. He told Rosemary he no longer believed in God, or life after death, but the prospect of dying seemed to frighten him. He voiced doubts about the foundation and his pledge to leave it all of his wealth. None of his friends agreed with this proposal. Even Espinosa thought it too extreme. Pop asked Rosemary: "Am I doing the right thing?"[109]

Tugging him in the other direction were his lifelong work ethic and his guilty conscience over Mary. To endow the foundation with all his fortune was to establish a monument to her. It was a form of apology. It was also an attempt to ensure that easy access to riches did not corrupt his family.

The daughters did not share his frugality; it had become a family joke. Once, as a treat, he had taken them to New York. They saw the sights and took in a Broadway show, but what was recalled most often was a meal in a fancy restaurant. Frowning at the prices on the menu, Jenkins announced: "I think I'll have the hash."[110]

His daughters had enjoyed all the benefits of his fortune, from education at the best schools to cars and houses and low-interest loans to help their spouses in business. Yet what had his generosity achieved? Against his instincts, he had tried to cultivate Elizabeth in business, and she failed. She became an embarrassment with all her sleeping around. She often defied his wishes, and her younger sisters had followed suit. She became an embarrassment with all her sleeping around. She took refuge from unhappiness in alcohol, and that had helped to kill her. Then came poor Margaret: her marriage to Tom Poole, though longer-lasting than the three before, was failing. Like Elizabeth she drank, and like each of her sisters bar Jane she smoked heavily. Throat cancer was already taking hold.

Tita had fallen for that snake Robert Lord and wed against his counsel. On marrying a second time, she had again turned her back on him by declining his offer to find work for her new husband, Matt Cheney, in Puebla. Cheney then insisted they relocate to Arizona, but the move threw Tita for a loop. She too developed an alcohol dependence. Her new marriage would end in despair, for after eighteen years and two offspring, Cheney left her for another woman.

Mary, his fourth daughter, had defied him since she was young, with her extravagant purchases using his and others' accounts ("life is not just buying what you want but it's a big fight to be able to get what you need," he once wrote to her). The problem was compounded by her constant fabrications; Tita would describe her as a "pathological liar." She seemed to find happiness with Robert William, and together they had six children, but her husband turned to womanizing. Mary channeled her frustration with him into motherhood and compulsive shopping from the Sears catalogue. After their fifth child she had a nervous breakdown, and after their sixth she broke down again. Robert had her institutionalized at the Menninger Memorial Hospital in Kansas. Being suspicious of psychiatry, Jenkins soon brought her to Puebla, along with her youngest children. During the fall of 1961 tried to look after her, but Mary strained at his austere regimen. She hated his attempts to rein in her spending.

Mary returned to Los Angeles, but the following summer she began a second stint at Menninger, this time for six months, her father reluctantly footing the bill. Any progress proved temporary, and in years to come her marriage would only worsen. There was a long-term mistress and lovers on the side. She responded by spiting her husband: yet more frivolous purchases, chain-smoking, collecting cats. When Robert's infidelities became too much, she moved into a home of her own. Once the children were grown, she would take comfort in her cats, more and more of them, mostly strays. And when there was no longer room for the cats, she had a house for new arrivals built in her backyard: a twin-level brick affair, with air conditioning. She called it The Catatorium. Eventually the cats numbered 150.

The only happily married daughter was Jane. Pop loved spending time with her children, Rosemary and young John. He enjoyed weekend banter and games of chess with Ronnie. The Englishman had become a close friend, and they would laugh like boys at their attempts to out-cheat each other at cards. But with Jane, ever since she had come of age and learned to voice opinions, his relationship had been strained. Jane was the one who had taken care of her mother the most, reading to her as she lay in bed all those years. Now she felt the need to take care of Pop, to direct his diet and watch his health. Pop found her bossy; Jane found him dogmatic. She later reflected: "Everything our father said was the Will of God."

Jane and her father were separated by their similarities: both would tell the other what to do. In a token of his resentment—a quality gone from his business dealings but persistent in his private life—he refused to buy Jane a house. He had done so for the other girls, even for Tita.

If only, Jenkins felt, his daughters had been less headstrong and more responsible with money. If only, his daughters felt, their father had taken the time to talk with them.

His solitary visits to his wife's grave continued. Still he read aloud to her. Moribund with cancer, unsure of his legacy, distanced from his daughters, and wracked by guilt, Jenkins, like an American King Lear, had full cause of weeping.

THROUGH THE WINTER and spring of 1962 Jenkins kept working. His trips to Apatzingán were no longer so regular, but he made them when energy permitted. His main concern was to channel the rest of his wealth to the foundation, selling his stakes in partnerships and donating the proceeds. Maintaining a scrupulous accounting, he would call board meetings so that each donation be formally noted; he was setting an example for when he was gone. At a March 1962 meeting, he submitted a sum of $5 million, and in April 1963 he was able to donate $9 million. The foundation would soon tally an endowment of $60 million.[111]

In April, Jenkins visited the United States.[112] The tumor on his prostate had required an operation, performed at Dr. Meadows' Latin American Hospital. But his discomfort worsened, so he flew to the Mayo Clinic, and two more operations followed. Optimistically, the doctors assured him he had at least four years to live; perhaps they did not reckon with Jenkins's disinclination to rest. Knowing better, perhaps, Jenkins made some further tweaks to his will.

Although he managed a week-long trip to Apatzingán, he found he often had to take to bed. His sisters Mamie and Kate flew down to help look after him, as did Tita, but since he was well cared for, by his faithful cook Mía and by a dedicated nurse, Alicia Juárez, they simply kept him company. His sister Anne Bunztler, still running the American School, often visited, as did Margaret and Bill, both now living in Mexico City.

By June 1, Jenkins was in constant pain. There was still work to be done, so he insisted on another board meeting. Manuel Espinosa, Felipe García Eguiño, Manuel Cabañas, and Bill all met with him in his bedroom on the morning of June 3 to register his donation of another of the Puebla buildings he owned.[113]

Alicia Juárez did not leave his side. She was a trusted member of Jane and Ronnie's household, having helped to raise their children. She was also a Methodist, attending the same church that Mary had supported with donations in the 1920s. At one point, Jenkins asked her to recite Psalm 23, and so she did, in Spanish, and after each line he repeated the words in English: "The Lord is my shepherd; I shall not want. . . ."

The following day, a Tuesday, Jenkins awoke to the bells of the cathedral. News had reached Puebla of the death of Pope John XXIII. As he slipped in and out of consciousness that day, the bells continued to ring.

At one in the afternoon, he made a great effort to get up to relieve himself. As he returned from the bathroom he raised his hand to his chest and babbled something that Alicia could not catch. Very pale, he staggered to his bed. Alicia raised the alarm and sent the chauffeur to collect Dr. Meadows. Jenkins whispered to Margaret that she should summon Bill. Meadows arrived, accompanied by a cardiologist. They confirmed that he had suffered a heart attack.

Jenkins spent the next two hours between discomfort and agony. Bill had not yet arrived, but Margaret, Anne, Mía, and Alicia were with him, along with his grandson John, and so were his long-serving secretaries, Cabañas and Sevilla.

At 3:30 Jenkins had a second heart attack. "I'm dying! I'm dying!," he gasped in Spanish. He began coughing up blood. A few minutes later, his heart stopped altogether.

Archbishop Márquez appeared soon after. He asked the family to be allowed to pray for the eternal rest of the departed. Permission given, he knelt at the side of Jenkins's bed, clasped his hands, inclined his head, and prayed, emotionally and at length.

Later that afternoon, Espinosa arrived from Mexico City. The film mogul-turned-banker was now de facto head of the Mary Street Jenkins Foundation, and hence chief arbiter of how the profits from its huge endowment should be spent. One of his first actions was to open the foundation safe, retrieve the latest version of Jenkins's will, and forge the dead man's signature. Unsure to the end about some of the details—perhaps wondering whether leaving a little more to his daughters might somehow make amends—Jenkins had left it unsigned.

Jenkins's Earthly Afterlife

*In the United States, people understand that the rich man
is blessed by God to administer the community's resources.
In Mexico, this vision doesn't exist.*

JORGE VILLALOBOS, Director, Mexican Center for Philanthropy
(2007)

The Legendary William O. Jenkins

"The Legendary William O. Jenkins," declared *Excélsior*.[1] The headline encapsulated the tone of the obituaries: in Mexico City, in Puebla, even in the United States. The legend of which they spoke was of a somewhat obscure and quite extraordinary climb to wealth, made by an inscrutable man. Jenkins's life was becoming a hybrid of Gothic romance and Horatio Alger tale.

"Son of Modest Farmers, Jenkins Came to Amass more than 3,000 Million Pesos," chimed Puebla's *La Opinión*. Was that indeed the sum? The paper was following the estimate of *Time*, which had put it at $200 million to $300 million. *El Universal* claimed a more modest worth, equivalent to $40 million. *El Sol de Puebla*, after consulting with the Jenkins Foundation, reported the fortune at close to 1 billion pesos, or $80 million. Either way, as *The New York Times* put it, Jenkins was "reputed to be the wealthiest man in Mexico."[2] "Mister Jenkins was not always well understood," said *Novedades*, the paper in which he had held a stake. "His life unfolded in mystery," agreed *Excélsior*; several times it cited Jenkins's reticence to discuss his story. Like the other obituarists, this author had to rely on the recall of friends, like Manuel Espinosa and Gregorio Walerstein, whose grasp of the American's early years was prone to error. In places the press augmented the legend it was claiming to demystify.[3]

"Only He Himself Could Relate the True Story of his Life," ran the most honest of the headlines. Published in *El Sol de Puebla* and penned by veteran reporter Luis Castro, this obituary was the lengthiest and most careful. Castro admitted that much of the story was unknown and much else owed to rumor. Repeatedly he gave Jenkins the benefit of the doubt, and he defended him against the old self-kidnapping charge.

Castro also gave ample record of Jenkins's local philanthropy. Perhaps it was this that persuaded the writer to be kind, for altogether the charitable imprint that Jenkins had left was huge. He had financed the building of two Red Cross hospitals in Puebla City, other hospitals elsewhere in the state, and a soon-to-be-opened Cancer Institute. He had built a second Alpha Club, now Puebla's top sports facility, where the monthly fee of $1.20 was low enough for those of middle income. He had cofunded Puebla's American School and paid for an extension at the Palafoxian Seminary. This was to say nothing of the five Schooling Centers he had helped build, another seventeen or so smaller schools he had financed, and the water works and covered markets he had subsidized, all of which Castro forgot, or lacked space, to mention.

El Sol soon reported that the Mary Street Jenkins Foundation had disbursed 86.6 million pesos, close to $7 million, so far. The sum was slightly greater than the state of Puebla's annual budget. Over the next quarter century, employing the model that Jenkins introduced of donating the profits from its investments, the foundation would make gifts of more than $150 million.[4]

WHILE THE PUBLIC was reading about Jenkins in the morning paper, five of his friends convened at his home and voted on appointments for the foundation's board.[5] First to be named was his closest friend, the dental surgeon Sergio Guzmán, who rose from alternate to full member, joining the sugar industrialist Felipe García Eguiño and Jenkins's private secretary Manuel Cabañas. Promoted to vice president was Jenkins's grandson William Anstead Jenkins, better known as Bill. Rising to the presidency was the man who served for twenty-five years as Jenkins's right hand, first in the film industry and then in banking, Manuel Espinosa Yglesias.

Still excluded from the foundation was Jenkins's other key partner. Gabriel Alarcón was reinventing himself as a multi-industrialist and publisher. In 1965 he would founded a newspaper that raised the bar for Mexican media, both in its full-color technical quality and in its slavishness toward the PRI. Called *El Heraldo de México*, it announced its commitment to journalistic integrity by splashing its debut front page with a photograph of the president—who declared himself the paper's "first reader"—and an editorial in praise of itself. *El Heraldo* would help Alarcón restore his battered image, and it certainly promoted his real estate firms, but it probably made no money.[6]

Next in order of foundation business was a catalogue of Jenkins's assets. An inventory would be no mean feat, for most of his wealth had yet to be ceded to the foundation, and much of it was held by frontmen. There was urgency too, for what had not been ceded was liable for taxation by the US government, and given the American's wealth and fame, auditors from the IRS could arrive any day. That month the board met six times (more than for all of 1962), and there were further meetings with Jenkins's notary, Nicolás Vázquez, as the directors rushed to make asset sales and get papers in order. When the IRS agents did show up, they spent several days looking over Jenkins's books but found nothing left in his name. They departed empty-handed.

Some of Jenkins's frontmen posed a bigger problem. This should not have been so, for in addition to the notarial records, Jenkins had jotted all of his investments in the little black book that he kept in his office safe. Every covert arrangement was registered. In many cases the frontmen were board members themselves, or their sons, and transfers to the foundation were mostly straightforward. But others, though more or less loyal to Jenkins, felt little or no bond with his board. Recovery of lands in Michoacán and Puebla's Matamoros Valley proved especially tricky. In the former case, Espinosa recruited the agriculture minister to press recalcitrant frontmen into parting with their tracts. At Matamoros, much of the land was held by Facundo Sánchez, the former Atencingo field manager whom Jenkins had retained to farm his sugar and melon crops. By one account, when the foundation dispatched an envoy to talk to Sánchez, the poor man was scared off back to Puebla, his car riddled with bullet holes.

There were even holdouts within the family. Son-in-law Robert William had made a success of his Los Angeles pasta factory, in which Jenkins's estate held an outstanding credit of $476,000. At his death, Robert would be worth $40 million. But when Bill Jenkins tried to redeem his grandfather's loan, he managed only to get $60,000 back. A million-dollar loan to Ronnie Eustace went similarly unpaid.[7]

Although the foundation had told *El Sol* that Jenkins's fortune was roughly $80 million, when the charity's official history came to be written, it was said to have been endowed with $60 million. Assets that frontmen refused to release, unpaid loans to business partners, and disputed lands that had to be sold for less than market value presumably accounted for the difference.

But there was no resistance from the Jenkins family. They had long ago come to terms with the patriarch's iron resolve. Whatever their feelings in private, in public they stated their agreement with the will and their desire it be effected without any obstacle.[8]

PUEBLA CITY HONORED its adopted son in style. On the morning of June 6, while a private funeral service was taking place at the family home, thousands were converging downtown to bid William Jenkins farewell.[9] At 11 AM, five hours after people began to line the streets, the procession commenced. Led by children from the American School and ambulances from the Red Cross, flanked by motorcycle riders from the state highway patrol, the cortege included a hundred cars as well as the Cadillac hearse. It took more than an hour to traverse the two miles to the French Cemetery, and at the approach the mourners passed through an honor guard of children from the Boy Heroes Schooling Center.

The crowd exceeded 20,000, news reports concurred. One noted that many were "roughly dressed peasants." Had they all come of their own volition? The party included representatives from Atencingo, presumably bussed up on the orders of Lorenzo Cue, the friend to whom Jenkins had sold the mill. As for all the others: How many of them were in mourning, as opposed to merely curious or present under the orders of bureaucrats and union bosses looking to curry favor? Perhaps some were grateful for the education they had received at schools the old gringo had funded. Perhaps others were one-time employees of his textile mills and movie theaters who felt that they owed Jenkins their jobs. The newspapers did not say. Their focus was on the size of the spectacle and the names of the very important who attended.

Well-peopled funerals for the powerful were a Mexican tradition. Under Porfirio Díaz, whose regime organized 110 state funerals, displays of public honoring were orchestrated to foster national unity among a socially fragmented populace. On the face of it, the crowds turning out for Jenkins showed a persistence of the old hierarchies of race and class that the Revolution had failed to eradicate. But the deference of workers and peons no longer ran as deep as when Jenkins first set foot in Mexico.[10] The numbers attending his procession—along with the large police presence to coordinate them—suggested that Puebla's city fathers were trying to preserve an antique social pyramid.

At the French Cemetery, resting place for Puebla grandees, only family members and the most powerful were allowed into the Jenkins family enclosure. Here William Jenkins was buried, just as he had willed, next to his wife. Manuel Espinosa and Gabriel Alarcón were present, as was Governor Antonio Nava Castillo. Dozens of Puebla nabobs and politicos and Mexico City businessmen (their names dutifully recorded by the press) had to wait outside.

For several years, on the anniversary of Jenkins's death, a new ritual would take place. At the Palafoxian Seminary the archbishop would offer a mass for the repose of his soul, then the governor, the mayor, and family members would convene at his grave, joined by representatives of the Jenkins Foundation, the American School, the Alpha Clubs, and so on. Espinosa would give a speech about the foundation's achievements (peppering his discourse with figures), and the press would record the proceedings (probably in exchange for payment). Modest versions of this ritual would endure for four decades.[11]

And so Pueblans would be goaded to think that while Don Guillermo was no longer with them in person, he remained with them in spirit. His fortune was providing for their betterment. Thanks to this legacy, and thanks to the leadership of the governor and other men who knew best, all was right with the world.

NAVA CASTILLO DID not in fact last long as governor. In 1964, his heavy-handed repression of a second student movement and his crass attempt at self-enrichment by creating a milk-distribution monopoly in which he had a stake caused massive and sustained protest. By late October, President López Mateos saw no option but to replace him.

Yet during his twenty-one months in office, Nava had started to lift Puebla out of two decades of economic stagnation. Unlike his four predecessors, whose failure to lure investors smacked of complacency, Nava drew up a well-conceived industrial policy, enacting an investment law with training centers to support it. His efforts heralded a new industrial dawn, and that autumn Volkswagen announced an $80 million auto plant outside Puebla City. Steel giant Hylsa would follow a few years later. These changes embodied a post-Jenkins era. Puebla ceased to be a state in which political and economic stagnation went hand in hand.[12]

From a national perspective, by contrast, Jenkins's passing symbolized no watershed. To some extent that was a testimony to his legacy, as a pillar of the PRI's right wing. The model he had helped create—a symbiosis of political and business monopolies, adhering to a US-friendly conservatism—was well entrenched. Two events within months of his death testified to this. In July 1963, Mexico returned to the US bond market after an absence of fifty-three years. Mexico's economy was sufficiently stable and capital-friendly, its policies sufficiently nonthreatening, for the United States to grant this seal of approval. Then, in November, López Mateos unveiled as his successor the interior minister—and former protégé of Maximino—Gustavo Díaz Ordaz.[13]

Despite gestures of Cold War nonalignment and further nationalizations of industry, Díaz Ordaz was fundamentally pro-business and increasingly intolerant of dissent. As a result, the seedlings of discontent planted by the rail workers' strike of 1958, watered by the Cuban Revolution, and nurtured by student protests in Puebla and other cities during the early 1960s would blossom into a major civil rights movement in summer 1968. Protesting authoritarian rule, Mexico's students would take to the streets as never before. That autumn, as the movement threatened to spoil the president's plan of showcasing his modernized nation while hosting the Olympic Games, the state would crack down, again as never before. At an October 2 rally in the Mexico City neighborhood of Tlatelolco, where once the Aztecs had fought their last stand against the Spaniards, dozens if not hundreds of students would fall to army gunfire.[14]

The Politics of Philanthropy, Revisited

Manuel Espinosa's ascent as head of the Jenkins Foundation, Mexico's largest private charity, caused an unadmitted change in its philosophy. After the death of Mary, Jenkins's gifts had mostly followed two principles: they should better the lot of the poor, via the building of schools and hospitals, and they should do so in Puebla; for the foundation's first decade, 90 percent of its giving targeted projects in the state.[15] Espinosa sidelined these principles. Donations increasingly benefitted the education of the wealthy. Puebla remained the main recipient of Foundation monies in the 1960s, but during the 1970s Espinosa prioritized high-profile schemes in Mexico City, seeking political capital and protection for his bank.

Espinosa grasped the foundation's helm at time of *entente cordiale* between the private sector and the state. Still, it behooved Espinosa to make a grand gesture of support for López Mateos, so it would be readily apparent to everyone in government that the Foundation was an ally. Thus the first donation made on Espinosa's watch was a $1.4 million pledge to help pay for the technical colleges the Education Ministry was rolling out nationwide.[16]

While the grant echoed Jenkins's interest in education, it marked a switch of emphasis from Puebla and a public cozying up to the president. On August 1, 1963, Espinosa joined López Mateos at the opening of a technical college in Mexico City. He sat with the president and other dignitaries on a platform, and after a couple of speeches he gave one of his own: the foundation would pay for six more colleges, wherever the president should order them built.[17] While Espinosa had taken over the Banco de Comercio nine years before, and while he had made pronouncements on economic policy, he had never been able to scotch the rumors that he had done so as Jenkins's puppet. The rumors irked Espinosa terribly, for he took great pride in having separated their interests and struck out alone.[18] This day, not two months after his mentor's death, marked a triple victory: Espinosa became a public figure in his own right, a visible friend of the president, and a famed philanthropist.

For the rest of his life, Espinosa effectively *was* the foundation. The board simply followed his will. None of the others had anything like his force of personality or acumen: Bill Jenkins was just thirty-one and reliant on Espinosa, with whom he had partnered in an insurance firm; García Eguiño was an old man who would live only three more years; Cabañas had spent his professional life asking no questions; and Guzmán had never taken much interest in money.

An early display of Espinosa's iron will involved Jenkins's pet megaproject, the Cancer Hospital. The foundation had already spent $1.7 million on it. The building was almost ready and the main equipment purchased. That August, the health minister visited the premises and declared that it would be the best cancer hospital in Latin America.

Within a year Espinosa had frozen it. Then he nixed it altogether. In his view, a hospital was too costly to be run as a charity. He felt the same about the city's Latin American Hospital, which Jenkins had subsidized since the 1920s; in time he let the Health Ministry take it over. His objections were not arbitrary. In his last years Jenkins had lost his Midas touch, and his philanthropic grand designs, like his proposed orphanage for a thousand children, were prone to fantastical thinking. While a Puebla cancer hospital could have been joint-managed with the state government, to Espinosa's free-market way of thinking private-public partnerships were a risk. Like most of Mexico's business elite, Espinosa and Jenkins had agreed that governments were full of crooks. Still, in shelving the cancer hospital, he was flouting his friend's wishes.

The Jenkins family was upset, and upset turned to anger when Espinosa finally opted, in 1984, to turn the idle building into a Best Western hotel. Jane, by then Jenkins's eldest surviving daughter, would say she never forgave him.[19]

ESPINOSA WAS FAR more interested in education than health. At Mexico's politically fractious universities, Jenkins's fortune promised him the means to help guide the right side to victory. His first concern was at home. Activism at the Autonomous University of Puebla (UAP), having grabbed the headlines in 1961 and 1964, caused consternation among Puebla's elites, not least because two decades of economic stagnation had left it lagging behind the clans of Guadalajara and Monterrey. Efforts to lure outside companies might falter if the state remained a hotbed of radicalism.[20] Whether or not Espinosa planned a unified strategy, what emerged was a two-pronged effort to counteract the activist left of the UAP.

In 1964 Espinosa moved to establish good relations with the university, now under the rectorship of Manuel Lara y Parra, a moderate liberal. The following year he offered $4.8 million, by far the foundation's biggest pledge to date, for the building of a whole new campus—something Jenkins had mooted in 1960. Again the offer was controversial: Espinosa and Lara y Parra had to counter a storm of protest from both the left, which viewed the foundation with disdain, and the right, which considered the UAP a den of communism, unworthy of largesse. But the gift was confirmed with fanfare on the second anniversary of Jenkins's death, in tandem with the laying of a foundation stone.[21] The ceremony set a precedent: for years to come Espinosa would ensure that Foundation initiatives were publicly recognized each fourth of June.

Soon after, Espinosa began to meet with Ray Lindley, president of a college for US expatriates that was branching out to include Mexicans. Founded in 1940 as Mexico City College, Lindley had rebranded it the University of the Americas. Espinosa promised he would donate $5 million, far more than Lindley was soliciting, on the condition he change its name into Spanish—hence Universidad de las Américas (UDLA)—and build its new campus in Puebla.[22]

At face value, both commitments seem altruistic: roughly equal donations that would benefit the youth of Puebla. They more or less complied with the foundation's charter. Jenkins had not much cared to support private education, but he would surely have approved of the UDLA, as a promoter of US-Mexican fellowship. As early as 1925 he had expressed interest in fostering ties through education, as an antidote to "the feeling of distrust and fear that prevails in many circles of Mexico toward Americans."[23] However, the "University City" of the UAP and the Puebla campus of the UDLA, by far the foundation's largest projects of the 1960s, represented above all a political strategy: to weaken the student left and bolster the right.

At the UAP, the main facilities stood at the heart of Puebla City. Its signature building, a grand sixteenth-century palace called the Carolino, stood only two blocks from the Cathedral, and these two places had served as rallying points for rival crowds in the early 1960s. By erecting a University City for the UAP amid fields on Puebla's southern outskirts, Espinosa and the state authorities were shifting most students a few miles away, where they might cause less trouble. Further, Espinosa was sending a signal: moderate rectors like Lara y Parra would receive financial support; socialists and communists would not.

Many students and academics were only too aware of Espinosa's agenda, and Jenkins Foundation support was roundly resented by some. At the laying of the University City foundation stone, the law student chosen to speak on behalf of the students declared that no thanks was owed, since William Jenkins had made his fortune exploiting the workers of Atencingo; money that had come from the people was now returning to it.[24]

At the UDLA, what stood out was the formula of financing. When Lindley had first approached Espinosa, he already held a pledge from the US Agency for International Development (USAID); the agency would supply $2 million if Lindley could find matching gifts. Once Espinosa offered $5 million, the USAID committed an equal amount, and in 1971, a year after the UDLA opened its doors, both backers gave another $5 million apiece, funding a business school and other facilities.[25] For Espinosa, the stated goal was to provide Puebla with an institution of excellence, a local answer to the Monterrey Technological Institute. For the USAID, founded by President Kennedy, the gifts conformed to its general mandate of supporting economic growth in the developing world. And both parties had ulterior motives.

Unlike Mexico City, Guadalajara, and Monterrey, Puebla offered no private university, no incubator for future Catholic business leaders. The UDLA might provide one—and a counterweight to the left-leaning UAP.

Espinosa felt the private sector should orient education toward the goals of capitalistic development, professional training, and free trade. To ensure its ideological loyalty, Espinosa insisted with Lindley upon a covert proviso: he would hold veto power over faculty appointments.[26]

Very likely, the US government was moved by concerns with communism. The worry was not only the UAP student body, with its left-leaning majority, but the institution as a whole. By 1967, when the UDLA foundation stone was laid, the UAP had seen enrollment double in four years to 10,000.[27] With its spiraling numbers and its victory against Governor Nava Castillo, it consolidated its status a center of power. Its rectorship could serve as a launch pad for a campaign for mayor or even for governor.[28]

The UDLA, therefore, might have served in addition as a listening post for the CIA, as several of its academics have alleged. There were precedents both local and global. Jenkins had maintained links with US intelligence, however informal, helping sabotage Mexico City's Russian film festival in 1954 and, it seems, keeping CIA agent Phil Roettinger informed about the Puebla political elite. As for the USAID, in the 1960s its programs sometimes gave cover for CIA operations. US alarm about communism in Mexico, heightened after the Cuban Revolution, would persist into the 1970s.[29]

ESPINOSA NEXT APPLIED his counterweight approach in Mexico City, where President Díaz Ordaz was worried about campus radicalism at the National University (UNAM).[30] The sums Espinosa gave furthered his divergence from Jenkins's mandate to favor Puebla. In the capital, he aided three conduits of more or less conservative ideology, each involving the Church. One was the Jesuit-run Iberoamerican University, to which he channeled $300,000 in 1966. Another was the University Cultural Center, a meeting place for Catholic youth near the UNAM, designed by a Dominican friar as a bulwark against campus Marxism. Between 1966 and 1974 the foundation granted it start-up and operating funds of more than $2 million.[31]

Above all, Espinosa pumped millions of Jenkins's dollars into the Anáhuac University. Along with other leading industrialists, he transformed it from a small private college into a bulwark of conservatism and the campus of choice for the offspring of the capital's business elite. Established in 1964, the Anáhuac was the brainchild of Father Marcial Maciel, founder of the congregation the Legionaries of Christ. The following year, the foundation approved an initial donation toward a new campus, located in the wealthy suburbs west of Mexico City. Its $1.6 million gift covered a quarter of the budget.

The Anáhuac took a great leap when the new campus, designed for 12,000, opened in 1968. The ceremony took place on the fifth anniversary of Jenkins's death. The press made no mention of Jenkins himself, presumably as no speeches referred to him. Espinosa, however, commanded the spotlight as the day's chief speechmaker. Evidently he felt that the date was signal enough to the Jenkins family that their forebear's memory was being honored. He focused instead on calling the government and his fellow bankers to facilitate loans to students, following the educational model of the United States.[32]

The foundation approved another $5 million in 1969, helping the Anáhuac add more buildings. Further hefty donations would follow over sixteen years, making for a total of some $15 million, around $70 million in today's currency. What proportion of overall Anáhuac funding came via Espinosa is not known, but his starring role at the inauguration suggests he was its biggest initial supporter. The most detailed investigation of the Legionaries and their donors has called Espinosa "the economic soul of the Anáhuac University since its foundation."[33]

Why such generosity? The Anáhuac offered an education that entirely contrasted with that at the UNAM. Long the great training ground of the political and business elite, the UNAM was now deeply associated with leftist activism and anti-authoritarianism; its students led the protests of 1968 that ended with the pre-Olympic massacre. Legionaries founder Maciel presented his order to its benefactors as a bulwark against communism. At the same time, the Anáhuac offered a Catholic education distinct from that of the Jesuits' Iberoamerican University, which although more prestigious was not as safe a bet for Espinosa. Some Jesuits were advocating "liberation" for the poor, from poverty and political marginalization. This current, gaining popularity throughout Latin America, would soon have a name: Liberation Theology.[34]

Maciel preached a less threatening gospel. His charisma and cult of personality—Legionaries called him "Our Father," took a vow never to criticize him, and deemed him a living saint—helped him convince the rich to part with large sums. One wealthy supporter would eventually admit that Maciel was adored by the rich because he made them feel as if "Christ loves them more than other people, and is using them as part of a divine plan." The remark suggests another reason why Espinosa gave so much: vanity. In what was clearly a cherished moment, a family memoir includes a photograph of Espinosa receiving a medal from Maciel.[35]

As so often the case with Espinosa's donations, there was in addition a business motive. The elite cachet that came with generous support for the Legionaries, along with his membership of the Anáhuac board, brought Espinosa closer to wealthy families from the Monterrey elite that had yet to do business with the Banco de Comercio.

It would be wrong to label Espinosa's support for the Anáhuac—or for the UDLA—as entirely self-interested. Whatever his elitist traits, Espinosa believed in the principle of social mobility and in education as its great facilitator. Very likely Jenkins had been an influence here: his own trajec-tory had served as testimony, as had his lifelong support for schooling, regardless of the race or class of the beneficiaries. Espinosa made clear in his inauguration day speech that he did not want to see the Anáhuac educate the rich alone. He called on business leaders, many of them pres-ent in the audience, to award scholarships to their employees and their employees' children, for Mexico had great need of well-trained personnel.[36]

IN 1970, WITH accession of President Luis Echeverría, Espinosa shifted his philanthropic goals. Under both Echeverría and his successor, José López Portillo, Espinosa found it politic to steer Jenkins's cash toward Mexico City. What the writer Octavio Paz would describe as a "philan-thropic ogre"—the PRI-led state that made gifts to the people with one hand and smacked ingrates with the other—had entered an irascible and self-indulgent middle age. Anything could happen, so it made sense to curry favor and cater to demagogic whims.[37]

Echeverría's gargantuan dreams included a new complex for the National Cardiology Institute. Here the foundation made its biggest grant yet, $10 million, which covered almost half the cost.[38] The institute already had an international reputation and the new site would enhance that. Its excellence aligned with Echeverría's rhetoric about "national dignity" and proud "Third Worldism." After nearly six years of planning, construction began in time for Echeverría to lay the foundation stone. Then, a few weeks before leaving office, the president insisted on inaugurating the building too, three years before its completion.[39]

A gift for a new Basilica of the Virgin of Guadalupe likewise appealed to Echeverría's taste for size and spectacle. Conceived to seat 10,000, the building was designed by Mexico's most famous grand-scale architect, Pedro Ramírez Vázquez. It would give Mexico City another signature building and another boost to tourism, a sector the state had prioritized for growth. Business leaders donated to a budget that during construction more than doubled to $25 million. In 1976, when the Basilica was inaugurated, some $5 million had still to be raised. By giving $2 million in foundation funds, Espinosa supported Echeverría's scheme of great works.[40]

The result of such support for presidential monumentalism is hard to gauge. But an era of friction between state and capital certainly turned out well for the Banco de Comercio (soon rebranded Bancomer), which continued to grow under Espinosa's astute leadership. The donations may have reaped specific reward in Echeverría's final year, when Espinosa had a strike on his hands back home. Puebla had remained a cualdron of student activism. A two-year struggle over the direction of the UAP had culminated in a street battle with police that left five students dead. The celebrated poet Efraín Huerta was moved to vilify the city's infamous late American: "The specter of Jenkins howls and caterwauls," he wrote, in "Puebla Possessed." Another unpopular governor was forced to resign.[41]

So great was the polarization, it affected even the UDLA. Many faculty and staff were dismayed at plans to curb humanities in favor of vocational programs. They disdained the new rector, an arch-conservative bent on steering enrollment further toward the Mexican elite. In April 1976 they struck, and the stoppage would last five months. Following the rhetorical tradition dating from the pro- and anti-Cuba marches fifteen years before, positions escalated in their stridency. The strikers demanded the removal not only of the administration but also of "the bourgeois element" in the student body. Echeverría's record of tolerating, even cultivating, radical speech gave them hope. Espinosa's ability to shape education looked dreadfully exposed.

After that summer's general election, however, federal authorities clamped down on the critical left. Soon the UDLA strike was brought to a close too, its administration firing all the strikers. Perhaps Echeverría would have sided with Espinosa anyway: after years of inflationary spending and capital flight, he was about to yield to the inevitable and devalue the peso, so he may have wished to shore up private-sector support. But Espinosa's loyalty—in contrast with the vocal opposition of many industrialists—surely inclined Echeverría to help him out.[42]

Espinosa was nonetheless glad to see the back of Echeverría. He sensed that with his departure the threat of a seizure of Bancomer had disappeared.[43] With José López Portillo came a shift in style. The new president seemed less unpredictable, more affable, less threatening to

business. However, he shared with Echeverría a belief in destined greatness: Mexico's and his own. This meant a continuity in grand populist
gestures and megaprojects. Owing to a recent oil discovery, it also meant
an accentuation of debt-driven development, which would yield yet higher
inflation. As he had done under Echeverría, Espinosa preached fiscal
responsibility. Convinced of his secondary vocation as a declaimer before
the press, he needed to carry on buying political space in which to be critical. So Bancomer continued to serve the needs of the state, and the foundation continued to bankroll giant projects in the capital.

Chief of these was a restoration of the colonial city center, coupled with
the excavation of a huge Aztec temple, the Templo Mayor. The project elicited a joint pledge from the foundation, which gave $22 million to restore
a host of buildings, and Espinosa himself, who gave $10 million to the
more glamorous restoration of the temple.[44] Espinosa made his gift via his
Amparo Foundation, set up in 1979 in memory of his wife. The charity
echoed Jenkins's example and used a similar structure. (In years to come,
many magnates in Mexico would set up endowment-based foundations.)
However, Espinosa endowed his with just $22 million, a minor part of
his wealth. He had never agreed with the American's blanket approach to
disinheritance.[45]

This was the year, 1980, that Espinosa's star peaked. In August he
invited López Portillo to open a new headquarters for Bancomer, which
had finally surpassed Banamex as Mexico's top bank. The building was a
gleaming horizontal complex of glass and concrete for 6,500 employees,
costing $87 million. Espinosa then posed before its vast indoor courtyard
for *Town & Country*. In a special edition on "Mighty Mexico," the US lifestyle magazine referred to Espinosa as "Mexico's wealthiest citizen," its
"biggest philanthropist," and a "self-made man."[46]

Yet all of Espinosa's moves—five or six years of cozying up to the president and offering him advice—ultimately proved in vain. In early 1982, after
a collapse in global oil prices, López Portillo was forced to devalue the peso.
His debt-financed house of cards began to tumble. At last, amid immense
capital flight, he reacted by expropriating all of Mexico's private banks,
Bancomer included. On September 1 he used his State of the Nation speech
to announce the confiscation, tearfully blaming the bankers for facilitating
the exit of capital, a factor in his suspension of international debt payments
ten days before. There was plenty of blame to share, but a consensus would
emerge that the president had scapegoated the banks for a disaster largely
courted through his regime's prodigal borrowing and spending.[47]

The bank seizure, the most drastic demonstration of presidential power since the oil nationalization of 1938, showed emphatically the boundaries of business-sector influence and politicized philanthropy in particular. The postrevoutionary symbiosis between state and capital seemed to have snapped. Then the new president, Miguel de la Madrid, obstructed Espinosa's designs elsewhere, causing him to announce his resignation from business entirely in 1985. He sold off his insurance company and other firms, mostly to his friend Carlos Slim.[48]

Within a decade, Mexico's richest magnate and leading financier had lost his wife, his bank, and his chance to reinvent himself as a multi-industrialist. Though seventy-six, Espinosa was still full of ideas and in vigorous health. The Jenkins Foundation was the only endeavor, and the only opportunity for greatness, he felt to be left to him.

Espinosa in Jenkins's Footsteps

Although neither is known to have voiced the idea, Manuel Espinosa Yglesias was possibly the son that Jenkins wished he had had.[49] First as his right-hand man and fellow monopolist, then as keeper of his philanthropic flame, Espinosa had much in common with Jenkins—perhaps more than either would have admitted. Both were preternaturally intelligent and gifted with numbers. Both cherished dreams of business empire and possessed the stamina and skill to see them realized. Both were early risers, happy to invest long hours conducting business, even to the neglect of their families.

They were equally power-mongers. Though neither entered politics, they imposed a rigid hierarchy within their businesses and sought sway in their wider environments. They resisted the unionization of their employees but rewarded hard workers with added responsibility regardless of their social backgrounds. They placed their financial muscle in the service of conservative ideology, whether by supporting the right wing of the ruling party or by bolstering capitalistic and Catholic institutions to counter the radical left.

Their family lives showed similarities too. In Mary Street and Amparo Rugarcía, they chose wives with a marked sense of social decorum. They sent their daughters to foreign boarding schools: the Jenkins's five girls went to Los Angeles; the Espinosas's three girls went to England, while their son attended college in Spain. Though traditional patriarchs, they both gave their eldest daughters, Elizabeth and Amparín, responsibilities in business. Mary and Amparo predeceased their husbands by many years, leaving them to nurse guilty consciences. Each man set up a foundation in their memory, but the unease never left them.

Espinosa honored his father's memory and attributed to him his start in business. But he remained a provincial player until he allied with Jenkins. Their association would endure for twenty-five years. That meant a quarter century of mentorship.

Jenkins had of course adopted his grandson Bill, but the boy was twenty-two years Espinosa's junior. It was clear to Jenkins that Espinosa was much nearer to him in ambition and intellect. It was also clear that Espinosa took after him more closely than did his other protégé, Gabriel Alarcón, whose temper was hotter and whose edges were rougher.

Espinosa was an admirer of the United States, and in middle age he learned decent English. He would tell his daughter Amparín that he liked the Americans' straightforward way of doing business. After moving to Mexico City, he became Jenkins's chief liaison with the federal authorities. Unlike Jenkins, he was happy to socialize with politicians. When Espinosa sought to remake himself as a banker by acquiring Bancomer, Jenkins overcame his reservations and lent him full support. Espinosa continued to visit Don Guillermo—as he respectfully addressed Jenkins—most weekends, to make a report and ask his advice. Each December 25 he would visit to wish him a happy Christmas. Jenkins's leading protégé, with nine years of success at Bancomer under his belt and a growing public profile, he was the board's unanimous choice to head the foundation, just as its founder had wished.[50] When his wife objected, worried that the Black Legend of William Jenkins would haunt him by association, Espinosa replied it would be unfair to turn the position down as Jenkins had always treated him well.

Espinosa nonetheless put great stock in appearances. So he countered the Black Legend when he could; earlier, he had tried in vain to convince Jenkins to dictate his memoirs.[51] Jenkins's lack of interest in public relations made for a rare contrast between them.

Another concerned other women. Early on, Espinosa could scarcely believe that Jenkins remained faithful to his wife, bedridden in distant California. He and Jenkins were making great strides in the film industry, with all the access to eager starlets that such power implied; Espinosa liked tall blondes. He hired a private investigator to tail Jenkins, seeking evidence of a mistress, but there was none. The producer Gregorio Walerstein was similarly struck by Jenkins's disinterest in dalliances. In later life Espinosa would tell Rosemary Eustace that there were two things her grandfather had never done: he never killed a man and he never cheated on Mary.

And yet, for all the loyalty and proximity between the two, the younger man was afflicted with resentments. Just as much of what had driven Jenkins was an ardent desire to prove himself to snobbish in-laws, Espinosa shouldered a chip of his own. In a country whose captains of industry were preponderantly tall and white, Espinosa was short (about five-foot-five) and *mestizo*-looking. He had been conscious of his aspect even as a boy, for while his brothers had inherited the fairer complexion of their mother, Manuel bore the somewhat indigenous features of his father's line. Observing how his mother favored her whiter sons, Manuel learned to be engaging to try to win her affection. Unimposing in appearance but dynamic and iron-willed, calculating and distrustful but able to charm, Espinosa came to be judged by some as having a Napoleon complex. Ronnie Eustace would jokingly refer to him as "Napi."

Espinosa was highly sensitive to such slights. Some came from Jenkins himself, who was fond of jocular terms of abuse and at times called him *Chaparro* (Shorty) or, when he made a rare mistake, *Pendejo* (Dumb-ass). To Manuel this was humiliation. But the resentment went still deeper. By the late 1940s, when Espinosa was building COTSA into Mexico's most powerful theater chain, Jenkins was starting to work half days, spending more time with family and friends. It seemed to Espinosa that he was doing twice the work for a half share in the business. Very likely this irritant helped him rationalize the purchase of Bancomer stock, behind Jenkins back, that put the American in the awkward position of majority owner. Espinosa rightly calculated that Jenkins would remedy the problem by letting him run the show.

After Jenkins's death, Espinosa led the eulogies. At the 1964 unveiling of the technical colleges the foundation underwrote, in the presence of López Mateos, Espinosa's speech focused squarely on Jenkins as philanthropist. To establish the foundation's bona fides and publicize its founder's wishes, he quoted extensively from Jenkins's will. Thereafter he mentioned him much less. Later speeches combined accounts of foundation giving with Espinosa's personal vision for education and the economy. With so many ceremonies taking place on a fourth of June, Jenkins was still being honored. But the date was merely a dash of symbolism to keep the Jenkins family happy, while Espinosa pursued his own ends.

AFTER DEALING WITH the loss of his bank and the surrender of his industrial assets—a tortured stretch of two or three years, during which the foundation disbursed little—Espinosa did revive one aspect of Jenkins's vision: Puebla returned to the center of his attention.

A major trigger was the prospect for Puebla City of recognition as a UNESCO World Heritage Site. The historical downtown would need a major makeover, including the repair of ancient buildings. Mayor at the time was Jorge Murad, whose 1983 election had been doubly momentous. It crowned the ascendance of the city's Lebanese, and it occurred amid electoral fraud not seen in several decades. Indeed, ruling-party use of "alchemy," in municipal, state, and eventually federal elections, became heavy-handed during the 1980s, as the opposition PAN was buoyed by the mess that the PRI had made of the economy. In Puebla, the PAN fielded a strong challenger and the poll was followed by weeks of protests at the PRI's dirty tricks. Thus the World Heritage initiative had dual motives: to garner prestige and facilitate tourism, and to legitimize Murad and smoothen the road for his PRI-designated successor.[52]

Espinosa was not an immediate supporter. Perhaps he remained too resentful of President De la Madrid. But in January 1986, after talks with Governor Guillermo Jiménez Morales, he came through, pledging $10 million. The sum advanced Puebla's UNESCO drive and, Espinosa hoped, won favor with the governor, who was well-connected at the federal level.[53]

In 1987, in a triumph for Espinosa and for Puebla, UNESCO bestowed upon the city the coveted status of World Heritage Site. The foundation's gift was not quite in line with Jenkins's wishes—other than the temporary spike in jobs, there was little direct benefit for the poor—but UNESCO recognition gave a great boost to civic pride and promised to lift tourism as well, with further job creation ensuing. A year earlier, with the restoration work in full swing, the PRI enjoyed a much easier victory in the contest for Puebla mayor.[54]

At heart, Espinosa craved the spotlight that he had lost as Mexico's most powerful banker. So he tried to remake himself as Mexico's most powerful philanthropist. He tightened his grip on the foundation by naming his daughters Lupe and Ángeles to its board. Rosemary Eustace, who was close to Espinosa at the time, became acutely conscious of her grandfather's absence from his speeches. She observed how people would approach Espinosa and hail his generosity, as though the foundation's gifts were his own; he would make no attempt to correct them. Newspaper columnists extolled him as a "hero" for the support of "his" money. It struck

Rosemary that Espinosa was trying to obliterate the man who had been his second father.[55]

At the same time, Espinosa dreamed of recovering ownership of Bancomer. President De la Madrid's pursuit of neoliberalism would likely lead to the privatization of the banks. If Espinosa supported the PRI by helping combat the PAN in Puebla, he might gain the favor of whomever succeeded De la Madrid, putting himself in a good position to bid for Bancomer. As it turned out, the president's successor was Carlos Salinas; Puebla's Jiménez Morales was close to him—he would join the Salinas cabinet in 1991—and able to lobby on Espinosa's behalf.[56]

But the strategy failed. The Salinas administration determined that while the banks should be auctioned off, as would be carried out in 1991–1992, they should not return to their previous owners. Salinas did not want the privatization to seem like a restoration. For one thing, bankers of Espinosa's generation were still tarnished in the public mind as *sacadólares* (dollar removers), unpatriotic elites who had sped their savings out of Mexico in 1982 and helped others do the same, exacerbating the collapse.[57]

In the wake of the bank sell-off, Espinosa gave an extensive interview to *Proceso*, an ardently left wing journal he would not have stooped to address before. The gist of his interview was reflected in the story's headline: "In this century, no one has lost as much as I." Espinosa would carry this sense of victimhood to his grave.[58]

In one sense, he was right. Of all those affected by the bank expropriation, Espinosa had been hardest hit. While his Banamex counterpart owned just a small fraction of its stock, Espinosa held a working majority of Bancomer stock, and state compensation undervalued such stakes.[59] But Espinosa was also exaggerating the damage to his overall worth, evincing another trait he shared with Jenkins. While his wealth never drew the notice of the *Forbes* list, by the end of the decade, according to close friends, he was worth a billion dollars. Still, Espinosa's sense of betrayal was understandable. Despite a lifetime's support for the ruling party, despite a brilliant record in business, three presidents in a row had spurned him.

And so the jealousy with which he conducted foundation business grew worse, and tensions with the Jenkins family boiled over. In the past, Espinosa had effectively bought their loyalty: allowing Bill to bring his wife onto the board, giving his sons Guillermo and Roberto executive posts at Bancomer, and selectively liberalizing the terms of Jenkins's will. Whereas one clause granted educational expenses to his grandchildren, Espinosa offered them to some of the great-grandchildren too. While another clause allowed Bill and Jenkins's daughters $1,000 per month should need arise, Espinosa made the payments automatic and increased them over time.[60]

By nature, Bill had always preferred to avoid confrontation. Now, however, he shared his cousin Rosemary's concern that Espinosa was overreaching and disassociating the foundation from its founder. When Bill tried to take a more active role, Espinosa shunned him. On one occasion he told him: "You're stealing my limelight."[61]

Above all, Espinosa seemed bent on dominion over the UDLA. When he transferred its land and buildings to the books of the foundation, Bill suspected that this move was a stopgap, the final aim being to transfer the UDLA to Espinosa's Amparo Foundation, along with all the other Jenkins Foundation assets. During the governorship of Mariano Piña Olaya (1987–1993), Espinosa had made monthly Foundation payments of $100,000 to the state for vaguely defined "public works"; to Bill these were little more than bribes, intended to gain Piña Olaya's approval of dubious maneuvers. The distrust was mutual: Espinosa told friends he suspected the Jenkins family wished to sell the UDLA and hide the proceeds.

The final straw for Bill was Espinosa's declaration in 1995 that he was moving aside to become foundation vice-president and naming his daughter Ángeles in his place. Bill and his wife quit the meeting in protest, refusing to return. A year later, Espinosa expelled the couple from the board. Bill brought suit, and the matter would remain unresolved until 2002 when Bill and his family assumed control.[62]

The UDLA stayed under the foundation's wings. Whatever his motive for transferring its assets, Espinosa saw the university as the jewel in his philanthropic crown. Under his guidance it grew in stature. He elicited new support for it; Carlos Slim was said to have donated $1 million. Strikingly for a man reputed to be a dictator, Espinosa gave the rector, the Yale-educated economist Enrique Cárdenas, ample rein to run things as he saw fit. The UDLA came to be known as a generous employer, populated by a talented and well-paid faculty, and the student body included a fair proportion of scholarship students from modest backgrounds. With its strengths in vocational programs such as business, the UDLA fulfilled Espinosa's vision of a Mexican training ground for the international marketplace.[63]

Cárdenas would honor Espinosa for his decades of commitment with an event at the UDLA in 1999. By now, the foundation had supported the university with a total of $98 million. Espinosa had recently turned ninety, and the day would mark his final visit to the campus. President Ernesto Zedillo led the homage. Along with several cabinet members he sang Happy Birthday to Manuel, and in his speech Zedillo hailed him as an "exceptional businessman, a determined builder, a good and generous Mexican."[64]

ESPINOSA'S FINAL YEARS were not happy ones. He wrestled with loneliness and fretted about his reputation. He had three historians write his biography but did not care for the result.[65] Instead he compiled a memoir, calling it *Bancomer: Achievement and Destruction of an Ideal.*

The book emits surprising flashes of candor, including accounts of dealings with Jenkins that make clear his having acted for self-gain. But it is broadly an exercise in self-justification, laced with righteous anger against the government from 1970 on. It treats his association with Jenkins as that of a go-getter paired with a lumbering money manager, whose biggest deals relied on the younger man's foresight and élan. In such passages Espinosa is guilty—as they say in Mexico—of "throwing himself flowers" and "putting cream on his tacos."[66]

The memoir says little about his personal life, yet it was clear to close observers that his zest for power had left him a solitary man. A longtime friend later noted how his cultivated air of authority—low of voice, straight of stare, obstinate, blunt, quick-witted—earned the admiration of his peers but left employees fearful. The biography he refused to publish contrasted him with his Bancomer predecessor, Salvador Ugarte, who developed a wide social circle: "Espinosa, with his dryer character, preferred the spheres of economic and political influence, maintaining few personal friendships. He was something of a cunning and willful lone wolf."[67]

Only rarely during his lifetime did Espinosa let his guard down. In 1991 he opened a Puebla art museum that memorialized his wife: the Amparo Museum.[68] Its lobby was dominated by a Diego Rivera portrait of Amparo. The famous muralist rendered her a beauty: a movie-star redhead in a black ball gown with violet and claret trim, along with Rivera's signature white lilies for a backdrop. Next to it was a plaque, inscribed with Espinosa's words: "This Amparo Museum carries the name of my wife, a beautiful and humane woman, who always loved me."

Who always loved me. The self-absorbed turn of phrase set society tongues a-wagging. Was this the work of a guilty conscience? Were the rumors about Amparo true? They were true indeed. Espinosa's wife had killed herself, sixteen years before. Driven to drink by Espinosa's serial

affairs with actresses and other women, isolated by his ferocious work regimen, she had taken an overdose of sleeping pills. Espinosa then covered
the matter up.

His desolation ran yet deeper. Like Jenkins, he had urged his children
to marry people from wealthy families who would not love them for their
money. He pressed them into matches that suited his interests; they complied and their marriages all failed. He urged his son to follow him in
business, but Manuelito was no Manuel. Inheriting little of his father's
drive or discipline, he comported himself as a "junior"—a bon vivant rich
kid—with an eye for strippers and a nose for cocaine. He had a sparkling
sense of humor, a polite and easy manner, and retinue of mostly useless
friends. While his mother spoiled him, his father scolded him. Manuel
gave him an executive position and put him on the Bancomer board—but
to little effect. Manuelito's vices prompted successive wives to leave him.
Manuel's browbeating persisted too.

One day in 1996—after Manuelito's third partner left, taking their two
girls with her—Espinosa arrived at his son's house to pick him up for
an event. There was another argument, then Manuelito went upstairs.
Waiting below, Manuel heard a bang. His son had shot himself.

Then there was a third suicide: a son of his daughter Ángeles. And
with Ángeles herself, who had acquired her father's Machiavellian streak,
there were dealings that sowed further bitterness. Being in charge of the
Jenkins Foundation was not enough for her ambitions. Long jealous of
her prettier and more popular sisters, she poured enough poison in her
father's ear to prompt him to rewrite his will, leaving a greater share for
her. Coincidentally or not the children of Jenkins's second protégé, Gabriel
Alarcón, would also tangle over their inheritance. Family members even
attempted to have each other jailed.[69]

Espinosa died in June 2000, aged ninety-one, just weeks after his
memoir appeared. On the cover, the man who was once Mexico's richest
loomed disconsolate from a black background, as though in mourning
for himself. At his funeral mass in Puebla, the organist played "My Way."

Jenkins too had endured a lonely and guilt-ridden widowerhood. But
at least he had the good-humored likes of Sergio Guzmán and Ronnie
Eustace for company. He had reneged on his material promises to Mary,
but he did not bear the added guilt of serial infidelity. In love with the business of business, he long neglected his daughters, but he tried to make
amends by spending time with them after he turned seventy; this was too
little, too late, yet he ensured they would not squabble over his fortune by

arranging to give it all away. Espinosa followed in Jenkins's footsteps but some of his stumblings were his own.

A few months before he died, a friend visited him at the home he had retired to in Cuernavaca. Located in the florid lowlands south of the capital and blessed with a perfect climate, the town had functioned as the summer retreat of the Aztec emperors. Hernán Cortés built his private palace there. Alexander von Humboldt, the Romantic-era naturalist, dubbed Cuernavaca "The City of Eternal Spring." The last Shah of Iran, deposed from his throne, found exile among the spacious homes and walled gardens of its American community.

It was not a place of comfort for Espinosa. He lived alone, ruminating.

"My wife committed suicide, my son committed suicide, my grandson committed suicide," he told his guest. "I am the guilty one. I am *sick* with power."

Jenkins Legends, White and Black

Except in Puebla, where it is the rare taxi driver who lacks a retort at the mention of his name, Jenkins has receded from the public imagination. Few besides historians and elderly elites recall him. But like a character from Cervantes his name still resurfaces in the national conversation, whether as historical actor or caricature.

In 2013 it happened with the eruption of further infighting at the Jenkins Foundation, this time between family members; news reports about the spat persist to this day.[70] In 2014 the popular novelist Francisco Martín Moreno claimed on national radio that some of the drug-cartel violence in Michoacán had its roots in Jenkins's legacy: under Cárdenas, Jenkins had acquired a hacienda called Nueva Italia and later turned it over to Espinosa and Alarcón. They administered it poorly and left its villages impoverished. What choice had the sons of these poor farmers but to emigrate to the United States or stay on as marijuana growers and meth producers?[71]

Like Martín Moreno's spurious anecdote, which garbled several historical threads and mined a rich vein of blaming the United States for Mexico's cartel problems, most stories about Jenkins are gringophobic—but not all, for Jenkins has always had his defenders. From the day he died, polarized views pervaded the press and public opinion. Impartial observers were few.

The obituaries had facilitated a White Legend. They marveled at Jenkins's wealth, lauded his philanthropy, and usually buried his darker deeds. *El Sol de Puebla* had called him "A brilliant figure, a typically North American product, a prodigious intellect in business able to turn a peso that fell into his hands into a million." As well as dwelling on his donations, it noted how he ran an empire with an office staff of three and it praised his thrifty ways: "he even sent his tennis shoes to be re-soled."[72]

The few critical obits, in the leftist press, pulled their punches. "He was 85 but he worked as though he were 20," admitted *La Opinión*. "No one believes in his goodness, but neither can anyone confirm that he was a bad man," minced *El Día*.[73]

Reluctance to speak ill of the recently deceased may have been unusually pronounced in Jenkins's case. His endowment of the foundation gave people pause. Marte Gómez, the finance minister who had tussled with Jenkins over his tax evasion in the 1930s, wrote to a friend: "It's harder to impoverish the rich than to enrich the poor. This was exactly so with Jenkins. He made many sacrifices—his virtue, among other things—to amass one of the greatest fortunes in Mexico, if not the greatest, but later he had no difficulty [in bequeathing it] to a trust that could bring happiness to thousands of needy people."[74]

Then came the events that Espinosa arranged to commemorate Jenkins's death. For each of the next five years, at least, there was occasion for publicly recalling the man's generosity, as foundation stones were laid and facilities inaugurated. In 1965, Puebla's Alpha Clubs began an annual William O. Jenkins Commemorative Games that continue today. Less well-off students could attend the UDLA and other colleges on Jenkins Scholarships.[75]

The White Legend has never disappeared, thanks to foundation activities. But the Black Legend became preponderant. It is what most Mexicans have wanted to hear.

IN THE PUBLIC sphere, the arts, and academia, all kinds of people found it useful to evoke Jenkins name or recycle myths about him. Some did so to make a political point, others to dress up a novel, still others to indulge their disdain for Americans, capitalists, or both.

An eminent publisher set a mark in 1964 when it issued a national encyclopedia; through six editions it became a standard reference work. Its entry on Jenkins recorded unreservedly that his kidnapping was a hoax. When Enrique Cordero y Torres, dean of the Puebla chroniclers, published his *Biographical Dictionary of Puebla*, he devoted by far the lengthiest entry to Jenkins. Cordero made much of the "self-kidnapping," the murder of Atencingo labor leaders, and the Alfonso Mascarúa killing. He called the

American's foundation a tax dodge and quoted a lot of vitriol from the *Black Book of Mexican Cinema*.[76]

After López Portillo seized the banks in 1982, many lawmakers welcomed his move. Edmundo Jardón of the Communist Party likened the bankers to Sicilian mafia. He assailed Bancomer by linking it with Jenkins, "a delinquent . . . who kidnapped himself trying to create problems for the government." He was an accumulator of money, a creator of an empire. It was Jenkins who had Atencingo activist Porfirio Jaramillo killed, and Jenkins, along with Alarcón, who planned the murder of Mascarúa.[77]

Jardón's speech captured the mood of the left toward Jenkins and its zeal to resurrect him for political mileage. In 1980, after Espinosa announced foundation support for restoring the capital's colonial center, news magazine *Proceso* ran a Jenkins profile that resembled a Black Legend compendium. Its headline claimed that President Abelardo Rodríguez had expelled him from the country. Its text offered juicy allegations as fact and revived the "kidnapping fortune" myth: that Jenkins had connived and founded his empire with the ransom.

The feature was less an investigation than a catalogue of villainy, designed to attack the Mexico City government for accepting "dirty money." Mayor at the time—unmentioned in the article—was the notoriously self-enriching Carlos Hank González, a PRI veteran. These were still the days when the press could not criticize politicians by name unless they were known to be out of favor with the president. Castigation of Jenkins served as a proxy for critique of a politician who was not only ethically suspect but also a ruling-party conservative.[78]

In 1985 Jenkins gained a new lease of life as the Bad Gringo archetype thanks to *Tear This Heart Out*, a historical novel about Maximino Ávila Camacho (here, Andrés Ascencio). Lending it credibility was the fact that the author, Ángeles Mastretta, was a granddaughter of Sergio Guzmán, Puebla mayor under Maximino and Jenkins's best friend. As Mastretta would reveal, the novel's sexual shenanigans and business chicanery were the stuff of household gossip when she was young. Various misdeeds involve an American partner of Ascencio's, a certain Mike Heiss. The Heiss-Jenkins parallels are obvious. One of Ascencio's "associates and protégés," Heiss is a "loud gringo" who "during Carranza's time had hatched a plot for his own kidnapping"; he proceeded to use "the money his government paid for rescuing him from himself" to get started in business. Mastretta's novel struck critics and readers as remarkably authentic. It would sell a million copies and be translated into multiple languages.[79]

Tear This Heart Out was filmed in 2008, in a lavish production said to be Mexico's most expensive to that date. It was a box-office hit, and press coverage reminded readers that Heiss was Jenkins. In 2012 Jenkins appeared on the big screen again, in *The Fantastic World of Juan Orol*, a biopic about a B-movie director of the Golden Age. The key financier with whom Orol deals is a smug and sinister American who goes by the name Don Guillermo. And 2016 saw the release of a documentary based on Contreras Torres's *Black Book of Mexican Cinema*, which once again argued that the Golden Age had been killed off by Jenkins.[80]

Mastretta's novel was neither the first involving Jenkins nor the last. A fanciful history of Atencingo appeared in 1980: *Harvest of Hatreds, Bitter Sugar*. Authored by a former accountant at the mill, it embellishes in its depiction of Jenkins as cruel overlord and offers an unreliable chronology. Still, the UAP published it as a primary document, and some historians saw fit to cite it, quoting as fact its authorial inventions. In 1993, Rafael Ruiz Harrell offered his minutely researched recreation *The Kidnapping of William Jenkins*, with its unorthodox reading of the famous episode as a genuine abduction. The kidnapping was then the departure point for a 2003 novel, *Conspiracy in The Arcadia*. Set in a grubby world of Mexican high politics, the tale assumes the traditional "self-kidnapping" thesis.[81]

Black Legend Jenkins also featured in the history books. The Mexican state established that the Revolution, whatever its factional complexities, was to be remembered in nationalistic terms.[82] Jenkins served that purpose, fitting nicely into the narrative of economic nationalism. His persona also fit the dependency theory narrative, which holds colonial-era Spain and Portugal, nineteenth-century Britain, and twentieth-century United States—their governments often serving the interests of their merchants—responsible for many of Latin America's ills. Popular in political circles as of the 1960s, especially on the left, dependency theory seeped into Mexican and US academia and for decades colored much of the writing on US-Mexican relations.[83]

Mexican historical interest in Jenkins has chiefly concerned the kidnapping. The tone was set in 1960, with one of the first official histories of the Revolution. Intended for colleges, it devoted four pages to the abduction, and its unequivocal verdict was that Jenkins had concocted it. Central to its argument, the account quoted a published letter of confession from the lead kidnapper, Federico Córdoba, claiming Jenkins had suggested the caper. In fact, Córdoba had denounced the letter as a fake, planted by the Puebla government, but the book omitted that part. Most subsequent histories followed suit, with an equally one-sided marshalling of evidence.[84]

A prominent politician then embarked on a mammoth documentary record of the Revolution. Volume 18 included the kidnapping, and, rather than fomenting debate, it offered a single document: a case summary from a propaganda organ of the Carranza regime. Since the 1970s, millions of students have used as a textbook the *General History of Mexico*. At first it described Jenkins's abduction neutrally, but in 1981 the kidnapping became a "self-kidnapping," and it was added (falsely) that Jenkins could never prove his innocence.[85]

At Puebla's UAP, chief academic guardian of the Jenkins Black Legend, an overall case against the American appeared in a slender 2004 biography. Its author, Teresa Bonilla, had been darkening the narrative for years; features about Jenkins in *Proceso* and the Puebla press glibly quoted her. To Bonilla, Jenkins hailed from a nation marked by "fanatical adherence to new forms of religion, racism, and a great superiority complex"; these were "Protestant religions that judge human value in relation to the possession of material goods." Throughout a narrative replete with sweeping judgments, Jenkins is less a human being than a malignant force. His predatory loans and political friendships are treated as though Mexicans rarely or never acted likewise. In a triumph of ideology over evidence, Bonilla's bibliography includes scant primary sources but five works by Karl Marx.[86]

US researchers too have assumed the worst. In his sociological study *Atencingo*, David Ronfeldt mentions the "kidnapping fortune" story, having presumably heard it from his sugar-worker informants. Ronfeldt also says that Jenkins's sale of Atencingo was a pretense, a claim that seems based on local suspicions and that ignores his desire to invest in the more lucrative film sector. Both cases exemplify pitfalls in writing about Mexico's have-nots: ignoring how their testimony might be self-serving and failing to explore the motives of elites.[87]

Historian Stephen Niblo was yet more slipshod, such as when he accuses Jenkins of having refused to screen Allied propaganda at his Mexico City movie theaters in 1940. First, by implying this owed in part to his friendship with Maximino (who did hold Axis sympathies), he smears Jenkins as a fascist by association. Second, he fabricates evidence, for Jenkins had no theater circuit in the capital until the COTSA chain was born, in 1943. Niblo, whose general opinion of US influence in Mexico is gleefully negative, also claims that Jenkins held "the most reactionary political views that existed in Mexico," which he does not illustrate. He calls Jenkins "a caricature of the rapacious foreign exploiter," unaware that he is party to the caricaturing.[88]

Film histories show a similar readiness to vilify. Many rely on Contreras Torres's *Black Book* or later works that repeat its claims. Hence Jenkins often resembles one of the villains in the B-movies he financed. One popular film history includes an out-of-context photograph of Jenkins at night, stone-faced, holding a tall candle, like the sinister butler in a horror flick. The occasion was in fact the service of blessing at a Red Cross hospital he had financed.[89]

IN PUEBLA, JENKINS still casts a tall shadow. The capital's convention center is named for him, and plaques acknowledging his foundation's repair of churches and monuments pepper the city. Here, to praise Jenkins is to announce oneself as a conservative; to condemn him is to be a leftist and a patriot. Here the "kidnapping fortune" tale remains alive in public memory. Schoolteachers relay it, and at some institutions the American's guilt is almost an article of faith.

David LaFrance, a historian at the UAP, presented a paper on the kidnapping before some of his colleagues in 2004. Having studied the case more thoroughly than anyone, he concluded that Jenkins had not fixed his abduction. He added: "Popular memory has been allowed to mold the 'truth' of the case." His colleagues were quite upset. It was not for a historian to judge whether Jenkins were guilty, declared one; that was a job for the courts! Another felt LaFrance misread the evidence. A third accused him of replacing one myth with another. The editors of *Historia Mexicana* begged to differ. Mexico's top historical journal found the essay persuasive enough to merit publication. It then earned a prize from the Mexican Committee of Historical Sciences as the year's best article on twentieth-century history.[90]

Perhaps LaFrance's experiences reflected a turning of the tide: a lessening distrust of the United States in general. In 2007, when President Felipe Calderón obtained the $1.4 billion Mérida Initiative package from George W. Bush to aid his war on the drug cartels, the news proved less polemical than analysts predicted. In 2013, as President Enrique Peña Nieto unveiled and shepherded reforms of the energy sector, opening the long-sacrosanct oil industry to foreign investment, protest was unexpectedly low-key. Several decades of mass migration back and forth between Mexico and the United States have made it harder for ideologues to demonize Uncle Sam. Too many Mexicans have been there and seen him for themselves.[91]

Similar changes have permeated Mexico City's UNAM. In 2012 the storied bastion of the left published a two-volume history of US-Mexican relations. Privileging recent research, the authors recount that, in 1919, Jenkins "was imprisoned by the Pueblan authorities, who accused him, *with very scant evidence*, of having organized his kidnapping."[92]

Indeed the entire study shows a fresh analysis. It refuses to recycle the ancient idea that Mexico is merely the recurrent prey of a deceitful imperialist. It admits an imbalance of power in US-Mexican dealings but argues that this has long been mitigated by institutional relationships, bilateral coalitions, the US division of powers (as when President Wilson blocked Senator Fall's war-mongering over the Jenkins case), and also by the US Latino population. It declines to view the United States and its citizens through the distorting lens of gringophobia.

Epilogue

THE MIXED LEGACY OF WILLIAM O. JENKINS

*Every revolution ends with the creation of a new
privileged class.*

CARLOS FUENTES, *Where the Air Is Clear* (1958)

ONCE CARLOS SLIM became a household name, stories began to circulate about his wizardry with numbers. The man who was turning around Mexico's decrepit telephone monopoly, and in the process turning his stock portfolio into the most valuable in the world, could run his finger down a column of prices and effortlessly add them. He could read a company balance sheet with a facility that most can apply only to reading a clock. Pegged as the world's top billionaire between 2007 and 2013, Slim was quoted as saying: "The numbers, they talk to me." Among those who knew him, William Jenkins spurred similar anecdotes.

Mexico's richest individual of today has other things in common with this predecessor. As Jenkins was cementing his position as magnate of magnates in the 1940s, he acted as mentor to Manuel Espinosa Yglesias; Espinosa, the richest Mexican of the 1970s, in turn, became something of a mentor to Slim. Both Jenkins and Slim evinced a talent for buying at bargain prices, often when the blood (literally or metaphorically) was running in the streets and investors were fleeing the country. Both became masters of monopoly. And both, it seems, were adept at protecting and expanding their monopolies through political ties. That was demonstrably the case for Jenkins; for Slim, the notion remains nebulous, a matter of conjecture and conspiracy theory more than documented fact. Clearly each man owed his rise to two basic factors: entrepreneurial drive and knowing the right people. The question is not a matter of one or the other but where on the continuum between vision and privilege the explanation should lie.[1]

The business genealogy that links Jenkins with Espinosa and then with Slim is more than an interesting historical tidbit. It raises questions for modern Mexico about economic mobility and the strength or weakness of institutions (the law, regulators, and electoral democracy). In the cases of Jenkins and Slim, it suggests that, in the business sphere, the pros of being ethnically different outweigh the cons. It also raises questions about "crony capitalism," or rather the distinct but often parallel forces of symbiotic imperative and symbiotic convenience between political and business elites.[2] Given the trouble that Mexico has had in eradicating poverty, in developing a political system truly representative of the people, and in shaping a business culture that favors initiative and application over political connections, strength of kin, and tone of skin, these questions all merit closer examination. The story of William Jenkins is one attempt to provide answers to those questions, to fill in some of the blanks in understanding present-day Mexico and how it got that way.

More than forty years after his death, Jenkins's career reveals the formation of features that still dominate the social map of Mexico. It helps explain the country's unbalanced economic development, a decidedly capitalistic project even at the height of revolutionary rhetoric, and the relationships between state and capital, often cozy, sometimes tense, always undergirded by some kind of interdependence. It demonstrates the critical role of the regions in Mexico's economic and political development. And it illustrates the politicized tradition of casting the United States and its business leaders as enemies of national progress.

The 1940s and 1950s—when Jenkins reached his money-spinning zenith—were the era in which the mold of modern Mexico was set. As the state took its pro-business turn, Jenkins and industrialists like him gravitated to cronyism, insider lending, and monopolistic practice, driving a concentration of wealth. Only the persistence of revolutionary slogans and cultural nationalism masked the growing disparities. The social revolution, launched by the Constitution of 1917 and peaking with the expropriations ordered by Cárdenas, had reduced rural poverty and nurtured a substantial middle class. Yet from around 1940 to 1970, opportunities narrowed. Then, after a twelve-year interlude of big-spending populism, the anti-egalitarian trajectory resumed. Despite some success in poverty alleviation under Salinas (1988–1994) and Fox (2000–2006), a notoriously unequal distribution of income plagues Mexico still.[3]

In his adoptive state of Puebla, Jenkins's political and economic legacy was yet more divisive. His pact with Maximino Ávila Camacho helped found a dynasty that would endure under Maximino's acolytes until the 1960s. Ironically, this pro-business clique did little to cultivate the economy. With a lock on power, its conservatism was chiefly of the complacent variety. Governors selected more for reasons of favoritism and malleability than aptitude were unwilling to alter the status quo or court new investors. Puebla experienced more than twenty years of stagnation, which left lingering aftereffects. Despite its strong automotive sector, Puebla City still lags far behind Guadalajara and Monterrey as a center of industry.[4]

Also lingering is the iron-handed style of rule that Jenkins helped Maximino establish. In a 2007 article on the persistence of PRI autocrats in the provinces, *The Guardian* called Puebla "dinosaur territory for the last 78 years." Three years later, the state finally had an opposition governor, Rafael Moreno Valle of the PAN. However, Moreno Valle, the grandson of a PRI governor, had only switched to the PAN when passed over for a PRI candidacy for the senate. While he did succeed in raising economic growth higher than the national average, Moreno Valle used violence and intimidation to suppress dissent, co-opted most of Puebla's media, and spent heavily on self-promotion to enhance a future presidential bid.[5]

Jenkins's proximity to Puebla's governors had unfortunate side effects. It contributed to a public perception of American businessmen as "pernicious foreigners" and thus to the use of gringophobia as a staple of leftist-nationalist speech. This device has long persisted. The image of the gringo exploiter regained prominence during the North American Free Trade Agreement (NAFTA) debates of the 1990s. Political cartoons of the NAFTA era delighted in fearmongering. A frequent trope was the smiling Anglo businessman or wizened Uncle Sam, scheming to make off with Mexico's oil, even though an opening of the petroleum sector was never under negotiation.[6] This pandering to fears over Mexico's old symbol of economic sovereignty arguably did the nation a disservice, distracting attention from the more complex yet critical threat of subsidized US corn, whose tariff-free entry would cause the destitution and forced migration of millions of subsistence farmers and their families.

Mexican concerns about US investors do have historical legitimacy: for one thing, the precedent of profiteering oil and mining companies until the 1930s. Moreover, Mexico relies on the United States for three-quarters of its trade and investment. Still, warnings about grasping Americans can mask self-interested agendas, particularly in the business arena.[7] They can also betray a naiveté about geopolitics, a charge often leveled at leftist firebrand Andrés Manuel López Obrador, the most prominent user of nationalist rhetoric on the contemporary political scene. It should come as no surprise, now that foreign investors are starting to return to the oil industry, if the capitalist gringo bogeyman should reappear, pushing debate in a nationalist-populist direction.[8]

THE LIFE OF William Jenkins is not a closed book. As long as the Mary Street Jenkins Foundation operates, his legacy will impact the lives of many Mexicans, and the Jenkins name will resonate. This is especially the case in Puebla, where the foundation remains a major source of donations and therefore of news, most recently with its support for the International Museum of the Baroque, a vast cultural complex designed by Toyo Ito and inaugurated in 2016.[9] The foundation's crown jewel, the Universidad de las Américas (recently rebranded as the UDLA–Puebla or UDLAP), has been the top private university in the state since its founding and ranks as one of the best in the country.

Owing to occasional meddling by the foundation, that reputation has not come easily. Not unlike what happened in 1976, when an autocratic rector provoked a faculty strike that resulted in mass firings, infighting over the university's direction recurred in 2005–2007. Sixty faculty were fired, enrollment tumbled, and amid concerns about governance the UDLAP was put on probation by its US accreditation agency. Under the subsequent rectorship of Luis Ernesto Derbez, who had served under Fox as Minister of Foreign Relations, the UDLAP has regained its luster. After an independent board was installed to ensure autonomy from the foundation, full accreditation was regained and enrollment recovered to seven thousand. Since 2011 the London-based QS Intelligence Unit has consistently ranked the UDLAP among Mexico's top ten universities.[10]

The Anáhuac University—the other main academic beneficiary of Jenkins's fortune—has also grown in stature. For decades the Anáhuac was known as a networking site for rich "juniors," too dim or too lazy to enter a better college, who would go on to executive posts in their father's firms anyway. As of 1997, its name was sullied by a sequence of revelations about the sexual predations of its founder, Marcial Maciel. Donations to the campus suffered. But in recent years the Anáhuac has raised its reputation and diversified its study body. Close to 40 percent of its 12,000 students receive some kind of financial aid. Between 2011 and 2015, its QS ranking climbed from twenty-sixth to eighth among Mexican universities.[11]

Would Jenkins have been satisfied with the foundation's record overall? The question retains its relevance because the American's desire for the uses of his fortune was both affirmed in his own record of giving and made explicit in the foundation's statutes, which gave emphasis to charity, public education, and "people of modest resources."[12] The question also sheds light on the uneven practice of philanthropy in contemporary Mexico as a whole.

Although Jenkins's support for private education had only ever been piecemeal, the UDLAP generally stands as a fitting legacy. Its first incarnation, when Americans and Mexicans studied alongside each other, fulfilled a desire Jenkins long held to see mutual prejudices eroded through contact. A long slump in foreign enrollment was eventually somewhat compensated for by exchange programs with US universities. Espinosa's willingness to subsidize the campus allowed a good proportion of students to attend with scholarships. But since around 2005, when the foundation began trying to make the campus self-sustaining, financial support for low-income students has declined.[13] This would have disappointed Jenkins, who himself attended college on a scholarship.

At the primary and secondary level, Jenkins's support for public education has similarly become less visible, for Espinosa took donations in an emphatically private direction. The chief recipient was Puebla's American School. Certainly, those outlays honored Jenkins's commitment to a school his sister had founded. Today it serves Puebla's professional classes, although in keeping with Jenkins's vision the sons and daughters of all full-time employees, from teachers to janitors, can attend tuition-free.[14] But there would be no more major gifts for the building of large K–12 public schools, as Jenkins had made in the 1950s.

In the late 1990s the foundation began donating to the American School of Mexico City, the grandest prep school in the country, where the offspring of business and political elites rub shoulders with those of embassy personnel. In 2012 it gave the school $2 million for a Jenkins Foundation Wellness Center. The inauguration, with a ribbon-cutting by the US ambassador, was amply covered in the capital's society pages.[15] Given Mexico's enormous and chronic deficiencies in public education, it is hard to imagine William Jenkins making such a gift.

In culture, health, and sport, the other areas in which the foundation was charged with making a difference, Jenkins would probably be pleased with his legacy. Standing out are the Alpha Clubs, offering reasonably priced sporting facilities to nearly 20,000 members in Puebla: gyms and fitness centers, swimming pools, basketball courts, and soccer fields. While Espinosa rather neglected them, under Bill Jenkins—who assumed control of his grandfather's bequest in 2002—the sites have been refurbished and a fourth club added. Hundreds of talented children from low-income homes now benefit from the facilities, thanks to annual tryouts for scholarships.[16]

What would have dismayed its founder is his family's infighting over the direction and control of the foundation, which erupted in 2013.[17] Yet the foundation's governance problems, which date from the Espinosa era, are by no means unique. At heart, they reflect an enduring ambivalence in Mexico toward philanthropy. On the one hand, the country has little tradition of altruistic, disinterested giving. Of course, even the robber barons had ulterior motives: they hoped that their foundations would burnish their reputations and that their universities would promote their belief in unfettered capitalism. But they generally did not seek to profit from them on the sly.[18]

In Mexico, it is typically assumed that foundations seek above all to advance their creators' business interests. This attitude, cynical but often founded, in turn feeds a public reluctance to support nonprofit initiatives. A dismal record of alumni giving to private universities, including the UDLAP, is a case in point.[19]

In 1988 the philanthropist and retail magnate Manuel Arango founded the Mexican Center for Philanthropy (CEMEFI), aiming to promote corporate giving. CEMEFI has made strides in helping to create a favorable legal and tax environment, which has seen foundations and other nonprofits multiply in subsequent decades. But its staff and other advocates admit that Mexican philanthropy remains very weak. Within foundations, a lack of transparency and able personnel present major obstacles to its strengthening.[20]

Should the Jenkins family eventually opt for an independent board and a more formal and transparent giving agenda, the Mary Street Jenkins Foundation, which with an endowment of some $750 million remains one of the country's largest foundations, could help set the stage for a new era of Mexican philanthropy. Such an advance would constitute a fitting echo of what William O. Jenkins did, when he willed away his fortune and created Mexico's first endowment-based charity.

Acknowledgments

IN MEXICO IT is rare that business leaders or their families entrust a biographer with full access without demanding right of approval. The descendants of William O. Jenkins did just that, so it is to them above all that this book owes its existence. Seventeen members of the extended family took part, often granting multiple interviews. Our conversations were marked by great frankness, a tone set by Jenkins's last surviving daughter and her husband, Jane and Ronald Eustace of Puebla (both since deceased), and continued by two grandchildren, William A. Jenkins (recently deceased) and Rosemary Eustace Jenkins, both of Mexico City. No family member attempted to exert control over content, even though they knew that some of what I wrote might be uncomfortable for them to read. I offer my sincere thanks to each.

Thanks are due next to Sergio Guzmán Ramos and Manuel Mestre, who were similarly and frequently helpful. I also met more than once with Eusebio Benítez, former Atencingo employee and union leader; Enrique Cárdenas, former rector of the UDLAP; Alfonso Gómez Rossi, Puebla businessman and columnist; Francisco Pérez Vega, grandson of Manuel Pérez; Fernando Ramírez Camarillo, former mayor of Chietla; and Manuel Sánchez Pontón, dean of Puebla journalists. Each interviewee appears in the Bibliography, and I am grateful to all of them.

The development of this book was aided immensely by three generous historians. Alex Saragoza fostered my initial interest in Jenkins more than twenty years ago. Later, as my advisor at Berkeley, he introduced me to the seminal texts of modern Mexican history. David LaFrance offered guidance in Puebla and shared with me his prodigious collection of notecards, which saved me months of context-establishing work. His trilogy on revolutionary Puebla (with Part 3 in the works) constitutes the definitive history of this important state for 1908 to 1937. Mauricio Tenorio shepherded this project after I moved from Berkeley to Austin. He goaded my analysis in fruitful directions, such as exploring the parallels between US and Mexican history, and remained vigilant after his move to the University of Chicago.

Many other historians have played key roles in this project. I am particularly grateful to Margaret Chowning and Louis Segal at Berkeley and Jonathan Brown at UT Austin. Among faculty at the Oaxaca Summer Institute of 2001, I had guidance from William Beezley, John Hart, Gil Joseph, the late Paul Vanderwood, Mary Kay Vaughan, and Alan Knight, who has continued to provide insights since. I also owe thanks to UT faculty H. W. Brands, Richard Pells, and, for helping me understand the Mexico before typewriters, Susan Deans-Smith.

In Puebla, academics who were generous with advice begin with Leticia Gamboa Ojeda and include Guadalupe Cano, Gonzalo Castañeda, Francisco Gómez Carpinteiro, Alexis Juárez, Humberto Morales, John Mraz, José Luis Sánchez Gavi, and Blanca Santibáñez. In Mexico City, I received generous advice from Gustavo del Ángel and Aurora Gómez-Galvarriato and further help from Blanca de Lizaur and family, Graciela Márquez, Francisco Peredo, Gabriela Recio, María Eugenia Romero, Ilán Semo, and Elisa Servín.

My work has also been enriched with help and advice from Rob Alegre, Ryan Alexander, Ted Beatty, Dina Berger, Jeff Bortz, Jürgen Buchenau, Raymond Buve, Barry Carr, Greg Crider, Jay Dwyer, Michael Ervin, Seth Fein, José Galindo, Ariadna García, Susan Gauss, Paul Gillingham, Stephen Haber, Patrick Iber, Lance Ingwersen, Halbert Jones, Juliette Levy, Renata Keller, David Luhnow, David Maciel, Gladys McCormick, Sandra Mendiola, Pablo Mijangos, Nicole Mottier, María Muñoz, Aaron Navarro, Verónica Oikión, Wil Pansters, Pablo Piccato, Gretchen Pierce, Enrique Plasencia, Alejandro Quintana, Monica Rankin, Thom Rath, Anne Rubenstein, Gema Santamaría, Arthur Schmidt, Laura Serna, Ben Smith, Daniela Spenser, David Tamayo, Christy Tharenos, Aurea Toxqui, John Womack, Drew Wood, Eddie Wright-Ríos, and Eric Zolov.

Among archivists whose expertise was vital to this project stands out Roberto Beristáin, formerly of Mexico's national archive, the AGN; I was also aided there by Alberto Álvarez, Raimundo Álvarez, Erika Gutiérrez, José Zavala, and freelance researcher Ángeles Magdaleno. I received further help from Enrique Cervantes at the Biblioteca Nacional; Guadalupe Bracho at the Archivo Calles-Torreblanca; Alfredo Díaz at the Archivo Aarón Sáenz; and Juan Manuel Herrera at the Biblioteca Lerdo. In Puebla I was aided by Edmundo Bautista of the Jenkins Foundation, Alejandro

Pacheco, and Javier Quintana. In Michoacán, I had help from Arturo Herrera Cornejo.

Walter Brem at the Bancroft Library, Berkeley, and Adán Benavides at the Benson Collection, Austin, gave guidance over many years. In Tennesse, I was aided by Lyle Lankford of Public Affairs and Teresa Gray of Special Collections at Vanderbilt; genealogist Marilyn Parker in Shelbyville; and Anne Toplovich at the Tennessee Historical Society. At the US National Archives, I was greatly helped by Amy Reytar and at the University of Florida by Flo Turcotte of Special Collections and Keith Manuel. At Millsaps College, I enjoyed guidance and an introduction to Oxford University Press (OUP) from fellow biographer William Storey; sterling service from librarian Tom Henderson; and vital support from Eric and Kathi Griffin, George Bey, and Abigail Susik.

Since 2014 I have been blessed to work at the Center for Research and Teaching in Economics (CIDE) in Mexico. I am grateful both to the CIDE and to the National System of Researchers (SNI) for backing my research with substantial resources. I am especially thankful for support from my old friend Pablo Mijangos, my new friend Michael K. Bess, my research assistants Fernanda Fraga and Berenice Hernández, and my department head Luis Barrón.

My editors Susan Ferber at OUP and Enrique Calderón and Cynthia Chávez at Penguin Random House have been a pleasure to work with. I am especially grateful to Susan, for nudging me to make all the necessary cuts to what was once a Tolstoyan manuscript of 315,000 words. (Academic readers who wish I had said more about X will soon find me doing so in journal articles and edited-volume chapters; there are several already in the Bibliography.) My translator for the Spanish edition, Sandra Strikovsky, gave outstanding and very prompt service.

This book has benefitted greatly from the feedback of those who read all or parts of it. They begin with my UT colleagues Chris Albi, Byron Crites, Matthew Gildner, and Meredith Glueck and continue with Rob Alegre, H. W. Brands, Paul Garner, Susan Gauss, Paul Gillingham, Barbara Kastelein, David LaFrance, David Lida, Sandra Mendiola, Gretchen Pierce, and my brother Jon Paxman. Five kindly commented on the entire text: my father, Edward Pratt; the indefatigable Barry Carr and Ben Smith; and the anonymous reviewers for OUP.

Many friends gave me *posada* during research, writing, and conference trips: my family in England; Shayne McGuire and Alejandra Murga in Austin; Mirella Alegre in Hackensack; Bettina and Richard Collins in Los

Angeles; Alberto Sánchez in Montreal; Patty and Bill King in Shelbyville; Anne Wakefield and Ned Hoyt in Washington; and, in Mexico City, above all, *mis compadres* David Luhnow and Helena Wygard, and also Lucy Conger, David Lida, Barbara Kastelein, Elisabeth Malkin and Eduardo García, Jan Richards, Susana Seijas, Aurélie Semichon, the late Tony Wakefield, and Andrew and Ros Wygard. For support and friendship while living in Puebla, I thank Ana Salazar, Rodolfo García Hernández, Vero Centeno, and Trini Hernández.

For love, patience, and encouragement in the book's final stages, I am indebted to my wife, Itzel Antuna.

This book is dedicated to my father, my first teacher.

Notes

INTRODUCTION

1. Impressions of Jenkins in 1960 draw from multiple interviews with Jane Jenkins Eustace and Ronald Eustace, Puebla, 2001–2008; William Anstead Jenkins, Mexico City/Puebla, 2001–2012; Sergio Guzmán Ramos, Puebla, 2001–2009; Manuel Mestre, Mexico City, 2003–2009; and Manuel Sánchez Pontón, Puebla, 2006–2008.

2. Renata Keller, *Mexico's Cold War: Cuba, the United States, and the Legacy of the Mexican Revolution* (New York: Cambridge Univ. Press, 2015); Ana Covarrubias, "La política exterior," in *Adolfo López Mateos: Una vida dedicada a la política*, ed. R. Hernández Rodríguez (Mexico City: Colegio de México, 2015).

3. *Excélsior* (Mexico City), 8 Jun. 1960, 1; Enrique Krauze, *Mexico: Biography of Power* (New York: HarperCollins), 694.

4. *Política* (Mexico City), 1 Jun. 1960, 27–9; cf. 15 Jun., 9; 1 Jul., 9; 1 Aug., 11f.

5. Miguel Contreras Torres, *El libro negro del cine mexicano* (Mexico City: n.p., 1960), 409.

6. "Meet Mr. Jenkins," *Time*, 26 Dec. 1960, 25f.

7. Branscomb to *Time*, Nashville, 6 Jan. 1961, RG 300/Branscomb (hereafter, Branscomb Papers), Vanderbilt Univ., Box 362, File 2.

8. Cosío Villegas, "Mexico's Crisis" (1947), in *Is the Mexican Revolution Dead?*, ed. S. Ross (New York: Knopf, 1966).

9. See, e.g., Adolfo Gilly, *La revolución interrumpida* (Mexico City: El Caballito, 1971); Jean Meyer, *La revolución mejicana, 1910–1940* (Barcelona: DOPESA, 1973); Ramón Ruiz, *The Great Rebellion: Mexico, 1905–1924* (New York: Norton, 1980); John Womack, "The Mexican Revolution," in *Cambridge History of Latin America, Vol. V*, ed. L. Bethell (Cambridge: Cambridge Univ. Press, 1986); Mark Wasserman, *Persistent Oligarchs: Elites and Politics in Chihuahua, Mexico, 1910–1940* (Durham, NC: Duke Univ. Press, 1993).

10. Nora Hamilton, *The Limits of State Autonomy: Post-Revolutionary Mexico* (Princeton, NJ: Princeton Univ. Press, 1982); Alan Knight, "*Cardenismo*: Juggernaut or Jalopy?," *Journal of Latin American Studies* 26:1 (1994).

11. I elaborate on my concepts "symbiotic imperative" and "symbiotic convenience" in "Simbiosis imperativa y conveniente: la evolución del capitalismo de cuates en Puebla," *Istor* 68 (Spring 2017).

12. Hamilton, *Limits of State Autonomy*; Alex Saragoza, *The Monterrey Elite and the Mexican State, 1880–1940* (Austin: Univ. of Texas Press, 1988); Stephen Haber, *Industry and Underdevelopment: The Industrialization of Mexico, 1890–1940* (Stanford, CA: Stanford Univ. Press, 1989); Noel Maurer, *The Power and the Money: The Mexican Financial System, 1876–1932* (Stanford, CA: Stanford Univ. Press, 2002).

13. For the Porfiriato and 1920s, see Stephen Haber, Armando Razo, and Noel Maurer, *The Politics of Property Rights: Political Instability, Credible Commitments and Economic Growth in Mexico, 1876–1929* (Cambridge: Cambridge Univ. Press, 2003); for Alemán, see Stephen Niblo, *War, Diplomacy, and Development: The United States and Mexico, 1938–1954* (Wilmington, DE: SR Books, 1995), 221–44, and *Mexico in the 1940s* (Wilmington, DE: SR Books, 1999), 207–16, 253–303.

14. See, e.g., Jeffrey Rubin, *Decentering the Regime: Ethnicity, Radicalism, and Democracy in Juchitán, Mexico* (Durham, NC: Duke Univ. Press, 1997); Jürgen Buchenau and William Beezley, eds., *State Governors in the Mexican Revolution, 1910–1952* (Lanham, MD: Rowman & Littlefield, 2009); Paul Gillingham and Benjamin T. Smith, eds., *Dictablanda: Politics, Work, and Culture in Mexico, 1938–1968* (Durham, NC: Duke Univ. Press, 2014).

15. Knight, "*Cardenismo*: Juggernaut or Jalopy?," 100–5.

16. Wil Pansters, *Politics and Power in Puebla: The Political History of a Mexican State, 1937–1987* (Amsterdam: CEDLA, 1990): 88–95, 100–2, 106f; Susan Gauss, *Made in Mexico: Regions, Nation, and the State in the Rise of Mexican Industrialism, 1920s–1940s* (University Park: Pennsylvania State Press, 2010).

17. For example: Sergio Valencia Castrejón, *Poder regional y política nacional en México: El gobierno de Maximino Ávila Camacho en Puebla* (Mexico City: INEHRM, 1996); María Teresa Bonilla Fernández, *El secuestro del poder: El caso William O. Jenkins* (Puebla: UAP, 2004); *Proceso* (Mexico City), 11 Aug. 1980, 16–18.

18. The few studies of Mexican opinions of the United States include Alan Knight, *US–Mexican Relations, 1910–1940* (La Jolla, CA: Center for US–Mexican Studies, 1987), chs. III–V; Stephen Morris, *Gringolandia: Mexican Identity and Perceptions of the United States* (Lanham, MD: Rowman & Littlefield, 2005).

19. *The Economist*, 1 May 1993, 76.

20. María Inés Barbero, "Business History in Latin America," in *Business History around the World*, ed. F. Amatori and G. Jones (Cambridge: Cambridge Univ. Press, 2003), 333; David Winder, "Mexico," in *Innovation in Strategic Philanthropy*, ed. H. Anheier et al. (New York: Springer, 2007).

21. Conversation with Edmundo Bautista, Mary Street Jenkins Foundation, Puebla, 24 May 2006.

22. Interview with Pilar Pacheco, State of Puebla General Archive, Puebla, 27 Apr. 2006.

23. Jenkins to Juan Posada Noriega, Puebla, 22 Jun. 1943, Rosemary Eustace Jenkins Papers (hereafter REJP), held by R. Eustace Jenkins, Mexico City; Jenkins to Luis Castro (1948), quoted in *El Sol de Puebla*, 5 Jun. 1963, 1.

CHAPTER 1

1. *Bedford County, Tennessee: Family History Book* (Paducah, KY: Turner Publishing, 2002), 136, 331.

2. J. Jenkins Eustace and R. Eustace interviews, 2 Apr. and 27 Jun. 2001, 10 Apr. 2002.

3. *Bedford County*, 331; Allen Shoffner, *A Bicentennial History of Shofner's Lutheran Church* (Shelbyville, TN: n.p., 2008), 39–47.

4. *Excélsior*, 5 Jun. 1963, 5; *Novedades* (Mexico City), 5 Jun., 1; *El Sol de Puebla*, 5 Jun., 1; *La Opinión* (Puebla), 5 Jun., 1; *El Día* (Mexico City), 6 Jun., 3; *El Universal* (Mexico City), 7 Jun., 13.

5. Robert Corlew, *Tennessee: A Short History* (Knoxville: Univ. of Tennessee Press, 1981), 8, 11; *Historical Atlas of the United States* (New York: Henry Holt, 1953), 68–71, 90f; *Bedford County*, 7f.

6. *Bedford County*, 7–10.

7. The sketch of Rev. Jenkins's career draws on *Bedford County*, 101, 123, 136f, 331; Shoffner, *Bicentennial History*, 39–42; Richard Smith, "Pastor William Jenkins" (lecture), Shelbyville, 2 Jun. 1996.

8. James Blanks, ed., *The Shofner Family Genealogy* (Bountiful, UT: Family History Publishers, 1989), 1–4, 159; Margaret Shoffner DeMoss, *Shoffner Family History* (Tennessee: n.p., 1971), 10–19; *Bedford County*, 101, 136.

9. DeMoss, *Shoffner Family History*, 71; Joe Ingram, "An Educational History of Shelbyville, Tennessee, 1870–1954" (MEd thesis, George Peabody College, Nashville, 1954), 17.

10. Stephen Ash, *Middle Tennessee Society Transformed, 1860–1870* (Baton Rouge: Louisiana State Univ. Press, 1988), 74–7, 82, 143–74; Timothy and Helen Marsh, "Bedford County," and Larry Whiteaker, "Civil War," in *Tennessee Encyclopedia of History and Culture*, http://tennesseeencyclopedia.net/entry.php?rec=69 & rec=265.

11. Neal O'Steen, *Bedford County Civil War Transcriptions from Various Sources* (Knoxville, TN: n.p., n.d.), 102; *Tennesseans in the Civil War* (Nashville: Civil War Centennial Commission, 1964), I:329, II:364, 532, 582; Blanks, ed., *Shofner Family Genealogy*, 235; *Eighth Census of the United States* (Washington, DC: Bureau of the Census, 1860), Dist. 25, Bedford, TN; roll: M653-1239, 168; J. Jenkins Eustace interview, 2 Apr. 2001; interview with Allen Shoffner of Shelbyville, TN (by telephone), 30 Jul. 2012.

12. The sketch of John Whitson Jenkins draws on: Blanks, *Shofner Family Genealogy*, 225f, 247; DeMoss, *Shoffner Family History*, 79; Jerry Cook, *Historic Normandy* (Normandy, TN: n.p., 1976), 35, 76; J. Jenkins Eustace interview, 2 Apr. 2001; interview with Betty Shofner (JWJ's granddaughter-in-law), Shelbyville, TN, 11 Jul. 2004.

13. Connie Lester, *Up from the Mudsills of Hell: The Farmers' Alliance, Populism, and Progressive Agriculture in Tennessee, 1870–1915* (Athens: Univ. of Georgia Press, 2006), ch. 1; Corlew, *Tennessee*, 367–70.

14. Quoted in Shoffner, *Bicentennial History*, 43.

15. *Ninth Census* (Washington, DC: Bureau of the Census, 1870), Dist. 25, Bedford, TN; roll: M593-1514, 435.

16. Photograph of "The Jenkins School," n.d. (c. 1888), Mary Street Jenkins Papers (hereafter MSJP), held by Rosemary Eustace Jenkins, Mexico City; *Bedford County*, 332.

17. William Jenkins to Mary Street, Bedford Co., 30 Sep. 1899 (title indicated in letterhead), MSJP.

18. W. O. Jenkins's childhood draws on *Shelbyville Times-Gazette*, 5 Jun. 1963, 1 (obit.); *Nashville Tennessean*, 28 Jun. 1964, mag. 5; Jenkins to Street, 6 Sep. 1900, 14 Jul., 4 and 8 Aug. 1901, MSJP; Rosemary Eustace Jenkins, ed., *Tennessee Sunshine: Oscar's Love Letters to Mary* (Mexico City: n.p., 2012), 325; J. Jenkins Eustace interviews, 2 Apr. and 15 Aug. 2001; Shofner interview, 11 Jul. 2004.

19. Cash, *The Mind of the South* (New York: Vintage, 1991 [1941]), 150f.

20. H.W. Brands, *The Reckless Decade: America in the 1890s* (Chicago: Univ. of Chicago Press, 2002 [1995]), esp. 177–82, 329–35; Corlew, *Tennessee*, 368–70, 380.

21. On Jenkins's high-school years: Jenkins to Street, 2 Jul., 22 Dec. 1899, 25 Jun., 8 Jul. 1900, 11 Aug. 1901, MSJP; Eustace Jenkins, *Tennessee Sunshine*, 326; J. Jenkins Eustace interview, 2 Apr. 2001.

22. Laurence McMillin, *The Schoolmaker: Sawney Webb and the Bell Buckle Story* (Chapel Hill: Univ. of North Carolina Press, 1971); School Registry (1870–1935), The Webb School, Bell Buckle, TN, 89.

23. Mary's childhood draws on Helen Marsh and Timothy Marsh, eds., *Cemetery Records of Bedford County* (Shelbyville, TN: Marsh Historical, 1976), 268; Ann Street to Mary Street, 1895–97, Clear Water Harbor, FL, MSJP; *Lincoln Lineage* (Fayetteville, TN) 1:1 (1998), 17; School Registry, Webb School, 89, 94; J. Jenkins Eustace interview, 2 Apr. 2001. John William Street was born to a planter family in Mississippi that owned fifteen slaves; Henry and Mary Street, *The Street Genealogy* (Exeter, NH: News-Letter Press, 1895), 328–32; *Eighth Census* (1860), Tishomingo Co., MS; roll: M653 (slave schedule); *Ninth Census* (1870), Prentiss Co., MS; roll: M593-746, 415B.

24. Jenkins to Street, 13 Jun. 1899 to 24 Sep. 1901, MSJP. As subsequently, my references to the content of Mary's letters are based on quotations in and inferences from his.

25. Jenkins to Street, 13 and 23 Jun., 2, 11, 22 and 31 Jul., 8 Aug. 1899, MSJP.

26. Jenkins to Street, 11 Jul. 1899, MSJP.

27. Jenkins to Street, 30 Sep., 11 and 19 Oct., 22 Dec. 1899, MSJP; Marsh and Marsh, *Cemetery Records*, 313.

28. Ruth Miller Elson, *Guardians of Tradition: American Schoolbooks of the Nineteenth Century* (Lincoln: Univ. of Nebraska Press, 1964), 70, 75f, 101f, 154–61; Benjamin Keen, "The Black Legend Revisited," *Hispanic American Historical Review (HAHR)* 49:4 (1969).

29. In his junior-year finals, he scored 93 percent in history; Jenkins to Street, 13 Jun. 1900, MSJP.

30. John J. Anderson, *A Popular School History of the United States* (New York, 1880), quoted in Kyle Ward, *History in the Making* (New York: New Press, 2006), 154f. See also Elson, *Guardians of Tradition*, 331f.

31. Elson, *Guardians of Tradition*, 1–4; *Petersburg History* (Petersburg, TN: n.p., 1986), 59; R. K. Morgan obit., 2 Jul. 1935, Morgan School Museum, Petersburg, TN, Morgan Book 4; Landrith synopsis, 25 Mar. 1900, MSJP.

32. *The Shelbyville Gazette*, 5 Oct. 1899, 1.

33. Robert May, *The Southern Dream of a Caribbean Empire, 1854–1861* (Athens: Univ. of Georgia Press, 1989 [1973]), chs. IV and V; Frederick Rosengarten, *Freebooters Must Die!: The Life and Death of William Walker* (Wayne, PA: Haverford House, 1976), 211–16.

34. Andrew Rolle, *The Lost Cause: The Confederate Exodus to Mexico* (Norman: Univ. of Oklahoma, 1965).

35. Robert Holden, *Mexico and the Survey of Public Lands* (DeKalb: Northern Illinois Univ. Press, 1994), 14–16, 42–8; John Hart, *Empire and Revolution: The Americans in Mexico since the Civil War* (Berkeley: Univ. of California Press, 2002), chs. 4, 5, 6, and 8; William Beezley, "The Porfirian Paradigm," lecture, UC Berkeley, 6 Oct. 2001.

36. "Cooper, Henry," *Biographical Directory of the United States Congress*, http://biodisplay.pl?index=C000751; author's observation, Shelbyville, 8 Jul. 2004.

37. Ivie to J.W. Jenkins, 24 May 1900; Jenkins to Street, 30 May, 6 Jun., 5 and 17 Aug. 1900, 14 Jul., 20 Aug. 1901, MSJP.

38. Jenkins to Street, 6 and 13 Jun. 1900, MSJP.

39. Jenkins to Street, 30 May, 6, 20 and 29 Jun., 5 Aug. 1900, MSJP.

40. Jenkins to Street, 6, 17 and 29 Jun., 19 and 30 Jul., 9 Aug. 1900, MSJP.

41. Jenkins to Street, 25 Jun. 1900, MSJP.

42. Jenkins to Street, 29 Jun. 1900, MSJP.

43. Jenkins to Street, 19 Jul., 5, 17 and 24 Aug., 6 Sep. 1900, MSJP.

44. Jenkins to Street, 9 Aug. 1900, MSJP.

45. Corlew, *Tennessee*, 295, 337, 362f; Ash, *Middle Tennessee*, 82, 97f, 146; Lester, *Up from the Mudsills*, 18–20; *Lincoln Lineage* 1:1, 10f; Jack and June Towry, "Lincoln

County," in *Tennessee Encyclopedia of History and Culture*, http://tennesseeency-clopedia.net/entry.php?rec=789; Jenkins to Street, 31 Aug. 1901, MSJP; interview with Dick Poplin (Bedford County historian), Shelbyville, TN, 8 Jul. 2004.

46. "Will of John Whitaker," in Gwen Coble Whitaker, *Whitaker: A Line from Pleasant Garden* (Lewisburg, TN: n.p., 1991), 28f; *Seventh Census* (Washington, DC: Bureau of the Census, 1850), Subdiv. 2, Lincoln, TN, roll: M432-887, 19, 33; *Eighth Census* (1860), Dist. 7, Lincoln, TN; roll: M653-1261, 65, 70; *Membership Roster and Soldiers* (Tennessee DAR, 1985), 729; *Lincoln Lineage* 1:1, 12, 14, 17; Towry, "Lincoln County"; J. Jenkins Eustace interview, 2 Apr. 2001; interview with Lainey Rodes (Lincoln Genealogical Soc.), Fayetteville, TN, 9 Jul. 2004.

47. Jenkins to Street, 17 and 30 Aug. 1900, MSJP.

48. Paul Conklin, *Gone with the Ivy: A Biography of Vanderbilt University* (Knoxville: Univ. of Tennessee Press, 1985), ch. 1 (quotation: 17); Matthew Josephson, *The Robber Barons: The Great American Capitalists, 1861–1901* (Norwalk, CT: Easton Press, 1962 [1934]), esp. 315–25.

49. Quoted in Orison Swett Marden, *How They Succeeded* (Boston: Lothrop, 1901), 207.

50. Conklin, *Gone with the Ivy*, chs. 2 and 5 to 8; *Register of Vanderbilt University for 1899–1900* (Nashville, 1900), 3f, 7, 24; Jenkins to Street, 19 and 21 Jul. 1901, MSJP.

51. Corlew, *Tennessee*, 347f, 365; Lester, *Up from the Mudsills*, 10f, 170, 212f; Conklin, *Gone with the Ivy*, 129.

52. Don Doyle, *Nashville in the New South, 1880–1930* (Knoxville: Univ. of Tennessee Press, 1985), xiv, 63–7, 74–83, 235.

53. *Register for 1899–1900*, 31; *The Comet 1901* (Nashville: Vanderbilt Univ., 1901), 57; Jenkins to Street, 24 Aug. 1900, 8 Sep. 1901, MSJP; Tigert to Hill Turner, Gainesville, 25 Nov. 1944, John J. Tigert Papers, University of Florida (hereafter, Tigert Papers); Eustace Jenkins, *Tennessee Sunshine*, 326; J. Jenkins Eustace interview, 2 Apr. 2001. Vanderbilt also offered loans; *Register*, 32.

54. *The Comet 1901*, 58, 138, 237, 247; Jenkins to Street, 12 and 16 Sep. 1900, MSJP; Frank Houston, "Memorandum on Oscar Jenkins," 17 Jul. 1967, Alumni Relations (RG 935/Jenkins), Vanderbilt Univ.; Tigert to Turner, 25 Nov. 1944, Tigert Papers; "Guide to the John James Tigert Papers," http://web.uflib.ufl.edu/spec/archome/Seriesp8.htm.

55. Jenkins to Street, 16 Sep. 1900, MSJP; *The Comet 1901*, 64, 98; 4(Nashville, 1901), 146, 159; the Mexicans were José Díaz de León (engineering) and Rafael M. Ramos (dentistry).

56. Jenkins to Street, 16 Sep. 1900, MSJP; *The Comet 1901*, 55–8.

57. Fred Russell and Maxwell Benson, *50 Years of Vanderbilt Football* (Nashville: n.p., 1938), 16; Conklin, *Gone with the Ivy*, 137–42; Houston, "Memorandum on Oscar Jenkins"; *Nashville Banner*, 12 Nov. 1900, and *Nashville American*, 18 and 30 Nov. 1900, MSJP.

58. *The Comet 1901*, 57; *Register for 1899–1900*, 53; Tigert to Turner, 25 Nov. 1944, Tigert Papers; *Nashville Tennessean*, 28 Jun. 1964, mag. 16; Eustace, quoted in Eustace Jenkins, ed., *Tennessee Sunshine*, 326.

59. Jenkins to Street, 23 and 25 Dec. 1900, MSJP.

60. Peoples to Jenkins, Fayetteville, TN, 16 Feb. 1901, MSJP; Jenkins to Street, 20 Jun., 12 and 28 Jul. 1901, MSJP.

61. Stone to Jenkins, Fayetteville, TN, 30 Jun. 1901, Jenkins to Street, 25 Dec. 1900, 21 and 22 Jun. 1901, MSJP.

62. Jenkins to Street, 21, 22, 23, 26 and 28 Jun., 14 Jul., 4, 5 and 13 Aug. 1901, MSJP.

63. Jenkins to Street, 30 Jun., 2 Jul. 1901, MSJP.

64. Jenkins to Street, 7 Sep. 1901, MSJP.

65. Jenkins to Street, 8 Aug. 1901, MSJP.

66. Jenkins to Street, 11 Aug. 1901, MSJP; Mrs. Craik, *John Halifax, Gentleman* (1856); Max Weber, *The Protestant Ethic and the Spirit of Capitalism* (1905).

67. Jenkins to Street, 30 Jun., 24 and 19 Jul., 8, 11 and 18 Aug. 1901, MSJP; Maurice Thompson, *Alice of Old Vincennes* (1900).

68. Jenkins to Street, 20 Jun. 1900, MSJP; J. Jenkins Eustace interview, 2 Apr. 2001.

69. Jenkins to Street, 22, 23, and 30 Jun., 14 Jul., 8 Aug. 1901, MSJP.

70. Jenkins to Street, 18 Jul. 1901, MSJP.

71. Corlew, *Tennessee*, 361–4; Brands, *Reckless Decade*, ch. 6.

72. Jenkins to Street, 12, 15, and 28 Jul., 31 Aug., 1 Sep. 1901; "Shofner Reunion" (invitation), encl. in 28 Jul.

73. Jenkins to Street, 16 and 21 Jul. 1901, MSJP.

74. Jenkins to Street, 24 Jul. 1901, MSJP. William quotes much of Mary's preceding letter, which is lost.

75. Jenkins to Street, 2 Jul., 1 Aug. 1901, MSJP.

76. Jenkins to Street, 11 and 25 Aug. 1901, MSJP; alluding to Gen. 29:14–30, Jenkins writes Sarah but means Rachel.

77. Jenkins to Street, 20 Aug., 8, 9 and 13 Sep. 1901, MSJP.

78. Jenkins to Street, 28 Jul., 16 and 17 Sep. 1901, MSJP; J. S. Borgerhoff to Jenkins, Nashville, 16 Jul. 1901, MSJP.

79. Jenkins to Street, 17 Sep. 1901, MSJP.

80. Houston, "Memorandum"; *Nashville Tennessean*, 28 Jun. 1964, mag. 16; J. Jenkins Eustace interview, 2 Apr. 2001.

81. Jenkins to Street, 15 Jul., 24 Sep. (envelope) 1901, MSJP.

82. Marriage Certificate, Nashville, 26 Sep. 1901, MSJP; "Jenkins-Street," *Nashville Banner*, 27 Sep. 1901 (evening), 7; *Nashville Tennessean*, 28 Jun. 1964, mag. 16.

83. Helen and Timothy Marsh, *Tennesseans in Texas* (Easley, SC: Southern Historical Press, 1986), iii; Corlew, *Tennessee*, 190–3; Marilyn Parker (genealogist), Shelbyville, TN to author, 24 May 2004.

84. T. R. Fehrenbach, *The San Antonio Story* (Tulsa, OK: Continental Heritage, 1978), 140–59; Randolph Campbell, *Gone to Texas: A History of the Lone Star State*

(New York: Oxford Univ. Press, 2003), 307 (map); Marsh and Marsh, *Tennesseans in Texas*, 37f, 72, etc.; Street and Street, *Street Genealogy*, 329f.

85. Jenkins to Street, 24 and 31 Jul., 25 Aug., 6 Sep. 1901, MSJP; "There are two people . . .," 31 Jul.

86. *Shelbyville Times-Gazette*, 5 Jun. 1963, 2; *Nashville Tennessean*, 28 Jun. 1964, mag. 16.

87. *Nashville Tennessean*, 28 Jun. 1964, mag. 16; J. Jenkins Eustace interview, 2 Apr. 2001; Eustace Jenkins, *Tennessee Sunshine*, 326; Borgerhoff to Jenkins, 16 Jul. 1901, MSJP.

88. Chester Lloyd Jones interview of Jenkins, Puebla, 13 May 1918, Doheny Collection, Occidental College, Los Angeles, Series J, unmarked box, interview 765, 11630; J. Jenkins Eustace interview, 2 Apr. 2001.

89. On the popularity of the Guadalupe cult, c. 1900: D. A. Brading, *Mexican Phoenix: Our Lady of Guadalupe: Image and Tradition across Five Centuries* (Cambridge: Cambridge Univ. Press, 2001), ch. 12.

90. Jonathan Brown, *Oil and Revolution in Mexico* (Berkeley: Univ. of California Press, 1993), 7f, 29, 81, 87; Saragoza, *Monterrey Elite*, 71, 85.

91. John Hart, *Empire and Revolution*, chs. 3–8; Sandra Kuntz Ficker, "De las reformas liberales a la gran depresión," in Kuntz, ed., *Historia mínima de la economía mexicana, 1519–2010* (Mexico City: Colegio de México, 2012), 148–97; William Beezley, *Judas at the Jockey Club* (Lincoln: Univ. of Nebraska Press, 2004), ch. 1.

CHAPTER 2

1. The sketch of Porfirian Mexico draws on Friedrich Katz, "The Liberal Republic and the Porfiriato," in L. Bethell, ed., *Mexico Since Independence* (Cambridge: Cambridge Univ. Press, 1991); Michael Johns, *The City of Mexico in the Age of Díaz* (Austin: Univ. of Texas Press, 1997); Mark Wasserman, *Everyday Life and Politics in Nineteenth Century Mexico* (Albuquerque: Univ. of New Mexico Press, 2000), ch. 9; Paul Garner, *Porfirio Díaz* (London: Longman, 2001); Mauricio Tenorio and Aurora Gómez Galvarriato, *El Porfiriato* (Mexico City: FCE, 2006), ch. 1.

2. Charles A. Hale, *The Transformation of Liberalism in Late Nineteenth-Century Mexico* (Princeton, NJ: Princeton Univ. Press, 1989), ch. 7; Spencer, *The Principles of Sociology* (1895), quoted in S. J. Gould, *The Mismeasure of Man* (New York: W. W. Norton, 1996), 146; Gregory Gilson and Irving Levinson, eds., *Latin American Positivism* (Lanham, MD: Lexington Books, 2013), ix, 14, 53–6.

3. Sumner, *What Social Classes Owe to Each Other* (Caldwell, ID: Caxton, 1995 [1883]), 34–7, 114; Josephson, *Robber Barons*, 11f, 32f, 315–25; Saragoza, *Monterrey Elite*, ch. 3; Leticia Gamboa Ojeda, *Los empresarios del ayer: El grupo dominante en la industria textil de Puebla, 1906–1929* (Puebla: Univ. Autónoma de Puebla, 1985), ch. 3; Ann Blum, "Conspicuous Benevolence: Liberalism, Public

Welfare, and Private Charity in Porfirian Mexico, 1877–1910," *The Americas* 58:1 (2001); Johns, *Mexico City*, 53–7, 70.

4. William Schell, *Integral Outsiders: The American Colony in Mexico City, 1876–1911* (Wilmington, DE: SR Books, 2001), 73, 77f, 80–101; Paul Garner, *British Lions and Mexican Eagles: Business, Politics, and Empire in the Career of Weetman Pearson in Mexico, 1889–1919* (Stanford, CA: Stanford Univ. Press, 2011), 70–5; Hart, *Empire and Revolution*, 103f, 123, 201.

5. Schell, *Integral Outsiders*, 14–16, 50, 113f, 175; Hart, *Empire and Revolution*, chs. 6–8 (esp. 180–3, 195–200, 227–30, 260); Garner, *Porfirio Díaz*, 124–7, 130–3, 205–9; Mark Wasserman, *Pesos and Politics: Business, Elites, Foreigners, and Government in Mexico, 1854–1940* (Stanford, CA: Stanford Univ. Press, 2015), chs. 4 and 5.

6. Saragoza, *Monterrey Elite*, chs. 1 and 2; cf. Fehrenbach, *San Antonio Story*, 155.

7. Saragoza, *Monterrey Elite*, 41, 85, 218 fn 38.

8. Jenkins to Mamie Jenkins, Monterrey, 7 Oct. 1903, in Rosemary Jenkins Eustace, ed., *Tennessee Sunshine*, 366; Dept. of State, Bureau of Appointments, memo: "William Oscar Jenkins" [1918], Secretaría de Relaciones Exteriores, Archivo Histórico (hereafter, SRE), 42-26-95; *Time*, 26 Dec. 1960, 25; J. Jenkins Eustace interview, 2 Apr. 2001.

9. Jenkins to Jenkins, 7 Oct. 1903, in Jenkins Eustace, *Tennessee Sunshine*, 366f.

10. J. Jenkins Eustace interviews, 2 Apr. and 15 Aug. 2001.

11. Quoted by Kate Shofner, *Nashville Tennessean*, 28 Jun. 1964, mag. 17.

12. Jenkins to Arnold Shanklin, Puebla, 7 Jan. 1915, Records of US Dept. of State (NARA Record Group 59; hereafter, RDS), 812.00/14285; envelope embossed with "Minas Bonanza y Anexas / Guggenheim Exploration Co. / Hacienda de Bonanza, Zac.," n.d., MSJP; Marvin Bernstein, *The Mexican Mining Industry, 1890–1950* (Albany: State Univ. of New York, 1965), 49–56; Saragoza, *Monterrey Elite*, 30, 37f. On Porfirian railroads: John Coatsworth, *Growth Against Development* (DeKalb: Northern Illinois Univ. Press, 1981); Sandra Kuntz Ficker, *Empresa extranjera y mercado interno* (Mexico City: Colegio de México, 1995).

13. *Nashville Tennessean*, 28 Jun. 1964, mag. 17; Hart, *Empire and Revolution*, 135f.

14. For a 1905 move: Jenkins to Jack Stanford, Puebla, 19 Apr. 1939, *Mary Street Jenkins Foundation*, ed. Beatrice Trueblood (Mexico City: Fundación Mary Street Jenkins, 1988), 7; "Testimonio de la escritura de testamento público abierto otorgado por el señor don William O. Jenkins," Puebla (Notary Public 13), 29 Oct. 1958, papers of William A. Jenkins, Mexico City (hereafter, WAJP). For a 1906 move: Jenkins to Shanklin, Puebla, 7 Jan. 1915, RDS.

15. *Time*, 26 Dec. 1960, 25; Luis Castro, *El Sol de Puebla*, 5 Jun. 1963, 1 (obit.); Enrique Cordero y Torres, *Diccionario Biográfico de Puebla* (Puebla: Centro de Estudios Históricos, 1972), 345; Manuel Frías Olvera, *Los verdaderos ángeles de Puebla* (Puebla: Mabek, 1976), 347; Sergio Guzmán Ramos, *Hombres de Puebla* (Puebla: n.p., 1999), 52.

16. Jenkins to Stanford, in *Mary Street Jenkins Foundation*, ed. Trueblood, 7; Sandra Reyes Romero, "La industria bonetera en Puebla y sus empresarios extranjeros, 1900–1930" (MA thesis, Univ. Autónoma de Puebla, 2011), 36–8, 54; Registro Público de la Propiedad, Puebla (hereafter, RPP-Puebla), Libro 1 de Comercio, Tomo 2, foja 174.

17. *El Sol de Puebla*, 5 Jun. 1963, 3; *La Opinión* [Puebla], 5 Jun. 1963, 1; Cordero y Torres, *Diccionario Biográfico*, 345; Manuel Cabañas Pavía, *Datos Biográficos del señor William O. Jenkins* (Puebla: n.p., 1975), 23f; Frías Olvera, *Los verdaderos ángeles*, 347; Miguel Espinosa M., *Zafra de odios, azúcar amargo* (Puebla: Univ. Autónoma de Puebla, 1980), 22; Leticia Gamboa Ojeda, *Las actividades económicas: Negocios y negociantes en la ciudad de Puebla, 1810–1913* (Puebla: Educación y Cultura, 2010), 65. On Rasst: Tribunal Superior de Justicia del Distrito Federal, Siglo XX, Archivo General de la Nación (hereafter, AGN-TSJDF), Folios 018583, 112925, etc.; Archivo General Municipal de Puebla (hereafter, AGMP), 1905, Tomo 456, Leg. 3, 25–7; 1906, Tomo 463, Leg. 11, 139–89, etc.

18. Gamboa, *Los empresarios*, 31; Reyes Romero, "La industria bonetera," ch. II. On general trends in textiles: Haber, *Industry and Underdevelopment*, 54–8; Fernando Rosenzweig, "La industria," in D. Cosío Villegas, ed., *Historia moderna de México*, vol. 7 (Mexico City: Hermes, 1965), I:339–44.

19. Ernest Gruening, *Mexico and its Heritage* (New York: The Century Co., 1928), 59, 468; David LaFrance, *The Mexican Revolution in Puebla, 1908–1913* (Wilmington, DE: SR Books, 1989), xxxii–xxxiv, 68; Roderic Ai Camp, *Mexican Political Biographies, 1884–1934* (Austin: Univ. of Texas Press, 1991), 136.

20. Timothy Henderson, *The Worm in the Wheat: Rosalie Evans and Agrarian Struggle in the Puebla-Tlaxcala Valley of Mexico* (Durham, NC: Duke Univ. Press, 1998), 17f; Gamboa, *Los empresarios*, 153, 158, 166f, 192f; Horacio Crespo and Enrique Vega Villanueva, *Estadísticas históricas del azúcar en México* (Mexico City: Azúcar SA, 1990), 132–248; RPP-Puebla, Libro 3 de Comercio, Tomo 10, no. 8.

21. Stephen Haber et al., "Sustaining Economic Performance under Political Instability," in Haber ed., *Crony Capitalism and Economic Growth in Latin America* (Stanford, CA: Hoover Press, 2002), esp. 37–42; Haber, *Industry and Underdevelopment*, 29; Haber, et al., *Politics of Property Rights*, 42–51, 12–37. For a contrasting view, questioning (though not ruling out) the importance of investors' crony ties to politicians, see Wasserman, *Pesos and Politics*, esp. ch. 7.

22. Moisés González Navarro, *Estadísticas sociales del porfiriato, 1877–1910* (Mexico City: Sec. de Economía, 1956), 9, 123f.

23. Guy Thomson, *Puebla de los Angeles: Industry and Society in a Mexican City, 1700–1850* (Boulder: Westview Press, 1989), chs. 6 and 7; Rodney Anderson, *Outcasts in Their Own Land: Mexican Industrial Workers, 1906–1911* (DeKalb: Northern Illinois Univ. Press, 1976), 137f; Gamboa, *Los empresarios*, 30–3.

24. The sketch of Puebla draws on Luis Casarrubias Ibarra, *Mi Patria Chica: Curso elemental de Geografía del Estado de Puebla* (Puebla: Gobierno del Estado, 1990

[1910]); Leonardo Lomelí Vanegas, *Breve historia de Puebla* (Mexico City: FCE/ Colegio de México, 2001), ch. IX. Cf. Doyle, *Nashville*, 123 (Table 4) and ch. 4.

25. José Donato Rodríguez Romero, ed., *Datos Históricos del Templo Metodista "Emmanuel" de la Ciudad de Puebla* (Puebla: Iglesia Metodista de México, 2004), 66f; Mary S. Jenkins to Verniscia [surname unknown], Puebla, 1 Apr. 1922, MSJP.

26. Carlos Contreras Cruz and Columba Salazar, "Francisco de Velasco y la transformación de la ciudad de Puebla, 1906–10," in *Espacio y perfiles: Historia regional del siglo XIX*, ed. Contreras Cruz (Puebla: UAP, 1989); Enrique Cordero y Torres, *Historia compendiada del Estado de Puebla* (Puebla: Bohemia Poblana, 1965), III:66; interview with Javier de Velasco Matienzo (Francisco's grandson), Puebla, 19 Jul. 2007.

27. Anderson, *Outcasts*, chs. 3 and 4.

28. Anderson, *Outcasts*, ch. 5, 305; Alan Knight, *The Mexican Revolution* (Lincoln: Univ. of Nebraska Press, 1986), I:145–50, 169.

29. Coralia Gutiérrez Álvarez, "Inmigración y aculturación," in *Presencia española en Puebla*, ed. Agustín Grajales and Lilián Illades (Puebla: UAP, 2002; quotation: 201); Gamboa, *Los empresarios*, 124–6, 159–80; J. Jenkins Eustace interview, 2 Apr. 2001.

30. Wil Pansters, *Politics and Power in Puebla: The Political History of a Mexican State, 1937–1987* (Amsterdam: CEDLA, 1990), 31; Gastón García Cantú, "Testimonios de viajeros," in Varios Autores, *Puebla en la cultura nacional* (Puebla: Univ. Autónoma de Puebla, 2000); Cabañas Pavia, "Datos Biográficos," 13; E.H. Blichfeldt, *A Mexican Journey* (New York: Thomas Crowell, 1912), 176.

31. Thomson, *Puebla de los Angeles*, xvii–xxi, 14–26, 33–42, 74–8; Frances Ramos, *Identity, Ritual, and Power in Colonial Puebla* (Tucson: Univ. of Arizona Press, 2012), ch. 1; Alexander McGuckin, "La Clase Divina of Puebla: A Socio-Economic History of a Mexican Elite, 1790–1910" (MA thesis, Univ. of Alberta, 1995), 28–52, 76–89, 99.

32. Pansters, *Politics and Power*, 32; Lomelí Vanegas, *Breve historia de Puebla*, 67–9, ch. VII; García Cantú, "Testimonios"; interview with Bertha Cobel vda. de Chedraui, Puebla, 25 Mar. 2006.

33. John S. D. Eisenhower, *So Far from God: The US War with Mexico, 1846–1848* (Norman: Univ. of Oklahoma Press, 2000), 296–303; Lomelí Vanegas, *Breve historia de Puebla*, 191f.

34. Charles Macomb Flandrau, *Viva México!* (Urbana: Univ. of Illinois Press, 1964 [1908]), xiv, 222–9; cf. *New York Times*, 1 Jun. 1902, 31.

35. Jean-Pierre Bastian, *Los disidentes: Sociedades protestantes y revolución en México, 1872–1911* (Mexico City: FCE/Colegio de México, 1989), chs. 1–4; Gamboa, *Los empresarios*, ch. 3; McGuckin, "La Clase Divina of Puebla," 113–24; Gutiérrez Álvarez, "Inmigración y aculturación," 201f.

36. *La Opinión*, 5 Jun. 1963, 1; Cordero y Torres, *Diccionario biográfico*, 345; Frías Olvera, *Los verdaderos ángeles*, 347; Guzmán, *Hombres de Puebla*, 52.

37. Ida Altman, *Transatlantic Ties in the Spanish Empire* (Stanford, CA: Stanford Univ. Press, 2000), esp. ch. 2. On capitalism in New Spain, see also John Tutino, *Making a New World: Founding Capitalism in the Bajio and Spanish North America* (Durham, NC: Duke Univ. Press, 2011).

38. McGuckin, "La Clase Divina of Puebla," 92–100, 112–33; Leticia Gamboa Ojeda, "Los comercios de barcelonnettes y la cultura del consumo entre las élites urbanas," in *México Francia, Vol. II*, ed. Javier Pérez Siller and Chantai Cramaussel (Puebla: UAP, 2004). On Francophilia as a means to modernity, see Mauricio Tenorio, *Mexico at the World's Fairs* (Berkeley: Univ. of California Press, 1996), ch. 1.

39. Bertram Wyatt-Brown, *Honor and Violence in the Old South* (New York: Oxford Univ. Press, 1986), 16, 119–31.

40. Jones interview with Jenkins, 13 May 1918, Doheny Collection; John Tigert, quoted in *Nashville Banner*, 24 Dec. 1919, MSJP; *Time*, 26 Dec. 1960, 25; Cordero y Torres, *Diccionario Biográfico*, 345; J. Jenkins Eustace interview, 2 Apr. 2001; interview with Ana María and María del Carmen Díaz Rubín de la Hidalga (sisters), Mexico City, 1 Aug. 2001.

41. On the Mexican-American War from the Mexican perspective, see Josefina Vázquez and Lorenzo Meyer, *The United States and Mexico* (Chicago: Univ. of Chicago Press, 1985), ch. 3.

42. Hart, *Empire and Revolution*, chs. 3–9, esp. 260–2, 271f; Kuntz, "De las reformas liberales," 166–87.

43. Jan Bazant, "From Independence to the Liberal Republic, 1821–1867," in Bethell, ed., *Mexico since Independence*, 10f.

44. Charles Hale, *Mexican Liberalism in the Age of Mora, 1821–53* (New Haven, CT: Yale Univ. Press, 1968), 213; Gruening, *Mexico and its Heritage*, 199.

45. Knight, *US–Mexican Relations*, 41.

46. Garner, *Porfirio Díaz*, 123–7, 139; John Hart, *Revolutionary Mexico* (Berkeley: Univ. of California Press, 1997), 179; Michael Matthews, "*De Viaje*: Elite Views of Modernity and the Porfirian Railway Boom," *Mexican Studies* 26:2 (2010): 275; Mary Kay Vaughan, *The State, Education and Social Class in Mexico, 1880–1928* (DeKalb: Northern Illinois Univ. Press, 1982), 37f, 214; Beezley, *Judas at the Jockey Club*, 103f.

47. John Reid, *Spanish American Images of the United States, 1790–1960* (Gainesville, FL: Univ. of Florida Press, 1977), 154; Schell, *Integral Outsiders*, 42f, 138 (the cartoon appeared in *El Hijo del Ahuizote*, 1901).

48. Garner, *Porfirio Díaz*, 149–53, 182f; Roger Hansen, *The Politics of Mexican Development* (Baltimore: Johns Hopkins Univ. Press, 1974), 15–18.

49. Rodó, *Ariel* (Austin: Univ. of Texas Press, 1988 [1900]); Frederick Pike, *The United States and Latin America* (Austin: Univ. of Texas Press, 1992), 193–201.

50. Alfonso Reyes, "Rodó" (1917), in *Obras completas* (Mexico City: FCE, 1956); Sierra, *En tierra yankee* in *Obras completas*, ed. A. Yañez (Mexico City: UNAM,

1948 [1898]), Vol. 6; Reid, *Spanish American Images*, 262f; Laurence Prescott, "Journeying through Jim Crow," *Latin American Research Review* 42:1 (2007): 13–15.

51. Garner, *Porfirio Díaz*, 140.

52. Claudio Lomnitz, "Anti-Semitism and the Ideology of the Mexican Revolution," *Representations*, 110:1 (2010).

53. Frías Olvera, *Los verdaderos ángeles*, 347; Espinosa, *Zafra de odios*, 22.

54. Jenkins Eustace, ed., *Tennessee Sunshine*, 249, 259 (photo), 327.

55. Jenkins to Street, 25 Aug. and 1 Sep. 1901, MSJP; J. Jenkins Eustace interview, 2 Apr. 2001; interview with Tita Jenkins Cheney, Beverly Hills, CA, 18 Aug. 2002.

56. *Nashville Tennessean*, 5 Jul. 1964, mag. 8; *Mexican Herald*, 11 Jul. 1912, 2; telephone interview with Martha Gains (daughter of Donald Street), Fairfield Glades, TN, 28 May 2005.

57. Knight, *Mexican Revolution*, I:173f, 183f.

58. LaFrance, *Mexican Revolution in Puebla*, 45–50.

59. Knight, *Mexican Revolution*, I:122f, 175f, 189f; LaFrance, *Mexican Revolution in Puebla*, 49, 62–4.

60. LaFrance, *Mexican Revolution in Puebla*, xxxiii, 48, 65–8.

61. Óscar Flores, "Empresarios y diplomáticos españoles en Puebla durante el gobierno de Francisco León de la Barra," in *Presencia española*, ed. Grajales and Illades, 253f, 260; LaFrance, *Mexican Revolution in Puebla*, 76f, 184. On the targeting of Spaniards (more than Americans), see also: Knight, *US–Mexican Relations*, 62–7.

62. Knight, *Mexican Revolution*, I:201–4, 218; Garner, *Porfirio Díaz*, 219f.

63. Cabañas Pavía, *Datos Biográficos*, 24; J. Jenkins Eustace interview, 2 Apr. 2001. On macroeconomics and inequalities: Katz, "The Liberal Republic," 110f, 117f.; Kuntz, "De las reformas liberales," 156, 160–3, 197f.

64. The founding of Jenkins's mill, La Corona, draws on Leticia Gamboa Ojeda, "Para una historia de la rama textil: géneros de punto en la Cd. de Puebla," *Arqueología Industrial* 4:8 (2001): 3f; Jenkins to Stanford, in *Mary Street Jenkins Foundation*, ed. Trueblood, 7f; *Nashville Tennessean*, 5 Jul. 1964, mag. 8f; Cabañas Pavía, *Datos Biográficos*, 24f; Guzmán Ramos interview, 16 May 2005. Mexican textile automation took place from 1895 to 1910; Edward Beatty, *Institutions and Investment: The Political Basis of Industrialization in Mexico Before 1911* (Stanford, CA: Stanford Univ. Press, 2001), 115.

65. Archivo General de Notarías de Puebla (hereafter, Notarías-Puebla), NP 8, 1908, Vol. I, no. 136; *The Acosta Directory* (Mexico City: Francis J. Acosta, [1910]), 193, 277; *La Prensa* (Puebla), 24 Aug. 1918, 1; Jenkins to Elizabeth Jenkins, Puebla, 26 Dec. 1919, MSJP; J. Jenkins Eustace interview, 15 Aug. 2001.

66. Jeffrey Bortz, "The Revolution, the Labour Regime and Conditions of Work in the Cotton Textile Industry in Mexico, 1910–1927," *Journal of Latin American Studies* 32:3 (2000): 676f; Reyes Romero, "La industria bonetera," 26f, 37f.

67. Mario Ramírez Rancaño, *Directorio de empresas industriales textiles: 1900–1920* (Mexico City: IIS-UNAM, [1980]), 44f; AGMP, Indice de Expedientes, Vol. 18 (1911), Rasst/Exp. 3C.

68. Mario Trujillo Bolio, *Empresariado y manufacturera textil en la Ciudad de México y su periferia* (Mexico City: CIESAS, 2000), 147f; Ramírez Rancaño, *Directorio de empresas*, 35f, 58, 138, 142, 166; Reyes Romero, "La industria bonetera," 55.

69. Jenkins to Stanford, in *Mary Street Jenkins Foundation*, ed. Trueblood, 7; *Mexican Herald*, 23 Jun. 1914, 3; Gamboa, "Para una historia," 3; Stephen Haber, "Industrial Concentration and the Capital Markets: A Comparative Study of Brazil, Mexico and the United States, 1830–1930," *Journal of Economic History* 51:3 (1991).

70. RPP-Puebla, Libro 3 de Comercio, Tomo 12, 26 (16 Jan. 1913); cf. Notarías-Puebla, N.P. 1, 1907, Vol. 1, No. 69.

71. *Twelfth Census* (Washington, DC: Bureau of the Census, 1900), Hanford, Kings Co., CA, roll: T623-87, 16A (Biddle); *Fourteenth Census* (Washington, DC: Bureau of the Census, 1920), Armona, Kings Co., CA, roll: T625-101, 9A (Jenkins); School Registry (1870–1935), The Webb School, Bell Buckle, TN, 188; *Nashville Banner*, 25 Oct. 1919; Jenkins to Stanford, in *Mary Street Jenkins Foundation*, ed. Trueblood, 13; Shoffner, *Bicentennial History*, 39; Shofner interview, 11 Jul. 2004; telephone interview with Betty Asbury of Fresno, CA, 25 May 2005.

72. Jenkins to Street, 1 Sep. 1901, MSJP.

73. *Mexican Herald*, 26 Jun. 1912, 2; 11 Jul., 2; *Nashville Tennessean*, 5 Jul. 1964, mag. 9.

74. J. Jenkins Eustace interview, 2 Apr. 2001.

75. Jenkins to Stanford, in *Mary Street Jenkins Foundation*, ed. Trueblood, 8; Dorothy Ford Wulfeck, *Wilcoxson and Allied Families* (Naugatuck, CT: n.p., 1958), 154.

76. Knight, *Mexican Revolution*, I:2.

77. Knight, *Mexican Revolution*, I:323–5, 480–90; II:1–77.

78. Hart, *Empire and Revolution*, ch. 9; Henderson, *Worm in the Wheat*, 45; Cons. Gen. Shanklin to Sec. of State, Mexico City, 13 Oct. 1910, 22 Sep. and 25 Oct. 1911, 28 Jan. and 30 Aug. 1913, RDS, 125.61383, box 2324.

79. Shanklin to Sec. of State, 30 Aug. 1913, RDS, 125.61383.

80. See Jenkins's correspondence for Apr. 1914 to Mar. 1915, Foreign Service Posts of the Dept. of State (NARA Record Group 84), Puebla, 1911–1930, Vol. II; Graham Stuart, *American Diplomatic and Consular Practice* (New York: Appleton-Century, 1936), 343f, 429–35.

81. Bryan to Shanklin, Washington, 15 Sep., Shanklin to Sec. of State, 21 Sep. 1913, RDS, 125.61383.

CHAPTER 3

1. Jenkins to Arnold Shanklin, Puebla, 7 Jan. 1915, RDS, 812.00/14285.

2. John Womack Jr., *Zapata and the Mexican Revolution* (New York: Vintage, 1970), 122f, 171, 219–23, 242; David LaFrance, *Revolution in Mexico's Heartland: Politics,*

War, and State Building in Puebla, 1913–1920 (Wilmington, DE: SR Books, 2003), 63–6.

3. Linda Hall, *Álvaro Obregón, Power and Revolution in Mexico, 1911–1920* (College Station: Texas A&M Univ. Press, 1981), 103f.

4. On Gutiérrez, Jenkins was prescient: cf. Knight, *Mexican Revolution*, II:223; Hall, *Álvaro Obregón*, 105f.

5. Arnold Shanklin to State Dept., Veracruz, 9 Jan. 1915, RDS, 812.00/14285.

6. Testimony of Edwin R. Brown, US Senate Committee on Foreign Relations, *Investigation of Mexican Affairs: Preliminary Reports and Hearings* (Washington, DC: USGPO, 1920), II: 2083f.

7. LaFrance, *Heartland*, 127–30.

8. Mary Kay Vaughan, "Education and Class in the Mexican Revolution," *Latin American Perspectives* 11:2 (1975), 21; Evans, *The Rosalie Evans Letters from Mexico* (Indianapolis: Bobbs-Merrill, 1926), 81, 149f, 278, 285f.

9. *Rudyard Kipling's Verse* (Garden City, NY: Doubleday, 1929); Janice Lee Jayes, *The Illusion of Ignorance: Constructing the American Encounter with Mexico, 1877–1920* (Lanham, MD: Univ. Press of America, 2011): 197f.

10. Turner, *Barbarous Mexico* (Chicago: C.H. Kerr, 1911); Reed, *Insurgent Mexico* (New York: D. Appleton, 1914); Jayes, *Illusion of Ignorance*, 196f, 203, 205–8, 211–3.

11. Jayes, *Illusion of Ignorance*, 209f.

12. Gildardo Magaña to Lauro Otorno, 27 Aug. 1919, Archivo Histórico de la UNAM, Fondo Gildardo Magaña, Caja 30, 3. On Magaña's career: Womack, *Zapata*, 288–91, 347–69.

13. The State Dept. would raise Jenkins's rank to consular agent in 1918, after five years at the acting level; Robert Lansing, memo, Washington, 26 Feb. 1918, SRE, 42-26-95.

14. Palafox to Zapata, 29 Dec. 1914, AGN Colección Revolución, Caja 3/44.

15. LaFrance, "Revisión del caso Jenkins," *Historia Mexicana* 53:4 (2004), 924, 932–5; Magaña to Otorno, 27 Aug. 1919, Fondo Magaña, C. 30/3.

16. The definitive surveys of the Revolution in Puebla are LaFrance's twin volumes, *Mexican Revolution in Puebla* and *Revolution in Mexico's Heartland*.

17. Jenkins to Stanford, in *Mary Street Jenkins Foundation*, ed. Trueblood, 7f, 13 (table).

18. Jones interview with Jenkins, 13 May 1918, Doheny Collection; Isaac J. Cox to Albert B. Fall, Evanston, IL, 8 Dec. 1919, Albert B. Fall Collection, Huntington Library, Pasadena, CA (hereafter, Fall Collection), Box 84, file 15.

19. Robert McCaa, "Missing Millions: The Demographic Costs of the Mexican Revolution," *Mexican Studies* 19:2 (2003).

20. Womack, "The Mexican Economy during the Revolution, 1910–1920," *Marxist Perspectives* 1:4 (1978), 80–123; Haber, *Industry and Underdevelopment*, ch. 8. For a traditional reading, see e.g. John Chasteen, *Born in Blood & Fire: A Concise History of Latin America* (New York: W. W. Norton, 2011), 225.

21. Except where noted, these and the following figures are reproduced or deduced from Haber, *Industry and Underdevelopment*, 125 and 127 (Tables 8.1 and 8.3).

22. Jenkins to Shanklin, 7 Jan. 1915, RDS, 812.00/14285.

23. Jenkins to Stanford, in *Mary Street Jenkins Foundation*, ed. Trueblood, 8; Jones interview with Jenkins, 13 May 1918, Doheny Collection.

24. Haber, *Industry and Underdevelopment*, 125, 135f.

25. Gamboa, *Los empresarios*, 88–90, 97; LaFrance, *Heartland*, 137.

26. Gamboa, *Los empresarios*, 88–97; LaFrance, *Heartland*, 121; William Canada to State Dept., Veracruz, 19 Nov. 1914, RDS, 812.00/13915; Jenkins to Shanklin, 18 Nov. 1914, RDS, 812.00/14073.

27. LaFrance, *Revolution in Puebla*, 113f, 116, 122f, 161–6.

28. LaFrance, *Revolution in Puebla*, 162f. The *jefes políticos* were a Porfirian creation, charged with minimizing dissent and fixing elections. On their roles and tendencies, see Knight, *Mexican Revolution*, I:24–31.

29. Brands, *Reckless Decade*, ch. 4; cf. Priscilla Long, *Where the Sun Never Shines: A History of America's Bloody Coal Industry* (New York: Paragon House, 1989); Samuel Yellen, *American Labor Struggles: 1877–1934* (New York: Pathfinder, 1974).

30. Jenkins to Depto. Trabajo, Puebla, 8 Nov. 1915, AGN Departamento de Trabajo (hereafter, AGN-DT), Caja 102, 2; Guadalupe Cano González, "La remuneración obrera textil en Puebla: 1912–1921" (PhD diss., Univ. Autónoma de Puebla, forthcoming).

31. LaFrance, *Revolution in Puebla*, 161, 164; *Heartland*, 171f; Antonio Gómez to Sec. de Industria y Comercio, Puebla, 3 Oct. 1918, Cámara de la Industria Textil de Puebla y Tlaxcala, Fondo IV: Centro Industrial Mexicano (hereafter, CITPyT-CIM), Libro Copiador 5, 135f.

32. Ignacio Cardoso to Depto. Trabajo, Puebla, 29 Jul. 1915, CITPyT-CIM, Libro Cop. 1, 164; Ramírez Rancaño, *Directorio de empresas*, 18, 28f.

33. Dr. Bruce B. Corbin, quoted in US Congress, *Investigation of Mexican Affairs*, I:1456; Ernest Tudor Craig to Francis J. Kearful, New York, 8 Jan. 1920, Fall Collection, Box 76, file 26.

34. LaFrance, *Heartland*, 182f; Estela Munguía Escamilla, "Continuidad y cambio en la legislación educativa de las escuelas elementales públicas de Puebla, 1893–1928" (MA thesis, UNAM, 2003).

35. Gamboa, *Los empresarios*, 42. On Puebla investors' parochialism compared with Monterrey: Gonzalo Castañeda, "The Dynamic of Firms' Chartering and the Underlying Social Governance. Puebla," working paper, Univ. de las Américas, Puebla, 9 Oct. 2005.

36. Ramírez Rancaño, *Directorio de empresas*, 166, 169, 172f; revenues are inferred from taxes levied subsequently.

37. RPP-Puebla, Libro 3, Tomo 12, no. 67; Leticia Gamboa Ojeda, "Formas de asociación empresarial en la industria textil poblana," in *Los negocios y las ganancias,*

ed. Leonor Ludlow and Jorge Silva Riquer (Mexico City: Instituto Mora, 1993), 281, 284–7.

38. Aurora Gómez-Galvarriato and Aldo Musacchio, "Organizational Choice in a French Civil Law Underdeveloped Economy," working paper, CIDE, 2004, 6; Gamboa, *Los empresarios*, 9f, 166f, and "Formas de asociación," 286.

39. LaFrance, *Heartland*, 117f, 168; Jenkins to Elizabeth Jenkins, Puebla, 19 Oct. 1919, Mary Street Jenkins Papers (hereafter, MSJP), held by Rosemary Eustace Jenkins, Mexico City; Ignacio Cardoso to José Mariano Pontón, Puebla, 10 May 1917, CITPyT-CIM, LC 3, 120–8; CIM Report, Jan. 1921, CITPyT-CIM, LC 9, 172f.

40. Shanklin to Sec. of State, 3 May 1915, RDS, 125.61383; LaFrance, *Heartland*, 169; Hart, *Empire and Revolution*, 321–9; Knight, *Mexican Revolution*, II:402–4; J. Jenkins Eustace interviews, 2 Apr. 2001, 27 Jun. 2002.

41. *Nashville Banner*, 24 and 25 Oct. 1919; Mary S. Jenkins to Elizabeth Jenkins, Puebla, 10 Nov. 1919, MSJP.

42. Telephone interview with Martha Gains (daughter of Donald Street), Fairfield Glades, TN, 28 May 2005.

43. Jenkins to SRE, Puebla, 7 Dec. and 10 Dec (twice) 1917, SRE, 143-PB-41.

44. LaFrance, *Heartland*, 117, 164; Maurer, *Power and the Money*, 136–57, 183; Jorge Jiménez Muñoz, *La traza del poder: Historia de la política y los negocios urbanos en el Distrito Federal* (Mexico City: Dédalo, 1993), 120–22.

45. Jenkins to Stanford, in *Mary Street Jenkins Foundation*, ed. Trueblood, 8.

46. Cf. Theresa Alfaro-Velcamp, *So Far from Allah, So Close to Mexico* (Austin: Univ. of Texas Press, 2007), 9, 104, 137.

47. Sec. de Justicia to SRE, Mexico City, 16 Oct. 1916, SRE, 246-PB-6; Gov. Alfonso Cabrera to SRE, Puebla, 20 May 1918, SRE, 42-26-95.

48. The account of rural property speculation draws on Jones's 13 May 1918 interview with Jenkins, Doheny Collection, and Jenkins's 1939 letter to Stanford of the IRS in *Mary Street Jenkins Foundation*, ed. Trueblood, 7–9, 13. Where there are discrepancies, I favor the earlier, more frank account. Cf. Cox to Fall, 8 Dec. 1919, Fall Collection, Box 84, file 15.

49. SRE, 139-PB-39, 140-PB-11, 143-PB-41, 246-PB-6.

50. Maurer, *Power and the Money*, 142–5; Jiménez Muñoz, *La traza del poder*, 118–20.

51. Jones interview with Jenkins, 13 May 1918, Doheny Collection; Jenkins to Stanford, in *Mary Street Jenkins Foundation*, ed. Trueblood, 8.

52. Jenkins to Stanford, *op. cit.*, 13; SRE, Exps. 140-PB-11, 143-PB-41; Jenkins to Obregón, Puebla, 31 May 1923, AGN, presidential files of Obregón and Calles (hereafter, AGN Obregón-Calles), 823-O-1. Jenkins's wartime gain of $2.5 million represents some $50 million in today's terms.

53. A possible rival to Jenkins's claim is Sinaloa sugar baron B. F. Johnston; see later discussion.

54. Jones interview with Jenkins, 13 May 1918, Doheny Collection; *La Prensa* and *El Monitor* (Puebla), 14 Jun. 1919, 1.

55. Gamboa, *Los empresarios*, 148–59.
56. Henderson, *Worm in the Wheat*, 32f; Jenkins to SRE, Puebla, 15 Jul. 1918, SRE, 140-PB-11.
57. Womack, *Zapata*, 157f, 170, 183, 191, 235; Horacio Crespo, ed., *Historia del azúcar en México* (Mexico City: FCE, 1988), I:150f; David Ronfeldt, *Atencingo: The Politics of Agrarian Struggle in a Mexican Ejido* (Stanford, CA: Stanford Univ. Press, 1973), 8f; Friedrich Katz, *The Secret War in Mexico* (Chicago: Univ. of Chicago Press, 1981), 531–38.
58. Castañeda, "The Dynamic of Firms' Chartering," 17; interview with José Luis Vázquez Nava (son of Jenkins's notary Nicolás Vázquez), Puebla, 26 May 2006. "Mexico's original micro-financiers": the term owes to Juliette Levy; see *The Making of a Market: Credit, Henequen and Notaries in Yucatan, 1850–1900* (University Park: Pennsylvania State Univ. Press, 2012).
59. Jenkins to Stanford, in *Mary Street Jenkins Foundation*, ed. Trueblood, 8f, 13. On the Viuda de Conde firm: Gamboa, *Los empresarios*, 170f, 204, 241–54.
60. Díaz Rubín de la Hidalga interview, 1 Aug. 2001; Gamboa, *Los empresarios*, 124, 154, 205, 215; Crespo and Vega Villanueva, *Estadísticas históricas*, 97, 238.
61. LaFrance, *Revolution in Puebla*, 77, 184, 195; Knight, *Mexican Revolution*, I:213, 219; Jenkins to Obregón, Puebla, 24 Jan. 1922, AGN Obregón-Calles, 818-J-4.
62. LaFrance, *Heartland*, 137f; cf. LaFrance, *Revolution in Puebla*, 77.
63. Jenkins's move to acquire Atencingo is first reported in *Excélsior*, 8 Oct. 1920, 1.
64. See, e.g., Hernández, *Proceso*, 11 Aug. 1980, 17; Bonilla Fernández, *El secuestro del poder*, 117–20; Henderson, *Worm in the Wheat*, 86f.
65. Crespo, ed., *Historia del azúcar*, I:188–96, 200–4, 249; McGuckin, "La Clase Divina of Puebla," 35–40, 90f; Gamboa, *Los empresarios*, 148–59.
66. Haber, *Industry and Underdevelopment*, 70, 208 n7; Paolo Riguzzi, "The Legal System, Institutional Change, and Financial regulation in Mexico, 1870–1910," in *The Mexican Economy, 1870–1930*, ed. Jeffrey Bortz and Stephen Haber (Stanford, CA: Stanford Univ. Press, 2002); Juliette Levy, "Notaries and Credit Markets in Nineteenth-Century Mexico," *Business History Review* 84:3 (2010).
67. Wyatt-Brown, *Honor and Violence*, 137.
68. LaFrance, *Heartland*, 118; Gamboa, *Los empresarios*, 205, 215.
69. Hans Werner Tobler, "La burguesía revolucionaria en México," *Historia Mexicana* 34:2 (1984), 213–37; Alicia Hernández Chávez, "Militares y negocios en la Revolución mexicana," *Historia Mexicana* 34:2, esp. 192–212; Hamilton, *Limits of State Autonomy*, 75f.
70. Carlos Fuentes, *The Death of Artemio Cruz* (New York: FSG, 1964).
71. Tobler, "La burguesía revolucionaria"; Alicia Hernández Chávez, *Historia de la Revolución Mexicana, vol. 16: La mecánica cardenista* (Mexico City: Colegio de México, 1979), 28–31; Abelardo Rodríguez, *Autobiografía* (Mexico City: n.p., 1962), 161–73; Gruening, *Mexico and Its Heritage*, 399–473.

72. See, e.g, Corinne Krause, *Los judíos en México* (Mexico City: Univ. Iberoamericana, 1987); Alfaro-Velcamp, *So Far from Allah*; Pablo Yankelevich, ed., *México, país refugio* (Mexico City: Plaza y Janés, 2002). On Slim's sale of Jenkins's products, e.g., *El Demócrata* (Mexico City), 27 May 1917, 8; *El Universal*, 5 Mar. 1922, 8.

73. Claudia Fernández and Andrew Paxman, *El Tigre: Emilio Azcárraga y su imperio Televisa* (Mexico City: Grijalbo-Mondadori, 2013), 57.

74. On Johnston (1865–1937): Hart, *Empire and Revolution*, 188f, 327, 357f, 524. On Wright (1876–1954): Schell, *Integral Outsiders*, 189, 191; Francisco Peredo Castro, *Cine y propaganda para Latinoamérica* (Mexico City: UNAM, 2013), 160, 301–15. On the majority of US investors: Hart, 304f, 370, 399.

75. Puebla's judicial records, held at the Archivo Judicial del Estado de Puebla, are organized by year only.

76. LaFrance, *Heartland*, 90–100, 104, 145–7, 152f; N. King to F.O., Mexico City, 6 Aug. 1919, Foreign Office records, National Archives, London (hereafter, UKFO), Series 369, doc. 1175:6; cf. Gruening, *Mexico and Its Heritage*, 497–505.

77. LaFrance, *Heartland*, 152f.

78. E. V. Niemeyer, *Revolution at Querétaro* (Austin: Univ. of Texas Press, 1974), 134–65.

79. Henderson, *Worm in the Wheat*, 86f; *La Opinión* (Puebla), 15 Dec. 1933, 1.

80. Henderson, *Worm in the Wheat*, 71, 87; Raymond Buve, *El movimiento revolucionario en Tlaxcala* (Tlaxcala: Univ. Autónoma de Tlaxcala, 1994), 242, 266; Jenkins to Stanford, in *Mary Street Jenkins Foundation*, ed. Trueblood, 13; "The Mexican Situation," *E-B Dealers Magazine* (Rockford, IL), [Dec.?] 1919, 15, MSJP.

81. Cordero y Torres, *Diccionario Biográfico*, 316–20; interview with Sergio Guzmán Ramos (son of Sergio B. Guzmán), Puebla, 17 Aug. 2001.

82. LaFrance, *Revolution in Puebla*, 156, and *Heartland*, 16; Camp, *Mexican Political Biographies, 1884–1934*, 145; Mestre interview, 16 Jul. 2003.

83. *Boletín del Club Alpha de Puebla*, nos. 1 (Jul. 1914) and 2 (Oct. 1915) and *Estatutos del 'Club Alpha de Puebla'* (1915), Eduardo Mestre Ghigliazza Papers, held by Manuel Mestre, Mexico City; W. O. Jenkins's Club Alpha share certificate (Jul. 1915), and "List of Shareholders of the Club Alpha de Puebla" (Apr. 1918), Sergio B. Guzmán Papers (hereafter, SBGP), held by Sergio Guzmán Ramos, Puebla; Mestre interview, 16 Jul. 2003.

84. Hart, *Empire and Revolution*, Part III, esp. 343–92, 399.

85. *The Thirties in Colour: Adventures in the Americas*, dir. Hina Zaidi (London: BBC Four, 2008); Wright to Abelardo L. Rodríguez, Mexico City, 4 Oct. 1932, Archivo Rodríguez at the Archivos Plutarco Elías Calles y Fernando Torreblanca (herafter, Calles-ALR), presidential series, Mexico City Country Club.

86. Jones interview with Jenkins, 13 May 1918, Doheny Collection; Knight, *Mexican Revolution*, II:313.

87. On venality of railroad officials under Carranza and Obregón: Gruening, *Mexico and its Heritage*, 318; Saragoza, *Monterrey Elite*, 120f. On landowners bribing (or

being shaken down by) Puebla officials: Knight, *Mexican Revolution*, II:468f; LaFrance, *Heartland*, 175. Puebla's Secretary of State refers to the Secretario General de Gobierno, the No. 2 official in state government.

88. Schell, *Integral Outsiders*, chs. 5–7, esp. 129–36, 143–5; Hart, *Empire and Revolution*, 189.

89. Flandrau, *Viva México!*, 222; Jayes, *Illusion of Ignorance*, 202f.

90. *Excélsior*, 5 Jul. 1918, 5.

91. Schell, *Integral Outsiders*, 61f.

92. Jones interview with Jenkins, 13 May 1918, Doheny Collection; Corbin, quoted in US Congress, *Investigation of Mexican Affairs*, I:1456; *El Monitor*, 4 Mar. 1919, 2; *Nashville Banner*, 24 Dec. 1919, MSJP; *The Vanderbilt Alumnus* 4:7 (1919): 213. The center, Alumni Hall, was erected in 1925.

93. Luke 12:48, KJV; Josephson, *Robber Barons*, 317–25.

94. LaFrance, *Heartland*, 181f; *El Monitor*, 30 Oct. 1918, 1, 13 Nov. 1918, 2f, 14 Nov. 1918, 1; CIM to Tesorero General, Puebla, 6 Dec. 1917, CITPyT-CIM, LC 3, 477. Jenkins's gift of 3,000 pesos would be $25,000 today.

95. Jones interview with Jenkins, 13 May 1918, Doheny Collection; Cox to Fall, 8 Dec. 1919, Fall Collection, Box 84, file 15; Evans to Daisy Pettus, Puebla, 30 Mar. 1918, Rosalie Evans Papers, Univ. of Virginia; Mary S. Jenkins to Elizabeth Jenkins, Puebla, 17 Oct. 1919, MSJP.

96. Jenkins to Elizabeth Jenkins, Puebla, 19 Oct. 1919, MSJP.

97. J. Jenkins Eustace interviews, 27 Jun. 2002, 30 Sep. 2005; interview with W. A. Jenkins, Mexico City, 9 Jun. 2003.

CHAPTER 4

1. The kidnapping narrative draws on Mary S. Jenkins to Elizabeth Jenkins, Puebla, 23 Oct., 4 Nov., 4 Dec. 1919, MSJP; Jenkins to J. Rowe, Puebla, 7 Nov. 1919, RDS, 125.61383/190; *Literary Digest* (NY), 21 Feb. 1920, 52–6.

2. The response to the kidnapping draws chiefly on Charles Cumberland, "The Jenkins Case and Mexican–American Relations," *HAHR* 31:4 (1951); David LaFrance, "Revisión del caso Jenkins," *Historia Mexicana* 53:4 (2004); *El Demócrata* (Mexico City), 22 Oct. 1919, 1.

3. On Hearst: David Nasaw, *The Chief: The Life of William Randolph Hearst* (New York: Houghton Mifflin Harcourt, 2001), 228f, 248f, 381; *El Demócrata*, 22 Oct. 1919, 1; *Excélsior*, 29 Nov., 5. On Myers: *New York Times*, 26 Oct. 1919, 1. On Taylor: David Glaser, "1919: William Jenkins, Robert Lansing, and the Mexican Interlude," *Southwestern Historical Quarterly*, 74:3 (1971), 346f. On Carranza and the United States: Douglas Richmond, *Venustiano Carranza's Nationalist Struggle, 1893–1920* (Lincoln: Univ. of Nebraska Press, 1983), 189–203.

4. Mestre interview, 22 Aug. 2007; cf. *Excélsior*, 29 Oct. 1919, 1; *Literary Digest*, 21 Feb. 1920, 54.

5. Dr. C. E. Conwell, sworn statement, in M. Hanna to G. Summerlin, Puebla, 26 Nov. 1919, RDS, 125.61383/262.

6. LaFrance, *Revolution in Mexico's Heartland*, chs. 5, 7, 8, 9, esp. 90–100, 145–7, 185–8.

7. *La Prensa*, 25 Oct. 1919, 1; *El Monitor*, 21 Oct., 4; cf. LaFrance, "Revisión del caso," 928.

8. *Excélsior*, 28 Oct. 1919, 1.

9. *El Universal*, 18 Nov. 1919, 1; Hanna to Summerlin, 26 Nov. 1919, RDS, 125.61383/262, encl. 7; *Literary Digest*, 21 Feb. 1920, 54.

10. Medina to Summerlin, 3 Nov. 1919, Mexico City, SRE, 16-28-1, pt. IV; cf. Cumberland, "Jenkins Case," 594f.

11. *Excélsior*, 15, 16, and 17 Nov. 1919, 1; *El Monitor*, 16 Nov., 1; *New York Times*, 17 Nov., 1.

12. Jenkins to Rowe, 7 Nov. 1919, RDS, 125.61383/190; Hanna to Summerlin, Mexico City, 29 Oct. 1919, RDS, 125.61383/161; Cumberland, "Jenkins Case," 592, 597; *Excélsior*, 28 Oct 1919, 1; 17 Nov., 8; *El Universal*, 18 Nov., 1.

13. *New York Times*, 14 Nov. 1919, 12; *Toledo Blade* et al. quoted in *Bulletin of the National Assn. for the Protection of American Rights in Mexico*, 20 Nov. 1919, Fall Collection, Box 84, file 15; Brown, *Oil and Revolution*, 235–7.

14. *El Demócrata*, 31 Oct, 1919, 1; 3 Nov., 9.

15. *El Monitor*, 20 Nov. 1919, 1; *Excélsior*, 20 Nov., 1; 2 Dec., 5; cf. LaFrance, "Revisión del caso," 945.

16. Mark Gilderhus, *Diplomacy and Revolution: US–Mexico Relations under Wilson and Carranza* (Tucson: Univ. of Arizona Press, 1977), 92–4, 98–100, and "Senator Albert B. Fall and 'The Plot Against Mexico,'" *New Mexico Historical Review* 48:4 (1973), 303–6; Knight, *Mexican Revolution*, II:358–60, 369–72, 379–92; Associated Press, 21 Nov. 1919 (in *Nashville Banner*, 22 Nov.); State Dept. bulletin, 21 Nov., RDS, 125.61383/172½.

17. Dimitri Lazo, "Lansing, Wilson and the Jenkins Incident," *Diplomatic History* 22:2 (1998), 186; Gilderhus, "Senator Albert B. Fall," 303–7.

18. John Wilson, *Maneuver and Firepower: The Evolution of Divisions and Separate Brigades* (Washington, DC: Center of Military History, 1997), 79–81.

19. Lazo, "Lansing, Wilson," esp. 177–9, 187; cf. Gilderhus, "Senator Albert B. Fall," 306f, and Robert Freeman Smith, *The United States and Revolutionary Nationalism in Mexico, 1916–1932* (Chicago: Univ. of Chicago Press, 1972), 157–74.

20. Lazo, "Lansing, Wilson," 187f; Cumberland, "Jenkins Case," 595f; Lansing memo, 28 Nov. 1919, RDS, 125.61383/201a.

21. Lazo, "Lansing, Wilson," 187; Gilderhus, *Diplomacy and Revolution*, 101.

22. Richmond, *Carranza's Nationalist Struggle*, 195–9.

23. Clifford Trow, "Woodrow Wilson and the Mexican Interventionist Movement of 1919," *Journal of American History* 58:1 (Jun. 1971), 50–6; Gilderhus, *Diplomacy and Revolution*, 89–92, 95.

24. Trow, "Woodrow Wilson," 46f, 54–7; Gilderhus, *Diplomacy and Revolution*, 96–9; US Senate Committee on Foreign Relations, *Investigation of Mexican Affairs* (Washington, DC: USGPO, 1920).

25. *New York World, New York American, Detroit Free Press, Grand Rapids Herald, Fargo Courier-News* quoted and cartoons reproduced in *Literary Digest*, 13 Dec. 1919, 11–13; *Los Angeles Times*, 1 Dec. 1919, 1; *Key West Citizen*: quoted in Machado and Judge, "Tempest," 18.

26. *New York Times* editions of 27, 28, 29 Nov. and 2, 4, 5, 6 Dec. 1919 all led with the Jenkins case.

27. LaFrance, "Revisión del caso," 938f; Cumberland, "Jenkins Case," 596–8. For international reactions, see also SRE, 16-28-1, pt. V, vol. 1.

28. *New York Times*, 4 Dec. 1919, 2; 5 Dec., 1.

29. Manuel Machado and James Judge, "Tempest in a Teapot? The Mexican–United States Intervention Crisis of 1919," *Southwestern Historical Quarterly*, 74:1 (1970), 13–19; Trow, "Woodrow Wilson," 64f; Lazo, "Lansing, Wilson," 188, 191; Smith, *Revolutionary Nationalism*, 165; Glaser, "1919," 340, 350.

30. *El Demócrata*, 25 Nov. 1919, 10; 3 Dec., 1; 4 Dec., 1; *Los Angeles Times*, 1 Dec., 1; *Excélsior*, 3 Dec., 1; *México Nuevo*, 5 Dec., cited in Glaser, "1919," 350.

31. Smith, *Revolutionary Nationalism*, 162–6; Lazo, "Lansing, Wilson," 189, 193.

32. *Literary Digest*, 21 Feb. 1920, 54.

33. Gilderhus, *Diplomacy and Revolution*, 102f; Glaser, "1919," 351–3; Trow, "Woodrow Wilson," 67–9; Smith, *Revolutionary Nationalism*, 166; *New York Times*, 9 Dec. 1919, 1.

34. F. J. Kearful to C. V. Safford, New York, 18 Dec. 1919, Fall Collection, Box 84, file 15; Womack, *Zapata*, 348–51; Gilderhus, *Diplomacy and Revolution*, 103–7, 111; Knight, *US–Mexican Relations*, 131.

35. Cumberland, "Jenkins Case," 598f, 602; *Excélsior*, 6 Dec. 1919, 1.

36. Cumberland, "Jenkins Case," 599–605; LaFrance, "Revisión del caso," 939f, 942; *El Monitor*, 5 Dec. 1919, 1; 13 Dec., 1; *La Prensa*, 1 Feb. 1920, 2; *Excélsior*, 9 Feb. 1920, 1; Wilbur Forrest (*NY Tribune*), US Senate, *Investigation*, II:2048f.

37. LaFrance, "Revisión del caso," 943; *New York Tribune*, reprinted in *Literary Digest*, 21 Feb. 1920, 52–6; *Los Angeles Times*, 13 Mar. 1920, 1–2.

38. Cumberland, "Jenkins Case," 604f; LaFrance, "Revisión del caso," 943f; *El Monitor*, 22 Nov. 1919, 1.

39. LaFrance, "Revisión del caso," 945; Roderic Camp, *Mexican Political Biographies, 1935–1993* (Austin: Univ. of Texas Press, 1995), 757f.

40. LaFrance, *Heartland*, 152f; Gruening, *Mexico and its Heritage*, 504f.

41. *New York Times*, 5 Dec. 1919, 1; *Literary Digest*, 13 Dec. 1919, 11; Jenkins to Jenkins, 20 Oct. 1919, in Summerlin to Lansing, Mexico City, 11 Feb. 1920, RDS 125.61383J41/53, encl. 10.

42. LaFrance, "Revisión del caso," 933–5; *Excélsior*, 16 Nov. 1919, 9.

43. LaFrance, "Revisión del caso," 929; LaFrance, *Heartland*, 187–95.

44. Womack, *Zapata*, 131, 148, 158; *E-B Dealers Magazine*, 1919, MSJP.

45. On Peláez, see Brown, *Oil and Revolution*, 256–306.

46. *New York Times*, 5 Dec. 1919, 1.

47. Hardaker to Norman King, Puebla, 8 Nov. 1919, National Archives, London, Foreign Office Series 371, 3836; Summerlin to Lansing, Mexico City, 31 Aug. 1920, RDS, 125.61383J41/71, encl.; Wilbur Forrest (*NY Tribune*), US Senate, *Investigation*, II:2048–50.

48. *New York Times*, 6 Jul. 1919, 7; 23 Jul., 3; 27 Jul., 3; 29 Jul., 3; 11 Aug., 5 (Carranza's order); 18 Aug., 1; 20 Aug., 3 (LaGuardia's resolution); 12 Sep., 17; 14 Sep., 5; *Los Angeles Times*, 1 Dec., 1.

49. On anti-Americanism, see e.g.: *New York Times*, 24 Jul. 1919, 4.

50. LaFrance, *Heartland*, 169, 185f, 199f, and "Revisión del caso," 929–31.

51. Gen. J. Barragán to Medina, Querétaro, 22 Oct. 1919, SRE, 16-28-1, pt. III; LaFrance, "Revisión del caso," 928, and *Heartland*, 147–50.

52. G. Narváez to Carranza, 25 Oct. 1919, Puebla, SRE, 16-28-1, pt. I. On its author, see LaFrance, *Heartland*, 101f, 133, 158.

53. LaFrance, "Revisión del caso," 930, 942–4; *La Prensa*, 1 Feb. 1920, 1–2; 22 Feb., 1.

54. Cabrera to SRE, Puebla, 20 May 1918, SRE, 42-26-95.

55. *El Monitor*, 7 Jul. 1919, 1 and 4; Jenkins to Summerlin, 13 Dec. 1919, Puebla, RDS, 125.61383J41/20.

56. Knight, *Mexican Revolution*, II:490–2; Krauze, *Biography of Power*, 369f, 389f.

57. Álvaro Matute, *Historia de la Revolución Mexicana, v.8: La carrera del caudillo* (Mexico City: Colegio de México, 1980), 56–61; Hall, *Álvaro Obregón*, 224–30; *El Universal*, 27 Oct. 1919, 1.

58. *Excélsior*, 22 Oct. 1919, 1, 23 Oct, 1; *El Demócrata*, 24 Oct., 1. On the leanings of the Mexico City papers: Álvaro Matute, *Historia de la Revolución Mexicana, vol. 7: Las dificultades del nuevo Estado* (Mexico City: Colegio de México, 1995), 264–9.

59. Quoted in Cumberland, "Jenkins Case," 592.

60. Others have read Carranza's role similarly: Womack, *Zapata*, 346f; Gilderhus, *Diplomacy and Revolution*, 100. On Bonillas, see e.g. *El Universal*, 26 Nov. 1919, 1; 5 Dec., 7; *Excélsior*, 26 Nov., 1; 27 Nov., 7; *El Demócrata*, 5 Dec., 1.

61. Medina to Cabrera, 24 Oct. 1919, Mexico City, SRE, 16-28-1, pt. III.

62. Cumberland, "Jenkins Case," 598f; Lazo, "Lansing, Wilson," 195 n41; *El Demócrata*, 5 Dec. 1919, 1; *Excélsior*, 6 Dec., 5, 10 Dec., 5; "The People of the State of New York against John S. Hansen" (indictment), 29 Dec. 1919, and *Denver Post*, 4 Mar. 1920, Fall Collection, Box 82, file 38.

63. LaFrance, "Revisión del caso," 946; further questions follow on 947f.

64. On Street's return to Tennessee; *Nashville Tennessean*[?], 25 Oct. 1919, Branscomb Papers, Box 362, file 1.

65. Jenkins to Rowe, 7 Nov. 1919, RDS, 125.61383/190; Special Mexican Claims Commission, Report (Washington, DC: USGPO, 1940), 612; Cumberland, "Jenkins Case," 606.

66. *El Demócrata*, 27 Nov. 1919, 2; LaFrance, "Revisión del caso," 937; Cumberland, "Jenkins Case," 596–8.

67. For exmple, F. Rivera and P. Ortega to Obregón, Lagunillas, Pue., 8 Apr. 1923, AGN Obregón-Calles, Exp. 818-J-4.

68. *Excélsior*, 22 May 1932, Dominical, 6, 15; *El Mundo* (Tampico), Jul. 1943, quoted in T. McEnelly to State Dept., Tampico, 12 Jul. 1943, RDS, 812.4061-MP/297; Open letter, Sindicato Héroes de Nacozari to Ruiz Cortines, Puebla, May 1956, AGN, presidential files of Adolfo Ruiz Cortines (hereafter, AGN ARC), 544.2/27; *Éxito* (Mexico City), 18–24 Oct. 1959, 4; *Time*, 26 Dec. 1960, 25. See also, e.g., *Hoy* (Mexico City), 29 Oct. 1949, 12f; *El Universal*, 18 Aug. 1951, 1; *El Universal*, 4 Jul. 1958, 14; Contreras Torres, *El libro negro*, 89–103; *Siempre!* (Mexico City), 17 Oct. 1962, 28.

69. *Excélsior*, 5 Jun. 1963, 5, 13; Cordero y Torres, *Diccionario Biográfico*, 346; J. Jenkins Eustace interview, 15 Aug. 2001.

70. Cordero y Torres, *Historia Compendiada*, III:457; *Time*, 26 Dec. 1960, 25; *La Opinión*, 5 Jun. 1963, 1, 6; *El Día*, 6 Jun., 3; Ángeles Mastretta, *Tear This Heart Out* (New York: Riverhead, 1997 [1985]), 28; Crespo, ed., *Historia del azúcar*, I:112; *Proceso*, 4 Nov. 1991, 22.

71. Jenkins to Stanford, in *Mary Street Jenkins Foundation*, ed. Trueblood, 13; Matute, *La carrera del caudillo*, 60; *El Monitor*, 31 Oct. 1919, 1.

72. Concluding the kidnapping was genuine: Cumberland, "Jenkins Case," 606, cf. Glaser, "1919," 344, Gilderhus, *Diplomacy and Revolution*, 99, and LaFrance, "Revisión del caso," 951. Withholding judgement: Womack, *Zapata*, 346–51, cf. Machado and Judge, "Tempest," Trow, "Woodrow Wilson," and Lazo, "Lansing, Wilson."

73. Bertha Ulloa, "La lucha armada (1911–1920)," in *Historia General de México*, ed. D. Cosío Villegas (Mexico City: Colegio de México, 1981 [3rd ed.]), II:1171, 1178–80; cf. Manuel González Ramírez, *La revolución social de México* (Mexico City: FCE, 1960), I:662–6; Luis Zorrilla, *Historia de las relaciones entre México y E.U.A.* (Mexico City: Porrúa, 1966), II:343f; Gustavo Abel Hernández Enríquez, *Historia moderna de Puebla. 1917–1920* (Puebla: n.p., 1986), 187–213; Álvaro Matute, *Las dificultades*, 60–7.

74. Ulloa, "La lucha armada," 1180.

75. Ruiz Harrell, *El secuestro de William Jenkins* (Mexico City: Planeta, 1992), 283–306.

76. See, e.g., Machado and Judge, "Tempest" (Bonillas's phrase appears in Fletcher to Lansing, Washington, 2 Dec. 1919, RDS, 125.61383/170½); Trow, "Woodrow Wilson," 51–61; Richmond, *Carranza's Nationalist Struggle*, 194–200; Gilderhus, *Diplomacy and Revolution*, 87–98, 103f. For the oil dispute per se, see Brown, *Oil and Revolution*.

77. A column on Jenkins's subsequent land accumulation would make this very claim; *La Opinión*, 11 Jun. 1937, 1.

78. Knight, *Mexican Revolution*, I:485–9, II:158–60, 350–2, and *US–Mexican Relations*, 32.

79. On postrevolutionary US investment: Sanford Mosk, *Industrial Revolution in Mexico* (Berkeley: Univ. of California Press, 1954); Julio Moreno, *Yankee Don't Go Home! Mexican Nationalism, American Business Culture, and the Shaping of Modern Mexico, 1920–1950* (Chapel Hill: Univ. of North Carolina Press, 2003).

80. Beatty, *Institutions and Investment*; Matute, *Las dificultades*, 264–8; Knight, *US–Mexican Relations*, 42.

81. Richmond, *Carranza's Nationalist Struggle*, 192–200; *El Pueblo*, 12 Aug. 1915, quoted in Richmond, 195.

82. John Mason Hart is the leading proponent of this view; see *Revolutionary Mexico*, chs. 4 and 5, and *Empire and Revolution*, chs. 3 to 8. On land ownership: Hart, *Revolutionary Mexico*, 47, 159, and *Empire and Revolution*, 260.

83. Knight, *US–Mexican Relations*, 49, 63–7.

84. Jenkins to Shanklin, 7 Jan. 1915, RDS, 812.00/14285; Jenkins to Shanklin, 18 Nov. 1914, 812.00/14073; LaFrance, *Heartland*, 91f; Knight, *US–Mexican Relations*, 49, 54f.

85. Moreno, *Yankee Don't Go Home!*, ch. 1; Paolo Riguzzi and Patricia de los Ríos, *Las relaciones México-Estados Unidos, 1756–2010* (Mexico City: UNAM, 2012), II:217–23, 234–41.

86. Crespo, ed., *Historia del azúcar*, I:114.

87. Smith, *Revolutionary Nationalism*, 190–228; Muñoz, *La verdad sobre los gringos* (Mexico City: Ediciones Populares, 1927); Embassy to State Dept., Mexico City, 2 Feb. and 5 Mar. 1927, RDS, 711.12/963 and /1025.

88. John Britton, "Redefining Intervention: Mexico's Contribution to Anti-Americanism," in A. McPherson, ed., *Anti-Americanism in Latin America and the Caribbean* (New York: Berghahn Books, 2006), 44–8.

89. Reid, *Spanish American Images*, 157–61, 269f; David Wilt, "Stereotyped Images of United States Citizens in Mexican Cinema, 1930–1990" (PhD diss., Univ. of Maryland, 1991), 295f, 314.

90. Still popular, the work remains in print: Vasconcelos, *La raza cósmica* (Mexico City: Porrúa, 2014).

91. Vaughan, *The State, Education, and Social Class*, chs. 7 and 8, and *Cultural Politics in Revolution: Teachers, Peasants, and Schools in Mexico, 1930–1940* (Tucson: Univ. of Arizona Press, 1997); Henry Schmidt, *The Roots of Lo Mexicano* (College Station: Texas A&M Press, 1978), chs. 4 and 5.

92. Bertram Wolfe, *The Fabulous Life of Diego Rivera* (New York: Stein & Day, 1963), 167; Vaughan, *Cultural Politics*, 38; Desmond Rochfort, "The Sickle, the Serpent, and the Soil," in *The Eagle and the Virgin: Nation and Cultural Revolution in Mexico, 1920–1940*, ed. Mary Kay Vaughan and Stephen Lewis (Durham, NC: Duke Univ. Press, 2006); A. Weddell to State Dept., Mexico City, 20 Oct. 1927, RDS, 711.12/1110; *Política*, 1 Jun. 1960, 29.

93. *El Demócrata*, 14 Aug. 1920; *El Heraldo*, 18 Aug. 1920; *Las Noticias*, 18 Feb. 1921 (Doheny); *Excélsior*, 7 Jun. 1960, 7 (Jenkins); cf. *Opinión Pública* (Mexico City),

1 Jan. 1959, cover (Axel Wenner-Gren), 15 Jul. 1962, 4 (Roberto García Mora), 15 Oct. 1962, 4 (film producers).

94. Wilt, "Stereotyped Images," 66 n. 67, 286; Carl Mora, *Mexican Cinema: Reflections of a Society, 1896–1980* (Berkeley: Univ. of California Press, 1982), 36–49.

95. Merle Simmons, *The Mexican Corrido as a Source of Interpretative Study of Modern Mexico* (Bloomington: Indiana Univ. Press, 1957), ch. XIX; Don Verdades, *Corrido del cine mexicano* (Mexico City: n.p., [1959]).

96. Pablo Yankelevich, "Extranjeros indeseables en México (1911–1940)," *Historia Mexicana* LIII:3 (2004), 693–744, and "Hispanofobia y revolución," *HAHR* 86:1 (2006), 47–9; *Los Derechos del Pueblo Mexicano* (Mexico City: Porrúa, 1978 [1967]), V:215–37 (esp. 220).

97. For example, the Emiliano Zapata Campesino Confederation requested President Rodríguez expel Jenkins, *por extranjero pernicioso*, due to his tax evasion; G. Bermejo to Rodríguez, Puebla, 29 Jun. 1934, AGN Rodríguez, 526.27/66.

98. *Mexican Folkways*, 18 Jun. 1927, 95.

99. Vázquez and Meyer, *United States and Mexico*, 127, 157; *La Prensa* (Mexico City), 16 Sep. 1932, 14.

100. Knight, "The United States and the Mexican Peasantry, circa 1880–1940," in D. Nugent, ed., *Rural Revolt in Mexico* (Durham, NC: Duke Univ. Press, 1998), 47; Krauze, *Biography of Power*, 474f.

101. Garner, *British Lions*, 170, 226–9; Martin R. Ansell, *Oil Baron of the Southwest: Edward L. Doheny and the Development of the Petroleum Industry in California and Mexico* (Columbus: Ohio State Univ. Press, 1998), chs. 3, 4 and Conclusion; Nasaw, *The Chief*, 58–60, 203; "Buckley, William Frank," *Handbook of Texas Online*, www.tshaonline.org/handbook/online/articles/fbu08.

CHAPTER 5

1. The planned move to LA draws on Rowe to Sec. of State, Mexico City, 28 Mar. 1919, RDS, 125.61383/113; Jenkins to Elizabeth Jenkins, Puebla, 26 Dec. 1919, MSJP; *Nashville Tennessean*, 8 Oct. 1920, Branscomb Papers, Box 362, file 1; Jenkins to Stanford, in *Mary Street Jenkins Foundation*, ed. Trueblood, 8f; *Los Angeles Times*, 4 Oct. 1953, II-1, 16; Eustace Jenkins, *Tennessee Sunshine*, 275; J. Jenkins Eustace interview, 2 Apr. 2001.

2. For the "official version" of the Revolution, e.g., Frank Tannenbaum, *Peace by Revolution* (New York: Columbia Univ. Press, 1933); Jesús Silva Herzog, *Breve historia de la Revolución mexicana* (Mexico City: FCE, 1960); Charles Cumberland, *Mexico: The Struggle for Modernity* (Oxford: Oxford Univ. Press, 1968). For the revisionist version, e.g., Gilly, *La revolución interrumpida*; Womack, "The Mexican Economy"; Wasserman, *Persistent Oligarchs*; Kuntz, "De las reformas liberales."

3. Maurer, *Power and the Money*, 160f, 173–7; Sylvia Maxfield, *Governing Capital: International Finance and Mexican Politics* (Ithaca, NY: Cornell Univ. Press, 1990), chs. 2–5; Emilio Zebadúa, *Banqueros y revolucionarios: La soberanía financiera de México, 1914–1929* (Mexico City: Colegio de México, 1994), chs. IV–VII; Luis Anaya Merchant, *Colapso y reforma: La integración del sistema bancario en el México revolucionario, 1913–1932* (Mexico City: Miguel Ángel Porrúa, 2002), ch. 3. On the bankers' alliance: Maxfield, 9.

4. Maurer, *Power and the Money*, 175; David Cannadine, *Mellon* (New York: Vintage, 2008), 348–51.

5. Compare, for Chihuahua: Wasserman, *Persistent Oligarchs*, ch. 5.

6. Francisco Javier Gómez Carpinteiro, *Gente de agua y azúcar* (Zamora: Colegio de Michoacán, 2003), 138; Jenkins to SRE, Mexico City, 26 Dec. 1921, SRE, Exp. 140-PB-11.

7. César Ayala, *American Sugar Kingdom* (Chapel Hill: Univ. of North Carolina, 1999), 65, 233.

8. *Excélsior*, 8 Oct. 1920, 1.

9. Gómez, *Gente de agua*, 318; Jenkins to SRE, Mexico City, 26 Dec. 1921, SRE, Exp. 140-PB-11; Jenkins to Obregón, Puebla, 24 Jan. 1922, AGN Obregón-Calles, Exp. 818-J-4.

10. Crespo, ed., *Historia del azúcar*, I:112, II:829; Gómez, *Gente de agua*, 322; Pedro Díaz Rubín et al. to SRE, Mexico City, 26 and 27 Dec. 1921, SRE, Exp. 38-PB-46; Díaz Rubín de la Hidalga interview, 1 Aug. 2001.

11. *Excélsior*, 5 Jul. 1922, 1; Buve, *El movimiento revolucionario*, 242, 266.

12. *La Opinión*, 15 Dec. 1933, 1 (obit.); RPP-Puebla, Libro 3 de Comercio, Tomo 17, no. 31 and T. 19, no. 82.

13. Hart, *Revolutionary Mexico*, 304f, 340; Jeffrey Bortz, "'Without any more law than their own caprice': Cotton Textile Workers and the Challenge to Factory Authority during the Mexican Revolution," *International Review of Social History* 42:2 (1997); Leticia Gamboa Ojeda, *La urdimbre y la trama* (Mexico City: FCE, 2001), chs. VII and VIII.

14. *El Monitor*, 9 Nov. 1920, 1; 13 Nov., 1; 14 Nov., 6; 28 Dec., 2; *La Crónica* (Puebla), 10 Nov. 1920, 1; 13 Nov., 1; Gamboa, *La urdimbre*, 311–8.

15. *El Monitor*, 10 Jan. 1921, 1; 2 Feb., 1; *Excélsior*, 2 Feb. 1921, 5; Reyes Romero, "La industria bonetera," 58.

16. Gruening, *Mexico and Its Heritage*, 349f; Leticia Gamboa Ojeda, "Momentos de crisis y recuperación en la industria textil mexicana, 1921–1932," *La Palabra y el Hombre* [Jalapa] (Jul. 1990), 23–53.

17. Jenkins to Stanford, in *Mary Street Jenkins Foundation*, ed. Trueblood, 13; *Lista general de industrias establecidas en la ciudad de Puebla* (Puebla: Depto. de Trabajo, 1921), 12f, AGN DT, Caja 279, Exp. 11; RPP-Puebla, L.1 de comercio, T. 7, nos. 8 and 9; Gamboa, *Los empresarios*, 130; Guzmán Ramos interview, 17 Jul. 2007. On

Abed: Alejandro Manjarrez, *Crónicas sin censura* (Cholula, Pue.: Imagen Pública, 1995), 369f, 375f.

18. Dawn Keremitsis, *La industria textil mexicana en el siglo XIX* (Mexico City: SEP, 1973), 235. On immigrant enclaves: Yankelevich, "Hispanofobia y revolución"; Alfaro-Velcamp, *So Far from Allah.*

19. Gaizka de Usabel, *The High Noon of American Pictures in Latin America* (Ann Arbor, MI: UMI, 1982), 20.

20. John W.F. Dulles, *Yesterday in Mexico: A Chronicle of the Revolution, 1919–1936* (Austin: Univ. of Texas Press, 1972), 3–16; Krauze, *Biography of Power,* 341, 384–9.

21. Crespo, ed., *Historia del azúcar,* II:822–28; Matute, *La carrera del caudillo,* 33, 39.

22. Jenkins to Obregón, Puebla, 24 Jan. 1922, AGN Obregón-Calles, Exp. 818-J-4; Gómez, *Gente de azúcar,* 162.

23. Cf. Luis González, *San José de Gracia* (Austin: Univ. of Texas Press, 1974), 186–9.

24. Crespo, ed., *Historia del azúcar,* I:114.

25. Crespo and Vega Villanueva, *Estadísticas históricas,* 238, 248, 257; Jones interview with Jenkins, 13 May 1918, Doheny Collection.

26. Presidencia to Jenkins, Mexico City, 28 Jan. 1922, AGN Obregón-Calles, Exp. 818-J-4; Mestre interview, 22 Aug. 2007. The pending regulations probably refer to the Agrarian Regulatory Law of 1922.

27. LaFrance, *Revolution in Mexico's Heartland,* 173; F. Lozano Cardoso (Sindicato de Agricultores) to Obregón, Puebla, 6 Feb. 1922, AGN Obregón-Calles, Exp. 818-C-43; *Excélsior,* 28 Jun. 1922, II-7.

28. Anita Brenner, *The Wind that Swept Mexico* (Austin: Univ. of Texas Press, 1996 [1943]), 71; M. Hanna to State Dept., Washington, 28 Dec. 1923, RDS, 812.00/266731½; Mestre interviews, 16 Jul. 2003, 22 Aug. 2007.

29. Dulles, *Yesterday in Mexico,* 94–98.

30. Knight, *Mexican Revolution,* II:24f; Jean Meyer, "Revolution and Reconstruction in the 1920s," in *Mexico Since Independence,* ed. L. Bethell, 204.

31. Crespo, ed., *Historia del azúcar,* I:110–6, II:815–7; Hart, *Empire and Revolution,* ch. 11, esp. 345–60.

32. Mestre to Obregón, Mexico City, 9 Jan. and 24 Mar. 1923, Obregón to Mestre, Mexico City, 14 Jun. 1923, Jenkins to Obregón, Puebla, 21 Jun. 1923, Obregón to Jenkins, 22 Jun. 1923, and Oficial Mayor to Jenkins, 25 Jun. 1923, AGN Obregón-Calles, Exp. 823-O-1; Anon. memo [1922], Fondo Álvaro Obregón of the Archivos Calles y Torreblanca (hereafter, Calles-FAO), Exp. 769, inv. 3645.

33. *Excélsior,* 5 Jul. 1922, 1; 7 Jul., II-7 (I discuss this episode in detail in the next chapter); Lozano to Obregón, Puebla, 18 Dec. 1922, AGN Obregón-Calles, Exp. 818-J-4.

34. Jenkins to Obregón, Puebla, 19 Feb. 1923, Obregón to Pres. CNA, Mexico City, 20 Feb., F. Rivera and P. Ortega, Lagunillas, Pue., to Obregón, 8 Apr., Obregón to Rivera and Ortega, 9 Apr., AGN Obregón-Calles, Exp. 818-J-4.

35. On Hispanophobia: Knight, *US–Mexican Relations*, 62–7. For *agrarista* and official targeting of Spaniards and their haciendas: Gov. Manjarrez to Obregón, Puebla, 26 Sep. 1922, AGN Obregón-Calles, Exp. 818-P-5; *Excélsior*, 28 Dec. 1922, 7; 22 Feb. 1923, 1; 2 Sep. 1924, 1; 2 Feb. 1925, 4; *El Universal*, 6 Nov 1929, 7; 2 Dec., 1.

36. Díaz Rubín de la Hidalga interview, 1 Aug. 2001; var. documents, AGN Obregón-Calles, Exp. 818-X-17.

37. Henderson, *Worm in the Wheat*, 37, 62, 68, 86, 105f. On Presno's wealth: Reyna Cruz Valdés and Ambrosio Guzmán Álvarez, *Casa Presno* (Puebla: Univ. Autónoma de Puebla, 2006), 45–8, 52f.

38. Gómez, *Gente de azúcar*, 101f, 110–13, 131–4.

39. Lomelí Vanegas, *Breve historia de Puebla*, 276f; Ronfeldt, *Atencingo*, 7f; Crespo, ed., *Historia del azúcar*, II:829; Gómez, *Gente de agua*, 138 (Table 1); Womack, *Zapata*, 76–82, 121–3, 126, 141, 152, 157, 175, 182f, 221–3, 249, 271–6, 281f, 292f, 393–6.

40. Report on Atencingo y Anexos, Mexico City, Mar. 1934, Registro Agrario Nacional—Puebla, Depto. Agrario, Exp. 1771-C, h. 88; L. Carden to F.O., Mexico City, 9 Dec. 1913, UKFO, Series 371, doc. 1679: 382.

41. Lozano to Obregón, Puebla, 6, 20 and 24 Feb. 1922, Sánchez to Obregón, Puebla, 15 Feb. 1922, Obregón to Sánchez, Mexico City, 16 Feb. 1922, Meré to Obregón, Puebla, 20 Feb. 1922, Partido Nacional Agrarista to Obregón, Mexico City, 18 Apr. 1922, AGN Obregón-Calles, Exp. 818-C-43.

42. Vda. de la Hidalga to Calles, Mexico City, 22 Dec. 1924, Lozano to Calles, Puebla, 20 Jan. 1925, Gonzalo Rosas to Calles, Izúcar, 5 May 1925, AGN Obregón-Calles, Exp. 818-C-43.

43. Gamboa, *Los empresarios*, 246–50; *Excélsior*, 11 Jun. 1922, II-7. The Conde firm's worth equalled $5 million.

44. Gamboa, *Los empresarios*, 153, 250, 253; Gómez, *Gente de azúcar*, 181; *Excélsior*, 29 Jan. 1923, II-7.

45. Crespo and Vega Villanueva, *Estadísticas históricas*, 28, 238; Ronfeldt, *Atencingo*, 11.

46. Dulles, *Yesterday in Mexico*, 175; Mestre interview, 16 Jul. 2003.

47. Kevin Starr, *Material Dreams: Southern California through the 1920s* (New York: Oxford Univ. Press, 1990), 78–85; "The Hollywood Sign," www.hollywoodsign.org.

48. Maurice Zolotow, *Billy Wilder in Hollywood* (New York: Limelight, 1996), 164f; *Los Angeles Times*, 4 Oct. 1953, II-1; J. Jenkins Eustace interviews, 2 Apr. 2001, 27 Jun. 2001.

49. Gruening, *Mexico and Its Heritage*, 468f.

50. Gruening, *Mexico and Its Heritage*, ix-xiii, 393–493. On the violence of the 1920s, cf. Heather Fowler Salamini (on Michoacán and Veracruz) and Gilbert Joseph (on Yucatán) in *Caudillo and Peasant in the Mexican Revolution*, ed. D. Brading (Cambridge: Cambridge Univ. Press, 1980); Wasserman, *Persistent Oligarchs*, ch. 3 (on Chihuahua).

51. I arrived at 16 governors using Enrique Cordero y Torres, *Cronología de: presidentes municipales de la Heroica Puebla de Zaragoza, gobernantes del estado . . .* (Puebla: Centro de Estudios Históricos, 1985), 25–7; Alicia Tecuanhuey, *Cronología política del Estado de Puebla, 1910–1991* (Puebla: Univ. Autónoma de Puebla, 1994); and newspapers. Cf. Camp, *Mexican Political Biographies, 1884–1934,* 428–45 (Chihuahua is ranked second with fourteen).

52. Henderson, *Worm in the Wheat,* 216–9.

53. Governors were supposed to submit recommendations from the state-level local Agrarian Commission to the National Agrarian Commission, which in turn sent them to the president for final approval and a definitive transfer of land; Susan Walsh Sanderson, *Land Reform in Mexico: 1910–1980* (Orlando, FL: Academic Press, 1984), 52–5.

54. Henderson, *Worm in the Wheat,* 96f, 102f, 106–8, 151, 197f, 213–5.

55. LaFrance, *Heartland,* 205f; Henderson, *Worm in the Wheat,* 163, 214; Dulles, *Yesterday in Mexico,* 128.

56. *Excélsior,* 27 Jun. 1920, 9; 28 Jun., 5; 4 Sep., 5; LaFrance, *Heartland,* 163–7, and "Las finanzas públicas y el desarrollo socioeconómico en el Estado de Puebla, 1910–1940," paper delivered at the Facultad de Economía, Universidad de las Américas, Puebla, 8 Apr. 2005.

57. LaFrance, "Las finanzas públicas"; *La Opinión,* 17 Jul. 1928, 1.

58. *El Monitor,* 8 May 1920, 1 (after Gov. Cabrera's exit); *Excélsior,* 9 Apr. 1921, 5 (after Sánchez Pontón); *Excélsior* and *El Universal,* 14 Apr. 1922, 1 (after J.M. Sánchez); *El Universal,* 13 Dec. 1923, 7 (after Manjarrez); 3 Nov. 1924, 5 (after Guerrero); 20 Jan. 1925, 1 (after Sánchez's second stint); *Excélsior,* 12 Jan. 1927, II-8 (after Tirado); *El Universal,* 5 Jul. 1927, 8 (after Montes).

59. *El Universal,* 20 Jan. 1925, 1; 5 Jul. 1927, 8; *Excélsior,* 4 Jul. 1927, 8; 5 Jul., 1; *La Opinión,* 9 Jun. 1955, 1; Henderson, *Worm in the Wheat,* 221.

60. Wasserman, *Persistent Oligarchs,* 142, 156 (cf. 37–49, 56–8); cf. *New York Times,* 24 Jun. 2013, A4.

61. *El Universal,* 5 Apr. 1925, II-1; *Periódico Oficial* (Puebla), 24 Dec. 1927, 53; *La Opinión,* 17 Jan. 1935, 5; Luis Aboites Aguilar, *Excepciones y privilegios: Modernización tributaria y centralización en México 1922–1972* (Mexico City: Colegio de México, 2003).

62. LaFrance, "Las finanzas públicas"; Gruening, *Mexico and Its Heritage,* 133; Crespo and Vega, *Estadísticas históricas,* 24f.

63. See, e.g., *El Universal,* 6 Jul. 1958, 7, 14; Contreras Torres, *El libro negro,* 92; *Proceso,* 11 Aug. 1980, 16–18; Donald Hodges, *Mexican Anarchism After the Revolution* (Austin: Univ. of Texas Press, 1995), ch. 2.

64. Henderson, *Worm in the Wheat,* 148–54, 176–8; Lomelí, *Breve historia,* 337–42, 344–9; Samuel Malpica, *Atlixco: Historia de la clase obrera* (Puebla: Univ. Autónoma de Puebla, 1989); Gregory Crider, "Material Struggles: Workers' Strategies during the 'Institutionalization of the Revolution' in Atlixco, Puebla, Mexico, 1930–1942" (PhD diss., Univ. of Wisconsin, 1996).

65. *Excélsior*, 30 Aug. 1925, 3; 4 Sep., 1; Mjr. E. L. N. Glass to State Dept., Mexico City, 15 Sep. 1925, Colección Embajada EU, Archivos Calles y Torreblanca (hereafter, Calles-CEEU), Series 100202, inv. 39.

66. *El Universal*, 19 Apr. 1921, 1; 6 Nov. 1929, 7; 29 Dec., II-9; *Excélsior*, 2 Sep. 1924, 1; 10 Jan. 1925, 1; "Informe," 15 Jan. 1926, Archivo del Congreso del Estado de Puebla (hereafter, ACEP), Libro 249, Exp. 1078; Henderson, *Worm in the Wheat*, 187–90, 193f, 214f.

67. J. Eustace Jenkins interview, 27 Jun. 2001; R. Eustace interview, 10 Apr. 2002. The fortnightly payroll was equal to some $100,000 today.

68. Interviews with Mario Ortega [pseud.], Atencingo, 9 Jul. 2005, and Eusebio Benítez, Atencingo, 22 Apr. 2006.

69. LaFrance, *Heartland*, 175–7; Henderson, *Worm in the Wheat*, 69; *La Opinión*, 8 Apr. 1930, 1; *El Universal*, 30 May 1935, 1; Sergio Valencia Castrejón, *Poder regional y política nacional en México: El gobierno de Maximino Ávila Camacho en Puebla (1937–1941)* (Mexico City: INEHRM, 1996), 35–7, 75f. Denials, e.g.: *El Universal*, 31 May 1935, 1. Examples elsewhere: Paul Friedrich, *Agrarian Revolt in a Mexican Village* (Chicago: Univ. of Chicago Press, 1977), 56; Heather Fowler-Salamini, *Agrarian Radicalism in Veracruz, 1920–38* (Lincoln: Univ. of Nebraska Press, 1978), 35–39,131f.

70. Strongmen emerged in the 1920s in San Luis Potosi (Saturnino Cedillo), Tabasco (Tomás Garrido Canabal), Tamaulipas (Emilio Portes Gil), Tlaxcala (Ignacio Mendoza), Veracruz (Adalberto Tejeda), Yucatán (Felipe Carrillo Puerto), and arguably Michoacán (Francisco Múgica), states that all had a lower than average turnover of governors; see Brading, ed., *Caudillo and Peasant*; cf. Camp, *Mexican Political Biographies, 1884–1934*, 428–45.

71. Jenkins to G. Summerlin, Puebla, 10 May 1920, RDS, 812.00/24101; Hardaker to N. King, Puebla, 20 May 1920, UKFO, Series 371, doc. 4494:50f; *El Monitor*, 8 May 1920, 1; *El Universal*, 18 Jun. 1920, 4; *Excélsior*, 4 Aug. 1920, 5.

72. LaFrance, *Heartland*, 77, 107, 160, 205–7; Womack, "Mexican Revolution," 198.

73. *Periódico Oficial*, 24 Dec. 1927, 53–74; M. Barrientos, report, 31 Dec. 1922, ACEP, Libro 224–1, Exp. 452.

74. James Wilkie and Edna Monzón de Wilkie, *México visto en el siglo XX* (Mexico City: Instituto Mexicano de Investigaciones Económicas, 1969), 266–9; Lomelí, *Breve historia*, 342; Daniela Spenser (biographer of Lombardo Toledano), email to author, 13 Nov. 2009.

75. W. A. Jenkins interview, 11 Nov. 2005; his assessment of Jenkins's US ties is borne out in the archival record (RDS, SRE, Tigert Papers, etc.) by a paucity of political friendships.

76. Laton McCartney, *The Teapot Dome Scandal* (New York: Random House, 2008); Mencken, "Politics," in *Civilization in the United States*, ed. H. Stearns (New York: Harcourt, Brace, 1922), 23f.

77. *El Universal*, 5 Apr. 1925, II-1, 16 Apr. 1925, 10; *Excélsior*, 11 Aug. 1925, II-7; *La Opinión*, 13 Sep. 1929, 1. Bravo made way for the elected Leónides Andreu Almazán in Feb. 1929.

78. *Excélsior*, 23 Aug. 1927, 8; *La Opinión*, 17 Jul. 1928, 1; Alejandro Manjarrez, *Puebla: el rostro olvidado* (Puebla: Imagen Pública y Corporativa, 1991), 107f; F. Lozano Cardoso to Legislature (herafter, Leg.), 18 Jul. 1921, ACEP, Libro 225, Exp. 478; Guzmán Ramos interview, 16 May 2005.

79. *El Universal*, 7 Dec. 1929, II-3; 14 Dec., II-3; *La Opinión*, 14 Nov. 1928, 1. Cf. Tigert to J. Daniels, Gainesville FL, 7 Sep. 1937, Tigert Papers.

80. J. Jenkins Eustace interview, 26 Jun. 2002; interview with Manuel Pérez Nochebuena, Puebla, 31 May 2006. On Abed: *La Opinión*, 3 Feb. 1928, 1; 13 Jan. 1933, 1; 14 Apr. 1937, 1; 24 Apr., 4; *Excélsior*, 28 Dec. 1931, II-1.

81. Michael Ervin (historian), email to author, 18 Dec. 2006; cf. Ervin, "The 1930 Agrarian Census in Mexico," *HAHR* 87:3 (2007), 568.

82. Ronfeldt, *Atencingo*, 8–10; Gómez, *Gente de agua*, ch. IV; Henderson, *Worm in the Wheat*, 86f; Mariano Torres Bautista, *La familia Maurer de Atlixco, Puebla* (Mexico City: Conaculta, 1994), 177–83.

83. *El Monitor*, 12 Jan. 1922, 1; Lomelí Vanegas, *Breve historia*, 272f, 278; Gamboa, *Los empresarios*, 153, 158. On the judiciary in the 1920s: Gruening, *Mexico and Its Heritage*, 498–505.

84. *Excélsior*, 5 Jul. 1922, 1; 7 Jul., II-6 (Manjarrez); 29 Jun. 1924, 1 (Guerrero); 4 Jan. 1925, 1 (Enrique Moreno).

85. Álvaro Matute, "Del Ejército Constitucionalista al Ejército Nacional," *Estudios de Historia Moderna y Contemporánea de México* VI (1977); Henderson, *Worm in the Wheat*, 100; David LaFrance, "The Military as Political Actor (and More) in the Mexican Revolution," paper delivered at LASA, San Juan, PR, Mar. 2006.

86. Lozano to Obregón, 24 Feb. 1922, AGN Obregón-Calles, Exp. 818-C-43; Jenkins to Tigert, Puebla, 21 Aug. 1927, Tigert Papers; G. Rosas Solaegui to Jefe Depto., Mexico City, 14 Dec. 1933, Dir. Gen. de Investigaciones Políticas y Sociales, AGN (hereafter, AGN DGIPS), Caja 66, Exp. 8; Mestre interview, 18 Jun. 2003.

87. Meré to Obregón, 20 Feb. 1922, AGN Obregón-Calles, Exp. 818-C-43; Gruening, *Mexico and its Heritage*, 319; Henderson, *Worm in the Wheat*, 100–2; Contreras Torres, *El libro negro*, 40; *El Universal*, 6 Jul. 1958, 14.

88. *Excélsior* 1 Oct. 1920, 5; *La Crónica*, 1 Oct. 1920, 4; Joseph Rickaby, *The Lord My Light* (London, 1915), personal collection of Rosemary Eustace Jenkins, Mexico City.

89. Pedro Vera y Zuria, *Diario de mi destierro* (El Paso, TX: Revista Católica, 1927); Margaret Branscomb to *Time* (magazine), Nashville, 21 Dec. 1960, Branscomb Papers, Box 362, File 2; J. Jenkins Eustace interviews, 27 Jun. 2002, 8 Jul. 2003, 20 Apr. 2005; W. A. Jenkins interview, 29 Sep. 2009.

90. Tecuanhuey, *Cronología política*, 39; *El Universal*, 24 Aug. 1924, 1; see also 25 Aug. 1924, 1.

91. On the tight bond between Puebla's Church and its business elite, including Jenkins, see José Luis Sánchez Gavi, *El espíritu renovado: La Iglesia Católica en México* (Mexico City: Plaza y Valdés, 2012), 81–6.

92. Henderson, *Worm in the Wheat*. On other luckless US landowners: Hart, *Empire and Revolution*, ch. 11.
93. Evans, *Rosalie Evans Letters*, 313; Alexander Weddell to State Dept., Mexico City, 27 Mar. 1927, RDS, 812.00/28297; Josephus Daniels, *The Wilson Era* (Chapel Hill: Univ. of North Carolina Press, 1946), Ch. XLIV.
94. I explore Jenkins's use of "soft power" in the next chapter.
95. Díaz Rubín de la Hidalga interview, 1 Aug. 2001; *La Opinión*, 28 Jun. 1932, 3.
96. Cruz Valdés and Guzmán Álvarez, *Casa Presno*, 30–6; *La Opinión*, 6 May 1932, 2.
97. *Excélsior*, 8 Nov. 1921, 1.
98. Leticia Gamboa Ojeda, *Au-delà de l'Océan: Les Barcelonettes à Puebla* (Barcelonette: Sabença de la Valéia, 2004), 287–301, 306f; RPP-Puebla, L.1 de comercio, T. 6, no. 102 (1919) and T. 7, nos. 182/183 (1927).
99. Jenkins to Tigert, Puebla, 24 Aug. 1924, 2 Apr. 1925, 21 Aug. 1927, Tigert Papers.
100. The $5 million reflects Atencingo Co. capital stock on 2 Jan. 1926 (see later discussion).
101. Crespo and Vega, *Estadísticas históricas*, 28; Espinosa Yglesias, "Introduction," 13.
102. Crespo, ed., *Historia del azúcar*, II:829; Gómez, *Gente de azúcar*, 323; Cordero y Torres, *Diccionario Biográfico*, 698f; Jenkins to SRE, Puebla, 11 Oct. 1924, SRE, Exp. 140-PB-11; Jenkins to Calles, Mexico City, 3 Mar. 1925, AGN Obregón-Calles, Exp. 818-X-18; J. Jenkins Eustace interview, 2 Apr. 2001; Velasco Matienzo interview, 19 Jul. 2007.
103. On Colón and Rijo: Vda. de la Hidalga to Calles, Mexico City, 22 Dec. 1924, G. Rosas to Calles, Izúcar, 5 May 1925, AGN Obregón-Calles, Exp. 818-C-43; C. Villafuerte to G.P. Serrano, Mexico City, 3 Jun. 1940, SRE, Exp. III-837–1; Gómez, *Gente de azúcar*, 298f. On Tatetla: Gamboa, *Los empresarios*, 253; Oficial Mayor to Jenkins, Mexico City, 25 Jun. 1923, AGN Obregón-Calles, Exp. 823-O-1; M. Jenkins to SRE, Mexico City, 19 Jun. 1928, SRE, Exp. 52-PB-53. On Teruel: E. Jenkins to SRE, Puebla, 26 Nov. 1927, SRE, Exp. 349-PB-7.
104. On Tolentino: Crespo, ed., *Historia del azúcar*, II:829; Cordero y Torres, *Diccionario Biográfico*, 443; Villafuerte to Serrano, 3 Jun. 1940, SRE, Exp. III-837–1. On Raboso: Torres, *La familia Maurer*, 84f, 177–83.
105. Ronfeldt, *Atencingo*, 10 (cf. Crespo, ed., *Historia del azúcar*, I:112; Pansters, *Politics and Power in Puebla*, 62; Lomelí Vanegas, *Breve historia*, 369; etc.); Reinhard Liehr, *Ayuntamiento y oligarquía en Puebla, 1787–1810* (Mexico City: SEP, 1971), I:15; Crespo, ed., *Historia del azúcar*, I:109–15, II:827f.
106. Cándido Gadea Pineda, *74 años de historia en la vida real de Atencingo* (Atencingo, Pue.: n.p., 1995), 4–18, 62–6; Ronfeldt, *Atencingo*, 10f; Gómez, *Gente de azúcar*, 148.
107. Henderson, *Worm in the Wheat*, 87; Cordero y Torres, *Diccionario Biográfico*, 346; Jenkins to E. Jenkins, Puebla, 19 Oct. 1919, MSJP; *La Opinión*, 27 Sep. 1928, 4 (ad); J. Eustace Jenkins interview, 15 Aug. 2001; Mestre interview, 18 Jun. 2003.

108. Ronfeldt, *Atencingo*, 10f; Crespo, ed., *Historia del azúcar*, I:113; AGN, Gobernación Siglo XX, Depto. de Migración (hereafter, AGN Migración), Españoles, Caja 187, Exp. 16; interviews with Francisco Pérez, José Manuel Pérez and Sara Vega de Pérez (relatives of Manuel Pérez), Puebla, 25 May 2006, and Georgina Luna, Atencingo, 18 Mar. 2006.

109. Ronfeldt, *Atencingo*, 10; Espinosa, *Zafra de odios*, 103; Gómez, *Gente de azúcar*, 147; J. Jenkins Eustace interview, 2 Apr. 2001; Luna interview, 18 Mar. 2006.

110. Felipe Ruiz de Velasco, *Historia y evoluciones del cultivo de la caña y de la industria azucarera en México* (Mexico City: Azúcar SA, 1937), 27f, 399–420; *Técnica Azucarera*, Feb. 1943, 25; Crespo, ed., *Historia del azúcar*, I:569f, 579; Crespo and Vega, *Estadísticas históricas*, 344–6, 331f; Ronfeldt, *Atencingo*, 11; Mestre interview, 18 Jun. 2003; Guzmán Ramos interview, 16 May 2005.

111. Mary S. Jenkins to Verniscia, 1 Apr. 1922, 28 Feb. 1927, MSJP.

112. Gómez, *Gente de azúcar*, 151; Ortega interview, 9 Jul. 2005.

113. Maurer, *Power and the Money*, 183–92; *Excélsior*, 14 Feb. 1923, II-7; *La Crónica*, 9 Mar. 1923 (ad).

114. RPP-Puebla, L.3 de comercio, T. 17, no. 118 (2 Jan. 1926).

115. Jenkins to Tigert, Puebla, 2 Apr. 1925, Tigert Papers.

116. Calles's chief misinterpreter was US Ambassador James Sheffield; Jürgen Buchenau, *Plutarco Elías Calles and the Mexican Revolution* (Lanham, MD: Rowman & Littlefield, 2007), 117f, 132f.

117. This is what Jenkins would argue to the IRS in 1939; *Mary Street Jenkins Foundation*, ed. Trueblood, 7–10.

118. This, again, is the argument Jenkins made to the IRS; *Mary Street Jenkins Foundation*, ed. Trueblood, 10–12.

119. Crespo, ed., *Historia del azúcar*, I:205, 253, 257, II:954f; Crespo, "The Cartelization of the Mexican Sugar Industry, 1924–1940" in *The World Sugar Economy in War and Depression*, ed. B. Albert and A. Graves (London: Routledge, 1988), 89f.

120. Jenkins to Tigert, Puebla, 21 Aug. 1927, Tigert Papers; Luis Ortega Morales, "La CTM en Puebla," *Boletín de Investigación del Movimiento Obrero* 10 (Dec. 1987), 102.

121. Crespo and Vega, *Estadísticas históricas*, 28f; Torres, *La familia Maurer*, 178–83.

122. Contreras Torres, *El libro negro*, 91f; Cordero y Torres, *Diccionario Biográfico*, 350–2; Ronfeldt, *Atencingo*, 9f, 14f, 44f; Espinosa, *Zafra de odios*, 149–52, 161–3; Gómez, *Gente de azúcar*, 31–5, 150f, 254, 381–3; Úrsulo Valle Morales, *El despertar democrático de Atencingo* (Atencingo, Pue.: n.p., 1984), 18.

123. Juan Oliver, quoted in Gómez, *Gente de azúcar*, 79, 410f; cf. 32–5, 140f.

CHAPTER 6

1. The 1922 shoot-out draws on Gil Vega to Gen. F. Mendoza, Lagunillas, Pue., 12 Jul. 1922, transcr. in Mendoza to Obregón, Tepalcingo, Mor., 22 Jul. 1922, AGN Obregón-Calles, Exp. 818-J-4; *Excélsior*, 28 Jun. 1922, II-7; 5 Jul. 1922, 1; 7 Jul. 1922, II-6, II-7.

2. Ronfeldt, *Atencingo*, 12–14.

3. Obregón to Mendoza, Mexico City, 14 Sep. 1922, AGN Obregón-Calles, Exp. 818-J-4; Womack, *Zapata*, 335–46.

4. *Excélsior*, 10 Nov. 1922, II-7; 15 Nov. 1922, 3; Jenkins to Juez Supernumerario Distrito, Puebla, 6 Nov. 1922, ACEP, Libro 231, Exp. 657.

5. *Excélsior*, 1 Dec. 1922, II-7.

6. Sidney Mintz, *Sweetness and Power* (New York: Penguin, 1985), ch. 2; Eduardo Galeano, *Open Veins of Latin America* (New York: Monthly Review Press, 1975), ch. 2.

7. Crespo, ed., *Historia del azúcar*, I:50–8, 200–4; Lomelí Vanegas, *Breve historia*, 276f; Cordero y Torres, *Historia compendiada*, III:44.

8. Hart, *Empire and Revolution*, 169.

9. Mark Wasserman, "You Can Teach an Old Revolutionary Historiography New Tricks," *Latin American Research Review* 43:2 (2008), 260–4; Tenorio and Gómez Galvarriato, *El Porfiriato*, esp. 12f, 83–8.

10. *Excélsior*, 28 Jun. 1922, II-7; Lomelí Vanegas, *Breve historia*, 276f.

11. Gómez, *Gente de azúcar*, 101–8.

12. Gómez, *Gente de azúcar*, 127f, 179f.

13. Womack, *Zapata*, 75–82, 393–404; LaFrance, *Mexican Revolution in Puebla*, 75–7.

14. LaFrance, *Heartland*, 89–114, 145–62.

15. Alan Knight and Wil Pansters, eds., *Caciquismo in Twentieth Century Mexico* (London: Institute for the Study of the Americas, 2006).

16. Alan Knight, *Mexico: The Colonial Era* (Cambridge: Cambridge Univ. Press, 2002), 12–14.

17. *Excélsior*, 10 Jul. 1924, quoted in Henderson, *Worm in the Wheat*, 178. On the role of land in cacique rule: Brading, ed., *Caudillo and Peasant*.

18. E.g., Womack, *Zapata*, 379–82, 385 (re. Zapata's son Nicolás); Henderson, *Worm in the Wheat*, 103 (Gov. Montes) and 221 (Gov. Sánchez).

19. Crump dominated Memphis politics from 1910 to c. 1948; G. Wayne Dowdy, *Mayor Crump Don't Like It: Machine Politics in Memphis* (Jackson: Univ. Press of Mississippi, 2006); Howse was mayor of Nashville for 1909–15 and 1923–38; Doyle, *Nashville in the New South*, 165–82.

20. Agent #6 to Sec. Gobernación, Mexico City, 30 Nov. 1928, AGN, Dirección General de Gobierno (hereafter, AGN DGG), Caja 289, Exp. 4.

21. Obregón to R. Gómez, Mexico City, 28 Jul. 1924, AGN Obregón-Calles, Exp. 121-W-B; Obregón to Gen. F.R. Serrano (Sec. Guerra), 2 Aug. 1924, AGN Obregón-Calles, Exp. 101-B-8.

22. Womack, *Zapata*, 357; Jenkins to SRE, 20 Apr. 1926, SRE, Exp. 140-PB-11; *Diario de los Debates de la Cámara de Diputados* (Mexico City), 21 Nov. 1927; Agent #6 to Sec. Gobernación, 30 Nov. 1928, AGN DGG, Caja 289, Exp. 4; *La Opinión*, 28 Jun. 1928, 4; 14 Aug. 1928, 1; 23 Aug. 1928, 5.

23. Jenkins to Calles, Puebla, 16 Jan. 1925, AGN Obregón-Calles, Exp. 818-M-9; *Excélsior*, 4 Jan. 1925, 1; 3 Feb. 1925, 1; Crespo, ed., *Historia del azúcar*, II:831.

24. *La Opinión*, 8 Oct. 1942, 2; Burgos to Rodríguez, Puebla, 22 Mar. 1933, and M. Hidalgo Salazar to Rodríguez, Puebla, 12 Jul. 1933, AGN, presidential files of Abelardo L. Rodríguez (hereafter, AGN ALR), Exp. 08/102; *Ixtahuac* (clipping, n.d.), AGN, presidential files of Lázaro Cárdenas (hereafter, AGN LC), Exp. 544.5/227.

25. Ronfeldt, *Atencingo*, 10; Crespo, ed., *Historia del azúcar*, II:828f; Gómez, *Gente de azúcar*, 147, 299.

26. Gómez, *Gente de azúcar*, 101f, 110–3, 134.

27. *Excélsior*, 9 May 1922, II-7; *La Opinión*, 14 Aug. 1928, 1; 23 Aug., 5; 27 May 1933, 1. Gómez, *Gente de azúcar*, 140. Similar tensions existed between the town of Tilapa and Jenkins's sugar estate Colón; 303–9.

28. The sketch of Celestino and Lola is drawn from Ronfeldt, *Atencingo*, 12–15; Gómez, *Gente de azúcar*, 325–38.

29. Conflicts between landowning ranchers and landless peasants were common; see e.g. Ian Jacobs, *Ranchero Revolt: The Mexican Revolution in Guerrero* (Austin: Univ. of Texas Press, 1983); Keith Brewster, *Militarism, Ethnicity, and Politics in the Sierra Norte de Puebla, 1917–1930* (Tucson: Univ. of Arizona Press, 2003).

30. Manjarrez to Leg., 24 Mar. 1923, Puebla, ACEP, Libro 231, Exp. 657; Gómez, *Gente de azúcar*, 323.

31. Ayaquica to Pres., Atlixco, 25 Apr. 1929, AGN EPG, Exp. 3/840; Burgos to C. López, [Chietla], n.d. [Apr. 1929], AGN LC, Exp. 544.5/227.

32. Ronfeldt, *Atencingo*, 15–17, 47, 51; Maria Teresa Ventura Rodríguez, "La organización sindical de los obreros azucareros en Puebla, México," paper presented at LASA congress, Rio de Janeiro, Jun. 2009. For a report on the Atencingo *sindicato blanco*, see: Rosas Solaegui to Jefe Depto., 14 Dec. 1933, AGN DGIPS, Caja 66, Exp. 8.

33. *La Opinión*, 12 Dec. 1931, 1; 9 Mar. 1932, 1; Andreu Almazán, "Memorias," *El Universal*, 4 Jul. 1958, 14; Hodges, *Mexican Anarchism*, 37, 42f.

34. Gómez, *Gente de azúcar*, 335.

35. Bonilla to Vega, 24 Apr. 1929, Cuautla; Burgos to López, [Apr. 1929], AGN LC, Exp. 544.5/227.

36. A. Romano and F. Ramos to Cárdenas, Chietla, 27 Nov. 1934, AGN LC, Exp. 544.5/227; Ronfeldt, *Atencingo*, 17.

37. *Puebla en cifras* (Mexico City: Dirección General de Estadística, 1944), 125; Crespo and Vega, *Estadísticas históricas*, 25, 28.

38. Mary S. Jenkins to Verniscia, 28 Feb. 1927, MSJP; Eustace Jenkins, *Tennessee Sunshine*, 329; J. Jenkins Eustace interview, 27 Jun. 2001; Guzmán Ramos interview, 15 Jul. 2005; Jane Jenkins's diary of 1931 (6 Mar.), REJP.

39. Crespo, ed., *Historia del azúcar*, I:113; Gómez, *Gente de azúcar*, 150f; interviews with Aurelio García Pliego, Atencingo, 18 Mar. 2006; Cruz Guzmán, Atencingo, 22 Apr. 2006; Ortega, 9 Jul. 2005; Benítez, 22 Apr. 2006.

40. F. Pérez, J. M. Pérez, and Vega de Pérez interview, 25 May 2006; Pérez Nochebuena interview, 31 May 2006.

41. Yankelevich, "Hispanofobia"; *El Universal*, 6 Nov. 1929, 7; 2 Dec. 1929, 1; 29 Dec. 1929, II-9; J. Ramírez to Sec. Particular, Rancho del Capire, 15 Nov. 1936, AGN LC, 404.1/5767; Mestre interview, 18 Jun. 2003.

42. Yankelevich, "Hispanofobia," 33f; A. Campos et al. to Ortiz Rubio, Chietla, 15 Jun. 1931, AGN, presidential files of Pascual Ortiz Rubio (hereafter, AGN POR), Exp. 1931-224-4794; *El Nacional* (Mexico City), 9 Oct. 1931, 1; Benítez interview, 22 Apr. 2006.

43. Interviews with Mestre, 18 Jun. 2003; Ortega, 9 Jul. 2005; García Pliego, 18 Mar. 2006; Benítez, 22 Apr. 2006. Cf. Friedrich Katz, "Labor Conditions on Haciendas in Porfirian Mexico," *HAHR* 54:1 (1974); Knight, *Mexican Revolution*, I:85–91.

44. Mintz, *Sweetness and Power*, 47–52; William K. Scarborough, *The Overseer: Plantation Management in the Old South* (Baton Rouge: Louisiana State Univ. Press, 1966), 67–75.

45. Fowler-Salamini, *Agrarian Radicalism*, 35–39, 131f; Wasserman, *Persistent Oligarchs*, 56, 72, 127. For Puebla: Valencia Castrejón, *Poder regional*, 35–7; various docs., AGN ALR, Exps. 540/40, 541.5/92 and AGN LC, Exps. 555.1/103, 556.7/7. On "white guards," compare "white unions," previously.

46. Ortega interview, 9 Jul. 2005; García Pliego interview, 18 Mar. 2006; Benítez interview, 22 Apr. 2006; Henderson, *Worm in the Wheat*, 164.

47. Gómez, *Gente de azúcar*, 322f; Emilio Maurer, quoted in Guzmán Ramos interview, 16 May 2005.

48. *Siempre!*, 6 Sep. 1961, 7; Gómez, *Gente de azúcar*, 151, 254; Ortega interview, 9 Jul. 2005; Alexis Juárez Cao Romero (sociologist), email to author, 16 Oct. 2007.

49. Secret police reports (cited here as AGN DGIPS) were first compiled on Atencingo in 1932.

50. Gadea Pineda, *74 años de historia*, 68f; Gómez, *Gente de azúcar*, 147; Torres, *La familia Maurer*, 177–83.

51. *La Opinión*, 10 Jun. 1934, 1; Gómez, *Gente de azúcar*, 336f; P.L. Romero to Cárdenas, Atlixco, 15 Mar. 1935, and F. Ramírez Villareal to Romero, Mexico City, 6 Apr. 1935, AGN Cárdenas, 546.2/19.

52. M. Sánchez and G. Bermejo to Rodríguez, Texmelucan, 31 Aug. 1934, A. Ceballos to Rodríguez, Chietla, 18 Sep. 1934, AGN ALR, Exp. 526.27/66; B. Vázquez to Cárdenas, Calantla, 21 Dec. 1936, AGN LC, Exp. Q/021/2666.

53. Untitled home movie, 1943, collection of R. Eustace Jenkins, viewed 4 Jul. 2003.

54. William Wiethoff, *Crafting the Overseer's Image* (Columbia: Univ. of South Carolina Press, 2006), ch. 4; Richard Follett, *The Sugar Masters* (Baton Rouge: Louisiana State Univ. Press), 173–8.

55. J. Jenkins Eustace interview, 27 Jun. 2001; R. Eustace Jenkins interview, 2 Aug. 2001.

56. W. A. Jenkins interview, 27 Jun. 2001. The notion that Latin America's peasants naturally incline to violence was standard among US observers and a common justification for harsh measures; cf. Greg Grandin, *The Last Colonial Massacre: Latin America in the Cold War* (Chicago: Univ. of Chicago Press, 2004), ch. 3.

57. Crespo, ed., *Historia del azúcar*, I:150–2; Ortega interview, 9 Jul. 2005; Luna interview, 18 Mar. 2006.

58. Atencingo anecdotes draw on interviews with Ortega, 9 Jul. 2005; García Pliego, 18 Mar. 2006; Benítez and C. Guzmán, 22 Apr. 2006. Henderson describes a similar landlord/manager dynamic; *Worm in the Wheat*, 168.

59. Ortega interview, 9 Jul. 2005.

60. Corbin, quoted in US Congress, *Investigation of Mexican Affairs*, I:1456; Cordero y Torres, *Historia compendiada*, I:236; Feland Meadows to J. Erwin, Puebla, 23 Jul. 1961, Mary Jenkins William Papers (herafter, MJWP), held by Susan Heflinger, Los Angeles; J. Jenkins Eustace interview, 27 Jun. 2002; R. Eustace interview, 8 Jul. 2003.

61. Interview with Fernando Ramírez Camarillo, Atencingo, 18 Mar. 2006; C. Guzmán interview, 22 Apr. 2006.

62. *Excélsior*, 11 Apr. 1921, 7; *La Opinión*, 9 Jul. 1934, 1, 20 Oct. 1937, 6.

63. Beezley, *Judas*, 26; Fernández and Paxman, *El Tigre*, 31, 301, 466; cf. Steve Stein, "The Case of Soccer in Early Twentieth-Century Lima," in *Sport and Society in Latin America*, ed. J. Arbena (Wesport, CT: Greenwood Press, 1988).

64. *Acción* (Puebla), 17 Jun. 1944, 2, 4; Ortega interview, 9 Jul. 2005. Photographs: Manuel Pérez and basketball team, Atencingo, c. 1930, collection of Vicente Lara Lara, Atencingo; "Aniversario de la Revolución," Atencingo, 20 Nov. 1946, and "La agrupación, comité local y los niños de José Lima," Chietla, 2 Sep. 1946, collection of Eufrasia de la Cuadra, Izúcar de Matamoros.

65. Gadea Pineda, *74 años de historia*, 52–61; Gómez, *Gente de azúcar*, 88, 371.

66. *La Opinión*, 20 Apr. 1931, 1; Gómez, *Gente de azúcar*, 156f, 175, 193f, 344f, 377. The school at Atencingo is depicted in a painting with the year "1928" above the schoolhouse door; collection of Eufrasia de la Cuadra, Izúcar de Matamoros. Prior to 1931, school-building laws had been left to the states, to highly varied outcomes; Dulles, *Yesterday in Mexico*, 514; Vaughan, *Cultural Politics*, 32f.

67. Gómez, *Gente de azúcar*, 157; photograph of Manuel Pérez Lamadrid opening school, Temaxcalapa, 30 Sep. 1934, and speech by Manuel Pérez Pena at school opening, Atencingo, 20 Nov. 1942, collection of Manuel Pérez Nochebuena, Puebla; Cyril Houle, "Some Significant Experiments in Latin-American Education," *Elementary School Journal* 49:2 (1948), 61–6.

68. *El Universal*, 12 Feb. 1930, II-3; Gómez, *Gente de azúcar*, 343–9, 357 and 375 (photos), 376–8.

69. Gómez, *Gente de azúcar*, 82f, 343f. For further alleged exchanges of favor, cf. 175, 193f, 347.

70. Luis Mora, quoted in Gómez, *Gente de azúcar*, 344 (cf. Melio Aguilar, 83); Ortega interview, 9 Jul. 2005.

71. *La Opinión*, 12 Jun. 1934, 3 (cf. 10 Jun., 1); Gómez, *Gente de azúcar*, 347.

72. Benítez interview, 18 Mar. 2006. Ortega recounted a similar personal experience; interview, 9 Jul. 2005.

73. *Puebla en cifras*, 78f; Vaughan, *State, Education*, 158.

74. Census questionnaire, Puebla, 5 Jul. 1938, Fondo Extranjería, AGMP, Exp. 7056 (7059); interview with Eufrasia de la Cuadra (daughter of Atencingo engineer), Izúcar de Matamoros, 9 Jul. 2005.

75. Vaughan, *State, Education*, chs. 4 to 7 (quotation: 236).

76. Vaughan, *Cultural Politics*, chs. 2 and 3; Stephen Lewis, *The Ambivalent Revolution: Forging State and Nation in Chiapas, 1910–1945* (Albuquerque: Univ. of New Mexico Press, 2004), chs. 5 and 9; Ronfeldt, *Atencingo*, 15.

77. *La Opinión*, 18, 25, 26 and 27 Apr. 1930, 1; 31 Aug. 1931, 1; *New York Times*, 26 Apr. 1930, 2; A. Scott Berg, *Lindbergh* (New York: Berkley Books, 1999), 172–5.

78. Camp, *Mexican Political Biographies, 1884–1934*, 14; Rogelio Sánchez López, "La institucionalización. Una historia de los derrotados. Puebla, 1929–1932" (Lic. thesis, Univ. Autónoma de Puebla, 1992), 59–73.

79. Pansters, *Politics and Power*, 49; Wilkie, *Mexican Revolution*, 188.

80. *El Universal*, 5 Feb. 1931, 1; Pansters, *Politics and Power*, 56; Sánchez López, "La institucionalización," 162–9; R. Cummings to State Dept., Mexico City, 8 Dec. 1931, RDS, 812.00/29673.

81. Ronfeldt, *Atencingo*, 10, 16; Pansters, *Politics and Power*, 49; Lomelí, *Breve historia*, 356f.

82. Crespo, ed., *Historia del azúcar*, I:252f, II:966; J. Vázquez Schiaffino (SRE) to A. Lane (Embassy), Mexico City, 22 Oct. 1930, and Amb. R. Clark to G. Estrada, Mexico City, 29 Nov. 1930, SRE, Exp. 42-26-95; *Periódico Oficial*, 6 Jan. 1931, 21f; G. Johnston and R. Cummings to State Dept., Mexico City, var. dates (4 Feb. 1931 to 17 Jan. 1933), RDS, 812.00/29540, 29603, 29631, 29648, 29684, 29714, 29740, 29800, 29823.

83. Jane Jenkins's diary of 1931 (entry of 6 Mar.), REJP.

84. On family matters: Jenkins to Tigert, Puebla, 1 Jun. 1937, Tigert Papers; Jane Jenkins's diaries of 1930–32, REJP; interviews with J. Jenkins Eustace, 2 Apr. 2001, 27 Jun. 2002; Cheney, 18 Aug. 2002; R. Eustace Jenkins, 8 Jun. 2005, 19 Jul. 2016.

85. On Higgins's activities: *New York Times*, 28 Aug. 1928, 16; 18 Sep. 1928, 60; 13 Jul. 1932, 14; 6 Dec. 1936, N8.

86. J. Jenkins Eustace interview, 15 Aug. 2001; Asbury interview, 25 May 2005.

87. Comisión Permanente Congreso Federal to Sec. Gobernación, Mexico City, 15 Mar. 1928, and J. García et al. to Sec. Gobernación, Puebla, 10 May 1928, AGN DGG, Series 2–384(18)6, Caja 17, Exp. 6; LaFrance, "Military as Political Actor."

88. Gómez to Almazán, 11 May 1929, Mexico City, Marte R. Gómez Archive, Mexico City, Correspondencia; *Excélsior*, 16 Jan. 1931, 7; 10 Jun., 7; *La Opinión*, 9 Mar. 1931, 1.

89. On Almazán's corporatist approach to governance, see Sánchez López, "La institucionalización," esp. 144–52; Vaughan, *Cultural Politics*, 63f; Miguel Ángel Pineda Ramírez, "Sucesión y Transición: Las elecciones para gobernador en Puebla, en 1932" (MA thesis, Instituto Mora, 2000).

90. *La Opinión*, 17 Jan. 1929, 1; 13 Sep. 1929, 1; *Periódico Oficial*, 27 Sep. 1929, 49.

91. *La Opinión*, 18 Jan. 1931, II-2 (1930 *informe*); cf. Crespo and Vega, *Estadísticas históricas*, 25, 28.

92. *La Opinión*, 11 Sep. 1931, 6; *El Nacional*, 9 Oct. 1931, 1; Campos to Ortiz Rubio, Chietla, 15 Jun. 1931, AGN POR, Exp. 1931-224-4794; Rosas Solaegui to Jefe Depto., 14 Dec. 1933, AGN DGIPS, Caja 66, Exp. 8; *La Opinión*, 14 Oct. 1939, 1.

93. N. Guerrero to Cárdenas, Mexico City, 8 Oct. 1931, AGN POR, Exp. 1931-24-6700; *Excélsior*, 3 Jan. 1932, II-7.

94. *El Universal*, 2 Feb. 1931, 1; *La Opinión*, 5 Feb. 1931, 1; 11 Nov., 1; Pineda Ramírez, "Sucesión y Transición," 42–8.

95. *La Opinión*, 4 Feb. 1931, 1; *El Universal*, 5 Feb. 1931, 1. The logo appears on all CCEZ correspondence; e.g. M. Hidalgo Salazar (Sec. Gen.) to Rodríguez, 12 Jul. 1933, AGN ALR, Exp. 08/102.

96. *La Opinión*, 13 Nov. 1931, 4; *Excélsior*, 2 Feb. 1932, 7.

97. J. Jenkins Eustace interview, 2 Apr. 2001.

98. M. Hidalgo Salazar to Calles, Puebla, 17 Feb. 1932, Archivo Plutarco Elías Calles of the Archivos Calles y Torreblanca (hereafter, Calles-APEC), Exp. 2, Leg. 4/8, Inv. 558, doc. 473; Partido Ignacio Zaragoza (flyer), Chietla, 7 Feb. 1932, P. Cardoso and M. Herrera Mercado to M. de León, Chietla, 10 Apr. 1932, and Agent 10 to Jefe Depto. Confidencial, Chietla, 12 Apr. 1932, AGN DGIPS, Caja 162, Exp. 1.

99. Pineda Ramírez, "Sucesión y Transición."

100. *La Opinión*, 4 Nov. 1932, 1.

101. Crespo, ed., *Historia del azúcar*, I:252f, II:966, 971f; interview with Purdy Jordan (great-nephew of Johnston), Mexico City, 19 Jul. 2005.

102. Nora Hamilton, "The State and the National Bourgeoisie in Postrevolutionary Mexico," *Latin American Perspectives* 9:4 (1982): 40f; Crespo, *Historia del azúcar*, I:119–24; Sáenz to Gómez, Mexico City, 12 Feb. 1934, Archivo Gómez, Correspondencia.

103. Crespo, ed., *Historia del azúcar*, II: 971f.

104. Carlos Moncada, *¡Cayeron! 67 Gobernadores derrocados (1929–1979)* (Mexico City: n.p., 1979), 73–81; Pansters, *Politics and Power*, 49; Lomelí, *Breve historia*, 356–8; *Excélsior*, 17 Dec. 1932, 1, 3.

105. Timothy Rives, "Grant, Babcock, and the Whiskey Ring," *Prologue* 32:3 (2000), 143–53; Mark Grossman, *Political Corruption in America* (Santa Barbara, CA: ABC-CLIO, 2003), 160f, 364f.

106. RPP-Puebla, L.3, T. 17; V. Islas González to Cárdenas, Chietla and Mexico City, 13 and 27 Mar. 1935, AGN LC, 432.1/34.

107. Charles Merz, *The Dry Decade* (Seattle: Univ. of Washington Press, 1969), 114f, 133f; cf. Robert Jones, *The Eighteenth Amendment and Our Foreign Relations* (New York: Thomas Crowell, 1933), ch. VIII.

108. Prohibition claims: Guzmán Ramos, *Hombres de Puebla*, 52; telephone interview with Paul Buntzler Jr. (nephew) of East Wenatchee, WA, 6 Jun. 2005; interviews with R. Eustace, 10 Apr. 2002; Ortega, 9 Jul. 2005; Cobel, 25 Mar. 2006. Among detractors: *El Día*, 6 Jun. 1963, 3; Ronfeldt, *Atencingo*, 11; Rigoberto Cordero y Bernal, *Maximino Ávila Camacho* (Puebla: n.p., 2012), 121. Jenkins's denials: *Nashville Tennessean*, 5 Jul. 1964, Magazine 13.

109. *Excélsior*, 16 Nov. 1932, 3; 1 Jul., 1933, 1; *Ixtahuac*, n.d. [1934]), 72, AGN LC, Exp. 544.5/227. Rodríguez's temperance campaign: Gretchen Pierce, "Sobering the Revolution" (PhD diss., Univ. of Arizona, 2008), ch. 2.

110. Various docs., 28 Jun. to 1 Oct. 1934, AGN ALR, 526.27/66; Islas González to Cárdenas, 27 Mar. 1935, AGN Cárdenas, 432.1/34; Cordero y Torres, *Diccionario Biográfico*, 346.

111. Jenkins to Stanford, in *Mary Street Jenkins Foundation*, ed. Trueblood, 10; *Excélsior*, 15 Sep. 1934, 1; 16 Sep., II-5; *El Universal*, 15, 16 and 19 Sep., 1; *La Opinión*, 15 Sep., 1.

112. Interviews with J. Jenkins Eustace, 2 Apr. 2001; Cheney, 18 Aug. 2002; Guzmán Ramos, 16 May 2005.

113. Krauze, *Biography of Power*, 431. Cf. José Alfredo Gómez Estrada, *Gobierno y casinos: El origen de la riqueza de Abelardo L. Rodríguez* (Mexicali: UABC, 2002); Buchenau, *Plutarco Elías Calles*, 163–5.

114. *La Opinión*, 14 May 1933, 1; 22 Sep. 1934, 1; 29 Sep., 1; 27 Feb. 1935, 3; 1 Oct., 1; *Excélsior*, 29 Sep. 1934, 3; various docs., 13 Mar. to 17 Jun. 1935, AGN Cárdenas, 432.1/34; Cordero y Torres, *Diccionario Biográfico*, 346; J. Jenkins Eustace interview, 2 Apr. 2001; interview with former Atencingo truck driver, Mexico City, 7 Apr. 2002.

115. Marte Gómez, *Vida política contemporánea: Cartas de Marte R. Gómez* (Mexico City: FCE, 1978), II: 516f; Guzmán Ramos, *Hombres de Puebla*, 52; Guzmán Ramos interview, 16 May 2005.

116. Mary Street Jenkins immigration records, AGMP-Extranjería, Exp. 7513; M.S. Jenkins to Verniscia, 28 Feb. 1927, MSJP; J. Jenkins Eustace interviews, 2 Apr. 2001, 8 Jul. 2003, 15 Mar. 2005; interview with Alicia ("Achi") Juárez, Puebla, 4 Oct. 2005.

117. M.S. Jenkins to Jane Jenkins, Puebla, 15 Jun. 1933, Jane Jenkins Eustace Papers, held by Rosemary Eustace Jenkins, Mexico City.

118. Jenkins to Tigert, Puebla, 1 Jun. 1937, and Tucson, 28 Dec. 1939, Tigert Papers; J. Jenkins Eustace interviews, 2 Apr. 2001, 27 Jun. 2001, 27 Jun. 2002.

119. Jenkins to Stanford, in *Mary Street Jenkins Foundation*, ed. Trueblood, 7; journal of Mary Street Jenkins, 1933–1939, MSJP.

120. Jenkins to Stanford, in *Mary Street Jenkins Foundation*, ed. Trueblood, 9f, 14; Zolotow, *Billy Wilder*, 164f; interview with J. Jenkins Eustace, 2 Apr. 2001.

CHAPTER 7

1. The sketch of Guzmán draws on interviews with his son Sergio Guzmán Ramos, 17 Aug. 2001 and 16 May 2005; Cordero y Torres, *Diccionario Biográfico*, 316–20; Guzmán Ramos, *Hombres de Puebla*, 45f; *La Opinión*, 16 Feb. 1937, 1; J. Jenkins Eustace interview, 15 Aug. 2001.

2. *Congreso del Estado: Legislaturas desde la I hasta la actualidad* (1999), unpublished binder, ACEP.

3. Alejandro Quintana, *Maximino Avila Camacho and the One-Party State* (Lanham, MD: Lexington Books, 2010), 41–4; Pansters, *Politics and Power*, 47f; Valencia Castrejón, *Poder regional*, 22–8.

4. Timothy Henderson and David LaFrance, "Maximino Ávila Camacho," in *State Governors*, ed. Buchenau and Beezley, 161. Cf. Luis Medina, *Historia de la Revolución Mexicana, vol. 18: Del cardenismo al avilacamachismo* (Mexico City: Colegio de México, 1978), 98–100, on Juan Andreu Almazán.

5. Henderson and LaFrance, "Maximino Ávila Camacho," 161; interview with Manuel Ávila Camacho López (son of Maximino), Mexico City, 16 Aug. 2006.

6. Chappell Lawson, *Building the Fourth Estate: Democratization and Media Opening in Mexico* (Berkeley: Univ. of California Press, 2002), chs. 3 and 8. Cf. *Historia de la Revolución Mexicana*, vols. 8–22 (Mexico City: Colegio de México, 1978–80); Valencia Castrejón, *Poder regional*; Adrian Bantjes, *As If Jesus Walked the Earth: Cardenismo, Sonora and the Mexican Revolution* (Wilmington, DE: SR Books, 1998).

7. Pineda Ramírez, "Sucesión y transición" (quotation: 91); Gustavo Ariza, *La candidatura del general José Mijares Palencia al gobierno del estado de Puebla* (Puebla: n.p., 1932), 66–70; Armando Romano Moreno, *Anecdotario estudiantil. Vol. 1* (Puebla: UAP, 1985), 203f.

8. Presentation cards, SBGP; Romano Moreno, *Anecdotario Vol. 1*, 204.

9. Guzmán Ramos interview, 16 May 2005; J. Stewart to State Dept., Mexico City, 7 Dec. 1938, RDS, 812.114 Narcotics/873. Jenkins's 40,000-peso gift would be worth $200,000 today.

10. Knight, "*Cardenismo*: Juggernaut or Jalopy?"

11. The 1936 election draws on Valencia Castrejón, *Poder regional*, ch. II; Pansters, *Politics and Power*, 50f.

12. Alicia Hernández Chávez, *Historia de la Revolución Mexicana, vol. 16: La mecánica cardenista* (Mexico City: Colegio de México, 1979), chs. I–III; Dulles, *Yesterday in Mexico*, 634–49; *La Opinión*, 29 Jan. 1935, 1; 2 Oct., 1.

13. *Excélsior*, 10 Apr. 1935, 1; 11 Apr., 3; 13 Jul., 1; *El Universal*, 30 May 1935, 1; 31 May, 1.

14. Camp, *Mexican Political Biographies, 1935–1993*, 86.

15. Valencia Castrejón, *Poder regional*, 47f; *La Opinión*, 29 Jan. 1936, 1; 30 Jan., 1; 13 Feb., 1; 8 Mar., 1. *La Opinión* also serialized the Bosques manifesto: 1 Mar. to 4 Apr., 3.

16. *La Opinión*, 24 Mar. 1936, 1; 2 Apr., 1; *Excélsior*, 24 Mar., 3. On PNR weakness: Bantjes, *As If Jesus*; Ben Fallaw, *Cárdenas Compromised* (Durham, NC: Duke Univ. Press, 2001).

17. Valencia Castrejón, *Poder regional*, 50–3; *La Opinión*, 7 Feb. 1936, 1; 29 Mar., 1; 2 Apr., 1; 25 Apr., 1.

18. *Excélsior*, 4 Feb. 1936, II-1; *La Opinión*, 4 Feb. 1936, 1, 28 Mar., 1; Gauss, *Made in Mexico*, 140–3.

19. *La Opinión*, 9 May 1936, 3; 24 Jul., 3; 7 Nov., 1; 29 Dec., 1; *Periódico Oficial* (Pue.), 31 Dec. 1935, XI–XLV.

20. Valencia Castrejón, *Poder regional*, 52.

21. *La Opinión*, 5 Apr. 1936, 1.

22. *La Opinión*, 6 Apr. 1936, 1; 30 Apr., 1; *El Diario de Puebla*, 1 May, 1; Dulles, *Yesterday in Mexico*, 676–8.

23. Lombardo Toledano, quoted in Wilkie and Monzón de Wilkie, *México visto en el siglo XX*, 266; *La Opinión*, 16 Apr. 1936, 1; 30 Apr., 1; 3 May, 1; 15 May, 1; *New York Times*, 14 May 1936, 13.

24. Niblo, *Mexico in the 1940s*, 326; Stewart to State, 7 Dec. 1938, RDS, 812.114 Narcotics/873; Friedrich Katz, "Mexico, Gilberto Bosques and the Refugees," *The Americas* 57:1 (2000), 8–12.

25. Knight, "*Cardenismo*: Juggernaut or Jalopy?," 84–6.

26. *La Opinión*, 16 Apr. 1937, 1; 16 Jan. 1939, 1; cf. 13 Jan. 1941, 1.

27. Gonzalo Bautista, *Los problemas de 1,300,000 mexicanos, de una unidad política de la patria y de una aspiración regional* (Puebla: n.p., 1940), 15; *La Opinión*, 20 Jan. 1936, 3; Richard Boyer and Keith Davies, *Urbanization in 19th-Century Latin America* (Los Angeles: UCLA Latin America Center, 1973), 37, 47.

28. Niblo, *Mexico in the 1940s*, 281–9; *La Opinión*, 24 Aug. 1938, 1; 24 Aug. 1939, 1.

29. Pacheco interview, 27 Apr. 2006.

30. Niblo, *Mexico in the 1940s*, 266f. Cf. Luis Medina, *Historia de la Revolución Mexicana, vol. 20: Civilismo y modernización del autoritarismo* (Mexico City: Colegio de México, 1979), 15; Valencia Castrejón, *Poder regional*, 76, 80.

31. J. Stewart to State Dept., Mexico City, 25 May 1939, RDS, 812.00/30744, 6; Stewart to State, 7 Dec. 1938, RDS, 812.114 Narcotics/873; Cordero y Bernal, *Maximino Ávila Camacho*, 104–6, 128–31, 139f; Ávila Camacho López interview, 16 Aug. 2006; W. A. Jenkins interview, 29 Mar. 2001.

32. The Atencingo expropriation takes its narrative from Ronfeldt, *Atencingo*, 16–37, and indicated coverage in *La Opinión*.

33. Hernández Chávez, *La mecánica cardenista*, 33–46, 176; Dulles, *Yesterday in Mexico*, 572–7; John Dwyer, *The Agrarian Dispute: The Expropriation of American-Owned Rural Land in Postrevolutionary Mexico* (Durham, NC: Duke Univ. Press, 2008).

34. Jenkins to Tigert, Puebla, 1 Jun. 1937, Tigert Papers.

35. *La Opinión*, 20 Aug. 1935, 1; 19 Sep., 1.

36. *La Opinión*, 25 and 28 May 1937, 1; Gómez, *Gente de azúcar*, 147, 334–6.

37. Lázaro Cárdenas, *Obras. Vol. 1: Apuntes 1913–1940* (Mexico City: UNAM, 1972): 366f; *La Opinión*, 25 May 1937, 5f; 11 Jun. 1937, 1.

38. Ávila Camacho to Cárdenas, Puebla, 30 Jun. and 13 Jul. 1937, AGN Cárdenas, Exp. 404.1/5767; Jenkins to John Tigert, Puebla, 28 Sep. and 6 Oct. 1937, Tigert Papers; Valencia Castrejón, *Poder regional*, 76f.

39. Pansters, *Politics and Power*, 57–9; Valencia Castrejón, *Poder regional*, 84f; *La Opinión*, 15 May 1936, 1.

40. Crespo, ed., *Historia del azúcar*, II:869.

41. *La Opinión*, 18, 28 and 31 Aug. 1937, 1.

42. Jenkins to Tigert, Puebla, 23 Aug. 1937, Tigert Papers; Daniels, *The Wilson Era*, ch. XLIV.

43. Jenkins to Tigert, Puebla, 14 Sep. 1937; Tigert to Daniels, Gainesville, FL, 7 Sep.; Daniels to Tigert, Mexico City, 14 Sep.; Tigert to Jenkins, 20 Sep.; Tigert to Davis, 23 Sep.; Rowe to Tigert, Washington, 1 Oct.; Anderson to Tigert, Washington, 7 Oct.; Tigert Papers.

44. Jenkins to Tigert, 28 Sep. and 14 Oct., 1937; Davis to Tigert, 28 Sep. and Oct. 1; Tigert to Davis, 4 Oct.; Anderson to Tigert, 13 Oct.; Tigert to Jenkins, 19 Oct., Tigert Papers; *Time*, 26 Dec. 1960, 25 (also cited in Ronfeldt, *Atencingo*, 18). On Jenkins's filing with the separate American-Mexican Claims Commission, see next chapter.

45. *Diario de los debates de la Cámara de Diputados*, XXXVII Leg., 1 Sep. 1937, 2–11; Crespo, ed., *Historia del azúcar*, II:855–7.

46. Jenkins to Tigert, 6 Oct. 1937, Tigert Papers.

47. *La Opinión*, 21 Dec. 1937, 1; 20 Jun. 1938, 1; Cárdenas, decree, [18 Jun.] 1938, AGN LC, Exp. 404.1/5767; Ronfeldt, *Atencingo*, 72. The 2,043 *ejido* members were distinct from another 2,150 or so who worked seasonally in the fields and 800 salaried workers employed at the mill.

48. Cordero y Torres, *Diccionario Biográfico*, 346; J. Jenkins Eustace interview, 27 Jun. 2001.

49. Ávila Camacho to Cárdenas, Puebla, 2, 8, 12 and 16 May 1939, AGN Cárdenas, Exp. 404.1/5767; *La Opinión*, 4, 7–10 and 21 May 1939, 1; J. Stewart to State

Dept., Mexico City, 9 May 1939, RDS, 312.115; Agent PS-1 to Jefe Depto., Mexico City, 2 Jun. 1939, AGN DGIPS, Caja 77, Exp. 3; Ronfeldt, *Atencingo*, 37–48.

50. Stewart to State, 7 Dec. 1938, RDS, 812.114 Narcotics/873.

51. Maximino to Leg., Puebla, 7 May 1940, and J. Pérez Moyano and P. Briones to Maximino, Puebla, 25 Jul. 1940, ACEP, Libro 321, Exp. 2336.

52. Crespo, ed., *Historia del azúcar*, I:111, II:876–80; María Eugenia Romero, "Azúcar y empresa: La United Sugar Companies," Asn. Uruguaya de Historia Económica, Montevideo, Jul. 2003. Cf. Hart, *Empire and Revolution*, ch. 12; Dwyer, *The Agrarian Dispute*, chs. 3 and 4.

53. Ronfeldt, *Atencingo*, 45–8; Crespo, ed., *Historia del azúcar*, I:258f; *Time*, 26 Dec. 1960, 25; Gustavo del Ángel interview with Manuel Senderos Irigoyen (former Bancomer shareholder), Mexico City, 7 Dec. 2006; interview with former Atencingo truck driver, Mexico City, 7 Apr. 2002.

54. Ronfeldt, *Atencingo*, 48; Camp, *Mexican Political Biographies, 1935–1993*, 157f; Campa, *Mi testimonio* (Mexico City: Ediciones de Cultura Popular, 1978), 117.

55. Stewart to State, 9 May 1939, RDS, 312.115, and 25 May, RDS, 812.00/30744, 6.

56. *La Opinión*, 9 Mar. 1932, 1; 24 Apr. 1937, 4; 6 Sep. 1938, 1; Ronfeldt, *Atencingo*, 49, 51; Gladys McCormick, *The Logic of Compromise in Mexico: How the Countryside Was Key to the Emergence of Authoritarianism* (Chapel Hill: Univ. of North Carolina Press, 2016), 113f, 117. For Doña Lola as heroine, see Ronfeldt, *Atencingo*, 12–36; Hodges, *Mexican Anarchism*, 37–43; Bonilla Fernández, *El secuestro del poder*, 129–31.

57. Jenkins to Tigert Family, Tucson, 28 Dec. 1939, Tigert Papers.

58. I explore Maximino's coopting of the Puebla press in "Changing Opinions in *La Opinión*," in P. Gillingham, M. Lettieri, and B. Smith, eds., *Journalism, Satire and Censorship in Mexico, 1910–2015* (Albuquerque: Univ. of New Mexico Press, forthcoming).

59. Valencia Castrejón, *Poder regional*, 72–94; Pansters, *Politics and Power*, 56–9, 100f; *La Opinión*, 3 Oct. 1939, 1; 14 Oct., 5; 16 Oct., 1; interview with Rómulo O'Farrill, Jr., Mexico City, 29 Jun. 2001.

60. Gonzalo N. Santos, *Memorias* (Mexico City: Grijalbo, 1986), 647, 822, 827–34; Quintana, *Maximino*, 108f; Cordero y Bernal, *Maximino*, 31, 53.

61. *Excélsior*, 2 Feb. 1937, 3; *La Opinión*, 2 Feb. 1937, 1; 7 Jan. 1938, 1.

62. *La Opinión*, 21 Dec. 1937, 1, 5, 6; ACEP, Libro 307, Exp. 2112; Libro 312, Exp. 2216; Libro 319, Exp. 2297; Libro 324, Exp. 2391.

63. *La Opinión*, 8 Jul. 1937, 3; 28 Aug., 1; 23 and 24 Aug. 1938, 1; 24 Aug. 1939, 1; *Variety* (New York), 30 Oct. 1940, 13; Guzmán Ramos interview, 16 May 2005.

64. Jesús Márquez Carrillo, *Cátedra en vilo* (Puebla: Univ. Autónoma de Puebla, 1992), 91–8; Romano Moreno, *Anecdotario Vol. 1*, 177–85, *Vol. 2*, 358–60; *La Opinión*, 10 May 1937, 3; 20 May, 1. On the Gold Shirts: John Sherman, *The Mexican Right* (Westport, CT: Praeger, 1997), 62–4, 73f.

65. Niblo, *Mexico in the 1940s*, 281.

66. *La Opinión*, 16 Nov. 1937, 1; 9 May 1940, 1; Gadea Pineda, *74 años de historia*, 83; O'Farrill interview, 29 Jun. 2001; interview with Felipe Bello Gómez (nephew of Julio López Sierra), Puebla, 8 Apr. 2005; Maximino to Leg., 24 Jun. 1938, ACEP, Libro 310, Exp. 2169; Manjarrez, *Puebla: el rostro olvidado*, 130.

67. Alan Knight, "Populism and Neo-Populism in Latin America, Especially Mexico," *Journal of Latin American Studies* 30:2 (1998).

68. *La Opinión*, 4 Feb. 1930, 1; 3 Jul. 1937, 1; 2 Mar. 1939, 1.

69. Dowdy, *Mayor Crump*; Roger Biles, *Memphis in the Great Depression* (Knoxville: Univ. of Tennesse Press, 1986), ch. 2; R. Eustace interview, 15 Aug. 2001.

70. Melvin Holli, *The American Mayor* (University Park, PA: Penn State Univ. Press, 1999); Ernesto Dal Bó et al., "Political Dynasties," 26 May 2006, http://ssrn.com/abstract=909251.

71. Guzmán's mayoralty and relationship with Maximino draws on Guzmán Ramos, *Hombres de Puebla*, 45f; R. Eustace interview, 15 Aug. 2001; Guzmán Ramos interviews, 17 Aug. 2001, 16 May 2005, 28 Nov. 2005.

72. *La Opinión*, 5 Jun. 1937, 1, 17 Dec., 1; Romano, *Anecdotario Vol. 1*, 186f; Miguel Ángel Peral to Cárdenas, Puebla, 25 Sep. 1935, AGN DGG, Caja 140, file 47; interview with Pedro Ángel Palou, Puebla, 11 Aug. 2009.

73. *La Opinión*, 14 Aug. 1937, 1.

74. Guadalupe Loaeza and Pável Granados, *Mi novia, la tristeza* (Mexico City: Océano, 2008), 159; "Sofía Álvarez," www.imdb.com/name/nm0959596.

75. *La Opinión*, 21 Jan. 1939, 1.

76. *La Opinión*, 13 Feb. 1939, 1.

77. Dwyer, *Agrarian Dispute*, 233.

78. Haber, *Industry and Underdevelopment*, 175–89; Maxfield, *Governing Capital*, 71f, 76–9; Hamilton, *Limits of State Autonomy*, 225–40; Mosk, *Industrial Revolution*, 64f.

79. Mora, *Mexican Cinema*, 36–49; De Usabel, *High Noon*, 129; María Luisa Amador and Jorge Ayala Blanco, *Cartelera cinematográfica, 1930–1939* (Mexico City: Filmoteca UNAM, 1980), 276; *Variety*, 16 Feb. 1938, 13.

80. *Allá en el Rancho Grande*, dir. Fernando de Fuentes, prod. Bustamante y Fuentes, 1936.

81. De Usabel, *High Noon*, 20; "Alma norteña," www.imdb.com/title/tt0229975; interviews with Guzmán Ramos, 23 Jul. 2005; Díaz Rubín de la Hidalga, 1 Aug. 2001; Cobel, 25 Mar. 2006.

82. The Espinosa–Jenkins ventures draw on Manuel Espinosa Yglesias, *Bancomer: Logro y destrucción de un ideal* (Mexico City: Planeta, 2000), 16–22; Marcos Águila, Martí Soler and Roberto Suárez, *Trabajo, Fortuna y Poder: Manuel Espinosa Yglesias* (Mexico City: Centro de Estudios Espinosa Yglesias, 2007), chs. II–IV; Amparo Espinosa Rugarcía, *Manuel Espinosa Yglesias* (Mexico City: n.p., 1988), 7–10.

83. Acting via his accountants and frontmen, Manuel Cabañas and Manuel Sevilla, Jenkins joined Alarcón in cofounding Cine Reforma SA on 4 Jul. 1938 and with

Cienfuegos in Cines Unidos SA on 23 Jul. 1938; RPP-Puebla, L. 1, T. 9, nos. 153 and 163.

84. Again acting via Cabañas and Sevilla, Jenkins cofounded Ultra-Cinemas de México SA on 29 Sep. 1938; RPP-Puebla, L. 1, T. 9, no. 174.

85. J. Jenkins Eustace interview, 15 Aug. 2001. A *prestanombres* would represent an investor's covert interests by putting his or her name to legal documents.

86. *Variety*, 25 Jan. 1939, 12; 10 Apr. 1940, 12; 19 Jun., 12; Mauricio Fernández Ledesma, "Todos los cines, el cine: historia de la exhibición cinematográfica en Guadalajara, 1895–1971" (Lic. thesis, ITESO, 2000), 167–71.

87. On tensions between Espinosa and Alarcón: interview with Óscar Alarcón (son of Gabriel), Mexico City, 15 Aug. 2007; J. Jenkins Eustace and R. Eustace interview, 27 Jun. 2001; O'Farrill interview, 29 Jun. 2001.

88. Familia Espinosa (unpublished manuscript, 1990), Centro de Estudios Espinosa Yglesias, Mexico City.

89. *La Opinión*, 12 Feb. 1928, 5; 9 Aug. 1931, 1; Cordero y Torres, *Diccionario Biográfico*, 346; interviews with Sergio Reguero (son-in-law of Alarcón's brother José), Puebla, 28 Mar. 2005, and Carmelita Larragoiti, Puebla, 29 May 2006; Guzmán Ramos, 17 Aug. 2001; Alarcón, 15 Aug. 2007.

90. Benjamin Smith, "Building a State on the Cheap," in *Dictablanda*, ed. Gillingham and Smith, 259; *Excélsior*, 19 Sep. 1928, 1, 11; Petition to Senate, Puebla, 3 Sep. 1928, Archivo Joaquín Amaro of the Archivos Calles y Torreblanca, Mexico City, Series 03-11, Exp. 3, leg. 45/66.

91. *La Opinión*, 27 Nov. 1939, 1.

92. Gustavo del Ángel, *BBVA Bancomer: 75 años de historia* (Mexico City: BBVA Bancomer, 2007), 78–80; Espinosa Yglesias, *Bancomer*, 35–7.

93. *Y esto tan grande se acabó: Testimonios y relatos de los trabajadores de la fábrica textil "La Trinidad"* (Tlaxcala: Gobierno del Estado, 1991), 181–4; RPP-Puebla, L. 3, T. 21, no. 23; Jenkins to Manuel Ávila Camacho, Beverly Hills, CA, 3 Jul. 1944, AGN, presidential files of Manuel Ávila Camacho (hereafter, AGN MAC), Exp. 432/220.

94. RPP-Puebla, L. 1, T. 9, nos. 38 and 150, and T. 10, no. 174; R. Eustace interviews, 8 Jul. 2003 and 15 Mar. 2006; Cobel interview, 25 Mar. 2006.

95. *La Opinión*, 4 Jul. 1932, 1; 14 Oct. 1939, 1; 9 Oct. 1940, 1; Libro de Registro de Socios, 3, Fondo VIII, CITPyT; RPP-Puebla, L. 3, T. 30, no. 46; Díaz Rubín de la Hidalga interview, 1 Aug. 2001; R. Eustace interview, 10 Apr. 2002.

96. Valencia Castrejón, *Poder regional*, 39. For Maximino's uncontested judicial appointments, see A. Durán et al to Leg., 11 Feb. 1937, ACEP, 301-I, Exp. 2053; Leg. to Ávila Camacho, 14 Apr. 1937, 303-II, Exp. 2077.

97. Paulo Antonio Paranaguá, ed., *Mexican Cinema* (London: British Film Institute, 1995), 9f; Peredo Castro, *Cine y propaganda*, 300f, 363. On the lack of appeals to US authorities: none appear within the RDS Name Indexes for 1940–1966 nor within RDS, Section 812.4061 (Mexico, Motion Pictures) for 1940 to 1949.

98. Santos, *Memorias*, 647; Stewart to State, 9 May 1939, RDS, 312.115; Knight, "The End of the Mexican Revolution?" in *Dictablanda*, ed. Gillingham and Smith, 52, 65n24.

99. *The Nashville Tennessean*, 24 Jan. 1948. Even supposing a misprint—that the loan was not $400,000 ($6 million today) but $40,000—the sum would have been enough to buy significant political capital.

100. Enrique Cordero y Torres, *Historia del periodismo en Puebla, 1820–1946* (Puebla: Bohemia Poblana, 1947), 524–51; Valencia Castrejón, *Poder regional*, 142–51; Niblo, *Mexico in the 1940s*, 79–89; Sherman, *The Mexican Right*, ch. 8.

101. Knight, "The End of the Mexican Revolution?," 54, 65n37; James Wilkie, "Review Essay on Stephan R. Niblo's Mythical View of Mexico," *Mexico and the World* 7:6 (2002).

102. Quintana, *Maximino*, ch. 5; Valencia Castrejón, *Poder regional*, 100–5, 152–61; Pansters, *Politics and Power*, 50–2, 100–2, 117, 149.

103. Pansters, *Politics and Power*, 63, 100–2, 118–20; Guzmán Ramos interview, 28 Nov. 2005; Palou interview, 11 Aug. 2009.

104. Krauze, *Biography of Power*, ch. 18; Manjarrez, *Crónicas sin censura*, 369f, 375f; Cordero y Bernal, *Maximino*, 70, 77f, 139–43.

105. Knight, "*Cardenismo*: Juggernaut or Jalopy?," 101–5; Saragoza, *Monterrey Elite*, 192–7; Bantjes, *As If Jesus*, 182–6; Krauze, *Biography of Power*, 441–6, 488f.

106. Frank Brandenburg, *The Making of Modern Mexico* (Englewood Cliffs, NJ: Prentice-Hall, 1964); Gilbert Joseph et al., eds., *Fragments of a Golden Age: The Politics of Mexico since 1940* (Durham, NC: Duke Univ. Press, 2001).

CHAPTER 8

1. Cienfuegos's killing draws on Romano Moreno, *Anecdotario Vol. 1*, 203–5; Antonio Deana Salmerón, *Cosas de Puebla* (Puebla: n.p., 1986), II:136–9; Urbano Deloya, *Puebla de mis amores* (Puebla: UAP, 2004), 145–51; Manuel Sánchez Pontón, "William Oscar Jenkins Biddle" (Puebla: n.p., 2007); Águila et al., *Trabajo, Fortuna y Poder*, 69–71; *La Opinión*, 3, 4, 6 and 21 Jan. 1941, 1; Sánchez Pontón interview, 15 May 2006.

2. Paxman, "Changing Opinions in *La Opinión*."

3. Lecona and Huidobro to Leg., Puebla, 29 Jun. 1937, and Guarneros and Youshimatz to Oficina Federal de Hacienda, Puebla, 9 Sep., ACEP, Libro 304, Exp. 2087; Huidobro et al. to Leg., 16 Jun. 1937, ACEP, Libro 304, Exp. 2090.

4. Guarneros et al. to Cárdenas, Puebla, 9 May 1938, ACEP, Libro 309, Exp. 2165; *La Opinión*, 15 May 1938, 1; 20 May, 1; Smith, "Building a State on the Cheap," 259.

5. See, e.g., Santos, *Memorias*, 647, 678, 683, 754f.

6. Sánchez Pontón, "Jenkins Biddle," 5; Cordero y Bernal, *Maximino*, 77f; RPP-Puebla, Libro 1 de Comercio, T. 9, no. 57.

7. Guzmán Ramos interview, 28 Nov. 2005.

8. RPP-Puebla, Libro 3 de Comercio, T. 24, no. 105 (Cine-Teatro Guerrero) and T. 25, no. 46 (Cines Unidos); Sánchez Pontón, "Jenkins Biddle," 5; Alarcón interview, 15 Aug. 2007.

9. L. Castillo Venegas, 24 Jul. 1954, AGN, Dirección Federal de Seguridad (hereafter, AGN DFS), Exp. 40-16-954, leg. 1, 258; Contreras Torres, *El libro negro*, 47; Bonilla Fernández, *El secuestro del poder*, 148.

10. Romano Moreno, *Anecdotario*, 203; Contreras Torres, *El libro negro*, 47–9; RPP-Puebla L. 3, T. 24, no. 105.

11. Rodrigo Fernández Chedraui, *Vivir de pie: El tiempo de Don Maximino* (Xalapa, VC: Las Ánimas, 2008), 80; *La Opinión*, 10 May 1942, 1.

12. Gustavo García and Rafael Aviña, *Época de oro del cine mexicano* (Mexico City: Clío, 1997); Charles Ramírez Berg, *Cinema of Solitude* (Austin: Univ. of Texas Press, 1992), 12–15; Carlos Monsiváis, "Mexican Cinema," in *Mediating Two Worlds*, ed. John King et al. (London: BFI, 1993), 142; Joanne Hershfield and David Maciel, "The Golden Age," in *Mexico's Cinema*, ed. Hershfield and Maciel (Wilmington, DE: SR Books, 1999), 33–6; Sergio de la Mora, *Cinemachismo* (Austin: Univ. of Texas Press, 2005), 76; García Riera, *Breve historia del cine mexicano* (Zapopan, Jalisco: Mapa, 1998), 120.

13. Berg, *Cinema of Solitude*, 5. Cf. *Variety*, 2 Jun. 1943, 12; 7 Jul., 19; Seth Fein, "Hollywood and United States–Mexican Relations in the Golden Age of Mexican Cinema" (PhD diss., Univ. of Texas at Austin, 1996), 563.

14. García Riera, *Breve historia*, 102, 150f; *Variety*, 19 Jun. 1940, 12, 10 Jul. 1946, 17, 7 Jun. 1950, 15; Fernández and Paxman, *El Tigre*, ch. 5.

15. *Variety*, 8 Jan. 1941, 74; Herbert Cerwin, *These Are the Mexicans* (New York: Reynal and Hitchcock, 1947), 274.

16. *Variety*, 10 Jul. 1946, 16; 28 Aug., 23; 29 Jan. 1947, 17; 9 Mar. 1949, 62; 7 Jun. 1950, 15; María Luisa Amador and Jorge Ayala Blanco, *Cartelera cinematográfica, 1940–1949* (Mexico City: UNAM, 1982), 377.

17. *Siempre!*, 8 Aug. 1953, 14; Espinosa Yglesias, "Introduction," 18; W. A. Jenkins interview, 15 Jul. 2003.

18. García Riera, *Breve historia*, 102–17. On a state-directed sector: Mora, *Mexican Cinema*, 52, 59; Michael Nelson Miller, *Red, White, and Green: The Maturing of Mexicanidad, 1940–1946* (El Paso: Texas Western, 1998), ch. 5.

19. *Anuario Financiero de México, 1942* (Mexico City: Asociación de Banqueros de México, 1943), 381f; Emilio García Riera, *Historia documental del cine mexicano* (Guadalajara: Univ. de Guadalajara, 1992), 2:236f; Espinosa Yglesias, *Bancomer*, 20; *Variety*, 28 Jan. 1942, 13.

20. Mora, *Mexican Cinema*, 59; García Riera, *Breve historia*, 121.

21. Espinosa Yglesias, *Bancomer*, 19; Águila et al., *Trabajo, Fortuna y Poder*, 80f; *Variety*, 12 Jan. 1944, 31; *Últimas Noticias*, 7 Jan. 1944, encl. in G. Ray to State Dept., Mexico City, 7 Jan. 1944, RDS, 812.4061-MP/303.

22. Espinosa Yglesias, *Bancomer*, 20–2, 35–7; Águila et al., *Trabajo, Fortuna y Poder*, 81–6; *Variety*, 11 Oct. 1944, 13; *Excélsior*, 30 Aug. 1956; G. Messersmith to State Dept. (encl. no. 3), Mexico City, 25 Feb. 1944, RDS, 812.4061-MP/305.

23. *Variety*, 2 Oct. 1946, 3; *Diario Oficial* (Mexico City), 7 Jul. 1944, 2–4; Niblo, *War, Diplomacy*, 214–7.

24. *Variety*, 20 Sep. 1950, 62; Alarcón interview, 15 Aug. 2007.

25. RPP-Puebla, L. 1, Tomos 9 to 17; Maxfield, *Governing Capital*, 85–7; W. A. Jenkins interview, 11 Nov. 2005.

26. *El Universal*, 13 Sep. 1944, 13; *Variety*, 4 Oct. 1950, 15. Technically the Jenkins Group became more of a monopsony (as the dominant renter of films) than a monopoly, for Espinosa and Alarcón's theaters competed.

27. Espinosa Yglesias, *Bancomer*, 36f. Cf. Calles ALR, Empresas, Circuito del Pacífico, SA.

28. J. Langston to Jenkins, Washington, 11 Oct. 1943, Records of the Boundary and Claims Commissions (NARA Record Group 76); American-Mexican Claims Commission, *Report to the Secretary of State* (Washington, DC: USGPO, 1948), 3f, 108, 110, 625; Dwyer, *Agrarian Dispute*, 259, 288n21. Jenkins's $2.27 million would be more than $30 million today.

29. Dwyer, *Agrarian Dispute*, chs. 2 and 3.

30. Dorothy Kerig, *El valle de Mexicali y la Colorado River Land Company, 1902–1946* (Mexicali: UABC, 2001), 309–11; *Utilization of Waters of the Colorado and Tijuana Rivers and of the Rio Grande* (Washington, DC: USGPO, 1946); *New York Times*, 9 Feb. 1945, 10; W. A. Jenkins interview, 16 Jun. 2005.

31. *Diario Oficial*, 31 Aug. 1934, 1159–63.

32. Ten such cartoons, dated between 1951 and 1959, are reproduced in the pages of Contreras Torres, *El libro negro*.

33. Interviews with O'Farrill, 29 Jun. 2001; R. Eustace, 27 Jun. 2001; O. Alarcón, 15 Aug. 2007.

34. Espinosa Rugarcía, *Manuel Espinosa Yglesias*, 13–15; Águila et al., *Trabajo, Fortuna y Poder*, 85–93; *Variety*, 12 Jan. 1944, 31; 14 Feb. 1945, 16.

35. T. McEnelly to State Dept., Tampico, 12 Jul. 1943, RDS, 812.4061-MP/297; *El Universal*, 13 Sep. 1944, 13; Mora, *Mexican Cinema*, 77; Fein, "Hollywood," 352; RPP-Puebla L. 1, T. 17, no. 52, and L. 3, T. 55, no. 57.

36. García Riera, *Historia Documental*, 2:237f; *Variety*, 11 Oct. 1944, 13.

37. Peredo Castro, *Cine y propaganda*, chs. III and IV; Seth Fein, "Hollywood," chs. 5 and 6.

38. Middlebrook, *Paradox of Revolution*, 162–71, 214f; Alan Knight, "The rise and fall of Cardenismo," in L. Bethell, ed., *Mexico since Independence*, 299, 310–12.

39. Pedro Salmerón Sanginés, *Aarón Sáenz Garza* (Mexico City: M. A. Porrúa, 2001), ch. VIII; Crespo, ed., *Historia del azúcar*, 255–9.

40. On Cárdenas loyalists in Ávila Camacho's cabinet: Niblo, *Mexico in the 1940s*, 88–91; Humberto Musacchio, ed., *Milenios de México* (Mexico City: Hoja Casa Editorial, 1999), 252 (Silvano Barba), 299 (Cárdenas himself).

41. Niblo, *War, Diplomacy*, chs. 6 and 8, and *Mexico in the 1940s*, ch. 5; Fernández and Paxman, *El Tigre*; Roderic Camp, *Entrepreneurs and Politics in Twentieth-Century Mexico* (New York: Oxford Univ. Press, 1989), 22f, 79.

42. The La Trinidad strike draws on *Y esto tan grande se acabó*, 189–94; Blanca Santibáñez, "El Estado y la huelga de 'La Trinidad'," *Boletín de Investigación del Movimiento Obrero* 8 (1985), 58–66; Jenkins to Ávila Camacho, Beverly Hills, CA, 3 Jul. 1944, AGN MAC, Exp. 432/220; RPP-Puebla, L. 3, T. 21, no. 23.

43. Middlebrook, *Paradox of Revolution*, 164; *Tiempo* (Mexico City), 19 May 1944, 32.

44. Middlebrook, *Paradox of Revolution*, 111f; *Excélsior*, 9 May 1944, 1; *El Universal*, 25 Jun., 1.

45. *El Universal*, 24 May 1944, 8; *La Opinión*, 3 Jun., 1, 4 Jun., 1, 9 Jun., 1; *El Universal*, 24 Jun., 1; *Excélsior*, 24 Jun., 1; *Acción* (Puebla), 1 Jul., 1; *El Popular* (Mexico City), 10 Jul., 1.

46. *El Universal*, 25 Jun. 1944, 1, 9 Jul., 1, 10 Jul., 1; *Excélsior*, 8 Jul., 1, 9 Jul., 1; *El Popular*, 9 Jul., 1, 10 Jul., 1; *Rebeldía* (Puebla), 9 Sep., 3; various to Ávila Camacho, 10–14 Jul. 1944, AGN MAC, Exp. 432/220.

47. Medina, *Del cardenismo al avilacamachismo*, ch. III; Niblo, *Mexico in the 1940s*, ch. 2.

48. Jenkins to Ávila Camacho, Beverly Hills, 3 Jul. 1944, AGN MAC, Exp. 432/220; *Excélsior*, 7 Jul. 1944, 1.

49. Cf. *New York Times*, 2 Oct. 1927, 10.

50. La Trinidad financial report, 30 Oct. 1946, AGN MAC, Exp. 432/220; *Excélsior*, 30 Aug. 1946, 1.

51. Mary's death and its impact draws on J. Jenkins Eustace to R. Eustace, Los Angeles, 18 and 28 Jan. 1944, in Eustace Jenkins, ed., *Tennessee Sunshine*, 279; H. Turner to Tigert, Nashville, 14 Nov. 1944, Jenkins to Tigert, Puebla, 3 Jan. 1945, Tigert Papers; interviews with J. Jenkins Eustace, 2 Aug. 2001 to 7 Jun. 2007; Cheney, 18 Aug. 2002; R. Eustace Jenkins, 4 Jul. 2003.

52. Jenkins to Tigert, 21 Aug. 1927, Tigert Papers; W. A. Jenkins interview, 22 Nov. 2000; interview with Joaquín Ibáñez Puget, Puebla, 9 Sep. 2005.

53. I. Marquina to Jenkins, 5 Mar. 1946, "Exploraciones Arqueológicas en Monte Albán. XIII temporada, 1944–45" and "XV temporada, 1946–47," WAJP.

54. Jenkins to Frank Houston, 18 Jan. 1947, Jenkins to Branscomb, 3 Aug. 1947, 25 Feb. and 8 Sep. 1948, 17 Jun. 1950, Branscomb Papers, Box 362, File 1; *Nashville Tennessean*, 24 Jan. 1948, 2; *Shelbyville Times-Gazette*, 7 Oct. 1969, 133.

55. Houle, "Some Significant Experiments," 65; Board Minutes, 7 Dec. 1950, Club Rotario de Puebla, Directorio Archivo 1950–51, Tomo I; Guzmán Ramos, *Hombres de Puebla*, 49; interviews with W. A. Jenkins, 27 Jun. 2002; Guzmán Ramos, 23 Jul. 2005; Buntzler, 6 Jun. 2005; Sergio Suárez (CEO, Fundación Alpha), Puebla, 9 Aug. 2012.

56. Fernández Chedraui, _Vivir de pie_, 508–23; Quintana, _Maximino_, 119–21; Deloya, _Puebla de mis amores_, 83; Cordero y Bernal, _Maximino_, 30f, 49, 88; _La Opinión_, 28 Oct. 1944, 1, 3 Nov., 1, 3 Dec., 1; _New York Times_, 18 Feb. 1945, 34; _Éxito_ (Mexico City), 18–24 Oct. 1959, 4; interviews with R. Eustace, 8 Jul. 2003; Guzmán Ramos, 23 Jul. 2005; Ávila Camacho López, 16 Aug. 2006; Rafael Artasánchez Bautista (grandson of Bautista), Mexico City, 28 Jul. 2005.

57. Crespo and Vega, _Estadísticas históricas_, 344–6, 331f; cf. Ronfeldt, _Atencingo_, 11.

58. Ronfeldt, _Atencingo_, 48f; F. and J.M. Pérez interview, 25 May 2006.

59. Pansters, _Politics and Power_, 55–9; Niblo, _War, Diplomacy_, 97f.

60. M. Rivera to Ávila Camacho, 17 Feb. 1946, Betancourt to Ávila Camacho, 27 Feb. and 5 Mar. 1946, AGN MAC, Exp. 432/704; _El Universal_, 22 Feb. 1946; _El Popular_, 22 Feb. 1946, 1; Valle Morales, _El despertar democrático_, 39–52, 103–7; Gadea, _74 años de historia_, 102–4; Ortega and Benítez interviews, 9 Jul. 2005, 18 Mar. 2006.

61. Pansters, _Politics and Power_, 101; Guzmán Ramos interview, 28 Nov. 2005.

62. Crespo, ed., _Historia del azúcar_, II:757, 762–4; Middlebrook, _Paradox of Revolution_, 113f, M. Rivera to Alemán, 20 Mar. 1952, AGN, presidential files of Miguel Alemán Valdés (hereafter, AGN MAV), Exp. 111/31724.

63. Knight, "The Rise and Fall of Cardenismo," 314f.

64. _El Popular_, 2 Aug. 1946, 3; Ortega interview, 9 Jul. 2005.

65. _La Opinión_, 2 Sep. 1946, 1; various documents, AGN MAC, Exp. 432/704, Case 6; Gadea, _74 años de historia_, 105–7; interviews with Ortega, 9 Jul. 2005; García Pliego, 18 Mar. 2006; C. Guzmán, 22 Apr. 2006.

66. Benítez interviews, 18 Mar. and 22 Apr. 2006.

67. Ronfeldt, _Atencingo_, 24–9, 50–5; McCormick, _Logic of Compromise_, 115–8.

68. Camp, _Mexican Political Biographies, 1935–93_, 57, 392; Medina, _Del cardenismo al avilacamachismo_, 190; Ronfeldt, _Atencingo_, 54.

69. Ronfeldt, _Atencingo_, 55–8; Presidential Resolution, Mexico City, 30 Jul. 1946, AGN MAC, Exp. 432/220; _Diario Oficial_, 29 Aug. 1946.

70. Jenkins to Ávila Camacho, 11 Sep. 1946, quoted in Ronfeldt, _Atencingo_, 58f.

71. Ronfeldt, _Atencingo_, 59–64; _La Voz de México_, 17 Nov. 1946, 4; cf. 24 Nov., 4.

72. Espinosa Yglesias, "Introduction," 18; Águila et al., _Trabajo, Fortuna y Poder_, 108–11; _La Opinión_, 5 Dec. 1946, 1; J. Jenkins Eustace and R. Eustace interview, 10 Apr. 2002.

73. Águila et al., _Trabajo, Fortuna y Poder_, 96f, 112. Between 1946 and 1948, Atencingo continued to belong legally to Jenkins, while Espinosa arranged for Cue to take majority ownership. Jenkins dissolved the Atencingo Company in Aug. 1947, though notarized papers were not presented at the Public Property Registry (suggesting the sale was imminent) until Jan. 1948; RPP-Puebla, L. 3, T. 37, no. 8. Cf. _La Opinión_, 18 Jul. 1949, 6 (final share purchase). The sale price of $7 million would equal some $90 million today.

74. Ronfedlt, _Atencingo_, 81–109; McCormick, _Logic of Compromise_, ch. 4; Hansen, _Politics of Mexican Development_, ch. 4.

75. Crespo, ed., *Historia del azúcar*, 975–87.

76. *Time*, 26 Dec. 1960, 25f.

77. Maxfield, *Governing Capital*, ch. 3; Alex Saragoza, *The State and the Media in Mexico* (forthcoming).

78. *Variety*, 17 Aug. 1938, 25; 16 Nov., 12; 30 Mar. 1949, 16; 18 Feb. 1948, 54.

79. Andrea Noble, *Mexican National Cinema* (London: Routledge, 2005), 76f; *La Opinión*, Dec. 1946.

80. Jenkins to Branscomb, 27 Nov. 1952, Branscomb Papers, Box 362, File 1; J. Jenkins Eustace interview, 2 Apr. 2001; Senderos interview, 7 Dec. 2006. Cf. Crespo, ed., *Historia del azúcar*, 258f.

81. On Maximino: Eduardo de la Vega, "Origins, Development and Crisis of the Sound Cinema (1929–1964)," in *Mexican Cinema*, ed. P.A. Paranaguá (London: British Film Institute, 1995), 91; Niblo, *Mexico in the 1940s*, 283–87; Cordero y Bernal, *Maximino*, 140. On Manuel: *Opinión Pública*, 15 Sep. 1962, 9; Niblo, *Mexico in the 1940s*, 289f. On Alemán: Niblo, *Mexico in the 1940s*, 290f; Krauze, *Biography of Power*, 555–7; Jenkins to Family, Puebla, 14 Jan 1955, MJWP.

82. Mora, *Mexican Cinema*, 42–51; Fein, "Hollywood," chs. 5 and 6; *Rebeldía*, 4 Aug. 1945, 3f.

83. On Cantinflas as "the essence of poverty, of expressive cleverness," see Carlos Monsiváis, "Cantinflas and Tin Tan," in *Mexico's Cinema*, ed. J. Hershfield and D. Maciel, 49–79; on Cantinflas as a vehicle for authoritarian containment, see Roger Bartra, *The Cage of Melancholy* (New Brunswick, NJ: Rutgers Univ. Press, 1992), 125–9.

84. Fein, "Hollywood," 423–61.

85. Fátima Fernández Christlieb, "El derecho de la información y los medios de difusión masiva," in *México, hoy*, ed. P. González Casanova and E. Florescano (Mexico City: Siglo XXI, 1979), 336; Miller, *Red, White, and Green*, 97; Ávila Camacho to Congress, 17 Jan. 1946, AGN MAC, Exp. 201.1/5.

86. Brenner, *Wind that Swept Mexico*, 102f.

87. José Luis Ortiz Garza, *México en guerra* (Mexico City: Planeta, 1989), 168–70; Fein, "Hollywood," 461–85. In 1946 the ratio was 420 US newsreels and shorts to 179 Mexican; *Variety*, 30 Jun. 1948, 16.

88. Fein, "Hollywood," 147–58, 461–9, 475–85; Ortiz Garza, *México en guerra*, 193; *Variety*, 11 Oct. 1944, 13; various documents, AGN MAV, Exp. 704.11/34; J.F. Azcárate, EMA annual report, n.d. [30 Mar. 1951], Calles ALR, Empresas, Exp. España-México-Argentina SA.

89. M. A. Ortega (IPS 15) to Jefe del Departamento, Mexico City, 11–12 Apr. 1944, AGN DGIPS, Caja 96, Exp. 1.

90. Anne Rubenstein, "Mass Media and Popular Culture in the Postrevolutionary Era," in *Oxford History of Mexico*, ed. Michael Meyer and William Beezley (New York: Oxford Univ. Press, 2000), 649; Agent C.15 to Dir. Gen. IPS, 3–9 Sep. 1948, AGN DGIPS, Caja 128, Exp. 9.

91. Ella Shohat and Robert Stam, *Unthinking Eurocentricism: Multiculturalism and the Media* (London: Routledge, 1994), 101–4.
92. *Variety*, 17 Jul. 1946, 12; 4 Dec., 1, 54; *Diario Oficial*, 18 Jul. 1943; Niblo, *Mexico in the 1940s*, 175f.
93. *Variety*, 23 Oct. 1946, 18; 30 Oct. 1946, 23; Berg, *Cinema of Solitude*, 39.
94. Messersmith to Corrigan, Mexico City, 10 Aug. 1945, RDS, 812.00/8-1045, 3.

CHAPTER 9

1. Jenkins in Acapulco draws on Eustace Jenkins, *Tennessee Sunshine*, 335–8, 342, 353–7, 361f, 372; *La Opinión*, 7 Dec. 1946, 1; *Mañana* (Mexico City), 4 Nov. 1950, 61; Jenkins to H. Branscomb, Puebla, 23 Jul. 1951, Branscomb Papers; Jenkins to family, 16 Apr. 1954, MJWP; interviews with Ron Lavender, Acapulco, 27 May 1994; J. Jenkins Eustace and R. Eustace, 2001–2005; Guzmán Ramos, 17 Aug. 2001; Artasánchez Villar, 23 Jul. 2005; Alarcón, 17 Aug. 2007.
2. Andrew Sackett, "Fun in Acapulco?," in *Holiday in Mexico*, ed. D. Berger and A. Wood (Durham, NC: Duke Univ. Press, 2010); Niblo, *Mexico in the 1940s*, 274f, 364.
3. On Eustace: Eustace Jenkins, *Tennessee Sunshine*, 324, 340; interviews with R. Eustace, 2 Apr. 2001, 8 Jul. 2003, 15 Mar. 2005; R. Eustace Jenkins, 4 Jul. 2003; Guzmán Ramos, 16 May 2005.
4. Libro de Actas, vol. 2, item 221, Mary Street Jenkins Foundation (hereafter, MSJF); *El Universal*, 16 Jan. 1955, 5 (ad); interviews with John Eustace Jenkins, Puebla, 20 Jul. 2004, 31 Jul. 2005; W. A. Jenkins, 11 Nov. 2005; Artasánchez Villar, 23 Jul. 2005.
5. On Alemán's years: Krauze, *Biography of Power*, ch. 18; Niblo, *Mexico in the 1940s*, chs. 4 and 5; Aaron Navarro, *Political Intelligence and the Creation of Modern Mexico, 1938–1954* (University Park, PA: Penn State Press, 2010).
6. *El Popular*, 23 Feb. 1947, 1; Cosío Villegas, "La Crisis de México," *Cuadernos Americanos*, Mar. 1947; Krauze, *Biography of Power*, ch. 18.
7. Cf. Reid, *Spanish American Images*, 48–57.
8. Interviews with Gonzalo Bautista O'Farrill, Puebla, 8 Sep. 2005; J. Jenkins Eustace, 15 Aug. 2001; W. A. Jenkins, 18 Jun. 2003; Mestre, 16 Jul. 2003; Cobel, 25 Mar. 2006; Artasánchez Villar, 23 Jul. 2005; Ibáñez Puget, 9 Sep. 2005. The sum of 500,000 pesos was then worth $58,000 (around $600,000 today).
9. *La Opinión*, 28 Mar. 1947, 3; W. A. Jenkins interview, 12 Oct. 2005; R. Eustace interview, 20 Apr. 2006.
10. Higgins (Armadora Automotriz SA) to Alemán, Mexico City, 20 Jan. 1947, and invitation to 18 Jun. 1947 inauguration, AGN MAV, Exp. 135.2/35; Higgins memo, 1 Apr. 1957, Ronald Eustace Papers (REP), held by Ronald Eustace, Puebla; R. Eustace interview, 10 Apr. 2002; W. A. Jenkins interview, 18 Jun. 2003.

11. Buntzler interview, 6 Jun. 2005. On VW de México: Gerhard Schreiber, *Eine Geschichte ohne Ende: Volkswagen de México* (Puebla: VW de México, 1998).

12. Jenkins to Guzmán, Puebla, 12 Jan. 1955, SBGP; Guzmán Ramos interview, 16 May 2005.

13. W. A. Jenkins interview, 18 Jun. 2003; Buntzler interview, 6 Jun. 2005.

14. Hansen, *Politics of Mexican Development*, ch. 4.

15. *La Opinión*, 7 Dec. 1946, 1; Cabañas Pavía, *Datos Biográficos*, 32f.

16. *La Opinión*, 3 Feb. 1951, 1; 7 May 1952, 1; M. Gula to Branscomb, D.C., 24 Mar. 1955, Branscomb Papers.

17. On the Adalberto García killing: AGN Gobernación, Series 2/102.2 (18): Asesinatos, Caja 50, Exp. 53; *La Opinión*, 8–12 Jan. 1949, 1; García Pliego interview, 18 Mar. 2006; C. Guzmán interview, 22 Apr. 2006.

18. Ronfeldt, *Atencingo*, 48, 91; Samuel Malpica, "La hegemonía de la CROM en Atlixco (1900–1948)" (MA thesis, Univ. Autónoma de Puebla, 1982), 111–38.

19. Jenkins to Branscomb, Puebla, 23 Jul. 1951, Branscomb Papers; Ronfeldt, *Atencingo*, 72; Gadea Pineda, *74 años de historia*, 135; interviews with W. A. Jenkins, 29 Mar. 2001; J. Jenkins Eustace, 27 Jun. and 15 Aug. 2001; Guzmán Ramos, 17 Aug. 2001 and 16 May 2005; C. Guzmán, 22 Apr. 2006; Vicente Lara Lara (local chronicler), Atencingo, 11 May 2006.

20. Ronfeldt, *Atencingo*, ch. 6; McCormick, *Logic of Compromise*, 128f.

21. *Política* (Mexico City), 1 Jun. 1960, 29; Ronfeldt, *Atencingo*, 82; "Arturo García Bustos," www.graphicwitness.org/group/bustosbio1.htm.

22. Photograph, collection of Ortega (pseud.), Atencingo. Neither the plaque nor Bustos's mural survive.

23. *El Popular*, 9 Jun. 1954, 5; Ronfeldt, *Atencingo*, 159; McCormick, *Logic of Compromise*, 124f, 130f.

24. David Sonnenfeld, "Mexico's 'Green Revolution,' 1940–1980," *Environmental History Review* 16:4 (1992).

25. Contreras Torres, *El libro negro*, 49.

26. The standard history of Mexican film in English, Mora's *Mexican Cinema*, devotes a few pages to Jenkins (76–78) but relies uncritically on Contreras Torres. So do García Riera, *Historia documental*, 4:7, 106f, 5:171, 6:7f, 7:10, 153f, 8:8, 9:7–10; Cordero y Torres, *Diccionario Biográfico*, 351f; García and Aviña, *Época de oro*, 32f; Jeffrey Pilcher, *Cantinflas & the Chaos of Mexican Modernity* (Wilmington, DE: SR Books, 2001), 137f, 171, 174.

27. Gabriel Ramírez, *Miguel Contreras Torres, 1899–1981* (Guadalajara: Univ. de Guadalajara, 1994); Peredo Castro, *Cine y propaganda*, 239–60; "Miguel Contreras Torres," www.imdb.com/name/nm0176472.

28. Bernard F. Dick, *Hal Wallis: Producer to the Stars* (Lexington: Univ. Press of Kentucky, 2004), 54f.

29. Ramírez, *Contreras Torres*, 95f, 98; W. A. Jenkins interview, 22 Nov. 2000.

30. *Hoy*, 29 Oct. 1949, 12f; various to Alemán, 1949, AGN MAV, Exp. 523.3/54.

31. García Riera, *Historia documental*, 3:223; Rodó, *Ariel* (see "Gringophobia" in chapter 2).

32. García Riera, *Historia documental*, 4:105–9; *Anuario Financiero de México, 1947* (Mexico City: Asn. de Banqueros de México, 1948), 135; *Variety*, 28 Jun. 1950, 13; 20 Dec. 1950, 53; *Siempre!*, 8 Aug. 1953, 14.

33. *Variety*, 12 Mar. 1947, 25; 21 Jul. 1948, 17; 1 Sep. 1948, 11; various correspondence, 17 Feb. to 21 May 1949, AGN MAV, Exp. 523.3/54.

34. *Hoy*, 29 Oct. 1949, 12f.

35. Niblo, *Mexico in the 1940s*, 49f, 160; Mora, *Mexican Cinema*, 78; Krauze, *Biography of Power*, 558.

36. Fein, "Hollywood," 600–5; cf. 338–42.

37. Contreras Torres to Alemán, Mexico City, 8 Dec. 1950, AGN MAV, Exp. 639/11585; Ramírez, *Contreras Torres*, 88–90, 93. The letter to Jenkins appeared on 20 Dec. 1950 in *Excélsior, El Universal*, and *La Prensa*.

38. Ramírez, *Contreras Torres*, 91–5; Fein, "Hollywood," 607f.

39. G. Ray to State Dept., Mexico City, 6 Oct. 1944, RDS, 812.4061-MP/10-644, 4f; Fein, "Hollywood," 608–15. Cf. Thomas Guback, *The International Film Industry* (Bloomington: Univ. of Indiana Press, 1969), ch. 2.

40. Contreras Torres, *El libro negro*, 53; *La Opinión*, 14 Oct. 1949, 1; *El Universal*, 2 Feb. 1951, 1; *Tiempo*, 27 Feb. 1953, 42.

41. *Variety*, 26 Nov. 1947, 15; interviews with R. Eustace, 27 Jun. 2001; O'Farrill, 29 Jun. 2001; interview with Amparo Espinosa Rugarcía (daughter of Espinosa Yglesias), Mexico City, 19 Jul. 2005. On Alarcón's shooting prowess: *La Opinión*, 21 Apr. 1936, 1; 25 Nov., 1.

42. *Variety*, 6 Aug. 1947, 14; 20 Oct. 1948, 3; 20 Sep. 1950, 62; 4 Oct., 15; Calles ALR, Empresas.

43. G. Ray to State Dept., 6 Oct. 1944, RDS, 812.4061-MP/10-644; *Variety*, 28 Jan. 1942, 13; 8 Dec. 1948, 54; 19 Jan. 1949, 54; García Riera, *Historia documental*, 2:237f, 3:221.

44. Interview with De Anda, 27–28 Nov. 1975, Mora-Palabra, PHO2/48, 28–30; "Raul de Anda," www.imdb.com/name/nm0025874/. Cf. *Variety*, 20 Sep. 1950, 62; Eduardo de la Vega, *Raúl de Anda* (Guadalajara: Centro de Investigación y Enseñanza Cinematográficas, 1989), 105f.

45. *Anuario Financiero de México, 1942*, 291f, and *1943*, 503f; Jenkins to Walerstein, Puebla, 25 Apr. 1953, Centro de Estudios Espinosa Yglesias, Archivo MEY (hereafter, CEEY), Caja 29, Exp. 1; interview with Walerstein, n.d., CEEY, Caja 29, Exp. 4; Águila et al., *Trabajo, fortuna y poder*, 130f. Cf. Neil Gabler, *An Empire of Their Own: How the Jews Invented Hollywood* (New York: Anchor, 1988).

46. Berg, *Cinema of Solitude*, 40; Águila et al., *Trabajo, Fortuna y Poder*, 127; *Variety*, 8 Jan. 1947, 179; 26 Oct. 1949, 17; *Siempre!*, 8 Aug. 1953, 14; interview with Eugenia Meyer (daughter of Walerstein), Mexico City, 8 Aug. 2007.

47. Díaz Rubín de la Hidalga interview, 1 Aug. 2001; Cobel interview, 25 Mar. 2006; R. Eustace Jenkins, email to author, 29 Nov. 2008.

48. Interview with Salvador Elizondo, 18 Jun. 1975, Mora-Palabra PHO2/27, 37f, 48f.

49. García Riera, *Breve historia*, 102, 121, 150, 185.

50. Libros de Juntas, Nacional de Drogas, consulted courtesy of Pablo Escandón Cusi, Mexico City, 24 Jul. 2006; Embassy to State Dept., Mexico City, 10 Mar. 1950, RDS, 102.11/3-1050; R. Eustace interview, 8 Jul. 2003. On Nafinsa: Mosk, *Industrial Revolution*, 242–9.

51. *El Universal*, 18 Aug. 1951, 1. On Alemán's exploration of reelection: Krauze, *Biography of Power*, 558–60.

52. Jenkins to Branscomb, Puebla, 27 Nov. 1952, Branscomb Papers, Box 362, File 1; Robert Armistead, "The History of Novedades" (MJ thesis, Univ. of Texas, Austin, 1964), 150f; Niblo, *Mexico in the 1940s*, 346f.

53. Saragoza, *The State and the Media*. Alemán covertly partnered O'Farrill in Mexico's first TV station, Channel 4; Fernández and Paxman, *El Tigre*, 72–8. For claims that Jenkins joined them: Contreras Torres, *El libro negro*, 51; Fernando Mejía Barquera, *La industria de la radio y la televisión y la política del Estado mexicano* (Mexico City: Fundación Manuel Buendía, 1989), 157.

54. *La Opinión*, 2 Dec. 1949, 2; 3 Dec., 1; R. Eustace interview, 15 Mar. 2006.

55. Gruening, *Mexico and Its Heritage*, 349f; Haber, *Industry and Underdevelopment*, 156–61, 180f; Gamboa Ojeda, "Momentos de crisis," 23–53; Aurora Gómez-Galvarriato, "The Political Economy of Protectionism," working paper, CIDE, 2001, 22–9.

56. Rosalina Estrada Urroz, *Del telar a la cadena de montaje: La condición obrera en Puebla, 1940–1976* (Puebla: UAP, 1997), 123; Pansters, *Politics and Power*, 81, 90; Guzmán Ramos, *Hombres de Puebla*, 109; interview with Rafael Artasánchez Bautista (nephew of Luis Artasánchez Romero), Mexico City, 28 Jul. 2005.

57. *La Opinión*, 18 Aug. 1945, 2; 28 Aug., 1; 1 Sep., 1; 2 Sep., 1; 30 Sep., 1; 18 Oct., 1; 22 Dec., 1; Espinosa Yglesias, "Introduction," 18; R. Eustace interview, 15 Mar. 2006.

58. Pansters, *Politics and Power*, 88–92; Lomelí Vanegas, *Breve historia de Puebla*, 373–5; Niblo, *Mexico in the 1940s*, 24–7, 35–8; Guzmán Ramos interview, 28 Nov. 2005.

59. *La Opinión*, esp. 1945–1962.

60. Estrada Urroz, *Del telar*, 124, 129; Board meetings, 13 Oct. 1943 and 19 Jan. 1944, Asociación de Empresarios Textiles (hereafter, CITPyT-AET), Libro de Actas de Juntas de la Directiva (LAJD), vol. 3. On the absence of Lebanese: LAJD, vols. 1–7 (1936–64), CITPyT-AET.

61. Gauss, *Made in Mexico*, ch. 4; Santos, *Memorias*, 650f, 822–4, 831–6; Niblo, *Mexico in the 1940s*, 164.

62. Gauss, *Made in Mexico*, ch. 4; Hansen, *Politics of Mexican Development*, 73; Crider, "Material Struggles"; Malpica, "La hegemonía," 111–38.

63. The elected leader, Jesús Díaz de León, was nicknamed *El Charro*, hence *charrazo*; on this episode, see: Middlebrook, *The Paradox of Revolution*, ch. 4;

Robert Alegre, *Railroad Radicals in Cold War Mexico* (Lincoln: Univ. of Nebraska Press, 2014), 57–63.

64. Malpica, "La hegemonía," 119–35; *Los días eran nuestros . . . Vida y trabajo entre los obreros textiles de Atlixco* (Mexico City: SEP, 1988), 241; interview with Marta Castro (daughter of *El Tiburón*, an Hernández gunman), Puebla, 3 Jul. 2005.

65. The sketch of Hernández draws on Miguel Ángel Peral, *Diccionario de historia, biografía y geografía del Estado de Puebla* (Mexico City: PAC, 1971), 195f; Flavio Barbosa Cano, *La CROM* (Puebla: UAP, 1981), 51–88; Denisse García Rodea, "Transición a la Democracia y fin del Caciquismo en el Municipio de Atlixco" (Lic. thesis, UDLA-Puebla, 2004), Anexo V; various docs. (1953–57), AGN ARC, Exp. 542.1/308.

66. *Los días eran nuestros*, 241; M. Castro interview, 3 Jul. 2005.

67. *La Opinión*, 17 Jul. 1949, 1; 27 Jul., 1; 1 Aug., 1.

68. *La Opinión*, 10 Oct. 1949, 1; 18 Oct., 1; 28 Oct., 1; 29 Oct., 1; 7 Nov., 1; 14 Nov., 1; 17 Nov., 1 and 6; 1 Dec., 1; 2 Dec., 2.

69. *La Opinión*, 3 Dec. 1949, 1; 6 Dec., 1; 8 Dec., 1; 13 Dec., 2; 14 Dec., 1. Striking at mills that had closed gave unions a chance to negotiate from greater strength, should owners wish to restart work.

70. *La Opinión*, 16 Dec. 1949, 1; 20 Dec., 1; 22 Dec., 1; 5 Jan. 1950, 1.

71. *La Opinión*, 17 Jan. 1950, 1; 18 Jan., 1; W. A. Jenkins interview, 27 Jun. 2002; R. Eustace interview, 6 Nov. 2008.

72. Interviews with Eustace, 15 Mar. 2006, 18 Jul. 2007; Artasánchez Villar, 23 Jul. 2005; Espinosa Yglesias, *Bancomer*, 22f, 37f. El León and (under holding co. CIMASA) La Concepción were registered as "La Quiebra de . . ." at association meetings until 1955/56; CITPyT-Asn., Libros de Actas de Asambleas Generales.

73. Except where noted, bankruptcy insights are from interviews with R. Eustace, 15 Mar. and 20 Apr. 2006, 18 Jul. 2007, and *La Opinión*, 27 Feb. 1953, 1.

74. Cf., for example, the case of a local wool mill: *La Opinión*, 18 Jun. 1953, 1; 6 Dec., 1; 16 Dec., 1.

75. Malpica, "La hegemonía," 136.

76. Gamboa, *Los empresarios*, 231–40; *La Opinión*, 2 Sep. 1945, 1; F. Pérez Vega interview, 25 May 2006.

77. Josué Villavicencio Rojas, *Industria y empresarios en Puebla, 1940–1970* (Puebla: UAP, 2013), 49f, 79–83; Pansters, *Politics and Power*, 90; Ibáñez Puget interview, 9 Sep. 2005; Sánchez Pontón interview, 3 Aug. 2007.

78. Pansters, *Politics and Power*, 88–91, 94f; Villavicencio, *Industria y empresarios*, 42–4, 141f, 212f; Samuel Malpica, *Metepec: La maquina urbana* (Puebla: UAP, 2002).

79. *El Universal*, 1 Feb. 1953, 1; 3 Feb., 1, 3; 4 Feb. 1; *Excélsior*, 1 Feb., 1; 4 Feb., 1.

80. *El Universal*, 4 Feb. 1953, 1; 5 Feb., 1; 6 Feb., 1; 8 Feb., 1; 9 Feb., 1; *Excélsior*, 5 Feb., 1; 6 Feb., 1, 6; 7 Feb., 1; 8 Feb., 1; 9 Feb., 6. Cartoon: 6 Feb., 6; cf. Frank Norris, *The Octopus* (New York: Doubleday, 1901).

81. *New York Times*, 8 Feb. 1953, 76; Krauze, *Biography of Power*, 601–4.

82. *Excélsior*, 8 Feb. 1953, 1; 9 Feb., 1, 6; *El Universal*, 18 Feb., 3, 9; Niblo, *Mexico in the 1940s*, 237.

83. *Excélsior*, 14 Feb. 1953, 1; *El Universal*, 14 Feb. 1953, 1, 6; Contreras Torres, *El libro negro*, 24, 179f; *Proceso*, 11 Aug. 1980, 16–18; Bonilla Fernández, *El secuestro*, 136.

84. J. Vázquez Schiaffino (SRE) to Arthur Lane (Embassy), Mexico City, 22 Oct. 1930, and Amb. Reuben Clark to Genaro Estrada, Mexico City, 29 Nov. 1930, SRE, Exp. 42-26-95; *Periódico Oficial*, 6 Jan. 1931, 21f.

85. Newspapers checked were *Excélsior* and *La Opinión*; interviews with J. Jenkins Eustace, R. Eustace, and W. A. Jenkins, 27 Jun. 2001. See also: SRE, Exp. 42-26-95; Fondo Extranjería, Archivo General Municipal de Puebla, Exp. 7056 (7059); var. letters, 28 Jun. to 1 Oct. 1934, AGN ALR, Exp. 526.27/66; Calles ALR, presidential series.

86. Krauze, *Biography of Power*, 431; *El Universal*, 21 Feb. 1953, 1.

87. *Siempre!*, 8 Aug. 1953, 14, 74; Contreras Torres, *El libro negro*, 237; *El Universal*, 3 Dec. 1953, 4. On *Siempre!*: John Mraz, "Today, Tomorrow, and Always," in *Fragments of a Golden Age*, ed. Joseph et al., 133–5.

88. Branscomb to Jenkins, Nashville, 7 May 1953, Branscomb Papers, Box 362, File 1; Fein, "Hollywood," 617.

89. Eric Zolov, *The Last Good Neighbor: Mexico in the Global Sixties* (Durham, NC: Duke Univ. Press, forthcoming).

90. Pansters, *Politics and Power*, 100f.

91. Niblo, *Mexico in the 1940s*, 351.

92. María Luisa Amador and Jorge Ayala Blanco, *Cartelera cinematográfica, 1950–1959* (Mexico City: UNAM, 1985), 355–63; De la Vega, "Origins, Development," 89f, and "The Decline of the Golden Age and the Making of the Crisis," in *Mexico's Cinema*, ed. J. Hershfield and D. Maciel, 171–4, 186–9.

93. García Riera, *Historia documental*, 8:7–17.

94. Jorge Ayala Blanco, *La condición del cine mexicano, 1973–1985* (Mexico City: Posada, 1986), 516f; García Riera, *Historia documental*, 3:109f, 220, 7:7–10; Berg, *Cinema of Solitude*, 5f, 41; De la Vega, "Decline of the Golden Age," 177–9; *El Universal*, 29 Aug. 1953, 1; 3 Dec., 4.

95. *El Universal*, 11–13 Aug. 1954, 1; *La Opinión*, 12 Aug. 1954, 1; L. Castillo Venegas, 24 Jul. 1954, AGN DFS, Exp. 40-16-954, leg. 1, 257f; var. letters, May-Aug. 1954, AGN ARC, Exp. 111/2855; Ignacio Moreno Tagle, *El caso Mascarúa* (Mexico City: n.p., 1955).

96. *Excélsior*, 18 Nov. 1951, 11-B; *El Universal*, 5 Feb. 1953, 4; *La Opinión*, 12 Aug. 1954, 1; var. documents, Jun./Jul. 1943, AGN MAC, Exp. 432/550; var. documents, Nov./Dec. 1951, AGN MAV, Exp. 621/28205.

97. *La Opinión*, 12 Sep. 1954, 1; 19 Sep., 1; 21 Sep., 1; *Síntesis* (Puebla), 18 Jun. 2007; interviews with R. Eustace, 20 Jul. 2004; Sánchez Pontón, 3 Aug. 2007; Emérita Migoya (niece of Alarcón), Mexico City, 26 Jul. 2007.

98. Various to Ruiz Cortines, AGN ARC, Exp. 111/2855; *New York Times*, 21 Sep. 1954, 12; *Síntesis*, 18 Jun. 2007.

99. *El Universal*, 14 Aug. 1954, 4; *La Opinión*, 3 Oct. 1954, 1, 7 Dec., 1; *La Prensa*, 8 May 1955, 2, 20; anon. to Enrique Rodríguez Cano, Mexico City, 9 May 1955, AGN ARC, Exp. 111/2855, Leg. 40. Cf. Sergio Aguayo, *La Charola: Una historia de los servicios de inteligencia en México* (Mexico City: Grijalbo, 2001), ch. 3.

100. *La Opinión*, 15 Dec. 1955, 1; *New York Times*, 16 Dec. 1955, 12; Xavier Olea Muñoz and Salterio Duque Juárez, *Trujeque, ante el tribunal de alzada* (Mexico City: n.p., 1955), 5, 87f; R. Eustace interview, 18 Jul. 2007.

101. Rodríguez, *Autobiografía*, 165–7; Calles ALR, Empresas.

102. *La Opinión*, 16 Mar. 1954, 1; 13 Aug., 1; 20 Aug., 1; 21 Aug., 1; 14 Sep. 1955, 1, 6, 7; 3 Oct., 5; 17 Aug. 1957, 5; Felipe Rayón Flores to Ruiz Cortines, Mexico City, 28 Aug. 1956, AGN ARC, Exp. 705.2/381; Contreras Torres, *El libro negro*, 339–49, 415; Ramírez, *Contreras Torres*, 106.

103. *Variety*, 3 Dec. 1958, 11.

104. *Variety*, 17 Aug. 1938, 25; 16 Nov. 1938, 123; 3 Dec. 1958, 11. According to affiliated producer Raúl de Anda, the Jenkins Group built (as opposed to buying or leasing) 200 to 300 venues; Mora-Palabra, PHO2/48, 29f.

105. Fernández and Paxman, *El Tigre*, 79.

106. Jenkins to Family, 9 Sep. and 13 Nov. 1954, MJWP; Sra. Del Arenal to López Mateos, Mexico City, 1 Mar. 1961, AGN, presidential files of Adolfo López Mateos (hereafter, AGN ALM), Exp. 444.1/144; *Time*, 26 Dec. 1960, 26.

107. L. Castillo Venegas, 26 Apr. 1954, AGN DFS, Exp. 9-232-954, leg. 1, h. 21; Espinosa Yglesias, *Bancomer*, 22f; Enrique Cárdenas Sánchez, *El largo curso de la economía mexicana* (Mexico City: FCE, 2015), 548f.

108. Jenkins, "Memorandum," Puebla, 2 Mar. 1951, Branscomb Papers, Box 362, File 1.

109. Mexican film exports declined from the mid-1950s: Rogelio Agrasánchez, *Mexican Movies in the United States* (Jefferson, NC: McFarland, 2006), 63–9, 131–9, 164–6; Robert McKee Irwin and Maricruz Castro Ricalde, *Global Mexican Cinema* (London: Palgrave/BFI, 2013), 13f, 148, 199.

110. *Variety*, 18 Jun. 1947, 15; 16 Jul., 16.

111. Fein, "Hollywood," 563, cf. 337–42; Thomas Schatz, *Boom and Bust: American Cinema in the 1940s* (Berkeley: Univ. of California Press, 1999), 13, 18–20, 343.

112. Federico Heuer, *La industria cinematográfica mexicana* (Mexico City: n.p., 1964), 176–81; Berg, *Cinema of Solitude*, 41.

113. García Riera, *Historia documental*, 3:109f, 220; De la Vega, "Origins, Development," 91; Berg, *Cinema of Solitude*, 5f, 37, 41. Cf. Thomas Schatz, *The Genius of the System: Hollywood Filmmaking in the Studio Era* (New York: Pantheon, 1988).

114. Heuer, *La industria cinematográfica*, 210. Heuer was writing in 1964; for his complete argument see 199–213.

115. I develop this argument further in "Cooling to Cinema and Warming to Television: State Mass Media Policy from 1940 to 1964," in *Dictablanda*, ed. Gillingham and Smith.

116. Amador and Ayala Blanco, *Cartelera cinematográfica, 1950–1959*, 357–62.

117. De la Vega, "Origins, Development," 90; Paranaguá, ed., *Mexican Cinema*, 42.

118. *Variety*, 1 Jun. 1966, 21; 5 Jan. 1972, 70; 9 May 1973, 217; Amador and Ayala Blanco, *Cartelera cinematográfica, 1950–1959*, 388–99, and 1960–1969, 476–89; Seth Fein, "From Collaboration to Containment," in *Mexico's Cinema*, ed. J. Hershfield and D. Maciel, 155.

CHAPTER 10

1. The foundation story draws on Espinosa Yglesias, "Introduction," 18, 21–3; Joseph C. Kiger, ed., *International Encyclopedia of Foundations* (New York: Greenwood, 1990), 170–4; Branscomb to Jenkins, Nashville, 6 Feb. 1952, Branscomb Papers; "Título para la 'Fundación Mary Street Jenkins,'" Puebla (Notaries Public 13 and 22), 18 Oct. 1954, MSJF.

2. J. Jenkins Eustace interview, 15 Aug. 2001.

3. R. Eustace interviews, 15 Aug. 2001, 15 Mar. 2006, 18 Jul. 2007; Buntzler interview, 6 Jun. 2005.

4. See e.g., RPP Puebla, Libro 1 de Comercio, T. 14, no. 180; T. 16, no. 16; T. 17, no. 32; T. 17, no. 52.

5. *La Opinión*, 15 Feb. 1953, 1; Harvie Branscomb et al., "Resolution by the Board of Trust of Vanderbilt University in memory of William Oscar Jenkins," 5 Oct. 1963, Branscomb Papers, Box 362, File 1.

6. *La Opinión*, 6 Nov. 1951, 1; 10 Nov. 1952, 1; *La Jornada del Oriente* (Puebla), 13 Jul. 2005, 10. Jenkins reportedly cofinanced five such schools; cf. Trueblood, ed., *Mary Street Jenkins Foundation*, 27.

7. *Hoy*, 5 Aug. 1950, 22–24; Thom Rath (historian), email to author, 3 Mar. 2016.

8. *La Opinión*, 16 Nov. 1952, 1; 2 Feb. 1953, 1; 14–16 Jan. 1955, 1.

9. *La Opinión*, 12 Jan. 1957, 1; 15–17 Jan., 1; *El Universal*, 16 Jan., 1; *La Jornada del Oriente*, 13 Jul. 2005, 10; D. Palma Gutiérrez to Director, 9 Jun. 1964, AGN DFS, Exp. 100-19-4-64, leg. 1, 14f.

10. Conversation with Purdy Jordan, Mexico City, 24 Feb. 2005; cf. Niblo, *Mexico in the 1940s*, 357n50.

11. Jenkins to Alemán, Puebla, 10 May 1950, AGN MAV, Exp. 568.3/160; I. Chávez to Jenkins, Mexico City, 10 Apr. 1951, Jenkins to Alemán, Puebla, 10 Jun. 1951, AGN MAV, Exp. 515/21187; *Sol de Puebla*, 5 Jun. 1963, 3.

12. Branscomb to Jenkins, Nashville, 6 Feb. 1952, and New York, 9 Dec. 1952, Branscomb Papers, Box 362, File 1; Vázquez Nava interview, 26 May 2006.

13. Jenkins to Carrillo Flores, 2 Jul. 1954, in *Mary Street Jenkins Foundation*, ed. Trueblood, 21.

14. Cordero y Torres, *Diccionario Biográfico*, 352; cf. *Proceso*, 4 Nov. 1991, 23; Bonilla, *El secuestro del poder*, 14.

15. Libro de Actas, vol. 1: 1, MSJF; Andrew Carnegie, *The "Gospel of Wealth" Essays and Other Writings* (New York: Penguin, 2006); Jenkins to E. Jenkins, Puebla, 26 Dec. 1919, MSJP.

16. AGN Migración, Estadounidenses, Caja 81, Exp. 70; *La Opinión*, 15 May 1954, 1; *Nashville Banner*, 5 Jun. 1963, 10; interviews with W. A. Jenkins, 27 Jun. 2002; R. Eustace Jenkins, 27 Jun. 2002, 8 Jun. 2005; Tita Cheney, 18 Aug. 2002; and J. Jenkins Eustace, 8 Jul. 2003, 30 Sep. 2005.

17. Higgins memo, 1 Apr. 1957, REP; Mary Jenkins to Jane Jenkins, Jilotepec, Mex., 20 Oct. 1950, MJWP; R. Eustace interviews, 10 Apr. 2002, 17 Jul. 2007.

18. *Variety*, 2 Oct. 1943, 3; *Los Angeles Times*, 17 Oct. 1946, 1; Jenkins to William, Puebla, 27 Oct. 1955, and Jenkins to Murray Hawkins, Puebla, 29 Oct. 1956, MJWP; interview with Susan Heflinger (daughter of Mary), Los Angeles, 18 Aug. 2002; Cheney interview, 18 Aug. 2002.

19. *San Francisco Chronicle*, 28 Feb. 1952; *Washington Post*, 28 Feb.; Cheney interview, 18 Aug. 2002; R. Eustace interview, 8 Aug. 2003; Diannah Morgan (daughter of Robert Lord), email to author, 10 Jun. 2003.

20. Jenkins to R. William, Puebla, 25 Nov. 1961, MJWP.

21. Libro de Actas, vol. 1: 1, 5, MSJF; W. A. Jenkins interview, 13 Apr. 2005.

22. RPP-Puebla, Libro 1 de Comercio, T. 17, nos. 31, 32, 33, 34, 35, 51, 114, 117, 119; interviews with Migoya, 26 Jul. 2007; R. Eustace, 1 Aug. 2007; Sánchez Pontón, 3 Aug. 2007.

23. M. Rangel Escamilla, 25 Feb. 1960, AGN DFS, Exp. 100-19-1-60, leg. 2, 6; D. Palma Gutiérrez, 9 Jun. 1964, AGN DFS, Exp. 100-19-4-64, leg. 1, 14f; Trueblood, ed., *Mary Street Jenkins Foundation*, 30, 164, 170f; *La Opinión*, 11 Jul. 1957, 1; 18–19 Oct., 1; 13 Jun. 1962, 1; 7 Jul., 1.

24. *Proceso*, 4 Nov. 1991, 23; Bonilla, *El secuestro del poder*, 14.

25. Jenkins to Posada, Puebla, 6 Jun. 1939, REJP. Posada later requested Jenkins's help with a book about Atencingo, and again he declined; Jenkins to Posada, 22 Jun. 1943, REJP.

26. Photo of Manuel Pérez Lamadrid opening school, Temaxcalapa, 30 Sep. 1934, and speech by Manuel Pérez Pena, Atencingo, 20 Nov. 1942, Manuel Pérez Nochebuena Papers, Puebla; J. Jenkins Eustace interview, 27 Jun. 2002.

27. *La Opinión*, 18 Oct. 1957, 1; 19 Oct., 6; Alfonso Sobero Nevares, *Apuntes históricos sobre el Teatro Principal* (Puebla: n.p., 1961).

28. G. Fuentes Coss et al. to López Mateos, Puebla, 14 Sep. 1959, AGN ALM, Exp. 404.1/1907; *Siempre!*, 6 Sep. 1961, 7; interviews with Sergio Reguero, Puebla, 28 Mar. 2005; Guzmán Ramos, 23 Jul. 2005; Artasánchez Bautista, 28 Jul. 2005; Vázquez Nava, 26 May 2006.

29. Flyer, "Puebla, Clama Justicia" (Sindicato Héroes de Nacozari to Ruiz Cortines), Puebla, May 1956, AGN ARC, Exp. 544.2/27; Pansters, *Politics and Power*, 106f; R. Eustace interview, 10 Apr. 2002.

30. The Bancomer takeover draws on Gustavo del Ángel Mobarak, *BBVA Bancomer: 75 años de historia* (Mexico City: BBVA Bancomer, 2007), 73–86, and Espinosa Yglesias, *Bancomer*, 22–31.

31. *Anuario Financiero 1940*, 133–7, 153f, 271–3, 276–8.

32. Hamilton, *Limits of State Autonomy*, 211f, 294–7. On the "hostile takeover": Del Ángel, *BBVA Bancomer*, 74.

33. Jenkins to Espinosa, Puebla, 16 Mar. 1954, CEEY, Caja 31, exp. 28; J. Eustace Jenkins interview, 31 Jul. 2005.

34. The $4 million is extrapolated from the value of Senderos's $10 million, plus an estimated premium for majority ownership.

35. *El Popular*, 6 Jun. 1955, 1; Espinosa to Jenkins, 16 Feb. 1961, in *Mary Street Jenkins Foundation*, ed. Trueblood, 23f; Hamilton, *Limits of State Autonomy*, 296n2; Espinosa Yglesias, *Bancomer*, 38–42; interview with Alexis Falquier (former consultant to Banamex), Mexico City, 27 Feb. 2005; Artasánchez Villar interview, 23 Jul. 2005.

36. *El Popular*, 6 Jun. 1955, 1. On insider lending at the Banco de Comercio: Del Ángel, *BBVA Bancomer*, 93f.

37. *El Popular*, 15 Nov. 1956, 1.

38. Alicia Ortiz Rivera, *Juan Sánchez Navarro* (Mexico City: Grijalbo, 1997); Espinosa Yglesias, *Bancomer*, 31–5, 50; cf. Del Ángel, *BBVA Bancomer*, 23f, 34.

39. Del Ángel, *BBVA Bancomer*, 26–8, 34, 68–70.

40. M. Basail de la Vía and J. M. Vertiz to DFS, Mexico City, 10 and 14 Jan. 1949, AGN DFS, Exp. 12-17-949, 4–6 and 49–53; index card, 26 Aug. 1949, AGN DFS, Exp. 25-12-949, 3.

41. *Opinión Pública*, Aug. 1959, 18; *Time*, 26 Dec. 1960, 26.

42. Espinosa Rugarcía interview, 19 Jul. 2005.

43. *El Universal*, 16 Jun. 1958, 25, 27; Eustace Jenkins, *Tennessee Sunshine*, 338–40.

44. Trueblood, ed., *Mary Street Jenkins Foundation*, 26, 108. The MSJF would donate 1.5 million pesos, 1958–66.

45. Navarro, *Political Intelligence*, 182–4; *Directorio de Empresas Industriales Beneficiadas con Exenciones Fiscales, 1940–1960* (Mexico City: Banco de México, 1961), 345; Jacob Bernstein, "What Goes Around . . .," *In These Times*, 12 Jun. 1995; W. A. Jenkins interview, 11 Nov. 2005.

46. L. Castillo Venegas, 13 Jul. 1954, AGN DFS, Exp. 11-4-54, leg. 3, 50f.

47. "Testimonio de la escritura de testamento público abierto otorgado por el señor don William O. Jenkins," Puebla (Notaries Public 13 and 22), 29 Oct. 1958, WAJP; *Novedades*, 8 Jun. 1963, 12.

48. RPP-Puebla, L. 1, T. 18, no. 101; Villavicencio, *Industria y empresarios*, 60.

49. R. Eustace Jenkins interviews, 20 Aug. 2001 and 27 Jun. 2002; J. Jenkins Eustace interview, 8 Jul. 2003.

50. Eric Zolov, "¡Cuba sí, yanquis no!," in *In from the Cold: Latin America's New Encounter with the Cold War*, ed. G. Joseph and D. Spenser (Durham, NC: Duke Univ. Press. 2008); Keller, *Mexico's Cold War*, chs. 2 and 3.

51. Stephen Niblo, "Progress and the Standard of Living in Contemporary Mexico," *Latin American Perspectives* 2:2 (1975), 109–11; Hansen, *Politics of Mexican Development*, ch. 4. On the Alemanist-Cardenist tug of war, see Rogelio Hernández Rodríguez, "La política," in R. Hernández Rodríguez, ed., *Adolfo López Mateos*, 234–9, 247–52.

52. Zolov, "*¡Cuba sí, yanquis no!*"; Pansters, *Politics and Power*, 109–17; *La Opinión*, 5 Jun. 1961, 1.

53. Moreno, *Yankee Don't Go Home!*; Fein, "Hollywood," chs. 5 and 6; Saragoza, *The State and the Media*.

54. Eric Zolov, *Refried Elvis: The Rise of the Mexican Counterculture* (Berkeley: Univ. of California Press), ch.1; Moreno, *Yankee Don't Go Home!*, ch. 7; Reid, *Spanish American Images*, chs. 9 and 10.

55. Cosío Villegas, "From Mexico," in *As Others See Us*, ed. F. Joseph (Princeton, NJ: Princeton Univ. Press, 1959); Muñoz, *La verdad sobre los gringos* (Mexico City: Ediciones Populares, 1961), 229–31; Carlos Fuentes, Prologue, in Rodó, *Ariel*, 14; Gabriel Antonio Menéndez, *Doheny, el cruel* (Mexico City: Bolsa Mexicana del Libro, 1958).

56. Wilt, "Stereotyped Images," 284, 286.

57. Vázquez and Meyer, *United States and Mexico*, 172–9; Keller, *Mexico's Cold War*, 60–72, 156–67.

58. See e.g., *Excélsior*, 15 Mar. 1955, 25; 11 Jul. 1960, 30; *El Popular*, 15 Nov. 1956, 1; *El Universal*, 22 Dec. 1957, 1; 4–6 Jul. 1958, 1; *Siempre!*, 10 Dec. 1958, 38f.

59. *Opinión Pública*, Aug. 1959, 16–20.

60. *Opinión Pública*, Jan. 1959, 2f (Wenner-Gren) and 7 (Suárez); 31 Jul. 1961, 2; 15 Sep. 1962, 9; 31 Oct., 3, 16.

61. *Éxito*, 18–24 Oct. 1959, 4; R. Eustace interview, 15 Jul. 2007.

62. Jacinto Rodríguez Munguía, *La otra guerra secreta* (Mexico City: Debate, 2007), 199, 205; Renata Keller, "Testing the Limits of Censorship? *Política* Magazine and Mexico's 'Perfect Dictatorship,'" in P. Gillingham, M. Lettieri, and B. Smith, eds., *Journalism, Satire and Censorship*.

63. *Política*, 1 Jun. 1960, 27–9; 15 Jun., 9; 1 Jul., 9; 1 Aug., 11f.

64. Contreras Torres, *El libro negro*; Ramírez, *Contreras Torres*, 106f; *Política*, 1 Jun. 1960, 27; 1 Aug., 11.

65. Don Verdades, *Corrido del cine mexicano*.

66. Abel Quezada, *Excélsior*, 7 Jun. 1960, 7.

67. *Excélsior*, 8 Jun. 1960, 1; cf. 9 Jun., 1, 6; *Política*, 15 Jun. 1960, 9.

68. Keller, *Mexico's Cold War*, 54–7, 105–12; Zolov, *Last Good Neighbor*.

69. Hansen, *Politics of Mexican Development*, 79f.

70. *Excélsior*, 9 Jun. 1960, 5.

71. *Excélsior*, 5 Jun. 1963, 14; W. A. Jenkins interview, 12 Oct. 2005. On Cárdenas's in Michoacán: Verónica Oikión Solano, *Los hombres del poder en Michoacán* (Zamora: Colegio de Michoacán, 2004), 364, 401, 445, 472–5, 480f.

72. *El Universal*, 30 Nov. 1960, 1; García Riera, *Historia documental*, 10:156; Krauze, *Biography of Power*, 660f.

73. *El Universal*, 1 Dec. 1960, 11, 29, 35; 2 Dec., 3 (etc.); *Time*, 26 Dec. 1960, 25; Espinosa Yglesias, *Bancomer*, 87–9.

74. Jenkins to Family, Puebla, 13 Nov. 1955, MJWP; Jenkins to Branscomb, Puebla, 10 Mar. 1961, Branscomb Papers, Box 362, File 2; García Riera, *Breve historia*, 211; Espinosa Yglesias, *Bancomer*, 58–77; Águila et al., *Trabajo, fortuna y poder*, 124–7, 139–45; W. A. Jenkins interview, 22 Nov. 2000; Alarcón interview, 15 Aug. 2007.

75. Alejandro Flores García, *Cinecompendio 1971–1972* (Mexico City: A Posta, 1972), 27, 38–43; Amador and Ayala Blanco, *Cartelera cinematográfica, 1960–1969*, 425–39.

76. Krauze, *Biography of Power*, 657, 661; Wilkie and Monzón de Wilkie, *México visto en el siglo XX*, 209.

77. González, *La querencia* (Morelia: SEP Michoacán, 1982), 107–60, esp. 109, 156f.

78. A. René Barbosa and Sergio Maturana, *El arrendamiento de tierras ejidales: Un estudio en Michoacán* (Mexico City: Centro de Investigaciones Agrarias, 1972), 46; Bill Alston (son of Wally), email to author, 19 Oct. 2014.

79. Libros de Ventas, Apatzingán, Registro Público de la Propiedad, Morelia (hereafter, RPP-Morelia), Tomo 44, nos. 6817–6826; *Excélsior*, 8 Jun. 1960, 1; *La Voz de Michoacán*, 5 Jul. 1961, 1; W. A. Jenkins interview, 29 Mar. 2001.

80. *La Voz de Michoacán*, 12 Jun. 1960, 5; 22 Jun., 5; 23 Jun., 1; Libros de Ventas, Apatzingán, RPP-Morelia, Tomo 44, no. 6850.

81. *La Voz de Michoacán*, 2 Jul. 1960, 1.

82. *La Voz de Michoacán*, 18 Jun. 1960, 1; Libros de Ventas, Apatzingán, RPP-Morelia, Tomo 49, nos. 7613, 7615, 7616; Oikión Solano, *Los hombres del poder*, 444f.

83. *Política*, 1 Jul. 1962, 31; Jenkins to Family, Puebla, 31 Jan. 1962, REJP; *La Opinión*, 5 Jun. 1963, 1; W. A. Jenkins interview, 12 Oct. 2005; Bill Alston, email to author, 1 Nov. 2014.

84. *Siempre!*, 17 Oct. 1962, 28f; 24 Oct., 24f.

85. *La Voz de Michoacán*, 5 Jul. 1961, 1; interview with Humberto Sánchez Gallegos, Apatzingán, 8 Aug. 2006. On pesticide ills in Mexico, see Angus Wright, *The Death of Ramón González* (Austin: Univ. of Texas Press, 2005).

86. W. A. Jenkins interviews, 10 Apr. 2002, 15 Jul. 2003; Sánchez Gallegos interview, 8 Aug. 2006; Carson, *The Silent Spring* (Boston: Houghton Mifflin, [Sep.] 1962).

87. *La Opinión*, 7 May 1952, 1; 28 Jul. 1956, 1; Jenkins to Socorro Sánchez, 27 Feb. 1960, REJP; interview with Socorro and Gloria Sánchez, Puebla, 8 May 2005.

88. *La Opinión*, 19 Oct. 1957, 1; F. Meadows to J. Erwin, Puebla, 23 Jul. 1961, MJWP; Cordero y Torres, *Historia compendiada*, I:237; Trueblood, ed., *Mary Street Jenkins Foundation*, 30.

89. Branscomb to Jenkins, Nashville, 21 May 1951, 24 Apr. 1962, Branscomb Papers; Jenkins to Family, 23 Oct., 3, 9 and 29 Nov. 1962, REJP; Mestre interview, 25 Feb. 2006.

90. The 1961 UAP conflict draws on Pansters, *Politics and Power*, 97–117, and David Tamayo, "¡Cristianismo sí! ¡Comunismo no!: Religion and Reform in the University of Puebla, 1961" (BA thesis, UC Berkeley, 2003).

91. Wil Pansters, ed., *La mirada del Fénix* (Puebla: UAP, 1996); Manuel Lara y Parra, *La lucha universitaria en Puebla* (Puebla: UAP, 2002); Humberto Sotelo Mendoza, *Crónica de una autonomía anhelada* (Puebla: UAP, 2004).

92. Lara y Parra, *La lucha universitaria*, 64f; Nicolás Dávila Peralta, *Las santas batallas* (Puebla: UAP, 2003), 114–8.

93. Rangel Escamilla, 27 Jul. 1960, AGN DFS, Exp. 100-19-1-60, leg. 2, 58; Alfonso Vélez Pliego, "La sucesión rectoral," *Crítica* (Puebla) 1 (1978), 59f; Alfonso Yáñez, *La manipulación de la fe* (Puebla: Imagen Pública y Corporativa, 2000), 27f.

94. The Puebla riot was not unique; for a similar occurrence in Morelia, see Zolov, "*¡Cuba sí, yanquis no!*"

95. *La Opinión*, 18 Apr. 1961, 1; Pansters, *Politics and Power*, 109f.

96. *La Opinión*, 5 Jun. 1961, 1; Dávila, *Las santas batallas*, 132–45. On Glockner: *La Jornada de Oriente* (Puebla), 9 Jun. 2009, supplement.

97. Eustace Jenkins, ed., *Tennessee Sunshine*, 352, 358f; *Política*, 15 Aug. 1961, 2; Yáñez, *La manipulación*, 152.

98. *La Opinión*, 26 Jul. 1961, 1; 1 Aug., 1; 5 Aug., 1; Guzmán Ramos interviews, 28 Nov. 2005, 9 Aug. 2009.

99. *La Opinión*, 27–29 Apr. 1961, 1; 17–20 Jun., 1; Dávila, *Las santas batallas*, 126f.; Yáñez, *La manipulación*, 182; Pansters, *Politics and Power*, 190n32; Bonilla, *El secuestro del poder*, 160f.

100. *Siempre!*, 16 Aug. 1961, 16f; Mraz, "Today, Tomorrow, and Always," 151f.

101. *Sobre los Sucesos de Puebla* (Mexico City: Movimiento de Liberación Nacional, 1961).

102. Unsigned summary (index card), 6 Oct. 1961, AGN DFS, Exp. 63-30-61, leg. 18, 87.

103. *Nashville Tennessean*, 28 Jun. 1964, 4f; "Martin Shofner, 1758–1838," plaque at Shofner Luthern Church, Thompson's Creek, Bedford County, Tennessee.

104. *Nashville Tennessean* 5 Jun. 1963, 6; Eustace Jenkins, ed., *Tennessee Sunshine*, 346f; Shofner interview, 11 Jul. 2004.

105. *La Opinión*, 23 Aug. 1962, 1; 10 Nov., 1; 20–21 Dec., 1; Pansters, *Politics and Power*, 52, 93f, 117; Lomelí Vanegas, *Breve historia*, 381–3; interview with Efraín Castro Morales, Puebla, 22 Jul. 2006; Sánchez Pontón interview, 3 Aug. 2007.

106. Krauze, *Biography of Power*, 634, 657–660, 674; Zolov, *Last Good Neighbor*.

107. Jane to Mary Jenkins, Puebla, 23 Apr. 1962, MJWP; Eustace Jenkins, ed., *Tennessee Sunshine*, 339.

108. Cheney interview, 18 Aug. 2002.

109. Espinosa Yglesias, "Introduction," 23; R. Eustace Jenkins interviews, 20 Aug. 2001, 4 Jul. 2003, 19 Jul. 2004.

110. On Jenkins's daughters and sons-in-law: Jenkins to Mary Jenkins, Puebla, 17 Oct. 1944, R. William to M. Hawkins, Los Angeles, 27 Dec. 1960, Meadows to Erwin, 23 Jul. 1961, Jenkins to Mary, 13 Apr. 1962, and R. William to Jenkins, 19 Jul. 1962, MJWP; "Testimonio" (will), 29 Oct. 1958, WAJP; *Excélsior*, 6 Jun. 1963, B4; Eustace Jenkins, *Tennessee Sunshine*, 340–3; interviews with J. Jenkins Eustace, 27 Jun. and 15 Aug. 2001, 8 Jul. 2003; R. Eustace Jenkins, 27 Jun. 2002, 8 Jun. 2005; Cheney, 18 Aug. 2002; Heflinger, 18–19 Aug. 2002; W. A. Jenkins, 21 Aug. 2007 and 27 Jul. 2009; R. Eustace Jenkins, email to author, 11 Sep. 2012.

111. Libro de Actas, vol. 1: 83, 91–97, MSJF; Trueblood, ed., *Mary Street Jenkins Foundation*, 7; interviews with Alicia Juárez, Puebla, 4 Oct. 2005; R. Eustace, 19 Jul. 2004; Bunztler, 6 Jun. 2005. The $60 million endowment would be worth some $500 million today.

112. On Jenkins's last weeks: *Shelbyville Times-Gazette*, 5 Jun. 1963, 2; *La Opinión*, 5 Jun., 1, 6; *El Sol de Puebla*, 5 Jun., 1, 4; *Novedades*, 8 Jun., 12; Urbano Deloya, "William Oscar Jenkins," transcript from *Puebla de mis amores*, XECD Radio (Puebla), 11 Mar. 1995, MSJF; Cheney interview, 18 Aug. 2002; Juárez interview, 4 Oct. 2005; J. Eustace Jenkins interview, 22 Aug. 2006.

113. Libro de Actas, vol. 1: 98f, MSJF.

CHAPTER 11

1. *Excélsior*, 5 Jun. 1963, 5.
2. *La Opinión*, 5 Jun. 1963, 1; *El Universal*, 5 Jun., 1; *El Sol de Puebla*, 6 Jun., 1; *New York Times*, 5 Jun., 39; cf. *Time*, 26 Dec. 1960, 25; *Nashville Banner*, 5 Jun. 1963, 1; *Nashville Tennessean*, 5 Jun., 1.
3. *Novedades*, 5 Jun. 1963, 1; *Excélsior*, 5 Jun., 5.
4. *El Sol de Puebla*, 5–6 Jun. 1963, 1; *La Opinión*, 1 Feb., 1; Trueblood, ed., *Mary Street Jenkins Foundation*, 7, 11.
5. Libros de Actas, vol. 1, 5 Jun. 1963, MSJF. Joining the board as an alternate member was Jenkins's notary, Nicolás Vázquez.
6. Fátima Fernández Christlieb, *Los medios de difusión masiva en México* (Mexico City: Juan Pablos, 1996), 31f, 51–4, 69–73; Rafael Rodríguez Castañeda, *Prensa Vendida* (Mexico City: Grijalbo, 1993), 93, 101f; Villavicencio, *Industria y empresarios*, 51f, 81f; *Síntesis* (Puebla), 18 Jun. 2007, 10.
7. *El Sol de Puebla*, 7 Jun. 1963, 1; Libros de Actas, vol. 1, 4 Sep., 5 and 18 Dec. 1963, MSJF; interviews with W. A. Jenkins, 29 Mar. and 27 Jun. 2001, 18 Jun. 2003, 11 Nov. 2005; R. Eustace, 15 Aug. 2001; Heflinger, 18 Aug. 2002; Guzmán Ramos, 2 Aug. 2007.
8. *Novedades*, 8 Jun. 1963, 12; Espinosa Yglesias, "Introduction," 7, 11.
9. *El Sol de Puebla*, 7 Jun. 1963, 1; *Novedades*, 7 Jun., 1; *El Universal*, 7 Jun., 7; *Nashville Banner*, 7 Jun.

10. Matthew Esposito, *Funerals, Festivals, and Cultural Politics in Porfirian Mexico* (Albuquerque: Univ. of New Mexico Press, 2010); Knight, *Mexican Revolution*, II: 519f.

11. *El Universal*, 5 Jun. 1968, 6; 5 Jun. 1971, 7; interview with Arthur Chaffee, Puebla, 11 Aug. 2009.

12. Pansters, *Politics and Power*, 93–5, 117–20; *La Opinión*, 1–3 Nov. 1963, 1; 11 Nov., 1; *Excélsior*, 31 Oct. 1964, 1; *Novedades*, 8 Nov., 1; Guzmán Ramos interview, 16 May 2005.

13. Smith, *Revolutionary Nationalism*, ix; *El Universal*, 4 Nov. 1963, 1; Krauze, *Biography of Power*, 634, 667–74.

14. Camp, *Entrepreneurs and Politics*, 24f; Krauze, *Biography of Power*, 694–731.

15. Palma Gutiérrez, 9 Jun. 1964, AGN DFS, Exp. 100-19-4-64, leg. 1, 12; Kiger, ed., *International Encyclopedia of Foundations*, 169–74.

16. Carlos Tello, *Estado y desarrollo económico: México 1920–2006* (Mexico City: UNAM, 2011), 361–7, 383–5, 401–17; Libros de Actas, vol. 1, 7 Aug. 1963, MSJF; W. A. Jenkins interview, 15 Jul. 2003.

17. Blas García Hernández to director, Mexico City, 1 Aug. 1963, AGN DFS, Manuel Espinosa Yglesias, Versión pública.

18. *El Popular*, 15 Nov. 1956; Espinosa, "Introduction," 23f; interview with Ramón Pieza Rugarcía (nephew of Espinosa), Puebla, 24 Aug. 2006; Artasánchez Villar interview, 23 Jul. 2005.

19. *El Sol de Puebla*, 5 Jun. 1963, 1, 4; *La Opinión*, 28 Aug., 1; Palma Gutiérrez, 9 Jun. 1964, AGN DFS, Exp. 100-19-4-64, leg. 1, 12; Trueblood, ed., *Mary Street Jenkins Foundation*, 30, 81; J. Jenkins Eustace interview, 2 Apr. 2001; Chaffee interview, 11 Aug. 2009.

20. Pansters, *Politics and Power*, 109–11, 118–20.

21. Libros de Actas, vol. 2, nos. 123, 184, 555, MSJF; *El Universal*, 5 Jun. 1965, 1, 7; Lara y Parra, *La lucha universitaria*, 121, 126, 149f, 237–56; *Tiempo Universitario* (Puebla), Sep. 2008, 5.

22. Enrique Cárdenas, *UDLA, una esperanza, una realidad: Don Manuel Espinosa Yglesias* (Cholula, Pue.: Fundación UDLA-Puebla, 2000), 16–21.

23. Jenkins to Tigert, 2 Apr. 1925, Tigert Papers.

24. Lara y Parra, *La lucha universitaria*, 121, 256; Guzmán Ramos interview, 23 Jul. 2005.

25. Cárdenas, *UDLA*, 20f, 35; Libros de Actas, vol. 4, no. 1367, MSJF.

26. Águila et al., *Trabajo, Fortuna y Poder*, 308–11; interview with Neil Lindley, Beaumont, TX, 13 Jul. 2013.

27. On leftist activism at the UAP in the 1960s, see Vélez Pliego, "La sucesión rectoral," 59–70; Pansters, *Politics and Power*, ch. V; Lara y Parra, *La lucha universitaria*, chs. III, V and VII; Yáñez, *La manipulación*; Dávila, *Las santas batallas*, ch. V. On enrollment: *Tiempo Universitario*, 9 Jul. 1998, 1.

28. Already, Rafael Artasánchez, rector 1954–56, had served as mayor in 1957–60, while another conservative, Gonzalo Bautista O'Farrill, rector 1953–54, would briefly serve as mayor and then governor in 1972–73.

29. Blum, *Killing Hope: US Military and CIA Interventions since World War II* (London: Zed, 2003), 142, 234; Samuel Schmidt, *The Deterioration of the Mexican Presidency* (Tucson: Univ. of Arizona Press, 1991), 134f; Keller, *Mexico's Cold War*, 223–8; off-record conversations with the author, Puebla, 2005–6.

30. Jaime Pensado, *Rebel Mexico: Student Unrest and Authoritarian Political Culture During the Long Sixties* (Stanford, CA: Stanford Univ. Press, 2013), ch. 8; Krauze, *Biography of Power*, 688–97.

31. Libros de Actas, vol. 2, no. 712 and vol. 3, no. 773, MSJF; Libros de Actas, vol. 3, nos. 744, 926 and 1172 and vol. 4. nos. 1465 and 1666, MSJF. On the CUC: www.cuc.org.mx/historia/.

32. Libros de Actas, vol. 2, no. 672, MSJF; *Excélsior*, 3 Dec. 1965, 1, 13; 5 Jun. 1968, 1, 10f; *El Universal*, 5 Jun., 1, 10. Espinosa's speech: www.ceey.org.mx/sites/default/files/1968-4.pdf.

33. *Mary Street Jenkins Foundation*, 29 (total gifts, 1972–86); Alfonso Torres Robles, *La prodigiosa aventura de los Legionarios de Cristo* (Madrid: Foca, 2001), 53; Ángeles Conde and David Murray, *The Legion of Christ* (North Haven, CT: Circle Press, 2004), 248f; Libros de Actas, vol. 3, nos. 1142 and 1217, vol. 4, no. 1907, etc., MSJF.

34. Jason Berry and Gerald Renner, *Vows of Silence* (New York: Free Press, 2004), 3, 159f.

35. Berry and Renner, *Vows of Silence*, 158–65, 170f, 256–8; *Wall Street Journal*, 23 Jan. 2006, 1; *National Catholic Reporter*, 16 Apr. 2010, 1; 30 Apr., 15; Espinosa Rugarcía, *Manuel Espinosa Yglesias*, 90. In 2006, Pope Benedict would remove Maciel from his ministry, following multiple revelations of his sexual abuse of seminarians.

36. *Excélsior*, 5 Jun. 1968, 10.

37. "The Philanthropic Ogre" (1979), in *The Labyrinth of Solitude and Other Writings* (New York: Grove, 1985); Krauze, *Biography of Power*, 747–9; Espinosa Yglesias, *Bancomer*, chs. 5 to 7; Águila et al., *Trabajo, Fortuna y Poder*, chs. IX and X; Del Ángel, *BBVA Bancomer*, 120–44, 160–9.

38. Libros de Actas, vol. 4, nos. 1504 and 1752, MSJF; Trueblood, ed., *Mary Street Jenkins Foundation*, 156–59.

39. Verissimo, *Mexico*, 163; Schmidt, *Deterioration*, 121–26; *El Universal*, 18 Oct. 1976, 1.

40. Libros de Actas, vol. 4, no. 1778, MSJF; Fernández and Paxman, *El Tigre*, 246–9.

41. GDA, *BBVA Bancomer*, 129–35; Pansters, *Politics and Power*, 129–31; Efraín Huerta, *Poesía completa* (Mexico City: FCE, 2014), 418f.

42. "Repression at UDLA," *Latin American Perspectives* 3:4 (1976): 2, 122; Schmidt, *Deterioration*, ch. 4; Krauze, *Biography of Power*, 747–51; interview with Edward Simmen (UDLA historian), Cholula, Puebla, 9 Aug. 2012.

43. Del Ángel, *BBVA Bancomer*, 128, 171f.

44. Libros de Actas, vol. 5, no. 2217, MSJF; Kiger, ed., *International Encyclopedia of Foundations*, 169, 174.

45. Kiger, ed., *International Encyclopedia of Foundations*, 169; Manuel Espinosa Yglesias, "Texto original del libro sobre la Fundación Amparo, prólogo," 1991, CEEY, Caja 40, II.A.3.a/1991-2.

46. Espinosa Yglesias, *Bancomer*, 124, 129; *Town & Country*, Nov. 1980, 227, 324f.

47. Stephen Haber et al., *Mexico Since 1980* (Cambridge: Cambridge Univ. Press, 2008), 57–65; Amparo Espinosa Rugarcía and Enrique Cárdenas Sánchez, eds., *La nacionalización bancaria, 25 años después* (Mexico City: Centro de Estudios Espinosa Yglesias, 2010; 3 vols.); Krauze, *Biography of Power*, 757–61.

48. Espinosa Yglesias, *Bancomer*, 166f, 171–93; Racial Trejo, *Carlos Slim: Vida y Obra* (Mexico City: Quién es Quién, 2013), 120–3, 131f; *Proceso*, 8 Apr. 1985, 28.

49. On Espinosa and Jenkins: Espinosa, "Introduction," 18–24; Espinosa Yglesias, *Bancomer*, 17–42; Enrique Cárdenas, *Manuel Espinosa Yglesias: Ensayo sobre su historia intelectual* (Mexico City: Centro de Estudios Espinosa Yglesias, 2006), 16–36; interviews with W. A. Jenkins, 2000–9; R. Eustace Jenkins, 2001–10; J. Jenkins Eustace and R. Eustace, 2002–5; Espinosa Rugarcía, 19 Jul. 2005; Gustavo del Ángel, Mexico City, 16 Jun. 2007; E. Meyer, 9 Aug. 2007; R. and G. Jenkins de Landa, 4 Nov. 2008; Paul Rich, Washington, 9 Jan. 2012; Enrique Cárdenas, Mexico City, 13 Aug. 2012; Álvaro Conde, Mexico City, 15 Aug. 2012.

50. Libros de Actas, vol. 1, 5 Jun. 1963, MSJF; cf. Águila et al., *Trabajo, Fortuna y Poder*, 171, 180–5.

51. Espinosa Yglesias, *Bancomer*, 70–2, 121–33; *Excélsior*, 5 Jun. 1963, 13.

52. Pansters, *Politics and Power*, 158–62; Miko Viya, *Puebla ayer* (Puebla: Cajica, 1989), 174–9; Lomelí Vanegas, *Breve historia*, 398–400.

53. Trueblood, ed., *Mary Street Jenkins Foundation*, 26f; Manjarrez, *Crónicas sin censura*, 343–5; Pansters, *Politics and Power*, 157; Libros de Actas, vol. 5, no. 2557, MSJF; W. A. Jenkins interview, 29 Jul. 2009.

54. Viya, *Puebla ayer*, 178, 187–93; Pansters, *Politics and Power*, 163.

55. Trueblood, ed., *Mary Street Jenkins Foundation*, 3; Manjarrez, *Crónicas sin censura*, 343–5; W. A. Jenkins interview, 29 Mar. 2001; R. Eustace Jenkins interviews, 2 Aug. 2001, 4 Jul. 2003.

56. Espinosa Yglesias, *Bancomer*, 195–209; *El Universal*, 9 Jun. 1990, 1; *Unomásuno*, 27 Apr. 1991, 17; W. A. Jenkins interview, 27 Sep. 2009.

57. Águila et al., *Trabajo, Fortuna y Poder*, 308, 317, 330f; interview with Gustavo del Ángel (by telephone), 2 Sep. 2010. On the bank auctions: Haber et al., *Mexico Since 1980*, 100–6.

58. Trejo, *Carlos Slim*, 170; *Proceso*, 22 Mar. 1993, 6–11; Espinosa Yglesias, *Bancomer*, 154, 181f.

59. Águila et al., *Trabajo, Fortuna y Poder*, 286–8; Espinosa Yglesias, *Bancomer*, 177f.

60. Trueblood, ed., *Mary Street Jenkins Foundation*, 3; "Testimonio," 29 Oct. 1958, WAJP, clause 14, parts (e) and (g); Cheney interview, 18 Aug. 2002; R. and G. Jenkins de Landa interview, 4 Nov. 2008.

61. W. A. Jenkins interview, 29 Jul. 2009.

62. *Reforma* (Mexico City), 24–25 Oct. 1996, 27A; 11 Mar. 1997, 25A; Libros de Actas, vol. 6, nos. 2689, 2720, 2745, 2767, 2878, 2909–20, 2881, 2898, MSJF; W. A. Jenkins interviews, 20 Aug. 2001, 27 Jun. 2002; Rich interview, 9 Jan. 2012.

63. *Chronicle of Higher Education*, 54:16 (14 Dec. 2007); Cárdenas, *UDLA*; W. A. Jenkins interview, 3 Mar. 2005; Cárdenas interview, 22 Sep. 2005.

64. Cárdenas, *UDLA*, 89, 101; *El Universal*, 15 Sep. 1999, 4; Rich interview, 9 Jan. 2012.

65. Águila et al., *Trabajo, Fortuna y Poder*; finished in 1994, the book was published after Espinosa's death, in 2007.

66. Espinosa Yglesias, *Bancomer*; Del Ángel interview, 16 Jun. 2007.

67. Cárdenas, *Manuel Espinosa Yglesias*, 35; Águila et al., *Trabajo, Fortuna y Poder*, 179.

68. Águila et al., *Trabajo, Fortuna y Poder*, 321f; *Art News*, Apr. 1994, 139.

69. *El Universal*, 20 Feb. 2008; *Reforma*, 4 Jun. 2012, 18 Apr. 2013. Gabriel Alarcón died in 1986.

70. For example: *Cambio* (Puebla), 12 Jun. 2013; *Reforma*, 11 Dec. 2013, neg. 10; *Proceso*, 29 Jun. 2014, 36–38; *Reforma*, 9 Dec. 2015, neg. 1; *Proceso*, 17 Apr. 2016, 35–7.

71. "La Otra Opinión," Imagen Radio, 15 Jan. 2014; cf. Susan Glantz, *El ejido colectivo de Nueva Italia* (Mexico City: INAH, 1974).

72. *El Sol de Puebla*, 5 Jun. 1963, 3 and 4.

73. *La Opinión*, 5 Jun. 1963, 1; *El Día*, 6 Jun., 3.

74. Gómez to Antonio Hidalgo, 24 Jul. 1963, in Gómez, *Vida política contemporánea*, II: 516f. Cf. Gadea Pineda, *74 años de historia*, 137f.

75. *La Jornada de Oriente*, 21 Aug. 2002, 7.

76. *Diccionario Porrúa* (Mexico City: Porrúa, 1964), 778f (and five subsequent editions to 1995); Cordero y Torres, *Diccionario Biográfico*, 346–52.

77. *New York Times*, 1 Oct. 1982, 2; *Diario de los Debates de la Cámara de Diputados*, 5 Oct. 1982, 85–7.

78. *Proceso*, 11 Aug. 1980, 16–18; José Martínez, *Las enseñanzas del profesor* (Mexico City: Océano, 1999).

79. Mastretta, *Tear This Heart Out*, 28f, 50–2, 72, 75–9, 83–7, 109–12, 270; *La Jornada*, 11 Jun. 1985, 25; *Nexos*, Apr. 1987, 5; *Vuelta*, Aug. 1987, 59; Bárbara Mújica, "Women of Will in Love and War," *Américas* 4 (1997), 36–43.

80. La Quinta Columna (Puebla), Sep. 2008 (laquintacolumna.com.mx); *Milenio*, 25 Nov. 2008; *Tear This Heart Out*, www.imdb.com/title/tt1130981; *El*

fantástico mundo de Juan Orol, www.imdb.com/title/tt2122443. The documentary is titled *La historia negra del cine mexicano*; www.cinetecanacional.net/php/detallePelicula.php?clv=14667.

81. Espinosa M., *Zafra de odios* (cited as history in Crespo, *Historia del Azúcar*, I:111; Hodges, *Mexican Anarchism*, 36; Bonilla, *El secuestro del poder*, 51f, 55, 103, 119, 130–4); Ruiz Harrell, *El secuestro*; Sealtiel Alatriste, *Conjura en La Arcadia* (Mexico City: Tusquets, 2003).

82. Thomas Benjamin, *La Revolución: Mexico's Great Revolution as Memory, Myth, & History* (Austin: Univ. of Texas Press, 2000), ch. 6.

83. Fernando Cardoso and Enzo Faletto, *Dependency and Development in Latin America* (Berkeley: Univ. of California Press, 1979). For a popularization, see Galeano, *Open Veins*; for a critique, see Stephen Haber, "Introduction," in Haber, ed., *How Latin America Fell Behind* (Stanford, CA: Stanford Univ. Press, 1997).

84. González Ramírez, *La revolución social de México*, I:662–66. Cf. Zorrilla, *Historia de las relaciones*, II:343f; Daniel Cosío Villegas, ed., *Historia general de México* (Mexico City: Colegio de México, 1976), 2:1178–80; Matute, *Las dificultades del nuevo Estado*, 60–71.

85. Isidro Fabela, ed., *Documentos históricos de la Revolución Mexicana* (Mexico City: Jus, 1970), 18:316–30; Bertha Ulloa, "La lucha armada," in D. Cosío Villegas, ed., *Historia General de México* (1976), 95, 108; (1981), 1171, 1178–80; the 2000 edition uses the same language: 819f.

86. Bonilla, *El secuestro del poder*, esp. 23, 49, 82f, 117–23. Cf. *Proceso*, 4 Nov. 1991, 22f; *Intolerancia*, 17 Nov. 2002, Semanario 8–13.

87. Ronfeldt, *Atencingo*, 9, 88.

88. Niblo, *Mexico in the 1940s*, 52, 283, 326; cf. also the spurious reference on 230.

89. See Ch. 9, note 26. Photo of Jenkins: García and Aviña, *Época de oro*, 32f; cf. *Ambiance* (Puebla), Jan. 2006, 88.

90. LaFrance, "Revisión del caso"; 951; "Presentación premios 2004," Comité Mexicano de Ciencias Históricas, www.mora.edu.mx; LaFrance, conversation with author, 21 Mar. 2006.

91. Jo Tuckman, *Mexico: Democracy Interrupted* (New Haven: Yale Univ. Press, 2012), 167, 206; Shannon O'Neil, *Two Nations Indivisible* (New York: Oxford Univ. Press, 2013), 27, 53–5; *Wall Street Journal*, 9 Sep. 2013, 11.

92. Riguzzi and De los Ríos, *Las relaciones México-Estados Unidos*, II:213 (emphasis mine), 592.

EPILOGUE

1. On Slim, see: *Wall Street Journal*, 4 Aug. 2007, 1; *New Yorker*, 1 Jun. 2009, 52–67; Andrew Paxman, "Slim Helú, Carlos," in *Iconic Mexico*, ed. Eric Zolov (Santa Barbara, CA: ABC-CLIO, 2015); Diego Enrique Osorno, *Slim: Biografía política del mexicano más rico del mundo* (Mexico City: Debate, 2016).

2. Paxman, "Simbiosis imperativa y conveniente."

3. Hansen, *Politics of Mexican Development*, ch. 4; *Growing Unequal? Income Distribution and Poverty in OECD Countries* (Paris: OECD, 2008); Tuckman, *Democracy Interrupted*, ch. 5; Mark Weisbrot, Stephan Lefebvre, and Joseph Sammut, *Did NAFTA Help Mexico? An Assessment After 20 Years* (Washington, DC: Center for Economic and Policy Research, 2014); "The Two Mexicos" (cover story), *The Economist*, 19 Sep. 2015.

4. According to a study by PricewaterhouseCoopers, measuring 2008 GDP in terms of purchasing-power parity, Mexico City generated $390 billion, Monterrey $102 billion, Guadalajara $81 billion, and Puebla $42 billion; "Global City GDP rankings, 2008–2025," http://pwc.blogs.com/files/global-city-gdp-rankings-2008-2025.pdf.

5. *Guardian*, 20 Dec. 2007, 5; Animal Político, 16 Oct. 2011, www.animalpolitico.com/2011/10/moreno-valle-contra-los-medios-en-puebla; Poblanerías, 13 Apr. 2015, www.poblanerias.com/2015/04/la-democradura-de-rmv-como-plataforma-presidencial/; *Libertad de expresión en venta* (Mexico City: Article 19/Fundar, 2015), 48–53.

6. Morris, *Gringolandia*, esp. chs. 4 and 8.

7. Note for example the gringophobic "Burton Helms" ad campaign by telephone company Telmex in 1996–97; *New York Times*, 14 Nov. 1996, 1; *Financial Times*, 31 Dec. 1996, 3.

8. George Grayson, *Mexican Messiah: Andrés Manuel López Obrador* (University Park: Pennsylvania State Univ. Press, 2007), 54f, 230, 244f. Cf. the *Proceso* cover story "La entrega," 10 Aug. 2014.

9. *El Sol de Puebla*, 12 Dec. 2015; Proceso (online), 4 Feb. 2016, www.proceso.com.mx/428951/moreno-valle-inaugura-su-museo-barroco-con-obras-prestadas.

10. *Chronicle of Higher Education*, 14 Dec. 2007 and 10 Oct. 2008; "QS University Rankings: Latin America," www.topuniversities.com/latin-american-rankings; interview with Luis Ernesto Derbez, Puebla, 8 Aug. 2012.

11. *National Catholic Reporter*, 16 Apr. 2010, 1; *Vida Anáhuac* (Mexico City), Mar. 2014, 8f; "QS University Rankings: Latin America."

12. "Título," 18 Oct. 1954, clause 3, MSJF.

13. Cárdenas, *UDLA, una esperanza*, 28f, 48f; Derbez interview, 8 Aug. 2012; Simmen interview, 9 Aug. 2012.

14. Trueblood, ed., *Mary Street Jenkins Foundation*, 148f; Chaffee interviews, 11 Aug. 2009, 28 Jun. 2016.

15. Libros de Actas, vol. 7: 3071 (17 Dec. 1999), MSJF; *El Universal*, 17 May 2012, Clase.In 34–36; *Reforma*, 20 May 2012, Sociales 4; *Quien* (Mexico City), Jun. 2012, 164f; W. A. Jenkins interview, 7 Aug. 2012.

16. Trueblood, ed., *Mary Street Jenkins Foundation*, 5, 169–75; Suárez interview, 9 Aug. 2012; www.clubalpha.com.mx/fundacion.php.

17. For sources, see ch. 11 fn 70.

18. Joel Fleishman, *The Foundation: A Great American Secret* (New York: Public Affairs, 2007), 26–45.
19. Telephone interview with Diana Campoamor (Hispanics in Philanthropy), 7 Sep. 2010; Derbez interview, 8 Aug. 2012.
20. David Winder, "Mexico," in H. Anheier, A. Simmons, and D. Winder, eds., *Innovation in Strategic Philanthropy* (New York: Springer, 2007); Nuno Themudo, *Nonprofits in Crisis: Economic Development, Risk, and the Philanthropic Kuznets Curve* (Bloomington: Indiana Univ. Press, 2013); interview with Carlos Cordourier (CEMEFI), Mexico City, 15 Aug. 2009; Campoamor interview, 7 Sep. 2010.

Bibliography

PRIMARY SOURCES

Archives

Archives in Mexico City

Archivo General de la Nación, Mexico City (AGN)
  Ramo Presidentes
  – Álvaro Obregón & Plutarco Elías Calles (Obregón-Calles)
  – Pascual Ortiz Rubio (POR)
  – Abelardo L. Rodríguez (ALR)
  – Lázaro Cárdenas (LC)
  – Manuel Ávila Camacho (MAC)
  – Miguel Alemán Valdés (MAV)
  – Adolfo Ruíz Cortines (ARC)
  – Adolfo López Mateos (ALM)
  Colección Revolución
  Departamento de Trabajo (DT)
  Dirección Federal de Seguridad (DFS)
  Dirección General de Gobierno (DGG)
  Dirección General de Investigaciones Políticas y Sociales (DGIPS)
  Gobernación Siglo XX
  – Departamento de Migración (Migración)
  – Gobernación
  Tribunal Superior de Justicia del Distrito Federal, Siglo XX (TSJDF)
Biblioteca Lerdo de Tejada, Mexico City
  Archivo Económico
  Fondo Reservado
Biblioteca Nacional, UNAM, Mexico City
  Archivo Histórico de la UNAM
  – Fondo Gildardo Magaña

Fondo Silvino González
Hemeroteca Nacional
Cineteca Nacional, Mexico City
Centro de Documentación
Fideicomiso Archivos Plutarco Elías Calles y Fernando Torreblanca, Mexico City
Archivo Torreblanca, Fondo Álvaro Obregón (Calles-FAO)
Archivo Joaquín Amaro (Calles-Amaro)
Colección Documental de la Embajada de Estados Unidos en México (Calles-CEEU)
Archivo Abelardo L. Rodríguez (Calles-ALR)
Instituto Mora, Mexico City
Archivo de la Palabra, Series PHO2: Cine Mexicano (Mora-Palabra)
Secretaría de Relaciones Exteriores, Mexico City (SRE)
Archivo Histórico

Archives in Puebla and Michoacán

Archivo del Congreso del Estado, Puebla (ACEP)
Libros Expedientes
Archivo General del Municipio de Puebla (AGMP)
Libros Expedientes
Fondo Extranjería
Archivo General de Notarías de Puebla (Notarías-Puebla)
Biblioteca Dr. Ernesto de la Torre Villar, Puebla
Cámara de la Industria Textil de Puebla y Tlaxcala (CITPyT)
Fondo IV: Centro Industrial Mexicano (CITPyT-CIM)
Fondo VI: Asociación de Empresarios Textiles de Pue. y Tlax. (CITPyT-AET)
Fondo VIII: Asociación de Empresarios Textiles & Cámara de la Industria Textil
Hemeroteca de Puebla
Registro Público de la Propiedad y del Comercio, Puebla (RPP-Puebla)
Libro 1 Matrículas de Comercio
Libro 3 Auxiliar de Comercio
Registro Público de la Propiedad, Morelia, Michoacán (RPP-Morelia)
Libros de Ventas (Apatzingán)

Archives outside Mexico

National Archives and Records Administration, Washington, DC (NARA)
Record Group 59: Records of the Department of State (RDS)
Record Group 76: Records of the Boundary and Claims Commissions
Record Group 84: Foreign Service Posts of the Department of State
Huntington Library, Pasadena, CA
Albert B. Fall Collection

Occidental College, Los Angeles, CA
    E.L. Doheny Collection (Doheny Research Foundation)
Public Library, Shelbyville, TN
    Bedford County Census Records
    County Cemetery Records
University of Florida, Gainesville, FL
    John J. Tigert Papers
University of Virginia, Charlottesville, VA
    Rosalie Evans Papers
Vanderbilt University, Nashville, TN
    Harvie Branscomb Papers
National Archives, Kew, London
    Foreign Office Records (UKFO)
        Series 369: Consular Dept., General Correspondence
        Series 371: Political Dept., General Correspondence

Collections of papers held privately

Archivo e Historia de la Iglesia Metodista de México A.R., Mexico City
Archivo Histórico Aarón Sáenz Garza, held by the Grupo Saenz S.A., Mexico City
Club Rotario de Puebla
    Directorio Archivo
Eduardo Mestre Ghigliazza Papers, held by Manuel Mestre, Mexico City
Manuel Espinosa Yglesias Papers, Centro de Estudios Espinosa Yglesias, Mexico
    City (CEEY)
Manuel Pérez Pena Papers, held by Manuel Pérez Nochebuena, Puebla
Marte R. Gómez Archive, held by Marte R. Gómez Jr., Mexico City
Mary Jenkins William Papers (MJWP), held by Susie Heflinger, Los Angeles, CA
Mary Street Jenkins Foundation, Puebla (MSJF)
    Libros de Actas
Mary Street Jenkins Papers (MSJP), held by Rosemary Eustace Jenkins, Mexico City
Nacional de Drogas (Nadro) Papers, held by Pablo Escandón Cusi, Mexico City
Ronald Eustace Papers (REP), held by Ronald Eustace, Puebla
Rosemary Eustace Jenkins Papers (REJP), held by Rosemary Eustace Jenkins,
    Mexico City
Sergio B. Guzmán Papers (SBGP), held by Sergio Guzmán Ramos, Puebla
William Anstead Jenkins Papers (WAJP), held by William Anstead Jenkins, Mexico City

Documents

American-Mexican Claims Commission. *Report to the Secretary of State.* Washington:
    US Government Printing Office, 1948.

Anuario Financiero de México, 1940–1947. Mexico City: Asociación de Banqueros de México, 1941–1948.

Census of the United States. Washington, DC: Bureau of the Census, 1850, 1860, 1870, 1900, 1920.

The Comet 1901. Nashville, TN: Vanderbilt University, 1901.

Don Verdades. *Corrido del cine mexicano.* Mexico City: n.p., [1959].

Department of State. *American Mexican Claims Commission: Report to the Secretary of State, with Decisions Showing the Reasons for the Allowance or Disallowance of the Claims.* Washington, DC: US Government Printing Office, 1948.

Register of Vanderbilt University for 1899–1900. Nashville, 1900.

Register of Vanderbilt University for 1900–1901. Nashville, 1901.

US Senate Committee on Foreign Relations, *Investigation of Mexican Affairs: Reports and Hearings.* Washington, DC: US Government Printing Office, 1920.

Memoirs

Cabañas Pavía, Manuel. *Datos Biográficos del señor William O. Jenkins.* Puebla: n.p., 1975.

Daniels, Josephus. *The Wilson Era.* Chapel Hill: University of North Carolina Press, 1946.

Deana Salmerón, Antonio. *Cosas de Puebla.* Puebla: n.p., 1986.

Deloya, Urbano. "William Oscar Jenkins." Transcript from *Puebla de mis amores,* XECD Radio, Puebla, 11 March 1995.

Deloya, Urbano. *Puebla de mis amores.* Puebla: Universidad Autónoma de Puebla, 2004.

Espinosa Rugarcía, Amparo. *Manuel Espinosa Yglesias: Perfil de un hombre con ideas modernas.* Mexico City: n.p., 1988.

Espinosa Yglesias, Manuel. *Bancomer: Logro y destrucción de un ideal.* Mexico City: Planeta, 2000.

Eustace Jenkins, Rosemary. *Tennessee Sunshine: Oscar's Love Letters to Mary.* Mexico City: n.p., 2012.

Flandrau, Charles Macomb. *Viva México!* Urbana: University of Illinois Press, 1964 [1908].

Gadea Pineda, Cándido. *74 años de historia en la vida real de Atencingo.* Atencingo, Pue.: n.p., 1995.

Guzmán Ramos, Sergio. *Hombres de Puebla: Semblanzas.* Puebla: n.p., 1999.

Houston, Frank. "Memorandum on Oscar Jenkins." 17 July 1967, Alumni Relations, Vanderbilt University.

Lara y Parra, Manuel. *La lucha universitaria en Puebla, 1923–65.* Puebla: Universidad Autónoma de Puebla, 2002 [1988].

Rodríguez, Abelardo L. *Autobiografía.* Mexico City: n.p., 1962.

Sánchez Pontón, Manuel. "William Oscar Jenkins Biddle." Puebla: n.p., 2007.

Santos, Gonzalo N. *Memorias.* Mexico City: Grijalbo, 1984.

Valle Morales, Úrsulo. *El Despertar Democrático de Atencingo.* Atencingo, Pue.: n.p., 1984.

Verissimo, Erico. *Mexico*. New York: Dolphin, 1962.

Viya, Miko. *Puebla ayer*. Puebla: Cajica, 1989.

Interviews

Alarcón, Oscar; son of Gabriel Alarcón and godson of Jenkins; Mexico City, 15 August 2007.

Alston, Bill; son of Apatzingán plantation manager Wally Alston; Laredo, TX (by telephone), 14 October 2014.

Artasánchez Bautista, Rafael; son of Rafael Artasánchez, mayor of Puebla (1957–60); Mexico City, 28 July 2005.

Artasánchez Villar, Luis; son of Luis Artasánchez and godson of Jenkins; Puebla, 23 July 2005.

Asbury, Elizabeth; daughter of Jenkins' brother Joe; Fresno, CA (by telephone), 25 May 2005.

Ávila Camacho López, Manuel; son of Maximino Ávila Camacho; Mexico City, 16 August 2006.

Bautista, Edmundo; Jenkins Foundation administrator; Puebla, 24 May 2006.

Bautista O'Farrill, Gonzalo; former governor of Puebla (1972–73) and son of Gov. Gonzalo Bautista Castillo (1941–45); Puebla, 8 September 2005.

Bello Gómez, Felipe; nephew of Tehuacán city councilor; Puebla, 8 April 2005.

Benítez, Eusebio; former mill employee and union boss; Atencingo, Puebla, 18 March 2006, 22 April 2006.

Buntzler, Paul Jr.; son of Jenkins' sister Anne; East Wenatchee, WA (by telephone), 6 June 2005.

Campoamor, Diana; president of Hispanics in Philanthropy, San Francisco, CA (by telephone), 7 September 2010.

Cárdenas, Enrique; rector of UDLA-Puebla, 1984–2001; Mexico City, 13 August 2012.

Castro, Marta; daughter of Antonio J. Hernández' gunman *El Tiburón*; Puebla, 3 July 2005.

Castro Morales, Efraín; Puebla historian and chronicler; Puebla, 22 July 2006.

Chaffee, Arthur; superintendent, American School of Puebla, 1970–2003; Puebla, 11 August 2009, 28 June 2016 (by email).

Cheney, Martha (Tita); Jenkins's fifth daughter; Beverly Hills, CA, 18 August 2002.

Cobel, Bertha; daughter of Jenkins's tennis partner Edmundo Cobel; Puebla, 25 March 2006.

Conde, Álvaro; Bancomer VP under Manuel Espinosa Yglesias; Mexico City, August 2012.

Cordourier, Carlos; former CEMEFI researcher; Mexico City, 15 August 2009.

De la Cuadra, Eufrasia; widow of Atencingo engineer; Izúcar de Matamoros, Puebla, 9 July 2005.

Derbez, Luis Ernesto; rector of UDLA-Puebla since 2008; Puebla, 8 August 2012.

Díaz Rubín de la Hidalga, Ana María and María del Carmen; daughters of former Atencingo owner Pedro Díaz Rubín; Mexico City, 1 August 2001.

Escandón Cusi, Pablo; CEO of Nacional de Drogas (Nadro) SA; Mexico City, 24 July 2006.

Espinosa Rugarcía, Amparo; daughter of Manuel Espinosa Yglesias; Mexico City, 19 July 2005.

Espinosa Yglesias, Manuel; Jenkins' principal business partner; Mexico City, 11 February 1994.

Eustace, Jane Jenkins; Jenkins' third daughter; Puebla, 2 April 2001 to 15 March 2006 (multiple interviews).

Eustace, Ronnie; son-in-law of Jenkins; Puebla, 2 April 2001 to 6 November 2008 (multiple interviews).

Eustace Jenkins, John; son of Jenkins's daughter Jane; Puebla, 20 July 2004 to 12 August 2009 (multiple interviews).

Eustace Jenkins, Rosemary; daughter of Jenkins's daughter Jane; Mexico City, 2 August 2001 to 9 July 2014 (multiple interviews).

Falquier, Alexis; former McKinsey executive; Mexico City, 27 February 2005.

Gains, Martha; daughter of Jenkins's cousin Annie Wells; Fairfield Glades, TN (by telephone), 28 May 2005.

García Pliego, Aurelio; former mill mechanic; Atencingo, Puebla, 18 March 2006.

Guzmán, Cruz; former millworker; Atencingo, Puebla, 22 April 2006.

Guzmán Ramos, Sergio; son of Sergio B. Guzmán; Puebla, 17 August 2001 to 9 August 2009 (multiple interviews).

Heflinger, Susan; daughter of Jenkins's daughter Mary; Los Angeles, CA, 18 and 19 August 2002.

Ibáñez Puget, Joaquín; son of Jenkins's lawyer Joaquín Ibáñez Guadalajara; Puebla, 9 September 2005.

Jenkins, William Anstead; adopted son of Jenkins and son of his daughter Margaret; Mexico City and Puebla: 22 November 2000 to 27 April 2015 (multiple interviews).

Jenkins de Landa, Guillermo; son of Jenkins's grandson William Anstead Jenkins; Mexico City, 4 November 2008, 30 July 2014.

Jenkins de Landa, Roberto; son of Jenkins's grandson William Anstead Jenkins; Mexico City, 4 November 2008, 29 July 2014.

Jordan, Purdy; great-nephew of Sinaloa sugar baron B. F. Johnston; Mexico City, 24 February 2005, 19 July 2005.

Juárez, Alicia; Jenkinses' family maid since 1949; Puebla, 4 October 2005.

Lara Lara, Vicente; chronicler and former teacher; Atencingo, Puebla, 11 May 2006.

Larragoiti, Carmelita; childhood friend of the Ávila Camacho and Alarcón families; Puebla, 29 May 2006.

Lavender, Ron; realtor; Acapulco, 27 May 1994.

Lindley, Neil; son of UDLA rector Ray Lindley (1962–72); Beaumont, TX, 13 July 2013.

Luna, Georgina; granddaughter and daughter of mill employees; Atencingo, Puebla, 18 March 2006.

Mestre, Manuel; son of Jenkins's lawyer Eduardo Mestre and godson of Jenkins; Mexico City, 18 June 2003 to 29 July 2009 (multiple interviews).

Meyer, Eugenia; daughter of film producer Gregorio Walerstein (active 1941–89); Mexico City, 8 August 2007.

Migoya Velázquez, Emérita; niece of Gabriel Alarcón; Mexico City, 26 July 2007.

Morgan, Diannah; daughter of Jenkins's son-in-law Robert Lord III; Los Angeles, CA (by telephone), 19 May 2003, 11 Oct. 2007.

O'Farrill, Rómulo Jr.; son of Jenkins's partner Rómulo O'Farrill; Mexico City, 29 June 2001.

Ortega, Mario (pseud.); former mill electrician; Atencingo, Puebla, 9 July 2005.

Pacheco, Pilar; former director, State of Puebla General Archive (AGEP); Puebla, 27 April 2006.

Palou, Pedro Ángel; chronicler and state functionary since 1960; Puebla, 11 August 2009.

Pérez, Francisco, José Manuel and Sara Vega de; grandsons and daughter-in-law of Atencingo manager Manuel Pérez Pena; Puebla, 25 May 2006, 6 November 2008.

Pérez Nochebuena, Manuel; grandson of Manuel Pérez Peña; Puebla, 31 May 2006, 17 August 2016.

Pieza Rugarcía, Ramón; nephew of Manuel Espinosa Yglesias; Puebla, 24 August 2006.

Poplin, Dick; Bedford County historian; Shelbyville, TN, 8 July 2004.

Ramírez Camarillo, Fernando; former mayor of Chietla and son of millworker; Atencingo, Puebla, 18 March 2006, 22 April 2006.

Reguero, Sergio; son-in-law of Gabriel Alarcón's brother José; Puebla, 28 March 2005.

Rich, Paul; former professor, UDLA–Puebla; Washington, DC, 9 January 2012, 6 January 2014.

Sánchez Gallegos, Humberto; junior administrator at Jenkins's cotton plantation; Apatzingán, Michoacán, 8 August 2006.

Sánchez Pontón, Manuel; journalist since 1944 and former editor of *La Opinión*; Puebla, 15 May 2006, 3 August 2007, 6 November 2008.

Shofner, Betty, Chris and Ann; daughter-in-law and grandchildren of Jenkins's sister Kate; Shelbyville, TN, 11 July 2004.

Simmen, Edward; former professor and college historian, UDLA–Puebla; Puebla, 9 August 2012.

Suárez, Sergio; CEO, Fundación Alpha (Alpha Clubs); Puebla, 9 August 2012.

Vázquez Nava, José Luis; son of Jenkins's notary Nicolás Vázquez; Puebla, 26 and 30 May 2006.

Velasco Matienzo, Javier de; grandson of Francisco de Velasco, Mayor of Puebla (1906–11) and of Andrés Matienzo, Mayor of Puebla (1913–14); Puebla, 19 July 2007.

Vélez Pliego, Alfonso; former rector, UAP (1981–87); Puebla, April 1994.

Newspapers and Magazines

Acción (Puebla)
Chronicle of Higher Education
La Crónica (Puebla)
El Demócrata (Mexico City)
El Día (Mexico City)
Diario de los Debates de la Cámara de Diputados (Mexico City)
Diario Oficial (Mexico City)
The Economist
Excélsior (Mexico City)
Éxito (Mexico City)
Hoy (Mexico City)
La Jornada de Oriente (Puebla)
Literary Digest (New York)
Los Angeles Times
Mexican Herald
El Monitor (Puebla)
Nashville Banner
Nashville Tennessean
National Catholic Reporter
New York Times
Novedades (Mexico City)
La Opinión (Puebla)
Opinión Pública (Mexico City)
Periódico Oficial (Puebla)
Política (Mexico City)
El Popular (Mexico City)
La Prensa (1917–1921: Puebla)
La Prensa (1928–present: Mexico City)
Proceso (Mexico City)
Rebeldía (Puebla)
Reforma (Mexico City)
Shelbyville Times-Gazette
Siempre! (Mexico City)
El Sol de Puebla
Tiempo (Mexico City)
Tiempo Universitario (Puebla)
El Universal (Mexico City)
Variety (New York)
La Voz de México
La Voz de Michoacán
Wall Street Journal

SECONDARY SOURCES (SELECTED)
Books

Águila, Marcos, Martí Soler and Roberto Suárez. *Trabajo, Fortuna y Poder. Manuel Espinosa Yglesias, un empresario mexicano del siglo XX*. Mexico City: Centro de Estudios Espinosa Yglesias, 2007.

Alfaro-Velcamp, Theresa. *So Far from Allah, So Close to Mexico: Middle Eastern Immigrants in Modern Mexico*. Austin: University of Texas Press, 2007.

Amador, María Luisa, and Jorge Ayala Blanco. *Cartelera cinematográfica, 1930–1939*. Mexico City: Filmoteca UNAM, 1980.

Amador, María Luisa, and Jorge Ayala Blanco. *Cartelera cinematográfica, 1940–1949*. Mexico City: UNAM, 1982.

Amador, María Luisa, and Jorge Ayala Blanco. *Cartelera cinematográfica, 1950–1959*. Mexico City: UNAM, 1985.

Amador, María Luisa, and Jorge Ayala Blanco. *Cartelera cinematográfica, 1960–1969*. Mexico City: UNAM, 1986.

Anderson, Rodney. *Outcasts in Their Own Land: Mexican Industrial Workers, 1906–1911*. DeKalb: Northern Illinois University Press, 1976.

Ash, Stephen. *Middle Tennessee Society Transformed, 1860–1870*. Baton Rouge: Louisiana State University Press, 1988.

Bantjes, Adrian. *As If Jesus Walked the Earth: Cardenismo, Sonora and the Mexican Revolution*. Wilmington, DE: SR Books, 1998.

Barbosa Cano, Flavio. *La CROM: De Luis N. Morones a Antonio J. Hernández*. Puebla: Universidad Autónoma de Puebla, 1981.

Bedford County, Tennessee: Family History Book. Paducah, KY: Turner Publishing, 2002.

Beatty, Edward. *Institutions and Investment: The Political Basis of Industrialization in Mexico Before 1911*. Stanford, CA: Stanford University Press, 2001.

Beezley, William. *Judas at the Jockey Club, and Other Episodes of Porfirian Mexico*. Lincoln: University of Nebraska Press, 2004.

Berg, Charles Ramírez. *Cinema of Solitude: A Critical Study of Mexican Film, 1967–1983*. Austin: University of Texas Press, 1992.

Berry, Jason and Gerald Renner. *Vows of Silence: The Abuse of Power in the Papacy of John Paul II*. New York: Free Press, 2004.

Bethell, Leslie, ed. *Mexico Since Independence*. Cambridge: Cambridge University Press, 1991.

Blanks, James, ed. *The Shofner Family Genealogy*. Bountiful, UT: Family History Publishers, 1989.

Bonilla Fernández, María Teresa. *El secuestro del poder: El caso William O. Jenkins*. Puebla: Universidad Autónoma de Puebla, 2004.

Brading, David, ed. *Caudillo and Peasant in the Mexican Revolution*. Cambridge: Cambridge University Press, 1980.

Brands, H. W. *The Reckless Decade: America in the 1890s*. Chicago: University of Chicago Press, 2002.

Brenner, Anita. *The Wind that Swept Mexico*. Austin: University of Texas Press, 1996 [1943].

Brown, Jonathan. *Oil and Revolution in Mexico*. Berkeley: University of California Press, 1993.

Buchenau, Jürgen. *Plutarco Elías Calles and the Mexican Revolution*. Lanham, MD: Rowman & Littlefield, 2007.

Buchenau, Jürgen, and William Beezley, eds. *State Governors in the Mexican Revolution, 1910–1952: Portraits in Conflict, Courage, and Corruption*. Lanham, MD: Rowman & Littlefield, 2009.

Buve, Raymond. *El movimiento revolucionario en Tlaxcala*. Tlaxcala: Universidad Autónoma de Tlaxcala, 1994.

Camp, Roderic Ai. *Entrepreneurs and Politics in Twentieth-Century Mexico*. New York: Oxford University Press, 1989.

Camp, Roderic Ai. *Mexican Political Biographies, 1884–1934*. Austin: University of Texas Press, 1991.

Camp, Roderic Ai. *Mexican Political Biographies, 1935–1993*. Austin: University of Texas Press, 1995.

Cárdenas, Enrique. *UDLA, una esperanza, una realidad: Don Manuel Espinosa Yglesias* Cholula, Pue.: Fundación UDLA–Puebla, 2000.

Cárdenas, Enrique. *Manuel Espinosa Yglesias: Ensayo sobre su historia intelectual*. Mexico City: Centro de Estudios Espinosa Yglesias, 2006.

Conklin, Paul. *Gone with the Ivy: A Biography of Vanderbilt University*. Knoxville: University of Tennessee Press, 1985.

Contreras Torres, Miguel. *El libro negro del cine mexicano*. Mexico City: Hispano-Continental Films, 1960.

Cordero y Bernal, Rigoberto. *Maximino Ávila Camacho: El ejercicio absoluto . . . del poder*. Puebla: n.p., 2012.

Cordero y Torres, Enrique. *Historia compendiada del Estado de Puebla*. 3 vols. Puebla: Bohemia Poblana, 1965.

Cordero y Torres, Enrique. *Diccionario Biográfico de Puebla*. 2 vols. Puebla: Centro de Estudios Históricos, 1972.

Corlew, Robert. *Tennessee: A Short History*. Knoxville: University of Tennessee Press, 1981.

Crespo, Horacio, ed. *Historia del azúcar en México*. 2 vols. Mexico City: Fondo de Cultura Económica, 1988.

Crespo, Horacio, and Enrique Vega Villanueva. *Estadísticas históricas del azúcar en México*. Mexico City: Azúcar SA, 1990.

Cruz Valdés, Reyna and Ambrosio Guzmán Álvarez. *Casa Presno: Historia y rehabilitación de una residencia*. Puebla: Universidad Autónoma de Puebla, 2006.

Dávila Peralta, Nicolás. *Las santas batallas: El anticomunismo en Puebla*. Puebla: Universidad Autónoma de Puebla, 2003.

Del Ángel Mobarak, Gustavo. *BBVA Bancomer: 75 años de historia*. Mexico City: BBVA Bancomer, 2007.

De Usabel, Gaizka. *The High Noon of American Pictures in Latin America*. Ann Arbor, MI: UMI Research Press, 1982.

Dowdy, G. Wayne. *Mayor Crump Don't Like It: Machine Politics in Memphis*. Jackson: University Press of Mississippi, 2006.

Doyle, Don. *Nashville in the New South, 1880–1930*. Knoxville: University of Tennessee Press, 1985

Dulles, John W. F. *Yesterday in Mexico: A Chronicle of the Revolution, 1919–1936*. Austin: University of Texas Press, 1972 [1961].

Dwyer, John. *The Agrarian Dispute: The Expropriation of American-Owned Rural Land in Postrevolutionary Mexico*. Durham, NC: Duke University Press, 2008.

Elson, Ruth Miller. *Guardians of Tradition: American Schoolbooks of the Nineteenth Century*. Lincoln: University of Nebraska Press, 1964.

Espinosa M., Miguel. *Zafra de odios, azúcar amargo*. Puebla: Universidad Autónoma de Puebla, 1980.

Estrada Urroz, Rosalina. *Del telar a la cadena de montaje: La condición obrera en Puebla, 1940–1976*. Puebla: Universidad Autónoma de Puebla, 1997.

Fehrenbach, T. R. *The San Antonio Story*. Tulsa, OK: Continental Heritage, 1978.

Fernández, Claudia, and Andrew Paxman. *El Tigre: Emilio Azcárraga y su imperio Televisa*. Mexico City: Grijalbo-Mondadori, 2013.

Fernández Chedraui, Rodrigo. *Vivir de pie: El tiempo de Don Maximino*. Xalapa, VC: Editorial Las Ánimas, 2008.

Frías Olvera, Manuel. *Los verdaderos ángeles de Puebla*. Puebla: Mabek, 1976.

Gamboa Ojeda, Leticia. *Los empresarios de ayer: El grupo dominante en la industria textil de Puebla, 1906–1929*. Puebla: Universidad Autónoma de Puebla, 1985.

Gamboa Ojeda, Leticia. *La urdimbre y la trama: Historia social de los obreros textiles de Atlixco, 1899–1924*. Mexico City: Fondo de Cultura Económica, 2001.

García, Gustavo, and Rafael Aviña. *Época de oro del cine mexicano*. Mexico City: Clío, 1997.

García Riera, Emilio. *Historia documental del cine mexicano*. 18 vols. Guadalajara: Universidad de Guadalajara, 1992.

García Riera, Emilio. *Breve historia del cine mexicano*. Zapopan, Jalisco: Mapa, 1998.

Garner, Paul. *Porfirio Díaz*. London: Longman, 2001.

Garner, Paul. *British Lions and Mexican Eagles Business, Politics, and Empire in the Career of Weetman Pearson in Mexico, 1889–1919*. Stanford, CA: Stanford University Press, 2011.

Gauss, Susan. *Made in Mexico: Regions, Nation, and the State in the Rise of Mexican Industrialism, 1920s–1940s*. University Park, PA: Penn State Press, 2010.

Gilderhus, Mark. *Diplomacy and Revolution: US–Mexico Relations under Wilson and Carranza*. Tucson: University of Arizona Press, 1977.

Gillingham, Paul, and Benjamin T. Smith, eds. *Dictablanda: Politics, Work, and Culture in Mexico, 1938–1968*. Durham, NC: Duke University Press, 2014.

Gillingham, Paul, Michael Lettieri, and Benjamin T. Smith, eds. *Journalism, Satire and Censorship, 1910–2015*. Albuquerque: University of New Mexico Press, forthcoming.

Gilly, Adolfo. *La revolución interrumpida*. Mexico City: El Caballito, 1971.

Gómez Carpinteiro, Francisco Javier. *Gente de azúcar y agua: Modernidad y posrevolución en el suroeste de Puebla*. Zamora: Colegio de Michoacán, 2003.

González Ramírez, Manuel. *La revolución social de México: I. Las ideas, la violencia*. Mexico City: Fondo de Cultura Económica, 1960.

Grajales, Agustín and Lilián Illades, eds. *Presencia española en Puebla: Siglos XVI–XX*. Puebla: Universidad Autónoma de Puebla, 2002.

Gruening, Ernest. *Mexico and its Heritage*. New York: The Century Co., 1928.

Haber, Stephen. *Industry and Underdevelopment: The Industrialization of Mexico, 1890–1940*. Stanford, CA: Stanford University Press, 1989.

Haber, Stephen, Herbert S. Klein, Noel Maurer, and Kevin J. Middlebrook. *Mexico Since 1980*. Cambridge: Cambridge University Press, 2008.

Hall, Linda. *Álvaro Obregón: Power and Revolution in Mexico, 1911–1920*. College Station: Texas A&M University Press, 1981.

Hamilton, Nora. *The Limits of State Autonomy: Post-Revolutionary Mexico*. Princeton, NJ: Princeton University Press, 1982.

Hansen, Roger. *The Politics of Mexican Development*. Baltimore: Johns Hopkins University Press, 1974.

Hart, John Mason. *Revolutionary Mexico: The Coming and Process of the Mexican Revolution*. Berkeley: University of California Press, 1997.

Hart, John Mason. *Empire and Revolution: The Americans in Mexico since the Civil War*. Berkeley: University of California Press, 2002.

Henderson, Timothy. *The Worm in the Wheat: Rosalie Evans and Agrarian Struggle in the Puebla-Tlaxcala Valley of Mexico, 1906–1927*. Durham, NC: Duke University Press, 1998.

Hernández Chávez, Alicia. *Historia de la Revolución Mexicana, vol. 16: La mecánica cardenista*. Mexico City: Colegio de México, 1979.

Hernández Rodríguez, Rogelio, ed. *Adolfo López Mateos: Una vida dedicada a la política*. Mexico City: Colegio de México, 2015.

Hershfield, Joanne, and David Maciel, eds. *Mexico's Cinema: A Century of Film and Filmmakers*. Wilmington, DE: SR Books, 1999.

Hodges, Donald. *Mexican Anarchism after the Revolution*. Austin: University of Texas Press, 1995.

Jayes, Janice Lee. *The Illusion of Ignorance: Constructing the American Encounter with Mexico, 1877–1920*. Lanham, MD: University Press of America, 2011.

Jiménez Muñoz, Jorge. *La traza del poder: Historia de la política y los negocios urbanos en el Distrito Federal*. Mexico City: Dédalo, 1993.

Johns, Michael. *The City of Mexico in the Age of Díaz*. Austin: University of Texas Press, 1997.

Joseph, Gilbert, Anne Rubenstein, and Eric Zolov, eds. *Fragments of a Golden Age: The Politics of Mexico since 1940*. Durham, NC: Duke University Press, 2001.

Josephson, Matthew. *The Robber Barons: The Great American Capitalists, 1861–1901*. Norwalk, CT: Easton Press, 1962 [1934].

Keller, Renata. *Mexico's Cold War: Cuba, the United States, and the Legacy of the Mexican Revolution.* New York: Cambridge University Press, 2015.

Kiger, Joseph, ed. *International Encyclopedia of Foundations.* New York: Greenwood, 1990.

Knight, Alan. *The Mexican Revolution: Vol. 1: Porfirians, Liberals and Peasants.* Lincoln: University of Nebraska Press, 1990.

Knight, Alan. *The Mexican Revolution: Vol. 2: Counter-Revolution and Reconstruction.* Lincoln: University of Nebraska Press, 1990.

Knight, Alan. *US-Mexican Relations, 1910–1940: An Interpretation.* La Jolla, CA: Center for US-Mexican Studies, UCSD, 1987.

Krauze, Enrique. *Mexico: Biography of Power.* New York: HarperCollins, 1997.

LaFrance, David. *The Mexican Revolution in Puebla, 1908–1913.* Wilmington, DE: SR Books, 1989.

LaFrance, David. *Revolution in Mexico's Heartland: Politics, War, and State Building in Puebla, 1913–1920.* Wilmington, DE: SR Books, 2003.

Lester, Connie. *Up from the Mudsills of Hell: The Farmers' Alliance, Populism, and Progressive Agriculture in Tennessee, 1870–1915.* Athens: University of Georgia Press, 2006.

Lomelí Vanegas, Leonardo. *Breve historia de Puebla.* Mexico City: Fondo de Cultura Económica / Colegio de México, 2001.

Manjarrez, Alejandro. *Puebla: El rostro olvidado.* Cholula, Pue.: Imagen Pública y Corporativa, 1991.

Manjarrez, Alejandro. *Crónicas sin censura.* Cholula, Pue.: Imagen Pública y Corporativa, 1995.

Marsh, Helen, and Timothy, eds. *Cemetery Records of Bedford County.* Shelbyville, TN: Marsh Historical, 1976.

Marsh, Helen, and Timothy. *Tennesseans in Texas.* Easley, SC: Southern Historical Press, 1986.

Mastretta, Ángeles. *Tear This Heart Out.* Translated by Margaret Sayers Peden. New York: Riverhead, 1997 [orig. *Arráncame la vida.* Mexico City: Cal y arena, 1985].

Matute, Álvaro. *Historia de la Revolución Mexicana, vol. 8, 1917–1924: La carrera del caudillo.* Mexico City: Colegio de México, 1980.

Matute, Álvaro. *Historia de la Revolución Mexicana, vol. 7, 1917–1924: Las dificultades del nuevo Estado.* Mexico City: Colegio de México, 1995.

Maurer, Noel. *The Power and the Money: The Mexican Financial System, 1876–1932.* Stanford, CA: Stanford University Press, 2002.

Maxfield, Sylvia. *Governing Capital: International Finance and Mexican Politics.* Ithaca, NY: Cornell University Press, 1990.

McCormick, Gladys. *The Logic of Compromise in Mexico: How the Countryside Was Key to the Emergence of Authoritarianism.* Chapel Hill: University of North Carolina Press, 2016.

Medina, Luis. *Historia de la Revolución Mexicana, vol. 18: Del cardenismo al avilacamachismo.* Mexico City: Colegio de México, 1978.

Middlebrook, Kevin. *The Paradox of Revolution: Labor, the State, and Authoritarianism in Mexico*. Baltimore: Johns Hopkins University Press, 1995.

Miller, Michael Nelson. *Red, White, and Green: The Maturing of Mexicanidad, 1940–1946*. El Paso: Texas Western Press, 1998.

Mora, Carl. *Mexican Cinema: Reflections of a Society, 1896–1980*. Berkeley: University of California Press, 1982.

Moreno, Julio. *Yankee Don't Go Home! Mexican Nationalism, American Business Culture, and the Shaping of Modern Mexico, 1920–1950*. Chapel Hill: University of North Carolina Press, 2003.

Morris, Stephen. *Gringolandia: Mexican Identity and Perceptions of the United States*. Lanham, MD: Rowman & Littlefield, 2005.

Mosk, Sanford. *Industrial Revolution in Mexico*. Berkeley: University of California Press, 1954.

Nasaw, David. *The Chief: The Life of William Randolph Hearst*. New York: Houghton Mifflin Harcourt, 2001.

Navarro, Aaron. *Political Intelligence and the Creation of Modern Mexico, 1938–1954*. University Park, PA: Penn State Press, 2010.

Niblo, Stephen. *War, Diplomacy, and Development: The United States and Mexico, 1938–1954*. Wilmington, DE: SR Books, 1995.

Niblo, Stephen. *Mexico in the 1940s: Modernity, Politics, and Corruption*. Wilmington, DE: SR Books, 1999.

Oikión Solano, Verónica. *Los hombres del poder en Michoacán, 1924–1962*. Zamora: Colegio de Michoacán, 2004.

Ortiz Garza, José Luis. *México en guerra: La historia secreta de los negocios entre empresarios mexicanos de la comunicación, los nazis y EUA*. Mexico City: Planeta, 1989.

Pansters, Wil. *Politics and Power in Puebla: The Political History of a Mexican State, 1937–1987*. Amsterdam: CEDLA, 1990.

Paranaguá, Paulo Antonio, ed. *Mexican Cinema*. London: British Film Institute, 1995.

Peredo Castro, Francisco. *Cine y propaganda para Latinoamérica: México y Estados Unidos en la encrucijada de los años cuarenta*. Mexico City: UNAM, 2013.

Quintana, Alejandro. *Maximino Ávila Camacho and the One-Party State: The Taming of Caudillismo and Caciquismo in Post-Revolutionary Mexico*. Lanham, MD: Lexington Books, 2010.

Ramírez, Gabriel. *Miguel Contreras Torres, 1899–1981*. Guadalajara: Universidad de Guadalajara, 1994.

Ramírez Rancaño, Mario. *Directorio de empresas industriales textiles, 1900–1920*. Mexico City: IIS-UNAM, [1980].

Reid, John. *Spanish American Images of the United States, 1790–1960*. Gainesville: University of Florida Press, 1977.

Richmond, Douglas. *Venustiano Carranza's Nationalist Struggle, 1893–1920*. Lincoln: University of Nebraska Press, 1983.

Riguzzi, Paolo and Patricia de los Ríos. *Las relaciones México-Estados Unidos, 1756–2010*. Mexico City: UNAM, 2012.

Rodó, José Enrique. *Ariel*. Austin: University of Texas Press, 1988 [1900].

Romano Moreno, Armando. *Anecdotario estudiantil*. Vol. 1. Puebla: Universidad Autónoma de Puebla, 1985.

Ronfeldt, David. *Atencingo: The Politics of Agrarian Struggle in a Mexican Ejido*. Stanford, CA: Stanford University Press, 1973.

Ruiz Harrell, Rafael. *El secuestro de William Jenkins*. Mexico City: Planeta, 1992.

Saragoza, Alex. *The Monterrey Elite and the Mexican State, 1880–1940*. Austin: University of Texas Press, 1988.

Saragoza, Alex. *The State and the Media in Mexico: The Origins of Televisa* (forthcoming).

Schell, William. *Integral Outsiders: The American Colony in Mexico City, 1876–1911*. Wilmington, DE: SR Books, 2001.

Schmidt, Samuel. *The Deterioration of the Mexican Presidency: The Years of Luis Echeverría*. Tucson: University of Arizona Press, 1991.

Sherman, John. *The Mexican Right: The End of Revolutionary Reform, 1929–1940*. Westport, CT: Praeger, 1997.

Smith, Robert Freeman. *The United States and Revolutionary Nationalism in Mexico, 1916–1932*. Chicago: University of Chicago Press, 1972.

Street, Henry and Mary. *The Street Genealogy*. Exeter, NH: News-Letter Press, 1895.

Tecuanhuey, Alicia. *Cronología política del Estado de Puebla, 1910–1991*. Puebla: University Autónoma de Puebla, 1994.

Tenorio Trillo, Mauricio and Aurora Gómez Galvarriato. *El Porfiriato: Herramientas para la historia*. Mexico City: Fondo de Cultura Económica, 2006.

Thomson, Guy. *Puebla de los Angeles: Industry and Society in a Mexican City, 1700–1850*. Boulder: Westview Press, 1989.

Torres Bautista, Mariano. *La familia Maurer de Atlixco, Puebla*. Mexico City: Conaculta, 1994.

Trejo, Racial. *Carlos Slim: Vida y Obra*. Mexico City: Quién es Quién, 2013.

Trueblood, Beatrice, ed. *Mary Street Jenkins Foundation: Mexico 1954–1988*. Mexico City: Fundación Mary Street Jenkins, 1988.

Tuckman, Jo. *Mexico: Democracy Interrupted*. New Haven, CT: Yale University Press, 2012.

Valencia Castrejón, Sergio. *Poder regional y política nacional en México: El gobierno de Maximino Ávila Camacho en Puebla (1937–1941)*. Mexico City: Instituto Nacional de Estudios Históricos de la Revolución Mexicana, 1996.

Vaughan, Mary Kay. *The State, Education and Social Class in Mexico, 1880–1928*. DeKalb: Northern Illinois University Press, 1982.

Vaughan, Mary Kay. *Cultural Politics in Revolution: Teachers, Peasants, and Schools in Mexico, 1930–1940*. Tucson: University of Arizona Press, 1997.

Vázquez, Josefina and Lorenzo Meyer. *The United States and Mexico*. Chicago: University of Chicago Press, 1985.

Villavicencio Rojas, Josué. *Industria y empresarios en Puebla, 1940–1970: Una aproximación a la historia económica regional*. Puebla: Universidad Autónoma de Puebla, 2013.

Wasserman, Mark. *Persistent Oligarchs: Elites and Politics in Chihuahua, Mexico 1910–1940*. Durham, NC: Duke University Press, 1993.

Wasserman, Mark. *Everyday Life and Politics in Nineteenth Century Mexico*. Albuquerque: University of New Mexico Press, 2000.

Wasserman, Mark. *Pesos and Politics: Business, Elites, Foreigners, and Government in Mexico, 1854–1940*. Stanford, CA: Stanford University Press, 2015.

Wilkie, James, and Edna Monzón de W. *México visto en el siglo XX: Entrevistas de historia oral*. Mexico City: Instituto Mexicano de Investigaciones Económicas, 1969.

Womack, John, Jr. *Zapata and the Mexican Revolution*. New York: Vintage, 1970.

Wyatt-Brown, Bertram. *Honor and Violence in the Old South*. New York: Oxford University Press, 1986.

Yáñez Delgado, Alfonso. *La manipulación de la fe: Fúas contra carolinos en la universidad poblana*. Puebla: Imagen Pública y Corporativa, 2000.

Y esto tan grande se acabó: Testimonios y relatos de los trabajadores de la fábrica textil "La Trinidad". Tlaxcala: Gobierno del Estado, 1991.

Zolotow, Maurice. *Billy Wilder in Hollywood*. New York: Limelight, 1996.

Zolov, Eric. *The Last Good Neighbor: Mexico in the Global Sixties*. Durham, NC: Duke University Press, forthcoming.

Zorrilla, Luis. *Historia de las relaciones entre México y E.U.A.* Mexico City: Porrúa, 1966.

Articles and Chapters

Cumberland, Charles C. "The Jenkins Case and Mexican-American Relations." *Hispanic American Historical Review* 31:4 (1951): 586–607.

De la Vega Alfaro, Eduardo. "Origins, Development and Crisis of the Sound Cinema (1929–1964)." In *Mexican Cinema*, edited by Paulo Antonio Paranaguá. London: British Film Institute, 1995.

De la Vega Alfaro, Eduardo. "The Decline of the Golden Age and the Making of the Crisis." In *Mexico's Cinema: A Century of Film and Filmmakers*, edited by Joanne Hershfield and David Maciel. Wilmington, DE: SR Books, 1999.

Espinosa Yglesias, Manuel. "Introduction." In *Mary Street Jenkins Foundation: Mexico 1954–1988*, edited by Beatrice Trueblood. Mexico City: Fundación Mary Street Jenkins, 1988.

Gamboa Ojeda, Leticia. "Momentos de crisis y recuperación en la industria textil mexicana, 1921–1932." *La Palabra y el Hombre* [Jalapa] (July 1990): 23–53.

Gamboa Ojeda, Leticia. "Formas de asociación empresarial en la industria textil poblana." In *Los negocios y las ganancias*, edited by Leonor Ludlow and Jorge Silva Riquer. Mexico City: Instituto Mora, 1993.

Gamboa Ojeda, Leticia. "Para una historia de la rama textil: Géneros de punto en la Cd. de Puebla." *Arqueología Industrial* 4:8 (2001): 3–4.

Gilderhus, Mark. "Senator Albert B. Fall and 'The Plot Against Mexico.'" *New Mexico Historical Review* 48:4 (1973): 299–311.

Glaser, David. "1919: William Jenkins, Robert Lansing, and the Mexican Interlude." *Southwestern Historical Quarterly* 74:3 (1971): 337–56.

Gutiérrez Álvarez, Coralia. "Inmigración y aculturación." In *Presencia española en Puebla*, edited by Agustín Grajales and Lilián Illades. Puebla: Universidad Autónoma de Puebla, 2002.

Houle, Cyril. "Some Significant Experiments in Latin-American Education." *The Elementary School Journal* 49:2 (1948): 61–66.

Katz, Friedrich. "The Liberal Republic and the Porfiriato." In *Mexico Since Independence*, edited by Leslie Bethell. Cambridge: Cambridge University Press, 1991.

Knight, Alan, "The Rise and Fall of Cardenismo, c. 1930-46." In *Mexico Since Independence*, edited by Leslie Bethell. Cambridge: Cambridge University Press, 1991.

Knight, Alan, "*Cardenismo*: Juggernaut or Jalopy?" *Journal of Latin American Studies* 26:1 (1994): 73–107.

Knight, Alan. "The End of the Mexican Revolution?" In *Dictablanda: Politics, Work, and Culture in Mexico, 1938–1968*, edited by Paul Gillingham and Benjamin T. Smith. Durham, NC: Duke University Press, 2014.

Kuntz Ficker, Sandra. "De las reformas liberales a la gran depresión." In *Historia mínima de la economía mexicana, 1519–2010*, edited by Kuntz. Mexico City: Colegio de México, 2012.

LaFrance, David. "Revisión del caso Jenkins: la confrontación del mito." *Historia Mexicana* 53:4 (2004): 911–57.

Lazo, Dimitri. "Lansing, Wilson and the Jenkins Incident." *Diplomatic History* 22:2 (1998): 177–98.

Machado, Manuel and James Judge. "Tempest in a Teapot? The Mexican-United States Intervention Crisis of 1919." *Southwestern Historical Quarterly* 74:1 (1970): 1–23.

Meyer, Jean. "Revolution and Reconstruction in the 1920s." In *Mexico Since Independence*, edited by Leslie Bethell. Cambridge: Cambridge University Press, 1991.

Morse, Richard. "The Heritage of Latin America." In *The Founding of New Societies*, edited by Louis Hartz. New York: Harcourt, Brace, 1964.

Mraz, John. "Today, Tomorrow, and Always: The Golden Age of Illustrated Magazines in Mexico, 1937–1960." In *Fragments of a Golden Age: The Politics of Mexico since 1940*, edited by Gilbert Joseph, Anne Rubenstein, and Eric Zolov. Durham, NC: Duke University Press, 2001.

Paxman, Andrew. "Cooling to Cinema and Warming to Television: State Mass Media Policy from 1940 to 1964." In *Dictablanda: Politics, Work, and Culture in Mexico,*

1938–1968, edited by Paul Gillingham and Benjamin T. Smith. Durham, NC: Duke University Press, 2014.

Paxman, Andrew. "Slim Helú, Carlos." In *Iconic Mexico*, edited by Eric Zolov. Santa Barbara, CA: ABC-CLIO, 2015.

Paxman, Andrew. "Changing Opinions in *La Opinión*: Maximino Ávila Camacho and the Puebla Press, 1936–1941." In *Journalism, Satire and Censorship in Mexico, 1910–2015*, edited by Paul Gillingham, Michael Lettieri, and Benjamin T. Smith. Albuquerque: University of New Mexico Press, forthcoming.

Paxman, Andrew. "Simbiosis imperativa y conveniente: La evolución del capitalismo de cuates en Puebla." *Istor*, forthcoming.

Santibáñez, Blanca. "El Estado y la huelga de 'La Trinidad.'" *Boletín de Investigación del Movimiento Obrero* 8 (1985): 58–66.

Smith, Benjamin T. "Building a State on the Cheap: Taxation, Social Movements, and Politics." In *Dictablanda: Politics, Work, and Culture in Mexico, 1938–1968*, edited by Paul Gillingham and Benjamin T. Smith. Durham, NC: Duke University Press, 2014.

Tobler, Hans Werner. "La burguesía revolucionaria en México." *Historia Mexicana* 34:2 (1984): 213–37.

Trow, Clifford. "Woodrow Wilson and the Mexican Interventionist Movement of 1919." *Journal of American History* 58:1 (1971): 46–72.

Turner, John Kenneth. "Slaves of Yucatán." *American Magazine*, October 1909, reprinted in Turner, *Barbarous Mexico*. Austin: University of Texas Press, 1990.

Ulloa, Bertha. "La lucha armada (1911–1920)." In *Historia General de México*, edited by Daniel Cosío Villegas. Mexico City: Colegio de México, 1981.

Vélez Pliego, Alfonso. "La sucesión rectoral, las lecciones de la historia y las tareas actuales del movimiento universitario democrático." *Crítica* (Puebla) 1 (1978): 41–90.

Womack, John Jr. "The Mexican Economy during the Revolution, 1910–1920: Historiography and Analysis." *Marxist Perspectives* 1:4 (1978): 80–123.

Yankelevich, Pablo. "Hispanophobia y revolución: Españoles expulsados de México (1911–1940)." *Hispanic American Historical Review* 86:1 (2006): 29–60.

Zolov, Eric. "*¡Cuba sí, yanquis no!* The Sacking of the Instituto Cultural México-Norteamericano in Morelia, Michoacán, 1961." In *In from the Cold*, edited by Gilbert Joseph and Daniela Spenser. Durham, NC: Duke University Press, 2008.

Unpublished Works

Castañeda, Gonzalo. "The Dynamic of Firms' Chartering and the Underlying Social Governance. Puebla." Working paper, Universidad de las Américas–Puebla, 2005.

Crider, Gregory. "Material Struggles: Workers' Strategies during the 'Institutionalization of the Revolution' in Atlixco, Puebla, Mexico, 1930–1942." PhD diss., University of Wisconsin, Madison, 1996.

DeMoss, Margaret Shoffner. *Shoffner Family History*. Tennessee: n.p., 1971.

Fein, Seth. "Hollywood and United States–Mexican Relations in the Golden Age of Mexican Cinema." PhD diss., University of Texas, Austin, 1996.

García Rodea, Denisse. "Transición a la Democracia y fin del Caciquismo en el Municipio de Atlixco." Lic. thesis, Universidad de las Américas–Puebla, 2004.

Malpica, Samuel. "La hegemonía de la CROM en Atlixco (1900–1948)." MA thesis, Universidad Autónoma de Puebla, 1982.

McGuckin, Alexander. "La Clase Divina of Puebla: A Socio-Economic History of a Mexican Elite, 1790–1910." M.A. thesis, University of Alberta, 1995.

Pineda Ramírez, Miguel Ángel. "Sucesión y Transición: Las elecciones para gobernador en Puebla, en 1932." MA thesis, Instituto Mora, 2000.

Reyes Romero, Sandra. "La industria bonetera en Puebla y sus empresarios extranjeros, 1900–1930." MA thesis, Universidad Autónoma de Puebla, 2011.

Shoffner, Allen. *A Bicentennial History of Shofner's Lutheran Church*. Shelbyville, TN: n.p., 2008.

Smith, Richard. "Pastor William Jenkins." Lecture, Shelbyville, TN, 2 June 1996.

Tamayo, David. "*¡Cristianismo sí! ¡Comunismo no!* Religion and Reform in the University of Puebla, 1961." BA thesis, University of California, Berkeley, 2003

Wilt, David. "Stereotyped Images of United States Citizens in Mexican Cinema, 1930–1990." PhD diss., University of Maryland, 1991.

Index

Abed, Miguel, 9, 143, 159, 164, 242, 300

Acapulco, 240–1, 256, 279–83, 299; Jenkins's home and guests in, 2, 264, 280, 282–3, 297, 304, 326, 330, 348

Agrarian Commissions (Local and National), 100, 147–8, 160, 163, 173, 175, 182, 222, 224

agrarian reform. *See* expropriation of Jenkins's land

agraristas, in conflict with Jenkins, 144–8, 159–60, 167, 170–3, 175, 181–3, 187–8, 198–9, 204, 206, 221–2, 225; in conflict with others, 148–50, 153–6, 164, 165–6, 180; making deals with Jenkins, 178–80, 222

Aguirre, José (Pepe), 283

Aguirre Berlanga, Manuel, 123

Ahuehuetzingo, Puebla, 193–5

Alamán, Lucas, 61

Alarcón, Gabriel, 208, 226, 242, 300, 326, 333, 341, 342; as Jenkins's partner, 235–7, 246–8, 253, 255–7, 292–7, 313, 315, 317, 320, 331, 334, 343; and the Mascarúa murder, 311–2, 326, 383; post-Jenkins career, 360–1, 363, 374, 380, 381

Alarcón, Herminia de, 312

Alarcón, Óscar, 282

Alatriste, Baraquiel, 121

alcohol, production by Jenkins, 92, 158, 168, 205–8, 226, 320, 322; production in the United States, 36–7, 205

Alemán Valdés, Miguel, 7, 230, 267; as partner of Jenkins, 273, 299; as president, 242, 275–6, 277–8, 280, 283–4, 291–5, 300–1, 307, 309–10, 321, 331, 341; dealings with Jenkins, 277–8, 297–8, 322

Alemanists, 309, 337–8

Allá en el Rancho Grande (film), 234, 250

Almazán. *See* Andreu Almazán

Alpha Club, Puebla, 2, 98–9, 192, 212, 264, 283, 336, 363; branches built by the Jenkins Foundation, 326, 360, 382, 392–3

Alston, Wally, 344

Álvarez, Sofía, 232

American School, of Puebla, 193, 264, 357, 360, 363–2, 392; of Mexico City, 392

Amescua, Ernesto, 328, 331

Anáhuac University, 368–70, 391

Anda, Raúl de, 296, 317

Andreu Almazán, Juan, 95, 198, 240–2, 258

Andreu Almazán, Leónides, 198–9, 201–5, 213–4, 216, 217, 230–1, 240–1

Anstead, Robert, 199–200, 263

Apatzingán, Michoacán, 340–3, 344–7, 348, 357, 361

Applegate, Rex, 334

Arango, Manuel, 393

Arenas, Domingo, 80

Ariel (book), 62–3, 132, 292, 339

Ariza, Ramón, 173–4

Armamex, 334

Artasánchez, Luis, 281–2, 345

Artasánchez, Luis (son), 282, 330

Artasánchez, Rafael, 327

Atencingo, Ejidal Cooperative Society of, 225–6, 268–71, 289–90, 326

Atencingo, Hacienda, 65–6, 89, 144–50, 156, 160–70, 177, 193, 289; Jenkins's purchase of, 92–4, 139–41; violence at, 147, 170–4, 185, 225, 268

Atencingo Company (sugar mill), 168–70, 192–3, 202, 220, 222, 225–7, 265–6, 269–70, 290; sale of, 270–1

Atencingo System (sugar estates), 166–70, 175, 179, 181, 184, 187, 189, 198–9, 202–3, 207; expropriation of, 221–7, 229

Atlixco, Puebla, 80, 108, 118–9, 155, 174, 184, 215–6, 288, 302–3; textile mills of, 82, 141, 192, 216, 265; textile mills owned by Jenkins, 238, 299–306

automotive industry, Jenkins's investments in, 228, 285–6, 298

Ávila Camacho, Manuel, 212, 217; as candidate for president, 240–2, 298; as president, 241, 251–2, 257, 267, 275–6, 310, 338; dealings with Jenkins, 248–50, 254–5, 258–62, 269–71, 272–3, 277

Ávila Camacho, Maximino, 8, 11, 212–3; as candidate for governor, 212, 215–9, 223; as governor, 218–33, 240–2, 245–8; dealings with

Jenkins, 214, 221–7, 237, 239; as minister of communications, 217–8, 220, 248, 262, 265; as partner of Jenkins, 220–1

Ávila Camacho, Rafael, 215, 233, 350; as governor, 12, 270–1, 310, 321–2, 327, 349

Ávila Camacho López, Manuel, 221

Ávila Camacho political machine, 4, 240–2, 209–10, 306, 309–10, 349, 351, 353; Jenkins's support of, 214, 216–7, 241, 321, 327, 348–9, 389–90

Ayaquica, Fortino, 155

Azcárraga Vidaurreta, Emilio, 95, 257, 272, 295–6, 299, 315, 333

Azcárraga Vidaurreta, Gastón, 95, 252

Bailleres, Raúl, 328, 330–2

Banco de Comercio (Bancomer), 238, 252, 254, 272, 304, 314, 340, 377; Jenkins's takeover of, 328–32, 375; under Espinosa's ownership, 365, 370–2, 374, 377, 379–80; *see also* nationalization

Banco Mercantil de Puebla, 238

Banco Nacional de México (Banamex), 138, 252, 328, 372, 377

Bank of Ejidal Credit (Banjidal), 225, 345–6

Bank of Montreal, 168, 238

banking sector, 43, 52, 88–9, 91–4, 95, 137–8, 168, 328; *see also* nationalization

bankruptcy, 150, 164–5, 200–1, 293; Jenkins's use of, 299–305; of the Puebla government, 81, 137, 152–4

Barba González, Silvano, 339

Batista, Fulgencio, 233

Bautista, Gonzalo, 245, 248, 265, 301, 310

Bautista O'Farrill, Gonzalo, 285, 349

Bedford County, TN, 13–19, 25, 28, 36,
40, 69, 70, 78, 264, 352–3
Benítez, Eusebio, 194, 268
Betancourt, Carlos, 267, 288, 301,
303–4, 310
Beteta, Ramón, 332
Biddle Jenkins, Betty (mother of
William J.), 17–18, 21
Biddle, Joseph, 69
*Black Book of Mexican Cinema, The (El
libro negro del cine mexicano)*, 3–4,
291, 341, 382–3, 384, 386
Blanco Moheno, Roberto, 346
Bonanza Mines (Zacatecas), 49, 75
Bonilla, Teresa, 385
Bonilla, S. M., 183–4
Bonillas, Ignacio, 112, 122–3, 127, 129
border. *See* US-Mexican border
Bosques, Gilberto, 213–19
Brandon, Gerald, 118
Branscomb, Harvie, 4, 264, 283, 348
Bravo Izquierdo, Donato, 152, 158–9,
201, 212
bribery. *See* corruption
Britons and British influence, 13, 14, 48,
61, 192, 233
Bryan, William Jennings, 72
Buckley, William F., 135
BUDA Group, 328–32
Buntzler, Anne. *See* Jenkins, Anne
Buntzler, Paul, Jr., 286
Buñuel, Luis, 317
Burgos, Sabino P., 179–81, 183–4, 187,
188, 221
Bush, George W., 386
business elite, Jenkins as member
of, 8, 156–8, 190, 198, 287, 333,
362–3, 365–6; national, 6–7, 44–5,
60, 137–8, 176, 213, 251–2, 287,
337, 368–9; in Puebla, 51–2, 54–9,
70, 85, 152, 180, 201–2, 205, 213–4,
218–9, 239, 298–9, 301, 349–50,
362, 366

Cabañas Pavía, Manuel, 207, 238,
248, 287, 327, 358; on Jenkins
Foundation board, 325, 357,
360, 365
Cabrera, Alfonso, 97, 100, 102, 140, 156;
and Jenkins's kidnapping, 108–10,
114, 117–27
Cabrera, Luis, 97, 114, 123–4
caciques (local political bosses), 120,
155, 178–81, 183–4, 203, 215–17,
221–2, 227, 241, 270, 290,
303, 351–2
Cadena de Oro (exhibition circuit),
295–6, 313
Calderón, Felipe, 386
Calderón, Fanny, 56
California, 69, 87–8, 105, 136–7, 165,
209–10, 214, 254, 261–2, 323, 374;
Jenkins's assets in, 69, 136, 151,
169, 200–1, 227, 254
Calipam sugar plantation, Puebla, 52,
165, 177
Calles, Plutarco Elías, 95, 138, 150, 153,
168, 198, 201, 204–5, 213; in conflict
with Cárdenas, 215, 217, 221
Camarillo, Lauro, 213
Campa, Valentín, 227
campaign donations, by business
elites, 214, 278; by Jenkins, 214,
216–7, 327
Campos, Dolores (Doña Lola), 179,
182–4, 197–99, 204, 221–2, 225,
227, 268, 289
Campos, José, 172–3
Canteli, Indalecio, 238, 303, 305
Cantinflas. *See* Moreno, Mario
Capone, Al, 205, 331
Cárdenas, Enrique, 378

Cárdenas, Lázaro, 202, 222; as president, 3, 5–8, 212, 214–7, 219, 233–4, 237, 239–42, 245, 246, 275, 287, 298; presidential dealings with Jenkins, 189, 221–5; subsequent career, 259, 322, 338, 342, 342, 352, 354; subsequent dealings with Jenkins, 341–3, 345

Cardenists, 234, 269, 309, 337–8, 342, 352

Cargill, William, and Cargill Lumber, 43, 147

Carnegie, Andrew, 10, 29, 84, 159, 319, 323

Carrancistas, 74–6, 86, 97–8, 130, 140, 161, 291; as Puebla governors, 75, 80–1, 97, 108, 153, 157; *see also* Alfonso Cabrera

Carranza, Venustiano, 73, 80–1, 87; character of, 116, 120, 140, 144; and Jenkins's kidnapping, 106–27, 129, 189, 383, 385; as president, 91, 93, 97, 105–24, 129–30, 146, 198

Carrillo Flores, Antonio, 323, 331–2

Carson, Rachel, 347

Casares, Adolfo, 285

Casasús family, 333

Cash, W. J., 18–19

Caso, Alfonso, 264

Castro, Cesáreo, 161

Castro, Fidel, 3, 309, 337–8, 349–50

Castro, Luis, 359–60

Catholic Church, Jenkins's relations with, 101–3, 161–2, 194, 196, 280, 287–8, 332–3, 349–50, 358; Jenkins Foundation's relations with, 363, 368–70; national-level, 199, 319, 331, 337; in Puebla, 55–6, 58, 81, 162, 246, 348–52

caudillos, 46, 51, 156, 231–2, 242

CCEZ (Emiliano Zapata Peasant Confederation), 180, 203–4, 206–7, 216, 231

Cedillo, Saturnino, 147, 242

centralization of power, 46, 106, 153–4, 284, 309–10

Chandler, Harry, 254–5

Cheney, Matt, 355

Chietla, Puebla, 93, 177, 181, 204; clashes with Jenkins, 144–5, 172–3, 179–84, 186, 188, 195, 202, 221–3

Chumacero, Blas, 222–4, 227

CIA (US Central Intelligence Agency), 334, 368

CIM (Mexican Industrial Center, Puebla), 84–5

Cienfuegos, Jesús, 214, 235–7, 244–8, 311

Claims Commission, Special Mexican, 124, 224; American-Mexican, 224, 254

Clavijero, Francisco Javier, 56

CNC (peasant confederation), 269

Coahuila, 97, 161, 221

Cobel, Edmundo, 238, 285

Cold War, 2–3, 283, 320, 334, 337–9, 348–52, 364, 368

Colorado River Land Company (CRLC), 254–5, 272

Commercial Company of Puebla, 69, 75, 107

communal lands, 44, 65, 144, 174, 176, 180–1; *see also ejidos*

communism, 115, 183, 203, 219, 234, 270; *see also* Cold War, Marx

Comte, Auguste, 45, 59

La Concepción (La Concha; mill), 238, 299–301, 303–6

Concha, Manuel, 214

Conde de Conde, Ángela, 92, 148–50, 166

Conde y Conde brothers, 99, 164

Congress, federal, 146, 155, 179, 215, 293–5; Puebla, 158, 226, 228, 246, 288, 289; US, 29, 113, 116, 117, 121, 158, 264 (*see also* US Senate)

Conklin, Paul, 29–30

Constitution of 1917, 108, 112, 122, 131, 141–2, 202, 255, 343; Article 33, 133–4, 203, 246; and land ownership, 97, 130, 144, 162, 250, 254, 283

consular agent, Jenkins as, 71–2, 79, 98, 105, 110, 115, 118–19, 121–2, 129, 146, 162–3; Jenkins ceases to be, 199, 308

Contreras Torres, Miguel, 291–2, 294–5, 315–7, 339, 341, 384, 386

Coolidge, Calvin, 223

Cooper, Henry, 24–5

Cordero y Torres, Enrique, 126, 220, 382–3

Córdoba, Federico, 106–7, 111, 118, 120–1, 125, 384

La Corona (mill), 67–9, 73–4, 76, 81–8, 95, 101–2, 104, 126, 237; sale of, 141–2, 168

corruption, under Díaz, 44, 46, 51–2, 65, 100–1; during the Revolution, 97, 100–1, 161; postrevolutionary, at the federal level, 94–5, 141, 204, 207–8, 284, 307, 311; postrevolutionary, in Puebla, 152, 154, 163, 179, 206–7, 220, 230, 232, 241, 290, 340–1, 363, 378; in the United States, 10–11, 158, 231–2

Cortés, Hernán, 174, 381

Cosío Gómez, Moisés, 270

Cosío Villegas, Daniel, 5, 284, 338

Coss, Francisco, 75

COTSA (exhibition circuit), 252–3, 256, 271, 273, 313, 329, 375, 385

cotton production, Jenkins's investments in, 254–5, 342–3, 344–6

Cristero War, 161–2, 199, 213

CROM (labor confederation), 141–2, 198, 215–6, 228, 231, 259–61, 267, 288–9, 299–306

crony capitalism. *See* symbiotic convenience and symbiotic imperative

Crump, Edward, 10, 179, 231

CTM (labor confederation), 215, 227, 260–1, 266–7, 289, 301–3

Cuba, 19, 61, 111, 113, 166, 172, 174, 233, 234, 353; Revolution of 1959 in, 2–3, 309, 337–9, 342, 348–51, 364, 368, 371

Cue, Lorenzo, 270, 362

Cué, Luis, 214

Cuernavaca, 381

Cumberland, Charles, 127

Daniel, Jack, 36–7

Daniels, Josephus, 112, 223–4, 338

Davis, Norman, 223–4

Davis, Richard Harding, 79

De Antuñano, Estevan, 53

De Fuentes, Fernando, 234

De la Hidalga, Vicente and family, 148–9, 177, 180–1

De la Huerta, Adolfo, 131, 182, 211, 234

De la Madrid Hurtado, Miguel, 373, 376

De Landa family, 333

De Mier family, 333

De Novara, Medea (Herminne Kindle Futcher), 292

De Velasco, Francisco, 54, 99, 166

Del Río, Dolores, 250, 275

debt peonage, 45, 79, 148, 176–7

Department, Agrarian, 222, 269–70; *see also* Ministry of Agriculture

Department of Labor, 85, 142; *see also* Ministry of Labor

Derbez, Luis Ernesto, 391

Díaz, Félix, 80, 111

Díaz, Porfirio, 3, 24, 42, 46, 51, 55, 58, 60–1, 64–6, 80, 93, 99, 176; *see also* Porfirian age

Díaz Ordaz, Gustavo, 4, 241, 302,
353–4, 364; as president, 364, 368
Díaz Rubín, Ángel, 92, 177, 238,
Díaz Rubín family, 65–6, 92–3, 99,
139–41, 177
Díaz Rubín, Pedro, 93, 148, 238
Díaz Soto y Gama, Antonio, 146, 155,
179, 181
Disney, Walt, 275
Doheny, Edward L., 43, 90, 97, 113, 120,
129, 133, 135, 339
Domínguez, Augusto, 328, 331
Doña Lola. *See* Campos, Dolores
Dorticós, Osvaldo, 337

Echeverría Álvarez, Luis, 370–2
economy (national), the, 5–7; under
Díaz, 42–5, 66, 176; during
the Revolution, 81–2, 94–7;
postrevolutionary, 134, 138, 199, 218,
233–4, 242–3, 249, 258; post-1945,
284, 287, 337, 364, 389
economy (Puebla), the, 51–3, 81–3, 153–5,
219, 228, 241–2, 299–300; post-
1945 stagnation of, 300–1, 306,
363, 389–90
education. *See* illiteracy, schools
ejidos (communal farms), 144–5, 155,
222, 224–6, 268–70, 342, 345
elections, national, 8, 46, 71, 122,
157, 218; in Puebla, gubernatorial,
8, 204, 212–8; in Puebla,
municipal, 183, 204, 327
elites. *See* business elite, Porfirian elites
Elizondo, Salvador, 297, 317
entrepreneurship, 52, 58–9, 233, 284,
300, 306, 388; as practiced by
Jenkins and associates, 66–8,
85–7, 96–7, 145–7, 166–7, 255–6,
272–3, 286
Espinosa, Celestino, 172–3, 179, 181–2
Espinosa, Rafael, 182–3, 188

Espinosa Bravo, Ernesto, 121, 235–6
Espinosa Rugarcía, Amparo (Amparín),
332, 373–4
Espinosa Rugarcía, Ángeles, 376, 378, 380
Espinosa Rugarcía, Guadalupe, 376
Espinosa Rugarcía, Manuel
(Manuelito), 380
Espinosa Yglesias, Amparo Rugarcía de,
372, 373–4, 379–80
Espinosa Yglesias, Manuel, 11, 270,
289, 300, 332–3, 343, 344–5, 355,
359, 381, 388–9; as Jenkins's film
sector partner, 235–7, 246–8, 251–3,
255–7, 292–3, 295–7, 313, 315, 317,
320, 334; as Jenkins's partner in
banking, 328–32; at the Mary Street
Jenkins Foundation, 325, 357–8,
360–1, 363–73, 382–3, 392–3;
parallels with Jenkins, 373–81
Euless, Mary, 15–17
Eustace, Ronnie, 281–2, 285, 303–5, 324,
335, 341, 356, 357, 361, 375, 380
Eustace Jenkins, John, 356, 358
Eustace Jenkins, Rosemary, 281, 336,
354–5, 356, 375–8
Evans, Rosalie, 77, 102, 156, 162, 190
Excélsior (newspaper), 261, 294, 306–9,
341–2, 359
expropriations, 135, 147–8, 150, 153, 163,
198, 254; of Jenkins's land, 108, 145,
147, 169, 198–9, 221–7

Fall, Albert, 10, 106, 109–17, 120, 123,
129, 146, 158, 387
Fayetteville, TN, 20–1, 27, 33, 38
Federal Security Directorate (DFS), 283,
312, 331–2, 334
Félix, María, 293, 297
Film Bank, 251–3, 257; post-
nationalization (as the National
Film Bank), 292, 294, 296–7,
310–11, 315–7, 329

film industry (Mexican), exhibition in, 54, 233–7, 244–7, 249–54, 255–7, 271–3, 276, 306–7, 309, 312–3, 334, 385; local distribution in, 235, 250, 292–6; production in, 234, 250–2, 257, 273–5, 277, 291–3, 296–7, 307, 310–11, 315–8, 343–4 (*see also* newsreels)

film industry (US, including distribution), 143–4, 234, 250–1, 256–7, 273–8, 291–8, 312, 315–6, 344

Film Laws of 1949 and 1952, 293–5, 317

Flandrau, Charles Macomb, 57–8, 100

Ford, Henry, 132, 134

Fox, Vicente, 389, 391

French immigrants and French influence, 45, 53, 59, 155,

Franco, Francisco, 95, 246, 352

FROC (Puebla labor federation), 215–6, 222–3, 228, 231, 260

frontmen (*prestanombres*), Jenkins's use of, 235–6, 238, 248, 251, 258, 283, 289, 320, 325–6, 344–6, 361–2; politicians' use of, 220, 273, 299

Fuentes, Carlos, 94, 388

Galicia de Pérez Salazar, Loreto, 88

García, Adalberto, 266, 288–9

García, Amelia (Mía), 162, 281, 283, 348, 357–8

García Bustos, Arturo, 290

García Eguiño, Felipe, 325, 357, 360, 365

García Riera, Emilio, 250

Garduño, Eduardo, and the Gardño Plan, 310–11, 313, 317

Gavaldón, Roberto, 317

Germans and German influence, 13–15, 40, 48, 50–1, 156, 167, 264

Getty, Paul J. and wife, 209–10

Gildred, Theodore, 252, 256

Glockner, Julio, 350, 352

Gómez, Marte R., 206–8, 382

Gómez Carpinteiro, Francisco, 177

Gompers, Samuel, 114

González, Luis, 344

González de la Vega de Zevada, Josefina, 88

governors, in general, 8, 52, 95, 242; of Puebla (collectively), 96, 138–9, 151–5, 156–60, 175, 231–2, 241, 327, 390

Granat brothers (Oscar and Samuel), 334

Grant, Ulysses, 46, 205

Green Revolution, the, 291, 346–7

gringophilia, 131, 146–7, 275, 277–8, 338

gringophobia, 9–10, 60–3; during the Revolution, 114–5, 128–30; after the Revolution, 129, 131–35, 233, 257, 290–3, 308–9, 314; during the Cold War, 309, 337–44, 348–52; today, 381, 385–7, 390–1

Grovas, Adolfo, 252

Grovas, Jesús, 257, 296, 317

Gruening, Ernest, 151–2

Guadalajara, 8, 52–3, 86, 213, 219, 328, 366–7, 390; Jenkins's investments in, 235–6, 253, 256

guardias blancas; see private militia

Guerrero, Alberto, 152

Guerrero, Vicente, 60

Guggenheim, Meyer, 43, 49

Gutiérrez, Eulalio, 75–7, 79

Guzmán, Daniel, 211

Guzmán, Fernando, 108–9, 118

Guzmán, Roberto, 211, 234

Guzmán, Sergio B., 98, 208, 211–2, 214, 234, 281, 286, 380, 383; as mayor of Puebla, 232–3; on Jenkins Foundation board, 325, 360, 365

Guzmán, Sergio, Jr., 286, 298, 345

hacienda owners (*hacendados*). *See* Porfirian elites

Hanford, CA, 69, 137, 169, 201, 353

Hank González, Carlos, 383
Hansen, J. Salter, 117, 123–4
Hardaker, William, 75, 98, 107,
     120–1, 141
Harding, Warren, 10, 146
Harris, Isham, 24–5
Hearst, William Randolph, 25, 43, 97,
     135, 277; newspapers of, 106, 113,
     115, 129
Henderson, John, 205
Hernández, Antonio J., 301–6
Hernández, Vicente, 302
Heuer, Federico, 316
Higgins, Lawrence, 200, 228,
     285–6, 323–4
Hill, Benjamín, 95
Hitler, Adolf, 217
Hollywood. *See* film industry, US
Hoover, Herbert, 117
Houston, Frank, 30–1, 39
Houston, Sam, 40
Howse, Hilary, 179
Huerta, Efraín, 371
Huerta, Victoriano, 71–3, 78–80, 89, 99,
     110, 128–9, 181
Humboldt, Alexander von, 381
Huntington, Collis, 43

Ibáñez, Joaquín, 285
illiteracy, 3, 45, 85, 157, 197, 219
immigrants. *See under* Jewish,
     Lebanese, Spanish, US
indigenous Mexicans (*indígenas*), 23,
     42, 44–5, 52, 58–9, 100, 132, 140,
     170, 174; as revolutionaries, 64–5,
     77–8, 90; *see also agraristas*, debt
     peonage
industrialization, 44–5, 47–8, 134,
     249, 338; Import-Substitution
     Industrialization, 298
Infante, Pedro, 250, 274–5, 297
Investments of Puebla Company, 169

irrigation, 174, 220, 254–5; at Atencingo,
     65, 139, 166–7, 187–8, 199; in
     Michoacán, 342, 345
Iturbide, Aníbal de, 330–1
Ivie, Charles, 25, 39

Jackson, Andrew, 46
Jaramillo, Porfirio, 186, 227, 268–71,
     290, 383
Jaramillo, Rubén, 268,
Jardón, Edmundo, 383
Jenkins, Anne (later, Buntzler; sister
     of William J.), 18, 21, 63, 69, 104,
     353, 357–8; and American School of
     Puebla, 193, 264, 357
Jenkins, Elizabeth (daughter of William
     J.), 48, 87, 103, 106–7, 115, 136, 200,
     208, 228, 282, 323–4, 355; role in
     Jenkins's businesses, 252–3, 254,
     285, 373
Jenkins, Jane (daughter of William J.),
     88, 136, 185, 199–200, 203, 208–9,
     262–3, 281, 336, 354–6, 366
Jenkins, Joe (brother of William J.), 18,
     201, 353
Jenkins, John Whitson (father of
     William J.), 17–18, 20–2, 33, 36–8,
     41, 63, 69, 200–1
Jenkins, Kate (later, Shofner; sister of
     William J.), 18, 39, 47, 283, 353, 357
Jenkins, Mamie (later, Moore; sister of
     William J.), 18, 21, 33, 47–8, 69,
     201, 283, 352–3, 357
Jenkins, Margaret (daughter of William
     J.), 63, 199–200, 208–9, 263, 280,
     324, 335, 355, 357–8
Jenkins, Mary (daughter of William
     J.), 184–5, 200, 209, 228, 324–5,
     355–6, 361
Jenkins, Mary Lydia Street (wife of
     William J.), courtship, 19–22,
     25–8, 31–4, 34–41; and Jenkins's

kidnapping, 104–7, 109, 115, 119–20, 124; in Mexico, 42–3, 47–50, 59, 71, 75, 102, 143, 168, 208, 282, 336; in the United States, 63, 87–8, 136–7, 189, 199–200, 208–9, 227–8, 262–5

Jenkins, Percy (Jake; brother of William J.), 18, 39

Jenkins, Ruth (sister of William J.), 18, 63, 69, 201, 283, 353

Jenkins, Tita (daughter of William J.), 185, 200, 209, 228, 263, 324–5, 335, 354–7

Jenkins, William (grandfather of William J.), 13–18, 336

Jenkins, William Anstead (Billy or Bill; grandson of William J.), 200, 208–9, 282, 332–4, 335, 347, 354, 357–8; adopted as Jenkins's son, 263, 374; at the Mary Street Jenkins Foundation, 325, 357, 360–1, 365, 377–8, 392–3

Jenkins de Landa, Guillermo, 377

Jenkins de Landa, Roberto, 377

Jenkins Group (film cartel), 248–9, 255–7, 271–3, 277, 291–4, 306–11, 320, 341, 343; degree of industry control, 252–3, 257, 295–8, 313, 315–8

Jewish immigrants, 50–1, 88–9, 95, 133, 218, 230, 238, 244–5, 296; *see also* Leon Rasst

Jiménez Morales, Guillermo, 376–7

Johnston, B. F., 9, 96, 100, 170, 204, 226, 254, 267

Jones, Chester Lloyd, 90–1, 100–2

Juárez, Alicia, 357–8

Juárez, Benito, 24, 54, 57–8, 61

Kennedy, Diego, 98, 141, 148, 155

Kennedy, Diego, Jr., 141, 172–3

Kennedy, John Fitzgerald, 2, 337, 348, 349, 367

kidnapping of Americans, 87, 121

kidnapping of Jenkins, 9, 104–12, 119–24; as part of Jenkins Black Legend, 125–9, 189, 207, 223, 257, 382–6

Kipling, Rudyard, 77

Kirkland, James, 29

Knight, Alan, 8, 70, 130, 146

Krauze, Enrique, 284

Kullmann, Edgard, 197–8

Kurián, Samuel, 244–5

labor, 44, 54–5, 59, 258, 300; at Atencingo, 183, 191–6, 202–3, 223, 266–71, 288–9; in the textile sector, 84–5, 141–3, 215–6, 259–62, 265, 299–306; *see also* strikes, women

LaFrance, David, 124, 386

LaGuardia, Fiorello, 121

Lagunillas, Puebla, 141, 166, 172–3, 177, 179, 181–3, 186, 188, 194

Landa Irízar, Elodia Sofía de (Chacha), 332–4, 354, 378

Landa y Escandón, Guillermo de, 333

landowners. *See* Porfirian elites

land reform. *See* expropriation of Jenkins's land

Lane, Franklin, 112

Lansing, Richard, 106, 109–12, 115–18, 123, 129

Lara de Miera, Lucrecia, 88

Lara y Parra, Manuel, 366–7

Larrazolo, Octaviano, 114

Latin American Hospital, Puebla, 101, 107, 192, 321, 347, 357, 365

laws, 193, 252, 258, 329; governing labor, 85, 193, 268, 304, 340; governing land use, 24, 91, 100, 148–50, 172, 175, 176–7, 222; *see also* Constitution of 1917, Film Laws

Lebanese immigrants, 51, 89, 95–6, 143, 156, 159, 242, 301, 306, 376

Leduc, Renato, 350

Legorreta, Luis, 252
El León (mill), 299–301, 303–6
Lerdo, Miguel, 176
Leyva Velázquez, Gabriel, 269
Lima, José, 268
Limantour, José and family, 46, 333
Lincoln County, TN, 19–20, 28, 70
Lindbergh, Charles, 197
Lindley, Ray, 366–8
Llera de la Hidalga, Herlinda, 148–9,
    166, 180
loans, Jenkins's, in the business sector,
    81, 137, 143, 164, 235–6, 238, 256,
    284–7, (*see also* predatory lending);
    to the federal government,
    298, 313; to politicians, 240; to
    Puebla *caciques*, 178–80; to Puebla
    governments, 108, 157, 202, 230
Lodge, Henry Cabot, 113
Lombardo Toledano, Vicente, 153, 157–8,
    215–6, 224, 266, 302
London, Jack, 78
López, Crescenciano, 183
López Mateos, Adolfo, 2–3, 316, 327–8,
    337, 339, 352, 353–4, 363–4; dealings
    with Jenkins, 343–4, 345; dealings
    with the Jenkins Foundation, 327,
    364–5, 375
López Obrador, Andrés Manuel, 390–1
López Portillo, José, 370–2, 383
Lord, Robert, III, 324–5, 355
Los Angeles, 136–7, 165, 169, 208,
    217, 227, 234, 254, 262, 277, 361;
    Jenkins's family in, 103, 106, 137, 165,
    262, 199–201, 203, 208, 228, 265,
    324–5, 335, 356; Jenkins's mansion
    in, 105, 136, 151, 168, 209–10
Lozano Cardoso, Francisco, 121

Maciel, Marcial, 368–70, 391
Madero, Francisco, 64–6, 73, 80, 218; as
    president, 70–1, 82–3, 86, 128, 138

Magaña, Gildardo, 79, 80, 111, 117,
Manjarrez, David, 172–3
Manjarrez, Froylán, 149, 152, 172–3, 182
María Candelaría (film), 275, 277, 279
Márquez, Francisco, 222–3
Márquez, José Ignacio, 280
Márquez, Manuel L., 230
Márquez, Octaviano, 287–8,
    349–50, 358
Martínez, Mucio P., 51–3, 64–6, 80,
    98, 231; business ventures of, 51–2,
    92, 160, 177
Marx, Karl, and Marxism, 132, 183, 351,
    368, 385
Mary Street Jenkins Foundation,
    319–20, 322–3, 325–7, 329, 333,
    335–6, 343, 355, 357, 382–3; under
    Manuel Espinosa Yglesias, 358,
    359–780, 381–3; under Ángeles
    Espinosa Rugarcía, 378, 380, 392;
    under W.A. Jenkins, 381, 391–3
Mascarúa, Alfonso, 311–12, 319, 326, 382–3
Mason, Gregory, 100–1
Mastretta, Ángeles, 126, 244, 383–4
Matamoros (Izúcar de), Puebla, 159, 174,
    177, 179, 230, 322, 326
Matamoros Valley, Puebla, 139, 146–50,
    168, 170–1, 175–8, 181–3, 189,
    288–9, 361; as Jenkins's sugar
    domain, 165–6, 168, 175, 184, 193,
    204, 222, 230
Matienzo family, 164
Maurer family, 150, 155, 166, 170, 188
Maurer, Roberto, 155–6, 190
Maximilian, Archduke (Emperor of
    Mexico), 24, 57, 61
Maycotte, Fortunato, 161
Mayer, Louis B., 275, 277
Mayo Clinic, 208, 348, 353
McKinley, William, 44
Meadows, Feland, 192, 347, 357–8
Medina, Hilario, 109, 112, 114

Mellon, Andrew, 138

Mendoza, Francisco, 173

Méndez de Gavito, Adela, 164

mestizos, 44–5, 58–9, 71, 77, 178, 375

Mestre, Eduardo, 98–9, 106–7, 109, 118, 121, 145–7, 150, 285

Mestre, Manuel, 285

Metepec mill, Puebla, 82, 302, 305–6

Mexicali, Baja California, 254–5, 283

Mexican-American War (US Intervention), 9, 22, 60–1,

Mexican Center for Philanthropy (CEMEFI), 359, 393

Mexican views of the United States, 57–8, 62, 275; *see also* gringophilia, gringophobia

Mexico City, 46, 52, 73, 95, 219, 251, 276, 277, 300, 313, 317, 332–3, 351; Jenkins's investments in, 68, 81, 86, 88–9, 168, 252–4, 256, 285–6, 292, 295, 334; Jenkins's philanthropy and foundation works in, 322, 333, 364–5, 368–71, 383, 392

Meyer, Jean, 147

Michoacán (state), 285, 342–3, 381; Jenkins's investments in, *see* Apatzingán

Mijares Palencia, José, 204–5, 213–6, 219, 241

mines and mining, 42, 47–9, 61, 75, 84, 130

Ministry of Agriculture, 147, 269

Ministry of Communications, 217–8, 220, 241

Ministry of Defense, 126, 212

Ministry of Finance (Hacienda), 138, 149, 206–7, 215, 232, 320, 322, 331

Ministry of Foreign Relations (SRE), 88, 308; and the Jenkins kidnapping, 108, 118, 123

Ministry of the Interior (Gobernación), 189, 289, 294

Ministry of Labor (Trabajo), 260–1

Ministry of Public Education (SEP), 132–3, 196, 215, 365

Miranda y Gómez, Miguel Darío, 333

Mitchell, Julio, 109, 118–19, 122, 128

modernization, as political project, 42, 45, 54, 131, 157, 159, 176, 280, 292, 322, 364; by Jenkins in textile sector, 53, 66–7, 335; textile sector's reluctance toward, 143, 286, 300–1, 306

monopoly and monopolistic practice, 10, 19, 52, 138, 272–3, 284, 298, 313, 316, 337, 388; by Jenkins, 68–9, 248–9, 255, 272, 287, 291–4, 295–6, 299, 306–13, 341 (*see also* Jenkins Group); by politicians, 51, 199, 213, 363

Monroe, James, 101

Monte Albán, 5, 264

Monterrey, 8, 14, 41–2, 47–9, 57, 219, 366–7, 370, 390; Jenkins's investments in, 293

Montes, Manuel P., 152–4

Morales Conde family, 143, 238, 259, 262

Morelos, 65, 73, 117, 148–9, 178–9, 183, 185, 222, 227, 268, 338–9; sugar-growing in, 65, 91, 148, 190, 224

Moreno, Francisco Martín, 381

Moreno, Mario (Cantinflas), 251, 274, 297

Moreno Valle (Rosas), Rafael, 390

Morgan, J. P., 43, 132

Morlet, Héctor, 282

Morones, Luis Napoleón, 141–2, 152, 198, 300–2

Movement for National Liberation (MLN), 342, 352, 354

Múgica, Francisco, 242

Mulberry, TN, 19, 20, 27

Muñoz, Ignacio, 131, 338–9

Murad, Jorge, 376

Mussolini, Benito, 218, 230

Myers, Henry, 106

Nacional de Drogas (Nadro), 298, 328
Nacional Financiera (Nafinsa), 251, 255, 272, 276, 298
Napoleon III, 24, 57
Nashville, 14, 16, 30–2, 38–40, 48, 54, 179
nationalism, 9–10, 60–1, 130–1, 143, 169, 362, 384; Carranza's use of, 106, 110, 116, 123–4, 130; in Mexican film, 234, 272, 275, 291–2; *see also* gringophobia
nationalization, of banks, 372–3, 383; of the electricity sector, 344; of Jenkins's movie theaters, 318, 343–4; of oil, 134–5, 233, 344; *see also* expropriations
National Sugarworkers' Syndicate (SNA), 266–7
Nava Castillo, Antonio, 353, 363, 368
Negrete, Jorge, 251, 274
news media, Mexican, 47, 61, 108–10, 123, 125, 133, 260–2, 270, 293, 308–10, 330–1, 339–41, 343, 345–6, 359–61, 381–3 (*see also Excélsior, Novedades, Política, Siempre!, El Universal*); in Puebla, 106, 121–2, 126, 240, 245 (*see also La Opinión, El Sol de Puebla*); US, 4, 23, 106, 109–10, 113–15, 118, 125–6, 252, 277, 359
newsreels, 275–6, 298
New York, 62, 123, 206, 224, 355
Niblo, Stephen, 220, 385–6
notaries, 92, 321, 334–5, 344, 349, 361
Novedades (newspaper), 273, 299, 359

Obregón, Álvaro, 98, 118, 138; as businessman, 95, 147; dealings with Jenkins, 75, 79, 139, 144–50, 175; as president, 7, 80, 91, 124, 138, 140–1, 153, 198
O'Farrill, Rómulo, 230, 248, 281, 300, 327, 333; as Jenkins's partner, 228, 237, 299

oil, companies, 42–3, 112–3, 120, 128–30, 131–5; *see also* nationalization
La Opinión (Puebla newspaper), 216, 228, 237, 265, 287, 300–1, 303–4, 359, 382, 443n58
Orizaba, 53, 55, 311
Orozco, Pascual, 66
Orr, Carey, 114
Ortega, Fausto, 327, 349–50, 353
Ortiz Mena, Antonio, 343
Ortiz Rubio, Pascual, 202

Padilla, Ezequiel, 267, 275, 309
Palafox, Manuel, 213–4
Palavicini, Félix, 77
PAN (National Action Party), 331–2, 376–7, 390
Pani, Alberto, 138, 276
Pax Porfiriana, 46, 57, 93, 174
Paz, Octavio, 370
Pearson, Weetman, 61, 135
peasant organizations, 180, 183; *see also* CCEZ
peasants. *See agraristas*, debt peonage, indigenous Mexicans
Peláez, Manuel, 111, 120–1
Peña Nieto, Enrique, 386
Peoples, Henry, and Peoples & Morgan's School, 19–23, 25–6, 30–1, 38
Peralta, Alejo, 300
Pérez, Fernando, 266, 268–9, 288
Pérez, Manuel, as agronomist and manager, 141, 166–8, 192–3, 225, 265–6; as local dictator, 170, 175, 182–3, 188, 184–90, 194–5, 202, 222
Pérez Treviño, Manuel, 221
Pershing, John, 117, 129
peso devaluation, during Revolution, 82, 89–90; of 1938, 233; of 1954, 311, 314, of 1982, 371–2
philanthropy, 17, 45, 359, 393; Jenkins's acts of, 101–2, 159, 192–5, 230, 264–5,

287, 319–22, 347–8, 352–3, 381–2; *see also* Mary Street Jenkins Foundation
Piña Olaya, Mariano, 378
PNR (National Revolutionary Party), 201–5, 213–7, 221, 240
Poinsett, Joel, 60
Política (magazine), 341, 345, 350
political chiefs (*jefes políticos*), 46, 83
Polk, James Knox, 60
Poole, Tom, 324, 335, 355
populism, 175, 179, 198–9, 201–5, 218, 228–33, 317, 370–2, 391
Porfirian age (*porfiriato*), 44–7, 52, 55, 59, 92, 100, 138, 154, 177, 242, 287; *see also* Pax Porfiriana
Porfirian elites, 44–5, 59, 65–6, 71, 164; dealings with Jenkins, 70, 88–94, 99, 139–40, 148, 160, 164, 176–7, 180, 333
Portes Gil, Emilio, 198
Posada Noriega, Juan, 326
predatory lending, 9, 87–94, 96–8, 137, 139–41, 160, 166, 170, 180
Presno, Marcelino, 148, 155, 164
prestanombres. See frontmen
press. *See* news media
PRI (Institutional Revolutionary Party), at national level, 213, 242, 283–4, 327–8, 331–2, 337–8, 342, 360, 370; division within, 2–3, 10, 307–10, 354, 363–4; in Puebla, 12, 327, 376–7
private militia (*guardias blancas*), 155–6, 161, 170, 187, 215–6, 266–7
PRM (Party of the Mexican Revolution), 240, 242
Protestants and protestanism, in Jenkins's upbringing, 13–16, 22–3, 29, 34, 36, 159, 336; in Mexico, 43, 54, 101, 192, 208, 332, 357; as viewed in Mexico, 58, 61, 288, 385
public works, Jenkins's financing of, 68, 159, 207, 230, 321, 322, 326, 351; *see also* schools

Puebla (state), 8, 51–4; during the Revolution, 65, 80–1, 89–93, 117; following the Revolution, 137, 151–6, 299, 306; *see also* economy (Puebla)
Puebla City, 8; before the Revolution, 50, 52, 54–9, 64–5; during the Revolution, 64–5, 71, 73–6, 79–80, 89, 97–9, 101–2, 105, 109, 126; following the Revolution, 153, 207, 215–6, 219, 232, 235–7, 244–6, 288, 300, 321–2, 360, 390; Jenkins's investments in, 69, 141, 143, 228, 248, 285, 287; Jenkins's philanthropy and foundation works in, 101–2, 159, 192, 264, 287–8, 322, 360, 367–8, 376, 391–3; *see also* economy (Puebla)
Puig, José Manuel, 131

Querétaro, 68, 85–6, 141, 302, 314

racism, Mexican, 44–5, 65, 95, 196, 282; US, 22, 28, 77–8, 110, 112–14, 116
railroads (Mexican), 41–4, 48–9, 60–1, 82, 100, 174, 301; at Atencingo, 166, 184, 206
Ramírez Vázquez, Pedro, 370
Rasst, Leon, 50–1, 58–9, 66–8, 127
Reed, John, 77
Rees, Annie, 20, 33, 36, 39
Rees, John and family, 20–1, 26–8, 31–4, 37–41, 70,
Revueltas, José, 293
Reynaud, Adrian, 164
Riach, J. C., 142
Rivera, Diego, 132–4, 379
roads and highways, 68, 159, 207, 230, 280; Panamerican Highway, 314, 324
robber barons, 10, 29, 45, 101, 319, 393
Robert, Sébastien, 68
Rockefeller, John D., 10, 29, 69, 132, 134, 159, 263, 323

Rockefeller, Nelson, 233, 275–7
Rodó, José Enrique, 62, 132, 292, 339
Rodríguez, Abelardo, 95, 165, 276, 294,
        307–8, 383; as president, 206–7;
        rivalry with Jenkins in film,
        296, 312–3
Rodríguez, Franco, 345
Rodríguez, Margarito, 172–3
Roettinger, Phil, 334, 368
Rojas, Rafael, 121, 153, 256–7
Ronfeldt, David, 385
Roosevelt, Franklin D., 117, 163, 224,
        233, 275, 338
Roosevelt, Theodore, 40, 61–2, 138
Rothschild, Baron Nathan M., 73, 96
Ruiz Cortines, Adolfo, 295, 306–7,
        309–14, 317, 328, 332, 341;
        dealings with Jenkins, 310, 313–4,
        322, 327
Ruiz Harrell, Rafael, 127, 384

Sáenz, Aarón, 95, 165, 276; as sugar
        magnate, 199, 204, 226, 237, 259,
        267, 270, 278, 333
Salinas de Gortari, Carlos, 377, 389
San Antonio, 14, 39–41, 43, 47
San Luis Potosí, 81, 89, 147, 150, 242
San Martín Valley, Puebla, 90–1, 148,
        154, 164
Sánchez, Abelardo, 351
Sánchez, Facundo, 191, 285, 289, 361
Sánchez, José María, 146, 149, 152–4
Sánchez, Manuel, 289–90,
Sánchez-Navarro, Juan, 331, 333
Sánchez y Paredes, Enrique, 102–3, 161
Santos, Gonzalo N., 242
schools, Jenkins's financing of, 85,
        192–8, 207, 264, 319, 321–2, 327
Senderos, Manuel, 329–31
Serdán, Aquiles, 64–5, 80
Serna, Clemente, 272
Sevilla, Manuel, 238, 248, 358
Shanklin, Arnold, 71, 75–6

Shelby, Jo, 24
Shelbyville, TN, 14–16, 23–5, 28,.
        264, 335
Shofner, Martin and family, 15–16, 36,
        38, 352–3
Sidar, Pablo, 197
Siempre! (magazine), 308, 346, 351–2
Sierra, Justo, 62
Signoret, Leon, 164
Sinaloa, sugar production in, 96, 100,
        170, 204, 206, 226
sindicato blanco (company–controlled
        union), 183, 259
Skipsey, Harold, 168
Slim, Julián, 95
Slim Helú, Carlos, 95, 373, 378, 388
social Darwinism, 45
Sociedad Anónima (SA), the, 86–7
El Sol de Puebla (Puebla newspaper), 311,
        349–50, 359–60, 382
Spanish immigrants and influence, 22,
        51–2, 55–6, 58–9, 86, 95, 125, 303;
        as landowners, 65–6, 90–2; as
        targets of xenophobia and violence,
        97, 129–30, 134, 148, 186, 190,
        244–8, 340
Spanish-American War, 19, 61, 77, 112
Spencer, Herbert, 45
Stanford, Leland, 29
Stewart, J., 220–1, 225–7
Stillman, James, 43
Street, John William and family, 20
Street, Donald, 20, 63, 67, 70, 74–5, 88,
        105, 142, 353
Street, Hugh, 20, 26–7, 37, 39–40,
        63, 69–70
strikes, 54–5, 83–4, 141, 215, 217, 219, 241,
        258, 302, 337, 364, 371; at Jenkins's
        businesses, 83–5, 142, 203, 259–62,
        270, 302, 303–4, 311
student movements, national, 337,
        364, 368; in Puebla, 230, 348–51,
        363, 364, 367, 371

Suárez, Manuel, 9, 340
sugar production, 140, 143, 174, 226; *see also* Atencingo, Atencingo System, Morelos, Sinaloa, Veracruz
Sumner, William Graham, 45
Sunset Boulevard (film), 210
Supreme Court (Mexican), 118–9, 260–1, 295, 309
symbiotic convenience, 6–7, 400nn1; at the federal level, 52, 249–50, 258–9, 271–2, 284, 298, 313–4, 320, 332, 363–4, 373, 389; at the state level, 52, 218–20, 228, 241–2, 286, 304, 320
symbiotic imperative, 6–7, 400nn1; at the federal level, 52, 137–8, 249, 259, 389; at the state level, 52, 137–9, 152, 205, 218, 242

Taft, William, 62
tax avoidance and evasion, by Jenkins, 68, 169, 205–8, 235, 251, 253, 320–2, 341, 361; in Mexico (general), 53, 88, 154, 237, 296; in the United States, 15, 18, 36
Taylor, J. W., 106
Tear This Heart Out (Arráncame la vida), 126, 244, 383–4
Tehuacán, 159, 230, 238
Téllez Vargas, Pedro, 311
Tennessee, 2, 10, 13–40, 63, 78, 113, 335–6, 352–3; parallels with Mexico, 10, 53, 99, 239, 140, 179, 190, 231, 239
Texas, 22, 24, 39–41, 62, 64, 95, 114, 206
textile industry, 50–1, 53–5, 81–3, 87, 141, 306; Jenkins's investments in, 66–9, 81, 141–3, 238–9, 286, 335 (*see also* La Concepción, La Corona, El León, La Trinidad)
Thielheim, Arturo, 50–1, 66

Thompson, David E., 100
Tigert, John, 31–2, 39, 165, 168, 221, 227, 263, 265; lobbies US government, 223–4
Tirado, Claudio N., 152–3, 158–9
Tlaxcala, 82–3, 89, 98; see also, La Trinidad
Treviño, Jacinto B., 307–9
La Trinidad (mill), 143, 238, 258–62, 269, 271, 302
Trouyet, Carlos, 330–1
Trujillo, Francisco, 260–1
Truman, Harry S, 275, 277
Tucson, Arizona, 208–9, 227–8, 262
Turner, John Kenneth, 44, 77

Ubera, Juan, 119–20
Ugarte, Salvador, 238, 328, 331, 333, 379
Ulloa, Bertha, 127
UNAM (National Autonomous University of Mexico), 368, 369, 387
unions. *See* labor, CTM, CROM, FROC
United States, influence in Mexico, 192, 196, 338–9 (*see also* film industry, US); intervention in Mexico, 117, 119, 129; investment in Mexico, 42–3, 54, 60–2, 69, 132, 145, 233, 338; relations with Mexico, 106, 110–7, 127, 257, 277, 338; views of Mexico, 22–3 (*see also* racism)
El Universal (newspaper), 207, 261, 294, 306–9, 312, 333, 359
University of the Américas (UDLA–Puebla), 366–8, 370, 371, 378–9, 382, 391–2, 393
University of Puebla (UAP), 229–30, 348–52, 366–8, 371, 384–6
urbanization, 54, 239, 274, 313, 317
US Agency for International Development (USAID), 367–8

US Civil War, 16–17, 18, 22, 24, 28, 40, 47, 59
US immigrants and expatriates, 43, 46–8, 55, 96, 99–101, 112, 238, 252, 366
US Internal Revenue Service, 18, 81, 83, 87, 90, 226, 285, 320, 361
US-Mexican border, 40–3, 66, 95, 114–5, 206, 254–5
US Senate, 206, 255; Foreign Relations Committee (Fall Committee), 76, 113, 117
US State Department, 71, 75, 82, 163, 294; and the Jenkins kidnapping, 109, 115, 117, 121; and the Atencingo expropriation, 224–6, 239
Utay, Simon, 238

Valencia, Daniel V., 118–9
Vanderbilt, Cornelius and family, 29, 31
Vanderbilt University, 4, 21, 25–6, 29–32, 37–41; Jenkins's donations to, 101, 264, 352; Jenkins on board of trustees, 264, 314; *see also* Branscomb, Harvie
Vasconcelos, José, 132
Vázquez, Nicolás, 321, 327, 349, 361
Vega, Gil, 173, 179, 183–4, 194, 221–2
Velázquez, Fidel, 227, 261
Vera y Zuria, Pedro, 161–2, 196
Veracruz, 24, 53, 54–5, 57, 71, 78, 117, 120, 242, 279, 299; Jenkins's investments in, 235, 244, 247, 253; sugar production in, 145, 169, 174, 206
Villa, Francisco (Pancho), 65, 73, 77–80, 87, 111, 117, 123, 129, 138, 144; theft of Jenkins's property, 75, 79, 82
Villasana, Vicente, 256–7
violence, electoral/political, 152, 198, 216, 240; rural, 65, 77, 137, 153,
155–6, 161, 170–4, 199, 225, 288–9; urban, 215–6, 223, 228, 244–8, 303–4; used by (or alleged of) Jenkins or his associates, 152, 183, 185, 170, 188–9, 310–12
Volkswagen de México, 286, 363

Walerstein, Gregorio, 296, 317, 359, 374
Walker, William, 23–5
Washington, 113, 123, 197, 223–4, 324; *see also* United States, relations with Mexico
Washington, George, 46
Webb School, TN, 20, 31, 69
Weber, Max, 34
Wenner-Gren, Axel, 9, 340
Whitaker, John (Peg-leg) and family, 28, 40
Wilder, Billy, 210
William, Robert, 324, 355–6, 361
Wilson, Woodrow, 78, 111–17, 130, 138, 387
Wishñack, Sam, 296
women, 45, 50–1, 347, 374; as Jenkins's employees, 67, 83–5, 102, 142, 192, 340, 346; as property owners, 88–9, 148–50, 165–6
workers. *See* labor
World War I, 99, 122, 134
World War II, 143, 226, 242, 251, 274, 277, 292, 315, 338; impact on Jenkins's businesses, 239, 258–9, 299–300
Wright, Harry, 96, 99
Wyatt-Brown, Betram, 94

Young, Andrew, 25, 38–9

Zapata, Emiliano, 65, 71, 73, 75, 78–9, 120, 138, 149, 175, 290
Zapatistas, 73–79, 86, 91, 108, 111, 124, 149, 181, 190; destruction of property by, 80, 82, 91–2, 166;

exacting protection money, 75, 80, 120, 122, 179; after the Revolution (former officers), 155, 163, 173, 178–9, 198, 213; after the Revolution (soldiers and sympathizers), 145–6, 148, 155, 175–84, 187

Zaragoza, Ignacio, 57

Zedillo, Ernesto, 379